Right-sizing the State

Right-sizing the State

The Politics of Moving Borders

Edited by

BRENDAN O'LEARY

IAN S. LUSTICK

THOMAS CALLAGHY

OXFORD
UNIVERSITY PRESS

OXFORD

UNIVERSITY PRESS

Great Clarendon Street, Oxford OX2 6DP

Oxford University Press is a department of the University of Oxford.
It furthers the University's objective of excellence in research, scholarship,
and education by publishing worldwide in

Oxford New York

Athens Auckland Bangkok Bogotá Buenos Aires Cape Town
Chennai Dar es Salaam Delhi Florence Hong Kong Istanbul Karachi
Kolkata Kuala Lumpur Madrid Melbourne Mexico City Mumbai Nairobi
Paris São Paulo Shanghai Singapore Taipei Tokyo Toronto Warsaw

and associated companies in Berlin Ibadan

Oxford is a registered trade mark of Oxford University Press
in the UK and in certain other countries

Published in the United States
by Oxford University Press Inc., New York

© the several contributors 2001

The moral rights of the author have been asserted

Database right Oxford University Press (maker)

First published 2001

British Library Cataloguing in Publication Data

Data available

Library of Congress Cataloging in Publication Data

Rightsizing the state: the politics of moving borders/edited by Brendan O'Leary, Ian s. Lustick, and
Thomas Callaghy.

p. cm.
Includes bibliographical references and index.
1. Boundaries. 2. Territory, National. I. O'Leary, Brendan.
II. Lustick, Ian, 1949– III. Callaghy, Thomas M.
JC323.R54 2001 320.1'2—dc21 2001031167

ISBN 0–19–924490–1

10 9 8 7 6 5 4 3 2 1

Typeset by Hope Services (Abingdon) Ltd.
Printed in Great Britain
on acid-free paper by
T. J. International Ltd.,
Padstow, Cornwall

ACKNOWLEDGEMENTS

The Editors would like to thank the contributors for their hard work, patience, and intellectual stimulation. This volume derives from conferences sponsored by the Social Science Research Council of the USA (1997) and a session at the American Political Science Association (1998), which all the participants and two of the editors would insist owed most to the organizational and inspirational efforts of Ian Lustick. The completion of the volume owes much to informal 'e-mail seminars' amongst all the contributors between 1997 and 1999. The Editors express warm appreciation on behalf of all the contributors to the Social Science Research Council of the USA. Tom Callaghy and Ian Lustick thank the University of Pennsylvania for its institutional support. Brendan O'Leary likewise thanks the London School of Economics and Political Science, especially Jane Pugh and her colleagues in the drawing office, and the United States Institute of Peace for research assistance. Dominic Byatt, Amanda Watkins, and their colleagues at Oxford University Press have been most helpful, as were the anonymous independent readers of our manuscript. We would like to thank other participants at our conferences who aided us through constructive criticisms of the chapters that materialize here. They include the late Professor James Bulpitt of Warwick University, Dr Hussein Adam of the United States Institute of Peace, Dr. Hillel Frisch of the Hebrew University of Jerusalem, and Professor Ilan Peleg of Lafayette College, Pennsylvania.

Contrary to two conventions the Editors have sorted their names in reverse alphabetical order, and refuse to take total responsibility for the good work that is here. We are, however, in keeping with a good convention, responsible for any remaining defects.

Brendan O'Leary, London
Ian Lustick, Philadelphia
Tom Callaghy, Philadelphia
August 2000

CONTENTS

FIGURES

TABLES

NOTES ON CONTRIBUTORS

Thomas M. Callaghy is Professor of Political Science at the University of Pennsylvania. He has written extensively on Africa and comparative and international political economy His books include *South Africa in Southern Africa: The Intensifying Vortex of Violence* (Praeger: 1983); *The State-Society Struggle* (Columbia University Press: 1984); and *Hemmed In: Response to Africa's Economic Decline* (New York: Columbia University Press 1993). Currently he is working on a book on the Paris Club as one prism through which to analyse the evolution of international economic governance over the last fifty years.

Ümit Cizre is Associate Professor of Political Science in the Department of Political Science, Bilkent University, Ankara, Turkey. Her publications include a book in Turkish on the relationship between the Turkish military and the chief political platform of the Turkish right (the Justice Party of the 1960s and 1970s), and an edited book in Turkish on military dictatorships and the women's movements in Latin America. She has published a number of articles in international journals, such as 'The Anatomy of the Turkish Military's Autonomy' in *Comparative Politics*; 'Kemalism, Hyper-Nationalism and Islam in Turkey' in *History of European Ideas*; 'Historicizing the Present and problematizing the Future of the Kurdish Problem' in *New Perspectives on Turkey*; 'Kurdish nationalism from an Islamist Perspective: The Discourses of Turkish Islamist Writers' in *Journal of Muslim Minority Affairs*; and 'Parameters and Strategies of Islam-State Interaction in Republican Turkey' in *International Journal of Middle Eastern Studies*. Her research interests include theories of nationalism, the military in politics, democratic control of armed forces, the changing meaning of security and its nexus with domestic politics and globalization, and human rights policies.

Ian S. Lustick is Professor of the Political Science Department at the University of Pennsylvania where he holds the (Richard L. Simon) Merriam Term Chair in Political Science. His publications include *Arabs in the Jewish State; Israel's control of a National Minority* (University of Texas Press: 1980); *State-Building Failure in British Ireland and French Algeria* (University of California Press: 1985); *For the Land and the Lord: Jewish Fundamentalism in Israel* (Council on Foreign Relations: 1988); and *Unsettled States, Disputed Lands: Britain and Ireland, France and Algeria, Israel and the West Bank-Gaza* (Cornell University Press: 1993). His articles on ethnic conflict, Middle East politics, American foreign policy, social science methodology, and organization theory have appeared in many journals, including the *American Political Science Review*, *World Politics*, *Foreign Affairs*, *Cornell Journal of International Law*, and *International Organization*. He is a founder and past president of the Association for Israel Studies and currently serves as President of the Politics and History Section of the American Political Science Association. His current research applies an agent based computer simulation model to the relationship between globalization and identitarian conflict.

Marc Lynch is Assistant Professor of Political Science in the Department of Political Science, Williams College, Williamstown, Massachusetts. He received his Ph.D. from Cornell University, and was a postdoctoral fellow at the University of California, Berkeley. His publications include *State Interests and Public Spheres: The International Politics of Jordan's Identity* (Columbia University Press: 1999). His research interests include international public spheres, Arab politics, and ethnic conflict. He is currently writing a book on the international politics of sanctions on Iraq.

Alexander J. Motyl is Associate Professor of Political Science and Deputy Director of the Center for Global Change and Governance at Rutgers University, Newark, USA. He is a specialist in Russian, Ukrainian and post-Soviet regimes as well as in nationalism, empires, and revolutionary change. His publications include *Will the Non-Russians Rebel? State, Ethnicity, and Stability in the USSR* (Cornell University Press: 1987), *Sovietology, Rationality, Nationality: Coming to Grips with Nationalism in the USSR* (Columbia University Press: 1990), *The Post Soviet Nations: Perspectives on the Demise of the USSR* (Columbia University Press: 1992), *Thinking Theoretically about Soviet Nationalities: History and Comparison in the Study of the USSR* (Columbia University Press: 1992); *Revolutions, Nations, Empires: Conceptual Limits and Theoretical Possibilities* (Columbia University Press: 1999); and most recently *The Encyclopedia of Nationalism* (Academic Press: 2000). His forthcoming book, *Imperial Ends: The Decay, Collapse, and Revival of Empires*, will appear in 2001 (Columbia University Press).

Vali Nasr is Associate Professor of Political Science at the University of San Diego and Faculty Associate at the von Grunebaum Center for Near East Studies at UCLA. He has written extensively on Pakistan's politics and the role of ideology and state-society relations therein, including *Mawdudi and the Making of Islamic Revivalism* (Oxford University Press: 1996) and *The Vanguard of the Islamic Revolution: the Jama'at-i Islami of Pakistan* (Tauris: 1994).

Denise Natali is a private consultant, adjunct fellow at the Center for Strategic and International Studies (CSIS), and member of the Advisory board of the Washington Kurdish Institute (WKI) in Washington DC. Her various publications and lectures have focused on the Kurds, self-determination, and conflict resolution. She would like to thank the United States Institute of Peace for financial support for this research project.

Brendan O'Leary is Professor of Political Science and Convenor of the Department of Government at the London School of Economics and Political Science, UK. His authored, co-authored and co-edited books include *Theories of the State* (Macmillan: 1987), *The Asiatic Mode of Production* (Blackwell: 1989), *The Future of Northern Ireland* (Oxford University Press: 1990), *The Politics of Ethnic Conflict Regulation* (Routledge: 1993), *Northern Ireland: Sharing Authority* (IPPR: 1993), *The Politics of Antagonism* (2nd ed. Athlone: 1996), *Explaining Northern Ireland* (Blackwell: 1995), and *Policing Northern Ireland* (Blackstaff: 1999). The author of numerous articles on nationalism, ethnic conflict regulation, Northern Irish, Irish and British politics, he has acted as a constitutional consultant for the European Union and United Nations on Somalia, and for British, Irish and American politicians on Northern Ireland. His current research interests include constitutional engineering in divided territories and national self-determination.

Gurharpal Singh is the CR Parekh Professor of Indian Politics and Director of the Centre for Indian Studies at the Department of Politics, Hull University, England. He received his Ph.D. from the London School of Economics and Political Science. The founding co-editor of the *International Journal of Punjab Studies*, he is the author of numerous articles and reports on South Asian ethnic politics, political corruption and electoral politics. His books include *Communism in Punjab: A Study of the Movement up to 1967* (Ajanta Publications: 1994), *Punjabi Identity: Continuity and Change* (Manohar: 1996), *Region and Partition: Bengal, Punjab and the Partition of the Subcontinent* (Oxford University Press: 1999), and *Sikh Religion, Culture and Ethnicity* (Curzon: 2000).

Oren Yiftachel teaches political geography and public policy, and is head of the Department of Geography at Ben Gurion University of the Negev, Beer-Sheva, Israel. He is also a research fellow at the Negev Centre for Regional Development. He studied urban and regional planning and political geography in Australian and Israeli universities. He is the author of *Planning a Mixed Region in Israel: The Political Geography of Arab-Jewish Relations in the Galilee* (Avebury: 1992), and *Planning as Control: Policy and Resistance in a Divided Society* (Pergamon: 1995), co-editor of *Ethnic Frontiers and*

Peripheries (Westview: 1998) and *The Power of Planning: States, Control, Identities* (Kluwer Academic: forthcoming), and the author of numerous articles in geographical and social science journals on ethnic relations, territory and democratic stability.

Stephen Zunes is Associate Professor of Politics and co-ordinator of the Peace and Justice Studies Program at the University of San Francisco. He is the co-editor (with Lester Kurtz and Sarah Beth Asher) of *Nonviolent Social Movements: A Geographical Perspective* (Blackwell: 1999) and of a forthcoming book with Syracuse University Press on the conflict over Western Sahara.

Introduction

Brendan O'Leary

> Our century has witnessed one successful de-territorialisation of nationalism: everyone knows now that the power and prestige of a nation depends on its annual rate of growth and its economic clout, and *not*, on how much of the map it manages to paint with its own colour. A further de-territorialisation . . . would be eminently desirable. But it will be exceedingly difficult: the entire weight of romantic literature is on the side of the fetishisation of landscape, of national culture as expressed in land-use and in its territorial delimitation.
>
> Ernest Gellner (1997: 107–8)

Was Ernest Gellner correct to conclude that the last century bore testimony to the partial de-territorialization of nationalism? Will this new century occasion the political de-fetishization of landscapes? These questions do not permit easy answers. A comparison of the political map of the world in 1900 with that of 2000 is most instructive—see Figs. 1.1 and 1.2. In 1900, empires dominated most of the earth's surface: the Austro-Hungarian, the Belgian, the British, the Chinese, the Dutch, the French, the German, the Italian, the Ottoman, the Russian, the Spanish, and the Portuguese empires held most of Africa, the Middle East, Asia, Australasia, and Oceania under direct and indirect rule. By 2000 these empires had gone or had been reduced to rumps, and the significantly named United Nations had nearly 200 member-states. In an interval of just one hundred years the initial map had been torn up by two world wars. Before, during, and just after the first the Austro-Hungarian, Chinese, German, Ottoman, Russian, and Spanish empires were wholly or partly destroyed, and their cores converted into precarious republics. The second world war saw off renewed German imperialism with a fascist face, and its Italian and Japanese allies and equivalents, but it so weakened most of the remaining empires that the de-colonization of their remaining 'possessions' occurred almost as fast as their nineteenth century conquests. The forty years from 1948 until 1988 saw the astonishing rise and fall of communist regimes around the Russian pioneer. At their peak they governed over one and a half billion people, in the USSR, Eastern and South-Eastern Europe, China, Indo-China, and parts of Africa, and they had loyal and critical supporters throughout most of the rest of the world. Initially these regimes appeared as curious amalgams: provincial jurisdictions of a cosmopolitan homogenizing salvationism and the client-states of an old-style imperialism in new clothes. But they proved fissiparous, polycentric, and incubators of nationalism. Eventually, under the weight of what was ironically referred to as their internal contradictions, all bar the Chinese, Vietnamese, Laotian, and North Korean versions collapsed during and after 1989, bringing renewed territorial turbulence in their debris.

In short, in the twentieth century borders were moved, re-moved, taken, re-taken, and abandoned, and peoples were moved, re-moved. and slaughtered on an epic scale. Given this recent history it would be more than arrogant to presume that we can foretell the history of the next century. Can we, however, know something more modest: the causes and consequences of the politics of moving borders? It would be remarkable if the territoriality of states was immune to the variables that have shaped modernity, and it is with this thought in mind that the next chapter commences.

The joint interest of the contributions to this book is in the efforts of state élites, and their challengers, to 'right-size' their states. By 'right-sizing' we do not mean the objective alignment of state borders to conform to some aesthetic of perfect organization, such as a racial or 'natural' geographic ideal, though such aesthetic convictions exist, and have existed, both in malign and benign forms. There is no world-historical Archimedian point from which one might declare the objective political correctness of a given set of territorial jurisdictions. By 'right-sizing' we refer to the preferences of political agents at the centre of existing regimes to have what they regard as appropriate external and internal territorial borders. The motivations that determine these preferences are, as we shall see, many and varied.

On an imperfect analogy with business enterprises the contributors to this volume think that state élites may be conceived as having five ways of externally 'right-sizing' their states. They can:

(1) *'up-size'* through take-overs;
(2) *stabilize* their borders;
(3) *'down-size'* through reducing their territories;
(4) *ally*—while retaining their former spatial configuration within federalizing or confederalizing unions; or lastly
(5) *merge*—through assimilationist or integrationist unification or re-unification, which may be thought of as 'upsizing by consent'.

These distinct strategies are capable of multiple permutations: for example state managers might simultaneously up-size by conquering one piece of territory, down-size from an imperial commitment, and stabilize a boundary with another state through an 'international' treaty.

Collectively and individually we address what we identify as 'right-sizing' efforts through using, and, where necessary, improving, contemporary theories of the state, of nationalism, and in comparative political analysis. We took as our starting points Ian Lustick's theory of state expansion and contraction, and the taxonomy of modes of regulating national and ethnic conflict, developed by John McGarry and Brendan O'Leary (Lustick 1993; McGarry and O'Leary 1993; O'Leary 1995). We also assume the general merits of modernist theories of nationalism.

Thinking about 'right-sizing', and possible territorial constitutional transformations of states, takes us outside the conventional prisms of much recent theorizing about the state, and indeed points us to older and neglected literatures,[1] for example on the rise and decline of kingdoms and empires. Max Weber's famous definition of the state appears to illustrate an important and historically strange restriction in its last clause. The best known of his definitions is that presented in *Politics as a Vocation*, namely, 'a human community that (successfully) claims the *monopoly of the legitimate use of physical force* within a given territory' (Weber 1977 (1918): 78, emphasis in original). The definition assumes a *given* territory. But surely territories are not given? Surely they are made, and re-made? Surely they are, in our contemporary parlance, variables, rather than constants? Perhaps Weber's phrasing accidentally occluded something of great importance, and which he recognized, not least in the wake of the negotiations at Brest-Litovsk, namely that successful statehood requires successful claims to a given territory? These questions pose others: can states remain themselves, at least in part, if their territories vary? Are states' identities, at least in part, independent of their territories? These are just some of the questions prompted by Ian Lustick's work that are explored further below.

The word territory itself repays inspection (Baldwin 1992; Gottmann 1975). It comes from the Latin noun *territorium*—the land surrounding a town and under its jurisdiction. In turn that derives from the verb *terreor*, to frighten, through *territor*, one who frightens, through to *territorium*, a place from which people are 'frightened off'. The etymology of territory is therefore the same as that of terrorist. That should be no surprise given that states

---

[1] Notable exceptions in historical and political sociology include the work of Charles Tilly and his associates and the late Samuel Finer (Tilly 1975, 1992 (1990); Finer 1974, 1975, 1997a, b, c). In political geography there is also a lively literature neglected by political scientists: Gottmann (1973); Kristoff (1959); Murphy (1996); Sack (1986); and Taylor (1994).

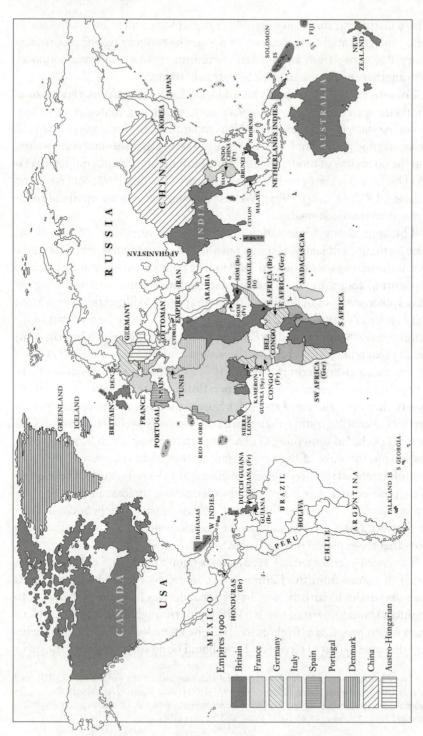

FIG. 1.1 The political map of the world, 1900

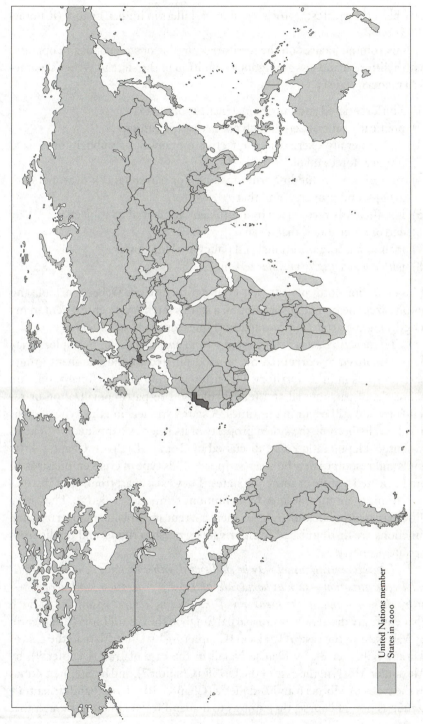

FIG. 1.2 The political map of the world, 2000

United Nations member
States in 2000

have been the greatest terrorists and mass-killers in human history (Rummel 1997 (1994)).

This volume focuses on the territorial variable of statehood, and operates with a different and less ambiguous definition of the state to Weber's, namely: a modern state is

(1) a differentiated and impersonal institution that is
(2) politically centralized though not necessarily unitary;
(3) that generally exercises an effective monopoly of publicly organized physical force and of
(4) authoritatively binding rule-making (or sovereignty) over persons, groups, and property; and that
(5) is sufficiently recognized by a sufficient number of its subjects,
(6) and of other states, that it can
(7) maintain its organizational and policy-making powers
(8) *within a potentially variable territory*.

This definition both corrects well-known difficulties in Weber's formula and emphasizes the potential variation in a state's territory. Each element in my lengthy eight-part definition suggests typical crises of statehood.

1. *A state may cease to be differentiated and impersonal*. For example, it may be personalized or corrupted by, or subordinated to, the dominant group, party, or person in its territory. De-differentiation and personalization are hallmarks of patrimonial and feudal rule, and re-patrimonialization or re-feudalization still occur in our times. A state experiencing this type of crisis may literally become the stolen property of its ruler, as happened in General Mobutu's kleptocratic Zaïre, discussed by Tom Callaghy in Chapter 4. Its lands and resources may be asset-stripped. This type of crisis emphasizes an oft-neglected feature of authentic states. They exist apart from, or in abstraction from, their current and, by definition, temporary ruler(s). They have differentiated public offices from their current incumbents. Governmental functions are distinguished from private ownership rights, and public from private property.

2. *A state's centralization may be challenged, either by those demanding radical decentralization—such as home rule, autonomy, federation, confederation— or by those demanding the break-up of the existing centre*. Examples of such challenges are discussed by Gurharpal Singh in the case of India (Chapter 5), by Vali Nasr in the case of Pakistan (Chapter 6), by Ümit Cizre in the case of Turkey (Chapter 8), by Denise Natali in the case of Iraq (Chapter 9), by Alexander Motyl in the case of the USSR (Chapter 7), and by Stephen Zunes in the cases of Morocco and Indonesia (Chapter 10). To demand decentralization is not, of course, the same as to demand fragmentation, though that

accusation is often made. To demand the break-up of the existing centre is most often not to prescribe a 'centreless' society, but rather to prefer at least two different centres with fully centralized state capacities.

3. *A state's sovereignty may be challenged.* Sovereignty, since the times of Bodin, Grotius, and Hobbes, the possession of supreme, hierarchical, integrated, and implicitly homogeneous law-making authority within a territory, has been seen as *the* mark of statehood, that which distinguished the new states of Europe from the Papacy and Holy Roman Empire (Bodin 1992 (1583); Hobbes 1968 (1651)).[2] A challenge to a state's sovereignty may be internally made by regionally, ethnically, religiously, or class-based organizations. Singh's analysis of contemporary India, Nasr's audit of Pakistan, Cizre's appraisal of Turkey, Natali's exploration of Iraq, Motyl's inspection of the former Soviet states, and Zunes's comparative evaluation of Morocco and Indonesia provide samples of the first three challenges. The contesting of a state's sovereignty may, however, derive externally, from other states, especially from 'great powers'. Iraq and Serbia experienced aerial pulverization, of disputed accuracy, at the hands of the USA and its allies in the 1990s. The challenge to a state's sovereignty may come from inter-statal organizations, such as the UN, which has not recognized Moroccan sovereignty in Western Sahara, did not recognize Indonesian sovereignty in East Timor, and has not recognized Israeli sovereignty over the West Bank and Gaza. External challenges may also derive from confederal organizations with federalist ambitions, such as the challenges posed by the court of the European Union to its member-states' traditional prerogatives. Internal and external challenges to sovereignty normally have territorial implications, but caveats must be entered: increases in the porosity of borders, much emphasized by globalization theorists, may not be challenges to sovereignty, for example, they may merely mark increases in legally authorized trade or immigration.

4. *A state's monopoly of organized physical force may be challenged.* This feature of the state was the one Weber's definition emphasized. The modern European state developed out of the successful struggle of absolutist rulers to disarm feudal nobilities, to de-fortify and demilitarize 'private' aristocratic military power, to crush pirates, and to dispense with or decommission mercenaries (Thomson 1994). Likewise in their encounters with segmentary societies, European empires and their post-colonial successors have sought to break the self-reliant military autonomy of tribes without rulers, especially of nomads. Internally, challenges to a state's monopoly of organized physical force may now be posed by paramilitaries, guerrillas, mafiosi, and

[2] Lucid and fascinating discussions of sovereignty and positive law-making in defining the state and politics exist in the German language jurisprudence of Hermann Heller, Carl Schmitt, and Hans Kelsen (Heller 1927; Heller and Niemeyer 1961; Schmitt 1985; Kelsen 1945).

'militiamen', as has been the case with the toppling of Mobutu's Zaïre (Chapter 4), the Kashmiri Intifada and Sikh revolt against the Indian state (Chapter 5), the Baluchis intermittent campaigns in Pakistan (Chapter 6), the PKK's challenge to Turkey (Chapter 8), multiple Kurdish and Shi'ite challenges to Iraq (Chapter 9), the Chechens' and Dagens' insurrections against the Russian federation (Chapter 7), and Palestinian paramilitary activities in Jordan (Chapter 11) and Lebanon (Chapter 12). Externally such challenges may take the direct form of invading armies, navies, and air forces, as has been the case with Zaïre (Chapter 4), Iraq (Chapter 9), in India's aiding and abetting of the partitioning of Pakistan in 1971 (Chapters 5 and 6), and Turkey's partition of Cyprus. Alternatively, assorted paramilitaries may operate with external assistance in cross-border incursions, as has happened in Kashmir (Chapter 5), and in Kurdish areas of Turkey (Chapter 8).

5. and 6. *A state may cease to be recognized.* Recognition lies at the heart of modern conceptions of the corporate identity of states (Ringmar 1996). The motivation to recognize a state by its own citizens may range from prudent acceptance to full-hearted legitimacy. Recognition of a state by its peers, other states, is, however, critical to state building and survival. De-recognition may happen internally, as occurred with Zaïre (Chapter 4) and, most remarkably, in the power-deflation of the Soviet Union (Chapter 7). It may happen externally, as indeed also happened with Zaïre and the Soviet Union. There are, of course, anomalous cases where states are not internally recognized but continue to be territorially externally recognized, for example no other state may formally dispute the territorial boundaries of the relevant collapsed state (Jackson 1990). Somalia is perhaps the exemplary case (Lewis *et al.* 1995), Chad may be another.[3] The opposite anomaly also occurs: 'states' may be internally recognized but not externally recognized. This may prove to be the case with Kosovo, and Somaliland.

7. *A state's policy-making powers within its territorial domain, especially its fiscal extractive capacities and steering abilities, may be constantly challenged and renegotiated by non-state agents, and by other states.* States have central governments, and usually they have local governments. These governments and their policy-making powers are subject to a range of internal and external constraints. The supposition that governments are losing their political capacities to be autonomous policy-makers at home was the stock-in-trade of some theorists of state crises in political science and sociology in the 1960s and 1970s (Dunleavy and O'Leary 1987). In the 1990s emphasis was placed on the idea that governments have increasingly become external economic

---

[3] States may respect the recognition of the borders of collapsed states. Other agencies are not so law-abiding. Large-scale waste-dumping and violations of fishing and other maritime rights occur off the coast of Somalia.

and social policy-takers rather than policy-makers because of the impact of globalization and the development of the institutions of global governance (Held 1991; Held and McGrew 1993).

8. *A state's territory and its territorial governance may be challenged, that is demanded, invaded, endangered, or protested by a range of agents.* Secessionists or anti-colonial movements are major agencies in this respect: the Kosovo Liberation Army, for example, seeks Kosovo's full exit from the rump Yugoslavia. Multiple potential secessionists exist in the Democratic Republic of the Congo (Chapter 4); some Kurds in Iran, Turkey (Chapter 8), and Iraq (Chapter 9) want to secede from their respective states; most Kashmiri Muslims wish to break away from the Indian Union (Chapter 5); and the peoples mobilized by the Polisario and by Fretilin devoutly wish, or wished, to be free from the enthusiasts for a Greater Morocco and a Greater Indonesia (Chapter 10). Conquerors are obvious major challengers to settled borders: the Moroccan and Indonesian invasions of newly independent polities, left vulnerable by the departing Spanish and Portuguese empires (Chapter 10), showed that this mode of up-sizing has not gone out of fashion. The destabilizing consequences of imperial overreach is an ancient topic in political reflection. Established political institutions, it is often argued, may be incapable of managing newly conquered lands: famously claimed of Republican Rome (Syme 1974 (1939)), some think it true of Israel's expansion into what was Jordanian territory in 1967.

Theories of the state in the second half of the twentieth century varied considerably in the emphases and explanations they gave to these eight possible crises of statehood. During the cold war the overwhelming focus of political science and political sociology in liberal democracies was on legitimacy, fiscal, 'governance', or 'steering' crises—what I have labelled type 7 crises. This was as true of rational choice as of pluralist, Marxist, and élite theorists. In international relations, by contrast, the dominant focus was upon external incursions on sovereignty and policy-making autonomy, particularly in the domains of military security and of international political economy. With the exceptions of the Marxists' emphases on class struggle, and the realists' concern for the stability of the formal and informal Soviet and American empires, the other feasible crises of statehood implied in some of the elements of our definition attracted much less intellectual interest.

This disciplinary intellectual myopia had several sources. The stability occasioned by the apparent freezing of state borders after the blood-soaked 'tidying-up' at the end of World War II, and the generally territorially ordered pattern of decolonization of the European empires that followed in its wake, were important sources of intellectual rigidity (Mayall 1990). Just as absolutism had acted as the incubator for European nation-state formation, so it appeared that European empire-building had acted as the incubator for new post-colonial states. Another source was the apparent linkage of all domestic conflicts and civil wars to the wider theatre of the Cold War between Leninist communism and democratic capitalism (Halliday 1986 (1983)). But these exculpatory sources no longer obtain, and political scientists, especially in comparative politics and international relations, must now pay much greater attention to the other crises of statehood, especially those that affect the state's territorial configuration. This volume reflects this shift and wishes to consolidate it.

Any general theory of 'right-sizing' the state must address two interrelated questions.

1. *What factors, from the perspective of central governing élites, govern the right-sizing of the state's domestic and external territorial shape?* A general theory must account for the broad incentives that have affected the territorial goals of managers of states and cognate political organizations, such as kingdoms, empires, and city-states, throughout the ages (see Chapter 2). These incentives will determine whether state officials prefer to expand, maintain, or contract their external frontiers or borders—an important distinction—or to merge them with others. The incentives which affect the internal spatial configurations of political institutions must also be identified.

2. *Which factors govern the right size of the state's despotic (coercive) and infrastructural (policy-making, extractive, allocative, and distributive) powers?*[4] Any general theory must account for the (broad) incentives that affect political élites', and their challengers', views and actions on the right domestic share, weight, and capacity of central political institutions compared with other domestic political and civil institutions.

The chapter which follows, and most of the essays in this volume, work on the first agenda—on the external and internal territorial shape of the state, particularly on its external shape—but they do not entirely neglect the second agenda, not least because its concerns can rarely be isolated from the former. Indeed the language of 'reshaping' the state, as opposed to its 'right-sizing', is used by most contributors to distinguish the second agenda from the first. By *reshaping* they refer both to the *internal* transformation of states' territorial jurisdictions and competencies, *and* the size, shape, weight, and capacity of central and local governmental institutions. 'Reshaping' strategies, such as expanding or contracting central governmental capacities, or changing from an acceptance of consociation to drive for integration, may be

---

[4] The distinction is Michael Mann's (Mann 1984).

preferred to the five 'right-sizing' options outlined above; but they may, of course, also be combined with them.

The concentration of most of our contributors on the first agenda is justified because most contemporary theories of the modern state have primarily focused on how autonomous, resourceful, and powerful central political institutions are, and should be (e.g. Alford 1975; Alford and Friedland 1985; Dunleavy and O'Leary 1987; Hall 1986a, b; Hall and Ikenberry 1989; Mann 1984, 1986, 1993). By contrast, as Ian Lustick has observed, the external territorial demarcation of states has not been explored in anything like the same depth, or with the same degree of comparative analysis (Lustick 1985, 1987, 1993, 1995, 1996). The same is true of the internal borders of states. These may matter as much as external borders: internal borders delimit areas of jurisdiction, as any citizen of a federation or confederation knows, and they may be autonomous 'states-in-waiting'. This neglect of the territorial dimension of statehood in recent political science and sociology does not mean, of course, that we are in uncharted intellectual waters. As Oren Yiftachel reminds us in Chapter 12, political geographers have long insisted that the territoriality of states has its own causal importance and consequences, and there are traditions in public administration (e.g. Smith 1985) and in diplomatic history of examining the governance of territory and the rise and fall of empires and great powers (e.g. Kennedy 1988). These literatures deserve greater attention within political science in the view of the contributors to this volume, but we also think they may be improved, but whether we do so is not for us to judge.

This book contributes, we hope, to correcting the complacent neglect of the territorial dimension of statehood in recent theories and applications of political science, and in the adjacent fields of political history and political sociology. The contributors assume that territory is a variable, not a given; something contested and contestable, rather than something natural. Borders can be changed both internally and externally; and indeed should sometimes be changed, both internally and externally. We have not, however, written a charter for secessionists or, by contrast, for unionists; nor have we sought to provide a platform for territorial 'stabilitarians' or 'libertarians', or for 'federalists' or 'unitarians'—though, no doubt, some of our arguments will be read in this manner. What follows is an analysis of the different status and salience that territories have had for political rulers and masses through time, in the stages of world-history, in inter-national/inter-state systems, and especially in our times (Chapter 2). Collectively we have framed our accounts of nationalism within a broadly Gellnerian prism, and we have sought to employ a common vocabulary. In the work of Ian Lustick we have found one framework through which the contemporary dynamics of state contraction and expansion may be profitably analysed. Neither he nor the rest of us think that his are the last words on the subject, and in the concluding chapter Lustick responds to the difficulties and opportunities occasioned by his and our arguments. The case studies, from Chapters 4 through to 12, focus largely on Africa, South and South East Asia, the Middle East, and the Commonwealth of Independent States. But we do not think that our discussions only have pertinence in the lands beyond the European Union and the USA. Far from it. Centre-stage in what follows are the relationships between nationalized and nationalizing publics and the borders of states. These are features of our planet's political systems; they are not civilizational or regional preoccupations, even if there may be different civilizational or regional temporalities. We are confident, if that is the right word, that the 'right-sizing', 'right-shaping' and the 'right-peopling' of states are not matters that will go away in our lifetimes, or yours. The politics of moving borders fascinates not just because borders move, but because they move our contemporaries, and our selves, to passionate intensities and bloody antagonisms that demand our rational and morally constructive attention.

REFERENCES

Alford, Robert. (1975). Paradigms of Relations between State and Society. In Lindberg, Leon, Alford, Robert, Crouch, Colin, and Offe, Claus (eds.), *Stress and Contradiction in Modern Capitalism: Public Policy and the Theory of State.* Lexington, MA: Lexington Books.

—— and Friedland, Roger. (1985). *Powers of Theory: Capitalism, the State and Democracy.* Cambridge: Cambridge University Press.

Baldwin, Thomas. (1992). The Territorial State. In Gross, Hyman, and Harrison, Ross (eds.), *Jurisprudence: Cambridge Essays.* 207–30. Oxford: Clarendon Press.

Bodin, Jean. (1992) (1583)). *On Sovereignty.* Cambridge: Cambridge University Press.

Dunleavy, Patrick, and O'Leary, Brendan. (1987). *Theories of the State: The Politics of Liberal Democracy.* London and New York, NY: Macmillan and Meredith Press.

Finer, Samuel E. (1974). State-building, State Boundaries and Border Control. *Social Science Information.* 13(4–5): 79–126.

—— (1997a). *The History of Government. Vol. I: Ancient Monarchies and Empires.* I Oxford: Oxford University Press.

—— (1997b). *The History of Government. Vol. II: The Intermediate Ages.* II Oxford: Oxford University Press.

—— (1997c). *The History of Government. Vol. III: Empires, Monarchies and the Modern State.* III Oxford: Oxford University Press.

—— (1975). State and Nation Building in Europe: the Role of the Military. In Tilly, Charles (ed.), *The Formation of National States in Western Europe*. Princeton, NJ: Princeton University Press.

Gellner, Ernest. (1997). *Nationalism*. London: Weidenfeld and Nicolson.

Gottmann, Jean. (1973). *The Significance of Territory*. Charlottesville, VA: University of Virginia Press.

—— (1975). The Evolution of the Concept of Territory. *Social Science Information*. 14(3/4): 29–47.

Hall, John A. (1986a). *Powers and Liberties: the Causes and Consequences of the Rise of the West*. Harmondsworth: Penguin.

—— (ed.) (1986b). *States in History*. Oxford: Basil Blackwell.

—— and Ikenberry, G. John. (1989). *The State*. Minneapolis, MN: University of Minnesota Press.

Halliday, Fred. (1986 (1983)). *The Making of the Second Cold War*. London: Verso.

Held, David. (1991). Democracy, the Nation State and the Global System. In Held, David (ed.), *Political Theory Today*. Oxford: Polity.

—— and McGrew, Anthony. (1993). Globalisation and the Liberal Democratic State. *Government and Opposition*. 26(2): 261.

Heller, Hermann. (1927). *Die Souveränität, ein Beitrag zur Theorie des Staats- und Völkerrechts*. (Max-Planck Institut für Ausländisches Offentliches Recht und Völkerrecht, Heidelberg. Beitrag, etc. Heft 4.)

—— and Niemeyer, Gerhart. (1961). *Staatslehre*. 2., unveränderte, Aufl. Leiden: A. W. Sijthoff.

Hobbes, Thomas. (1968 (1651)). *Leviathan*. Penguin English Library. Harmondsworth: Penguin.

Jackson, Robert H. (1990). *Quasi-States: Sovereignty, International Relations, and the Third World*. Cambridge: Cambridge University Press.

Kelsen, Hans. (1945). *General Theory of Law and the State*. New York, NY: Russell and Russell.

Kennedy, Paul. (1988). *The Rise and Fall of the Great Powers: Economic Change and Military Conflict from 1500 to 2000*. London: Unwin Hyman.

Kristoff, Ladis. (1959). The Nature of Frontiers and Boundaries. *Annals of the Association of American Geographers*. 49: 269–82.

Lewis, Ioan, Mayall, James, Barker, John, Brett, Teddy, Dawson, Peter, McAuslan, Patrick, O'Leary, Brendan, and Von Hippel, Karin. London School of Economics and Political Science (1995). *A Study of Decentralised Political Structures for Somalia: A Menu of Options*. London: European Union.

Lustick, Ian. (1985). *State-Building Failure in British Ireland and French Algeria*. Berkeley, CA: University of California Press.

—— (1987). Israeli State-Building in the West Bank and Gaza Strip: Theory and Practice. *International Organisation*. 41(1): 151–71.

—— (1991). *Unsettled States, Disputed Lands: Britain and Ireland, France and Algeria, Israel and the West Bank-Gaza*. Ithaca, NY: Cornell University Press.

Lustick, Ian. (1995). What Gives a People Rights to a Land? *Queen's Quarterly*. 102(1): 53–68.

——— (1996). Hegemonic Beliefs and Territorial Rights. *International Journal of Intercultural Relations*. 20: 479–92.

Mann, Michael. (1984). The Autonomous Power of the State: Its Origins, Mechanisms and Results. *European Journal of Sociology*. 25(2): 185–213.

——— (1986). *The Sources of Social Power: A History of Power from the Beginning until A.D. 1760. I* Cambridge: Cambridge University Press.

——— (1993). *The Sources of Social Power: The Rise of Classes and Nation States 1760–1914. II* Cambridge: Cambridge University Press.

Mayall, James. (1990). *Nationalism and International Society*. Cambridge: Cambridge University Press.

McGarry, John, and O'Leary, Brendan (eds.). (1993). *The Politics of Ethnic Conflict Regulation: Case Studies of Protracted Ethnic Conflicts*. London and New York, NY: Routledge.

Murphy, Alexander B. (1996). The Sovereign State System as Political-Territorial Ideal: Historical and Contemporary Considerations. In Biersteker, Thomas J., and Weber, Cynthia (eds.), *State Sovereignty as Social Construct*. 81–120. Cambridge: Cambridge University Press.

O'Leary, Brendan. (1995). Regulating Nations and Ethnic Communities. In Breton, Albert, Galeotti, Gianluigi, Salmon, Pierre, and Wintrobe, Ronald (eds.), *Nationalism and Rationality*. 245–89. Cambridge: Cambridge University Press.

Ringmar, Erik. (1996). *Identity, Interest and Action: A Cultural Explanation of Sweden's Intervention in the Thirty Years War*. Cambridge: Cambridge University Press.

Rummell, Rudolph J. (1997 (1994)). *Death by Government*. London and New York, NY: Transaction Publishers.

Sack, Robert. (1986). *Human Territoriality: Its Theory and History*. Cambridge: Cambridge University Press.

Schmitt, Carl. (1985). *Political Theology: Four Chapters on the Concept of Sovereignty*. Cambridge, MA: MIT Press.

Smith, Brian C. (1985). *Decentralization: The Territorial Dimension of the State*. London: Allen & Unwin.

Syme, Ronald. (1974 (1939)). *The Roman Revolution*. Oxford: Oxford University Press.

Taylor, Peter J. (1994). The State as a Container: Territoriality in the Modern World-System. *Progress in Human Geography*. 18(2): 151–62.

Thomson, Janice E. (1994). *Mercenaries, Pirates and Sovereigns: State-Building, and Extraterritorial Violence in Early Modern Europe*. Princeton, NH: Princeton University Press.

Tilly, Charles. (1992 (1990)). *Coercion, Capital and European States, A.D. 990–1992*. Oxford and Cambridge, MA: Basil Blackwell.

——— (ed.) (1975). *The Formation of National States in Western Europe*. Princeton, NJ: Princeton University Press.

Weber, Max. (1977 (1918)). Politics as a Vocation. In Gerth, Hans H., and Mills, C. Wright (eds.), *From Max Weber: Essays in Sociology*. 77–128. London: Routledge.

2

The Elements of Right-Sizing and Right-Peopling the State

Brendan O'Leary

> As you know it is always the powerful who dictate what the borders will be, never the weak. Thus we must be powerful.
>
> Slobodan Milosevic, speaking to the Serbian
Parliament in April 1991 (cited in Cigar 1995: 42).

> This era does not reward people who struggle in vain to redraw borders with blood.
>
> President William Jefferson Clinton, speaking in Pakistan, March 2000
(cited in *Economist* Editorial 2000: 18).

States are, of course, more than territories with borders. They also encapsulate peoples, be they citizens, subjects, immigrants, refugees, or metics. And the relationships between borders and peoples are profoundly interdependent. 'Right-Sizing' and 'right-peopling' may be the two most important imperatives of successful state-builders and state-managers. It makes sense therefore to locate the general elements of a broad theory of right-sizing the state within social and political frameworks that address

(1) the distinctiveness of borders in our modern world;
(2) the pivotal nature of nationality and ethnicity which makes public officials deeply concerned with 'right-peopling' their states; and
(3) territorial expansion, maintenance, and contraction which oblige public officials to consider 'right-sizing', if only tacitly.

I would like to thank Tom Callaghy, Ian Lustick, John A. Hall, David Held, John McGarry, and Margaret Moore, and all the contributors to this volume, for their comments on a previous draft of this chapter. They can be held culpable for whatever merits it has.

These elements can be found respectively in the work of Ernest Gellner, in the literature on national and ethnic conflict regulation, and in the work of Ian Lustick.

The Distinctiveness of our States and our World

Three major stages in human history are identified in Gellner's philosophy of history, namely *foragia*, *agraria*, and *industria*, and two episodic revolutionary transformations, namely the *neolithic* and the *industrial* (Gellner 1964, 1983, 1988a, b). Each stage has characteristic forms of production, coercion, and cognition. The three stages apply to world-history as a whole because not every historic human collectivity has been through all three. Perhaps hundreds of thousands of human collectivities were wiped out in foragia—by nature, by their rivals, or, later on, by agrarians and industrials. Likewise perhaps thousands were destroyed in agraria—by nature, by their rivals, or, later on, by industrials. Industrial societies are much less numerous than foragian or agrarian entities, and are not likely ever to number exponentially more than presently exist. But industria is inexorably absorbing, or destroying, the last remnants of foragia and agraria. This triadic conception of history has obvious implications for theories of the state, their peoples, their sizes, and their external and internal territorial markings.

Foragia

Foragia is a state-free zone, both in space and time. Hunters and gatherers and nomads do not require statal organization, though nomads can be state-makers. Foragers are acephalous anarchists and are egalitarian in a brutal if not always Hobbesian way; arbitration is performed by holy men rather than governors (Gellner 1969). Foragers are not easily taxed; their mobility and lack of fixed properties make them free. Foraging collectors are, at least potentially, pacific; nomads, however, are more likely to be thieves and thugs. In a solely foragian world nomads recognize prey and roam through landscapes, but they do not have political borders. Physical or weather zones that affect the consumption of their herds, by contrast, are of major importance. Likewise, hunters and gatherers slash, burn, and roam, but do not settle permanently, and do not have territories, or borders in our senses—though they may confine their slashing, burning, and roaming to specific 'natural' locations. Foragers, in short, do not 'right-size' because they have no states, though they have to right-size their populations, or nature will do that task for them in her characteristically maternal way. The political theory of the

Stone Age demonstrates in short that we are not genetically given to organizing ourselves through sovereign political borders. Given the age of the human species, we are, most likely, genetically adapted to being hunters, opportunistic foragers, and shepherds. We have no trans-historical 'territorial imperative'.

Agraria

Agraria by contrast, has statal characteristics. Stationary populations formed, and reformed, throughout the post-neolithic millennia. 'Caging theory' synthesizes the perspectives of those who see the origins of the state in conquest, and those who see its origins in the defence of property (O'Leary 1989: 309–16). The first victims of the state were trapped when clusters of population developed beside great rivers—made possible by alluvial agriculture. Their comparative wealth permitted incipient urbanization, but made them vulnerable to conquest by militarized nomads, who could control them and extract resources from them, confident that their subjects could, or would, no longer return to the wild.[1] A complementary tale suggests that the incipient cities, aware of the annual pillages, regular sacks, and incessant rapes of the nomads, learned to defend themselves, and thereby invented rudimentary statal forms.

The major form of production, agriculture, creates fixed investment in fertile land that can be captured. The state begins, so to speak, as a granary rather than as a slaughterhouse. The exemplary political form of agraria, what Gellner termed the 'agro-literate empire', is significantly assisted by its most important cognitive techniques, writing and counting, monopolized by castes of specialists. Agraria is in this respect, and many others, profoundly inegalitarian; and made so by the scarce surplus of extractable resources, and by the pervasive lack of (social) cognitive power on the part of most of its populations. It is typically severely caste-ridden: people are hunted and gathered, shepherded and 'domesticated', ranked and sorted, generally tied to the land by force and dependency, and, not least, by ignorance. Stocks in slavery and serfdom do well. Social mobility, horizontal and vertical, is extremely limited.

The typical agro-literate empire had external frontiers, not borders in our sense, and perpetually faced the question of 'right-locating' those frontiers. Its most sharply delineated political borders were internal: structured by past conquests and fiscal imperatives. An empire was characteristically based on a

---

[1] The *Book of Genesis*, which gets most big things wrong, has Cain, 'a tiller of the ground', killing Abel 'a keeper of sheep'. It is more likely that the transition from foragia to agraria saw Abel and his fellow nomads form states through 'shepherding' the Cains and putting them to work.

dualist form, the basis of the distinction between 'high' and 'low' politics. A 'core' or 'court' made claims to numerous farms, estates, and cities—in which craftsmen lived and between which merchants roamed. It did so through intermediaries, tax-farmers, and officials, while leaving the multiple peripheries—subjects, and their subjects—to various forms of limited self-government. The core, through its generally thieving intermediaries, extracted from these peripheries whatever share of rents, tributes, and taxes it could.

Agraria was the time of the thugs who called themselves the best: nobles, or aristocrats. They were by training, maximally predatory, their rapacity limited only by four general social constraints.

1. The first was set by the limits to fiscal or tributary extraction. Beyond certain thresholds peasants, serfs, and slaves could not deliver surpluses to lords and overlords without counter-productive demographic attrition, colloquially known as death, or mass flight. Beyond another threshold, urban merchants and craftsmen migrated, if they could, to less inhospitable empires, or they abandoned their precarious occupations and returned to the land, if they could. Rational emperors controlled the rapacious propensities of their intermediaries—fleecing their subjects in ways that encouraged them to believe that being a sheep was not so bad after all. It was not for nothing that mercantilists thought that people were wealth, and that mercantilist rulers sought to limit, and indeed forbid, emigration.[2] In agraria right-peopling was about having a high volume human herd.

2. The second limit was set by military logistics. The agro-literate empire found the maintenance and use of standing armies and navies enormously costly: they comprised the overwhelmingly largest component of the imperial 'budget' (Mann 1984). The scope of imperial power was doubly circumscribed by limits to fiscal extraction to sustain its military prowess, and by the potentially ruinous consequences of imperial overreach (Kennedy 1988).

3. The third was 'civilizational'. An agro-literate empire, which began as a city-state, or from the fusion of nomadic conquerors with city-states, found it profitable, and indeed imperative, to expand and conquer all the urban literates and extractable surplus-producing agrarians that lay within the range of its military capacity. It had to expand or die at the hands of its rivals, but there was a limit to expansion. It was rational to expand until the empire was entirely surrounded by foragers and nomads—some of which, over time, were progressively acculturated, assimilated, or in a word, civilized. The marchlands, where the militarized barbarian nomads roamed, marked the

---

[2] An emigration tax, 'Free or Departure Money', was imposed on the estates of would be migrants from Germany until the early nineteenth century (Enzensberger 1990: 119).

limits to rational conquest and incorporation. No stable and reliable taxation could be garnered from the marchlands; and incorporating them threatened 'imperial overreach'.

4. The last constraint was normative. Though the authenticity and efficacy of the taboos and restraints that world-religions placed upon rulers varied across time, space, and individuals, they were not null, and partially inhibited the ambitions of kings and emperors, embedding tacit wisdom about the limits of sustainable rule, and telling them which lands could be justly conquered, and which peoples justly enslaved or killed.

The 'laws of motion' of the agro-literate empire suggested a logic of right-shaping the imperial apparatus and right-locating the imperial frontiers. Autonomy to imperial officials, tax-farmers, or feudal aristocrats had to be circumscribed, to prevent loss of fiscal resources and to inhibit fiscal rebellions, and not least to constrain the incipient emergence of rival courts. The extractors of resources from fiscal units, which sometimes had sharply delimited borders, were rotated, or required to have their demesnes regularly re-approved; or were subjected to overlapping and competitive jurisdictions, likely to be carved out under weak courts.

Frontiers, by contrast, had to be organized according to military and civilizational priorities.[3] Immediately contiguous rival agrarian empires had to be conquered, incorporated or destroyed; if not, they would do it to you. *Carthago delenda est*, that was Scipio and the prophets of agraria. Frontiers had to be defended 'in depth', not as neat territorial lines. Physical barriers that blocked entry, such as daunting mountains, rivers, swamps, and deserts, were excellent protections. In this sense the frontiers of agraria were 'natural'—that is, natural to agraria. They were pitched at the interface with barbarians who generally continued to dwell and roam in the aforementioned mountains, rivers, swamps, and deserts. If necessary, walls and fortifications were built to provide surveillance and to engage in punishment-raids (massacres) on those nomads who lay within inexpensive striking-range. Military governors in frontier-regions had to be family court-members, or were regularly redeployed to prevent them acquiring imperial ambitions above their station. Precious resources were not wasted in attempting to subdue inaccessible foragians.

The governing imperatives of right-shaping and right-sizing the agro-literate empire were therefore straightforward:

---

[3] The late Samuel Finer argued that 'In Britain we call a hard line, which marks out sovereign territory, a frontier; we call a blurred, fluctuating, and debatable area a border (the Latin *limes*). The Americans use the terms in exactly the reverse sense' (1997: 10). This has not been my experience of English usage across both sides of the Atlantic, but usage here will be what Finer terms American, or rather Irish and American.

(1) to expand courtly extractive capacity to the limits of fiscal, military, and civilizational possibilities; and

(2) to divide and rule, or regularly restructure the imperial apparatus, especially its tax-extractors and generals, if only to prevent their vampire-like thirsts from leaving insufficient blood-supplies for the court.[4]

What is striking to modern, or industrial, eyes is that the agro-literate empire, Roman or otherwise, did not require the governed to be co-cultural with the governors. The 'right people', apart from those at the court, did not require any particular cultural characteristics, other than being agrarians. The culturally homogeneous empire, and conversely, the culture which possessed its own territorial kingdom co-extensive with that of its influence, were seldom found in agraria. On the contrary, the cultural differentiation of diverse layers of the population, including the rulers, was highly functional for the imperial rulers, and, according to Gellner, was seldom resented and often warmly approved—if only by the diverse scribes who worked for the ruler(s). The agro-literate empire looked like a painting by Kokoschka, a riot of diverse points of colour (Gellner 1983: 139). Though the picture as a whole has a pattern, in its details it is not easy to see it. The peripheries are multiple, various, culturally heterogeneous: only the imperial court and its frontiers give overarching meaning to the whole.

Industria vs. Agraria

Industria differs radically from agraria. Its peoples have escaped the Malthusian trap. Its most fortunate—liberal democratic welfare capitalist—

---

[4] *The Grand Strategy of the Roman Empire* is a superb exposition of the imperatives facing the exemplary agro-literate empire in European history (Luttwak 1999 (1976)). Luttwak identifies three systems of Roman imperial security strategy: for the periods of expansionism, territorial stabilization and sheer survival respectively. Each 'integrated diplomacy, military force, road networks, and fortifications to serve a common objective' (ibid. 4) The initial Julio-Claudian system, like its successors, was based on a careful economy of force. There was no demarcated imperial frontier and no system of fixed frontier defences; nor were the legions housed in permanent fortresses. The legions were not deployed to defend the adjacent ground but rather 'to serve as mobile striking forces' (ibid. 18). 'There was no *limes*, in its later sense of a fortified and guarded border': [the word] described a route of penetration cut through hostile territory rather than a 'horizontal' frontier (ibid. 19). In short, the first grand strategy involved the absence of perimeter defence. Within a zone of direct control disposable and concentrated forces were available for wars of conquest and the intimidation or 'suasion' of clients. Beyond this core was a zone of client states that were responsible for their own security, and beyond them (stateless) client tribes—and in these sectors Roman diplomacy operated vigilantly. In its second phase of strategic development the Roman Empire came to resemble the modern state—in its territoriality, in the incorporation of the client states and tribes within the zone of direct Roman governance, and in the evolution of a permanent, 'scientific' frontier defence, maintained through a network of fortifications. Had Rome been wholly successful it may have become the first modern state—it is no accident that the state-builders of early modern Europe did so within its long cultural and institutional shadow (Anderson 1974).

peoples continue to experience sustained economic growth across generations, cumulative and positive-sum growth. Wealth no longer lies primarily in land or landed serfs, slaves, and debtors. Wealth is capital, produced in goods and services—increasingly in weightless and invisible media—produced by literate and numerate urban peoples, engaged in an exceedingly complex division of labour. These peoples are, however, actually or latently, culturally homogenized. To Gellner they resemble a painting by Modigliani: with sharp blunt artificial lines, and with relatively rare clashes of colours and blurring of lines (ibid. 139–40). They have modern borders, though the lines are generally not created by artists but rather by great powers, genocidal officials, ethnic cleansers, and coercive assimilationists. Occasionally treaties that reflect authentic agreements created them. In fact, treaties on maritime borders are the most Modigliani-like, blunt, artificial lines, created with rational zig-zags suited for the granting of rectangular oil and mineral exploration rights.

Agrarian societies too had complicated divisions of labour but, by comparison, they had little cultural homogeneity. Agrarians expressed and recognized their identities in their social status. They were not co-nationals. Co-nationality, at least in Gellner's theory, requires the egalitarianism of industria. A nationality must not only be conscious of itself, but convinced that the ethnic boundary which separates itself from others ought to be a political one—that the boundaries of nationality should also be the borders of the state or a political unit, and, above all, that at least some of the rulers of the state should be of the same nationality as the ruled. Foreigners are generally unwelcome—though calibrated immigration programmes are possible and widespread—especially as rulers.

So, industria is both statal and national. The officials of the successful industrial state are infrastructural managers and maintenance engineers, and may be (should be) much less rapacious predators than their agro-literate imperial predecessors; and this despite the fact that they have much more potential power. The industrial state, because of the technology it can deploy or command, is potentially more despotic, pervasive, brutal, and appalling than any of its agrarian predecessors, and it has displayed these traits many times in the century just gone,[5] its most politically and economically

---

[5] No barbarians, not even Genghis Khan and his hordes, are guilty of the magnitude of mass murder of modern state-killers. The genocidal rulers (and their collaborators) of Nazi Germany, of late Ottoman Turkey, of modern Burundi and Rwanda, and the politicidal Marxist-Leninist rulers of the USSR, the Balkans, China, Korea, and the Horn of Africa are 'democidal' killers, mass murderers of peoples on a historically unprecedented scale (Rummel 1997 (1994)). Rummel names the Soviet Union, Communist China, Nazi Germany, and the Kuomintang Chinese regime as 'dekamegamurderers', and describes two of the states discussed in this book—Turkey, Chapter 8, and Pakistan, Chapter 9—as amongst the 'lesser megamurderers'.

successful exemplars succeed because they are not merely the instruments of rapacious élites. In industria a high-quality, high-productivity set of culturally homogenized thoroughbreds is preferred by rational rulers to the mass herd of agraria.

Industria is statal in a much sharper territorial way than the loose agglomerates and dual polities of agraria. Modern states have borders—precise cartographically represented lines, entrenched in bilateral and multilateral treaties, which specifically demarcate their territories from those of other states. Sometimes these cartographic statements are physically expressed in electric fences and walls, but they are more often signified by border posts and patrols on land, at sea, and in the air. By contrast, pre-modern or pre-statal systems had 'frontiers', that is, their cores were surrounded by military zones in which they disputed and faced the enemy. Frontiers were zones of conflict rather than demarcated lines or borders. They were not tightly specified. Even where Roman and Chinese emperors built walls these represented military bases rather than strict borders; they sought, successfully, to exercise manifest power as well as influence well beyond the walls manned by their armies.[6]

The contrast between an ideal typical modern state and an agro-literate empire is immediate and striking: in the modern state the economic, administrative, and internal military domains of the state are, in principle, identical. Within its well-bordered territory the grip of the state, and its extractive and policy-making agencies, is presumptively of equal and uniform capacity; and there is, in principle, no differentiation between an inner and outer military frontier. Sovereignty is territorially uniform; no zones are recognized in which state-sanctioned law does not apply: 'no go' zones are an abomination. That is what is meant when it is said that a state's internal sovereignty is recognized.

It is not essential that the modern state's territory be a single, contiguous geographical land mass, though this option is preferred by nationalist image-makers, and by generals keen on 'natural' lines of defence. But military industria, at the limit, tends towards the abolition of geography. States can be composed of a mainland and islands, and part of an island, for example the rump of the British Empire styles itself the United Kingdom of Great Britain and Northern Ireland. Another state can separate the state's territory, as Canada separates Alaska from the continental USA, and Quebec may one day separate the rest of Canada into two halves. Nor need the state be the exclusive sovereign of all its territory: condominiums are possible, though

---

[6] The history of imperial China suggests that the internal integration of its successive empires before the fifteenth century was profoundly limited (Lattimore 1940 (1988)). The parallels with the Roman Empire are evident (see e.g. Lintott 1993: esp. ch. 3).

rare entities. But these are qualifications. The territorial attributes of a respected and self-respecting state require some exclusively delimited area in which it enjoys a monopoly of sovereignty.

The optimal specimens of industria, from the perspective of prosperity and stability, are national-statal. Many thinkers tacitly or explicitly assume that industria will, eventually, be cosmopolitan, and that nationalism is merely a phenomenon of the transition from agraria to global industria (e.g. Held 1990). If Gellner was right, they are wrong. Nationalism exists and will persist because it is a necessary component even of mature industria; and is expressed perhaps especially acutely in the more representative and democratic political systems that are its accompaniments.

Gellner's account of why we industrials are mostly nationalists is well known, and need only be brutally summarized here.[7] Agrarian village-communities possessed neither the means nor the incentives for literacy, or abstract communication. There was a marked discontinuity between High Culture and Low Culture, or between High Tradition and Little Tradition. The political relationship between the two varied from one civilization to another, but there was a general pattern: a discontinuity between high, literate, education-transmitted spiritually formulated culture, and a low oral culture, transmitted without much or any assistance from full-time cultural specialists or prescriptive and codified educators. Industria is different. For the great majority 'work' involves the interpretation, selection, and transmission of messages, not the direct transformation of nature. High or literate or education-transmitted culture is the pervasive possession of the overwhelming majority. Citizens owe their employability, cultural participation, and status as civic equals to skills that can only be acquired by passing through a continuous all-embracing educational system, operating in a standardized linguistic or cultural medium. The most important possession of the modern person is access to that shared literate high culture. It is this that makes her predisposed to be a nationalist, not least because that high culture is some particular high culture, with expectations about the typical traits displayed by bearers of that culture—be they oral sounds, skin pigmentation, religion believed by ancestors, or whatever.

If this story is broadly correct, industria provides systemic incentives for two forms of social boundary-drawing: between high-cultured populations and those still in agraria and foragia; and between rival high-cultured populations. These are, implicitly, the latent bases of territorial political borders in industria, if Gellner's interpretation of modernity is essentially correct. If it is, then these latent bases constrain the ambitions of those concerned to

[7] For the theory's nuances and for criticisms see O'Leary (1998 and forthcoming).

'right-size' their states. It suggests that there will be ethnic and national cleavages that 'right-sizers' can adjust, manipulate, and attempt to restructure—but public officials do not have the wholesale autonomy suggested by naïve social constructionists; they 'receive history' in ways that they do not choose.

It is easiest to understand the first potential border: it is analogous to that which existed at the civilizational frontiers between agrarians and foragians. The second border, by contrast, has material and cultural foundations of a different order. Industria, as Trotsky argued, arrives in combined and uneven forms—creating enormous disparities in wealth, and in economic and political power. Antagonisms develop at the interfaces between more and less developed populations. Excluded or offended élites in backward regions may opt for protectionist development. They may perceive advantages to secession—instead of competing in a rigged game with their rivals with a more and or better established educational tradition, they can have their own states: a poor thing but our own. '*Sinn Féin*: ourselves alone', that is early industria and its prophets. The setting up of separate political units linked to standardized educational systems becomes a systemic imperative in industria, the strongest marker of the second border. That border, of course, is not merely a reflection of past or imagined material inequality; it may also be the result of the denial of recognition on the part of co-industrials who should recognize the relevant nation as of equivalent status to their own, but fail to do so. Group-arrogance and group-resentment do not disappear in industria: they take a national rather than a caste form.

This is the bare bones of the Gellnerian tale. The standardization of productive activities in industria encourages a set of internally homogeneous, externally differentiated political units, which are simultaneously cultural and political. The state is a protector of a culture; the culture is the symbolism and legitimization of the state. The number of these pure national-statal units is far smaller than that of the earlier cultural differences between peoples. Their borders now reflect, in part, the limits of some of the major high agrarian cultures, and in part, Gellner said, the points of friction 'which became septic' in the course of uneven industrial development. Minor cultural units and nuances tend to disappear; but major ones become very significant politically.

This reasoning recognizes the vigour of political nationalism in industria, and focuses not on the ownership, or control, of capital as the source of deep conflict, but rather on the nature and implications of the types of cultural skills and activities involved in modern forms of production and of social closure on life-chances (see also Parkin 1979). These are the key sources of ethno-national conflict. The theory accounts for why nationalism is so very salient in our age, and why the social prominence of cultural nuance has diminished, whilst at the same time the political significance of the few surviving cultural boundaries has greatly increased.

Four implications follow for any general theory of 'right-sizing' and 'right-peopling' the state:

1. *Optimal industrial states are not systematically driven to expand to incorporate all industrial civilized peoples.* There are systemic inhibitions on imperial expansion and these are not merely normative. The primary sources of wealth in industrial states lie in the productive skills of their peoples; not in the 'raw land' or 'raw materials' found in, or under, grounds and oceans. The industrial state, *qua* infrastructural manager, is likely to be more successful in harnessing the skills of its people if they are its nationals—and this sets an important constraint on the appropriate borders of an efficient nation-state. The wealth of nations is their (relatively free) co-nationals; whereas the wealth of emperors is (tied people) on their estates.

This proposition implicitly accepts Schumpeter's rather than Hobson's or Lenin's argument about nineteenth-century territorial imperialism—that it was a cultural hangover, a phenomenon of the transition from agraria to industria, and not a reliable guide to the future of mature industria. The first industrials, emulating their predecessors, behaved like emperors and their aristocracies, remorselessly expanding their domains, even though it often made little industrial or capitalistic sense to do so, and even though they created costly forms of governance. The territorial imperialism of the successful European, Asian, and American states of the nineteenth and twentieth centuries was not, however, intrinsically rooted in the systemic logic of industrial society—though their respective military successes certainly were.

This does not mean that any one should deny that several states or empires sought, by war and other means most foul, to incorporate much of the modernized planet within their formal jurisdiction: the British Empire did not grow in a fit of benign sleepwalking. This ambition was pursued in the last century notably by Nazi Germany and by the USSR—at least in its revolutionary self-presentation before the years of peaceful co-existence. But they were defeated. Had Hitler succeeded, industria could have developed, so to speak, as a global South Africa under apartheid—a global racial hierarchy writ-large. But he did not. Perhaps we have been the beneficiaries of a lucky accident, but then perhaps not. Amongst other things, nationalism in other industrial states, the efficiency imperatives of industria, and the greater economic and military effectiveness of liberal democratic capitalist states, have combined to check this prospect. In short, nationalism both insists upon, and helps to preserve, plural industrial states; and industrial states can be at their most economically efficient and most militarily competent when they are national and liberal democratic. National legitimacy, enhanced by democratic mechanisms, is the open secret of stable government in industria. The numerous empires that have expired in the last two centuries suggest that this political system faced intrinsically unmanageable dilemmas in managing the transit to modernity (Lieven 1999).

2. *The nation-state is the exemplary form of the modern state.* Still more parts of the world are set to emulate this form, even though many, indeed most, states are not presently mono-ethnic or mono-national in character, and even though many may be engaged in interstate organizations or confederal unions. Nevertheless, we can expect an increasing proportion of states to have a more than titular dominant nationality. In turn, this suggests that the issues arising from the widespread existence of national and ethnic minorities present the greatest challenges to state-managers, even in the best functioning liberal democratic industrial states. For political élites in heterogeneous states the appropriateness of their borders—external and internal—will be fundamentally determined by the answer to the question: how do we manage (or eliminate) our national and ethnic minorities?

3. *The apparent rootedness of nationalism in the repercussions of industrial civilization suggests that facile cosmopolitanism will not do—either as ethics or as enlightenment.* The appeal of cultural ('national') identity is not a delusion spread by what Hobsbawm inaccurately and derisively calls the lesser-examination passing classes (Hobsbawm 1990), or by what others call muddled romantics. The Gellnerian message is powerful: the appeal of nationalism is rooted in the conditions of modern industrial life, and cannot be conjured away, either by sheer good will and the preaching of a spirit of universal brotherhood, or, for that matter, by the co-ordinated imprisonment of all extremists and the re-education of all romantics.

4. *It follows that the external borders of states in industria are subject to pressures from two sources.* One is endogenous, stemming from the imperatives of organizing a legitimate and effective industrial culture. Political managers learn that it is easiest to have borders which encompass willing potential co-nationals—that is, the *Staatsvolk* and whatever voluntary national allies it may have forged in history, plus voluntary migrants willing to shed some of their original culture in return for equal citizenship. They will, conversely, learn that it is problematic to have borders which encompass rival nationalities living within their homelands—or at least their homelands within 'historical standard time', that is, the time necessary for amnesia to suppress inconvenient national history/memory—or borders that fail to encompass all actual or potential co-culturals and co-nationals —that is, the unredeemed or 'lost' nationals living in *irredentas*. These are endogenous pres-

sures because they will be felt within the domestic political system—whether it is democratic or not.

These pressures interact with exogenous ones flowing from the interstate-system. That system is not one in which all states are nation-states, yet; but all states, with varying degrees of hypocrisy, must pretend to be so. It is the Westphalian system modified by its encounters with nationalisms. It places normative constraints upon state-managers' considerations about their borders. It behoves them to avoid blatant breaches of the territorial integrity of other recognized states. *There is also, so to speak, a formal normative check on territorial expansion without representation.* Borders cannot, it is said by international law, be moved by force. They can only be moved by consent—presumably of the affected people(s) and the affected state(s). There is also a formal normative constraint on contraction: international law prohibits the expulsion of citizens from their states, and thereby, it is hoped, normatively checks any prospective 'down-peoplers' who might wish to offload their responsibilities for certain peoples within their current borders. The Westphalian system has been modified to pay lip-service to national self-determination, at least for regions that were the overseas possessions of European empires, but by and large it remains the case that states combine to criticize, if not always to sanction, coercive transformations of borders, whether they be ethno-nationally motivated or not.

The foregoing are the formal pieties of 'international' 'law'—in which all states are nominally equal. These pieties are most often breached by superpowers or regional powers, or by their proxies, as realists observe. Thus the USA assisted Israel's illegal—under international law—annexations, occupations, and invasions of Jordanian, Palestinian, Lebanese, and Syrian territories, while mobilizing a coalition of western powers to liberate—though not democratize—the oil-producing Kuwaitis from their co-national conquerors in Iraq (Finklestein 1996: ch. 3). Similarly, there was little 'international'—that is, western—protest at India's militarized absorption of Goa, Kashmir, and various princely states, as one can read in Gurharpal Singh's discussion in Chapter 5; or, as Stephen Zunes observes in Chapter 10 at Indonesia's conquest of West Irian and East Timor.

These grim tales are not, however, proof that international law provides no constraints on the managers of superpowers or regional powers. The conquering actions of Indonesia, India, and China have been glossed as historically justified retributions for the (alleged) dismemberment of these regions by European imperialists, apologies that, naturally enough, have no purchase with the East Timorese—see Chapter 10, Muslim Kashmiris—see Chapter 5, or Tibetans (Karmel 1995–6). But they are nevertheless suggestive. Superpowers and regional powers must employ the vocabulary of national self-determination even when they betray its voluntarist and consensual premises. Perhaps, as more states join the ranks of the industrialized democratic states, present hypocrisies may be replaced by effective moral codes. The reason for this hope is not mere optimism. The European and American industrialized democratic nation-states have had a half century, and some would claim longer, in which no sovereign border has been permanently adjusted except by consent: sea-borders have been adjudicated and arbitrated; and land-borders are potentially open to adjustment by democratic headcounts, as proved by the reintegration of the Saar into West Germany, the later reunification of Germany, the potential secession of Quebec, and possible reunification of Ireland.

We live in Gellner's world. Industria is sweeping away the remnants of agraria and foragia. We call it globalization, when that term is deployed in a well-specified way. Frontiers have everywhere given ground to the borders of industria, even in the people-free Antarctica. Kokoschka's riotous colours have given way to Modigliani's linear bluntness. What right-sizing strategies, as regards their borders—be they external or internal—can be adopted by managers, in the presence of ethno-national differences within their existing sovereign territory, or if they have co-nationals beyond their sovereign territory? The answers involve simple but often deadly choices over the right peoples and the right borders.

Ethno-National Strategies for Industrial and Industrializing States

The condition in which state managers confront their peoples and their borders is explored in the literature on national and ethnic conflict regulation.[8] They can choose, within constraints, to eliminate or to manage ethnonational differences. They have four domestic grand strategies for *eliminating* differences:

(1) genocide;
(2) ethnic expulsion;
(3) territorial elimination, such as permitting secession, active decolonization or partition; and
(4) political homogenization, in the form of integration—eliminating culture from the political domain by treating all as civic equals—or assimilation (encouraging acculturation and eventual fusion).

---

[8] See *inter alia* Connor (1994); Esman (1994); Horowitz (1985); Horowitz (1989); Lijphart (1977); and Nordlinger (1972).

They also have four grand strategies for *managing* differences:

(1) control;
(2) arbitration;
(3) territorial management through autonomy—home rule or devolution—
    or federation; and
(4) consociation.[9]

Some of these strategies have no immediate implications for the right-sizing of external borders. Three of the eight seek to eliminate differences within existing borders, and are what one would expect from Gellnerian theory, namely genocide, ethnic expulsions, and similitude through integration or assimilation. Let us call these 'right-peopling' homogenization strategies, where 'right' has no sense of approval on our part. Two of the eight strategies seek to manage differences through opposing principles of group-relations: domination (control) or equality (consociation). Both have significant implications for the placement of the internal political borders of the state. Arbitration seeks to manage differences within the relevant state but its territorial logics need elaboration. Explicitly territorial strategies naturally have immediate implications for the location of state borders—internal borders in the case of management strategies, such as autonomy or federation, and external borders in the case of elimination strategies, such as permitting secession, active decolonization or partition. I shall deal with these plain right-sizing strategies last. Let me deal first with the alternatives to right-sizing.

'Right-Peopling' Within Borders

The most extreme 'solutions' to ethnic difference are the most abhorrent: genocide and expulsion. Regrettably they have not proven sufficiently abhorrent to prevent some power élites from engaging in these extreme modes of right-peopling.

Genocide

Genocide is the systematic killing of a race or kind, and involves the intentional mass killing of very large numbers or proportions of unarmed or disarmed civilians of a community who share real or alleged ascriptive national or ethnic traits,[10] or the indirect physical destruction of such a community

---

[9] These strategies are not mutually exclusive; they may be found in combinations and targeted at the same ethnic group(s), or, alternatively, different strategies may be aimed at different ethnic groups within the same state.

[10] Harff's term 'politicide' should be employed for the politically motivated systematic mass killing of people who may or may not share ascriptive traits, and Rummel's 'democide' is the best general term for the mass murder of peoples.

through the deliberate termination of the conditions which permit its biological and social reproduction.

Genocides in the twentieth century have been perpetrated within up-sizing states, such as Nazi Germany, involuntarily down-sizing empires, such as Ottoman Turkey, and states that show no overt desire to adjust their external borders, such as Burundi and Rwanda. Despite the infamy won by the Nazi holocaust it is wishful thinking to assume that genocide has become unthinkable.[11] Since 1945 there have been partial genocides perpetrated in the Soviet Union—of the Chechens, the Ingushi, the Karachai, the Balkars, the Meskhetians, and the Crimean Tartars[12]—Burundi, Rwanda, Iraq, Paraguay, Indonesia, Nigeria, Equatorial Guinea, Uganda, and the former Yugoslavia.

Organized 'right-peopling' through extermination by state officials[13] is more likely to occur when:

(1) an empire is being constructed and maintained, and genocide is used as a conscious policy of land acquisition, terrorization, and encouragement of mass flight, for example the killings of the Herrero in South West Africa and of the native peoples of the Americas and Australasia;

(2) an empire is being contracted into a nation-state, for example the Young Turks' treatment of the Armenians during World War 1;

(3) an ethno-national, racial, or religious community is left vulnerable in an intense phase of nation-building, especially one that lacks geo-political resources—such as its own institutions of self-rule, or links with a state in which its co-culturals are dominant or influential—and, perhaps especially, if it possesses economic superiority and cultural identifiability in conditions of industrialization, but lacks military and political power, for example Jews, Ibos, Armenians, overseas Chinese;

(4) an ethno-national, racial, or religious community is left vulnerable within a disintegrating system of control, whether organized by an empire or by a party-dictatorship, for example the orphaned national minorities in Yugoslavia;

---

[11] In a moment of high optimism McNeill (1986: 71) argued that Hitler's genocides of Jews, Gypsies, and Slavs had decisively tainted advocacy of the ideal of ethnic unity within an existing state, though he stopped short of using the term 'irreversibly'.

[12] Some believe that these were cases of internal expulsions because Stalin's express intention was to remove these peoples from militarily sensitive areas, and not to kill them. However, by the 'indirect destruction' element in our definition they count as partial genocides.

[13] 'Frontier genocide', by contrast, is likely to occur when settlers, possessed of technologically superior resources, displace natives from access to land. A concomitant of colonization and conquest, it occurs on the frontiers between industrial and agrarian, or between industrial and foragian peoples—sometimes with and sometimes without state sanction. 'Frontier-genocides' occurred in all the parliamentary colonies of the British empire which became the 'white dominions'.

(5) the relevant state is not democratic, or not stably democratic; and
(6) when other right-peopling or right-sizing strategies have been ruled out.

Three points need elaboration. State officials, we may hopefully presume, embark on genocide only when other options are ruled out, either on pragmatic or ideological grounds. The Nazi Judeocide was motivated by what Goldhagen calls 'eliminationist anti-Semitism', but others were targeted for mass death who were not 'Semites', and the scale and historic continuity of anti-Semitism in the German nation as a whole may reasonably be doubted (Finkelstein and Birn 1998). It was the rapid victories of Hitler's armies in the East and the ruling out of the options of expulsion and transfer of Jews to Madagascar which led to the systematic planning of the 'final solution' (Browning 1992). Up-sizing in this case facilitated genocide. Public officials may decide that certain communities are mortal threats to the life and culture of the *Staatsvolk*, and that they cannot be integrated or assimilated. They will not, almost by definition, cede authentic territorial autonomy or sovereignty to such peoples because they are considered mortal threats. And since third parties are not trusted to manage such threats, decision-makers with this mentality are left three options: control, expulsion, and genocide. If control is considered too difficult or costly then the extreme options may be considered, especially under the cover of war.

Secondly, genocide is often used in accompaniment with an expulsion strategy, as has been the case with Slobodan Milosevic's wars in Bosnia and Kosovo. Partial genocide is executed to compel the target group to flee across the sovereign borders. Genocide can also occur partly as a result of 'failures' in expulsion policies, for example the Nazis embarked upon the 'final solution' after conquering territories, such as Poland, which had received Jews already expelled from the Reich.

Thirdly, territorial sovereignty, *de facto* rather than *de jure*, gives state officials the capacity to commit genocide on their own soil. Some have argued that the coalition against Hitler would never have come together 'had he been satisfied with killing his own fellow citizens' (Enzensberger 1990: 65). It is wrong in ethics, and now in fact, to argue that sovereignty gives the state the legal right to commit genocide, but it has been a matter of immorality and of fact that interventions to prevent genocides almost never happen, except as a by-product of other motivations for intervention. An up-sizing state, expanding through war, risks intervention against its genocidal practices because it is expansionist, far more than a contracting state or, so to speak, a stationary state. The intervention in East Pakistan by India—see Chapters 5 and 6—and in Kosovo by NATO are exceptions that confirm this rule—though Milosevic's elimination of Kosovo's autonomy and subjection of its population was portrayed, to some extent accurately, as Serbian expansionism. The intervention against Saddam Hussein's Iraq was not sparked by his genocidal massacres of Kurds but by his conquest of his co-ethnic Arab neighbours in Kuwait.

The conditions just specified that promote genocide are facilitative, rather than necessary. A necessary condition seems to be the presence of a racial, ethnic, or religious ideology which sanctions a non-universalist conception of the human species, and makes mass murder easier to accomplish, something akin to what Goldhagen identifies as 'eliminationist anti-Semitism', though he exaggerates its popular resonance. Such an ideology may be more important than a state's technological capacities for managing mass-killings, as it is the disciplined beliefs of the killers, rather than their instruments, which may best account for the scale of genocides.

Some have argued that ideological, as opposed to imperial, genocides are modern: beginning in the religious wars of the Middle Ages they have been carried further by the spread of nationalist and Marxist-Leninist doctrines. But this is partly contestable. The rise and fall of empires in modern times is the primary factor in explaining the conditions that facilitate genocide, and genocide is not 'modern', although it occurs in modern times. This proposition links back to previous arguments. If the numbers expand of industrial states that have learned the wastefulness of imperialism then we may *hope* for a reduced incidence of genocide.

Expulsion

Ethnic expulsion is a right-peopling strategy, the intended, direct or indirect, forcible movement by state officials, or sanctioned paramilitaries, of the whole or part of a community from its current homeland, usually beyond the sovereign borders of the state.[14] A population can also be forcibly 'repatriated', or pushed back towards its alleged 'homeland', as happened to blacks during the high tide of apartheid in South Africa.[15] We may distinguish two paradigm forms: creating 'Siberian exiles', that is, coerced transfers within a state or empire, and 'creating refugees', that is, the expulsions of populations

---

[14] Not all refugees, of course, are expellees.

[15] Forced mass-population transfers must be distinguished from agreed 'population exchanges'—e.g. those between Greece and Turkey after the war of 1919–22—the populations which move never consider such moves to be voluntary, but their fate must be distinguished from those unilaterally compelled to move. The expulsion of citizens or those who should be citizens should be distinguished from the deportation of illegal immigrants—the latter is not ethnic expulsion in the relevant sense. And lastly, ethnic expulsions must be distinguished from policies which promote differential out-migration of a target group—the latter is associated with 'control', see below. Though indirect and intentional these policies do not have the same immediately coercive character.

beyond the sovereign border. Examples of the former include the treatment of indigenous peoples throughout the world; the Irish Catholics moved by Oliver Cromwell to Connaught during 1649–50 and after; and national minorities within the Soviet Union. Examples of the latter include the expulsion of the *Volk Deutsch* from Eastern Europe after World War II; of Palestine's Arab population during the formation of Israel in 1948; of Jews from Arab states in the 1950s; of Uganda's Asians by Idi Amin; of the Greek-Cypriot community of Northern Cyprus in 1974; and, more recently, of communities within Bosnia, Croatia, and Kosovo.

The circumstances under which ethnic expulsions are contemplated are not different from those which have occasioned genocide, but the incidence of expulsions has been much higher, notably in Europe, and the number of persons affected by this incidence has also been higher. The *World Refugee Survey 1993* estimated a total of 26 million international refugees and displaced persons at the end of 1992, of which some 23 million were attributable to ethno-national conflicts (Gurr and Harff 1994: 171, n. 1). Since then about 5 million people have at one time or another been expelled from their homelands within the former Yugoslavia. One interpretation of refugee flows can be found in the work of Aristide Zolberg and his colleagues who argue that the secular transformation of the world of empires into nation-states is accompanied by the formation of refugee populations (Zolberg 1983; Zolberg, Suhrke, and Aguayo 1989; see also Trazi 1991). Their thesis is simple: nation-building homogenization causes refugees. A similar argument is advanced by Michael Mann, who argues that ethnic expulsions are the 'dark side of democracy', the most undesirable consequence of the modern practice of vesting political legitimacy in 'the people' (Mann 1999).

Wars, civil wars, and state-collapses; colonial expansion, decolonization, and wars of national liberation—all these give rise to expulsions, as do totalitarian regimes, and exclusivist ideologies or philosophies. The pragmatic justifications of expulsions are that they are necessary on security grounds: to prevent actual or potential 'fifth columnists' betraying part or all of the relevant territory; to facilitate national liberations or secessions by establishing facts on the ground;[16] and to obtain strategically vital land and resources. They are often motivated by revenge or retribution.

Expulsions have long-run consequences. The turmoil in the Soviet Union after the start of *glasnost* and *perestroika* was partly the outcome of forced mass-population transfers executed by Lenin and Stalin and their successors, as Alexander Motyl's discussion indicates in Chapter 7. Violence in the contemporary Caucasus is, in part, the result of similar policies pursued by

---

[16] 'Induced population transfers' to dilute natives are a form of control (see below).

Tsarist and Ottoman emperors. The forced creation of a Palestinian 'diaspora' of expellees helped precipitate the destabilization of Jordan (Chapter 11), the Lebanon (Chapter 12), and Kuwait, and ensures that deep antagonism persists between Israelis and Palestinians. As Marc Lynch shows in Chapter 11, the status of the Palestinian refugees in Jordan remains a fundamental question in Jordanian politics, affecting the status of Jordan's borders and citizenship debates. The 'refugee question' as it is euphemistically described, for example by Peretz (1993), will shape all future debates about the political forms to emerge from any durable Middle East process, especially the prospects of a fully sovereign Palestine in West Bank and Gaza, and of a Palestinian-Jordanian confederation.

The sole moral merit to expulsion is that it is better to be expelled than killed. Even those expulsions regarded as 'rough justice' merit condemnation: up to 16 million Germans were expelled from Eastern Europe between 1945 and 1948 (De Zayas 1994, 1977/1989, 1989). Expulsions facilitate genocidal assaults on vulnerable populations and encourage the likelihood that the victims will suffer from famine. They violate human rights and egalitarian political philosophies. Nevertheless, where peoples believe that their homelands have been stolen from them it becomes thinkable, if not justifiable, for their political élites to support and lead masses who think that retribution is in order. The leaders of new states, established after the breakdown of empires, are likely to contemplate expulsion policies, not least because their successful implementation will minimize the dangers of what might otherwise become the bases of secessionist or irredentist movements.

Right-Peopling without Murder or Deportation: Integration and Assimilation

Right-peopling the state has led several states to embrace genocide and ethnic expulsions as forms of what is revealingly called 'internal hygiene' or 'cleansing'. These horrors have ensured that the overwhelming preponderance of member-states and candidate members of the European Union now have a dominant titular nationality (Mazower 1998: ch. 2 and Tables 1–2; Mann 1999), what I call a *Staatsvolk*. But states have most frequently and less shamefacedly pursued rather different homogenization policies: integration or assimilation.

Whereas *assimilation*, through fusion or acculturation, seeks to eliminate public and private differences between people's cultures, *integration* stops at the public domain, permitting private cultural differences to be sustained. Integrating or assimilating minority national or ethnic communities into a new transcendent identity can be deployed to stabilize a new state, to inhibit secession, or to consolidate an expanded state or recently contracted state. The presence of all these motivations is discussed by Ümit Cizre in the case of Turkey in Chapter 8. Combinations of integration or assimilation have been the official aspiration of liberal leaders in the USA, the African National Congress in South Africa, and the democratic left in those European countries seeking to include their new immigrant communities. The democratic right has also advocated integration and assimilation: the difference between the right and the left has been in the degree of concern for the relevant dominant nationality and minorities respectively.

Integrationists favour reducing the differences between ethnic communities, ensuring that the children of the (potentially rival) communities go to the same schools, socializing them in the same language and conventions, encouraging desegregationist public and private housing policies, and ensuring that the workplace is ethnically integrated through outlawing discrimination. Liberal integrationists promote bills of rights with equal rights for individuals, rather than communities. Assimilationists' policies go further. They favour the merging of ethnic identities into one already established identity, *acculturation*, for example a French identity; or into a new one, *fusion*, for example a Soviet identity. Proof of success is large-scale intermarriage across ethnic boundaries which leads first to their blurring and then to their eradication. Integrationists and assimilationists in democratic or open regimes support 'catch-all' political parties, arguing against ethnic political parties, and shun policies that might show up politically salient differences between communities.[17] They may even, as in the case of the Turkish state, outlaw ethnic parties (Chapter 8).

Integration or assimilation strategies are characteristic of states engaged in nation-building, and those with very numerically small minorities, and which therefore feel no need to grant generous forms of autonomy. Homogenization of either form may be driven by high-minded motives: ethnic pluralism may be associated with racism, sectarianism, parochialism, narrow-mindedness, and chauvinist bigotry. Thus the French state has declared that Article 27 of the International Covenant on Civil and Political Rights[18] is not applicable in France, because France has no minorities, and to admit the existence of minorities is to admit discrimination (Thornberry 1995: 21). Sometimes, however, integrationism and assimilation are merely coercive, as the Kurds of Turkey and of Iraq can testify (Chapters 8 and 9).

---

[17] Integrationists and assimilationists are especially sceptical about consociational arrangements which they believe entrench ethnic divisions and reward divisive political leaders—in my view this drives Lustick's criticisms of the work of Lijphart (Lustick 1997).

[18] To wit: 'In those States in which ethnic, religious or linguistic minorities exist, persons belonging to such minorities shall not be denied the right, in community with the other members of their group, to enjoy their own culture, to profess and practice their own religion, or to use their own language'.

The targets of homogenization respond in various ways, partly as a function of their perceptions of the motives lying behind the policies. Migrants, in principle, may be willing to adapt their cultures to their new host country and accept a new civic identity (integration) or acculturate (assimilation). Often integrationist or assimilationists projects are aimed at uniting (moderately) different communities against a common foe. Denise Natali in Chapter 9 shows how Kurds in pre-independent Iraq could be won over to an integrated anti-colonial struggle only to find themselves regarded by some Arabist nation-builders as surplus to requirements if they remained Kurds. Marc Lynch, in Chapter 11, addresses a fascinating integrationist challenge. Jordan, a state in transit from agraria, presides over pools of people with shared cultural heritages, but very different recent political pasts, that of being indigenous natives or expelled refugees. Its political élite does not know whether it can successfully pursue a Jordanization strategy in the face of resistance from both Palestinian and Jordanian publics as long as the sovereignty of Palestine remains an open question.

Mutually agreed integration or assimilation projects have reasonable prospects of success. They can, however, be blocked by strata of the *Staatsvolk*. Moreover, where minority communities seek more than individual fair play or equal opportunity, and insist on autonomy or self-government, or where no external threat can induce pan-community unity, integration or assimilation policies may fall on stony ground, tempting state-managers towards more extremist elimination strategies including partition, decolonization, and secession, or persuading the respective protagonists to seek some other form of conflict management including federal and consociational strategies. Assimilation or integration on contested homeland(s), however high-minded, does not work easily where it involves tacit or actual coercive assimilation on one community's terms: if one community's language, culture, religion, and national myths are given precedence then this may be regarded as *ethnocide*, the destruction of a people's culture as opposed to the physical liquidation of its members. This complaint is the standard one raised by the indigenous movements of the world, the last of the foragians. It is also the complaint of Iraqi and Turkish Kurds—see Chapters 8 and 9.

Integration and assimilation require some coercion: compulsory educational homogenization and the imposition of standard cultural codes are the Gellnerian preconditions of full citizenship. Even apparently balanced and transcendent strategies of integration or assimilation encounter significant resistance: as with Yugoslav and Soviet communism. These efforts may encounter double resistance: from minorities who see them as thinly disguised forms of cultural hegemony, and from the dominant communities who see these transcendent or pan-ethnic identities as detrimental to their cultures: consider some Serbs' and Russians' views of 'Yugoslavism' and 'Sovietism'—see Chapter 7. Resistance to unwanted assimilation or integration projects is likely to be very high and can provoke ethnic revivals and secessionism in response, as has occurred in India, Pakistan, Turkey, and Iraq—see Chapters 5, 6, 8, and 9.

Some political engineers recommend the development of catch-all political parties to break down the salience of ethnic cleavages, that is, electoral integration. The onset of a debate around these issues in Jordan is discussed by Marc Lynch in Chapter 11. Jordanian exclusionists have done their best to try to prohibit the organization of parties with overt Palestinian identities and agendas. The belief that one can generate integrationist parties either through coercion or through heroic acts of will, is, however, fundamentally utopian if the relevant communities have already been mobilized behind different conceptions of nationalism (Barry 1991: 146). This is not a lesson yet learned by the Turkish political and judicial class that outlaws ethnic parties, especially Kurdish ethnic parties, in the hope of generating integration through cross-ethnic parties—see Ümit Cizre's analysis in Chapter 8.

The internal normative territorial logic of integration and assimilation is straightforward: ethnicity, language, religion, and history should not count in administrative theory and practice; internal borders should not publicly recognize ethnicity or, alternatively, all should recognize only one ethnic culture, that of the *Staatsvolk*. Uniform, rationalist, managerial prefectures are preferred when nations need to be built from above. The Jacobin way of dealing with the *ancien régime*, the organizational extermination of territorial particularism, is the preferred model of integrationist and assimilationist nation-builders, such as the Kemalists in Turkey discussed by Cizre—see also Gellner (1994). Integrationists and assimilationists pursue this territorial logic even within federations. In the United States 'in general . . . there is little coincidence between ethnic groups and state boundaries' (Glazer 1983: 276). The formation of the federation as a constitutionalized institution preceded the great expansion in the USA's internal ethnic diversity, and new states were generally only created and then added when they had WASP or assimilated white majorities.[19] English-speaking whites were the creators of every state 'writing its Constitution, establishing its laws, ignoring the previously settled American Indians, refusing to grant any [autonomy] rights to blacks, and making only slight concessions to French and Spanish speakers in a few states' (ibid. 284). Internal territorial homogenization, when it works, mightily assists the homogenization of peoples.

---

[19] There were some exceptions to this pattern as Glazer (1983) points out.

Managing Differences

But suppose state managers decide, or are forced to recognize, that 'right-peopling' homogenization strategies are neither feasible nor desirable. If they decide against down-sizing, through permitting decolonization or secession, then their primary choice is between managing ethno-national differences in either a hierarchical or egalitarian fashion.

Control

The former option points towards *'control'*: the most common system of managing conflict practised in multi- or bi-ethnic states, especially in the transit from agraria to industria.[20] Coercive domination and élite co-option amongst the controlled are the themes. Controllers attempt to suppress divisions between ethnic communities, but in a partial manner, on behalf of the *Staatsvolk*, the titular dominant nationality. Their control is 'hegemonic' if it makes an overtly violent ethnic contest for state power 'unthinkable' or 'unworkable' on the part of the subordinated communities.

Control need not rest on the support of the largest ethnic community.[21] What is necessary is to have the relevant coercive apparatuses: thus ethnic minorities in Burundi, Fiji (after 1987), Liberia (before 1980), and South Africa (until 1990–1) were able to sustain control because of their control over security and policing systems. Sunni Arabs have retained control over Kurds and Shi'ites in Iraq—see Chapter 9. Control appears less feasible in liberal democracies or open regimes because they permit, indeed facilitate, group organization and mobilization; and so ethnic contests for state power become 'thinkable' and 'workable'. Irish nationalism was facilitated by the democratization of the United Kingdom (O'Leary and McGarry 1996: ch. 2). Ethnic nationalism was encouraged by *glasnost* in the Soviet Union—see Chapter 7. Bengali nationalism was facilitated by Pakistan's first state-wide elections—see Chapter 6. The liberal may conclude that parliamentary democratization spells doom to systems of control. But it is not so: controllers can surmount the difficulties.

---

[20] The concept was pioneered in a brilliant analysis by Ian Lustick (1979, 1987). Others use the term slightly differently (O'Leary and Arthur 1990; O'Leary and McGarry 1996: chs. 3 and 4).

[21] There is a key difference in coercive authoritarian regimes which practise control. In authoritarian empires no grand objective is pursued to eliminate ethnic difference—although they may sponsor world-religions that propagate transcendent identities. By contrast, in communist systems a new transcendent identity was proclaimed: intended to eliminate ethnic differences as irrelevant to people's identities as citizens. Though the policies of Communist parties primarily focused on suppressing the overt politicization of ethnic differences they had some success in generating Soviet—see Chapter 6—and Yugoslav identities.

To do so they must organize the dominant group and disorganize the dominated. The most obvious method is to monopolize liberal democratic institutions by a minority of the state's population and disenfranchise the rest. Citizenship and representative government are confined to the *Herrenvolk*, as in the former Rhodesia and apartheid South Africa. Minority-control within regions is common: consider Serbian domination of Albanians in Kosovo (1987–99), or the treatment of the majority Bengalis in what was East Pakistan (1947–71)—see Chapter 6.[22] But control can also be exercised in states in which the entirety of the relevant state's adult population has formal access to citizenship. Democracy in its most primitive meaning is 'majority-rule', and where 'majorities' constantly fluctuate then it is an agreeable decision-rule, strongly preferable to the kind of minority-rule practised by emperors, dictators, or one-party regimes. But where there are two or more deeply established ethnic communities, and where the members of these communities do not agree on the basic institutions and policies the regime should pursue, or where the relevant communities are not internally fragmented on key policy-preferences in ways which cross-cut each other, then 'majority-rule' can easily become the instrument of control.

When simple majoritarian institutions in the electoral system and the legislature are implemented in multi-ethnic or bi-communal societies they may lead either to the consolidation of control, or to state-fragmentation through the development of civil war and secessionist movements. Northern Ireland (1920–72), the deep South of the USA (c. 1870–c. 1964), and Israel (1948–), are examples of regions or full sovereign states where formal majoritarian democracy co-existed with control over the relevant minority. In such systems the dominant bloc monopolizes the police and judicial systems, manipulates the franchise to consolidate its domination, practises economic discrimination in employment and the allocation of public expenditures, and institutional discrimination against the minority's cultural and educational system(s), and ruthlessly represses minority-discontent. Democratic government is therefore no guarantee of liberty for national or ethnic minorities.

Some, however, maintain that systems of control may be normatively defensible—for example, Lustick (1979)—primarily because they are often the only alternative to continuous war, and because consociations may not be possible. This perspective is open to the challenge that it represents a form of 'might makes right' reasoning.[23] Universalizing Lustick's argument would lead one to maintain—as some do—that the dictatorial CPSU and the

---

[22] Unlike Northern Ireland, Rhodesia, and South Africa, all of which have seen forms of settler control, Fiji and Malaysia are, or are becoming, forms of native control.

[23] This reasoning appears to be taken further in one of Lustick's less well-known papers (Lustick 1995). He does not agree.

Yugoslav League of Communists were justified precisely because they suppressed ethnic conflict in the Soviet Union and Yugoslavia, that one-party states in Africa and Asia are similarly defensible, and that the reimposition of Ba'athist control over the Kurds is preferable to continuous civil war in Iraq. In any case the options in any conflict are rarely simply between those of control and continuous inter-ethnic war, although there will usually be political entrepreneurs seeking to advance precisely this argument. Some options, such as federalism, autonomy, consociation, and arbitration, have some record of success in stabilizing societies in ways that are compatible with liberal democratic norms, whereas control is easily convertible into the execution of genocide, expulsions, and other major violations of human rights. 'Down-sizing' options may be normatively more desirable than the imposition of control, as Lustick would certainly agree. If the down-sizing is moderately well executed then it should ensure that more people can enjoy legitimate self-government than would be the case under control. Under control systems the subordinated seek to 'internationalize' their plight, and thereby threaten the stability of the relevant regime as well as the regional and local international order, for example the Kurds and the Palestinians. Systems of control are vulnerable to external losses of support from liberal democratic states, and to internal corrosion through the costs that they generate. If a system of control breaks down, its practices will have added to the accumulated stock of ethnic grievances. Repression sidelines moderates, bolsters extremists and obstructs prospects for future accommodation, as Singh demonstrates has been true in the Punjab—see Chapter 5. Lastly, one might even argue in a realist fashion, although the evidence would need fastidious appraisal, that wars may 'sort matters out' more successfully than exercising control, and even create incentives for post-war co-operative behaviour.

Whatever one's judgement of these arguments, state managers preserve (or create) systems of control when there are incentives to do so. Settler regimes, or regimes built from the descendants of settlers who have preserved their differences from the natives, are the most likely candidates. New 'nationalizing states' (Brubaker 1996), especially those with large and allegedly or actually unassimilable national minorities, are also strong contenders, for example the former states of the Soviet Union—see Chapter 7.

The territorial instruments of control systems are designed to avoid down-sizing. Two stratagems are very widely used: population redistribution, and gerrymandering (see e.g. Connor 1984a: esp. ch. 9; O'Leary and McGarry 1996: ch. 3). Demographic control takes two primary forms, which can be combined: encouraging settlers to migrate into the homelands of groups targeted for control, and encouraging the out-migration of the group targeted for control. Gerrymandering, by contrast, takes the form of restructuring internal electoral or provincial borders to weaken or disorganize the targeted group(s). A national or ethnic homeland may be divided by fresh internal electoral or provincial borders, or it may be diluted by being partially or wholly encapsulated within other internal/provincial borders. Demographic control and gerrymandering may be regarded as alternatives—if people cannot be induced to move across a border the border can be moved, if borders cannot be changed peoples can be moved—but they can also be combined to disorganize targeted groups. Walker Connor's telling analysis of the USSR, China, Yugoslavia, Romania, and Vietnam demonstrates how pervasive were (or are) demographic and gerrymandering control policies in Marxist-Leninist regimes. Variations on these strategies can also be found in liberal democratic control regimes, for example in Northern Ireland (O'Leary and McGarry 1996: ch. 3). Settler-infusion strategies have been integral to Israeli state-building (Lustick 1987, 1993); of Morocco's attempts to make the Western Sahara its own; and of Indonesia's attempts to stabilize its conquest of East Timor—see Chapter 10. The Turkish State's forced urbanization of Kurdish villagers, by contrast, involves moving the natives.

Huge costs in the maintenance of control may encourage state or sub-state managers to contemplate routes to reform. There are three: considering national integration, which involves an agreement to lose formal governmental power, as happened with the apartheid regime in South Africa; moving towards a consociational bargain, as has happened with some unionists in Northern Ireland; or contemplating granting limited forms of self-government, as with Israel's recent moves on the West Bank and Gaza. In such circumstances public officials will be strongly concerned that such reforms may be stepping stones towards a complete reversal of power-relations. If all such reforms are deemed unthinkable or unworkable that leaves open the options of 'right-peopling' through genocide and expulsion, or through down-sizing, an admission of defeat.

Consociation

The most obvious antonym of control is consociation. Here differences are managed amongst equals rather than among castes in a hierarchy. Consociational or power-sharing principles, prefigured in the work of the Austro-Marxists (Hanf 1991) but first articulated in political science by Arend Lijphart, operate at the level of an entire state, or within a region of a state (Lijphart 1968, 1969, 1977). They were invented or reinvented by Dutch politicians in 1917 through till the 1960s, and by Lebanese politicians between 1943 and 1975. Malaysian politicians experimented with consociation between 1955 and 1969, Cypriots between 1960 and 1963, Fijians on and off between 1970 and 1987, and Northern Irish politicians for a brief spell in 1974. Presently the Lebanese are attempting again to rebuild a consociational settlement, as Yiftachel notes in Chapter 12, as are the Northern Irish, with British and Irish encouragement, though their precarious consociational settlement has subtle confederal dimensions (O'Leary 1999).

Consociational democracies usually have four features (Lijphart 1977):

1. *Grand coalition government* which incorporates the political parties representing the—or at least some of the—main segments of the divided society, or *government by more than a simple majority or plurality* which guarantees an inclusive executive and legislative.
2. *Proportionality rules* apply, generally, throughout the public sector: each ethnic partner in the consociation is proportionally represented in the legislature(s), in the executive, the judiciary, the civil service, and the police—the core institutions of the state. Proportionality applies both to public employment and public expenditure. Proportionality might also apply in private sector employment.
3. *Community autonomy* norms operate. Consociational partners are given self-government over those matters of most profound concern to them. In most ethnic conflicts these issues revolve around language, education, religion, culture, and the expression of national identity. Ideally consociational autonomy differs from autonomy under federal or devolved systems because members of each community have their autonomy respected irrespective of where they live and work—in short it need not be territorially confined to one section of the state or region. One can think of it as 'community federalism', or 'corporate federalism' in contrast to territorial federalism. The most obvious examples of the principle are denominationally or linguistically organized education systems.
4. Constitutional *vetoes* for minorities are entrenched. These may take various forms. In Belgium weighted majorities are required before some legislation becomes law—see Chapter 12. If Bills of Rights are established, with supreme courts to uphold them, and if these bills entrench individual as well as communal rights, they can provide an effective way of entrenching minority rights.

Consociational principles are based upon the acceptance of equal ethnic pluralism, at least amongst the partners to the bargain. They aim to secure the rights, identities, freedoms, and opportunities of the partner ethnic communities, and to create political and other social institutions that enable them to enjoy the benefits of equality without forced assimilation, and with only limited integration—common formal citizenship. They do not oblige people to be schooled or housed together, although they do imply a commitment to proportionality in political and legal institutions and possibly to proportionality in economic work-organizations, since these arenas are the ones in which ethnic differences are likely to produce violence, instability, and perpetuation of conflict. Proponents of consociation maintain that in some zones of ethnic conflict the relevant populations effectively have a simple choice: between consociational democratic institutions or having no meaningful democratic institutions. The Lebanon's delicate consociational compromise was destabilized by Israel and Syria in 1975–6 and by the impact of the expelled Palestinian 'diaspora', and is presently being reconstructed after a painful and protracted civil war—see Yiftachel's discussion in Chapter 12. Another case is Northern Ireland (O'Leary 1999).

Consociational arrangements do not require academic experts: they are constantly reinvented by politicians. Consociational settlements require politicians to have the necessary motives, autonomy, and incentives to construct such compromises and the appropriate external environment (see McGarry and O'Leary 1995: 311–55; Nordlinger 1972). By no means all consociational experiments have proven successful, as the cases of Cyprus and Lebanon, discussed by Yiftachel in Chapter 12, and Northern Ireland may yet indicate. But some of them have. The case for consociation is that it involves the self-government of the relevant communities, that it can manage residentially intermingled or proximate populations, and that it is better than most of the alternatives: coercive integration or assimilation, control, bloody partition, secessionist warfare, expulsions, and genocide.

To work, consociational systems require at least three fundamental conditions to be present. First, the rival ethnic segments must not be unreservedly committed to immediate or medium-term integration or assimilation of others into 'their' nation, or to the creation of their own nation-state. Secondly, successive generations of political leaders must have the right motivations to sustain the consociational system. The leaders of the rival communities must fear the consequences of ethnic war, and desire to preserve the economic and political stability of their regions. They must believe they are incapable of governing on their own or establishing control. Their motivations may be self-interested or high-minded, but without them there is no prospect of producing and sustaining a consociational arrangement. Thirdly, the political leaders of the relevant ethnic communities must enjoy some political autonomy themselves—so that they can make compromises without being accused of treachery. If they lack confidence—for example because external irredentists outbid them—they will not be prepared to engage in hard bargaining. This condition may not only require restraint on the part of external élites outside the affected area but also within the relevant ethnic communities. This condition is most exacting, and is made more excruciating by a fundamental dilemma in constitutional design.

Proportional representation systems, which go with consociational practices, create incentives for extremist ethnic leaders to compete for office confident that they will not lower the overall support for their bloc, but each minority's extremists may lack the incentive to moderate their demands. The dangerous phenomenon of outflanking is latent in all proportional representation systems.[24] Thus we may say that a consociational settlement requires that each community be internally politically stable in a way which promotes compromise.

These are demanding requirements. If they are not present, as they have not been at crucial junctures in the history of Lebanon, Northern Ireland, Malaysia, Cyprus, and Fiji, then authentic consociational experiments break down. An even more depressing conclusion is also possible, though not foreordained. Consociational practices work to calm ideological, religious, linguistic, or ethnic conflicts, but do so much more easily if these conflicts have not become the bases of separate national identities. Consociation, in short, may only be practicable in moderately rather than deeply divided societies.

How does consociation relate to right-sizing; what are the territorial dimensions of consociation? State-managers may contemplate either:

(1) localized consociational settlements in ethnic frontier zones, for example where settlers and natives historically mixed; in places such as Northern Ireland where British and Irish intermingle in a former settler colonial site; or the South Tyrol where Austro-Germans and Italians are intermingled; or

(2) system-wide consociation when ethnic pluralism is pervasive throughout the state's territory.

The former option has important implications for internal right-sizing. State managers must try to ensure that the relevant provincial jurisdiction, and any internal jurisdictions within it, are acceptable to the parties to the consociational bargain. And they must manage the asymmetries that will flow between the jurisprudence and public policy of the local consociation— where collective rights may be better protected—and the rest of the integrated or assimilated state. In system-wide consociations ethnic concentrations may make 'ethno-federalism' feasible—when territorial and ethnic autonomy coincide—while strictly consociational arrangements are kept for ethnically heterogeneous regions.

---

[24] By contrast, in plurality-rule electoral systems, which are more congruent with control, a dominant party may have no incentive to appeal to minorities.

Outside Management—Arbitration

Arbitration is the least theorized form of ethnic conflict-management, except in international relations (Hoffman 1992). The best way to understand arbitration is in contrast with control and consociation—as set out in Table 2.1 which extends and modifies Lustick's (1979) contrast between control and consociation. The term covers both external and internal modes of arbitration (McGarry and O'Leary 1993).[25]

Arbitration requires a 'neutral', bipartisan, or multipartisan umpire, that is conflict-regulation by agents other than the directly contending parties. The 'disinterestedness' of the arbiter makes it possible to win the acquiescence if not the enthusiastic support of the contending ethno-national communities. An arbiter provides governmental effectiveness where war might otherwise prevail. Arbitration is distinguishable from *mediation* because the arbiter makes the relevant decisions, whereas mediators merely facilitate. The arbiter pursues the common interests of the rival segments in the relevant society as s/he perceives them; regulates their political exchanges and presides over élites who have variable incentives to engage in responsible and co-operative behaviour. Arbitration, in principle, can establish the conditions for longer-term democratic conflict-resolution. The prerequisite is that the major ethnic segments broadly accept the arbiter's claim to neutrality.[26]

Internal arbitration can be executed by individuals not from the main antagonistic communities, for example Nyerere in post-independence Tanzania; by statesmen who are widely seen to transcend their origins, for example Tito in Yugoslavia; or who can claim a connection with all the major communities, for example Stevens in Sierra Leone. Arbitration can be performed by institutions, such as courts, and even kings, as the Jordanian monarchy has sought to show—see Chapter 11. A political party can also perform it. One-party states claim to absorb members of all ethnic communities and to regulate their rival aspirations, such as the Ba'athist party in Iraq

---

[25] External arbitration includes both 'co-operative internationalization' and forceful intervention by a self-appointed umpire concerned to establish stability. To count as arbitration any external third-party intervention must display procedural neutrality of some kind—many interventions, of course, are indistinguishable from efforts to establish control. Imperial powers, especially prior to their departure, present themselves as arbiters.

In legal literature, adjudication is used to refer to neutral third-party intervention, coupled with an imposed decision, while arbitration can often involve non-neutral third parties such as commercial arbitrators pushing the parties towards compromise

[26] Within any community there will be activists who will challenge the neutrality of any arbiter, and there will always be co-opted 'Uncle Toms and Aunty Thomasinas' who proclaim the benign impartiality of the most blatantly partisan government.

and Syria, but it is difficult to distinguish such regimes from control systems. In a polyarchy, arbitration can be performed by a pivotal political party, one judged to be sufficiently disinterested to be able to organize a cross-ethnic bloc or chair a cross-ethnic coalition. The Indian Congress party long claimed to be a fair arbiter in the states of the Indian Union, a claim that has become steadily threadbare in the years since Nehru's death—see Chapter 5. A single external agent or a bipartisan or a multipartisan authority can perform external arbitration. Co-operative internationalization, for example through the United Nations' peacekeeping and peacemaking forces, has been performed with intermittent success in Cyprus, parts of the Middle East, Africa, and the Balkans. It is usually a sign that the relevant conflict is seen as internally insoluble and as a threat to the security of an entire region.[27] But the adjudication of the International Court of Justice shows that there are instruments for multi-party arbitration of ethnic conflicts, should states choose to develop them. Bipartisan arbitration at its fullest involves two states sharing sovereignty over a territory in the form of a condominium.[28] But it can also involve a bilateral agreement in which one state maintains sovereignty over a disputed region but consults with a neighbouring interested state over law and public policy in that region, and grants the non-sovereign neighbour a role as guardian of an ethnic minority within the relevant region.

One example is the cross-border Anglo-Irish Agreement signed in 1985 (O'Leary and McGarry 1996: ch. 6). The Italian and Austrian governments in 1946 came to a similar agreement over South Tyrol, ensuring the German-speaking community 'complete equality of rights with the Italian-speaking inhabitants within the framework of special provisions to safeguard the ethnic character and the cultural and economic development of the German-speaking element', though it took many years before the agreement was implemented (Wolff 2000). Other bilateral agreements over contested regions and national minorities existed in inter-war Europe until they were washed away in the tidal wave of Nazi up-sizing (Macartney 1934).

Arbitration has no obvious territorial imperatives: but its existence suggests a stalemate in territorial claims and counter-claims. Internal arbiters may organize a multi-ethnic federation on balance of power principles, as Tito did in Yugoslavia. They may establish multiple asymmetric forms of

[27] Churchill observed of the Balkans that it produces more violence than it can consume domestically, one reason why it has been the site of external interventions (Buchanan 1991: 2).

[28] For the merits of this idea in some situations see O'Leary and McGarry (1996: ch. 8), and O'Leary *et al.* (1993). A condominium over the West Bank between Israel and Jordan was advocated by some, especially those concerned to blunt the radical edge of Palestinian nationalism. As Marc Lynch observes in Chapter 11 one of the purposes of the Intifada was to render such an idea unworkable.

TABLE 2.1. *Comparing control, consociation, and arbitration*

Regime/Facets	Control	Consociation	Arbitration
1. Interests protected	Interests of the dominant	Common interests of the consociational partners	Common interests of groups as perceived by the arbiter
2. Linkages between groups	Extraction by the dominant from the dominated	Exchanges between groups	Regulated exchanges
3. Bargaining	Unilateral imposition is norm: hard bargaining is a sign of collapse	Bargaining is a sign of health: proportionality norms operate	Threats/bargains made to/with arbiter rather than directly with other groups
4. Role of official regime	Partisan: supports dominant titular nationality	Cipher: registers/ processes the consociational bargain(s)	Umpire
5. Normative justification	Ideology of dominant group	Common welfare/peace	Necessity
6. Relations between élites	Asymmetric: subordinated choose between co-option and rebellion	Responsible/ co-operative	May be irresponsible
7. Metaphor	Puppeteer manipulating puppet	Balancing scale	Judge in family quarrels

autonomy within otherwise unitary systems. External arbiters, by contrast, usually hold territory 'in trust', pending a political settlement—an arrangement which may come to resemble imperial government.

Managing Existing Borders

Two internal territorial principles for managing conflict-regulation, namely autonomy and federalization, are compatible with egalitarian liberal democratic norms. Another external egalitarian principle, confederalism, enables clubs of states to share specific functions jointly while preserving important sovereign prerogatives and their existing territorial configurations.

Autonomy

Autonomy—or home rule, or devolution, or regionalism, or cantonization—grants territorial rights of self-government to communities within binational or multinational or polyethnic states. Under autonomy the relevant state is subjected to an internal division in which political power is devolved to at least one—conceivably very small—other political unit. This grant of autonomy may be distinctive or asymmetrical with autonomy rights being different for different nations, regions, or ethnic communities, or uniform and symmetrical with all nations and regions treated alike.

Autonomy must be distinguished from mere administrative decentralization, common in homogenized unitary states: it is built upon the recognition of national and ethnic difference, though it may be combined with some other forms of functional or spatial decentralization. The Kingdom of Spain, after the fall of Franco, and the recent devolutionary programme in the United Kingdom of Great Britain and Northern Ireland, are examples of formally asymmetrical grants of autonomy within decentralized unitary states that are acquiring a *de facto* federal character (Hazell and O'Leary 1999).

Autonomy arrangements are usually designed to create nationally or ethnically homogeneous units where majority rule is practically coterminous with the self-government of the relevant community.[29] Where ethnic conflict is high then the further local division of existing governmental units to create homogeneity may be followed, as in the case of the Bernese Jura in Switzerland (Voutat 1992). Autonomy is intended to restructure the sites of ethnic conflict and competition into smaller and more manageable units: a negotiable form of 'limited internal secession.' Under 'rolling devolution', policing and judicial powers can be gradually devolved to those areas where the population express a wish to exercise such powers, and where it is judged that the experiment had some prospects of success.

Autonomy is, however, fraught with potential difficulties, notably in the drawing and policing of appropriate units of government in heterogeneous or mixed areas, winning consent for them, and facing the ever-present threat that policing and judicial powers might be used as preparation for creating 'liberated zones'. Asymmetrical forms of autonomy may also generate resentments—be they fiscal or representative—in other parts of the state, threatening the relevant union. Yet granting autonomy may also stave off secessionists—by recognizing the relevant ethno-national identity, and by

---

[29] Autonomy can be designed to achieve a local form of consociation between rival ethno-national communities, especially where, as in the South Tyrol and Northern Ireland, the communities are so intermingled that a neat division is not possible.

putting the onus on secessionists to prove that independence is better than the *status quo* (Lapidoth 1997).[30]

Federalism

Federalism is similar but not coterminous with autonomy as a device for regulating multinational or polyethnic states. In a genuine federation both the central and the provincial governments enjoy constitutionally separate competencies, although they may also have concurrent powers. Unlike the forms of autonomy found in unitary or union states the central or union government of a federation usually cannot unilaterally alter the constitution—constitutional change affecting competencies requires the consent of both levels of government. Therefore federations automatically imply codified and written constitutions, and normally bicameral legislatures—in which the federal as opposed to the popular chamber may disproportionally represent, that is overrepresent, the smallest provinces.

Federations are usually built from confederations by state-managers who maintain that only an autonomous federal government can perform certain necessary functions that confederations find difficult to perform, especially a unified defence and external relations policy (Riker 1964). Multinational or ethno-federalists maintain that if the provincial borders between the components of the federation match the boundaries between the relevant national, ethnic, religious, or linguistic communities, that is, if there is a 'federal society' mapping onto a federal state, then federalism may be an effective conflict-regulating device because it has the effect of making an ethnically heterogeneous society less heterogeneous through the creation of more homogeneous subunits. However, of the seven large-scale genuine federations in long-term western democracies, only three achieve this effect: those of Belgium, Canada, and Switzerland. The federations of Australia, Austria, Germany, and the USA do not achieve this effect, and therefore federalism cannot be used to explain the relative ethno-national tranquillity of Australia, post-war Austria and Germany, and the post-1860s USA—where past genocides, integrationism/assimilation, and a dominant *Staatsvolk* may be more

---

[30] 'Pseudo-autonomy' is a form of control. The South African National Party established a number of barren 'homelands' for blacks in an ultimately unsuccessful attempt to delegitimize their demands for power at the centre. Successive Israeli governments have offered Palestinians forms of permanent autonomy that no representative Palestinian could embrace.

There also exists a grey area in territorial management of ethnic differences often found in conjunction with arbitration. International agreements can entrench the territorial autonomy of certain ethnic communities, even though the 'host state' does not generally organize itself along federalist principles: e.g. the agreement between Italy and Austria guaranteeing the autonomy of South Tyrol, or the agreement between Finland and Sweden guaranteeing the autonomy of the Åland islands.

important in explaining stability. In Belgium, Canada, and Switzerland the success of federalism in conflict-regulation, such as it is, has been based upon the historic accident that the relevant ethnic communities are quite sharply geographically segregated. Post-independence India, especially after the reorganization of internal state borders along largely linguistic boundaries, is an example of deliberate engineering to match certain ascriptive criteria with internal political borders—see Chapter 5.

Federalism is less successful for communities that are so dispersed, or small in numbers, that they cannot control federal units or provinces, for example Quebec anglophones, Flemish-speakers in Wallonia, francophones in Flanders, blacks in the USA, indigenous peoples in Australia, India, and North America. Indeed one reason federalism proved insufficient as a conflict-regulating device as Yugoslavia democratized was because there was insufficient geographical clustering of the relevant ethnic communities in relation to the existing borders.

There is a more subtle view that is rarely defended (see Horowitz 1985: chs. 14 and 15). It suggests that federations can and should be partly designed to prevent ethnic minorities from becoming local provincial majorities. The thought is that federalism's territorial merits may lie in enabling it to be used as an instrument to prevent local majoritarianism, and the attendant risks of local tyranny or secessionist incentives. Designing provincial borders, on this argument, should be done almost on 'balance of power' principles—proliferating where possible the points of power away from one focal centre, encouraging intra-ethnic conflict, and creating incentives for inter-ethnic co-operation by designing provinces without majorities, and for alignments based on non-ethnic interests. This logic is extremely interesting but empirical support for Horowitz's argument seems so far confined to the rather uninspiring case of independent Nigeria, and in most actually existing federations the redrawing of provincial borders deliberately to achieve these results could probably only be implemented by dictators.[31]

State-managers develop multi-ethnic federations for a variety of reasons. They have often evolved out of multi-ethnic colonies—to bind together the coalition opposing the imperial power. Federation may have been promoted by the colonial power in an attempt to sustain an imperial system and developed a dynamic of its own, as was true of Canada and India. A history of common colonial government usually creates élites—soldiers, bureaucrats and capitalists—with an interest in sustaining the post-colonial territory, as has

---

[31] Belgium may be an interesting exception: the Brussels region, created in the new Belgian federation, is neither overtly Flemish or Wallonian, and perhaps the existence of this heterogeneous region helps stabilize inter-ethnic relations in Belgium as a whole, because without Brussels, Flanders will not secede, and there is little prospect of Brussels obliging Flanders.

been true of Indonesia. Large federal states can often be sold economically—they promise a larger single market, a single currency, economies of scale, reductions in transactions' costs, and fiscal equalization. Lastly, they can be marketed as geopolitically wise, offering greater security and protection than small states.

Unfortunately federalism has a poor track-record as an ethnic conflict-regulating device, even where it allows a degree of minority self-government. Democratic federations have broken down throughout Asia and Africa, with the possible exception of India—though consider Singh's arguments in Chapter 5. Federal failures may occur because minorities continue to be out-numbered at the federal level of government. The resulting frustrations, combined with an already defined boundary and the significant institutional resources flowing from control of their own province or 'state', provide con-siderable incentives to attempt secession—see Motyl's reflections in Chapter 7. Secessionist breaks from federations may invite harsh responses from the rest of the federation: the disintegration of the Nigerian and American fed-erations were halted only through millions of deaths. India, the most suc-cessful post-colonial federation, faces vigorous secessionist movements on its frontiers, especially in Kashmir and Punjab, and Canada is perennially threatened with the secession of Quebec. The threat of secession in multi-ethnic federations is such that Nordlinger (1972) excluded federalism from his list of desirable conflict-regulating practices—and the recent emergent principle of international law that permits the disintegration of federations along the lines of their existing territorial units would appear to confirm this worry (Horowitz 1998). Integrationist nation-builders in Africa have dis-trusted federalism precisely for this reason. It was no accident that Mobutu only offered federalism as a model for Zaïre as his power collapsed (Chapter 4). African state-builders' antipathy to federalism is now matched amongst the intellectuals of Eastern Europe who regard it as a recipe for secession, given the Czechoslovakian, Yugoslavian, and Soviet experiences. Federa-tions have been especially fragile in bi-ethnic societies. With the possible exception of Belgium there is not a single case of successful federalism based upon dyadic or two-unit structures (Vile 1982).[32] Even relatively successful multi-ethnic federations appear to be in permanent constitutional crises: the divisions of powers must be constantly renegotiated as a result of technolog-ical advances, economic transformations, and judicial interventions.

My own research suggests that there may well be a law of federations, to wit, a stable democratic majoritarian federation requires a *Staatsvolk*—more

---

[32] Even the Belgian federation technically has four subunits, though it is built around a dualist ethno-linguistic division, and the EC has helped sustain the unity of Belgium.

technically, the politically effective number of ethno-national groups must be less than 2 on the ethno-national index, defined as the reciprocal of the relevant Herfindahl–Hirschman concentration index. This argument, elaborated fully in O'Leary (forthcoming), appears to be confirmed in all stable democratic federations to date. The theory underlying it is that a stable democratic federation must have a *Staatsvolk*, a national people who are demographically dominant, not necessarily a majority, and who must be the co-founders of the federation. The law has a corollary: a federation without a *Staatsvolk*, or, more technically, a multicultural federation which registers about 2 or more effective cultural groups on the relevant ethno-national index, must use supplementary consociational practices if it is to persist as a democratic federation. This is a hypothesis: a claim that consociational institutions are a necessary supplement to preserve democratic federations where there is no *Staatsvolk*.

What the law and hypothesis state may be the necessary conditions for stability in democratic multicultural federations. In liberal democratic systems the population-share of an ethno-national group can be taken as a reasonable proxy for its *potential* electoral power. A majoritarian federation must have a *Staatsvolk*, a people sufficiently confident about their place in the state that they believe that they can afford to make territorial concessions to smaller peoples. The theory also suggests that if there is no *Staatsvolk* then federalism alone, of whatever internal territorial configuration, will not be enough to sustain stability. Consociational devices will be required if the state is to be democratic, and control devices if it is to be undemocratic.

Confederation

State-managers may conceivably 'up-size' to regulate ethnic and national differences. Interstate agreements to establish confederations would, of course, mean that the confederation as a whole would be more heterogeneous than any of its member-states. Confederations have often been justified as means of resolving historic national and ethnic antagonisms (see Elazar 1994). For example, the European Union has been defended as a forum that resolved all the security and ethno-territorial disputes between France and Germany; as a mechanism that facilitated the possible and actual resolution of British–Irish and Italian–Austrian border questions; as a means through which the Northern Irish nationalists, the Tyrolese germanophones and the Basques may be interlinked with their co-nationals and co-ethnics in transfrontier and functional cross-border programmes and institutions; and as a decision-making site through which multinational member-states will be encouraged on functionalist logic to permit a fuller flourishing of internal regional autonomy.

But one must enter strong caveats about these arguments. As Horowitz has put it

It is . . . no accident that international integration [what I call confederation] has come to very little on a world scale. There are many reasons for this, but ethnic diversity has contributed at least its fair share. The decisive fact is that for every ethnic group that enthusiastically favours unification with a neighbouring country or countries, there is another group that vehemently and often violently opposes the idea. In ethnically divided societies, international integration becomes a central aspect of ethnic arithmetic, comparable in potency to those divisive issues, the census, immigration policy, birth rates and birth control . . . it is difficult to determine just where irredentism leaves off and international integration begins.

(Horowitz 1985: 593, 595)

Among many examples, he cites how the Kurds in Iraq have forced the relevant regime in power to back off from efforts to unite with other Arab states—see also Chapter 9. As for the European Union, its success as a conflict-regulating device may in large measure be because the bulk of its members are predominantly homogenized nation-states, and that the bleak history of wars, expulsions, and genocides of this century have left many fewer possible sites of ethno-territorial antagonism for them to dispute (Mazower 1998). Groups with overt or covert irredentist ambitions may support entry into the European Union but member-states' motivations for 'upsizing' have largely lain within the domains of security and economic policy.

Confederation may, of course, ease the pain of 'down-sizing' and/or partition. The Jordanian élite's decision to sever its claims to the West Bank, discussed by Marc Lynch in Chapter 11, carefully did not preclude the possibility of a confederation with a sovereign Palestine—to be subsequently freely negotiated. Irish nationalists in both parts of Ireland have consistently sought to build all-Ireland confederal relationships, either to dampen the impact of partition, or with the explicit intent of seeing such confederal relationships as a first step towards reunification. What may make the British-Irish Agreement over Northern Ireland of 1998 institutionally unique is the agreement in principle to have partly balancing forms of confederal relations, one set that link Northern Ireland to the Republic of Ireland through a North-South Ministerial Council, and another that link Northern Ireland to all the political jurisdictions of Great Britain and the Republic of Ireland (O'Leary 1999). Neither proposal, the Palestinian-Jordanian confederation, nor the all-Irish and British-Irish confederal dual protection model, have yet been fully implemented.

Down-Sizing External Borders: Secession, Partition and Decolonization

If co-operative up-sizing to manage ethno-national differences is discounted by most political élites what then of down-sizing? The sharpest forms of territorial down-sizing public officials may consider are to impose partition, to permit secession, and to decolonize. They may combine elements of all three. Let us consider the first two in some detail as modes of right-sizing.

Partition

A partition should be understood as an externally proposed and imposed *fresh* border cut through at least one community's national homeland, creating at least two separate units under different sovereigns or authorities. That is how Irish, Greek, Indian, and Palestinian nationalists understand the partitions of Ireland, Cyprus, India, and Palestine. Partitions create new states or territories.[33] Sovereign or Great Powers execute partitions—though local parties may affect them. Partitions are always regarded by at least one 'loser' as an imposition, a violation.

Arend Lijphart, however, has argued that there can be an acceptable partition where it is negotiated by all of the affected groups rather than imposed; when it involves a fair division of land and resources; and where it results in homogeneous, or at least substantially less plural, independent countries (Lijphart 1984). But I submit that agreed border adjustments that meet these three conditions would not match the normal sense of what a partition involves. Lijphart's agreed 'partition' looks more like an ideally negotiated decolonization, or a secession with some border-adjustments. Lijphart, however, is not alone in believing that acceptable partitions are feasible and worthy of consideration by policy-makers.

Jan Tullberg and Brigitta Tullberg have argued that borders should be drawn to leave as few people as possible in the 'wrong' state (Tullberg and Tullberg 1997). A fair rule, they think, is that an equal number of people from each group should be wrongly placed. They argue that the partitioning border ought to be as 'natural' as possible. For 'transfers' of peoples they propose three principles: each state should be responsible for accepting people of its own nationality; each state should be entitled to evict members of the other group; and each individual may emigrate to the 'right' state. They propose that an agreed partition should require two-thirds support within the group wishing to separate. Critics have little difficulty in demonstrating that the

---

[33] Local partitions involve the deliberate, fresh re-structuring of local and regional governments on ethno-territorial lines, either in pursuit of control or to assist ethno-federalism.

Tullbergs' proposals are more morally and politically problematic than they imagine (see for example McGarry and Moore 1997), not least their ideal of natural borders.

Partitions as brutal or radical surgery on existing polities were once normal features of the warring European states-system, when territories were the 'real estate' of monarchs rather than the 'national lands' of citizen-peoples. The successive partitions of Poland between the Tsarist, Habsburg, and Hohenzollern dynasties were paradigm cases. The partition of Africa in the late nineteenth century was the last large-scale shameless division of territories by imperialists of this ilk—thirty new colonies and protectorates and 10 million square miles of territory were 'sliced up like a cake' in half a generation (Pakenham 1991). Henceforth, at least within the heartlands of industria, partitions have paid lip-service to the principle of nationalities—the carve-up of the losing Ottoman, Hapsburg, and German empires after the Great War registered this shift. The post-World War II partitions of Germany, Vietnam, and Korea formally respected the principle of self-determination even while sundering the relevant territories during the cold war. Where capitalism or communism triumphed the relevant partition was shortly overturned, as in the cases of Germany and Vietnam respectively: Korean unification will follow shortly upon the collapse of North Korean communism.

After the dismemberment of losing empires in the Great War and of losing nation-states in the Second and the Cold Wars, the major partitions of this century have taken three forms. The first, partition with decolonization, has been a British specialty, for example Ireland (1920–1), the Indian subcontinent (1947), and Palestine (1948). In each case the partition was preceded by planning of both a benign and malign kind.[34] The second is the partition consequent upon an irredentist (or 'rescuing') invasion, for example Turkey's partition of Cyprus in 1974. There is a case for seeing the 'line of control' in Kashmir in the same way. The third type of partition accompanies the internationalization of an ethnic conflict, for example the likely partition of Bosnia and of rump Yugoslavia—between Serbia, Kosovo, and possibly Montenegro.

Partitions accompanying decolonization display a marked bias in favour of minorities that supported the imperial power—thus Ulster Unionists and Israeli Zionists won more territory than their numbers might have warranted (Frazer 1984), and the Muslims of British India won the strikingly bifurcated state of Pakistan—see Chapter 9. Any further formal partition of

[34] See *inter alia* Fraser (1984); Gwynn (1950); Hassan (1993); Johnston (1976); Kumar (1997a, b); Laffan (1983); Mansergh (1978); Masalha (1993); Page (1982); Shlaim (1990); Singh (1987/90); Singh (1997).

Palestine is likely to be biased in the interests of the post-1967 Israeli settlers. Irredentist or 'rescue' partitions have remained rare, not least because they violate international norms against territorial seizures, but quasi- or unofficial partitions, by contrast, may be the wave of the future if NATO repeats some of its recent interventions, and if more 'collapsed states' materialize in Africa.

Partitions are facilitated if empires or states collapse, if there are some historic administrative borders that provide some cover for disguising what is otherwise experienced as 'fresh cut', and if there are territorial concentrations of ethno-national communities that will defend the new cut. The motivations that drive partitions are usually straightforward: to

(1) preserve as much territory for the core of a down-sizing state or empire;
(2) placate losing settler colonialists, or formerly dominant minorities;
(3) arbitrate the differences between allegedly or actually irreconcilable native communities; and
(4) hive off the unwanted or undesirable.

Partitions are essentially contested arrangements. Until 1988 the PLO refused to consider the partition of Palestine—calling the idea 'filastinian'. Right-wing parties in Israel still refuse to contemplate the partition of 'Eretz Israel' by an international border—'autonomy', of a very constrained type, is the limit to which they will go. The Jordanian monarchy, as Marc Lynch recounts in Chapter 11, had considerable difficulty in accepting the irreversibility of the partition of Jordan occasioned by the Israeli victory of 1967. Irredentist or unificationist movements on the part of the perceived losers normally accompany partitions of nations—as opposed to empires. These may take the form of militarized or paramilitarized conflict, or more peaceful moves to establish functional or confederal cross-border co-operation, to repair or heal the 'wound'.

Partition has its advocates who believe it may resolve ethnic conflict by allowing divorce between those ethnic communities which do not wish to live together, but the trouble is that partition rarely accomplishes a 'clean divorce', that is, bringing into being nationally homogeneous or harmonious states (see Horowitz 1998: 190–3). Pakistan, 'twice the product of partition, is testimony to the propensity of new cleavages to supplant the old' (Horowitz 1985: 591)—see Vali Nasr's discussion in Chapter 6.

When do state officials contemplate partitions? Rarely, and mostly of states that are not theirs! Let us therefore confine our attention to cases in which officials are considering their own core state, and not where they are partitioning territories to be subsequently independently governed by others. One answer is that they contemplate partition only when obliged to do so.

States resist contraction, it is said, in the way that a human being resists dismemberment. But this metaphor is correct if and only if states regard all their territories as intrinsic parts of their identity. Plainly the historical record suggests that some territories are more expendable, more suitable for load-shedding than others. States will, it seems, adjust their external borders if the benefits from doing so outweigh the costs; and sometimes they will do this because they also respect the normative principle of national self-determination.[35] On the benefit side of the calculus it is plain that contracting the sovereign borders may have the advantage of creating a more nationally homogeneous and legitimate rump-state—as has been publicly argued by Jordanian exclusionists—see Chapter 11. Down-Sizing therefore offers the prospect of a more functional industrial state. It sheds the load of governing a recalcitrant or rebellious people, and all the military, administrative, and redistributive costs that they impose on the *Staatsvolk*. These arguments are likely to be reinforced with ballot boxes—if they have access to them—and by bombs by at least some of the recalcitrant and rebellious peoples. Lastly, down-sizing allows the prospect of respect for the principle of national self-determination, leading to good neighbourly relations between the successor states. These arguments were obviously persuasive to Czech élites in 1990–2, as they were once attractive to Swedish élites in 1905, and to Malaysian élites in 1965.

The costs of contracting the core state must also be considered. These include *inter alia* the blows to national pride and prestige caused by cutting off part of what was regarded as the state's territory, the losses of legitimacy for power élites held culpable for such load-shedding, the loss of manpower and other taxable resources, and the formation of new and perhaps less defensible land and sea borders. The political management costs will be especially problematic, and difficult to calculate, when 'a clean partition' is not feasible.

Secession

Secession is something that states permit or accept, it is not something that states do: secession is an action of regions or provinces. Secession is generally down-sizing without the voluntary consent of the centre. After World War II successful secession was relatively rare. Between 1948 and 1991 only one new state, Bangladesh, was carved out of an existing state, out of the bizarre format of Pakistan Mark 1. By contrast, in the same period, the decolonization of the European and USA controlled imperial territories in Asia, the Middle East, Africa, and Latin and Caribbean America produced the

---

[35] Self-determination can in principle be exercised to agree to integration with the state and its *Staatsvolk*, to assimilation, or to federation and autonomy—for exemplary contemporary discussions see Moore (1998).

majority of states in the world today. Interestingly, these were not, in general, regarded as secessions. The collapse of the communist regimes of Ethiopia, Yugoslavia, and the Soviet Union in 1989–91 has precipitated another round of secessionist state-building efforts, though on some interpretations these should also be read as decolonizations.

Despite their difficulties in achieving their goals in the twentieth century, secessionists have not gone away, and they still impact on the state system (Heraclides 1992). Some Iraqi Kurds still hope that they may get the chance to build Kurdistan under the umbrella of an American supervised domination of Northern Iraq; the KLA has similar ambitions after NATO's conquest of Kosovo. There are secessionist or semi-secessionist[36] movements in Europe, for example amongst the Basque, Corsican, Northern Irish nationalist, Scottish, Slovak, and Welsh peoples; in Canada, amongst the Quebecois; in Africa, the Polisario movement in the western Sahara, the Dinkas of the southern Sudan, and a variety of communities in the Horn of Africa; in the new republics of the Commonwealth of Independent States— see Chapter 7; and in central and south Asia, the Khalistan movement for a Sikh homeland, the Kashmiri independence movement, the Tamil Tigers of Sri Lanka; the Tibetans in communist China, and the multiple ethnic secessionists of Myanmar.[37]

The principle of national self-determination moves these organizations and peoples against regimes that they portray as empires. The principle famously begs four questions: who are the people with this right? What are the borders within which they should exercise self-determination? What constitutes consent for change? Will the exercise of the right produce a domino-effect in which national minorities within seceding territories will seek self-determination for themselves?

In what were Yugoslavia and the Soviet Union these questions were not academic. In what was the Soviet Union it was eventually accepted that each of the former republics had the right to self-determination, but there was no such agreement about peoples trapped within republics which they would rather not be within. Most of the former Soviet republics are ethnic minefields. There are many hard cases in seeking to apply the doctrine of self-determination: Northern Ireland, Quebec, Punjab, Kashmir, Sri Lanka. In moderately complex cases the principle seems indeterminate. As Ivor

---

[36] Semi-secessionist movements describes those seeking to leave one state to unite or reunite with another. Strict secessionists seek to create an independent state. States that seek to up-size to complete their nation-stateness are properly irredentist; semi-secessionists are unificationists (positive) or irredentists (negative).

[37] While the Israeli–occupied territories of the West Bank and the Gaza Strip are not legally part of the Israeli state the Palestinian population there want to secede from Israeli political control.

Jennings remarked 'On the surface [the principle of self-determination] seem[s] reasonable: let the people decide. It [i]s in fact ridiculous because the people cannot decide until somebody decides who are the people' (Jennings 1956: 56). Exercising the principle is theoretically straightforward when there is no large or disgruntled ethnic minority within the relevant region affected by the proposed new independent state *and* when the seceding area includes the great majority of those who wish to leave. There are some cases where these optimum conditions have applied: Norway's secession from Sweden, and Iceland's from Denmark. More often than not the exercise of secessionist self-determination to achieve independence will create orphans, bereft of their parent nation (McGarry 1998).

There have been some ingenious answers to Jennings's question about who decides who are the people, and where. One is that every (self-defined) area within a liberal democratic state should be given the right to secede, provided the same right is extended to every sub-area within the proposed secessionist territory (Beran 1984, 1988, 1990, 1993). This argument answers the accusation that self-determination creates a dangerous domino-effect by saying that there is nothing wrong with allowing a state to fragment on the principle of self-determination; and the fact that the seceding units themselves should grant the right of self-determination within their borders should put a prudential check on the aspiration to seek self-determination in territorially problematic zones. Philosophical engagement with these arguments is now widespread (Moore 1998; O'Leary 1996).

But state officials, in general, are not liberals with their territories. The right of secession seems unlikely to be entrenched in many modern liberal democratic constitutions,[38] and it is likely to continue to have a bad press amongst liberals and socialists.[39] In part this is a geopolitical legacy. The cold

[38] One liberal democracy to have granted the right of secession is the United Kingdom. In 1949 it granted the right of secession to the Northern Ireland parliament, and in 1985 it granted the right of the people of Northern Ireland to become part of the Republic of Ireland, reinforced in the 1998 *Northern Ireland Act*. This right, as Irish nationalist critics point out, was not one which the local majority of unionists were ever likely to choose—though demographic change *may* eventually remove the unionist veto. Another liberal democracy to follow suit has been Canada: in 1998 its Supreme Court in a complex judgement ruled that Quebec has the right to secede if there is a 'clear' majority in a 'clear' question in a referendum on secession. Ethiopia, which has liberal democratic aspirations, also has a secessionist clause but does not seem keen to have anyone exercise it after Eritrea's departure. The right of secession was fictionally embodied in successive Soviet constitutions, even though the Bolsheviks had ruthlessly reconquered the territories of the Tsarist Russian empire.

[39] Liberals and socialists favour lax divorce laws, but their arguments against secession have a remarkable isomorphism with those deployed against the legalization of divorce. The dangers posed to children by divorce are analogous to those posed to minorities; the reduced incentives to work-out differences between marriage-partners are analogous to those intended to establish a workable accommodation between ethnic communities; and the likelihood that one partner will benefit more

war elevated the stability of states' borders into a necessity: rather than face nuclear confrontation the two superpowers respected the borders of the other's client-states, at least in Europe. But with the collapse of the cold war, there is now much greater room for successful secession and the alteration of borders artificially frozen by the strategic interests of the superpowers—as the reunification of Germany and the fragmentation of the Balkans suggests.

In many parts of the world, especially those still in transit to industria, the claims and counter-claims of unionists, federalists, and exponents of national self-determination remain likely to produce violence. Whether implementing a claim for secessionist independence is straightforward or not, the proposal is likely to encourage key élites in the affected states to behave in chauvinistic and warlike ways: the peaceful secessions of Iceland from Denmark, or Norway from Sweden were exceptional. Ian Lustick's argument that secessionists are mostly regarded as treasonous people by unionists has full historic purchase.

What can be said of a general nature about the circumstances under which secessions are likely to be successfully executed? Two external phenomena matter: the nature of the interstate system—is it permissive or restrictive?; and the aftermath of wars—which often lead to territorial departures, often without any considerations of consent. Internally, national groups in Gellner's industria will continue to seek full self-determination, in the form of independent statehood, for a variety of reasons. They may be motivated by a reaction against ethnic discrimination and humiliation, by the pragmatic expectation that the new nation-state will have greater economic and political freedom, by the wish to have a state in which different public policies will be pursued, by the desire for power and prestige amongst nationalist élites, or to protect a given ethnic culture from extinction. Not much of a very general nature can be successfully sustained about the economic circumstances or motivations of full-scale ethnic secessionist movements (Connor 1984). Secessions are demanded both by economically advanced groups—for example Basques, Catalans, Ibos, Lombards, Sikhs, and Tamils—and by economically backward communities—East Bengalis, Karens, Kurds, and Slovaks; and secessionist communities can be located in either backward or advanced regional economies (Horowitz 1985: 229 ff.). There are good arguments for rejecting 'direct causal relationships between regional economic disparity and ethnic secession' (ibid. 235).

Enthusiasm for self-determination flows most powerfully from the democratization of the world. Democratization means that the people are to

than another from divorce is analogous to the argument that the better-off should not be allowed to secede in order to obtain material advantages.

rule. The statist declares that the people are all those who are legitimately resident in a given state or political unit's borders (the civic nationalist); the nationalist that they are the nation (the ethnic nationalist). In happy cases such as Iceland, these two answers approximately coincide; in most cases they do not. The definition and championing of the people are, in most polities, up for grabs, or for hegemonic definition, as others prefer to put it, and the possibility of fragmentation enters into the fabric of any state where ethnic and civic nationalisms point to different populations as composing *the* nation. Once democratization poses the issue of the definition of the right people a clustered set of issues automatically follows: the most important of which are the definition of citizenship, the possession of the franchise, the organizational structure of the state, and the state's borders. These issues create incentives for political entrepreneurs to make party-building and vote-winning efforts out of ethnic cleavages—whether at the foundation of the state or afterwards. Politicians in multi-ethnic states have multiple incentives to manipulate ethno-national politics, as Randolph Churchill chose to play the Orange card in the UK in the 1880s. It is not possible to immunize the democratic process to exclude these issues. They are always there for mobilization by the oppressed or the opportunist or both. Those who lose out politically under existing state-arrangements and policies, whoever they may be, may always choose to try to redefine the rules of the game. If there are any economic differences between communities in a liberal democratic state,[40] then class and ethnicity may become reinforcing divisions—leading to the creation of parties with different ethnic constituencies. Where political parties are representative of all ethnic communities then party competition raises no immediate threat of destabilization, but this case will be unusual.

Democratization therefore increases the likelihood that political agents will pursue secessionist self-determination for their ethno-national or ethno-religious community, and thereby destabilize the borders of existing multinational and multi-ethnic states. But three important qualifications to this proposition are in order.

1. Border destabilization is likely to be contained if the relevant state or region exists in a milieu of other liberal democratic states. In the twentieth century liberal democracies, or at least it is now conventionally argued this way in the 'democratic peace' literature, rarely went to war against one another. Whether the complete avoidance of wars between democratic states is a systemic feature of industrial liberal democracies is not

---

[40] There will almost inevitably be such differences, whether or not they flow from discrimination, historic advantages/disadvantages, or differing cultural traits or preferences which give some groups an advantage in the relevant division of labour.

something about which there is definitive evidence, but wars between such entities are much less likely than wars between democracies and non-democracies, or between non-democracies and non-democracies. Spreading democracy is, however, no panacea for territorial stabilitarians: 'democracy' *per se* cannot stop all secessionist politics; indeed, as I have suggested it can encourage it.

2. There are historic, political, and sociological factors which mute the destabilizing effects of democratization upon multinational and multi-ethnic states, and may inhibit the impetus to territorial break-up, either at the moment of democratization or later. These factors include a pre-industrial history of good inter-ethnic relations at élite level; a unification of the opposition to an authoritarian or control regime before it breaks down; the internal territorial segregation of ethnic groups that may permit territorial autonomy or federal self-government—'good fences make good neighbours'; demographic dominance by a *Staatsvolk*, where the large ethno-national community group is sufficiently secure not to fear the minority or minorities, and may behave in a generous way; and demographic stability, where one or more groups are not outgrowing one another.

3. Liberal democratic states have flexible and accommodative methods for managing national and ethnic minorities—as we have seen with respect to autonomy, federalist, and consociational arrangements. Their swift, effective, and generous deployment can make it difficult for independence movements to win mandates for break-up—because it is always possible to emphasize the benefits of Union, compared with the risks of independence. To do so the relevant political centre must minimally demonstrate that the union recognizes the potentially secessionist nation(s) as (a) full co-partner(s), that the union is a co-prosperity sphere; and, not least, that the union is the best means of protecting the security of the relevant nation.

Lustick's Theory of Statal Expansion and Contraction

Partitions and secessions are often run together in the political science literature (see for example Horowitz 1985; McGarry and O'Leary 1993: ch. 1), and decolonizations and secessions are often treated as synonyms. All three involve the restructuring of sovereign territorial borders and the 'downsizing' of at least one polity, so it is not senseless that they are merged for analytical, normative, and comparative purposes. But there are subtle, though important, differences between the three concepts.

There is firstly the issue of agency: partitions are carried out 'from outside and above'; decolonization is carried out 'from within and above' by the recently dominant core state or empire; whereas secession is executed 'from within and below'. There is secondly the question of what is being partitioned, or decolonized, and what is seceding from what. A national homeland is partitioned. A colony is decolonized by a retiring empire. A region, province, or member-state secedes from a state, a union state, a federation, or a confederation. Then, thirdly, there is the relations between the parties involved in partition, secession, and decolonization. Partition is necessarily imposed on its victims. Decolonization is seen as accompanying the emancipation of a previous inferior. Secession is the departure of an equal. A nation is liberated from an empire through decolonization; a region, province, or state breaks from a state.

Do these phrasings merely amount to a matter of partisan ethno-national 'position' and the rhetoric apposite to that position? Do 'losers' call the territorial restructuring partition? Do winners and graceful losers call it decolonization? Do losers claim that secessionists (separatists) have left them, while winners claim that they have been liberated from an empire? Ian Lustick argues that rhetorical issues are at stake, but that they are of genuine, almost symptomatic, significance—see Lustick (1993) and Chapter 3. In particular, he maintains that when the political élites at the core of a state are freely prepared to disengage from a territory they necessarily regard that territory in a colonial manner. They do not then see the territory in question—at least any longer—as a fundamental, permanent, and defining feature of the political body. It can be done without; 'disengagement' can be considered. By contrast, when the territory is seen as fully incorporated into the core, as fundamental, as a permanent and a defining component, as a vital organ of the state, then a demand for independence on the part of that territory is treated as secessionist, that is, treasonous. Lustick uses these insights to develop a theory that is used, developed, or criticized, in the contributions that follow from Chapter 4.

The core of the theory suggests that both state expansion and state contraction have two thresholds: 'a regime threshold' and 'an ideological hegemony' threshold. Take state expansion first. When a state expands into a given territory Lustick posits that this will create an 'incumbency stage', in which the territory is regarded as like a colony, capable of being disengaged from. It is weakly institutionalized. The status of the territory in the minds of political élites at the centre is entirely negotiable. But once the 'regime threshold' is crossed the status of the territory changes: to question its locus as part of the political system is now to precipitate a struggle over 'regime integrity'. A second threshold may then be crossed: that of ideological hegemony. The territory is now regarded as so integral to the meaning of the state that its status is unquestionable; it is unthinkable for political élites to consider its status as merely a question of interests, costs, and benefits. It has become part of the identity of the state.

State contraction follows a reverse trajectory. A territory's status may lose its ideologically hegemonic character, as part of the very identity of the state: it becomes a place apart. It may then be subjected to legitimate debate over the interests, costs, and benefits attaching to its continuing membership of the polity. Lastly, it may lose its regime status, and become available if not automatically scheduled for disengagement. Lustick treats these different thresholds as 'non-linear'. They can be reversed and a state can shift from the last to the first stage in catastrophic jumps.

The theory appears to imply that the difference between a state and an empire is fundamentally a question of legitimacy in the minds of the central power élite. Where a state has so incorporated territories that their status is unquestionable, when their nature is unchallenged from within the dominant political class, then state-building has been successful: the relationships between the original core and the acquired territory lose their imperial character; imperialism is rendered historic, and indeed subject to historical amnesia. By contrast, when a territory's status loses its ideologically hegemonic character then the state's relationship to that territory may be regarded by some of its dominant political class as imperial or colonial. The theory suggests that examining the public discourses of politicians at the centre, the ways in which they define and regard outlying territories, provide the best empirical indicators of the status of the relevant territories, that is, whether they are in the ideological hegemony, regime, or incumbency stages, and whether any particular threshold is being neared.

The theory is richer than the skeletal framework sketched here and Lustick elaborates it with power and eloquence in the next chapter. It has explanatory promise, and both normative and strategic resonance. The theory has micro-foundations, in so far as Lustick places the status of territories within the (transformable) constraints and preferences of ambitious politicians intent on obtaining or maintaining power. He believes that hegemonic beliefs about the nature of territories cannot be too far removed from 'reality', and he sketches a range of means through which politicians can develop strategies for crossing or reversing the two key thresholds. For example, in state-contraction they may engage in the 'rechannelling' of territorial politics through

(1) problem decomposition;
(2) regime recomposition;
(3) coalition realignment;
(4) organizing a change in the preference orderings of their followers and publics.

The subtlety of these arguments are best read in the original—but see Chapter 3.

What of difficulties? At first glance Lustick's theory appears entirely power-élite centred, ignoring the autonomous agency and reflective capacities of mass publics, the historic ethno-national character of the territories in question, or their status in Gellner's stages of history: foragia, agraria, or industria. Synthesizing the views of its critics, in reviews, at our meetings, and in our e-mail seminars, five principal difficulties with the theory can be identified (see also Kissane 1996), some of which are addressed by Lustick in his conclusions to this volume.

1. The first two objections are based on conceptual history. Lustick uses the Gramscian notion of ideological hegemony, originally developed for inter-class relations, to address the status of territory in the minds of a ruling political class—or indeed a ruling political nation. This transformation not only involves a tacit shift from class to ethno-national relations, but also, and more importantly, appears not to address the status of the peripheral territories in the eyes of their native inhabitants. Lustick addresses this challenge indirectly, in so far as he acknowledges that nationalist dissent and violence may be palpable features of reality that preclude 'ideologically hegemonic' conceptions of the relevant territory being held at the metropolitan centre— but the suggestion remains that in his thinking political constructions of reality at the metropolitan core are determinant in the last instance. This implicit argument is criticized by Oren Yiftachel in Chapter 12, and is replied to by Lustick tacitly in Chapter 3 and explicitly in Chapter 13. The status of Gramsci's own views on these matters is an interesting issue in the history of political thought, but is not treated here. What matters substantively is whether analyses of ideology, legitimacy, and hegemony can be successfully transferred from the field of class to the field of ethno-territorial politics.

2. Lustick's redefinition of the distinction between a state and an empire as something determined, in effect, in the minds of the metropolitan political class does not persuade those who regard empires as exemplars of agraria, or of early industria, that are being phased out by remorseless modernization. Critics of Lustick's theory would argue that the distinction between modern states and empires rests essentially upon the issue of mass nationalist legitimacy rather than upon the conceptions of the metropolitan power-élite.

Empires are conventionally contrasted with states in the following ways. Empires are necessarily 'large'. Empires are brought into existence by conquest. In an empire an identifiable core territorial unit—a city-state, or a national state—or ethnic/communal unit exerts domination, without mass consent, over other territorial or ethnic units (see for example Finer 1997: 8). Empires rarely achieve administrative or other forms of homogenizing integration. Some areas are subject to direct rule from the centre; others to indirect rule. Citizenship is not, in principle, universally granted to legal residents or subjects. Lastly, empires are 'star-shaped': the centre controls and co-ordinates peripheries that cannot co-ordinate with other peripheries.

Lustick's perspective, by contrast, privileges the view of the centre in determining whether a political system is a state or an empire. This may be a necessary corrective to much previous literature, but, as several contributors point out, it may not allow sufficiently either for the structural differences between states and empires that I have just highlighted, or for the strategic powers, efforts, and conceptions of peripheral agents.

The twentieth century was in some respects testimony to the power of the weak in the imperial periphery rather than to the power of ideological hegemony at the centre. The British and French were forced from some of 'their' territories after the failures of their armies to carry out successful counter-insurgencies, for example in Algeria and Ireland. The Dutch in Indonesia, the Belgians in Africa, the Spanish in Latin America, the Pacific and North Africa, and the Portuguese in Africa were all obliged to evacuate some of their colonies because of the direct costs of military pressure from insurgencies. The USA and the USSR failed to win hearts, minds, or decisive military victories in Vietnam and Afghanistan. The Vietnamese could not hold Kampuchea; the Ethiopians could not keep Eritrea; the Israelis, despite formidable weaponry could not hold southern Lebanon, at least not at an acceptable price. Lustick, of course, treats such insurgencies as 'palpable' disconfirming evidence against ideological beliefs being propagated at the centre, evidence which may change the ideological status of the territories in question from that of integrated to colonial or occupied territories. His critics nevertheless insist on the autonomous efficacy of peripheral agents in moving the borders of sovereignty, whatever the state of minds and mentalities at the imperial centre.

3. In any case Lustick's conception of what political discourse at the centre indicates about the status of a given territory may be more problematic than he suggests. This point is subtly made by Marc Lynch in Chapter 11 where he suggests that Lustick takes for granted a stable and somewhat open 'public sphere' within his core states. The 'non-discussability' of the idea of autonomy or independence for a territory or region, for example the denial of the existence of Kurds and a Kurdistan question in official Turkey—see Chapter 8—is after all, an indication of an exclusionary, militaristic control system, rather than of a successful integrated state-building project. Moreover, the very fact that the status of a territory may not be discussible by the power élite may make its members and their supporters less constitutionally flexible, and the relevant natives more, rather than less, determined

to go for independence rather than autonomy. In short, it is a strange form of ideological hegemony that renders the domination of the *Staatsvolk* more vulnerable to challenge from peripheral nationalities and ethnic communities.

4. Lustick's theory does not directly address the relevance of the historical form of the incorporation of a given territory into a state, unlike his earlier work which emphatically emphasized the co-existence of native and settlers as the key blockage to the successful permanent incorporation of a territory (Lustick 1985). Surely, we may want to argue, that it matters whether the relevant territory was acquired through conquest, through partition, through treaty, after a catastrophe, or through some permutation of these experiences? Were native élites co-opted or deleted, or did the centre's strategy vary? Were the inhabitants of the territory at the time of state-formation foragians, agrarians, or industrials? Were the conquerors or settlers agrarians or industrials? Did genocide, expulsion, and/or coercive assimilation accompany the incorporation? Were settler colonialists planted in large, medium, or small numbers, and were they territorially concentrated or dispersed? Lustick's historical work on Ireland, Algeria, and Palestine (1985, 1993) shows that he is fully aware of the importance of these matters but arguably they are not fully incorporated within the theory presented in this work, nor in his book.

5. Lastly, Lustick appears not to want to concede the independent impact of nationalism upon the morphology of states, for example the concentration or dispersion of historically constituted ethno-national groups in given regions; and the salience of ethnic groups' identification with principles of national self-determination in a democratizing and nationalizing world, the world of Gellner's industria. In Chapters 3 and 13 Lustick recognizes the independent efficacy of norms in international law, and the evolving inter-state system, in determining the morphology of states, but he does not see these as in turn independently grounded in the power of nationalism as the principle of legitimacy in the modern world. The autonomy of politics should, of course, be a heuristic principle amongst political scientists, but perhaps in this theory it is overdone.

Readers will come to their own judgements as to the merits of these criticisms of Lustick's work. Few will doubt, however, that he has provided a lucid, fertile, and intelligent theory for the comparative analysis of the right-sizing of the state. To those unpersuaded of the research programme begun here, the riposte is not that it is ideal. Our answer is simple: provide us a better one.

68   *Brendan O'Leary*

REFERENCES

Anderson, Perry. (1974). *Lineages of the Absolutist State*. London: New Left Books.
Barry, Brian. (1991). *Democracy, Power and Justice: Essays in Political Theory I*. Oxford: Clarendon Press.
Beran, Harry. (1984). Liberal Theory of Secession. *Political Studies*. 32: 21–31.
—— (1988). More Theory of Secession: A Response to Birch. *Political Studies*. 36: 316–23.
—— (1990). Who Should be Entitled to Vote in Self-Determination Referenda? In M. Warner, and R. Crisp (eds.), *Terrorism, Protest and Power*. 152–55. Aldershot: Edward Elgar.
—— (1993). Border Disputes and the Right of National Self-Determination. *History of European Ideas*. 16(4–6): 479–86.
Browning, Christopher R. (1992). *The Path to Genocide: Essays on Launching the Final Solution*. Cambridge: Cambridge University Press.
Brubaker, Rogers. (1996). *Nationalism Reframed: Nationhood and the National Question in the New Europe*. Cambridge: Cambridge University Press.
Buchanan, A. (1991). *Secession: The Morality of Political Divorce from Fort Sumter to Lithuania and Quebec*. Boulder, CO: Westview Press.
Cigar, Norman. (1995). *Genocide in Bosnia. The Policy of 'Ethnic Cleansing'*. College Station, TX: Texas A&M University Press.
Connor, Walker. (1984a). *The National Question in Marxist-Leninist Theory and Strategy*. Princeton, NJ: Princeton University Press.
—— (1984b). Eco- or Ethno-Nationalism? *Ethnic and Racial Studies*. 7 (October): 342–59.
—— (1994). *Ethnonationalism: The Quest for Understanding*. Princeton, NJ: Princeton University Press.
De Zayas, Alfred-Maurice. (1994). *A Terrible Revenge: The Ethnic Cleansing of the East European Germans, 1944–50*. New York: St Martin's Press.
—— (1977/1989). *Nemesis at Potsdam: The Expulsion of the Germans from the East: Background, Execution, Consequences*. London/Lincoln, NB: Routledge and Kegan Paul/ University of Nebraska Press.
—— (1989). A Historical Survey of Twentieth-Century Expulsions. In A. Bramwell (ed.), *Refugees in the Age of Total War*. 15–37. London: Unwin and Hyman.
Economist Editorial. (2000). No Hope for Kashmir?, *The Economist*. 356: 18–19.
Elazar, Daniel. (1994). *Federalism and the Way to Peace*. Kingston, Ontario: Queen's University Press.
Enzensberger, Hans Magnus. (1990). *Civil Wars: From L.A. to Bosnia*. New York, NY: The New Press.
Esman, Milton. (1994). *Ethnic Politics*. Ithaca, NY: Cornell University Press.
Finer, Samuel E. (1997). *The History of Government I: Ancient Monarchies and Empires*. Oxford: Oxford University Press.
Finkelstein, Norman G. (1996). *The Rise and Fall of Palestine: A Personal Account of the Intafada Years*. Minneapolis, MN: University of Minnesota Press.

—— and Birn, Ruth Bettina. (1998). *A Nation on Trial: The Goldhagen Thesis and Historical Truth*. New York, NY: Owl Book Editions.

Fraser, Thomas G. (1984). *Partition in Ireland, India and Palestine: Theory and Practice*. London: Macmillan.

Gellner, Ernest. (1964). *Thought and Change*. London: Weidenfeld and Nicolson.

—— (1969). *Saints of the Atlas*. London: Weidenfeld and Nicolson.

—— (1983). *Nations and Nationalism*. Oxford: Basil Blackwell.

—— (1988a). *Plough, Sword and Book: The Structure of Human History*. London: Collins-Harvill.

—— (1988b). *State and Society in Soviet Thought*. Oxford: Basil Blackwell.

—— (1994). Kemalism, *Encounters with Nationalism*. 81–91. Oxford: Basil Blackwell.

Glazer, N. (1983). Federalism and Ethnicity. The American Solution. In N. Glazer (ed.), *Ethnic Dilemmas, 1964–82*. 274–92. Cambridge, MA: Harvard University Press.

Goldhagen, Daniel Jonah. (1997). *Hitler's Willing Executioners: Ordinary Germans and the Holocaust*. London: Abacus.

Gurr, Ted Robert, and Harff, Barbara. (1994). *Ethnic Conflict in World Politics*. Oxford: Westview.

Gwynn, Denis. (1950). *The Partition of Ireland, 1912-25*. Dublin: Browne and Nolan.

Hanf, Theodor. (1991). Reducing Conflict Through Cultural Autonomy: Karl Renner's Contribution. In U. Ra'anan, M. Mesner, K. Armes, and K. Martin (eds.), *State and Nation in Multi-Ethnic Societies: The Breakup of Multi-National States*. 33–52. Manchester: Manchester University Press.

Hassan, Mushirul (ed.). (1993). *India's Partition: Process, Strategy and Mobilization*. Delhi: Oxford University Press.

Hazell, Robert, and O'Leary, Brendan. (1999). A Rolling Programme of Devolution: Slippery Slope or Safeguard of the Union? In R. Hazell (ed.), *Constitutional Futures: A History of the Next Ten Years*. 21–46. Oxford: Oxford University Press.

Held, David. (1990). The Decline of the Nation State. In S. Hall, and M. Jacques (eds.), *New Times: The Changing Face of Politics*. 191–204. London: Lawrence and Wishart.

Heraclides, Alexis. (1992). *The Self-Determination of Minorities in International Politics*. London: Frank Cass.

Hobsbawm, Eric. (1990). *Nations and Nationalism since 1870: Programme, Myth, Reality*. Cambridge: Cambridge University Press.

Hoffman, M. (1992). Third-Party Mediation and Conflict-Resolution in the Post-Cold War World. In J. Bayliss, and N. Rengger (eds.), *Dilemmas in World Politics: International issues in a Changing World*. 261–86. Oxford: Oxford University Press.

Horowitz, Donald. (1985). *Ethnic Groups in Conflict*. Berkeley, CA: University of California Press.

Horowitz, Donald. (1989). Ethnic Conflict Management for Policymakers. In J. P. Montville (ed.), *Conflict and Peacemaking in Multiethnic Societies*. 115–30. Lexington, MA: Heath.

—— (1998). Self-Determination: Politics, Philosophy and Law. In M. Moore (ed.), *National Self-Determination and Secession*. 181–214. Oxford: Oxford University Press.

Jennings, Ivor. (1956). *The Approach to Self-Government*. Cambridge: Cambridge University Press.

Johnston, R. E. (ed.). (1976). *The Politics of Division, Partition and Reunification*. New York, NY: Praeger.

Karmel, Solomon M. (1995–6). Ethnic Tension and the Struggle for Order: China's Policies in Tibet. *Pacific Affairs*. 68(4): 485–508.

Kennedy, Paul. (1988). *The Rise and Fall of the Great Powers: Economic Change and Military Conflict from 1500 to 2000*. London: Unwin & Hyman.

Kissane, Bill. (1996). Review of Ian Lustick's Unsettled States, Disputed Lands: Britain and Ireland, France and Algeria, Israel and the West Bank-Gaza. *Nations and Nationalism*. 2(1): 144–6.

Kumar, Radha. (1997a). *Divide and Fall? Bosnia in the Annals of Partition*. London: Verso.

—— (1997b). The Troubled History of Partition. *Foreign Affairs*. (Jan–Feb.): 22–34.

Laffan, Michael. (1983). *The Partition of Ireland, 1911–25*. Dundalk: Dundalgan Press.

Lapidoth, Ruth Eschelbacher. (1997). *Autonomy: Flexible Solutions to Ethnic Conflicts*. Washington, DC: United States Institute of Peace Press.

Lattimore, Owen D. (1940 (1988)). *Inner Asian Frontiers of China*. Oxford: Oxford University Press.

Lieven, Dominic. (1999). Dilemmas of Empire 1850–1918. Power, Territory and Identity. *Journal of Contemporary History*. 34(2): 163–200.

Lijphart, Arend. (1968). *The Politics of Accommodation*. Berkeley, CA: University of California Press.

—— (1969). Consociational Democracy. *World Politics*. 21 (January).

—— (1977). *Democracy in Plural Societies: A Comparative Exploration*. New Haven, CT, London: Yale University Press.

—— (1984). Time Politics of Accommodation: Reflections—Fifteen Years Later. *Acta Politica*. (1): 9–18.

Lintott, Andrew. (1993). *Imperium Romanum: Politics and Administration*. London: Routledge.

Lustick, Ian. (1979). Stability in Deeply Divided Societies: Consociationalism Versus Control. *World Politics*. 31(3): 325–44.

—— (1985). *State-Building Failure in British Ireland and French Algeria*. Berkeley, CA: University of California Press.

—— (1993). *Unsettled States, Disputed Lands: Britain and Ireland, France and Algeria, Israel and the West Bank-Gaza*. Ithaca, NY: Cornell University Press.

—— (1995). What Gives a People Rights to Land? *Queen's Quarterly*. 102(1): 53–68.

—— (1997). Lijphart, Lakatos and Consociationalism. *World Politics*. 50 (October): 88–117.

Luttwak, Edward. (1999 (1976)). *The Grand Strategy of the Roman Empire: From the First Century A.D. to the Third*. London: Weidenfeld and Nicolson.

Macartney, C. A. (1934). *National States and National Minorities*. London: Oxford University Press.

Mann, Michael. (1984). The Autonomous Power of the State: Its Origins, Mechanisms and Results. *European Journal of Sociology*. 25: 185–213.

—— (1999). The Dark Side of Democracy: The Modern Tradition of Ethnic and Political Cleansing. *New Left Review*. May/June (235): 18–45.

Mansergh, Nicholas. (1978). *Prelude to Partition: Concepts and Aims in Ireland and India*. Cambridge: Cambridge University Press.

Masalha, N. (1993). *Expulsion of the Palestinians: The Concept of 'Transfer' in Zionist Political Thought, 1882–1948*. London: I. B. Tauris.

Mazower, Mark. (1998). *Dark Continent: Europe's Twentieth Century*. Harmonds-worth: Allen Lane The Penguin Press.

McGarry, John. (1998). Orphans of Secession: National Pluralism in Secessionist Regions and Post-Secession States. In M. Moore (ed.), *National Self-Determination and Secession*. 215–32. Oxford: Oxford University Press.

—— and Moore, Margaret. (1997). The Problems with Partition. *Politics and the Life Sciences* (September): 18–19.

—— and O'Leary, Brendan. (1995). *Explaining Northern Ireland: Broken Images*. Oxford, Cambridge, MA: Basil Blackwell.

McNeill, William H. (1986). *Polyethnicity and World History: National Unity in World History*. Toronto: Toronto University Press.

Moore, Margaret (ed.). (1998). *National Self-Determination and Secession*. Oxford: Oxford University Press.

Nordlinger, Eric A. (1972). *Conflict Regulation in Divided Societies*. Cambridge, MA: Center for International Affairs, Harvard University.

O'Leary, Brendan. (1989). *The Asiatic Mode of Production: Oriental Despotism, Historical Materialism and Indian History*. Oxford and New York, NY: Basic Blackwell.

—— (ed.). (1996). Symposium on David Miller's *On Nationality*. *Nations and Nationalism*. 2(3): 407–52.

—— (1998). Gellner's Diagnoses of Nationalism: A Critical Overview *or* What is Living and What is Dead in Gellner's Philosophy of Nationalism? In J. A. Hall (ed.), *The State of the Nation: Ernest Gellner and the Theory of Nationalism*. 40–90. Cambridge: Cambridge University Press.

—— (1999). The Nature of the British-Irish Agreement. *New Left Review*. 233 (January–February): 66–96.

—— (forthcoming). An Iron Law of Federations? A (neo-Diceyian) Theory of the Necessity of a Federal Staatsvolk, and of Consociational Rescue. The 5th Ernest Gellner Memorial Lecture. *Nations and Nationalism*.

O'Leary, Brendan and Arthur, Paul. (1990). Introduction: Northern Ireland as the site of State- and Nation-Building Failures. In J. McGarry, and B. O'Leary (eds.), *The Future of Northern Ireland*. 1–47. Oxford: Oxford University Press.

—— and McGarry, John. (1996). *The Politics of Antagonism: Understanding Northern Ireland*. London and Atlantic Heights, NH: Athlone.

—— Lyne, T., Marshall, J., and Rowthorne, B. (1993). *Northern Ireland: Sharing Authority*. London: Institute of Public Policy Research.

Page, David. (1982). *Prelude to Partition: The Indian Muslims and the Imperial System of Control 1920–1932*. Oxford: Oxford University Press.

Pakenham, Thomas. (1991). *The Scramble for Africa*. London: Weidenfeld and Nicolson.

Parkin, Frank. (1979). *Marxism and Class Theory: A Bourgeois Critique*. London: Tavistock Press.

Peretz, Don. (1993). *Palestinians, Refugees and the Middle East Peace Process*. Washington, DC: USIP Press.

Riker, William H. (1964). *Federalism: Origin, Operation, Significance*. Boston, MA: Littlebrown.

Rummel, Rudolph J. (1997 (1994)). *Death by Government*. London and new York, NY: Transaction Publishers.

Shlaim, A. (1990). *The Politics of Partition: King Abdullah, the Zionists and Palestine, 1921–53*. Oxford: Oxford University Press.

Singh, Anita Inder. (1987/90). *The Origins of the Partition of India 1936–1947*. Delhi: Oxford University Press.

Singh, Gurharpal. (1997). The Partition of India as State Contraction: Some Unspoken Assumptions. *Journal of Commonwealth and Comparative Politics*. 35(1): 51–66.

Tarzi, Shah M. (1991). The Nation-State, Victim Groups and Refugees. *Ethnic and Racial Studies*. 14(4): 441–52.

Thornberry, Patrick. (1995). The UN Declaration on the Rights of Persons Belonging to National, or Ethnic, Religious and Linguistic Minorities: Background, Analysis, Observations, and an Update. In A. Phillips, and A. Rosas (eds.), *Universal Minority Rights*. 13–76. Abo and London: Institute of Human Rights Abo Akademi University and Minority Rights Group International.

Tullberg, Jan, and Tullberg, Brigitta S. (1997). Separation or Unity? A Model for Solving Ethnic Conflicts. *Politics and the Life Sciences*. 16(2): 237–48.

Vile, Maurice J. C. (1982). Federation and Confederation: The Experience of the United States and the British Commonwealth. In D. Rea (ed.), *Political Co-operation in Divided Societies*. 216–28. Dublin: Gill and Macmillan.

Voutat, Bernard. (1992). Interpreting National Conflict in Switzerland: the Jura Question. In J. Coakley (ed.), *The Social Origins of Nationalist Movements: The Contemporary West European Experience*. 99–123. London: Sage.

Wolff, Stefan. (2000). Managing Disputed Territories, External Minorities, and the Stability of Conflict Settlements. Unpublished Ph.D. thesis, University of London.

Zolberg, Aristide R. (1983). The Formation of New States as a Refugee-Generating Process. *Annals of the American Academy of Political and Social Science*. 467 (May): 24–38.

—— Suhrke, Astri, and Aguayo, Sergio. (1989). *Escape from Violence: Conflict and the Refugee Crisis in the Developing World*. Oxford: Oxford University Press.

3

Thresholds of Opportunity and Barriers to Change in the Right-Sizing of States

Ian S. Lustick

Strategic decisions to reduce the size, scope, and/or ambitions of organizations, including states, in order to enhance future prospects, are among the most difficult and least well understood choices made in collective life. In political life they are often honoured as courageous, or 'statesmanlike', when successfully implemented. More often, however proposals to consider such policies are rejected as cowardly, as reflective of an absence of faith or self-confidence, and as evidence that someone else could do a better job securing the interests of the collective. Accordingly it may be assumed that most politicians who consider such policies advisable would yet hesitate or even refuse to make their inclinations public. It is precisely because policies oriented toward contraction and retrenchment are, *ceteris paribus*, so unlikely to be attractive as political platforms and so likely to be suppressed in normal political discourse, that we need to make special efforts to focus on the potential of this kind of right-sizing.

The O'Leary/McGarry Taxonomy and Its Relationship to Theories of State Contraction

We can begin by noticing the somewhat hidden role that contraction plays in four of the eight techniques Brendan O'Leary and John McGarry identify for stabilizing polities threatened by disruptive, polarizing conflicts (O'Leary 1995). They divide these into four elimination strategies and four management strategies. The elimination strategies are genocide, expulsion, partition/separation, and integration/assimilation. The management strategies are control, arbitration/third party intervention, federation/cantonization, and consociation. An alternative way to classify these same eight techniques or strategies is to distinguish those which would not require decision-makers to reduce the scope of state authority from those which assume that the state will be right-sized, specifically that the territorial or functional scope of state institutions will be reduced. Some of these strategies, in other words, assume state contraction; others do not. The strategies that require either territorial or functional contraction are partition/separation, arbitration (third party intervention), federation/cantonization, and consociationalism. The strategies that do not entail state contraction are genocide, expulsion, integration/assimilation, and control.

Of these non-contractionist strategies, O'Leary and McGarry, and most other observers, oppose genocide, expulsion, or control as techniques for eliminating internal conflicts because the cures may be worse than the disease. Meanwhile commitments to cultural diversity militate against assimilation—forcible or voluntary—as an option, while the entrenched prejudices and fears associated with protracted conflicts tend to reduce prospects for mutually satisfying policies of integration. Attention is thus naturally and appropriately concentrated on the remaining strategies for the amelioration or elimination of such disputes. Each of these, however, is based on expectations of state contraction.

But no effective policy of state contraction can be devised, and there can be no expectation that such a policy could be implemented successfully, without a theory of how it is that states do or can contract. Of course, entertaining territorial partition or regional separation as an option for the management of conflict, means asking what the results of such a policy would be on the long-term prospects for stable relations between the two states, for example in creating irredentism, or subjecting remaining minorities to discriminatory policies in the now smaller, more homogeneous, but still divided polities. However it is equally important to ask how a decision can be made to give up something—in this case territory—which does not stand in danger of being physically taken away in the absence of such a decision? Under what circumstances do states take decisions which entail short-term risks and costs even major disruptions, on the basis of long-term calculations of the general interest?

If arbitration or third party intervention is entertained, it is not enough to ask about ensuring objectivity by the arbiter. One must also ask about the circumstances under which a polity can agree to relinquish a substantial portion of its sovereign authority, thereby 'contracting' its political domain, if not necessarily its geographical extent. If federation or autonomy are entertained, one must not only ask questions about the particular institutional mechanisms appropriate for binding semi-independent units together and the cultural environment within which such mechanisms may or may not be able to function effectively. One must also ask about the conditions—apart from the threat of force—under which a state would be able to produce a decision to change its constitution so as to transfer to formerly subordinated groups, substantial powers and resources. Finally, if consociationalism is entertained, it is not enough to ask whether the particular authority structures and cultural dispositions identified as conducive to consociationalism are present in the various population segments. One must also ask about the dynamics that would lead a unitary, non-consociational polity, characterized by commitments to civic homogeneity and a relatively centralized state structure operating across cultural divides in economic, educational, and other sectors, to transform itself into a state exercising much less cross-cultural authority in many fewer sectors.

The general question must therefore be posed: how can and do states 'down-size' themselves by shrinking the ambit of their authority—a contraction that may be defined functionally as in consociationalism, territorially as in partition, or as some combination of both: likely in federative or cantonal schemes, possible as a result of arbitration?[1]

The point is that although our focused interest in this project is on the opportunities and constraints associated with *territorial* changes in the shape of the state, this effort can be seen as bearing directly on the other, often functionally, contraction-oriented stabilization strategies depicted by McGarry and O'Leary. For whatever theoretical claims we may make about the process of state right-sizing with respect to territorial borders, these will *either* translate more or less readily into hypotheses and expectations about federalist, consociational, or third-party intervention strategies, *or* we will be presented with evidence that something theoretically distinctive attaches to the kind of political processes associated with 'territorial' expansion or contraction.

Expansion versus Contraction: Analysis of a Theoretical Prejudice

Edward Gibbon summarized his explanation for the decline and fall of the Roman Empire by writing that it was 'the natural and inevitable effect of immoderate greatness.' The causes of destruction, he observed, 'multiplied with the extent of conquest; and, as soon as time or accident had removed the

---

[1] To pose the problem this way is not to assert that state expansion is never desirable. To try to explain or design policies for contraction requires theories, preferably reversible ones that address both state expansion and contraction.

artificial supports, the stupendous fabric yielded to the pressure of its own weight.' Though Gibbon has passed out of fashion, most explanations for the failure, collapse, decline, or disappearance of the (western) Roman Empire share a notion of a state which had overreached its capacities in the face of increasingly difficult challenges. But these explanations beg what might seem to be the obvious question of why those governing the sprawling empire did not seek to preserve their state by reducing its burdens, that is by con-tracting it.[2]

While it is virtually impossible even to count the books and articles written about the demise of the Roman Empire or about the economic, strategic, political, ideological, and cultural forces which impelled Rome toward its 'immoderate' size, few scholars have even posed the question of why Rome did not prudentially shrink its domain to conform to available resources. The absence of this question in the vast historiography on the Roman world is particularly striking in view of the praise often registered by scholars of ancient Rome for Hadrian's state contraction policy. Realizing in the early second century that Trajan's conquests in the East were too extensive for Rome to maintain, Hadrian boldly chose to relinquish those provinces, there-by consolidating Roman rule behind less ambitious frontiers in the Near East. Similar calculations lay behind the construction of 'Hadrian's Wall' along a more southern line in Britain than previous emperors had tried to defend. Despite approval for this specific set of judgements and policies, there has been little if any effort to understand Hadrian's policy as a strategy of 'limited state contraction,' a conceptualization which would enable broad-er questions to be asked about the conditions under which he was able to con-template and effectuate a strategic option which other emperors seemed either to ignore or avoid.

I believe it is neither coincidence nor academic custom which explains why this same pattern, of interest in expansion, decline, or collapse, but not in contraction, is present in the literature on nineteenth and early twentieth

[2] The same can be said of the literature on the Ottoman Empire. Great attention has been paid to the fate of alternative projects for redefining the nature of the empire as strategies to save it during the eighteenth, nineteenth, and twentieth centuries, but virtually none to the question of whether or why before World War I, no efforts were made to adapt by strategic contraction. Although I am not equally familiar with the relevant literatures, I would hypothesize that similar patterns of research characterize scholarly traditions pertaining to other empires, such as the Austro-Hungarian and the Tsarist Empires. It is also relevant to note that in the sophisticated treatments of organizational evolution, growth, and development, the overwhelming tendency has been to study expansion of organizations and the reasons for their failure or collapse, rather than to study patterns of strategic contraction. See, e.g. the seminal book by J. D. Thompson, *Organizations in Action*, which systematically considers the reasons for organizational growth as a strategic response to envi-ronmental circumstances and survival requirements but not once entertains the possibility of strate-gic contraction as an adaptive response to a threatening task environment (Thompson 1967).

century European imperialism and its results. Here again the dominant questions, which have guided scholars, from Hobson and Lenin to Schumpeter, Staley, Robbins, Arendt, and Said, have focused on the economic, strategic, political, cultural, and ideological causes of imperial expansion. Another smaller, but still substantial literature on the causes and timing of the retreat or collapse of these empires appears under the heading of 'decline' or 'decolonization.' As with Rome, so too with European imperialism, few scholars have posed the question of why the greatly enlarged states did not contract themselves effectively at a pace which could have secured their continued rule of still large but more realistically designed domains. Therefore, although we have studies which compare the dynamics of European imperial expansion to those of Roman expansion, or which compare the Roman 'collapse' with the decline of European empires, there is no literature which seeks to learn about the rigidities of European imperial rule from the Roman Empire's failure to contract with the same opportunism with which it expanded.[3]

One reason, of course, for the greater prominence of expansion as opposed to contraction in the relevant literatures is that instances of strategic expansion—that is enlargement of a polity's territorial domain as an intended result of policies implemented for that purpose—far outnumber those of strategic contraction—that is purposeful reduction in a polity's territorial domain.[4] But noting this vast discrepancy in the appearance of expansionary and contractionist episodes leads to the question: why should it be that expansion occurs so much more frequently than contraction? A deceptively simple answer to this question is that it is easier to expand than to contract. I say 'deceptively simple' because this answer conceals within itself a theory of states as institutions, and of asymmetric processes of institutionalization and deinstitutionalization, including images of state contraction as a process which is not, simply, the converse of state expansion.

The Shape of States: Institutionalizing and Deinstitutionalizing Territorial Boundaries

We must begin with a concept of a state as a special kind of institution. An institution is a framework for social action which elicits from those who act within it expectations of regularity, continuity, and propriety. Such a frame-

---

[3]   See e.g. Doyle (1986: 92–8); Brunt (1964–5); and Miles (1990).
[4]   This definition of state contraction excludes the collapse, destruction, or dismemberment of polities effected despite, or without reference to, the strategic calculus of ruling élites.

work is institutionalized to the extent that those expectations are reliably reproduced. Institutionalization is a process by which change in the rules of political competition becomes increasingly disruptive and decreasingly likely to be part of the strategic calculus of competitors within the institutional arena. States are special institutions. They are the institutions that enforce property rights and provide order sufficient to permit people within their purview to design and build other institutions. The boundaries of states, both internal boundaries between state authority and other kinds of authority within a specified territory, and external boundaries, between territories falling within the ambit of state authority and those which do not, are crucial components of the set of stable expectations which, ultimately, constitute the state as an institution.

The evolution of Wessex and then England into Great Britain, then into the United Kingdom of Great Britain and Ireland, and most recently into the United Kingdom of Great Britain and Northern Ireland, illustrates the fundamental fluidity of states as regards their territorial and cultural composition.[5] But if the morphological variability exhibited by 'Britain' and 'the United Kingdom' indicates the need for a dynamic conception of the state, the long time periods through which such discontinuous shifts in size and shape manifest themselves suggest the need to temper awareness of fluidity with expectations that change in the contours of states will not respond smoothly to marginal changes in patterns of popular loyalty, economic interest, élite ideology, or even military strength.

What endows the nominal border of a state with long-term political significance? Study of the dynamics of state expansion and contraction requires a fairly precise answer to this question—one that combines the notion of ultimate fluidity with the expectation of sluggishness and discontinuity in patterns of border change.

Considering a state as an institution, that is, as an established set of expectations, suggests that borders of states describe boundaries between political arenas within which it is believed that available power resources will be mobilized according to *different* sets of norms and legal arrangements. State borders are politically important because they serve as a constraint which advantage certain groups and rival élites within the state at the expense of others. Substantial changes in the territorial shape of a state represent institution transforming episodes. Struggles over the size and shape of the state must accordingly be understood as struggles over the 'rules of the game.' Boundaries specify who and what are potential participants or objects of the

---

[5] Concerning long-term fluctuations in the shape of the British and French states see Lustick (1985: 1–16).

political game and who and what are not. Different borders have different demographic implications and different political myths associated with them. The territorial shape of a state thus helps determine what interests are legitimate, what resources are mobilizable, what questions are open for debate, what ideological formulas will be relevant, what cleavages could become significant, and what political allies might be available.

Territorial expansion or contraction can be expected to trigger shifts in the distribution of power within a state by changing the resources available to different groups and, ultimately, by changing prevailing norms and legal arrangements to correspond with the interests of newly dominant groups. Accordingly, unless the border of the state is accepted as an immutable given, different groups within the state will, under some circumstances, adjust their perceptions of what the proper border of the state should be in light of the implications of different borders, or different principles of inclusion and exclusion, for those groups' chances to achieve and/or maintain political power.

The usefulness of this formulation is that it suggests both the long-term variability of state borders—flowing from the essentially subjective nature of popular beliefs and linked ultimately to constellations of economic benefit, social status, and political interest—and the potential for stability in the size and shape of states that can attend deeply embedded, widely shared, and uncontested beliefs. It is, in fact, much more useful for analysing change in the size and shape of a state than Weber's standardly cited definition of the state, including as it does a reference to state authority 'within a given territory'.[6]

As events during the last decade in Europe, Asia, Africa, and the Middle East conclusively demonstrate, territorial boundaries are far from being a given of a state's existence. Indeed the territorial shape of a state, *qua* institution, is one of its most salient *contingent* dimensions. Understanding patterns of change and stability in the territorial composition of a state thus entails analysis of processes of institutionalization and deinstitutionalization. To be sure, change in the size and shape of states is commonly attributable to success or failure in armed conflicts—a sudden loss or acquisition of territory that in itself does not reflect the institutionalizable character of borders. But the loss of a territory in war does not necessarily mean its permanent separation from the defeated state. Nor does conquest of a territory necessarily lead to its political integration. With respect to territorial expansion and contraction as a *political* problem, a problem of the shaping of an institution, it is precisely those cases where *force majeure* was not decisive in the determination of

---

[6] For an analysis of the pernicious effects of Weber's definition see Lustick (1993: 3–4).

outcomes, or where it is not expected to be decisive, which are of the greatest interest.

As suggested by the studies in this volume, a well-developed concept of state contraction, and a well-supported theory of how states can strategically contract, territorially or functionally, would have important policy implications. They could, for example, have helped the former Soviet Union preserve itself in smaller boundaries or transform itself in an orderly manner. Considering struggles such as those that are or have been occurring in the Kurdish areas of south-eastern Turkey, between Muslims and non-Muslims in Sudan, between Sahrawis and Moroccans in the western Sahara, Irish nationalists and British unionists in Northern Ireland, Azeris and Armenians in Ngorno-Karabakh, Tibetans and Chinese in Tibet, Russians and Chechens in Chechnya, Russians and Tatars in the Crimea, Israelis and Palestinians in the West Bank and Gaza, Hindus and Muslims in Kashmir, Sinhalese and Tamils in Sri Lanka, etc., such a theory could also help assess the feasibility of consolidating existing or enlarged boundaries as opposed to contracting the state as part of a process leading to less violence and fewer threats to international security.

A Two Threshold Image of Territorial State-Building and State Contraction

Recognizing states and state boundaries as institutions does not itself suggest a solution to the problem of why there should be such a huge discrepancy in the occurrence of state expansion vs. state contraction. Solving this problem requires elaborating a theory of institutions consistent with this pattern and which links the continuous, gradual, linear processes which strengthen or weaken pressures toward expansion or contraction, to discontinuities in these processes.

In one sense the territorial shape of states changes in sudden and drastic ways. Ireland was annexed as an integral part of the United Kingdom on 1 January 1801. The twenty-six counties of the Irish Free State left the authority of the British state on 5 December 1922. France made Algeria three departments of France in 1848. France officially recognized Algerian independence on 3 July 1962. Within a few short years the Soviet Union relinquished control of vast areas in central Asia, the Caucuses, and eastern Europe, to become 'Russia.' On the other hand, the political pressures and psychological processes leading up to these transformations and consequent upon them were cumulative and gradual—pushing the British, French, and

Soviet/Russian states toward expansion or contraction without being reflected simultaneously with the presence of those pressures by proportionate changes in boundaries.

In the building of states, as in the building of any institution, the process by which positively valued and stable expectations are produced or destroyed includes both continuous and discontinuous elements and both political and psychological aspects. These facets of institutionalization and deinstitutionalization processes can be located in relation to one another if the continuous aspects of institution-building, including gradually increasing propensities to expect norms, rules, and boundaries to be adhered to and symbols to be honoured, are understood to surround two distinct thresholds. These thresholds mark discontinuities in the process of institutionalization, dividing it into three stages. Movement from one stage to another entails a shift in the order of magnitude in the scale of political conflict that would surround efforts to change a particular institution along a salient dimension.

The metaphor of threshold is key. It describes a mechanism for modelling an expansionary process that can be reversed, but only, once either threshold has been crossed, at the cost of much greater dislocation than the same amount of movement in the expansion direction. The image of threshold is meant to suggest a kind of ratcheting effect. Once accomplished as the result of cumulative pressures in the direction the gears are pointing in, moving 'backward' is still possible, but only by risking damage to or destruction of the machine (the institution) itself.

Drawing on this asymmetric model of expansion and contraction, the expansion of an already existing state to include another piece of territory can be portrayed as a sequence of changes in the character of political conflict within the core state that would attend efforts to *disengage* from the new territory. More precisely, the scale of the internal political dislocation which the political class within the core state expects to be associated with efforts to disengage from an outlying territory measures the extent to which that territory has been built, or integrated, into the central state. State contraction involves reducing the scale of the internal political dislocation that would be associated with disengagement, while state expansion involves increasing it. The 'regime' and 'ideological hegemony' thresholds divide political conflicts pertaining to the territorial shape of the state into three types or stages, linked to one another in Guttman-scale fashion. These stages correspond to struggles over incumbency; incumbency and regime integrity; and incumbency, regime integrity, and ideological hegemony (see Figure 3.1).

Conflict at the incumbency stage, over a government policy designed to achieve disengagement from a closely held territory, might be intense. Indeed the political future of incumbents and their rivals may be at stake in

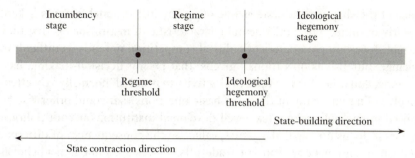

Fig. 3.1 State-building and state contraction

any effort to move toward disengagement. But if competition is limited to political bargaining, threats to bolt from the ruling coalition, or electoral campaigns, etc., it is easily contained within the political institutions of a developed polity. In such conflicts the rules of the allocative game are not the issue. Neither the integrity of the regime, nor the underlying balance of power enshrined by state institutions is threatened. The scale and content of struggles over separation of the territory from the state would challenge neither the structure of state institutions, nor the underlying beliefs and identities of the state's population. It is precisely for this reason that such conflict can be interpreted to mean that integration of the peripheral territory into the state-building core is in its early stage.

The territory can be considered much more closely integrated into the core state if proposals for disengagement from the territory raise in the minds of competitors for political power, not only the danger of losing coalition partners, partisan advantages, or career opportunities, but also the real possibility of violent opposition and the mounting of extra-legal challenges to the authority of state institutions. By struggling over the right of the state to determine the fate of the relationship between the core and the no-longer-so-peripheral territory, the protagonists bear witness to the drastically different status of that territory. Clearly, state-building has proceeded much further if conflict over disengagement is conducted about the 'rules of the game', that is, about state institutions, and not within them. At this 'regime' stage of political struggle over the inclusion or exclusion of the territory, the issue is not only 'Should the state, for its own interests or the interests of those it is deemed to represent, disengage from the territory?', but also 'Should the future of the territory as a part of the state be legitimately entertained as a question of interests, costs, and benefits, by government officials or by participants in the wider struggle for power in and over the state?'

The need to think in terms of *two* thresholds dividing the process of territorial state-building into three kinds of political situations is apparent is the idea of the shape of the state as one of its key institutional features is kept clearly in mind. The fundamental characteristic of institutions is that they establish certain parameters of political competition not only as difficult to change, but also as operational 'givens' that permit decision-making, bargaining, and other forms of political activity to proceed 'normally.' By effectively ruling out many of the most basic questions that could otherwise be raised in any political context, well developed institutions permit political actors to focus on particular issues, calculate the consequences of different outcomes, and make appropriate trade-offs. The establishment of a belief as common-sense, as necessarily true, has the effect of privileging it—of protecting it from re-evaluation in the face of events or pressures that might otherwise affect it, and of diverting political responses to strains associated with the state of affairs it describes. This agenda-shaping aspect of deep-seated, unquestioned beliefs represents a qualitatively different kind of protection against deinstitutionalization than the incumbency or regime-level concerns of political actors. The way that embedded beliefs shape outcomes by excluding certain questions from appearing before the public as relevant, or even meaningful, is what Antonio Gramsci emphasized in his study of how hegemonic beliefs, that is, maximally institutionalized norms, set limits to the rational pursuit of self-interest.[7]

When maximally institutionalized, I understand the territorial expanse of the state—its borders—to be the boundaries of the institution (the state) which people within it expect/presume to be permanent, proper, and unquestioned features of their public life. The incorporation of a particular territory into a core state is as fully institutionalized as it can be only when its status as an integral part of the state, not as a problematically occupied asset, becomes part of the natural order of things for the overwhelming majority of the population whose political behaviour is relevant to outcomes in the state. Operationally, the territorial expanse, or shape, of a state has been institutionalized on a hegemonic basis when its boundaries are not treated by competing political élites within it as if those boundaries might be subject to change. If typical political discussions imply that such change might be advisable or possible, and certainly if debate rages over whether a particular area and its population are or are not to be considered integral parts of the

---

[7] Though most interpreters of Gramsci have focused on the application of his notion of hegemony to inter-class relations, there is ample evidence in his work that he viewed state borders as capable of being established as hegemonic beliefs. This is a central concern in those portions of his *Prison Notebooks* known as 'Notes on Italian History', 'The Modern Prince,' and in his treatment of the Sardinian question. 'Even the geographical position of a national state,' he wrote, 'follows (logically) the structural innovations, though reacting on them to a certain extent (to the extent precisely to which superstructures react on the structure, politics on economics, etc.)' (Gramsci 1957: 164).

state, the state-building process with respect to that boundary and territory is plainly incomplete.

We may therefore think of two different thresholds that must be crossed by a state if some outlying territory is to be incorporated on as permanent a basis as possible. The first threshold is the 'regime threshold' (see Fig. 3.1)—the point at which a government interested in relinquishing the areas finds itself more worried about civic upheavals, violent disorders, and challenges to the legitimate authority of governmental institutions than with possible defections from the governing coalition or party. The second, ideological hegemony threshold signals a deeper kind of institutionalization, though it still does not represent an intrinsically irreversible state of affairs. This stage begins when the absorption of the territory ceases to be problematic for the overwhelming majority of citizens of the central state, that is, when hegemonic beliefs prevent the question of the future of the territory from occupying a place on the national political agenda. The presence of such beliefs is revealed when, in public, ambitious politicians systematically avoid questioning, even by implication, the permanence of the integration of the territory.

The ideological hegemony threshold divides political struggles over the authority of the state to determine the fate of the territory (regime stage), from a political context within which no serious contender for political power finds it advisable to refer to the area as if its permanent incorporation as a part of the state had not been decided. At this ideologically hegemonic stage of state-building, its least reversible stage, advocacy of 'disengagement' would be expected to produce, not vigorous intra-institutional competition, nor polarized and possibly violent political struggle, but a discourse marked by all but universal rejection of the idea as impossible, unimaginable, absolutely unacceptable, and certainly irrelevant. Real movement toward 'disengagement' or 'state contraction'—now more appropriately labelled 'secession'—would, at this stage, require raising fundamental questions about the community's sense of itself and its rightful political domain. The political unpalatability of raising such necessarily iconoclastic questions, and the difficulty of waging a successful political struggle within or against state institutions by doing so, is what ultimately defends the integrity of the new and larger state. It is the absence of struggle about the shape of the state that indicates its successful institutionalization.[8]

---

[8] Technically this is not quite the case, as is evident from French beliefs about Algeria's status before WWII. In the absence of significant sources of strain, the particular borders of a state need not appear on its political agenda even if the conception of those borders has not been institutionalized on a hegemonic basis.

State-building, or expansion, is thus conceived of as a process of entanglement between the centre and the acquired territory. As it proceeds the nature and scale of the disruption expected to be associated with ever cutting the relationship increase. Élites first develop particular, incumbency-related interests in preserving central state control over the territory. Then images of the result of disengagement come to include threats to the regime of the central state which accompany and eventually overshadow incumbency concerns. Subsequently the larger conception of the state, including the acquired territory, may become part of the common sense of political life. This hegemonic level of institutionalization is attained as politicians who might otherwise have reason to oppose permanent incorporation of the target territory adopt vocabularies and rhetorical strategies which imply presumptions of its inclusion within the state. State contraction is conceived as a process of moving 'backward' through these thresholds, first by legitimizing public discussion of disengagement as a credible or sensible option, then by eliminating from public debate and private calculation the threat of challenges to the legal order should a coalition favouring disengagement be in a position legally to implement its preferences, and then by forming a winning coalition favouring a policy of disengagement and capable of implementing it.

Theorizing Institutional Expansion and Contraction

The framework presented here can help address a wide range of important conceptual, theoretical, and policy problems resulting from previous failures to recognize 'state contraction' as a distinctive political phenomenon. It does this by conceiving of boundaries as institutional features of states and by imagining two thresholds within a process of institutionalization producing asymmetric processes of expansion and contraction. But the framework is not itself a theory of how the transformations from one level or stage of institutionalization to another are accomplished, or of what consequences are associated with different processes and mechanisms used to move across these thresholds in the state-expanding or state-contracting direction. The bulk of my book, *Unsettled States, Disputed Lands* (Lustick 1993), is devoted to the elaboration, testing, and refinement of two clusters of propositions for the partial accomplishment of these tasks.

Adopting Gramscian terminology, and drawing some inspiration from his observations for the development of these theories, I analyse political struggles around regime thresholds as 'wars of manoeuvre' and struggles around ideological hegemony thresholds as 'wars of position.' Theoretical propositions about how thresholds are crossed in each direction spring from consideration of the implications of asymmetry in the requirements of movement across the same threshold in different directions, and the logic of different strategies available for winning, or surviving, the sharper struggles to move through these thresholds in the state-contracting direction.

A useful way to appreciate the special challenges of theorizing institutional contraction is to consider the problem of understanding reversal of certain kinds of 'state' changes in physical domains. Again, political transformations that I refer to as threshold crossings involve non-linear changes in the amount of internal disruption associated with contracting out of a particular territory or functional sector. As asymmetric thresholds, they conform in patterns of behaviour surrounding them to the hysteresis effect described in many branches of the natural sciences. A susceptible piece of metal, for example, exposed to a magnetic field of increasing strength, will exhibit a rapid increase in the alignment of its atoms to correspond to the magnetic field until it is 'saturated' with magnetism, that is, fully 'magnetized.' But if the field's strength is decreased, and even reduced to zero, the magnetization of the metal decreases only very slowly, dropping away suddenly and falling back to zero only after the strength of the magnetic field is reduced well *below* zero, that is, only when it becomes a negative magnetic field. In other words, not only does gradual increase in one variable (strength of the magnetic field) produce a qualitative, or 'state' change, in another variable (magnetization of the susceptible object), but the implications for change in the level of magnetization of the object depend strongly on the 'history' of changes in that level. The same amount of reduction in the strength of the magnetic field, *at the same level of strength of that field*, will have a much smaller effect on the level of magnetization if it occurs during the process of 'demagnetization' than if it occurs as part of a process leading up to the saturation point. Conversely, the same amount of increase in the strength of the magnetic field, *at the same level of strength of that field*, will have a much larger effect on the level of magnetization if it occurs during the process leading up to the saturation point, than if it occurs during the process of demagnetization.

What this suggests for the dynamics of state institutionalization over acquired territories—or for the dynamics of any institutionalization/deinstitutionalization process—is that disjointed and incrementalist processes that give rise to increasing numbers of cross-'border' transactions, increasingly interpenetrating legal codes, increasing economic, social, military, and natural resource interdependencies, and increasing numbers of 'settlers,' would produce a rising curve describing the cost of disengaging from the territory. The notion of a threshold is that at a certain point along this curve its slope would rise so steeply that the resources and risks of dislocation associated with reversing the direction of the relationship would no longer be proportional to the amount of reversal producible by the devotion of such resources or the assumption of these risks. An order of magnitude, or qualitative shift in the scale of the problem would thereby be observed—a consequence of what can very appropriately be called an 'emergent property' of a dynamical system.

The asymmetry of the 'threshold' thereby crossed can be seen as expressed in two ways. First, consistent with the principle of hysteresis, the amount of political pressure required to move the problem in a state-building or state-contracting direction would vary, near the threshold, with the 'history' of that movement. To the 'right' of the regime threshold, for example, the same amount of political pressure would produce much less movement if that movement were part of a 'historical' process of deinstitutionalization than if it were part of a 'historical' process of institutionalization. To the 'left' of the threshold, the reverse would be true—though the difference would not be as spectacular. Second, one can expect that although purposeful activity to increase the level of institutionalization can add to the efficacy of processes leading to the crossing of the threshold from the incumbent stage to the regime stage, or from the regime stage to the ideological hegemony stage, the ratio of such 'design' activity to disjointed and evolutionary processes will be much greater in successful efforts to cross thresholds in the deinstitutionalization (state contracting) direction than in the institutionalization (state expanding) direction. In other words, emergent properties can crystallize—meaning institutionalizing thresholds can be crossed—through the cumulative interaction of many separately produced activities, but the removal of an emergent property (deinstitutionalizing) is much less likely to simply 'evolve' and is much more likely to require calculated strategic effort.[9]

The hypotheses I have developed concerning movement across the two institutional thresholds reflect these asymmetries. Since they largely pertain to available élite strategies, they focus more on deinstitutionalization than institutionalization. This makes sense to the extent that embedding an enlarged border of a state more deeply into the institutional framework of a polity—crossing the regime and hegemonic thresholds in the state-building direction—is more likely to be attainable incrementally, via the sheer weight and number of accumulated practices, than is crossing thresholds in the other direction—dis-embedding a state border that has become intimately interconnected with the constitutional and legal order of that state or deconstructing a reigning hegemonic belief—processes more likely to require strategic élite calculation and action.

---

[9] For an accessible and effective introduction to closely related topics of emergence, complexity, and evolution see Holland (1998). For a more wide-ranging treatment see also Dennett (1995).

Another set of hypotheses pertains to the changing intensity and substantive focus of political competition as the level of institutionalization of the problem varies—moving toward one threshold or another, moving away from one threshold or another, proximate to one threshold on one side or the other, or located beyond what may be considered the 'phase transition' space surrounding the threshold. In *Unsettled States, Disputed Lands* (Lustick 1993) I suggested four strategies élites inclined toward state contraction could use to recross the regime threshold, and presented them as mechanisms for 'rescaling' the problem—in that study, the problem of disengaging from an outlying territory. As rescaling mechanisms, each strategy presents a logically available technique for increasing the likelihood that efforts to remove regime-threatening aspects from problems will not be deterred by the prospect of regime-disturbing events and/or that efforts actually made in this direction will be implemented successfully. These rescaling mechanisms are (1) problem decomposition, (2) regime recomposition, (3) coalition realignment, and (4) change in preference orderings.

1. Decomposition of the problem entails dividing the problem into pieces to reduce or eliminate regime-threatening aspects. This could be accomplished either by spatially or materially dividing the problem so that, for example, only the parts that do not threaten regime stability are addressed. Alternatively, it could entail temporal division of the problem—what I have called 'serial decomposition,' better known as 'salami tactics.' Thus if disengagement from a particular territory raises threats to regime stability, one way to proceed toward that objective while lowering or eliminating risk to the regime is to separate either the territory, or the process of disengagement, into parts. By 'decomposing' the problem, a 'partial disengagement'—either temporary or permanent—might be achieved which would arouse only incumbent-level opposition. If the remaining portions of the territory or the process might still trigger regime-level opposition to further movement toward disengagement, the crisis thus precipitated would be less severe.

2. The yearning for bold and far-seeing leadership and a strong determined state, as a solution for seemingly intractable and polarizing political problems, is a staple of political debate in democracies experiencing deep divisions, and protracted, polarized conflict. The theoretical basis for the 'regime recomposition' strategy implicit in this yearning is the reconstitution of authority relations. By centralizing and introducing more hierarchy in the structure of authority for making crucial choices, access to the decision process is substantially reduced. This kind of regime recomposition can broaden the range of policies capable of being endorsed by state institutions. Whether officially acknowledged as a change in regime or not, the paralysis produced by the domination of blocking veto-groups or negative

majorities, based in part on the fear of regime stability, will more likely be overcome.

3. Coalition realignment is a third mechanism. Indeed a situation of stalemate, whether in the midst of a regime crisis or simply in the context of ordinary, incumbent-level competition, might always be broken if one or more segments on one side of the political divide become convinced that a different set of alliances, with groups on the other side, would be a more efficacious route to their distinctive objectives. Although the polarization of political competition characteristic of wars of manoeuvre makes such shifts less likely than the more fluid patterns of interaction which normally prevail in democratic states, charismatic leadership, the presence of groups with strong commitments on issues orthogonal to the substantive question(s) perceived by most competitors as crucial, and/or the appearance of an overarching external threat, could provide the basis for dramatic realignments.

4. Neither problem decomposition nor regime recomposition necessarily entails change in the individual preferences of politicians or citizens. Assuming stable preferences, problem decomposition is a strategy for changing the question to which those preferences are applied, while regime recomposition is a strategy for making the preferences of some more determinative than those of others. But people can and do change their minds. Impressive events, persuasive arguments, or the skilful presentation or information can strip an 'insoluble problem' of its regime-threatening aspects by effecting substantial changes in both absolute and relative preference orderings.

The logic of each of these rescaling mechanisms has been explained in a way that indicates their theoretical independence of one another. However my research has suggested that although one or another may be the anchor for a more complex array of methods to move 'backward,' as it were, through the regime threshold, certain combinations of these strategies seem particularly potent. For example, a regime recomposition strategy may well set the stage for a dramatic showdown between a legally strengthened state and a regime-threatening opposition ready to fight outside the state's legal or constitutional boundaries. In this context, change in preferences, through pedagogical use of the spectre of 'civil war' to highlight the costs of opposition to government policy, may be a particularly promising path to deinstitutionalization—this was the combination of strategies, along with serial decomposition of the Algerian problem, that de Gaulle used to address the Algerian problem. Another combination of strategies that can work, and was used in the British-Irish case, is to base the rescaling effort on spatial decomposition—the division of Ireland—and then realign coalitions, leaving off hardliners on either side.

Two other clusters of propositions relate to explaining which mechanism, or combination of mechanisms, is more likely to be adopted in what circumstances and what consequences are likely to be associated with accomplishment of regime-to-incumbent level deinstitutionalization according to one strategic pathway or another. For example, if the coalition of groups opposing deinstitutionalization of central state rule over the outlying territory includes substantial elements of the military, especially of the officer corps, regime recomposition will be less likely to be chosen as an anchoring mechanism and less likely to succeed if it is chosen—this is what made de Gaulle's performance all the more remarkable, and highlights the relative timidity of the Rabin government in Israel. Geographic separation of the central state and the disputed territory implies, *ceteris paribus*, that confrontations with settlers inside the outlying territory will be more violent since those settlers will have more to lose from disengagement. To the extent that settlers are spatially concentrated within specific zones, the attractiveness and workability of problem decomposition as an anchoring mechanism is enhanced. To the extent that politically-salient groups operate within the central state whose perceived interests are orthogonal to the dispute over the disposition of the territory, strategies based, in whole or in part, on coalition realignment are made more likely and more workable.

An interesting implication of the asymmetric nature of the threshold effects discussed above is that there will likely be a striking contrast between disengagement struggles occurring to the right of the regime threshold compared with those occurring to the left of the threshold. To the right of the regime threshold, conflicts will likely be long and tumultuous. But once an issue is relocated to the left of the regime threshold, it resolves quickly, with a strong likelihood of disappearing within the metropolitan political arena or becoming mixed among a host of other 'normal' political disputes. This effect is to be expected as a result of the enormous surplus of political pressure required to strip a dimension of the state of its regime-level institutionalization. Where disengagement does occur the forces necessary to accomplish the prior change in the scale of the problem are so much larger than those required to formulate and enforce an actual decision to disengage—within the incumbent stage—that the process of disengagement itself is likely to be politically anticlimactic. More particularly, strategies which attempt to move quickly and decisively through the regime threshold in the deinstitutionalization direction will, if successful as rescaling mechanisms, precipitate much more rapid movement toward actual policies of disengagement—within the incumbent level stage—than will strategies associated with mechanisms—anchored in spatial or serial decomposition—which do not entail building up the amount of political pressure necessary to overcome semi-legal and illegal opposition to disengagement.

A very powerful set of propositions can be based on the expectation that rescaling strategies entailing large risks of severe regime crises may have as their eventual payoff both a more complete removal of the issue from the agenda of the central stage, but also a more stable outcome within the outlying territory. The logic of this latter expectation is that the new polity, moving toward its autonomous future, can do so with less need to overcome its own 'regime threatening' opposition to the kind of severe compromise associated with a core rescaling strategy based on problem decomposition and minimization of political stress within the core. There may be, as I have suggested, a kind of law of the conservation of risk and suffering (Lustick 1994: 43). If Britain avoided a real risk of civil war in 1914 by decomposing the Irish problem as the basis of its rescaling strategy, it did so with the consequence of an all-out civil war in Ireland and at the long-term cost of being burdened by the festering issue of Northern Ireland's disposition (McGarry and O'Leary 1995; O'Leary and McGarry 1996). If France, under de Gaulle, endured perilous and violent confrontations with anti-regime coalitions of settlers, military commanders, and right-wing politicians, it yet managed rather quickly and completely to free itself of the incubus of the Algerian question. One implication is that Israeli governmental choices regarding how generously to respond to Palestinian demands, and how forthrightly to face up to regime-challenging opposition from Israeli settlers, religious, and right-wing political groups, will partially determine whether Israel will suffer from a 'Northern Ireland' type problem for decades to come, or whether, as in France, a sharper display of strength at the centre will result in a more radical, but more complete and more stable set of political arrangements in both Israel and Palestine.[10]

Theory pertaining to wars of position, that is, to struggles over the construction or deconstruction of hegemonic beliefs, relates to the dynamics of competition among aspiring hegemonic projects and the struggles between intact hegemonic discourses and counter-hegemonic efforts. A fully developed theory of this kind would specify, at some useful level of abstraction, the necessary and sufficient conditions for constructing, defending, or removing hegemonic beliefs as well as systematic expectations about the relationship between variation in the accomplishment of those outcomes and patterns of subsequent political and cultural change. What I have suggested in this domain builds on Gramsci, who did considerably more systematic thinking

[10] For my analysis of Rabin's 'rescaling' strategy and my predictions for the Israeli-Palestinian case using the theories tested in the British and French cases, see Lustick (1993: 385–438).

about wars of position than wars of manoeuvre, but it remains only an incomplete and very partial attempt to build such a theory.

From a Gramscian perspective, hegemonic conceptions provide stabilizing distortions and rationalizations of complex realities, inconsistent desires, and arbitrary distributions of valued resources. They are presumptions that exclude outcomes, options, or questions, from public consideration; thus they advantage those élites well positioned to profit from prevailing cleavage patterns and issue definitions. That hegemonic beliefs do not shift fluidly with changing realities and marginal interests is what makes them important. That they require *some* correspondence to 'objective' realities and interests is what limits their life and the conditions under which they can be established and maintained.

Studying the dynamics of competition among hegemonic projects and explaining patterns of success and failure can be understood as a probe into the dynamics of 'wars of position'—political struggle over what ideas and values will be accepted by leading strata of a state as the 'concrete fantasy' which will achieve hegemonic status. Though subtle, non-violent, and conducted as much in the press and in educational and religious institutions as in the political arena, the outcome of such struggles are of far-reaching importance. For whatever particular interpretation of reality is contained in the set of conceptions enshrined as hegemonic, will decisively advantage certain groups by privileging their particular preferences and attitudes as unassailable assumptions of community life.[11] In *The Modern Prince* Gramsci attempted to generalize about the patterns such struggles display, and the factors that determine the outcome of competition among hegemonic projects. The result of his effort, though limited, is suggestive. New hegemonic projects develop, fundamentally, because of 'incurable contradictions' between reigning beliefs and underlying conditions (Gramsci 1957: 166).

---

[11] As noted, wars of manoeuvre are to be distinguished from wars of position. The former—surrounding the regime threshold—refer to the direct clash of interests associated with acute crises, when governments or regimes can change hands as a result of illegal or semi-legal actions by political groups. Gramsci used these military metaphors mainly to explain why the Russian Revolution, characterized by a short sharp seizure of power, had not and would not be repeated in the industrial states of Europe and America. In these countries authority structures were well-institutionalized and elaborately legitimized by an ideologically and culturally integrated civil society. Before state power itself could be seized, the state would have to be successfully confronted on the ideological plane and deprived of its hegemonic resources—see Femia (1987: 50–5, 305–9).

In my use of Gramsci's metaphors and concepts I move from his predominant emphasis on a revolutionary process conceived as devoted to the transformation of an entire political system to a focus on struggles over one particular constitutive and constituted element of the state—its territorial shape. For a systematic argument for why and how Gramsci's concept of hegemony should be seen as applicable to discrete dimensions of political life, rather than necessarily centred in a comprehensive, class-based formula for apprehending social reality see Laclau and Mouffe (1985: 69, 86–7, 136–44).

This circumstance undermines the self-confidence of state élites and ruling groups and weakens the ability of prevailing conceptions to limit entry of new kinds of questions into the public domain. But a war of position cannot be inaugurated or conducted without conflicting ideas. Intellectuals, according to Gramsci, play a key role in producing these ideas. As candidates for hegemonic status, these ideas camouflage particular distributions of power by linking them to commonsensical, established myths, symbols, and categories. The substance of a successful hegemonic conception, says Gramsci, is not arbitrary. It presupposes a 'stubborn reality' to which the formulas it contains can convincingly be seen to correspond. If its purpose and function is to advance or consolidate the position of particular groups, still the 'consent,' acquiescence, or agreement it elicits from relatively disadvantages groups must be based on 'a certain balance of compromises' (Gramsci 1957: 154–5).[12] Implicit here is the notion that only by arranging at least a modicum of satisfaction for the groups from whom consent is required and a minimum correspondence between objective conditions and ideological pictures, can hegemonic conceptions fulfil their primary function, namely the containment and political neutralization of latent tensions which, if unleashed, would threaten the power of those whose interests the conceptions serve.[13]

Political and ideological entrepreneurship is the transmission belt that carries ideas with hegemonic potential forward into the political arena. It is practised by bold leaders, intellectuals, and the organizations they build or control: 'Ideas and opinions are not "born" spontaneously in the brains of each individual; they have had a centre of formation, of radiation, or propaganda, of persuasion, a group of men or even a single individual who has elaborated and presented them . . .' (Gramsci 1957: 183). Of course most people who challenge basic assumptions of their community's political life fail. Whether because of their own shortcomings, the solidity of prevailing beliefs, or the ineffectiveness of their ideas, their likely fate is to be dismissed as either cranks or criminals. Still, the inventors and promoters of hegemonic projects are people who understand the decisive importance of 'reclothing political questions in cultural forms.' (ibid: 147). By shaping the cognitions and values of élites and masses these entrepreneurs seek to (re)define the allowable boundaries and the appropriate stakes of political competition. In this they show their understanding of Gramsci's primary dictum: 'Whatever one does, one always plays somebody's game, the important thing is to seek in every way to play one's own game, i.e. to win completely' (ibid: 152).

---

[12] Gramsci also says that there must be an economic component.

[13] For a fascinating attempt to establish the extent of 'exploitation which can, or cannot, be contained by hegemonic conceptions, see Przeworski (1980).

I have sought to distil and reformulate Gramsci's ideas on these matters as follows. Overthrowing an established ideologically hegemonic conception or explaining its breakdown requires:

(1) a severe contradiction between the conception advanced as hegemonic and the stubborn realities it purports to describe;
(2) an appropriately-fashioned alternative interpretation of political reality capable of reorganizing competition to the advantage of particular groups;
(3) and dedicated political-ideological entrepreneurs who can operate successfully where fundamental assumptions of political life have been thrown open to question, and who see better opportunities in competition over basic 'rules of the game' than in competition for marginal advantage according to existing rules.

Obviously, to establish a belief as hegemonic, or successfully defend its status as such, requires *at least* substantial correspondence between the claims of the belief and the political realities it purports to describe; the absence of a widely accepted basis for an alternative interpretation; *or* the absence of political entrepreneurs capable of profiting from its overthrow or breakdown.

These hypotheses are considerably more refined for explaining the requisites of breakdown and defence of existing hegemonic beliefs than for their construction. In other words, corresponding to the asymmetry of the threshold, it is, so far at least, and based on both the inferential logics associated with hegemony and available empirical evidence, possible to say more about the necessary conditions for deinstitutionalizing a hegemonic belief than it is about the necessary conditions for institutionalizing hegemony. In neither case do I claim an ability to specify sufficient conditions.

However I have suggested some propositions pertaining to wars of position, which relate to but are not logical extensions of the core hypotheses listed above. consistent with the insights into the political dynamics of discursive fields, as suggested by Michel Foucault and operationalized by Katherine Verdery (Verdery 1991) and others, it appears that 'new ideas' promoted to reinterpret gross discrepancies in accordance with a counter-hegemonic effort may act powerfully and indeed most saliently as foils serving the purposes of defenders of the *status quo* rather than as direct facilitators of the counter-hegemonic élites. At the same time it appears that the temptation of established interests to exploit popular prejudice by acknowledging, warning of, and even exaggerating the support available for counter-hegemonic ideas may play a crucial role in the failure to establish dominant conceptions as 'hegemonic'. This was apparent in the British Unionist Party's use of the Irish Home Rule issue and of anti-Irish sentiment in Britain to deprive the Liberals of working class support between 1885 and 1906. Temptations to exploit the issue by stressing the evil consequences of its all-too-possible implementation made it impossible to promote the idea that incorporation of Ireland into the United Kingdom was a foregone conclusion. Formulas of cultural relativism and economic realism eventually helped legitimize and rationalize French disengagement from Algeria. Their main importance, however, in the mid-1950s, was the opportunity they offered de Gaulle and his supporters to cast the struggle over the fate of the Fourth Republic as a contest, eminently winnable by de Gaulle, over whether such ideas were not indeed an embarrassment to France and whether the Fourth Republic would have to be replaced by a Gaullist-designed regime capable to restoring and maintaining French 'grandeur' (Lustick 1993: 149–60). Yet another example of this dynamic has been apparent in Israel, where the right-wing's use of the Labour Party's putative 'willingness to divide Jerusalem' has weakened the principle of an indivisible Israeli capital by repeatedly reminding Israelis of how precarious is Israel's hold over the Arab sections of the city (Lustick 2000).

An important question in analysing hegemonic projects within *superordinate* states pertains to relations of domination between those states and other communities/territories. To what extent is it possible to build or sustain a hegemonic belief concerning such a relationship within the core state unless it is also experienced as hegemonic within the *subordinated* community? Evidence from my own work so far is mixed on this question. British beliefs that Ireland was an integral part of the United Kingdom were hegemonic during the first half of the nineteenth century, although explicit opposition to British rule was widespread in Catholic Ireland. Israel was also successful in promoting and sustaining a hegemonic belief in the western and central Galilee and the Little Triangle—Arab majority territories captured in 1948—as integral parts of the State of Israel. On the other hand, a powerful coalition in favour of *Algérie française*, in control of the state and ready to commit huge resources to the prosecution of an all-out war effort, failed to enshrine its claims as hegemonic inside France. In Israel, successive annexationist governments, allied with settlers and an array of right-wing, fundamentalist, and religious parties, sought to establish the 'Whole Land of Israel' principle as politically hegemonic inside Israel. They were making impressive progress toward this objective until the Palestinian *Intifada* (1987–93) impelled many Israelis to rethink their commitments and prevented almost all Israelis from experiencing Israeli rule of 'Judea, Samaria, and the Gaza District' as unproblematically permanent and natural. As noted, this hegemonic project failed—or at least has not yet succeeded—even with respect to 'united Jerusalem.'

These outcomes raise the possibility that the asymmetries surrounding the two thresholds are not identical. Perhaps it is nearly as difficult to establish a belief as hegemonic, at least under conditions such as those prevailing in the French and Israeli-Palestinian cases, as it is to strip an existing hegemonic belief of its hegemonic status. There are indeed reasons to think that workable hegemonic conceptions will require substantial elements of strategic design. In neither the French nor the Israeli (West Bank/Gaza) case did the hegemonic project within the dominant communities contain the kind of compromise with the subordinated classes or groups that Gramsci suggests is necessary for stabilizing the hegemonic order. While Arabs in the Galilee and the Little Triangle were made Israeli citizens—thereby enjoying real, albeit partial, access to a wide range of benefits—citizenship status was not granted to the mass of Algerian Muslims, nor to the Arabs of the West Bank, Gaza, nor even to those of east Jerusalem.

Two additional points are worth making regarding the difficulty of constructing hegemonic beliefs to naturalize central state rule over disputed territories. Because of the enormous power-differential that typically exists between the core state and outlying territories, or at least because of the appearance within the core state of an enormous power-differential, there is a likelihood that coalitions within the core favouring more expansive images of the proper ambit of the state will win out over more modest, but more realistic, ambitions. Failures that inevitably attend pursuit of these extravagant objectives—late nineteenth century British ambitions to consolidate a world-circling 'Greater Britain,' post-World War II French efforts to transform its Asian, Middle Eastern, and African empire into a hexagon dominated 'French Union,' and Revisionist/Fundamentalist efforts in Israel to establish Jewish sovereignty over all territories captured in the 1967 war—severely compromise the ability to convincingly characterize substantially scaled-down versions as natural, inevitable, and common-sensical, rather than simply 'the most we might be able to get'. Related to this point is the circumstance that principles of self-determination, mass politics, and democracy are becoming hegemonic within international political culture and that states are increasingly permeable to ideas, arguments, and to mass-media and internet-delivered information. It is therefore increasingly difficult, and perhaps impossible, for a modern state—at least one advancing itself credibly as a democracy—to shield its citizens from information and insistent questions that require political superordination of one people over another to be defended in terms that inevitably expose and reinforce the hegemonic project's contingency and problematic character.

In any event, whether the hegemonic threshold is intrinsically more difficult to pass in the state-building direction as imagined within the theory

I have advanced of 'asymmetric thresholds,' or whether, with respect to this particular kind of hegemonic project at this historical moment, constructing such beliefs as hegemonic is particularly difficult, the result is similar. Across the globe we can expect that relationships of domination between a central state and an outlying territory that have passed the regime threshold, but not the ideological hegemony threshold, will experience repeated oscillations. If the problem of the outlying territory cannot be removed from the central state's public agenda through the establishment of an intrastate hegemonic belief, changing constellations of power, internationally and within both the core and the periphery, will periodically produce pressures to stabilize the relationship through disengagement. But these pressures will push the problem up against the regime threshold, where élites will usually be deterred from following through on the necessary rescaling measures. Failure to rescale the problem will leave it intact. Dormant for a while, as it moves away from the 'phase transition' zone to the right of the regime threshold, it will return, in the absence of hegemony and with changing particular circumstances, to destabilize the system again. Absent forcible external intervention or a massive change in the balance of coercive capability between the core and the periphery, this cycle will recur unless or until right-sizing is achieved. To stabilize the relationship the ruling strata will either have to take the risks necessary to deinstitutionalize rule of the outlying territory across the regime threshold, or adjust the content of its hegemonic project sufficiently to correspond with the stubborn realities of demands by peoples in both the centre and the periphery, and with internationally hegemonic norms.

Conclusion: Opportunities and Barriers

The views of those who closely follow protracted and polarizing disputes of the sort that have afflicted Sri Lanka, Kashmir, Northern Ireland, the West Bank, the western Sahara, Kurdistan, Cyprus, southern Sudan, and the former Yugoslavia, cluster around two poles. On one side a tendency crystallizes to view the past as having led, after some tragic turning point, to an inexorably dismal future. On the other hand, there are those whose rationalist confidence or idealist faith in a mutually satisfying outcome blind them to the enormous obstacles that real historical processes have placed in the path of that tantalizing resolution. The theoretical approach to right-sizing the state advanced here is in part an effort, not to deny the validity of these two perspectives, but to invigorate them by offering conceptual tools and guiding ideas that can help link the insights and knowledge associated with them to the processes which lie beyond their conceptual horizons.

From the perspective of observers who emphasize entrenched interests and irreversible institutional facts as barriers to any creative efforts to ameliorate disputes, the notion of threshold constitutes a kind of opportunity. Both analytically and emotionally it suggests the possibility of sudden, substantial, and even transformative change. The crucial element is to develop a base of knowledge, accumulated and refined through cross-cultural comparison, about the dynamics of these thresholds and the signs reflecting their political proximity. Only thus can they be the basis for reasoned and realistic action rather than faith-based commitments.

On the other side are those fixated on the irrationality or even insanity of violence-prone disputes and the intellectual availability of arrangements that could alleviate or eliminate them. This kind of attitude can lead to a severe under-appreciation of the enormous barriers to changes—changes that might, in some abstract sense, reflect the long-term interests or forces at work. For these actors and observers the theory's institutionalization thresholds are important for two different reasons. First, no resolution of a conflict can be achieved, and no effective action toward its achievement can be plotted, unless a path from 'here' to 'there' is understood as politically viable by élites willing and able to carry out the necessary policy changes. But no design of these pathways will be possible if the sometimes sharply, sometimes slowly changing slopes of the terrain to be traversed are not well mapped and if the political tasks at different points along the way are not distinguished from one another.

Another contribution of this theory to political right-sizing is that once deinstitutionalization has been accomplished, and a wider array of options is made feasible by the transformation of hegemonic or regime-level problems into incumbent-level problems, processes of reinstitutionalization will be required. So even for those whose immediate interest may be in down-sizing—territorially or functionally—they will also need to think, eventually, of how the new smaller or more limited sectoral authority structure can be institutionalized, that is, moved across the regime and then hegemonic thresholds in the state-building direction.

The amount of work to be done on these problems is enormous. The hypotheses adumbrated here are but beginning points for the inquiries that are necessary, both empirical and theoretical/conceptual, if real progress is to be made. Among the most important empirical questions are the degree to which the routinization processes of hegemonic construction and the accumulation of vested interests that eventually produce regime-level institutionalization can be theorized; whether hypotheses developed for the study of territorial boundary institutionalization can find support, that is, can do useful explanatory work, with respect to functional or sectoral 'right-sizing';

and whether progress can be made toward refining and testing rather broadly stated propositions about deinstitutionalization, developed in relation to the British, French, and Israeli cases, using data generated from other cases. On the theoretical side I have suggested that using the complex adaptive system notion of 'emergent property,' and a variety of other analytic tools borrowed—with caution!—from complexity and evolutionary theory, will prove extremely useful for the production of new ideas about institutionalization, its requisites, and its consequences.

REFERENCES

Brunt, P. A. 1964–5. 'Reflections on British and Roman Imperialism'. *Comparative Studies in Society and History*, 7.

Dennett, Daniel C. 1995. *Darwin's Dangerous ideas.* New York, NY: Simon & Schuster.

Doyle, Michael W. 1986. *Empires.* Ithaca, NY, and London: Cornell University Press.

Femia, Joseph V. 1987. *Gramsci's Political Thought: Hegemony, Consciousness, and the Revolutionary Process.* Oxford: Clarendon Press.

Gramsci, Antonio. 1957. *The Modern Prince and Other Writings.* New York, NY: International Publishers.

Holland, John H. 1998. *Emergence: From Chaos to Order.* Reading, MA: Helix Books.

Laclau, Ernesto, and Mouffe, Chantal. 1985. *Hegemony and Socialist Strategy: Towards a Radical Democratic Politics.* London: Verso.

Lustick, Ian S. 1985. *State-Building Failure in British Ireland and French Algeria.* Berkeley, CA: University of California Press.

—— 1993. *Unsettled States, Disputed Lands: Britain and Ireland, France and Algeria, Israel and the West-Bank-Gaza.* New York, NY: Cornell University Press.

—— 1994. 'Necessary Risks: Lessons for the Israeli-Palestinian Peace Process from Ireland and Algeria'. *Middle East Policy* 2/1: 41–59.

—— 2000. 'Yerushalayim and al-Quds: Political Catechism and Political Realities'. *Journal of Palestine Studies*, 30/1: 5–21.

McGarry, John, and O'Leary, Brendan. 1995. *Explaining Northern Ireland: Broken Images.* Oxford and Cambridge, MA: Basil Blackwell.

Miles, Gary B. 1990. 'Roman and Modern Imperialism: A Reassessment'. *Comparative Studies in Society and History*, 32: 629–59.

O'Leary, Brendan. 1995. 'Regulating Nations and Ethnic Communities'. 245–89 in *Nationalism and Rationality*, edited by Albert Breton, Gianluigi Galeotti, Pierre Salmon, and Ronald Wintrobe. Cambridge: Cambridge University Press.

—— and John McGarry. 1996. *The Politics of Antagonism: Understanding Northern Ireland.* London and Atlantic heights, NJ: Athlone.

Przeworski, Adam. 1980. 'Material Bases of Consent: Economics and Politics in a

Hegemonic System'. 21–65 in *Political Power and Social Theory: A Research Annual*, edited by Maurice Zeitlin. Greenwich, CT: JAI Press.

Thompson, James D. 1967. *Organization in Action*. New York, NY: McGraw-Hill.

Verdery, Katherine. 1991. *National Ideology under Socialism: Identity and Culture in Ceausescu's Romania*. Berkeley, CA: University of California.

4

From Reshaping to Resizing a Failing State?
The Case of the Congo/Zaïre

Thomas M. Callaghy

> The country's unity is not in danger. This is the most durable achievement of my political career. Everybody will have to learn a lesson in this war: the Zaïrians are welded together by their national feeling. . . . There was no Zaïre before me, and there will be no Zaïre after me.
>
> Mobutu Sese Seko, April 1997 (Grill 1977)

> We talk about changing the head of state, but we have no state.
>
> Francesca Bomboko, a Zaïrian political analyst in Kinshasa, April 1997
> (cited in *Foreign Broadcast Information Service*, 28 April 1997)

> [Zaïre's people are in] a gripping and epic-making contest (that aims to) give a new birth to their country. . . . As Africans, we have a vision, a hope, a prayer about will come in the end. We see a Zaïre perhaps with a new name, a Zaïre which shall be democratic, peaceful, prosperous, a defender of human rights and an exemplar of what the new Africa should be, occupying the geographic space that it does at the heart of our Africa . . . as Africans, we would like to believe that we know that at the end, what all of us will see, thanks to the wisdom of the Zaïrian people themselves, is not the heart of darkness but the light of a new African star.
>
> South African Deputy President Thabo Mbeki, April 1997
> (Duke 1997a)

> Mr. Kabila has failed us and we need to set out a new vision for the Congo. A vision based on the future of all Congolese, regardless of their tribal affiliation. Instead of putting in place a government of national unity, Mr. Kabila has put in place a government composed of members of his family.
>
> Rebel statement, August 1998 (Reuters 1998e)

This is not a Banyamulenge [Tutsi] struggle. It is a struggle of all Congolese. This is not a struggle of Rwandans who want to colonise the country. It is the struggle of all Congolese.

Rebel leader, August 1998 (Holman 1998)

The Rwandan Tutsi want to establish a Tutsi empire in the Congo. Last time we were sick of Mobutu and so we welcomed the rebels here. But this time it's different. We're ready to take arms if they come here.

Congolese student, Kinshasa, August 1998 (Onishi 1998)

We have to be concerned about our security before everything, about our development, certainly after the terrible trials which this country has seen. [But] talk of annexing Kivu makes no sense whatsoever.

Rwandan leader Paul Kagame, Kigali, Rwanda, August 1998 (Reuters 1998d)

If the rebels do not succeed in rapidly taking control of the whole country and if Kabila exerts his authority in part of Congo, a partition is not excluded. It is necessary to pay attention to the alliances before one can cry victory for one camp or another.

Kengo wa Dondo, former Prime Minister under Mobutu, Brussels, August 1998 (Reuters (1998c)

The international community remains silent, a silence that is becoming more and more a silence of complicity.

Kabila minister, Kinshasa, August 1998 (Malu-Malu 1998b)

Over the last few years, Central Africa, especially its Great Lakes region, has been the crucible for dramatic and often tragic conflict and change.[1] It has

---

[1] This paper was first written in May 1997 just as the first Congolese civil war was ending. It was revised as war rages and gets more complicated by the day. The victor of the first civil war, Laurent Kabila, renamed Zaïre the Congo, and created the 'Third Republic'. I use Zaïre to refer to the Mobutu regime and the Congo to refer to the Kabila regime. The revision takes into account the performance of the Kabila regime and changes in the region. It is written in the light of Ian Lustick's theory, outlined in Chapter 3 of this volume. I want to thank the following: Vikash Yadav, Michele Commercio, and Jeanette Lee for their wonderful research assistance; Michael G. Schatzberg, Leonardo Villalón, John F. Clark, Winsome Leslie, Robert Bartlett, and Jeffrey Herbst for providing me with unpublished manuscripts and other materials; and all the current and former US and World Bank officials, military officers, Congressional staffers, academics, research institute scholars, and representatives of private volunteer organizations and the press who engaged in spirited and sometimes contentious discussion of the situation in Zaïre during the meeting of the nineteenth American Assembly on 'Africa and US National Interests', at Arden House, Harriman, New York, 13–16 March 1997. I must also acknowledge the extraordinary resources of the Internet—it is an amazing experience to follow the course of two civil wars in Central Africa in such detail and from such a variety of sources and viewpoints. This tells us a good deal about wars of position and manoeuvre at the end of this century.

experienced genocide in Rwanda; a Tutsi invasion of Rwanda by a Uganda-supported army that successfully overthrew the Hutu government; and the flight of that government and its army, as well as large numbers of Hutu people into Zaïre—one of the most complex failing states in Africa. Out of these events erupted a totally unexpected civil war with strong regional backing and no major external intervention, which resulted in the collapse of the brutal but ineffective regime of Africa's last and longest-ruling dictator, Mobutu Sese Seko. Then a little more than a year later a new 'civil war' erupted with the aim of overthrowing the new government of Laurent Kabila in Kinshasa. This time African states have lined up on both sides, leading to an even more explosive situation. We are only beginning to understand the nature, importance, and long-term consequences of these events.

In the preface to *Unsettled States, Disputed Lands* Ian Lustick laid out three central abstract problems of statehood: 'the presumptively permanent but actually contingent nature of state boundaries . . . the relationship between the internal complexion of states and their external shape and . . . the mysterious links between gradual processes of political metamorphosis and sudden transformations' (Lustick 1993). He mentioned Africa as one of the regions for which these issues are relevant in the post-Cold War world, and listed Zaïre as one of the states 'whose territorial shape is under pressure or may change as the result of hostile action, co-operative agreements, or both, within the next decade' (Lustick 1993: xii, 2).[2] Given the dramatic events that have unfolded before our eyes since 1996, how right he was. This chapter seeks to show why he was right.

The Argument

First, let us be clear what this chapter is *not* about. It is not an analysis of an attempt by a central ruling group in a relatively developed democratic[3] country to down-size or expand territory that is not in danger of being taken away

[2] He was also correct about the other African states he listed, Somalia, Liberia, and the Sudan. These issues are, of course, germane to all African states, many of which have been quietly failing for a couple of decades—see Herbst (1992).

[3] See Lustick, Chapter 3 above. Both Gramsci and Lustick developed their theories in the context of industrial countries—with modern princes—where 'authority structures are well-institutionalised and elaborately legitimised by an ideologically and culturally integrated civil society.' Gramsci noted that in these cases such change rarely comes about in short sharp seizures of power but from more slowly cumulative forces punctured by episodes of more discontinuous change. Gramsci was comparing such cases to that of the Russian Revolution. In the case of the Congo, the change came in a dramatic 'short sharp seizure of power,' but one, as we will see, that was preceded by a relatively coherent war of position designed to reshape a state that had been failing quietly for decades.

by force, or having to agree to relinquish sovereign functional authority within the existing political domain to resolve a conflict for the long-term general interest using a consciously adopted strategy and specific decisions to implement it. As Lustick puts it, 'It is precisely those cases where *force majeure* [is] not decisive in the determination of outcomes, or where it is not expected to be decisive, which are of the greatest interest'—see Chapter 3 above. This chapter seeks to see how the institutionalization and deinstitutionalization themes elaborated so well by Lustick can help us understand events in Central Africa today, and what these events might tell us about his theory. Unlike the rest of the chapters in this volume, this is about a failing or collapsing state. By elaborating an important but underexplored distinction Lustick makes between territorial and functional state contraction, this chapter explores the nature of 'reshaping' and 'resizing' and the relationship between them, and then applies this analytic perspective to the events that are shaking Central Africa to its foundations.

The chapter applies Lustick's analysis of institutionalization and deinstitutionalization to Mobutu Sese Seko's Zaïre. That failing state was subject to reshaping efforts by his opposition for over fifteen years. These efforts resulted in a strong war of position that pushed the country 'backwards' across the ideological hegemony threshold, but failed to move it across the regime integrity threshold because of a weaker war of manoeuvre. In this entire process, however, the issue was explicitly not down-sizing—although strong underlying ethno-regional tensions and resizing aspirations were never effectively eliminated by Mobutu—but rather political reshaping. The opposition was attempting to remove the incumbent leadership and reshape the rules of the game in a distinctly federal, even confederal—and allegedly democratic—direction in the midst of systemic processes of state failure and dramatic changes in regional and international dynamics.[4] This chapter shows how this ongoing conflict was affected by dramatic discontinuous trigger events that resulted from changes in the wider region, and the reactions to them of the Mobutu government and various regional and international agents within the more 'permissive' post-cold war context—despite the claims of a New World Order. Out of the interplay of these processes of reshaping and discontinuous change, resizing attempts have become entirely possible, especially if reshaping efforts fail to meet the expectations of key groups. Consequently, this chapter speaks to the possibilities of a more generalized process of resizing that might result from ongoing state failure in Africa.

[4] In the terminology used by Brendan O'Leary in Chapter 2, most of the opposition to Mobutu wanted a form of ethno-national conflict regulation based on the 'management of differences' through internal territorial autonomy.

Lustick reminds us that states are never 'finished' being 'built,' and never irreversibly in 'final' shape, and that their operation constantly impinges on their 'formation' or 'shaping.' State-shaping is a set of both continuous and discontinuous processes of institutionalization of political and psychological expectations of regularity, continuity, and propriety. What appears to be continuous 'path-dependent' change (North 1990) may, in fact, be shaken by 'punctuated equilibria' that dramatically alter the territorial configuration of states.[5] Processes that go unnoticed for decades may suddenly come into play and challenge 'immutable' realities, and 'we can expect that different groups will align their own perceptions of the proper border in light of the implications different borders, or different principles of inclusion and exclusion, may have for their chances to achieve and/or maintain political power' (Lustick 1993: 28–38). For boundaries

specify who and what are potential participants or objects of the political game and who and what are not. Different borders have different demographic implications and different political myths associated with them. The territorial shape of a state thus helps to determine what interests are legitimate, what resources are mobilizable, what questions are open for debate, what ideological formulas will be relevant, what cleavages become significant, and what political allies might be available.

(Lustick 1993: 41)

When the state is being 'right-sized,' Lustick argues that 'the *territorial or functional* scope of state institutions will be reduced'—a process of 'contracting out of a *particular territory or functional sector*' (see Chapter 3 above, emphases added). He goes on to note that 'State contraction [territorial or functional] is conceived as a process of moving "backwards" through [ideological hegemony and regime integrity] thresholds, first by legitimizing public discussion of disengagement as a credible or sensible option, then by eliminating from public debate and private calculation the threat of challenges to the legal order should a coalition favouring disengagement be in a position legally to implement its preferences, and then by forming a winning coalition favouring a policy of disengagement and capable of implementing it.' (ibid). Such a definition implies a staged process with a specific sequence, and increasing levels of struggle with no overlap, a linear order of unfolding. Theoretically, this may be the way that these complicated processes can be analysed most effectively, but in practice attempts at contraction are usually much more mixed, overlapping, and uneven processes, with the various

---

[5] Hendrik Spruyt nicely reminds us that we have bought our own myths about the nature, rise, and permanence of the state system as well as the relationship of states to nations. He has developed his own non-linear view of evolutionary change and institutional variation and selection (Spruyt 1995).

'stages' playing out simultaneously. I prefer to use the term arena for the incumbency, regime integrity, and ideological hegemony struggles, but, as will be indicated later, the notion of stages and the crossing of thresholds are central to an overall understanding of contraction as a process, and how it plays out in any given case.

Reshaping for me refers to attempts to alter the rules of the game without necessarily resizing the state, that is, altering its external borders. Both political and military opposition groups tried to reshape Zaïre without resizing it, but the very attempts to reshape the country unintentionally pushed the struggle 'backwards' across what Lustick calls the ideological hegemony threshold, thereby raising the possibility of eventual resizing if the expectations of contending domestic and external groups are not met. In short, the failure of ruling or opposition groups to prevent or control the reshaping process may lead to dramatic resizing. The reshaping process will be centrally affected by the ability of the contending groups to erect viable structures of control, establish effective new rules of the game—wars of manoeuvre—and spin persuasive ideas—wars of position—and it is strongly influenced by the regional and international contexts in which it operates.[6]

The Case and Its Implications: Zaïre/Congo in the Central African Cauldron

Wracked by multiple crises of order and identity in the 1960s, Zaïre became a highly personalized state ruled for over thirty years by a presidential monarch—Mobutu Sese Seko.[7] This authoritarian regime, built on the shifting sands of the Belgian colonial state, was quietly failing for much of its existence as it tried to maintain control of a mineral rich country the size of Western Europe, with over 250 ethnic groups speaking over 400 languages. It was simultaneously a soft, yet highly coercive state—a lame Leviathan (Callaghy 1987b). The state was weakened over time by the progressive but uneven patrimonialization of politics and the inherited colonial administrative apparatus, such that the performance of key functions slowly declined

[6] My own work has used the concept of 'domain consensus,' which 'is a set of mutually agreed upon expectations of what the state can and cannot do, which is based on ideological principles, bargaining and/or dominance. A domain consensus is not the same thing as legitimacy because its establishment may not be the result of voluntary agreement by the population. There are three types of domain consensus: normative, utilitarian, and coercive. Once a relatively stable domain consensus is established, it tends to decrease the amount of coercion and conflict necessary to maintain the dominance of the state', Callaghy (1984: 92) and *passim*; see also Callaghy (1980).

[7] On this entire period see Young (1965a, 1967, 1970, 1976a, b). Also see Verhaegen (1966, 1969); Mahoney (1983); Kalb (1982); Gibbs (1991); and Shatzberg (1991).

and in some cases disappeared completely. Corruption so permeated the system that the state was slowly hollowed out. The economy started to collapse in the middle 1970s, and the survival tactics of the informal economy spread. The control of the state was maintained by a 'national' army of occupation, by repeated external rescue efforts, and by the astute statecraft of an African Machiavelli. Mobutu as a presidential monarch created a doctrine that was a mélange of disparate, but in the beginning believable ingredients—he was the father who saved the nation from chaos in the 1960s by bringing order, dignity, and development.[8] Powerful customary notions of patrimonial authority, dignity, arbitrariness, grandeur, display, and the occult underpinned this hegemonic discourse.[9] An external support system was shrewdly maintained and exploited, founded on the geopolitical perceptions and perversions of the cold war, and the manipulation of 'national' and regional power rivalries.

By 1967 the country had achieved relative peace, but many of the major issues remained unresolved, in particular whether the state was to be a unitary or a federal/confederal one. A series of roundtable conferences were held over this issue during this period. The basic outlines of the complex interplay of ethnicity and regionalism, with roots well into the colonial and pre-colonial periods, were established—on this period see the magisterial account in Young (1965a). And they still have amazing resonance today. In fact, it is almost as if Mobutu's period of centralized unitary rule from 1967 to 1997 was a thirty year hiatus that settled very little, thereby demonstrating the power these shaping and sizing ethno-national forces have on élite and mass imagination and specific interests. As with a state's borders, such shaping issues are often never finally and definitively settled. It is striking that many of the same people involved in 'the troubles' of the 1960s were so prominent in 1996—Mobutu; Kabila—a Lumumba follower with Maoist roots; Christophe Gbenye and Nguza Karl-I-Bond, leaders of secessionist attempts in Stanleyville (Kisangani) and Katanga (Shaba) respectively; and lots of less well-known figures. In March 1997 in the middle of the civil war, one of them noted that 'it's a pursuit of a fight which started in those years,' while another asserted, 'I am one of those who started this, and I am one of those to finish it' (Duke 1997b). Kivu province, where Kabila eventually took refuge in the 1960s, remained one of the important flash points. Rwandan 'refugees' rioted in July 1965 in North Kivu for lack of representation, and the entire province remained the only active centre of armed resistance, albeit low grade, to the Mobutu regime.

---

[8] For a popular culture version of these discourses see the magnificent Fabian (1966).

[9] On the importance of the occult see the wonderful account in Schatzberg (1997a).

The peak of Mobutu's reshaping endeavour was reached in the late 1970s, less than a decade after the country was pacified after the turmoil of multiple secessionist attempts, wars of manoeuvre over federalism and confederalism, widespread but not well organized rebellions and uprisings, assassinations, and multiple international interventions. Yet even at its 'peak,' the Mobutu regime had to be rescued once more from external invasions in 1977–8 by military forces of the failed Katanga secession effort that had been maintained in good military form by the Marxist government in neighbouring Angola, and which used them to fight its own rebel movement, Jonas Savimbi's Unita.

In the early 1980s efforts to chip away at the dominant monarchical doctrine began to make headway as an internal opposition coalesced round a former Mobutu official—Etienne Tshisekedi, a Luba from the Kasai region. This process was aided by the opposition of the Catholic Church as the only major proto-state actor in Zaïre, by syncretic religious movements, by the safety net of the informal economy as it responded to the collapsing formal economy, by a massive debt problem, and failed efforts at economic reform— shepherded by increasingly baffled international financial institutions. Growing *de facto* regional autonomy, a growing popular culture that challenged the notions of personal power, and quietly shifting wider regional realities prised apart the basis of the regime. By the early 1990s, the Mobutuist lame Leviathan had become an archipelago state, both functionally and territorially—a group of islands of control and extraction which kept the stumbling system alive by focusing on the most easily profitable forms and locations of resource pillage.[10]

A watershed was reached in 1990 when Mobutu was forced by internal and external realities to announce that he would bring democratization to Zaïre, a process he thought he could control, as he had always been able to do. By this point, however, the political opposition had managed to push the political struggle 'backwards' over the ideological hegemony threshold into the regime integrity arena where reshaping battles really began, resulting in a national conference that continued the attack on Mobutuist hegemonic doctrines, and challenged the current rules of the game and, as a result, the incumbent élite. The intent of the opposition, however, was to reshape the state without resizing it, to push 'backwards' across the regime integrity

[10] One of the most astute journalistic observers of the civil war points to a parallel distancing of Mobutu from his own state as it shrank into an archipelago: '(Mobutu) appeared to have accepted a dilution of his role as long as the mineral revenues needed to keep his entourage in style kept rolling in. "During those seven years there was a gradual shift from Kinshasa to the river boat, from the river boat to Gbadolite (Mobutu's lavish palace in his native region of Equateur), from Gbadolite to the Riviera", says an ambassador', Wrong (1997a). On the notion of an archipelago see Reno (1994 and 1998: especially ch. 5).

threshold into the incumbency arena and bring Mobutu down. The dominant opposition group around Tshisekedi tried to defend a unitary conception of the state, but were buffeted by strong federalist, even confederalist pressures, resulting in a draft constitution that would have led to much greater autonomy for the regions and the eventual possibility of actual resizing.

Mobutu managed to manipulate this process for six years, preventing major changes in the regime's rules of the game or his incumbency and ruling élite, but his doctrines of legitimation were badly mangled in the process. In short, the basic control structure of the archipelago was maintained, surrounded by what Will Reno has called the 'shadow state' (Reno 1995). A call for authentic democratization by both internal and external actors was the weapon of choice. A vague and inclusive proposition, it did not challenge the external border of the state because a wide range of domestic, regional, and external agents could all envision their view of a reshaped Zaïre as fitting their expectations and interests—including highly confederalist ones. Since Mobutuist doctrines had been effectively challenged, however, each of the contending groups had a fall-back set of expectations that would be expressed if their expectations of power were not met. Then changing Zaïre's external borders might become a live option, resizing a real possibility. This is the case because moving to the left of Lustick's ideological hegemony threshold entails 'the abandonment of settled presumptions about the boundaries of the political community, [the possibility of] destabilization or central decision-making institutions, as well as challenges to the reputations and careers of governing politicians and their parties' (Lustick 1993: 185). In short, the three key issues delineated by Lustick in his preface to *Unsettled States, Disputed Lands* become inextricably mixed, illustrating

how intimately the territorial shape of the state [size in my usage], the character of the regime [shape in my usage] institutionalized within its borders, and the power position of the incumbent élites are linked to one another. It highlights the importance of treating the embeddedness of the shape [in both Lustick's and my senses] as one among many dimensions of its institutional coherence. It supports a view of institutionalization as a process of accumulating more fundamental kinds of expectations about limits on the possibility of change and seeing deinstitutionalization as a process of losing those expectations. It illustrates how the discontinuities of institutional construction . . . help explain how long-term cumulative processes of change [in this case, the interplay of slow state failure with partially fluid but not totally malleable territorially-based solidarities] can be translated quickly, chaotically, but in recognizable patterns, into nonlinear transformations. It also shows . . . how prevailing international norms and shifting balances of power influence outcomes in wars of position and manoeuvre by reinforcing or inhibiting the efforts of protagonists.

(Lustick 1993: 441)

As political struggles play out in different arenas, threshold struggles and movements across them in either direction can be kept analytically distinct, but in practice they are related in quite complex and uneven ways, sometimes even moving in different directions at the same time—as my case materials will demonstrate. To the left of the ideological hegemony threshold, resizing is contingent on the way reshaping processes play out. In other words, the territorial border of the state undergoing political reshaping is based on contingent expectations about the limits, or lack of them, on the possibilities for change in relation to perceived interests. Groups are willing to consider reshaping rather than resizing as long as they perceive that their interests can be achieved. When it becomes increasingly likely that reshaping will not serve those interests, resizing becomes a live option, if not always ultimately achievable. Whether any resizing attempt is successful depends primarily on the skill of the leaders in the complex wars of manoeuvre over reshaping, the strategies they choose, and their ability to carry them out.[11]

I will briefly illustrate this by looking at the performance of the Kabila regime in its first year. Given the long-term state decline sketched above, a shift from continuous but controllable and cumulative reshaping efforts by civilian opposition groups to a 'discontinuous' punctuated equilibrium reshaping effort through the dramatic emergence of an internal military challenge with strong regional backing should not have been surprising. Nevertheless, it was a surprise to almost everybody. However, it should not be assumed that this more dramatic form of reshaping will necessarily lead to resizing.

In the case of Zaïre, and of Africa more generally,[12] local realities have clashed with the post-cold war rhetorical shift of the major western powers from the 'containment' of communism to the 'enlargement' of the world's market democracies. This is partly because states themselves are at stake, not merely their ideological, institutional, or public policy orientations. In *Unsettled States, Disputed Lands*, Lustick discussed an analogy of absolutist state formation,[13] especially its distinctive ideologically hegemonic

---

[11] On various strategies, see Chapter 3 above. Considering the possible outcomes at the end of the first civil war in May 1997 I wrote in the first draft of this chapter: 'As with the civilian opposition, the military movement will pursue reshaping as long as it controls the process. Here again, when it becomes clear that it may not be able to do so, it may shift to a resizing strategy, and, with the possible assistance of regional and international actors, already have the military capability to carry it out. At the same time, if the reshaping effort of the military movement appears to threaten the interests of powerful domestic actors with control capabilities (incumbent elites or aspirant regional elites), they may shift to a resizing strategy, again with the possible assistance of regional and international actors.'

[12] See Lustick's nice discussion of African realities (1993: 441–5).

[13] David Laitin and I sketched this analogy.

conceptions, and wondered about the applicability of this historical analogy to Africa:

Reflecting Roman imperial, Christian, and monarchical notions of authority, these (European) conceptions appear to have provided a legitimizing framework for aggregating territories without simultaneously requiring a 'nation-building' effort to unite their populations. Similar if less salient conceptions are present in African political mythologies. But instead of receiving support externally, African leaders who style themselves as kings or 'emperors' stand in direct contradiction to internationally hegemonic norms of democracy and 'national self-determination.' The European-absolutist style path to national state formation may thus not be available in Africa.

(Lustick 1993: 445–6)

The striking fact is that for thirty years it was available, and, I will argue, the end of the cold war has not rendered patrimonial options fully inoperable. In a situation of extreme uncertainty and apparently unresolvable tensions and cross pressures, the Kabila regime reverted to type, and to the deeply embedded norms of the patrimonial administrative state. It is true that during the cold war, internationally hegemonic norms of democracy were suspended in the struggle with communism. But this allowed deeply-rooted African notions of patrimonial monarchical power to flourish, although to outsiders they may have appeared odd in the late twentieth century. The cold war power struggle made boundaries seem immutable, as Mobutu was repeatedly bailed out by external powers whose rhetoric and interests he manipulated brilliantly. But direct military intervention from the great powers on a major scale with the intention of maintaining a regime and its borders is far less likely now, and hence more room exists for regional factors and powers to operate. This is what US officials have called 'African solutions to African problems'—though perhaps with not quite the outcomes they expected.

External agents will still try to influence the outcome of reshaping processes in African states. In doing so, their own ambivalence, and continuing African realities will set up a complex set of contending forces. In important cases, major powers try to foster reshaping without resizing, and attempt to use their own norms to encourage it. These norms are not fully consistent, however, leading to ambiguous behaviour by external agents. The western vision of the simultaneous spread of democracy and market economies has internal tensions that are exposed against hard African realities (Callaghy 1993). External powers may be groping towards a half-way house, between economically devastating and highly personalized authoritarianism on the one hand and full democracy and neo-liberal economic reform on the other. This half-way house is best exemplified by the personalized one-party democracy of Yoweri Museveni's Uganda and, in a slightly different way, that of Jerry Rawlings in Ghana, both of whom have presided over impressive economic reform. They may represent a new generation of more effective African regimes increasingly integrated into the globalizing world economy. These half-way houses are certainly not fully democratic, however; and in my view they reflect the continuing importance and deeply-rooted nature of patrimonial notions of authority in Africa.

The short track-record of the Kabila regime has shown that establishing new, stable, and functional regimes in most of post-colonial and post-cold war Africa may be difficult indeed. The key ingredients that Gramsci believed necessary to break old hegemonic constructions and establish new ones may not be present (Lustick 1993: 123–4, and see Chapter 3 above). In much of Africa[14] severe contradictions between realities and ideological conceptions of those realities exist, but 'an appropriately fashioned alternative interpretation of political reality' is missing, especially one consistent with western norms and interests. Whether a new generation of African leaders and post-cold war western powers will find a mutually acceptable half-way house is open to question. The issue is whether African regimes can reshape productively with or without resizing.

Illustrative Episodes

In the spirit of Lustick's injunction that 'our objective should not be full accounts of the cases but better, more widely relevant answers to interesting questions' (1993: 451) I will now sketch more detailed elements of the Zaïre/Congo case that have relevance to our theoretical concerns.

Rise of an Internal Opposition: Wars of Position and Manoeuvre

The long, slow march by an internal opposition began in 1981 when a group of Legislative Council members issued an inflammatory manifesto calling for free elections in a multi-party system, and for Mobutu's resignation. Led by Tshisekedi, they became known as the 'Group of Thirteen'. They were arrested and treated very badly. In 1982 some of them formed a *de facto* second party, the *Union pour la Démocratie et le Progrès Social* (UDPS). Mobutu banned it immediately, and moved to co-opt and outmanoeuvre it, with some success. Under Tshisekedi's leadership, however, the UDPS survived, slowly became more radical in its demands, and it gained a mass following both in

---

[14] And perhaps central Asia—see Alexander Motyl's arguments in Chapter 7 of this volume.

Kinshasa and other parts of the country. Factionalism remained a major problem, as it always had been for the Zaïrian political class, and it was not clear how deep a sense of nationhood there was at the mass level.[15]

The effort of the opposition to challenge the doctrines of the regime began to bring dramatic results in January 1990 when Mobutu conducted a *'consultation populaire'* that was meant to indicate how popular he remained outside of Kinshasa. He toured the country asking his people to tell him about their sufferings, and invited everyone to put them in writing. He was shocked by the results that were massively hostile across all levels of society and areas of the country, and included direct personal attacks on him. Because of this intensifying internal opposition and post-cold war external pressure, Mobutu announced on 24 April 1990 that he was bringing a process of democratization to Zaïre. He maintained supreme confidence in his ability to control this process. Over one hundred parties, both pro- and anti-Mobutu, emerged within months. By the next year almost two hundred and fifty parties existed, many of them with heavy personalistic and ethno-regionalist tendencies. A consensus emerged on the need to convene a Sovereign National Conference to reshape the Zaïrian political system. From 1990 onwards the opposition fought a strong war of position and a weaker war of manoeuvre, largely through the National Conference which met intermittently from August 1991 through to December 1992. In 1992, one hundred and thirty two of the anti-Mobutu parties formed a united front called the *Union Sacrée* with Tshisekedi as its recognized leader.[16]

A Strong War of Position

The National Conference brought all types of groups together in a major national catharsis. A deep extension of the *'consultation populaire'*, it was a

[15] In the middle 1980s there was a major debate in US and to a lesser extend in European government and academic circles about the degree to which the Zaïrian population saw itself as part of a Zaïrian nation—something Mobutu had long claimed he created. As with most such debates, the line of argument was often influenced by the political outcome the participants wanted to see. Many government officials argued that there was not a mass sense of nationhood and, hence they argued that care should be taken not to let the opposition open again the Pandora's Box of the 1960s—despite Mobutu's claims to have created a nation. On the other hand, many academics and political activists argued that a sense of nationhood did exist and argued that the opposition should be given major support because the country would hold together, again ironically given their view of Mobutu. The debate was so fierce that the State Department finally commissioned an outside assessment of it. The judgement of the outside assessment was that such a mass sense of nationhood did indeed exist. I was asked to review the paper. I concluded that this was an incorrect assessment, arguing that a sense of patriotism existed among much of the élite and somewhat at the mass level, but that this clearly was not equivalent to a strong sense of nationhood and that even the sense of patriotism was no guarantee against resizing.

[16] On this period, see Willame (1992, 1994); Leslie (1993); Nzongola-Ntalaja (1994); Mbaya (1993); and Braekman (1992).

major move, and a victory in the war of position against the hegemonic discourses of the Mobutu regime.[17]

This war of position operated at three overlapping levels: that of the political class, an emerging civil society, and a mass popular culture. Members of the political class and Zaïre's rapidly growing civil society dominated the National Conference, with over 2,800 participants. Central to this civil society were the Christian churches, especially the Catholic Church as the major proto-state institution in the country. It had a long running struggle with the Mobutu regime. Also pivotal in the new vibrant civil society were other Christian churches, syncretic religious movements, and professional and human rights groups. All of them chipped away at Mobutuist discourses in their own way while being harassed by the government.[18]

In fact, the person voted to head the National Conference was Archbishop Onsengo Pasinya from Kisangani. Under his stewardship the one-third of participants who were strongly opposed to Mobutu seized control of the agenda and controlled the debates, which were carried live on radio and television. The debates attacked in all three arenas simultaneously—hegemonic discourses, regime institutions and norms, and incumbents, especially Mobutu. It had its most impressive success at the level of hegemonic discourse, but less at the institutional and incumbency levels because Mobutu's ability to influence and co-opt remained relatively strong. On the surface, these debates had a unitary state thrust to them, but strong currents of ethno-regionalism resurfaced when debates about a new constitution got underway. A federal structure emerged victorious, one with real resizing potential under the appropriate conditions. One seasoned observer noted: 'A la conférence nationale, l'ethnisme a trouvé son déguisement sous le label de géopolitique puis sous celui d'un "fédéralisme" défendu par la majorité des participants comme nouveau cadre constitutionnel adapté au pays' (Willame 1994: 136). The National Conference declared itself sovereign in August 1992, voted Tshisekedi the new Prime Minister, adopted a new federal constitution in October, and created a 453-member High Council of the Revolution as a provisional legislature. By the end of December 1992, the National Conference had concluded that Mobutu might be able to rule, but he would not be able to govern. It dissolved itself in favour of the new transitional government and the High Council.

[17] For a magnificent documentary record of these rich, vivid, and complex struggles to tear down the hegemonic discourse see Engunduka and Ngobaasu (1991a, b); and see de Dorlodot (1992).

[18] Given the complexity of Zaïrian society, it is fortunate that the country is not on the Islamic-Christian fault line in Africa. On the role of the churches see Callaghy (1987a); Boyle (1992); Kabongo-Mbaya (1991); and MacGaffey, W. (1992). On the rise and repression of civil society groups see Lawyers Committee on Human Rights (1990).

Attacks on Mobutuist hegemonic discourses also emerged over time at the mass level in the rich complexity and ambiguities of popular culture—in music, painting, dress, literature in local languages, and humour. In this effervescent popular culture, Mobutu was equated with the oppressor states of the Belgian Congo, and King Léopold II of Belgium's Congo Free State that preceded it. The popular culture included attempts to break the mass belief in Mobutu's perceived powers of magic. It included the manipulation of mass symbols by changing place names, refusing to use new 'pro-state' currency,[19] or to display Mobutu's picture in homes, schools, businesses, churches, and on clothing. These elements of the popular culture that attacked Mobutuist discourses pre-dated the rise of a powerful opposition, but were clearly reinforced and made bolder by it.[20] Lastly, the war of manoeuvre was greatly reinforced by the long-term consequences of patrimonialization that had turned Zaïre into a failing state.

A Weaker War of Manoeuvre

As a war of manoeuvre,[21] however, the National Conference and related activities were far less of a success, as Mobutu manipulated opposition effort with consummate skill, aided by the factional nature of the political class, and its ethno-regionalist inclinations. This was much too complex a process to explore here. Suffice it to say that from late 1992 onwards Tshisekedi and the 'radical' opposition, as it came to be called, attempted unsuccessfully to constitute itself as a parallel government. In response Mobutu dismissed Tshisekedi right after he was appointed Prime Minister the first and second times; bought-off and co-opted important members of the opposition; and created new institutions.

By early 1994 Tshisekedi was losing influence. A former associate notes that 'Tshisekedi destroyed the Mobutu myth and that is something that we all owe him. He weakened the system and triggered its decline. But psycho-

---

[19] During this period Zaïre was commonly referred to by the population as the Congo, as was the river. The Kabila government now refers to the territory it controls as the Democratic Republic of the Congo and issues a new currency called the Congolese franc. As one rebel official put it, 'The idea is to return to the pre-Mobutu names. He had no need to change them' (Reuters 1997a). In Luba-dominated Kasai Oriental, which managed to achieve an amazing degree of autonomy, the local administration printed 'real fake' zaïres in Argentina and Brazil to replace disintegrating notes and keep their rival currency going (Reuters 1997a). The US dollar also circulates as an alternative national currency.

[20] On the various elements of popular culture see Callaghy (1987a); on painting Fabian (1966); and on popular literature MacGaffey, W. (1982).

[21] According to Lustick, a war of manoeuvre implies semi-illegal and extra-legal challenges to the rules of the game, to the authority of institutions, including greater polarization and the possibility of civic upheavals and violent challenges to the integrity of the state, see Chapter 3.

logically, he is a demolition expert, not an architect. He cannot see a project through. He can only oppose' (Wrong 1997b). Mobutu had agreed to eventual transitional elections by 1997, in which he and his party would run, but by 1995 the opposition did not want elections so soon because they were not ready, having yet to do the hard organizational work of a real war of manoeuvre. In late 1996 Mobutu announced a new draft constitution which would have created a federal system of 26 provinces; Tshisekedi rejected it for a variety of reasons. A referendum was to be held on it in December, but the civil war started in late October. Mobutu clearly believed he could control a more fragmented Zaïre. In short, as Michael Schatzberg put it, Kobutu, like rulers in Kenya, Cameroon, and elsewhere 'hijacked' the democratic transition process (Schatzberg 1997c); see also McCormick (1994) and Komisar (1992). He still controlled revenue and coercion, and appeared to have won the war of manoeuvre in a post-cold war context in which he was still getting support from France and others. He was firmly intent on continuing to govern as well as rule.

Tshisekedi—who had earned the nickname of Moses—and much of the opposition attempted to rely on a strict legal formalism that merely manifested their weaknesses. Like most of the political class on both sides, they always looked to outsiders to do the hard parts. Mobutu and Tshisekedi ultimately looked to outsiders to save them, and, if they were not saved, then that was because of a plot by some group of outsiders. For example, in 1993 Tshisekedi said that 'we have called upon the international community to intervene . . . to ensure that the democratisation process put in place by the Sovereign National Conference is respected, given that Mobutu, by refusing to commit himself to this plan, is resorting to brute force' (Ross and Green 1993). In this sense, Zaïre was deeply scarred by the cold war. As one analyst observed in April 1997 just before the end of the civil war 'most Zaïreans have simply sat and waited to be liberated. Even now, when Mobutu is on his last legs, they expect someone else to bundle him onto the helicopter and do the job for them' (Wrong 1997b).

The slow but continuous process of state failure, leading to the logical terminus of the archipelago and the shadow state, progressively hollowed out the underpinnings of the Mobutu regime, underlining the collapse of the formal economy and the functional contraction of the administrative apparatus. This is a process general to Africa, but as always, one that is more intense in Zaïre.[22] Some analysts have considered African states to be only 'quasi-states,' artificially propped up by the international system. A longer

[22] For Africa generally see Callaghy and Ravenhill (1993) and Callaghy (1991). Also see the good analysis in Clapham (1996); Widner (1995); and Mazrui (1995).

historical perspective is required, however. Propped up they may have been, at least until recently, but states they certainly are and have been—in my comparative work I have characterized them as early modern states.[23]

Very few states actually collapse. Zaïre was, however, a seriously failing state, with terrible costs for its people. Since the late 1970s Zaïre has been in what seemed to be a perpetual socio-economic crisis. A popular saying of the middle 1980s was that 'if there is a world crisis, its centre must be in Zaïre'. The infrastructure was nearly gone; the formal economy had all but collapsed; and the real economy was now the informal economy. In short, social destitution was and is real and pervasive. In most places the state no longer performed even the basic function of official revenue collection, although officials often collected it for themselves, in massive corruption at all levels. A culture of survival based on the four Ps—patrons, pillage, prophets, and prayer—was all-pervasive.[24] Though the Mobutuist state managed to maintain its formal political dominance, in the undercurrents of the shadow state and the archipelago increasing degrees of informal autonomy were allowed in many parts of Zaïre. It was not surprising therefore that older regionalist tendencies re-emerged with some vigour in 'the four Ks'—Katanga (Shaba), Kasai, Kivu, and Kongo (Bas-Zaïre)—see Kalele-ka-Bila (1993).

As the state weakened, residents of Shaba began to think of themselves as Katangan again; the memories of the 1960 secession and the two invasions in 1977 and 1978 by Katanga *gendarmes* revived, reinforced by a renewed belief that Katanga could easily stand on its feet as an independent state. An ethno-regionalist trend also emerged, again aimed at Luba residents in the province. Two of the region's most influential politicians, Nguza Karl-I-Bond and Kyungu wa Kumwanz, both of whom had long established on-and-off-again ties with Mobutu, formed a regionalist party, Ufer. In 1992 Kyungu was the governor who set off the ethnic cleansing which forced hundreds of thousands of Luba out of Katanga and into the Kasai region. Explaining his ties to Mobutu, he said, 'Better a dying dictator than a permanent dictatorship of Kasaians', a reference to Tshisekedi's origins (Rosenblum 1997: 33, see also 3–4). Kyungu built a strong power base for himself, but became too powerful. He was arrested and replaced in 1995 allegedly for importing arms for a secessionist attempt.

The Luba are the dominant population in Kasai, which also attempted to secede in the early 1960s. They became a powerful ethnic diaspora, proudly

---

[23]   On the notion of 'quasi-states', see Jackson (1990); on the use of early modern states for Africa see Callaghy (1984); also see Zartman (1995).

[24]   See Kabongo (1986). On Zaïre's general crisis, see Nzongola-Ntalaja (1986) especially the section on survival strategies; MacGaffey, J. (1988, 1991); Sangmpam (1994); Young (1994); Weiss (1995); and Clark (1998).

referring to themselves as the 'Jews of Zaïre', and were viewed with suspicion by local populations. Tshisekedi is Luba, as are many of his followers. With Mbuji-Mayi as its capital, East Kasai in particular acquired considerable autonomy as its informal governors—Jonas Mukamba, head of Miba, the local state diamond para-statal, and Monsignor Tharcisse Tshibangu, Bishop of Mbuji-Mayi—walked a political tightrope with Mobutu. The region maintained its own currency, refusing to use 'pro-state' bills from Kinshasa, formed its own university, and lived off the diamond wealth not controlled by Mobutu. This process of 'creeping independence' began with the 1992 expulsions of Luba from Katanga. As one Luba intellectual put it, 'The kinds of secessionist movements that we have seen in the past are simply outmoded. Kasaians are as much a part of Zaïre as anyone else. But that Zaïre is not functional, and we realise that in order to survive we have to take responsibility for ourselves' (French 1996).[25]

Kongo regionalism in the far west also has old roots but had been relatively quiescent. As the Mobutu government continued to weaken, however, even the Bakongo began to revive autonomist sentiments, laced with irredentist/secessionist possibilities in regard to Angola.

Lastly, Kivu also has deep autonomist roots and always remained marginalized by the Mobutu government which distrusted it intensely. As the formal economy collapsed, the region turned eastward even more than in the past, especially under entrepreneurial Banande and Banyarwanda traders. It has the highest population density and the greatest pressures on the land. It was Kivu that was the site of the trigger for the dramatic discontinuous transformation of politics, opening the civil war.

Regional Transformation

Changing regional realities played a key role in transforming the Zaïre saga. Rwanda and Burundi were originally German colonies, although never effectively occupied. Within them the Tutsi, with strong pre-colonial power bases, were clearly dominant over the Hutu. As part of the 1885 Conference of Berlin settlement of the rules for the partition of Africa, a large number of the subjects of the Rwandan king ended up outside of Rwanda, most of them living in what is now Zaïre. A further convention was signed in 1910 between Germany, Belgium, and Britain under which four Rwandan territories were formally attached to the Belgian Congo and one to the British colony of Uganda. Belgium assumed control of the two German colonies during World

---

[25] See also *Africa Confidential* (1996).

War I, and officially acquired them as League of Nations mandate territories in 1924, creating an administrative union of its now three contiguous colonies in 1925. Early on the Belgians encouraged a policy of labour 'emigration' of both Tutsi and Hutu from Rwanda into the Congo to work on plantations in what is now Kivu. Rwanda became a UN Trust Territory in 1946, still under the Belgians, and the programme of formal labour migration ended only in 1955. Rwanda became independent in 1960 with a Hutu government, following major riots against the Tutsi in 1959 that pushed thousands of them into Zaïre. The Tutsi population in Kivu became known as the Banyarwanda in North Kivu, and the Banyamulenge in South Kivu, where much of the population was settled well before 1885.

Boundaries have not determined citizenship in these cases. The citizenship of these Congolese populations has long been a source of tension, with other ethnic groups in the region considering them 'foreigners.' At independence in 1960, Zaïrian citizenship was granted to all those who had been living in Zaïre for at least ten years, but those receiving citizenship on this basis were excluded from administrative positions in the 1960s, although they were allowed to vote in 1965 and 1967. In 1972 a new law of the Mobutu government reaffirmed this citizenship but said it applied only to those living in Zaïre continuously since 1 January 1960. In 1981, however, a further new law granted citizenship only to those who could prove that they had lived in Zaïre before August 1885! This law was never actively enforced, but it was much resented, especially as the Mobutu government established strong ties with the Hutu government in Rwanda. This anti-Tutsi political orientation was not confined to Mobutu. Similar sentiments were dominant among the Zaïrian opposition. Despite—or because of—the possibility of genuine elections at some point, the Banyarwanda and Banyamulenge were barred from participation in the National Conference, effectively upholding the 1981 bar to citizenship (Pabanel 1991; Human Rights Watch Africa 1996; Willame 1997: 3–4, 32–5; see also Callaghy 1984: 375–95, and *passim*).[26]

Over the years the Mobutu government frequently used force to put down rebellions of one sort or another in Kivu. During the country's relatively peaceful 1970–7 period, Kivu was the only place with active rebel activity. But in October 1990, Mobutu made a fateful decision to put troops in Rwanda to help the Hutu government fight the invading Tutsi army from Uganda. In 1992 the government sent troops to North Kivu, where over 50 per cent of the population is Banyarwanda, to put down a rebellion, but the soldiers looted and pillaged instead, sending 30,000 villagers into Uganda.

---

[26] I spent considerable time in Kivu in 1975 and witnessed much of the underlying tension. It is one of the most beautiful places in the world, and it has been very hard to watch events since 1996, although I certainly understand them far better than I would have otherwise.

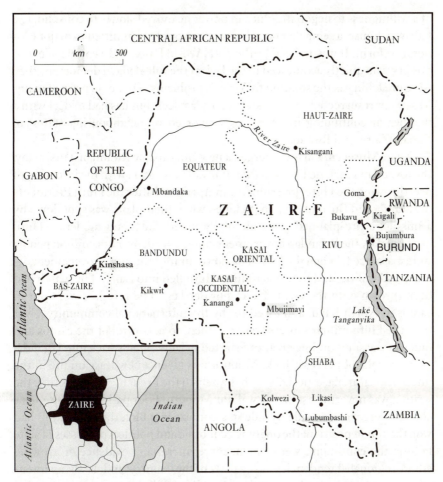

Fɪɢ. 4.1 Zaïre/Congo and the Great Lakes Region

Major ethnic conflict broke out the next year between local Hunde people and the Banyarwanda, in which thousands of the latter were killed. Clearly Kivu and the larger Great Lakes region more generally was a major zone of tension (see the map in Fig. 4.1). In the great ethno-territorial flux of this period, democracy was increasingly perceived by local populations to mean getting land back and expelling 'foreigners.'

In retrospect it is likely that the rise to power in 1982 of Yoweri Museveni in the failing state of Uganda through a locally developed military movement will be seen as a major watershed in the history of post-colonial Africa, an African solution to an African problem. Many Tutsi formed key elements of Museveni's army as he fought his way to power while giving the appearance of a willingness to negotiate. Once in power he moved slowly to consolidate a half-way house, a semi-democratic regime strongly committed to major economic reform. It was assisted by the IMF, World Bank, and a couple of major powers who quietly acquiesced in the lack of the full-fledged democracy they were preaching as the solution to Africa's problems. To the surprise of many, Museveni resurrected a failing state on its last legs, but has had to deal with a number of continuing insurgencies supported by neighbouring states, in Sudan, Zaïre, and Rwanda.[27]

Out of Museveni's army emerged a new and capable Rwandan Tutsi army, the Rwandan Patriotic Front (RPF). It invaded Rwanda with the intention of overthrowing the Hutu government. In April 1994 after the Hutu Presidents of Rwanda and Burundi were both killed when their plane was shot down by a missile, a pre-planned genocide of Rwandan Tutsi and moderate Hutu organized by the Rwandan government commenced; over one million people were massacred. When the RPF took power in July, the Hutu government, its army and militia, and over one million Hutu fled into Zaïre. The match had been thrown onto the Great Lakes powder keg. The refugees were put in camps in North Kivu, and cared for by the international community. Over time the Hutu military forces were rearmed, took control of the camps and much of the surrounding area, and started to launch raids back into Uganda.

In a stroke of perverse luck, Mobutu was given a new lease on life in the international arena, especially with the help of the French.[28] But this time the writing was nevertheless on the wall for Mobutu. Four paths of evolutionary change were running side by side in a context in which the opposition had won the war of position: the ongoing economic and political processes of state failure; the continuing war of manoeuvre; increasing evidence of growing ethno-regionalist tendencies in key parts of the country; and, lastly, an intensification of long-standing tensions in Kivu and the larger Great Lakes region.

Tensions rose considerably between Kivu officials, the Zaïrian army, and Hutu militia on the one hand, and elements of the local 'indigenous' popula-

[27] See Kasfir (1985: 169 ff., 1993); Gertzel (1990: 205–8, 231–2); Hansen and Twaddle (1991); Khadiagala (1995); Omara-Otunnu (1992); Brett (1995); and Museveni (1989). See also Kaplan (1987), an amazingly—and appropriately so—optimistic piece about Uganda, and the potentialities for positive transformation in Africa by the man later to write the famous or infamous—depending on your point of view—piece entitled 'The Coming Anarchy' (Kaplan 1994). When travelling in East Africa in November 1995, the name I found that emerged most commonly and with the most respect in conversations about the dilemmas of, and prospects for, political and economic transformation in Africa, was that of Yoweri Museveni. Many Africans now refer to the 'Museveni model', although it may be a little tarnished after Uganda's recent military activity.

[28] For the most balanced and complete work on the tragic Rwanda story, see Prunier (1995); also see Gourevitch (1996).

tion and the Banyarwanda and Banyamulenge on the other. South Kivu officials began to take an inventory of Banyamulenge property. Consequently the Banyamulenge started to arm themselves, at first mostly with weapons coming through Shaba (Katanga). Each family was encouraged to buy a Kalashnikov, which sold for the equivalent of about US$60.

At the same time, Zaïrian officials announced that long-resident Tutsi, some of those residency predated even the Belgian colonial state, were no longer considered 'Zaïrian' and thus had to vacate their lands. This triggered intense conflict as armed Tutsi struck back, encouraged and aided by the Rwandan and Ugandan governments. A major civil war began in October. As it spread in the face of a collapsing Zaïrian army—long unpaid, untrained, and undisciplined—other forces begin to enter the fray on both sides. On the government side were mercenaries recruited by the French, and forces of the Angolan opposition movement Unita, which had long been supported by Mobutu. On the rebel side, in addition to the Rwandan and Burundi Tutsi and some Ugandans, there were the Angolan government and its long-time Katangan allies, plus some assistance from Zambia and Zimbabwe. In addition, the rebels picked up eager recruits in each territory into which they moved. Using tactics developed during the 1960s rebellions, under Laurent Kabila the new AFDL—the Alliance of Democratic Forces for the Liberation of Zaïre—pushed north, west, and south, pushing the demoralized and pillaging Zaïrian army before it. The AFDL was warmly greeted at the mass level as it moved across Zaïre, Kabila being seen as a saviour. Just as the rebellions in the 1960s were seen as an effort to achieve a real 'second independence,' this civil war was seen as an attempt to get a 'third independence.' On 17 May 1997, Kabila's forces entered Kinshasa, and Mobutu fled, only to die soon afterwards never fully realizing what had happened.

The fall of Mobutu was a last rattle of the cold war, just as his rise was one of its first roars in Africa. External agents wanted to reshape Zaïre their way, and a variety of African agents want to reshape, and possibly resize, it according to their interests and desires.[29] Each of the region's states had reasons to support the rebellion. It was 'pay back' time. Uganda, Rwanda, and to a lesser extent Burundi, wanted to create a buffer zone against Hutu and other rebel forces that were bothering them. Angola greatly relished paying back for years of harassment by Mobutu but it was also a chance finally to close off Unita's pipeline to the outside world, and to begin to squeeze it—despite an Angolan peace accord Unita still controlled huge sections of the country.

Thus, the trigger to dramatic discontinuous transformation through a real war of manoeuvre was the treatment of 'foreigners' not regarded as part of

[29] See Davidson (1992); Callaghy (1995); and Young (1993).

the Zaïrian community of peoples. As one Zaïrian scholar put it, 'The problem of the Tutsi identity in Zaïre had existed for decades. If as a regime you
repeatedly challenge an ethnic group's existence and then do nothing to prepare for a backlash, you're asking for trouble.' Trouble they got. The perception of the Tutsi as invading foreigners was pervasive among the political
class in Kinshasa, which had brought down a Mobutu-appointed Prime
Minister because his mother was Tutsi. As one politician-businessman in
Kinshasa put it, 'A lot of people are saying we want Kabila to bring about
change, but we don't want him to take power. We want a real Zaïrean to lead
the country. We are not going to be ordered around by a bunch of Tutsis.'
(cited by Wrong 1997a).

From Kabila's 'Third Republic' to Renewed Civil War

Kabila banned all political parties and promised elections and full democracy
after a transitional period. He said: 'We are in the process of liberation'
(Davies 1997). This decision-making clearly followed the Museveni model.
In fact, Museveni advised precisely this:

In the case of Zaïre, there must be democratic elections at regular intervals, press
freedom and *perhaps* a beginning of the formation of a broad coalition government
including all parties. Elections must be conveniently held, but there must first be a
state to do so. There are certain state pillars, which are indispensable for the holding
of elections, and such structures do not seem to exist today. I am talking of the army,
the police, the justice system, and the civil service. This requires some time, so I
would advise a two or three-year period. Elections must be organized with all seriousness, to avoid elections which cause more unrest than peace'.

(Radio France Internationale 1997, emphasis added)

At the same time, Kabila made it very clear that he did not intend to resize
the state: 'The world should know what are the real issues in Zaïre. The
integrity of Zaïre is not an issue—no one is threatening that integrity'
(MSNBC 1997).

Kabila had a short honeymoon in his efforts to begin moving 'forward'
through the regime and ideological hegemony thresholds of institutionalization. One observer referred to Kabila's reshaping efforts as 'awkward
attempts to consolidate power and establish political legitimacy [that] bear an
eerie resemblance to the actions of his predecessor.' he issued a broad and
vague one-page constitutional decree for the 'Third Republic' that allocated
almost total power to himself. He lost friends on all fronts without losing enemies. Even his regional supporters began to back away seeing him 'as incon-

sistent, undependable and paranoid' (Rosenblum 1998: 193, 199),[30] although they expected him to live up to his promises to provide security in the north-east and to help control Unita in the south. Ironically, the regional support base that many believed to be Kabila's major pillar of support was quickly turning into a pillar of salt while he had very little legitimacy in the Congo.

Kabila faced a major dilemma: how to reshape a political system when his coming to power was viewed as a foreign invasion led by a widely unpopular ethnic group and regarded as foreign in most of the state, and without allowing the most legitimate political leader any room to challenge him. His dependence on his external backers made matters even worse, for he had promises to keep, and he did not fully trust his allies. This mistrust was mutual, because very shortly both Rwanda and Uganda began to manifest their displeasure. The Banyamulenge Tutsi threatened rebellion against Kabila in the east in March 1998.

Above all, Kabila made no effort to assume the legitimate mantle of the National Conference, which had been so central to the wars of position against Mobutu, most likely because he felt it would strengthen Tshisekedi. It proved to be a major lost opportunity, one stemming from the common practice of African leaders of falling back on the deeply embedded patterns of the patrimonial administrative state when facing severe uncertainty. He responded to his dilemma by moving relatives and members of his own Balubakati clan, ethnic group, and region into key positions. His cousin became Interior Minister, his brother-in-law army Chief of Staff, his son deputy army Chief of Staff, and his nephew the Justice Minister. At the same time he began to marginalize or ease Tutsi political officials out—a delicate and dangerous game with unclear political pay-offs for his reshaping and legitimation efforts, especially since he banned the major human rights group, harassed others, and eventually arrested Tshisekedi and sent him into internal exile.

Efforts by major western powers to reshape the Congo in a democratic direction were a complete failure. Probably because of major pressure from Rwanda, Kabila made every effort to stall and thwart the effort of the United Nations to investigate alleged massacres of Hutu during the civil war. Secretary General Kofi Annan finally suspended the effort in early April 1998, a fact that went almost unreported by the international media. This did, however, lose Kabila external friends and badly needed reconstruction resources, including from mineral firms with whom he had signed major agreements during the civil war.

---

[30] See also Oloka-Onyango (1997); Rosenblum (1997a); Evans (1997); Gourevitch (1997); Braeckman (1997); Schatzberg (1997b).

Rwanda, and to a lesser extent Uganda, have dilemmas of their own. They have security difficulties that they would like to resolve, and they felt that helping to overthrow Mobutu and installing a friendly government would allow them to do this. Consequently, they facilitated an incipient civil war but found that the Kabila government could not consolidate itself, largely because of their backing and the intense dislike of Tutsi in the Congo. At the same time they seem to have ruled out expansion of their own despite available war of position notions such as 'Greater Tutsiland'. Instead, while ruling out expansion, at least for the moment, the Rwandans, to use O'Leary's and McGarry's taxonomy of strategies for stabilizing a polity (O'Leary and McGarry 1995), have engaged in control while rejecting partition, expulsion, assimilation, genocide—although they are sparing no effort to eliminate Hutu opponents in Zaïre/Congo—federalization or autonomy, arbitration, and consociation.[31]

Expansion would be made more difficult because of the spatial distribution of the Tutsi in Kivu, and the intermixing with other groups that has existed for hundreds of years. To get the kind of buffer the Rwandans want would entail expansion and control, and would probably require the expulsion of non-Tutsis. Their reaction to these 'stubborn or objective realities', 'incurable contradictions', or underlying conditions will be key. Lustick notes that ideologically hegemony beliefs do not change fluidly with changing realities. The Rwandans may feel that for the moment they lack viable counter-hegemonic ideas, ones that would 'camouflage particular distributions of power by linking them to common-sensical established myths, symbols, and categories', ones that need to have some minimal correspondence with objective conditions (see Lustick Chapter 3 above).

With the failure of the Kabila government to live up to a host of expectations and with the prospect of losing even remaining control over it, the Rwandans and Ugandans decided to overthrow it. Kabila handed them the excuse. On 27 July 1998 he ordered all remaining soldiers to leave the Congo and begin harassing Tutsi generally. On 2 August Banyamulenge Tutsi in Kivu declared a rebellion against the Kabila government, and proceeded to take key towns in the east. In a bold and co-ordinated stroke, Tutsi troops still in the Congo seized a major airbase to the west of Kinshasa and started ferrying troops in by air. This allowed them to seize the Atlantic ports and begin a move toward Kinshasa, capturing the major Inga Dam in the process, and periodically plunging Kinshasa into darkness and cutting much of its water supply.

---

[31] See Brendan O'Leary's discussion in Chapter 2 above.

Kabila threatened Rwanda with full-scale war and accused it of attempting to create a 'Tutsi empire' by invading his country, adding that, 'Naturally little Rwanda and Uganda will not swallow Congo'. His Health Minister went further: 'They say the enemies of your enemy become your friends. Well, we are going to work with the Hutu to end minority power in Rwanda once and for all. We cannot let the massacres start up again, but Congo must come to dominate Rwanda, not vice versa.' Kabila's government worked to stir up similar feeling in the population, with some effect. One Kinshasa resident declared, 'We want weapons to go to Rwanda and kill Kagame. Nothing else will stop this humiliation of such a little nation invading Congo', while another declared, 'We want to fight to save our nation from the Rwandans. This is no time to debate the flaws of our leaders. Our country is about to be swallowed up' (Tucker 1998; French 1998b; Malu-Malu 1998a).

For their part the rebels accused Kabila of nepotism and corruption. One rebel statement said, 'Instead of putting in place a government of national unity, Mr. Kabila has put in place a government composed of members of his family'. High Tutsi officials and other members of Kabila's government, especially, Bizima Kahara, the Foreign Minister, soon joined the rebels. They attempted to paint a broad picture of the movement, with some success, including several well-known non-Tutsi opposition figures and a respected Bakongo exiled academic, Wamba dia Wamba. Professor Wamba offered to 'negotiate with Kabila. We could even negotiate a cease-fire with him, but he must first behave and he must stop running to his foreign friends for help because this is an internal Congolese matter.' Kabila refused (Mseta 1998; Reuters 1998a, b).

Having no effective army, Kabila turned to his southern neighbours who proved willing to help him despite his failure to live up to earlier promises. President Robert Mugabe became his most vocal defender, while the Angolans organized major support. Mugabe got into a major public spat with Nelson Mandela because the South Africans favoured a negotiated solution to the conflict. Mugabe sent planes and soldiers to aid Kabila, while the Angolans eventually entered the Congo at several points, trapping the advancing Tutsi forces, along with former Mobutu troops who had joined them, between the Angolan forces and Kinshasa. This raised the possibility that the Rwandans may have overreached and seriously underestimated the willingness of Kabila's other neighbours to assist him. Both Kigame and Museveni defended their actions, all the while denying major participation. A Rwandan statement declared that 'Rwanda reserves the right to get involved and to assist the Congolese people in their search for a lasting solution in whatever manner it deems appropriate', charging that Kabila had promoted ethnic hatred and regional bias and had failed to settle the issue of the nationality of ethnic Tutsi living in the Congo. Kagame asserted that he wanted a Kinshasa capable of controlling its eastern borders, 'We are a vulnerable little country. What is at stake is our survival, pure and simple, our existence.' For his part, Museveni declared that 'Uganda may be forced, after due internal consultations, to take its own independent action in the protection of its own security interests' and warned other African countries not to get involved (Kayigamba 1998; Reuters 1998d; Busharizi 1998). Uganda became deeply involved in the conflict in the Congo, both directly and through support of other military groups. A bizarre peace agreement was signed in Lusaka in July 1999 between the multiple contending parties; by early 2001 the agreement had not brought any end to this terrible conflict.

A competitive state system has indeed really come to Central Africa. Up to this point the Rwandans have not wanted to flout African and international norms about altering boundaries, or invading neighbours by expanding their territory, or creating a new state in Kivu, or even an effectively occupied buffer zone. Given the dynamics of the processes they have wittingly and unwittingly unleashed, they may change their minds about this. They have already proved their ability to find African solutions to African problems that greatly alter the existing rules of the African and international games. This may have been further fostered by events in the wider region, where Angola intervened to install a government in Congo-Brazzaville, and elsewhere in the world, where interventions have occurred in Somalia, the Balkans, and Central Asia. The failure of the Tutsi élites in Rwanda and Burundi, and of Kabila, to cope with their dilemmas has reinforced the difficulty of ameliorating the 'unresolvable' situation in the Great Lakes region of Africa, as well as ongoing disputes in the region such as the perpetual Angolan civil war with Unita.

Conclusion: Theoretical and Practical Implications

Let me suggest some theoretical implications from my case-study for Ian Lustick's theory of institutionalization and deinstitutionalization. First, by making more explicit his distinction between functional and territorial 'right-sizing' using the notions of reshaping and resizing, we may be in a better position to analyse the complex interplay of struggles over institutionalization in a wider range of cases.

Second, while battles over incumbency, wars of manoeuvre, and wars of position can be kept distinct analytically, they are often very mixed, uneven parallel processes that support and play off against each other in multiple and complex ways. To help sort this out analytically, I suggest the notion of arena for each of the three, while maintaining the notion of possible stages.

Conflicts can take place in each of the three arenas simultaneously, but usually at different levels of intensities and development. As a result, it is still important whether thresholds are crossed or not, when, how, in what direction, and with what relationship to struggles in the other arenas. For example, opposition groups may focus primarily on reshaping the state, with resizing remaining a relatively minor issue at first. Having lost political struggles in the incumbency arena, opposition groups that have been waging a war of position may shift their focus of activity to the regime arena by engaging in extra-legal activities. Whether they can effectively cross the regime threshold is likely to remain in doubt for some time. In the attempt to cross it, however, they may strengthen their situation in the war position and simultaneously weaken the ability of incumbents to carry on the struggle. The point is that using the notions of reshaping and resizing and three arenas rather than stages, and stressing the simultaneous and overlapping nature of struggles does not weaken the overall usefulness of thresholds, sequence or direction, for at some higher level of observation and analysis they allow an overall assessment which effectively promotes understanding and even prediction.

Lastly, to return to points made at the beginning of the paper, the Great Lakes region powerfully underlines Lustick's three points about:

1. '*the presumptively permanent but actually contingent nature of state boundaries*'. In this case the cracks in the African and international norms against changing boundaries, and even the creating of new states, demonstrates the observation. The same point should also hold for the larger processes of reshaping.

2. '*the strong relationship that exists between the internal complexion of a state and its external shaping*'. My case demonstrates that this is so, and especially illustrates the tendency of states 'to revert to type' under conditions of extreme insecurity—which makes productive reshaping of a failing state harder, while making resizing simultaneously more possible, chaotic, *and* harder to sustain and institutionalize. At the same time, these relationships underscore the importance of regional and international agents and processes. In this case the move of new and old leaders to allow the emergence of a truly competitive state system in Central Africa with all the risk it entails has created a new Africa inter-state system. The Pandora's Box that the continent's leaders have struggled so long to keep closed may have opened.

3. '*the mysterious links between gradual processes of political metamorphosis and sudden transformations*'. My case particularly highlights the relationship between the processes of state failure and the classic statecraft needs of state-building, along with the inclination and ability to act boldly in violation of reputed regional and international norms.

On the more immediate practical side, if the Congolese and Rwandan Tutsi lose the current struggle, the option of creating a new state in Kivu, or at least a fully occupied buffer zone, will become more of a possibility, if not a fully palatable option. It would take place in a regional economy that is increasingly integrated and coherent. On the other hand, if Kabila loses the civil war, then the secession of Katanga will become a more likely and palatable alternative, with support from its neighbours and other states in the region. That attempt would take place in a regional economy that has long had powerful linkages to the greater political economy of Southern Africa. But, it should be pointed out that the newly victorious government in Kinshasa—and Rwanda—would face the same dilemma that haunted the Kabila government. If a government of 'national unity' emerges out of some combination of military stalemate and negotiation/arbitration, older reshaping and resizing pressures for regional federation, and possibly full-fledged confederation, become more likely options. If Kabila 'wins' the civil war with major help from his southern neighbours, he will still confront a major legitimacy dilemma and desperate need for effective reshaping, although he could then take on the mantle of 'national saviour' *à la* Mobutu in the middle 1960s. He will still have promises to live up to, small but powerful enemies in the east, and strong remaining ethno-regional tensions that might, in the context of incomplete control, lead to the emergence of a variety of local or regional warlords who run gangster regimes without formal secession. Resizing of drastic kinds is thus still entirely possible, especially since domestic, regional, and international interests are not fully congruent.

Hendrik Spruyt reminds us about the great historical variety of states that we seem to have conveniently forgotten. His Braudelian view that stresses the importance of broad, contingent change in milieu, and his and Ian Lustick's emphasis on non-linear evolutionary change need to be remembered, especially in the African context where the variety of pre-colonial forms of polity is striking.[32] We will have to wait to see if Thabo Mbeki's April 1997 vision, hope, and prayer for the Congo come true; right now it does not seem likely.

Clearly, the limits of preventative diplomacy and humanitarian intervention are becoming more obvious with each declining or collapsing African state, and the ability of external agents to reshape regimes will be affected by the lessons learned from ongoing cases such as the Congo.[33] During the cold war, odd regimes could get away with things because of the nature of superpower competition. Unexpectedly for many observers, this remains the case

[32] See Spruyt (1995); also see Vansina (1996); and Herbst (1996).

[33] For an astute pessimistic view in regard to Zaïre before the civil war see Morrison (1995); also see Metz (1996). On the realities of international intervention, see Smock and Crocker (1995); Gottlieb (1993); Copson (1994); and Keller and Rothchild (1996).

because external powers will not intervene very often in a major way in the vaunted new world order. There will be more wars and other forms of large-scale violence in Africa, and the Congo may be turned into what one long-time observer has called 'a country, preyed on by neighbouring countries, soldiers of fortune, business groups, pieces of armies and private plunderers, while its people look on in disgust.' In criticizing his own government, one Congolese colonel said that 'Kabila made the mistake of counting on numbers rather than quality when he put together his army. They discarded the notion of elite corps and specialisation, destroying everything they found without distinction. The problem now is that our neighbours have serious armies with experienced units, and it is easy for them to dominate us.' (Zartman 1998, cited in French 1998). But whether the future of the Congo will match its recent sensational chaos will have a great deal to do with the reshaping and resizing strategies of both external and African agents in ongoing wars of position and manoeuvre, and the complex interactions between them (see Kaplan 1994; and Goldberg 1997).

REFERENCES

Africa Confidential. 1996. 'Kasai Takes Off: Diamonds and Ethnic Solidarity Explain the Prosperity in the Opposition Leader's Province', 19 January.

Boyle, Patrick. 1992. 'Beyond Self-Protection: The Catholic Church and Political Change in Zaïre', *Africa Today*, 39: 49–66.

Braeckman, Colette. 1992. *Le dinosaure: Le Zaïre de Mobutu*. Paris: Fayard.

—— 1997. 'Zaïre: Récits d'une prise de pouvoir annoncée', *Politique Internationale*, 76: 59–96.

Brett, E. A. 1995. 'Neutralising the Use of Force in Uganda: The Role of the Military in Politics', *Journal of Modern African Studies*, 33: 129–52.

Busharizi, Paul. 1998. 'Uganda Warns It May Enter Congo Conflict', *Reuters* [*Internet*], 22 August.

Callaghy, Thomas. 1980. 'State-Society Communication in Zaïre: Domination and Concept of Domain Consensus', *Journal of Modern African Studies*, 18: 469–92.

—— 1984. *The State-Society Struggle*. New York, NY: Columbia University Press.

—— 1987a. 'Politics and Culture in Zaïre', Ann Arbor, MI: Center for Political Studies, Institute for Social Research University of Michigan.

—— 1987b. 'The State as Lame Leviathan: The Patrimonial Administrative State in Africa', 87–116 in *The African State in Transition*, edited by Zaki Ergas. London: Macmillan.

—— 1991. 'Africa and the World Political Economy: Still Caught Between a Rock and a Hard Place', 41–68 in *Africa in World Politics*, edited by John Harbeson and Donald Rothchild.

Callaghy, Thomas. 1993. 'Vision and Politics in the Transformation of the Global Political Economy', 161–257 in *Global Transformation and the Third World*, edited by Robert Slater. Boulder, CO: Lynne Reiner Publishers.

—— 1995. 'Africa: Back to the Future?', 140–52 in *Economic Reform and Democracy*, edited by Larry Diamond and Marc F. Plattner. Baltimore, MD: Johns Hopkins University Press.

—— and Ravenhill, John. (eds.) 1993. *Hemmed In: Response to Africa's Economic Decline*. New York, NY: Columbia University Press.

Clapham, Christopher. 1996. *Africa and the International System: The Politics of State Survival*. Cambridge: Cambridge University Press.

Clark, John F. 1998. 'The Extractive State in Zaïre', 109–28 in *The African State at a Critical Juncture*, edited by Leonardo Villalón and Phillip Huxtable. Boulder, CO: Lynne Reiner Publishers.

Copson, Raymond W. 1994. *Africa's Wars and Prospects for Peace*. Armonk, NY: M. E. Sharpe.

Davidson, Basil. 1992. *Black Man's Burden: Africa and the Curse of the Nation-State*. New York, NY: Times Books.

Davies, Karin. 1997. 'Political Will May Win in Zaïre', *Associated Press* [*Internet*], 25 March.

de Dorlodot, Philippe. 1992. *Marche d'Espoir: Non-Violence pour la Démocratie au Zaïre*. Paris: L'Harmattan.

Duke, Lynne. 1997a. 'Stability and Democracy at Stake in Mobutu-Kabila Battle of Wills', *Washington Post* [*Internet*], 20 April.

—— 1997b. 'Violent Echoes of Zaïre's Past: Rebel Leadership Sprinkled With Veterans of '60s Uprisings', *Washington Post*, 13 March: A1.

Engunduka, A. Gbabendu, and Ngobaasu, E. Efolo. (eds.) 1991a. *Volonté de change-ment au Zaïre: vol. 1, De la Consultation Populaire vers la Conférence Nationale*. Parks: L'Harmattan.

—— (eds.) 1991b. *Volonté de changement au Zaïre: vol. 2. Archives 1990–91*. Paris: L'Harmattan.

Evans, Glynne. 1997. *Responding to Crises in the African Great Lakes*. Oxford: Oxford University Press.

Fabian, Johannes. 1996. *Remembering the Past: Painting and Popular History of Zaïre*. Berkeley, CA: University of California Press.

French, Howard. 1996. 'A Neglected Region Loosens Ties to Zaïre', *New York Times*, 18 September: A1, A12.

—— 1998a. 'Civilians Flee Congo's Capital in Fear of Rebel Advance', *New York Times*, 15 August.

—— 1998b. 'Top Fear in Congo Conflict: Wider Regional Violence', *New York Times*, 19 August.

Gertzel, Cherry. 1990. 'Uganda's Continuing Search for Peace', *Current History*, 89: 205–8, 231–2.

Gibbs, David G. 1991. *The Political Economy of Third World Intervention*. Chicago, IL: University of Chicago Press.

Goldberg, Jeffrey. 1997. 'Their Africa Problem and Ours', *New York Times Magazine*, 2 March: 32–77.

Gottlieb, Gidon. 1993. *Nation Against State: A New Approach to Ethnic Conflicts and the Decline of Sovereignty*. New York, NY: Council on Foreign Relations.

Gourevitch, Philip. 1996. 'Neighborhood Bully: How Genocide Revived President Mobutu', *The New Yorker*, 9 September: 52–7.

—— 1997. 'Letter from the Congo: Continental Shift', *The New Yorker*, 4 August: 42–55.

Grill, B. 1997. 'Zaïre: Mobutu Rules Out Giving In to Foreign Orders to Resign' (Interview), *Die Zeit*, 25 April.

Hansen, Bernt, and Twaddle, Michael. (eds.) 1991. *Changing Uganda: The Dilemmas of Structural Adjustment and Revolutionary Change*. London: James Currey.

Herbst, Jeffrey. 1992. 'Challenges to Africa's Boundaries in the New World Order', *Journal of International Affairs*, 46: 17–30.

—— 1996. 'Alternatives to the Current Nation-States in Africa', unpublished manuscript, Woodrow Wilson School, Princeton University.

Holman, Michael. 1998. 'Congo Revolt Fuels Fears of Growing Regional Instability', *Financial Times*, 6 August.

Human Rights Watch Africa. 1996. 'Zaïre: Forced to Flee, Violence Against Tutsis in Zaïre'. New York, NY: Human Rights Watch.

Jackson, Robert H. 1990. *Quasi-States: Sovereignty, International Relations and the Third World*. Cambridge: Cambridge University Press.

Kabongo, Ilunga. 1986. 'Myths and Realities of the Zaïrian Crisis', 27–36 in *The Crisis in Zaïre*, edited by Georges Nzongola-Ntalaja. Trenton: Africa World Press.

Kabongo-Mbaya, Philippe B. 1991. 'Protestantisme zaïrois et déclin du mobutisme', *Politique Africaine*, 41: 72–89.

Kalb, Madeline. 1982. *The Congo Cables: The Cold War in Africa from Eisenhower to Kennedy*. New York, NY: Macmillan.

Kalele-ka-Bila. 1993. 'Regionalist Ideologies', 17–42 in *Zaïre: What Destiny?*, edited by Mbyaya Kankwenda. Dakar: CODESRIA.

Kaplan, Robert D. 1987. 'Uganda "Starting Over" ', *Atlantic Monthly*, 259: 18–25.

—— 1994. 'The Coming Anarchy', *Atlantic Monthly*, 273: 44–76.

Kasfir, Nelson. 1985. 'Uganda's Uncertain Quest for Recovery', *Current History*, April.

—— 1993. 'Popular Sovereignty and Popular Participation: Mixed Constitutional Democracy in the Third World', *Third World Quarterly*, 3: 597–606.

Kayigamba, Jean-Baptiste. 1998. 'Rwanda Defends Right to Get Involved in Congo', *Reuters* [*Internet*], 21 August.

Keller, Edmond J., and Rothchild, Donald. (eds.) 1996. *Africa and the New International Order: Rethinking State Sovereignty and Regional Security*. Boulder, CO: Lynne Reiner Publishers.

Khadiagala, Gilbert M. 1995. 'State Collapse and Reconstruction in Uganda', 33–47 in *Collapsed States: The Disintegration and Restoration of Legitimate Authority*, edited by I. William Zartman. Boulder, CO: Lynne Reiner Publishers.

Komisar, Lucy. 1992. 'The Claws of Dictatorship in Zaïre: The "Leopard" Still Rules', *Dissent*, 39: 326–30.

Lawyers Committee for Human Rights. 1990. 'Zaïre: Repression as Policy: A Human Rights Report'. New York, NY: Lawyers Committee for Human Rights.

Leslie, Winsome J. 1993. *Zaïre: Continuity and Political Change in an Oppressive State*. Boulder, CO: Westview.

Lustick, Ian. 1993. *Unsettled States, Disputed Lands: Britain and Ireland, France and Algeria, Israel and the West-Bank-Gaza*. New York, NY: Cornell University Press.

MacGaffey, Janet. 1988. *Entrepreneurs and Parasites*. New York, NY: Cambridge University Press.

—— 1991. *The Real Economy in Zaïre*. Philadelphia, PA: University of Pennsylvania Press.

MacGaffey, Wyatt. 1982. 'Zamenga of Zaïre', *Research in African Literatures*, 13: 208–15.

—— 1992. 'Religion, Class and Social Pluralism in Zaïre', 133–51 in *Religion, State and Society in Contemporary Africa*, edited by Austin Ahanotu. New York, NY: Peter Lang.

Mahoney, Richard D. 1983. *JFK: Ordeal in Africa*. New York, NY: Oxford University Press.

Malu-Malu, Arthur. 1998a. 'Kabila Pledges Victory After Angola Talks', *Reuters* [*Internet*], 16 August.

—— 1998b. 'Power Cut Hits Kinshasa's Fuel, Water Supplies', *Reuters* [*Internet*], 18 August.

Mazuri, Ali A. 1995. 'The African State as Political Refugee', 9–25 in *African Conflict Resolution*, edited by David R. Smock and Chester A. Crocker. Washington, DC: United States Institute of Peace.

Mbaya, Kankwenda. 1993. *Zaïre: What Destiny?* Dakar: CODESRIA.

McCormick, Shawn H. 1994. 'Zaïre II: Mobutu, Master of the Game?', *Current History*, 93: 223–7.

Metz, Steven. 1996. 'Reform, Conflict, and Security in Zaïre'. Carlisle Barracks, PA: Strategic Studies Institute, Army War College.

Morrison, J. Stephen. 1995. 'Zaïre: Looming Disaster after Preventive Diplomacy', *SAIS Review*, 15: 39–52.

Mseta, Buchizya. 1998. 'Foreign Minister Joins the Rebels in Kabila's Congo', *Reuters* [*Internet*], 5 August.

MSNBC. 1997. 'Zaïre Factions Agree to Talk Peace', *MSNBC* [*Internet*], 28 March.

Museveni, Yoweri. 1989. *The Path to Liberation*. Kampala: Government Printer.

North, Douglas. 1990. *Institutions, Institutional Change and Economic Performance*. Cambridge: Cambridge University Press.

Nzongola-Ntalaja, Georges. (ed.) 1986. *The Crisis in Zaïre*. Trenton: Africa World Press.

—— 1994. 'Zaïre I: Moving Beyond Mobutu', *Current History*, 93: 219–22.

O'Leary, Brendan, and McGarry, John. 1995. 'Regulating Nations and Ethnic Communities', 245–90 in *Nationalism and Rationality*, edited by Albert Breton, Jean-Luigi Galeotti, Pierre Salmon, and Ron Wintrobe. Cambridge: Cambridge University Press.

Oloka-Onyango, J. 1997. 'Uganda's "Benevolent" Dictatorship in Africa', *Current History*, 96: 212–16.

Omara-Otunnu, Amii. 1992. 'The Struggle for Democracy in Uganda', *Journal of Modern African Studies*, 30: 443–64.

Onishi, Norman. 1998. 'Congo Rebels Cut Power and Water Again', *New York Times*, 18 August.

Pabanel, Jean-Pierre. 1991. 'La question de la nationalité au Kivu', *Politique africaine*, 41: 32–40.

Prunier, Gérard. 1995. *The Rwanda Crisis: History of a Genocide 1959–1994*. London: Hurst.

Radio France Internationale. 1997. 'Museveni States Ugandan Position on Zaïrian Crisis', *FBIS [Internet]*, 23 April.

Reno, William. 1994. 'International Actors and the Transformation of Decaying African States: "Greater Liberia" and Zaïre', *Annual Conference of the American Political Science Association*, New York, September.

—— 1995. *Corruption and State Politics in Sierra Leone*. Cambridge: Cambridge University Press.

—— 1998. *Warlords and African States*. Boulder, CO: Lynne Reiner Publishers.

Reuters. 1997a. 'Proliferating Currencies Divide Embattled Zaïre', *Reuters [Internet]*, 11 March.

—— 1997b. 'Welcome to Rebel-held Congo, No Zaïre', *Reuters [Internet]*, 8 April.

—— 1998a. 'Congo Rebel Leaders Says Kabila Talks Not Ruled Out', *Reuters [Internet]*, 19 August.

—— 1998b. 'Congo Rebels Announce New Anti-Kabila Front', *Reuters [Internet]*, 12 August.

—— 1998c. 'Ex-Congo Prime Minister Fears Congo Partition', *Reuters [Internet]*, 20 August.

—— 1998d. 'Rwanda's Kagama Defends Role in Kabila's Congo', *Reuters [Internet]*, 19 August.

—— 1998e. 'Upheaval in Zaïre To Go On Indefinitely', *Reuters [Internet]*, 21 April.

Rosenblum, Peter. 1997a. 'Endgame in Zaïre', *Current History*, 96: 193–205.

—— 1997b. 'Violence in Zaïre', 31–6 in *Zaïre: Predicament and Prospects*, edited by Jean-Claude Willame *et al.* Washington, DC: United States Institute of Peace.

—— 1998. 'Kabila's Congo', *Current History*, 97: 193–9.

Ross and Green. 1993. 'International Democracy Alert: Focus on Zaïre'. Washington, DC, 5 July.

Sangmpam, S. N. 1994. *Pseudocapitalism and the Overpoliticized State*. Aldershot: Avebury.

Shatzberg, Michael G. 1991. *Mobutu or Chaos? The United States and Zaïre, 1960–1990*. Latham: University Press of America.

Shatzberg, Michael G. 1997a. 'Alternate Causalities and Theories of Politics: Explaining Political Life in the Congo (Zaïre)', *Research and Knowledge in Africa*, Center for the Study of Cultures, Rice University, 6–9 November.

—— 1997b. 'Beyond Mobutu: Kabila and the Congo', *Journal of Democracy*, 8: 70–84.

—— 1997c. 'Hijacking Change: Zaïre's "Transition" in Comparative Perspective', 113–34 in *Democracy in Africa: The Hard Road Ahead*, edited by Marina Ottaway. Boulder, CO: Lynne Reiner Publishers.

Smock, David R., and Crocker, Chester A. (eds.) 1995. *African Conflict Resolution*. Washington, DC: United States Institute of Peace.

Spruyt, Hendrik. 1995. *The Sovereign State and Its Competitors*. Princeton, NJ: Princeton University Press.

Tucker, Neely. 1998. 'Congo's Leader Comes Close to Declaring War on Rwanda', *Philadelphia Inquirer*, 8 August.

Vansina, Jan. 1966. *Kingdoms of the Savannah*. Madison, WI: University of Wisconsin Press.

Verhaegen, Benoît. 1966. *Rébellions au Congo*. Brussels: CRISP.

Weiss, Herbert. 1995. 'Zaïre: Collapsed Society, Surviving State, Future Polity', 157–70 in *Collapsed States: The Disintegration and Restoration of Legitimate Authority*, edited by I. William Zartman. Boulder, CO: Lynne Reiner Publishers.

Widner, Jennifer A. 1995. 'States and Statelessness in Late Twentieth-Century Africa', *Dædalus*, 124: 129–53.

Willame, Jean-Claude. 1992. *L'automne d'un despotisme: Pouvoir, argent et obéissance dans le Zaïre des années quatre-vingt*. Paris: Karthala.

—— 1994. *Gouvernance et pouvoir: Essai sur trois trajectoires africaines— Madagascar, Somalie, Zaïre*. Paris: L'Harmattan.

—— et al. (eds.) 1997. *Zaïre: Predicament and Prospects*. Washington, DC: United States Institute of Peace Press.

Wrong, Michela. 1997a. 'End of an Era in Africa's Mineral Treasure House', *Financial Times*, 5 May: 4.

—— 1997b. 'Tshisekedi in Position for Zaïre's Endgame', *Financial Times*, 24 April.

Young, Crawford. 1965a. 'Federalism: The Quest for a Constitution, and Fragmentation: The New Provinces', 475–571 in *Politics in the Congo*, edited by Crawford Young. Princeton, NJ: Princeton University Press.

—— (ed.) 1965b. *Politics in the Congo*. Princeton, NJ: Princeton University Press.

—— 1967. 'Domestic Violence in Africa: The Congo', 120–42 in *Issues of Political Development*, edited by Charles Anderson, Fred von der Mehden, and Crawford Young. New York, NY: Prentice-Hall.

—— 1970. 'Rebellion and the Congo', 969–1011 in *Protest and Power in Black Africa*, edited by Robert Rotberg and Ali Mazrui. New York, NY: Oxford University Press.

—— 1976a. 'Ethnic Politics in Zaïre', 163–215 in *The Politics of Cultural Pluralism*, edited by Crawford Young. Madison, WI: Wisconsin University Press.

—— 1976b. *The Politics of Cultural Pluralism*. Madison, WI: Wisconsin University Press.

—— (ed.) 1993. *The Rising Tide of Cultural Pluralism: The Nation-State at Bay?* Madison, WI: University of Wisconsin Press.

—— 1994. 'Zaïre: The Shattered Illusion of the Integral State', *Journal of Modern African Studies*, 32: 247–63.

Zartman, William. (ed.) 1995. *Collapsed States: The Disintegration and Restoration of Legitimate Authority*. Boulder, CO: Lynne Reiner Publishers.

—— 1998. 'Congo: "A Carrion Country"', *Washington Post National Weekly Edition*, August.

5

Resizing and Reshaping the State: India from Partition to the Present

Gurharpal Singh

Introduction

In the comparative study of state expansion and contraction, the politics of moving borders, and ethno-nationalist movements for self-determination, India arguably occupies a distinctive and exceptional position. Established in the carnage of partition it appears to have evolved as a successful liberal democracy in one of the most plural and simultaneously underdeveloped societies in the world. This apparent success is even more striking given the complex range of external and internal threats confronted by the new state at independence. In half a century the Indian Union has emerged as the premier representative of a developing democracy with a population just now approaching one billion. But as the country passed through the fiftieth anniversary of its independence, there was profound pessimism as to whether the current state can survive for the next half-century. Gone are the old certainties of the Nehru-Gandhi dynasty, replaced by what the novelist V. S. Naipaul has called a 'million mutinies' (Naipaul 1990), with every 'vote-bank' and disgruntled ethnic and religious group making unmanageable demands on the political system. As the dominance of the Congress has declined, weak and unstable national governments have added to the sense of impending doom, voter disenchantment, and what Kohli has called a grow-ing crisis of 'governability' which afflicts nearly all aspects of Indian stateness and its political institutions (Kohli 1991). The most widely acknowledged distasteful manifestation of this decay has been the major corruption scan-dals that erupted between 1995 and 1997 and placed the whole political sys-tem on trial (Singh 1997b). At the same time the main beneficiary of Congress's decline and political uncertainty has been the right-wing Hindu revivalist Bharatiya Janata Party (BJP) that succeeded in forming a national government in March 1998. The BJP with its objective of a powerful Hindu state has emerged as a self-styled national saviour, promising to provide effective remedies for the multiple crises that now afflict the Indian Union.

The crisis of governability is most acute in India's borderlands, the peripheral regions away from the core Hindu and Hindi heartland of central India. Since the early 1980s violent secessionist movements in Jammu and Kashmir,[1] Punjab, and the north-eastern states have demonstrated that India has been engaged in internal wars, with almost 80,000 fatalities flowing from secessionist violence and counter-insurgency operations.[2] According to one source 50 per cent of the Indian Army has been tied down in dealing with Kashmiri, Sikh, and Assamese separatist activity while an overall 80 per cent is on constant alert for internal duties (Thandi 1996). The uprising in the Kashmir valley symbolizes growing *intifadas* against the Indian state which are attracting global interest. Although these borderland insurgencies have been contained by massive use of physical force, they show little sign of abating or being radically restructured within the framework of India's democracy. Not surprisingly, these struggles have generated a high degree of anxiety amongst India's political élites about the country's physical borders—an anxiety heightened in the media by a regular coverage of borderland violence 'against the nation' (Krishna 1994), and in border disputes with its co-nuclear neighbour Pakistan.

India's political élites have responded to these multiple crises by a confident reassertion of Indian 'exceptionalism': that is, they claim that India's secular, plural, multi-religious, multi-ethnic, and quasi-federal democracy has successfully contained the tiger of ethno-national secessionism. Consider, for example, the comments of J. N. Dixit, a former Foreign Secretary who has been influential in formulating India's foreign policy in the 1990s. Commenting on the Kashmir situation in light of comparative state collapses elsewhere, he noted:

India has observed with profound concern the disintegration of multi-lingual, multi-ethnic and multi-religious state structures like those of the former Soviet Union and Yugoslav Republic. The events which followed and the predicaments in which areas belonging to these states are now [in] should forewarn everybody about encouraging the break up of such state structures or advocating simplistic solutions which do not

---

[1] To highlight its legal claim to Kashmir, official Indian usage is always Jammu and Kashmir. For simplicity I shall use the designation Kashmir.

[2] This total is a 'guess-timate' between the underreporting in the official figures and the overreporting by protagonists. In Punjab the official death-toll is around 30,000, whereas human rights groups believe that the actual fatalities are nearer 45,000. Likewise in Kashmir the official figure is around 25,000, whereas Kashmiris put the total at 50,000. In the north-east, official figures put the death toll at around 10,000. See Thandi (1996) and Balagopal (1997).

comprehend the dynamics of such fragmentation of such societies. The situation in Bosnia, Georgia, Tajikistan, parts of Azerbaijan would be repeated ten times in the subcontinental land mass because of the size of the population involved, and the diversity and range of ethnic, linguistic and regional factors characterizing vast segments of these populations . . . A replication of the extensive and prolonged violence which has affected former Yugoslavia, republics of the former Soviet Union and countries of Africa, like Somalia and Sudan, can be anticipated if various quick fix solutions suggested for Jammu and Kashmir—and destabilising its link with India— are considered. India will certainly not have any part of this.

(Dixit 1994: 6–7).

Dixit's observations are significant not for the contextual distortions but as a statement of intent and belief. India has never been—and is unlikely to be— party to 'quick-fix' solutions for Kashmir, especially if they involve self-determination by the Kashmiris themselves. What is more disturbing is that for Dixit the comparative experience suggests that India's ethnic plurality can *only* be guaranteed by a form of statism informed by an enlightened élite, backed by a sizeable armed force engaged in counter-insurgency, and high levels of violence in the pursuit of a 'self-evident' truth. That such prescription is itself a form of ethnic oppression, or can be perceived as such in India's borderlands, is a proposition that Dixit is neither prepared to entertain, nor discuss.

If the political élite's perspective is clouded in rhetoric, then the academic literature on the subject is also an unhelpful guide. In the last decade there has been a proliferation of publications on Indian nationalism, subregional problems, ethnic conflict, and counter-insurgency—see Singh (1995a) for a survey of the literature. Much of this output, especially by analysts of Indian background, avoids problematizing the issue of borders, self-determination, and questions of nation and state-building in the peripheral regions—for examples see Varshney (1991) and contributions to the Special issue JAS (1997). Post-modernists, for example, in celebration of India's heterogeneity, diversity, and complexity have disembowelled regional ethnic identities, exposing them as imagined souls without bodies. Paradoxically the only academic approach which in some measure goes half way draws on heavy qualifications to rational choice theory, and advocates the need to politically accommodate with the segmental realities of Indian society (Mitra 1996). In the absence of a systematic approach, therefore, most analysts, like Paul Brass have formulated their own *ad hoc* rules about how the Indian state responds to movements for secession or autonomy from the Union (Brass 1991: ch. 5).

A group of scholars who are now explicitly beginning to address these issues have traditionally specialized on the politics and history of the peripheral regions, partition, ethno-nationalist movements and identity—see for example Samad (1995) and Talbot (1996). To some extent their enterprise has been spurred by the prospects of 'Back to the Future?': the growing academic and popular interest in the appropriateness of pre-partition political proposals for a decentralized, confederal, more loosely united India. These scholars are currently engaged in reworking their understanding of the partition to understand unmanageable ethnic conflicts, both within the periphery and the core; and more systematic work is also being undertaken on ethnicity, state secularism, and nation- and state-building (Ahmed 1996). My own research is located within this school of thought, and recently I have sought to illustrate the relevance of Ian Lustick's theory of state contraction and expansion (Lustick 1993) to the Indian subcontinent with reference to the partition and politics of separatist movements in the borderlands that it created.[3]

This chapter aims to further demonstrate the relevance of Lustick's theory by incorporating the insights of McGarry and O'Leary on national and ethnic conflict management (McGarry and O'Leary 1993), and introducing the revisionist debate about the ethnic character of the Indian state. This adaptation is necessary because separatist movements in the peripheral regions have generally been considered beyond the realms of 'normal politics' in India; and even though they have posed a serious challenge to the Indian state, and its ability to control them, these movements have yet to emerge on the negotiable political agenda at the centre; they have not crossed the ideological hegemony stage in the terms of Lustick's theory, let alone threatened to pass from the regime to the incumbency stage. This paradox arises because of the ethnic character of the Indian state, which is intimately shaped by the majority Hindu community, and the associated plurality of Hindi speakers. In the peripheral regions, where there is no majority of citizens from the *Staatsvolk*, Indian nation and state-building since 1947 has been sustained by what McGarry and O'Leary call 'hegemonic control'[4]—a

---

[3] In particular, I have focused on five areas of potential research: the weakness of national political institutionalization before 1947; the prospects of state contraction and provincial level politics between 1940–7; the national war for manoeuvre between the Congress and the Muslim League from 1945–7; post-partition state size and hegemonic beliefs in India and Pakistan; and post-1947 separatist movements and the prospects of 'right-sizing' the Indian and Pakistani states (Singh 1997a).

[4] The terms hegemony and hegemonic control are used distinctly. The distinction is necessary to grasp the difference between India's ethnic core and the peripheral regions. Our operational use of hegemony conforms to the common Gramscian reading as a 'sphere of cultural and ideological influence of pure consent' (Forgac 1988: 423). More particularly, it refers to the ideas of dominant élites ('hegemonic beliefs') within the ethnic core about boundaries, nationhood, and self-determination movements. Hegemonic control, on the other hand, refers to the peripheral regions and implies the use of coercion and consent, as well as the manipulation of consciousness, to exclude certain possibilities. When hegemonic control breaks down, overt coercion and domination ('control')

form of 'coercive and/or co-optive rule which successfully manages to make unworkable an ethnic challenge to state order' (McGarry and O'Leary 1993: 23).

The main argument of this chapter is that hegemonic beliefs about India's external borders were shaped by the partition in 1947. The existence of separatist movements in the peripheral regions, perversely, continues to rein-force rather than challenge these beliefs among political élites. Although the growing crisis of governability suggests that there is enormous scope for both resizing and reshaping the Indian state, under prevailing circumstances this potential is unlikely to be realized by separatist movements waging milita-rized self-determination struggles in the peripheral regions. There is more likelihood of change if there are fissures, cracks, and dissension within India's ethno-religious and ethno-linguistic cores accompanied by simultaneous demands for reshaping, or if élites within these ethnic cores recognize the need to either link or de-link the borderland struggles with the prospect of creating a more homogeneous core *à la* BJP—which has an unacknowledged interest in down-sizing—and/or undertake a fundamental restructuring involving substantial autonomy to the states—which may be in the interest of the left and centrist opposition to the BJP. Barring these two possibilities, or a combination of them, it is unwise to preclude the possibilities of an implosion triggered by continued political decay, uncertainty, and economic collapse.

In the rest of this chapter I illustrate the relevance of these propositions by examining: the hegemonic beliefs about state size and border deliberately entrenched by political élites after the partition; with reference to Kashmir, Punjab, and the north-eastern states, the response of the Indian centre when these beliefs have been violently contested; why these beliefs have not encountered sustained opposition within the ethno-religious and ethno-lingual core of the Indian state; the potential coalition of political forces and processes supportive of resizing and reshaping the Indian state; and the coali-tion of political forces and political processes opposed to resizing and reshap-ing the Indian state.

Post-1947 Hegemonic Beliefs about State Borders

It is an established conventional wisdom that partition provided the founda-tions of hegemonic beliefs about Indian nation and statehood. 'What the

replace it. Hegemonic control therefore is more than overt domination by ordinary means, see Lustick (1979). In the Indian case hegemonic control is certainly the more appropriate concept because in the peripheral regions formal democratic structures have provided the front for nation and state-building.

partition succeeded in doing,' Gupta has noted, 'was searing the lineaments of India's territorial boundaries deep into the national consciousness . . . [through] the popular sacralization of territory' (Gupta, D. 1996: 17). Nehru and the Congress had opposed colonial proposals for a united India on the grounds that they would lead to 'balkanization' and 'communalism'—concessions to the Muslim League—but, as power was transferred to two centralized dominions, the demographic realities of independent India—83 per cent Hindu—belied the confident belief in state secularism which had been used as an ideological weapon against the Muslim League. Nehru's own secularism had never been in doubt, but his leadership of the Congress, which accommodated the mainstream of Hindu nationalism, together with a predilection to use the Soviet model of national self-determination[5] chimed with majoritarian discourse on any future secession, division, or separation. In fact after 1947 any movement for autonomy or secession would be excoriated as partition, vivisection, and division of the country.

Logically, it could be argued that if the Congress's commitment to secularism was deep-rooted, it had little to fear from movements for self-determination, religious or otherwise. Since this was not the case it is appropriate at this juncture to introduce the revisionist debate about the ethnic character of the Indian state. Because the formalism of Nehruvian secularism and its coalescence with majoritarianism remained, until recently, unquestioned, most analysts of Indian politics have tended to take this commitment at face value (see for example Brass 1991). In line with the common view of Indian diversity, the idea of an overarching dominant ethnicity defined by Hinduism has been resisted on the grounds that there are cross-cutting cleavages of caste, religion, and language—see Manor (1996). Students of comparative nationalism, on the other hand, have been more sceptical of this view, and have highlighted the pan-Indian function of Hinduism that transcends linguistic and other barriers so the 'Hindus "speak the language" even when they do not speak the same language' (Gellner 1992: 109, n. 1). The public relations interpretation of the Congress as the leader of a non-nationalist

---

[5] The influence of the Soviet nationalities question on Nehru was considerable. Writing before 1947 he noted: 'The right of any well-constituted area to secede from the Indian federation or union has been put forward, and the argument of the USSR advanced in support of it . . . Before any such right of secession is exercised there must be a properly constituted, functioning, free India. It may be possible then, when external influences have been removed and real problems face the country, to consider such questions objectively and in the spirit of relative detachment, far removed from the emotionalism of today, which can only lead to unfortunate consequences which we will regret later. Thus it may be desirable to fix a period, say ten years after the establishment of the free Indian state, at the end of which the right to secede may be exercised through proper constitutional process and in accordance with the clearly expressed will of the inhabitants of the area concerned' (Nehru 1989: 534). In the event Nehru's commitment to the right of self-determination of Indian states after 1947 was more tactical than strategic—as his handling of Kashmir was to demonstrate.

'civilization' movement is largely anchored in a version of Hinduism produced by nineteenth-century German hermeneutics and romanticism which
celebrated the idea of Hindu tolerance. But what follows from this assertion,
as Embree has reminded us, 'is not toleration; rather all truths, all social practices, can be encapsulated within the society as long as there is a willingness to
accept the premise of encapsulation' (Embree 1990: 40). In short, India's
encapsulated secularism facilitated the primacy of the Hindu universe—in
which 'all religions are true'—and legitimized western, secular and élite rule
over a society steeped in folk religion.

The existence of cumulative cleavages in the borderlands—religion, language, and regional ethno-nationalisms—that were hostile to Congress's
political project even before 1947, and the renewed hostility to the country's
Muslims—13 per cent of the total population—following the destruction of
the Ayodhya mosque (1992), have led some to argue that it is more appropriate to view India as a *de facto* ethnic democracy (Singh 1995b). Indian
democracy, it is suggested, neither conforms to secularized majoritarianism—where the state encouraged acculturation and assimilation but allows
ethnic groups to maintain ethnicity in the private sphere, such as the USA's
model of integration—nor ethnically accommodative consociation where
ethnicity is publicly recognized as the basis for the organization of the state
which acts either as a register or an arbiter of ethnic groups—for example
Belgium. India, in contrast, appears to resemble a third variant, a form of
hegemonic control, namely, an 'ethnic democracy' which combines the
'extension of political and civil rights to individuals and certain collective
rights to minorities with institutionalized dominance over the state by one of
the ethnic groups' (Smooha 1990: 391). Whereas in some ethnic democracies
the process of 'institutionalization of dominance' is formal and explicit, in
India it is implicit and arises from unspoken assumptions about state secularism, the historical ascendancy of the Congress party, and the ever-present
threat of overt Hindu majoritarianism. Thus even though minorities have
asserted individual and collective rights, the recognition of these rights has
been based on a tactical accommodation with Hinduism.

Within India's ethnic democracy, more hard-line hegemonic control is
exercised over minorities, especially borderland minorities. Hegemonic control underpins the functioning of political and administrative structures; and
when it is challenged, contested or opposed, the Indian state regularly resorts
to coercion—here I redeploy the analysis of O'Leary and Arthur (1990).
Hegemonic control has also been used alongside internal partition—redrawing the boundaries of borderland states; co-option; the creation of tribal
zones and of special territories—and attempted integration and assimilation—for a wider discussion of these methods see McGarry and O'Leary

(1993) and O'Leary's Chapter 2 above. In sum, the methods of ethnic-conflict management followed by the Indian state since 1947 with special reference to the borderland states post a fundamental challenge to the assumptions of state secularism and the view of India as a multi-ethnic and pluralist democracy.

If partition created in-built hostility to secession, in the five decades since, the Indian state has consciously pursued a policy of state expansion to which most national political parties have willingly consented. In the name of national integration princely states, nominally independent after August 1947, were coerced into the Indian Union. The accession of Kashmir still remains shrouded in mystery but what is certain is that without the presence of Indian forces in the valley, this achievement would have been doubtful if not impossible. The Portuguese territories of Goa, Damn, and Diu were forcibly liberated and incorporated despite strong US pressure. In its northern border India has territorially integrated the former independent kingdom of Sikkim (1975), eroded the independence of Bhutan, and since 1950, has ensured paramountcy over Nepal which makes the latter's claim to independence resemble that of a dependent territory. India has also successfully taken part in 'state-breaking', or indeed an external partition, by dismantling the eastern wing of Pakistan in the war that led to the creation of Bangladesh in 1971. Most recently Indian peace-keeping forces were deployed in Sri-Lanka (1987–90), and only withdrawn after heavy casualties suffered by the Indian Army in the Jaffna peninsula.

In one example, however, state expansion was severely checked, resulting in the creation of new myths about the sanctity of borders. Nehru did not just accept the colonial border with China, but instigated a forward policy that the colonial administration had let lapse. Despite numerous proposals by the Chinese government for a negotiated settlement and joint demarcation of the border defined in colonial treaties, to which the Chinese government had not been party, Nehru persisted with the forward policy, thereby precipitating a war with China in 1962.[6] When this short border war resulted in a humiliating defeat the experience was used not for reflecting on the consequences of state expansion entailed in the forward policy: instead the mythology of the sacred Himalayas was further reworked into sanctifying the claimed borderlines. Indeed, Nehru and most Indian nationalists

---

[6] Most contemporary interpretations of the Indo-China war portrayed communist China as the aggressor. At the height of the cold war, when Nehru successfully portrayed India as the leader of the Non-Aligned Movement, this interpretation was readily accepted. In fact recent scholarship has shown that 'India led the world up the garden path', and demolishes the belief that 'India was the victim of Chinese aggression.' For one rigorous account see Maxwell (1970).

assumed, without verification, that the large imaginary north-eastern and north-western borders of the country (mainly defined by the McMohan Line) as determined by the colonial power would hold good in perpetuity. They gave no thought to the political repercussions of borders that straddle neighbouring countries across soft areas and societies lying on either side of the highly permeable interface. These rigidities prevented India from settling outstanding inter-national and regional issues within South Asia, involving small countries as well as large neighbours such as China. No other regional power in the world is held in greater suspicion by its neighbours than India.

(Sathyamurthy 1996: 23–4)

Against the backdrop of the war with China hegemonic beliefs about borders were formalized in declarations, statute, and a constitutional amendment to strengthen their application in the peripheral regions. During the war, parliament adopted a resolution to 'drive out the aggressors from the sacred soil of India, however long the struggle may be' (Thakur 1994: 76). To date this resolution has neither been revoked nor amended. An amendment to the *Indian Criminal Act* (1961) made it an offence punishable by imprisonment for three years to question by words, written or spoken, signs, or visible representation the territorial integrity of India. The sixteenth *Constitutional Amendment Act* (1963) in the interest of the sovereignty and integrity of India imposed restrictions on the rights to freedom of speech and expression, to assemble peaceably without arms, and to form associations. It further prescribed that all candidates seeking election to provincial and national parliaments had to affirm an oath of allegiance to uphold the sovereignty and territorial integrity of India. Although the validity of measures are regularly contested in peripheral regions, within India's ethnic core they have lost none of their resonance. In the 1984 general election campaign, for example, following the assassination of Indira Gandhi and the pogroms in Delhi against Sikhs, one of the most effective posters used by the Congress depicted the borders of India being moved to the outskirts of Delhi if the party was not re-elected.

Hegemonic Control: The Challenge of State Contraction in Kashmir, Punjab, and the North-Eastern States

Although India's momentum for state expansion in the peripheral regions has been cloaked in the language of state and nation-building, it has been unable to proceed without significant challenges. Much of the contemporary literature on this resistance situates it in terms of a desire for more autonomy *per se* against a centralizing state (see Brass 1991), or affirms the 'bell-curve' pattern in which these movements arise, accumulate momentum and then dissipate as their demands are co-opted, deflected or incorporated through participatory mechanisms (Kohli 1997). In essence, it is argued, the Indian state can continuously *restructure* the political demands of these movements. Such interpretations however fail to appreciate the continuity in secessionist demands, the coercive instrumentality of democratic structures in the regions where the secessionist demands arise, and the regular absences of political legitimacy of rule-bound behaviour that commands majority consent freely given and underpinned by normative agreement on how rules are constructed. Hegemonic control describes precisely the kind of accommodation that is suggested, but when such accommodation challenges hegemonic norms, overt coercion is frequently used, thereby undermining the fragile structures of institutionalization. Rigged elections, the nomination of a large proportion of 'independents', or outright boycotts of elections by regional parties, have not been uncommon (see Table 5.1). Thus Kashmir, Punjab, and the north-eastern states that have witnessed the frequent imposition of President's Rule—direct rule from New Delhi—khaki elections, counter-insurgency, and other methods of political closure, provide paradigms for this argument.

Kashmir

The story of Kashmir, the oldest unresolved conflict before the United Nations according to Butros Butros Ghali, is too familiar to require full narration. The decision of the Hindu prince of a Muslim majority province to accede to the Indian Union at the moment of partition resulted in hostilities between India and Pakistan, and a *de facto* division of the province in January 1949 along the case-fire line—for a useful summary see Puri (1993). The accession to India was softened by the concessions to Kashmiri nationalism embodied in Article 370 of the Indian Constitution that limited the powers of New Delhi to defence, communications, and foreign affairs. At the time of UN intervention in the dispute, Kashmiris saw this article as a transitional measure before the proper exercise of the right of self-determination. Nehru personally gave an open pledge to ensure that the 'fate of Kashmir is ultimately decided by the people' and accepted the Security Council resolution of 21 April 1948 that the question should be 'decided through the democratic method of a free and impartial plebiscite'. This commitment however soon waned as the Indian state first promoted the Kashmiri nationalists led by Sheikh Abdullah and then, subsequently in a *volte face* because of Hindu nationalist pressure in 1952–4, Nehru started the piecemeal integration of

TABLE 5.1. *Performance of regional parties in state assembly elections in peripheral regions of India since 1983*

| State (population) | Year | Votes for (%) | | |
		Regional Parties	Others and Independents	All-India Parties
Jammu & Kashmir (8 m)	1983	55.8	10.4	33.8
	1987[a]	36.7	37.5	25.8
	1996	[b]		
Punjab (20 m)	1985	37.9	11.9	50.2
	1992	5.2[c]	9.9	84.8
	1997	40.1	13.4	46.4
Mizoram (0.6 m)	1987	23.7	43.3	33.0
	1989	54.6	10.2	34.8
	1993	40.4	23.4	36.2
Munipur (1 m)	1984	22.1	43.1	34.8
	1990	35.2	6.3	58.5
	1995	42.6	8.2	49.2
Tripura (3 m)	1983	59.7 M	9.0	31.3
	1988	58.7 M	3.0	38.1
	1993	56.3 M	9.5	34.2
Assam (22 m)	1983	10.8[c]	29.0	60.2
	1985	55.0	15.0	30.0
	1991	33.6	24.3	42.1
Meghaalaya (1 m)	1983	49.3	25.5	27.7
	1988	47.4	20.0	32.6
	1993	44.1	21.3	34.6
Nagaland (1 m)	1987	60.0	0.0	40.0
	1989	44.4	4.2	51.5
	1993	33.1	20.9	46.4
	1998[c]			[d]
Arunachal	1984	41.0	11.5	37.5
Pradesh (0.8 m)	1990	2.2	20.5	77.6
	1995	0.0	25.9	74.1

[a] Election rigged in eyes of objective observers
[b] Election won by the regional National Conference
[c] Election boycotted by the principal party/parties
[d] Congress won 42 seats unopposed
M   State Unit of the Communist Party of India (Marxist) defined as a regional party

Source: Butler (1995); *The Sunday Tribune* (Chandigarh), 8 February 1998.

the province into the Union. Abdullah, the 'Lion of Kashmir', was interned for two decades while a compliant assembly, established by extensive vote-rigging, voted for the merger with India in 1956. Thereafter India's response to a renewed Security Council resolution (24 March 1957) calling for a 'free and impartial plebiscite conducted under the auspices of the United Nations' was to cover its integrationist intentions under the pretext of a cold war threat to its national security emanating from the US policy of encirclement, including a military alliance with Pakistan.

Three wars, one with China and two further engagements with Pakistan, and the emergence of India as a nuclear power in 1974 convinced Abdullah of the limits of the demand for Kashmiri sovereignty. Towards the end of his life he signed an accord with Indira Gandhi (1975) that accepted that Kashmir was a 'constituent unit of the Union of India' in return for the formal survival of Article 370—though its provisions were extensively diluted in the application of central powers to the state. For almost a decade Abdullah nurtured a political dynasty with his son Farooq taking over after his death in 1982. Farooq's reign was marred by the needs to straddle regional nationalism and the limits of autonomy imposed by New Delhi. His efforts to establish an all-India oppositional front for more autonomy resulted first in his dismissal, and subsequently, in his return to power in alliance with Congress in the rigged elections of 1987. It was these elections, and the denial of the growing support of the Muslim United Front, that triggered the Kashmiri *Intifada*. Thereafter the separatist groups—the Jammu and Kashmir Liberation Front and the Hizbul Mujahideen—transformed decades of ethnic oppression into a generalized uprising against the Indian state. Between 1990 and 1996, 25,000 people were killed in Kashmir, almost two-thirds of them by Indian armed forces; Kashmiris put the figure at 50,000 (Balagopal 1997). In addition 150,000 Kashmiri Hindus have fled the valley to settle in the Hindu majority region of Jammu. In 1991 Amnesty International (1992) estimated that 15,000 people were being detained in the state without trial.

The Indian state's response to the Kashmir crisis has been to resort to coercive measures that are justified according to four principles: that the insurgency is externally supported and directed by Pakistan against India; that it is rooted in Islamic fundamentalism which poses no serious threat to India's secularism; that the separatist movements have no legal or political claim to independence; and that the insurgency is a threat to India's overall security, territorial integrity, and nationhood (Dixit 1994: 1–6). In furtherance of these principles the Indian Army, paramilitaries, and lumpen counter-insurgents were unleashed against Kashmiri separatists to contain the violence and re-establish hegemonic control. After 1994 in response to world-wide concern about the violation of human rights in the province, central governments attempted to restart the political process by holding regional elections. In September 1996 elections were held for the state assembly for the first time since 1987. Conducted under the shadow of a khaki umbrella provided by the Indian forces they have seen the revival of Farooq in a campaign largely boycotted in the valley, with overall turnout less than 30 per cent (*India Today*, 31 October 1996). Farooq recognized the serious limitations to his legitimacy and joined the beleaguered United Front government in New Delhi to set up a commission to investigate the issue of autonomy from 1947 to the Indira-Sheikh accord of 1975. A sustained revival in the fortunes of the Farooq administration may lead to a gradual dismantling of the coercive apparatus but because the history of Kashmir suggests that 'periods of relative calm can turn overnight into outbursts of rage and violence without an end' (ibid). India's political élites are likely to proceed with extreme caution in this direction.

Punjab

The Punjab problem that emerged in the early 1980s posed a different challenge to hegemonic beliefs about state borders. In a sense Punjab has never been a 'disputed territory' like Kashmir, but the distinctive position occupied by Sikhs in pre-partition Punjab—and their hostility to the division of the province—led their leadership to seek special guarantees within the Indian Union. After partition the promise of such guarantees by Nehru was broken with the result that the Akali Dal—the main Sikh political party—sought to contest Nehruvian secularism by pursuing a campaign for the linguistic reorganization of the Punjab. Opposition to this campaign was marshalled largely by the Congress party which became the main instrument for exercising local hegemonic control, mobilizing Punjabi Hindus to declare Hindi as their mother tongue, thereby frustrating the numerical case for a Punjabi province.

Although a Punjabi state was eventually conceded (1966), this concession came under emergency conditions as a *quid pro quo* for the defence of Punjab during the Indo-Pakistan war (1965). Subsequently, linguistic reorganization was hemmed in by so many qualifications that it soon led to an autonomy movement organized by the Akali Dal around the Anandpur Sahib Resolution (ASR, 1973)—which called for New Delhi's powers to be limited to currency, defence, communications, and external affairs. This agitation eventually climaxed in Operation Blue Star (1984) in which the Indian Army stormed the Golden Temple (Singh 1987).

Coercive measures had been intermittently used in Punjab in the 1950s and 1960s but what distinguished the 1980s, especially after the failure of

Rajiv Gandhi to re-establish some degree of political normalcy, was the extent to which the central governments were prepared to use force to crush Sikh separatism. By conservative estimates something like 30,000 people were killed as a result of separatist violence and counter-insurgency operations by the security forces between 1981–93. The numbers of involuntary disappearances and illegal detainees remain unknown although the latter were estimated to vary from 20,000 to 45,000 (Thandi 1996: 165). At the height of the insurgency in the early 1990s, almost a quarter of a million military and paramilitary troops were engaged in counter-insurgency operations against groups campaigning for a separate Sikh state of Khalistan. These groups were not without significant support: in the 1989 all-Union elections their representatives or supporters won ten of the thirteen parliamentary seats from Punjab; and in June 1991 had the newly elected national Congress government not postponed the poll, the militants would certainly have won the assembly elections scheduled at the same time. In the event the Congress aborted these polls and held khaki elections in February 1992 that were boycotted both by the militants and moderate Sikh political leaders. The boycott resulted in a Congress 'triumph'—on a turn-out of 24 per cent—that was used as a pretext to intensify the war against separatism (Singh 1992). By the end of 1993 most leading separatists and their organizations had been eliminated, the moderates had been muzzled, and Punjab was being hailed as a 'model' for combating separatism (Singh 1996).

The overwhelming use of force against Sikh militants and moderates between 1981 and 1993 highlighted the limits of Sikh ethno-nationalism and the resolute determination of the Indian state to defeat it. But if separatism has been militarily defeated, and if hegemonic control defines the acceptable limits of contemporary Sikh nationalism, the latter remains a significant political force which in the latest assembly elections (February 1997) returned the Alkali Dal to power in a landslide. Interestingly while the demands of the Alkali Dal remain rooted in the ASR, the realities of operating within the limits of hegemonic control have drawn the party closer to an alliance with the BJP both regionally and nationally—the enemy of their enemy may become their friend. Such a tactical agreement is a product of the realities of political competition: it could, however, become the basis of redrawing boundaries, or resizing the Indian Union if the BJP decides to forego its ambition to create a continental Hindustan.

North-Eastern States

In the north-eastern states, Indian nation and state-building has always been bitterly contested. After fifty years of independence the region is still tormented by separatist insurrection, guerrilla warfare, and terrorism with some of the movements campaigning for independence dating from before 1947. The original inhabitants of the region, nearly half of whom are from aboriginal tribes, are uncertain of their place, whether within India or outside it. In a visit to the area in 1996, the former Prime Minister, H. D. Deve Gowda, acknowledged that people in the north-east feel New Delhi treats them like a stepmother and pledged to provide basic services to bring the region 'to the standards in the rest of the country.'

In August 1947 Nehru's response to movements in this region seeking self-determination was blunt: 'We can give you complete autonomy but never independence. No state, big or small, in India will be allowed to remain independent. We will use all our influence and power to suppress such tendencies' (Ali 1993: 31). Thereafter the strategic importance of this area for state expansion against China led to state-building and 'nation-destroying' as the inaccessible regions were brought within the parameters of New Delhi's rule. Where economic exploitation of the region's natural resources resulted in indigenous opposition to migration from the heartland, a variety of administrative and constitutional provisions were adopted to placate tribal sentiment—the creation of tribal zones and councils, of autonomous districts, Union territories and, eventually, new states.

According to one commentator, state-building in the face of separatist pressures has followed a three-step strategy: 'to fight the insurgency with military force for some time; then, when the rebels seem to be tiring, offer negotiations; and finally, when the rebels are convinced that no matter what the casualties are on either side, they are not going to be able to secede, win them over with the offer of constitutional sops, invariably resulting in power being given to them in the resulting elections' (Gupta, S. 1995: 25). Although the same commentator emphasises the capacity of the Indian State to control these movements, he is silent on numerous cases where constitutional rehabilitation has been followed by renewed struggles, violence, and endemic terrorism. Since the 1950s the history of Assam, Mizoram, Nagaland, Tripura, and Manipur is littered with 'accords' signed by New Delhi with separatists. In fact in Assam, as in Punjab, much of the resentment which fuelled the separatist movement was the failure of New Delhi to deliver on the regional accord signed in August 1985. This failure revived the fortunes of the United Liberation Front for Assam, resulting in the repeated deployment of the army to crush the movement.

Unlike Kashmir or Punjab, coercion tempered by minimal consent has been the main strategy by which India has maintained its hold on the north-eastern states. In this sparsely populated region what is surprising is not the willingness of the insurgents to accept hegemonic control—in the face of overwhelming odds—but their determination to sustain opposition to the Indian state for so long. Current developments suggest that these states have been far from pacified, or politically integrated into the Indian Union. If anything the emergence of a first generation of educated youth among these communities combined with a growing realization of India's 'internal colonialism'—Assam produces 70 per cent of India's oil, and the bulk of its tea— has strengthened the arguments for separatism.

Separatism within the Ethnic Core

If the argument advanced thus far, that India should be seen as an ethnic democracy, is valid, then it is necessary to address the issue of separatism in the ethnic core. Opponents of the classification of India as an ethnic democracy have pointed to the successful completion of federal linguistic reorganization in the 1950s and 1960s, and the containment of the separatist threat posed by the Dravida Munnetra Kazagham (DMK) in Madras (now Tamil Nadu) in the 1950s and 1960s. Separatism in the core and separatism at the periphery, they argue, follow similar trajectories (Mitra and Lewis 1996). Such interpretations overlook the fact that there are significant differences of *kind* rather than *degree* between the cases. Given India's immense diversity, size, and complexity, the question posed should perhaps be not *how* separatist movements have been contained but *why* many more such movements have not emerged in the heartlands for outright self-determination. One obvious answer is that these heartlands are the bedrock of the Indian democracy's power-structure, with the Hindi-belt providing almost 40 per cent of the MPs to the All-Union Parliament. West Bengal and the Dravidian South are, despite their cultural differences with the Hindi-belt, also intimately locked into this structure. In 1947, for example, the Bengali Hindu élite successfully sabotaged the emergence of an independent Bengal largely because of fear about Muslim majoritarianism in such a state. In this move the Hindu élite were supported by the national Congress High Command which sought a quick transfer of power to a centralized state (Bose 1991). Similarly it is mistaken to interpret the cultural advocacy of separatism by Tamils in the 1950s and 1960s as a movement for independent territorial statehood on a par with that demanded in the peripheral regions. Most of the demands of the DMK, the regional political party which led the movement, were for cultural and linguistic autonomy couched in anti-Brahminical rhetoric—Brahmins had traditionally dominated the regional Congress. Once the DMK established itself in power in 1967, the rhetoric of separatism was quietly forgotten and has not been rekindled even by the Tamil strife in Sri Lanka.

In contrast to the demands from the peripheral regions for linguistic reorganization and autonomy, the Indian state is remarkably responsive to such demands from the core—contrast the reorganization of Andhra Pradesh with Punjab and the north-eastern states; or the non-imposition of Hindi in Tamil Nadu, with the non-imposition of Punjabi in Punjab. Seen in this light it is perhaps appropriate to conjecture that some of the contemporary movements for reorganization of existing states within the core led by lower castes and tribals—Uttarakhand, Jharkhand, Chhatisgarh, Telengana, and Vidharbha: see the map in Fig. 5.1—will be conceded, whereas similar demands in the borderlands, for example in Gorkhland and Bodoland, are likely to be rejected, contested, or tactically conceded to undermine separatist movements.[7]

It is within the ethnic core that the BJP has established its power base. Since 1990 the party has ruled state governments in Uttar Pradesh—the largest and most populous state of 139 million—Delhi, Himachal Pradesh, Rajasthan, Gujarat, Madhya Pradesh and, with its allies, in Maharashtra. The BJP has also been making in-roads into Karnataka, Bihar, Kerala, Andhra Pradesh, and Punjab, where it rules in coalition with the Alkali Dal. This rapid growth transformed the BJP into the leading all-India party in the 1998 national elections, capturing 250 of the 545 seats with its allies. But if the BJP ideologues sometimes advocate a continental-wide Hindu state—including a form of outrageous irredentist 'wrong-sizing' that would incorporate Pakistan—the political reality is that it is essentially a Hindu constituency party, without much firm support outside the ethnic core. Where it does have such pockets of support, as in Jammu and Punjab, this is mainly from the borderland Hindus who have historically influenced Congress policy in these regions. Whether the compulsions of party-building pull the BJP in the direction of the ethnic core or ideological borderland politics remains to be determined. What is less in doubt, however, is that if the party is to emerge as the dominant all-India force, it needs to consolidate its support base further within and beyond the Hindi-belt.

The party-building factor may drive the BJP in two possible directions: like Russian nationalists, it may consider the advantages of resizing the Indian state without the troublesome peripheral nationalities; alternatively, like the Congress in its heyday, it may build regional alliances as the road to sustained electoral success. Whereas the former option is likely to preserve the ideological integrity of the party, the latter may lead to its reincarnation

---

[7] Interestingly the BJP in its manifesto for the 1998 elections supported the creation of new states within the ethnic core while advocating the abrogation of Article 370 and a hard line against terrorism, see India News Network Digest (1998).

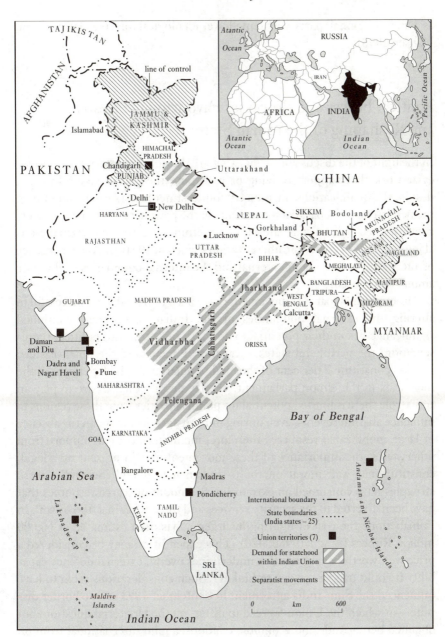

Fig. 5.1 The Indian Union

as a 'meta-regional' party with a mellower ideological tone (see Jaffrelot and Hansen 1998).

Political Forces and Processes Favouring the Resizing and Reshaping of the Indian State

In the light of the discussion so far, what are the political forces and process-es at work that support resizing or reshaping the Indian state? In brief, despite the qualifications introduced, four distinct factors can be identified: the persistence of separatist movements in the peripheral regions; the emer-gence of a neo-federalist debate within the ethnic core; the long-term region-al implications of economic liberalization started in 1991; and the emergence of alternative beliefs about external and the internal boundaries of the state among the non-élites.

Although the separatist movements have been remarkably unsuccessful in altering the external boundaries of the Indian state, their continued significance lies in their potential to do so. In resources and political repre-sentation, the peripheral states—Kashmir, Punjab, and the north-eastern states—constitute 7 per cent of the total population, and 7.8 per cent of the total seats in the Union parliament. Clearly despite their desire to play an active role there is limited potential for political parties from these regions to influence all-India events, even during minority governments. In the absence of large mobilizable resources therefore, including external support from other states, the importance of these movements lies in presenting a legal, constitutional, and moral mirror to Indian nationhood. Secondly, these struggles have consumed an extraordinary amount of scarce resources that have been diverted to the security services and the war against 'terrorism'. In Punjab alone the cost of fighting insurgency has been estimated at 60,000 million Rupees (Singh 1995b: 420). This expenditure may be considered a price well worth paying but if it undermines overall external defence capa-bility it could trigger serious rethinking. Such considerations seem to have influenced the Sino-India agreement in September 1993 on the border dis-pute—in which the Union 'agreed to differ' on the territorial question, but obtained better trade and economic relations, a joint international front on human rights, and China's neutrality on Kashmir (*India Today*, 30 September 1993). Finally, the separatist movements in the 1990s have been successful in globalizing their demands. The Kashmiri, Sikh, and Naga dias-poras have been active in lobbying governments, international agencies—the UN and INGOs—and human rights bodies with considerable effect. The brutal violations of human rights in Kashmir and Punjab by the security forces have focused international attention in a way that the separatist movements never succeeded in achieving. Both China and India supported each other at the UN-sponsored conference on human rights in Vienna (1993) against non-governmental (separatist) representatives in order to overcome their joint embarrassment in Tibet, mainland China, Kashmir, Punjab, and the north-eastern states.

The main momentum for reshaping the Indian state has come from the demand for territorial autonomy. Whereas in the peripheral regions the exercise of hegemonic control has often led to the rearticulation of separatism in the guise of seeking greater autonomy—Kashmir, Punjab—within India's ethnic core growing centralization has generated considerable demands for redefining federalism. To be sure, though the peripheral regions have been at the forefront of the campaign for autonomy, the ethnic core states and their political élites have rarely been forceful advocates of the former's case. Since the 1980s some political élites in West Bengal, Orissa, and Tamil Nadu have called for a new power relationship between the centre and the states, as well as a serious discussion of confederalism along the lines of the Cabinet Mission Plan of 1946 (Mukarji 1996). India's Defence Minister under the United Front government openly proposed new confederal arrangements embracing India and Pakistan (the *Sunday Tribune*, Chandigarh, 21 July 1996). Even *India Today*, a publication not noted for its radicalism, in an editorial pointed to the desperate need to reverse 'the five-decade long trend of centralisation'. This call was made with reference to the intentions of the framers of the Indian Constitution as spelt out in the Objective Resolution of 1946 to create a loose confederation in which the states would 'retain the status of autonomous units'. Although the partition strengthened the hand of the centralizers, the editorial continued, the 'time is indeed right to revert to the Objective Resolution and confer greater autonomy on the states' (15 September 1996). The election to the Union government in May 1996 of the national United Front, a coalition of over sixteen parties, most of whom were regionally based, represented the most significant development of this demand. In its Common Minimum Programme the United Front government committed itself to a radical reform of federalism, agreed to legislate on greater financial powers to the states, and devolve power in large areas of centrally administered programmes (*India Today*, 30 June 1996).

The sustained rise in regional party support in all-Union elections is likely to increase the possibilities that in the medium-term the relationship between the centre and the states will be restructured. However, the experience of the United Front government suggests that this will be a painful and slow process. General policy change since the 1980s has been pitifully slow:

the Sarkaria Commission (1987) on centre–state relations confirmed the *status quo*, proposing minor modifications to existing arrangements; and the period of National Front government (1989–91) was largely overtaken by other crises. Unless and until there is a substantial majority in New Delhi for new federal arrangements, the demand for autonomy is unlikely to make substantial headway.

In many ways the demand for greater autonomy to the states has also been strengthened by economic liberalization pursued since 1991. The Nehruvian view of the Indian state was underpinned by centralized planning on the Soviet model—which systematically eroded the limited constitutional powers of the states. Following the virtual financial collapse of the Indian state in 1991, a policy of economic liberalization was adopted which abandoned economic planning. Deregulation, disinvestment from public sector undertakings, and efforts to promote foreign investment have provided new opportunities for the states to generate and manage resources as central transfers of revenues to the states from New Delhi have been drastically reduced to meet the targets of the Union's fiscal deficit.[8] All states have been competing with each other to attract foreign investment. Some have been remarkably successful: Maharashtra, India's financial capital, has captured 17.5 per cent of all proposed inward investment. Maharashtra's state government has ambitious plans to emulate the success of Hong Kong and Singapore to become the 'financial nerve centre of Asia' (*India Today*, 31 December 1995). Similarly, Gujarat with its large (western) diaspora of Gujaratis has emerged as the front-runner for foreign investment, attracting 20.6 per cent of all inward investment (ibid). Other states, particularly the more populous, like Bihar and West Bengal, have shown little enthusiasm for the policy, or of attractiveness to foreign investors. All other things being equal, economic liberalization is likely to accelerate the development gap between the western and eastern states; and if the present growth and population patterns persist, this gap will become increasingly wider.[9] Given that more affluent states such as Punjab have traditionally been reluctant to subsidize the less developed ones, similar

---

[8] Between 1991 and 1996 central transfers to the states declined from 6 per cent of gross domestic product to 4.5 per cent (*India Today*, 30 June 1996). As a percentage of states' expenditure, the share of gross transfers from the centre has declined from 56 per cent in 1990–1, to 42.2 per cent in 1993–4 (*India Today*, 31 December 1995).

[9] Much discussion in the *Economic and Political Weekly*, India's leading intellectual journal, has focused on the increase in poverty *within* states as a result of economic liberalization. This tends to overlook the fact that poverty has been regionally concentrated, both before and after economic liberalization. In 1987–8, for example, Bihar and Uttar Pradesh accounted for 34 per cent of the population defined as poor—see Sen (1996: 2460). As these and other populous states—West Bengal, Madhya Pradesh, Andhra Pradesh, and Tamil Nadu—have been relatively unsuccessful in attracting foreign investment, the argument that interstate disparities will increase seems valid: it is reflected in their current income per capita.

movements for autonomy are likely to develop a bitter economic edge, especially if the growth is acquired as a result of external markets or inward investment. A vision of 'bloody and anarchic change'[10] ushered in by economic liberalization may not materialize until sometime in the future but the policies of some state governments in seeking to restrict internal migration and promote preferential treatment for the 'sons of the soil' is perhaps indicative of things to come.[11] Of course economic liberalization by itself may not provide the sufficient condition for separatism, particularly if the growth of all-India markets remains a powerful attraction, but rapid growth at the state level may intersect, as it has done so far, with demands for more powers for states to regulate their own affairs. Economic liberalization has reversed the economic logic that led to the creation of a centralized Union after partition. Increasingly, economic power is shifting to the states; and this process appears to be largely irreversible, as all major all-India political parties, including the BJP, are committed to the new industrial policy.[12]

Lastly, in contrast to hegemonic beliefs about state size and borders that are articulated by political élites and the establishment, surveys of public opinion suggest a more fluid picture about the range of alternative possibilities. Much of this is perhaps because of the emergence of a new generation for which the partition and the cold war are but distant events. It is also to some extent a reflection of a wider global reality in which borders are no longer perceived as sacrosanct. Indeed, Dixit himself expressed amazement at the response of college students 'up-and-down' the country to the break-up of the Soviet Union and Yugoslavia, who according to him, are demonstrating an unhealthy enthusiasm for the event repeating itself in India.[13] A poll carried out on the eve of talks between India and Pakistan showed interesting results. Asked what they felt about a solution to the Kashmir dispute, 51 per cent of those polled said the territory must be granted more autonomy within India, 35 per cent said that Kashmiris must decide their own future, and 14 per cent said the issue ought to be handed over to the United Nations (*India*

[10] Again within the columns of the *Economic and Political Weekly* there is much discussion of the potential political consequences of economic liberalization—usually equated with globalization—for India. See Kishnaswamy (1994) and Kothari (1995).

[11] 'Sons of the Soil' policies came to prominence in the 1970s because of increasing migration within Indian states (see Weiner 1978). Some transnational corporations operating in India have encountered strong political pressures to discriminate in favour of the 'sons of the soil' (interview with R. Bagga, Senior Executive with a multinational company specializing in power generation, 12 December 1997, London).

[12] Despite the BJP's rhetoric about 'self-reliance,' its economic policy does not seek to reverse economic liberalization but to adapt it to an Indian vision of globalization (*India Today*, 30 March 1998).

[13] These comments were made by Dixit at the Centre for Study of Indian Politics, University of Hull, 4 March 1996.

Network News Digest, 26 March 1997). In another poll published in *India Today* ahead of the fiftieth anniversary of India's independence, 36 per cent of the respondents said India would disintegrate into independent nations in the next fifty years, while 41 per cent said it would stay united (10 August 1997). Such surveys give the impression that for most Indians, peripheral separatist movements and the question of the unity of India are now emerging as secondary to issues of corruption, poverty, and insecurity (*India Today*, 15 March 1996). The rise of lower caste parties in the most populous states has further strengthened this trend by projecting bread-and-butter political issues to the fore.

The main difficulty facing the political forces and processes working towards resizing and reshaping the Indian state is establishing effective links between the fragments. Political élites in the peripheral regions have often spoken in the language of greater autonomy, but the ethnic core's mistrust of such language as a cover for separatism has contributed to disarticulating a genuine debate abut the nature of Indian federalism. In contemporary Indian politics there is only a small section among the enlightened political élites who recognize the need to decentralize as well as economically liberalize, to address the democratic deficit confronting the poor sections of society and the historically oppressed nationalities in the periphery.

Political Forces and Processes Opposing the Resizing and Reshaping of the Indian State

Against the factors favouring the resizing and reshaping of the Indian state's external and internal boundaries are substantial obstacles that will have to be overcome if the processes sketched above are to gain momentum. These include the rigidity of hegemonic beliefs, and their influence among the security forces; the Congress and the BJP; and the opposition of groups who are likely to become minorities in any such resizing and reshaping endeavours.

Despite the increasing scepticism within the public about India's borders, hegemonic beliefs as articulated by state representatives have shown a remarkable rigidity. Two recent examples will illustrate this fact. A newly arrived British High Commissioner to India inadvertently forgot to include the reference to Jammu in his informal party invitation to Kashmiris. This serious *faux pas* brought forth howls of protest within the Indian press, and among leading politicians righteous declarations were made that the whole of Kashmir—including Pakistani occupied territory—was legally part of the Indian state. In a second instance US Vice-President Albert Gore in a communication incorrectly referred to Punjab as Khalistan, resulting in diplomatic ruffled feathers which caused much ill-wind in the Indian Foreign Ministry. Yet if these incidents illustrate the lighter side with which these beliefs are held, their inculcation among the security services and the administrative élite—especially the Indian Administrative Service—has been systematic. Because the peripheral territories are on India's external borders and have been the sites of several wars they are seen as essential to the strategic defence of the country. This significance is perceived to be so fundamental that according to one source in 1990 the insurgency in Kashmir came close to triggering a nuclear exchange between India and Pakistan (Cortright and Mattoo 1996). The nuclear cold war between India and Pakistan has had the consequences of reinforcing the sanctity of existing state structures not necessarily because of perceptions of each other, but because it has made domestic challenges to concessions more vehement. The élite administrators and leading members of the security services have always demonstrated significant opposition to territorial change, either externally or internally. This is reflected in their public utterances—for example the writings of Jagmonah, the former Governor of Kashmir—and in every successive external treaty that India has signed since 1947. In short, dominant beliefs among the ruling élite about the sanctity of borders have been *overdetermined* by the consequences of partition—an experience, in some ways, shared by other states this century which have also been partitioned—for example Ireland, Palestine, Cyprus.

Second, notwithstanding the progress made by the United Front, which represented a pro-regional states 'third front' in national politics, the BJP and Congress still occupy influential positions. The Congress, though the weakest of the three all-India groupings, succeeded in undermining the United Front government in 1997, thereby precipitating a fresh round of parliamentary elections. As a party whose fortunes have been intimately connected with post-independence politics the Congress has traditionally responded in a belligerent way to any prospects of resizing. Despite the induction of Sonia Gandhi into the party's election campaign in 1998 and her subsequent elevation to the party leadership, Congress's share of seats in parliament actually declined, and the percentage of votes polled by it fell to a historic low of 25.4 per cent (*India Today*, 16 March 1998). Although a revival in the support for Congress in the short term seems unlikely—and in the long term cannot be ruled out—its ability to wreck and consume coalition governments (1979–80; 1989–91; 1996–8) suggests a remarkable capacity for survival. A substantial period in opposition might enable the Congress to 'reconstruct' itself as a party of the regions but this endeavour, if undertaken, will challenge the historic association of the Congress with the creation of the modern Indian state. In all probability the Congress, like the CPSU, will be a reluctant partner in resizing the state it founded and built.

The BJP, in contrast, openly despises the 'Congress culture' which it holds responsible for the country's difficulties. The party's meteoric rise from two parliamentary seats in 1984 to forming an all-India government in 1998, has coincided with a Hindu revival which has led the BJP aggressively to advocate a Hindu state, and Hindu cultural values to replace Nehruvian 'pseudo-secularism'—'pseudo-secular' in their eyes because it proclaimed western secularism for Hindus, while consolidating minority religious identities among Muslims, Sikhs, and Christians. Genuine secularism, according to the BJP, would avoid the western ideal and assert the primacy of Hinduism, a common shared value of 'all Indians'—Muslim, Sikh, Christians, and Hindus. Uncompromising ideological Hinduism is the BJP's formula for preserving India's cultural identity which it sees as threatened by the growing pressures of assimilation inherent in economic liberalization on the one hand, and regional insurgencies on the other.

These policies led the BJP to follow the politics of direct action which climaxed in the destruction of the Ayodhya mosque, and led to nation-wide clashes between Hindus and Muslims. Although Ayodhya precipitated the dismissal of the local BJP state government, the party recovered its momentum by stoking xenophobic fears against the cultural consequences of globalization following economic liberalization. After the 1994–5 state elections the BJP formed a short-lived all-Indian government (May 1996) and was the main beneficiary of political uncertainty gripping the Union. In the mid-term parliamentary elections of February 1998 the BJP achieved a landmark breakthrough which resulted from tactical alliances with regional parties.

Formally, the BJP programme supports the creation of a continental Hindu state with its more militant factions often calling for the dismemberment of Pakistan. The party, furthermore, has long supported the development of a nuclear programme, and has resisted the pressures on India to join the Nuclear Test-ban Treaty. The BJP has also been the most vociferous opponent of Article 370 that grants special status to Kashmir. Its 'solution' to the Kashmir question is to repeal Article 370, and integrate the valley into the Indian Union, both politically and culturally. Similar proposals are also offered for resolving the discontent of peripheral and non-peripheral minorities. Group rights guaranteed by the constitution, such as Muslim Personal Law, the BJP insists, should be removed because of the imperative of nation-building and cultural homogeneity.[14] Where ethnic boundaries

---

[14] These proposals were included in the BJP manifesto for the 1998 elections. See *India News Network Digest*, 7 February 1998.

between Hindus and non-Hindus are vague, the party calls for emotional empathy combined with systematic integration into the Hindu fold (Singh 1995a).

However, in the aftermath of all-Indian parliamentary elections in February 1998, the BJP appeared to have moderated its political outlook. In leading a thirteen-party coalition it agreed to a National Agenda for Governance which excluded three of the party's key manifesto commitments: the repeal of Article 370, a uniform civil code, and construction of a temple on the site of the Ayodhya mosque. The programme of the coalition was prominent on cultural nationalism—'India is to be built by Indians'—but lacked detail in defining the parameters of this nationalism, especially with reference to economic policy (*India Today*, 30 March 1998; *Asian Affairs* 2: 18 April 1998).

In light of these developments some commentators have viewed the emergence of the BJP as a moderate nationalist force, best epitomized by its parliamentary leader Vajpayee. Others have been more sceptical, suggesting the current moderation of the party is a 'mask,' a 'master strategy to wrest political power under false pretences' (*India Today*, 9 February 1998). Such a twin-tracking interpretation is supported by statements by senior party officials that its agenda is currently on 'hold' until the party can establish itself as the dominant party in India. The clearest indication of this is perhaps provided by the BJP's president L. K. Advani, also one of its leading ideologues, who has described the current situation as 'the transformation of an ideological movement into a mass-based party' (ibid).

Finally, since 1947 one of the main arguments used by New Delhi to resist the demands for resizing and reshaping the state is the potential opposition to such a policy from groups who would become minorities in any such reorganization. In the debate about separatism for Kashmir, for example, the right of self-determination for Buddhists in Ladakh and Hindus in Jammu is counterposed to the claims made by Muslims in the valley (Hewitt 1995). In the peripheral regions the existence of a large and politically powerful settler Hindu populations provides a constant source of support for ideological hegemonic beliefs about borders. These arguments were also skilfully exploited in the efforts to frustrate linguistic reorganization, and have been raised in opposition to new demands for creating further Indian states. To be fair, of course, there are, indeed, large minorities in some of the Indian states: in Punjab, for example, Hindus constitute 40 per cent of the total population; and in some smaller states the figure is even higher. Within the ethnic core the degree of diversity is less, but numerically it is not insignificant. Whether the existence of such minorities can reasonably continue to be used to deny decentralization, autonomy, or self-determination is a matter for debate. In an interesting proposal, one writer has suggested the use of Article 371 of the

Indian Constitution that allows for special provisions for individual states 'notwithstanding anything in the Constitution,' to allow states to formulate their own constitutions with entrenched provisions on amendment—two-thirds and individual and group rights—to protect their minorities (Mukarji 1996). This proposal is remarkable in that it draws directly from the suggestions made by the Cabinet Mission Plan (1946) for establishing a loose federation for a united India.

Conclusion

This chapter has attempted to argue that in the debates about state expansion and contraction, the politics of moving borders, and ethnicity it is mistaken to accept the thesis of Indian exceptionalism: that is, the notion that the Indian experience since 1947 suggests that it has developed a unique capacity for managing self-determination movements and ethnic conflicts without a fundamental revision of external borders. This view is ideologically prescriptive, theoretically untenable, and empirically incorrect.

The cost of sustaining an Indian Leviathan is the permanent militarization of the peripheral regions—punctuated with periods of hegemonic control—increasing uprisings, and global exposure of the brutal realities of India's democracy. Because the peripheral regions have commanded few political resources, their demands have failed to be articulated at the regime level. Indeed mainly because Nehru and other Congress élites were exceptionally successful in using the partition experience to embed beliefs about the new state's borders, the mere questioning of these beliefs became synonymous with subversion. The peripheral and core divide in which the latter was the main power base of the new state, moreover, reinforced this hegemony. If the self-determination movements in the peripheral regions served a function, they did so by displaying a distorted reflection to the logic of Indian nation and state-building. The methods used by the Indian state to manage conflicts in the peripheral regions revealed the hollow realities of its secularist credentials. But fifty years on, the environment that created the Indian state no longer prevails. The bankruptcy of Nehruvian economic planning has resulted in economic liberalization and growing demands for decentralization within the ethnic core. Such a development, if it gains momentum, holds considerable potential both for resizing and reshaping the Indian state. This potential will really become meaningful if links are established between the two processes. Although there are significant forces which oppose the pressures towards resizing, the strength of this opposition is perhaps more ideological than rooted in contemporary political realities. In many ways the rise of the BJP represents the most interesting potential for change—whether towards a continental assertion of Hinduism, or of a contraction to its core. The main paradox regarding state size and political competition in India in the late 1990s, almost a half a century after partition, is that after the fall of the Congress party that was so successful in creating India's hegemonic beliefs, state contraction offers enormous opportunities for new political élites but it remains difficult to escape from the trap that Congress has constructed. The emerging debate on the realities of partition and its implications for the present may perhaps mark the beginning of the effort to escape from this predicament.

REFERENCES

Ahmed, I. 1996. *State, Nation and Ethnicity in Contemporary South Asia*. London: Pinter Press.

Ali, S. M. 1993. *The Fearful State: Power, People and Internal Wars in South Asia*. London: Zed Press.

Amnesty International. 1992. 'India: Torture, Rape and Death in Custody'. London: Amnesty International.

Balagopal, K. 1997. 'Kashmir: Self-determination, Communal and Democratic Rights', *Economic and Political Weekly*, 2 November: 2916–21.

Bose, S. 1991. 'A Doubtful Inheritance: The Partition of Bengal', 130–43 in *The Political Inheritance of Pakistan*, edited by D. A. Low. London: Macmillan.

Brass, P. R. 1991. *Ethnicity and Nationalism: Theory and Comparison*. New Delhi: Sage.

Butler, D., Lahiri, A., and Roy, P. 1995. *India Decides: Elections 1952–95*. New Delhi: Books and Things.

Cortright, D., and Mattoo, A. 1996. 'Elite Public Opinion and Nuclear Weapons Policy in India', *Asian Survey*, 36: 545–60.

Dixit, J. N. 1994. 'Kashmir: The Contemporary Geo-Political Implications for India and Regional Stability and Security', *Conference on Kashmir*, 8 April 1994. London: School of Oriental and African Studies.

Embree, A. T. 1990. *Utopias in Conflict: Religion and Nationalism in Modern India*. Berkeley, CA: University of California Press.

Forgac, D. (ed.) 1988. *A Gramsci Reader*. London: Lawrence and Wishart.

Gellner, Ernest. 1992. *Postmodernism, Reason and Religion*. London, New York, NY: Routledge.

Gupta, D. 1996. *The Context of Ethnicity: Sikh Ethnicity in a Comparative Perspective*. Delhi: Oxford University Press.

Gupta, S. 1995. *India Redefines its Role*. Oxford: Oxford University Press and IISS.

Hewitt, V. 1995. *Reclaiming the Past?* London: Portland Books.

India News Network Digest. 1998. 'India News Network Digest', *The India Network Foundation* [*indnews@INDENET.ORG*] 7 February.

Jaffrelot, C., and Hansen, B. (eds) 1998. *The BJP and Its Allies*. Delhi: Oxford University Press.

Journal of Asian Studies. 1997. Special issue 'Community Conflicts and the State in India', 56.

Kishnaswamy, A. M. 1994. 'Between Friends', *Economic and Political Weekly*, 22 October: 2783–6.

Kohli, A. 1991. *Democracy and Discontent: India's Growing Crisis of Governability*. New York, NY: Cambridge University Press.

—— 1997. 'Can Democracies Accommodate Ethnic Nationalism? Rise and Decline of Self-Determination Movements in India', *The Journal of Asian Studies*, 56: 325–44.

Kothari, R. 1995. 'Globalization and Revival of Tradition: Dual Attack on model of Nation Building', *Economic and Political Weekly*, 22 March: 625–33.

Krishna, S. 1994. 'Cartographic Anxieties: Mapping the Body Politic in India', *Alternative*, 19: 507–21.

Lustick, I. 1979. 'Stability in Deeply Divided Societies: Consociationalism Versus Control', *World Politics*, 31: 325–44.

—— 1993. *Unsettled States, Disputed Lands: Britain and Ireland, France and Algeria, Israel and the West-Bank-Gaza*. New York, NY: Cornell University Press.

Manor, J. 1996. 'Ethnicity and Politics in India', *International Affairs*, 72/3: 459–75.

Maxwell, N. 1970. *India's China War*. London: Jonathan Cape.

McGarry, J., and O'Leary, B. 1993. 'Introduction: The Macro-Political Regulation of Ethnic Conflict', 1–47 in *The Politics of Ethnic Conflict Regulation*, edited by J. McGarry and B. O'Leary. London and New York, NY: Routledge.

Mitra, S. 1996. 'Sub-national Movements in South Asia: Identity, Collective Action and Political Power', 14–41 in *Subnational Movements in South Asia*, edited by S. Mitra and R. A. Lewis. Boulder, CO: Westview Press.

—— and Lewis, A. (eds.) 1996. *Subnational Movements in South Asia*. Boulder, CO: Westview Press.

Mukarji, N. 1996. 'Strengthening Indian Democracy', *Economic and Political Weekly*, 11 May: 1129–34.

Naipaul, V. S. 1990. *India: A Million Mutinies Now*. London: Heinemann.

Nehru, J. 1989. *The Discovery of India*. New Delhi: Signet Press.

O'Leary, B., and Arthur, P. 1990. 'Introduction: Northern Ireland as the Site of State- and Nation-Building Failures', 1–47 in *The Future of Northern Ireland*, edited by J. McGarry and B. O'Leary. Oxford: Oxford University Press.

Puri, B. 1993. *Kashmir: Towards Insurgency*. Delhi: Orient Longman.

Samad, Y. 1995. *A Nation in Turmoil: Nationalism and Ethnicity in Pakistan, 1937–1958*. New Delhi: Sage Publications.

Sathyamurthy, T. V. 1996. 'The State of Debate on Indian Nationalism', *25th Millennium Anniversary Conference Paper*, London School of Economics and Political Science, October.

Sen, A. 1996. 'Economic Reforms, Employment and Poverty: Trends and Options', *Economic and Political Weekly*, September.

Singh, G. 1987. 'Understanding the "Punjab Problem" ', *Asian Survey*, 27: 1268–77.

—— 1992. 'Punjab Elections: Breakthrough or Breakdown?', *Asian Survey*, 32: 988–99.

—— 1995a. 'Perspectives on Ethnic Conflict in Indian Politics', *Internationales Aesinforum*, 26: 233–48.

—— 1995b. 'The Punjab Crisis Since 1984: A Reassessment', *Ethnic and Racial Studies*, 18: 476–93.

—— 1996. 'Punjab Crisis Since 1984: Disorder, Order and Legitimacy', *Asian Survey*, 36: 410–21.

—— 1997a. 'The Partition of India as State Contraction: Some Unspoken Assumptions', *The Journal of Commonwealth and Comparative Politics*, 35: 51–66.

—— 1997b. 'Understanding Political Corruption in Contemporary Indian Politics', *Political Studies*, 45: 626–38.

Smooha, S. 1990. 'Minority Status in an Ethnic Democracy: The Status of the Arab Minority in Israel', *Ethnic and Racial Studies*, 13: 389–413.

Talbot, I. 1996. 'Back to the Future? The Punjab Unionist Model of Consociation Democracy for Contemporary India and Pakistan', *International Journal of Punjab Studies*, 3: 65–73.

Thakur, R. 1994. *The Politics of Economics of India's Foreign Policy*. London: Hurst.

Thandi, S. 1996. 'Counterinsurgency and Political Violence in Punjab, 1980–1994', 159–85 in *Punjabi Identity: Continuity and Change*, edited by G. Singh and I. Talbot. New Delhi: Manohar.

Varshney, A. 1991. 'India, Pakistan and Kashmir: Antinomies of Nationalism', *Asian Survey*, 31: 997–1019.

Weiner, M. 1978. *Sons of the Soil. Migration and Ethnic Conflict in India*. Princeton, NJ: Princeton University Press.

6

The Negotiable State: Borders and Power-Struggles in Pakistan

Vali Nasr

Changes in the territorial shape and size of states have not traditionally been treated as important to the unfolding of their politics. There is, however, increasing evidence that the threat of change in state borders, posed explicitly as well as implicitly, can occur within the framework of central or 'high' politics, and become one element among others in determining the outcome of struggles for domination between various political groups, state leaders, and social institutions. How political leaders manage that threat within the polity, and what consequences the 'politics of moving borders' may have on conduct of politics as a whole, development, regime stability, and the relations between state- and nation-formation pose important theoretical questions. Accommodating the malleability of borders within the framework of 'high politics' has broad and far-reaching consequences. It reveals much about the logic and conduct of politics in unstable, weak, or 'failed' states, where the political centre is unable, or unwilling, to thwart challenges to its territorial borders, and where changes in borders—'resizing' the state—is a live political issue.

Pakistan is a suitable case for examining some of these issues. It is a young state with little continuity in time, and low levels of institutionalization of its borders. It is comprised of disparate provinces, distinct ethnic, linguistic, and religious groups, and it has been continuously besieged with threats to its borders. It is, in fact, among the few states in which the borders are continuously 'reimagined'. The scope of this exercise has been such that ethnic posturing and negotiations over borders have become ingredients of 'high politics', albeit not always overtly. What actually is or should be Pakistan, and the relative power and position of its political centre, constituent provinces and peoples, and indeed where provinces and peoples begin and end, in one form or another, constitute the main axes along which political debates, strategies, alignments, agendas, and ideologies take their form.

Carved out of British India, Pakistan's conception of its territorial reality is very much influenced by the political dynamics of secessionism. Civil war, Indian intervention, and the separation of Bangladesh in 1971, a decade-long civil war in Baluchistan in the 1970s, and the continued eruption of ethnic tensions across the country, most recently in Sind, have confirmed that commitments to the stability of the state's borders and its political institutions have not been widely-shared. The malleability of borders has been and remains a pivotal political issue. In December 1997 on a ballot cast by a member of the legislature from North-West Frontier Province (NWFP) for new president, was written the slogan 'Down with Pakistan, up with Pakhtoonkhwa [Land of the Pathans]' (cited in *The Economist*, 10 January 1998: 32). A weak government at the centre, one that is unable to formulate and implement clear economic, strategic, or social policies, today rules Pakistan. The state is simultaneously confronted by a number of ethnic conflicts: a violent ethnic conflict in its largest city and financial nerve centre, Karachi, which began in 1985, and in 1996 alone claimed the lives of some 2,000 people; unrest in rural Sind; intermittent insurrection among Pathans in the NWFP; and smaller secessionist rumblings among the Baluch and Seraiki peoples.

This chapter aims to discern the nature of the linkage between, on the one hand, power élite interests and their perceptions of the malleability of state borders and recurring ethnic tensions, and, on the other, the pattern of state formation and policy-making. I want to explain how the power élite's interests and perceptions have found reflection in politics, manifesting social resistance,[1] or the attempt to override it; what political language have they adopted and what modes of political behaviour have they produced? What institutional framework is the result of the politics of negotiable borders? What are the determinants of negotiations over borders? How do politicians assess their options and formulate their strategies, and when and why are the key thresholds—in Lustick's senses—crossed or averted, hegemonic beliefs maintained or altered, and new parameters and conceptions of the state introduced?

Lustick's Theory of Resizing

The starting point for this chapter is Ian Lustick's theory of resizing borders and especially state contraction outlined in his *Unsettled States, Disputed*

---

[1] For theoretical discussion of the management of social resistance by states see Migdal (1988); and Migdal, Kohli, and Shue (1994).

Lands (1993) and in his contribution in Chapter 3 of this volume. Lustick argues that state expansion and contraction involves a process of political institutionalization and deinstitutionalization, and requires changes in hegemonic beliefs about the state and its borders. Consequently, changes in borders are tied to struggles over domination within that state, and can constitute an important element in competitions for power. State contraction, the focus of this chapter, involves shifts in the distribution of power and resources, and can alter norms and legal arrangements to the advantage of one political group (Lustick 1993: 38–9, and see Chapter 3 above). Changes in borders can amount to 'institution-transforming episodes' which involve struggles over the 'rules of the game' (ibid: 41). Lustick argues that this struggle can pass through three stages: first, among the governing élite; secondly, involving social groups as well, which may lead to a challenge to the ruling regime; and, lastly, conflict among the élite over the regime itself and hegemonic beliefs about the nature of the state and its society (ibid: 439). The process involves crossing key thresholds, which distinguish between levels of resistance to changes in borders. In the incumbent stage, change in borders threatens the ruling coalition alone, whereas in the regime stage it could undermine the ruling regime and produce violent opposition to state institutions. In the ideological hegemony stage, changes in borders are unimaginable without reformulating the definition of the state, and the self-conception of its citizens (ibid: 41–3). The incumbent stage occurs when there is the least degree of state formation—including in the territory in dispute—and hence is the least costly type of state contraction.

Lustick's theory serves as a valuable heuristic tool for interpreting the Pakistani case. The theory is, however, premised on prior state expansion. The cases that form the basis of his study—Great Britain and Ireland, France and Algeria, and Israel and West Bank/Gaza—all involved an already institutionalized 'core' and a peripheral territory that was acquired at some later point in time, but not fully integrated. Consequently, the debate over contraction is limited to the nature of the relationship between the institutionalized core and the territory that was acquired through expansion. Contraction does not, in principle, question the very existence of the core state.

Pakistan presents a different case. Here the territorial candidates for secession have not been later additions to an already institutionalized state, and none of the constituent territorial units are bound together to form a fully institutionalized state. Lustick's theory contends with a punctuated equilibrium, where periods of stability and consensus about borders are interrupted by struggles over contraction and the institutional transformations that it might entail. In Pakistan there is a fundamental lack of stability and equilibrium, and the process of contraction which began with the partition of India in 1947 is ongoing. In Pakistan, negotiations over borders occur on a continuous basis, so that the struggles over the 'rules of the game' have become an integral part of the political process, part of the rules of the game. The Pakistani case therefore expands the purview of Lustick's theory by exploring the implications of negotiations over the size and shape of the state where the levels of institutionalization of borders are low, and the hegemonic notion of the state is weak.

This chapter uses a broad framework for understanding the case of Pakistan, and the negotiations with East Pakistan and Sind during the critical period of 1969–71, in particular. It uses Lustick's theory as its anchor, but it will seek to expand the scope of the discussion about resizing the state by reflecting on the particularities of Pakistan. The paper will focus on negotiations over borders that led to the civil war of 1971 and the secession of East Pakistan—later Bangladesh—the institutionalization of Sind's special status in the state, and the routinization of ethnic posturing in high and low politics. The narrative will seek to identify variables that determined both the regime and the opposition's strategies, and the responses that they elicited, producing different outcomes in the cases of Sind and East Pakistan. It will explore both what accounts for the non-institutionalized character of the state, and the political opportunities and limitations that inhere in it.

This chapter argues that while state leaders have publicly treated the contraction of borders as unimaginable—as if Pakistan was in the ideological hegemonic stage—in practice negotiations over borders have occurred in the political arena—in the incumbent and regime stages. The public insistence on a stand appropriate to the ideological hegemony stage is necessitated by the non-institutionalized character of the state, whereas the acceptance of negotiations over borders demonstrates the limits of state power, and the nature of the socio-political pacts that undergird its authority. The tension that is inherent in the ideological posture of state leaders and their pragmatic political practices has provided both opportunities to manage challenges to borders, as in Sind, and to loss of territory, as in East Pakistan. It has also determined the possibilities and limitations before political agents, shaping their strategies in bargaining for power and over borders.

The career of one politician in particular, Zulfiqar Ali Bhutto (d. 1979), is central to our analysis. His rise to power was closely tied to negotiations over reshaping and resizing the state in Sind and East Pakistan respectively. The different strategies that he adopted in negotiating for Sind on the one hand, and controlling the state's response to negotiations over East Pakistan on the other, were based on a particularly intricate relationship between political interests and change in borders. These episodes point to the importance of key variables that govern both the outcome of negotiations over borders and their political consequences.

The 'Foundations' of the Negotiable State

Before examining the manner in which negotiations over borders has unfolded in Pakistan, it is important to look at what accounts for those negotiations' non-institutionalized character, and within that context, permissiveness to negotiating over borders, the relative power of the various agents, and the possibilities and constraints that have governed their decision-making. The story begins in the partition of British India.

The Legacy of Partition

Pakistan was the product of the contraction of the British imperial state in India in 1947.[2] Fear of marginalization in a Hindu-dominated India led many Muslims to conceive of Pakistan as an alternate political arena, one in which Muslim aspirations would not be limited by identity (Nasr 1995). In many ways the demand for Pakistan was a demand first for reshaping the prospective independent India, and only later became a demand for resizing it (Singh 1997). As Jawaharlal Nehru and the Congress party refused to countenance the demands which the Muslim separatist leader, Muhammad Ali Jinnah, and his Muslim League party put before the future Indian state, the Pakistan movement crossed both the ideological and regime thresholds, and the idea of the partition of India was eventually accepted by the Congress leadership with little impact on their positions of power.

Pakistan was, however, an ideal in search of a 'territory'. Although Muslim separatism was popular in those Indian provinces where Muslims had been a minority, Pakistan was created in the Muslim majority provinces of North Western India—Punjab, NWFP, Sind, Baluchistan, Western Kashmir—and East Bengal, where the prospects of Hindu domination did not evoke the same degree of anxiety. While all of these areas were predominantly Muslim, clear ethnic, linguistic, and cultural distinctions set them apart from one another, and indeed from the Muslim populations of the Muslim minority provinces. From its inception Pakistan had a pluralist character. The state was not associated with any one of its constituent parts; it was not built on a historic, continuous core; it rather defined a conglomeration of disparate territories lumped together to form a state. The legacy of Jinnah's 'give us what

---

[2] For examination of the rise of the Pakistan movement see Sayeed (1968), and Aziz (1967).

we demand, or we'll secede' discourse was predictable in a state in which some of the constituent units were reluctant participants and had few linkages with one another. It helped establish the threat of secession as a viable and efficacious political tool.[3] In many ways, Jinnah and the Muslim League's discourse during the inter-war years has been internalized in Pakistan's politics; it has become part of its rules and procedures, and has surfaced time and again in struggles for power and domination as an accepted mode of political behaviour.[4] It has defined the rules of the game in high politics, and still serves as a model for negotiating for power.

The consequence has been that Pakistan's borders have remained rather uninstitutionalized—to the left of Lustick's regime threshold, but not entirely in the incumbent stage. The reason for this classification is that the military's intervention, in 1958 and 1969, to prevent resizing can be seen as indicative of the kind of wars of manoeuvre, and challenges to government institutions and authority, characteristic of the regime stage. The prospect of change in borders, however, primarily threatens incumbents, though it still has wider repercussions because it keeps the political system in a constant boil, which leads to crippling instability.

Élite Interests and the Creation of Pakistan

The Pakistan movement culminated in a state only because its leadership was able to strike a bargain with the traditional rural élite of the provinces and territories that would constitute it—Sind, Punjab, and East Bengal in particular. The terms of the bargain made the oligarchy the clientelistic intermediaries in rural areas and in provincial politics, in return for which they delivered mass support to Pakistan. The oligarchy's continuing power in the new state would depend on keeping the Muslim League, state institutions, and national political structures and ideology out of their territories. To do this, the oligarchy would frequently resort to ethnic posturing, and would treat loyalty to Pakistan as a bargaining chip in its power play with the political centre.

In time, the political centre itself became important to the continued prominence of the oligarchy, and that class therefore developed an interest in staying within the framework of Pakistani politics, albeit on its own terms. In NWFP and Sind, the more radical ethnic parties, such as the *Khudai Khidmatgar* (God's Servants, later renamed, the National Awami Party,

---

[3] Gurharpal Singh argues that the Indian élite was deeply affected by the partition in their treatment of ethnic demands from peoples living in border regions—see Chapter 5 above.

[4] On the importance of recurrence of rules and procedures in determining the shape of politics see Koelble (1995: 233).

NAP) or *Jiye Sind* (Long Live Sind) mixed separatism with socialism, calling for national liberation in tandem with the abolition of feudalism. Consequently, the oligarchy began to rely on the political centre to resist the populist and redistributive pressures from separatist ethnic parties and limited the scope of the oligarchy's penchant for ethnic posturing. This shift became increasingly important as oppositional politics in the 1960s became more left-of-centre. The NAP, Jiye Sind, and the Baluch Student Federation, much like the Awami League in East Pakistan, began to talk of class war in the context of ethnic politics, thus pushing the landed élite closer to the political centre. By the same token, however, the oligarchy found it necessary to speak for ethnic aspirations, lest the separatist parties dominate the rural scene and use ethnic demands to undermine the oligarchy's control. Class interests, therefore, determined the posture of the oligarchy in Pakistani politics.

The importance of class interest was also evident in warding off the challenge of populist movements that may have cut across ethnic lines to define Pakistani politics in class cleavages. To prevent such an outcome, the oligarchy in the various provinces forged Pakistan-wide alliances, which in turn made the oligarchy a 'national' class. Its rhetoric would, however, harp on ethnic identity to prevent the peasantry from making common cause across provincial and ethnic boundaries (Nasr 1997). In so far as the oligarchy is part of the political establishment, its class interests and political goals have created a paradoxical situation, one in which the ruling regime includes agents whose political ethos is rooted in asserting independence from the state by questioning its authority and its borders. The political role of the oligarchy accounts for why negotiability of state borders continues to shape politics in Pakistan. The oligarchy conducted a successful war of manoeuvre, through which it kept alive certain assumptions about state borders, and by so doing has prevented a hegemonic notion of the state from taking root. It means that negotiations over state borders occur primarily within state institutions as opposed to over them, and that such negotiations occur on a continuous basis as routine politics with the consequent effect of instability alluded to earlier. Still, the incumbent position of the oligarchy suggests that Pakistan is on the edge of the regime threshold.

The paradoxical role of the oligarchy is epitomized in the career of Bhutto, who would play a central role in negotiations over borders in the 1969–71 period as both Pakistan's future Prime Minister and the spokesman of Sind. He was a member of the landed élite, represented their interests, and used the institutional frameworks that relate feudalism to ethnic posturing; but he was also a powerful member of the ruling regime and became the chief executive of the state.

The Dilemmas of a Weak State: 1948–71

Massimo D'Azeglio may well have been talking of the problem facing Pakistan's leadership in 1948 when he said, of post-Risorgimento Italy, 'We have made Italy, now we must make Italians.' Italy, however, had the advantage of having something like a single language, and a long history of ethnic assimilation. Pakistan's disparate units did not share either a common ethnic identity or a common language. In fact, the new state was immediately confronted with disputes over language. While most Pakistanis spoke Bengali, Urdu which was spoken by only 3.4 per cent of Pakistanis (Jahan 1972: 12) became the national language (Oldenburg 1985).

Millions migrated from the Muslim minority provinces to the two wings of Pakistan, settling among people who were their co-religionists, but who were not as enthusiastic about Pakistan, did not share their language and culture, nor those of the other provinces of the new state. The problem was evident at the highest levels. Many in the leadership of the ruling party, the Muslim League, were born and raised in provinces that had remained in India, and hence they had no territorial political base in their new country (Sayeed 1968: 206). The influx of the newcomers, and their domination of politics, seen in such measures as declaring Urdu the national language, raised the ire of the 'sons of soil', and precipitated ethnic tensions.

These problems were further aggravated by the fact that the provinces that comprised Pakistan had few linkages with one another, and had been tied to the economic grid of India, from which they were now cut. Some had been won over to the cause of Pakistan late in the game, and then only with the barest of majorities. In Muslim Bengal—later, East Pakistan—the League's support had been limited, so much so that on the eve of the partition Jinnah contemplated letting the Bengalis—later East Pakistanis—create their own Muslim state (Moore 1988: 133). Pakistan was therefore from the outset confronted with the problems of a weak hegemonic definition of the state and of a low level of institutionalization of its borders—liabilities that have not been effectively remedied over the past five decades.

Unlike India, Pakistan did not inherit the 'vice-regal' state. The new state did not have effective machinery of government, and enjoyed only limited authority in the various provinces. While state leaders favoured a strong central government, the oligarchy through whom they ruled favoured a weak centre (Amin 1988: 72).[5] Pakistan's new leaders attempted to reconstruct the

---

[5] This trend in fact predated partition. Muslim minority areas of India, from where the Muslim League drew its support, favoured a strong centre in Delhi with a strong Muslim party to represent their ideas. The Muslim majority areas, which became Pakistan, however, had no need for protection by a strong party in a strong centre, and in fact, favoured a weak centre (Barlas 1995: 157).

vice-regal state, but were unable to invest it with the authority that it had enjoyed under the British. Pakistan was therefore from inception a weak state, a 'lame leviathan' to borrow Thomas Callaghy's term in describing the patrimonial state of Zaïre (see Chapter 4 above).

The weak state was in no position to assert its primacy, or establish a hegemonic conception of itself, nor even to articulate a widely-shared conception of 'Pakistani-ness'. Early on, ethnic posturing became ensconced in the polity and its use in political negotiations became institutionalized. The state's officials would eventually propagate ideologies of national unity; but given their early loss of the war of manoeuvre with the oligarchy they would not succeed in altering the role of ethnicity in politics. Hence, the ethnic reality of Pakistani politics has belied the rhetoric of the state—one that has emphasized Islam and 'Pakistani-ness.' The state was seriously constricted by the legacy of the partition, the socio-political pact that produced the state in the first place, and by managing the institutional and ethnic heterogeneity of a core-less territory.

Pakistan has survived because there has been great power and international support for its borders, especially during the state's early years when the USA viewed it as an important part of the 'northern tier' strategy of containing the USSR. Otherwise Pakistan has remained intact, when it has, because of an uneasy equilibrium of internal forces. It has been besieged with ongoing crises of governability that have led to the weakening of its political centre and the collapse of law and order. The consequences confirm Lustick's conclusion that the failure to remove debates over borders from politics will lead to instability.

Debates Over Contraction: East Pakistan and Sind

The factors discussed above have kept progress toward a strong hegemonic definition of the state limited, as a result of which borders have remained generally uninstitutionalized—although, to the right of the incumbency threshold. Contraction, especially early in the state's history, was not about disengaging from a territory into which it had expanded, but questioning whether the state existed at all, and whether the contraction of British India should stop at Pakistan. Contraction was therefore more a problem of state survival than disengagement. Although many of the same forces and processes that Lustick has identified in state contraction are discernible in Pakistan, their working and impact is at times different.

The problem that confronted the political centre immediately after the partition was how to keep East Pakistan at bay, avoid its domination of

Pakistan politically and culturally, and to produce an ideology capable of keeping the country together under the control of the West Pakistani élite, Punjabis and Muhajirs for the most part. The dynamics of negotiations over the decolonization and partition of India led Jinnah to include Muslim Bengal in the demand for Pakistan, although that decision extended the borders of Pakistan beyond the power-base of the élite that was to rule it. The state was particularly susceptible to down-sizing because East Pakistan was separated from West Pakistan by the breadth of India, and was more populous than West Pakistan,[6] and the West was itself divided into ethnically distinct provinces—see Fig. 6.1. Immediately after the partition, the political centre faced a strong demand for reshaping the state and the distribution of power and resources in it: East Pakistan insisted on a greater share of economic investments and military expenditures, and greater representation for East Pakistani Bengalis in government service.[7] The centre rejected either the redistribution of resources and devolution of power to East Pakistan, or the contraction of the state to make its borders coincide with the power base of its ruling élite. Consequently, the Bengali population in the east, gradually but surely, crossed the low threshold of their loyalty to the state and demanded secession. Provincialism as a bargaining platform eventually became full-fledged secessionism, the demand for reshaping had become one for resizing.

The problems of East Pakistan for the power élite manifested themselves soon after independence in the constitution-making process that lasted some nine years. The debates over distribution of powers between West and East Pakistan, the question of a national language, and the role of Islam preoccupied the political élite.[8] Meanwhile, a host of *ad hoc* measures were adopted to manage the state. The polity became increasingly Islamicized, both because of the constitutional impasse and as a means of diverting attention from the stand-off between the two wings of Pakistan. The power élite nominated a series of Bengali Prime Ministers to appease East Pakistan. But East Pakistan was not satisfied with symbolic gestures. Hence, constitutional wrangling, manipulations, and negotiations became the order of the day. The Muslim League began to lose all support in East Pakistan, while attempts to cultivate a base of support for the Awami League in West Pakistan failed. The gradual polarization, which continued even after the promulgation of a constitution

[6] At the time of the first census in Pakistan in 1951 there were 41.9 million East Pakistanis and 33.7 million West Pakistanis (Jahan 1972: 25).

[7] Although East Pakistanis outnumbered West Pakistanis, East Pakistanis accounted for only 11% of the civil service and 1.5% of military officers (Jahan 1972: 25–7).

[8] On debates over the role of Islam see Binder (1961). On the issue of the role of East Pakistan in the state see Syed (1982).

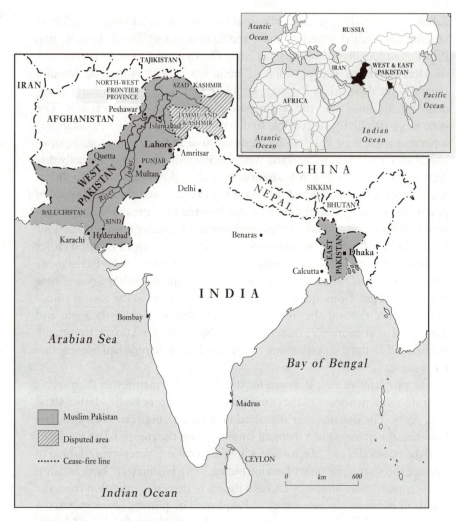

FIG. 6.1 West and East Pakistan

in 1956, weakened the centre. State leaders sought to resist East Pakistan's ascendance by reorganizing internal borders: West Pakistan's four provinces were amalgamated into one in the belief that in a two province state East Pakistan's numerical superiority would be less apparent than when it was by far the most populous of five provinces. The 'one-unit' conception of West Pakistan (1955–69) merely served to underscore the political, economic, and geographical chasm between East and West Pakistan. It was also unpopular with the smaller West Pakistan provinces who became sub-provincial divisions, and consequently, lost bargaining power with the centre (Samad 1995: 126–66). Moreover, West Pakistan as a whole was still less populous than East Pakistan.

The pressure to devolve power to East Pakistan gained momentum in the late 1950s. The rise to power of the popular Bengali politician, S. H. Suhrawardi, and his Awami League in 1956, for a time presented the possibility of assuaging East Pakistan without actually altering the balance of power between the two wings of the country. The success of this enterprise, however, would have required the Awami League to grow roots in West Pakistan to the detriment of the Muslim League, and Suhrawardi's own power-base would have eventually compelled him to devolve some power to East Pakistan. These realizations doomed the Suhrawardi government. After Suhrawardi left office in 1958 some began to contemplate, if not yet fully accept, some form of reshaping of the state. Although such a course of action would have advantaged the incumbents and the ruling regime in the long run, it posed short-run challenges. Reshaping and possibly resizing would have required changing the prevailing perception in West Pakistan that, as *the* Muslim homeland, the territorial boundaries of Pakistan were sacrosanct, and that West Pakistan's status as the political and cultural heart of Pakistan was inviolable. Negotiations over borders would have required politicians to come to terms with possible social resistance, and loss of legitimacy, power, and even access to high office. Jinnah's largely tactical decision to keep Muslim Bengal in the demand for Pakistan had become an albatross around the neck of his successors. Still, the resultant tensions could have been managed.

A segment of state leaders, notably in the military, and some among the right-of-centre and Islamist politicians viewed the question from the standpoint of Pakistan's security imperative. The military saw East Pakistani grievances as pro-India, in so far as they posed a threat to Pakistan's unity. The fact that some 20 per cent of East Pakistanis was Hindu were used to cast aspersions on all East Pakistani demands for autonomy and devolution of power. West Pakistanis also generally, and correctly, believed that East Pakistan had not been central to the Pakistan movement, and more controversially that its Bengali culture was 'Indic' and parochial, since it was not a part of the high culture of North-West Indian Muslim civilization that had supported Muslim rule in India, and had been closely tied to Muslim separatism. During General Ayub Khan's rule (1958–69) these viewpoints were translated into blatant anti-Bengali racism that justified the state's pro-West Pakistan policies. Finally, negotiating over the state with East Pakistan was seen in many quarters in West Pakistan as likely to engender a domino effect, a challenge to the existence of the state because it would encourage more assertive demands for reshaping from other provinces, most notably Sind.[9]

Sind is an important province. On its east it borders with India, and it provided West Pakistan with its only outlet to the sea to the south. Since 1971 it has been Pakistan's second most populous province, and its capital, Karachi—the country's first capital—has been its most populous city and most important commercial centre. Despite its importance to Pakistan, Sind has remained ill-at-ease with its inclusion in the new state. To begin with, the oligarchy in Sind, as in the Punjab, had supported the demand for Pakistan only to augment their power and serve their economic interests. In Sind, however, the rural élite were not as successfully integrated into the ruling order as was the case in Punjab, and as a result, they felt marginalized. The influx of millions of Muhajirs and Baluchis after 1947, Punjabis after 1965, and Pathans after 1979, moreover, made 'sons of the soil' versus migrant disputes central to the province's politics along with demands for autonomy from the centre.

Soon after the creation of Pakistan Muhajirs and Punjabis dominated the new state. The official language became Urdu, the language of the Muhajirs who also occupied a disproportionate number of central and provincial bureaucratic positions. It was therefore not long before Sindhi nationalists, in the Jiye Sind party and among the oligarchy, began to demand greater provincial autonomy, and at times separatism. Sind was then the seat of Pakistan government, where many of the migrants from India and leaders of the Pakistan movement had settled, and the commercial heart of the state. Consequently, Sind's demands for reshaping Pakistan, aired at the same time as those of East Pakistan, placed a great deal of pressure on the state. In particular, defending the rights of 'sons of the soil' before those of migrants implied rejecting the rhetoric of Pakistani and Islamic unity that had formed the basis of the state's foundation.

When it appeared that the politicians at the centre were no longer able to address the question of the relative power of provinces within the existing political framework, the military stepped in in 1958, to subdue East Pakistan and Sind, and to enforce the superiority of the Punjabi–Muhajir alliance by force (Ali 1983: 210–12). The military action undermined the ruling political order, and changed state institutions, and, as such, suggested that the question of borders was in the regime stage. The coup was tantamount to regime recomposition: doing away with democracy and concentrating power at the top to give more flexibility to the state to resist contraction. It initiated a

[9] Tariq Ali argues that the Punjabi and Muhajir ruling alliance was concerned with the possibility of a common cause between East Pakistan and the smaller provinces of West Pakistan (Ali 1983: 47–8).

pattern that would continue to recur in Pakistan. When the negotiability of the state's borders reaches the point of rupture the military and public officials resort to the use of force.[10] As Lustick has predicted, regime recomposition of this sort can galvanize and radicalize the opposition, the result of which can be civil war—see Chapter 3 above. The reactions in East Pakistan and Sind differed, however: a fact that draws attention to intermediate variables that determine the opposition's behaviour in the face of regime recomposition.

The military's action undermined the ideological basis of Pakistan. Between 1947 and 1958 the ruling regime had appealed to Islamic solidarity to keep the country's disparate provinces together and give meaning to the concept of Pakistan. This had led to the incremental 'Islamicization' of national political discourse, and culminated in the 'Islamic' constitution of 1956. The military opposed the greater role of Islam in public life, and in the definition of the state. Once in power, they defined Pakistan as a secular Muslim state, whose existence was justified above all else in socio-economic terms (Nasr 1994: 147–65). Not only would this prove untenable as a basis for Pakistani state- and nation-building, it would serve to underscore the grievances of East Pakistan and Sind.

The Ayub Khan regime sought to end the debate over reshaping the state, and to dissociate that debate from politics. It failed on both counts, for it attempted to do so by asserting the power of the centre—which was in West Pakistan and Punjab—at the cost of East Pakistan and Sind. The suspension of negotiations with East Pakistan and Sind and of efforts to placate the two provinces, which had hitherto occurred through the open political process, translated into blatant disparities in distribution of resources and power between East and West Pakistan, and between Punjab and Sind, pushing both East Pakistan and Sind in the direction of secessionism. The assertiveness of the ruling regime transformed the provinces' demands for reshaping into ones for resizing the state. The ultimate failure of Ayub Khan was that his political agenda did not include a commitment to contracting the state's borders to conform to the ruling regime's power-base in West Pakistan, and even Punjab. He rather sought to assert the merits of a unified Pakistan that his own bias towards West Pakistan, and towards Punjab within it, had effectively undermined. In addition, his industrialization strategy created a new vested interest, exporters and industrialists whose fortunes were tied to the inequitable economic relations between the two wings of Pakistan, and who would complicate state contraction further at the juncture of 1969–71.

---

[10] For a discussion of the paradox of use of force in weak states in Africa see Young and Turner (1985: 405).

Ayub Khan's attempt to alter the basic calculus of Pakistan's politics eventually faltered in 1969, and henceforth, the negotiability of state borders would resurface. But his dictatorship witnessed greater political centralization. This regime recomposition increased the ability of the state to exercise force in contending with ethnic challenges, but failed to defuse or diffuse tensions. In fact, the social and economic policies of the military government increased ethnic grievances, and led to greater political tension and a polarization of the political scene. Economic growth and industrialization favoured Punjab at the cost of the other provinces of West Pakistan, and West Pakistan as a whole at the cost of East Pakistan. The business élite—Punjabis and Muhajirs for the most part—amassed great fortunes, as did senior civil servants and high-ranking members of the armed forces—all dominated by Punjabis—while the middle class and poor, especially in East Pakistan, lost ground. On the eve of the civil war of 1971 twenty-two families, all West Pakistani, controlled 75 per cent of all industrial assets, 80 per cent of banking, and 70 per cent of insurance (ul-Haq 1976: 7–8). Six West Pakistani commercial houses controlled 40 per cent of industries, 32 per cent of industrial production, and 81 per cent of jute exports in East Pakistan (Zaheer 1994: 144). These realities help account for the radicalization of Bengali nationalism, and the popularity of Sheikh Mujibur Rahman and the Awami League's 'six-point' plan for East Pakistan's autonomy.

Partial defeat in the Kashmir war with India in 1965 greatly weakened the Ayub regime, and opened the door for challenges to its authority from various quarters. The Awami League entered the fray by putting forth demands for provincial autonomy that would have transformed Pakistan into a confederation. Each unit would have its own constitution, control over resources and investment expenditures, and they would be loosely tied together. The plan initiated a struggle over the institutions of the state, most notably, its constitution. The plan and the opposition to it would involve serious and violent confrontation.

The 'six-point' plan was placed before the central government at a time when it was under pressure from a pro-democracy movement and from the rise of leftist activism in opposition to its industrialization strategy in West Pakistan. The military regime was unable to formulate a clear strategy for contending with East Pakistan's demands, especially because it had great bearing on ethnic tensions in Sind, which were also on the rise. In Sind too, the Ayub era had strengthened separatism. After West Pakistan became one unit, Sindh nationalist parties, Jiye Sind in particular, concluded that Sind was destined for a secondary status under 'Muhajir-Punjabi imperialism' (Syed, G. 1974). That Karachi, and hence, the Muhajirs benefited greatly from Ayub Khan's industrialization plans, and that Punjabis were given grants of newly irrigated lands in Sind, added to the sense of siege in the province. Nationalists began to demand separation. However, Sind did not have the demographic and geographic advantages of East Pakistan, and was under the sway of the landed élite whose class interests kept them tied to the oligarchy in other provinces and the powers-that-be at the centre. Consequently, in Sind it was not the secessionists that were politically dominant, but Bhutto, one of the province's largest landowners, who championed the cause of Sind within the framework of Pakistani politics.

Why secessionism prevailed in one province and not in the other is critical to understanding the nature of linkages between political interests and the negotiability of borders, on the one hand, and the role of key variables in determining the scope and extent of those negotiations. Throughout the 1960s Jiye Sind demanded the end of the one-unit scheme, and the recognition of Sindhi as an official provincial language. By 1967 Sindhi students had resorted to protest that produced clashes with authorities, and nationalists had raised the banner of secession. Bhutto took note of the growing popularity of the movement. He had witnessed what ethnic posturing had done for the Awami League's popularity in East Pakistan, but understood that separatism would not be successful in Sind. It could, however, serve as a strong bargaining chip with the political centre. Bhutto made the strategic choice of not making common cause with separatists in East Pakistan to maximize gains for Sindhi nationalism, although a Bengali alliance could have reduced the manoeuvrability of the political centre. Although both Bhutto's Pakistan Peoples Party (PPP) and the Awami League were left-of-centre, rooted in local nationalism, and demanded provincial autonomy, Bhutto chose to create an alliance with the political centre against East Pakistan, maximizing his own political interests. That he developed a base of support in Punjab between 1967 and 1971, owing to his populism, was important in this regard because it made his rise to the helm in Pakistan a possibility, and the alliance with the Awami League less attractive.

Through alliances with other Sindhi landlords, Bhutto was able to outmanoeuvre anti-Pakistan Sindhi nationalist parties, and to gain control of Sindhi politics. His gambit marginalized the secessionists in that province, and yet incorporated Sindhi nationalism with his own drive for power at the centre. Between 1967, when Bhutto launched his drive for power, and 1971, when he assumed power, he followed the interesting strategy of running as a national politician in Punjab, and a provincial one in Sind (Amin 1988: 121–2). In Punjab, Bhutto stood as the statesman who had resigned from Ayub Khan's cabinet over the Tashkent agreement of 1966, which marked the end of the Indo-Pakistan war of 1965, and who opposed reshaping the state in favour of East Pakistan. He therefore appealed to the Punjab's apprehensions about the Indian threat and the loss of control to Bengalis. In Punjab, he was, moreover, the champion of the poor. His populism proved resonant in that province, providing the Sindhi oligarch with his political opportunity.

In Sind he appropriated the rhetoric of the separatists favouring some reshaping of the state in favour of Sind but he shied away from anti-Pakistan vitriol. He promised Sindhis a greater share of power in Sind, as well as in the central government, through appropriation of land from non-Sindhis and its redistribution to the 'sons of the soil'; the appointment of Sindhis to high office in the province and at the political centre; and greater redirection of investment from Karachi—where Muhajirs and Punjabis dominated—to interior Sind (Kennedy 1980). Throughout his campaign for power, he championed the Sindhi language, which became an official language of the province in 1973 (Amin 1988: 144–8). The impact was to harness the energies of Sindhi nationalism, but they were encapsulated in his campaign for power.

Unlike Jiye Sind, which was as anti-Punjabi as it was anti-Muhajir, Bhutto focused on the Muhajirs alone. To be a player at the centre he could not be anti-Punjabi, the province in which his party did very well in the 1970 elections. Still, to speak for Sind he had to focus on an ethnic bugbear. The Muhajirs would serve that purpose well. An anti-Muhajir stance would give him Sindhi nationalist credentials without alienating Punjab. In the process he weakened separatist Sindhi parties, and by defining Muhajirs in plainly ethnic terms Bhutto consciously sought to drive a wedge between Muhajirs and Punjabis, who until then had jointly dominated Pakistan's politics, to the advantage of the Sindhis. What he proposed was a Punjabi-Sindhi alliance that would catapult him to power and would marginalize the Muhajirs: Punjab would be guaranteed its supremacy and Sindhis would be placated at the cost of the Muhajirs.

Bhutto conducted a sophisticated game of political brinkmanship, keeping pressure on the state by demanding reshaping in favour of Sind, but opposing any such reshaping in favour of East Pakistan. The consequence was that he institutionalized a new arrangement between the state and Sind. Responding to the different realities that governed the negotiations between the two provinces and the state, he engineered different outcomes just as he served his own position of power. His strategies reveal the variables that were at work and the close linkage between political interests and negotiations over borders.

Bhutto and the Contraction of Pakistan

The rise of ethnic tensions in East Pakistan and Sind, combined with rising socio-economic tensions and opposition to authoritarian rule across Pakistan led to a second regime recomposition in 1969. In that year Ayub Khan handed over power to the Pakistan military under the command of General Yahya Khan (1969–71). The military imposed martial law on Pakistan, but promised elections in short order. The Yahya Khan interlude would prove decisive for Pakistan because it would settle the two most serious negotiations over the state's borders, one through civil war and secession, and the other through the accommodation of Bhutto's political agenda.

The 1970 Election and Its Aftermath

The East Pakistan debacle followed Pakistan's first general elections, held soon after the collapse of Ayub Khan's regime.[11] When Pakistan went to the polls in December 1970 Bengali grievances against the central government were already threatening the unity of the country. Sheikh Mujibur Rahman and the Awami League had mobilized support around their 'six-point' plan, which, in effect, demanded a confederation between the two wings of the country, in which the eastern wing would receive parity and broad autonomy.[12] The elections produced deeply polarizing results in which the Awami League won 160 of the 162 National Assembly seats allocated to East Pakistan—of the total of 300—but won no seats in West Pakistan, whereas Bhutto's PPP won 81 of 138 seats allocated to West Pakistan, and no seats in East Pakistan. The PPP won most of its seats in rural Sind—but not in Karachi where Muhajirs denied Bhutto victory—and Punjab, and also won the provincial assembly elections in the two provinces, but it did poorly in NWFP and Baluchistan. The PPP clearly dominated in West Pakistan's two most important provinces, but could not claim to represent all of West Pakistan, at least not in the manner that the Awami League could in East Pakistan. The election results gave the Awami League an absolute majority in the National Assembly, which would have allowed it to form a government on its own.

Bhutto understood that the polarization between East and West Pakistan, and the greater size of the vote in East Pakistan, meant that if the election

---

[11] Brendan O'Leary and John McGarry have pointed to a strong correlation between sudden democratization and successful secessionism, which holds true in the case of Pakistan as well (O'Leary and McGarry 1995), and see Chapter 2 above.

[12] For the specifics of the 'six-point' plan and their implications see Sisson and Rose (1990: 19–21).

results were to determine the government a West Pakistani politician would not stand a chance of leading the country. He was quite open about the fact that he had no intention of serving as the permanent opposition.[13] Bhutto believed that his victory in Punjab and Sind made him the chief spokesman of West Pakistan, and he was not going to be denied his 'right' to play *a*, if not *the*, central role in the changes that lay ahead—not by the Awami League, and not by the military. In his own words: 'Punjab and Sind are bastions of power in Pakistan. Majority alone does not count in national politics. No government at the centre could be run without the co-operation of the PPP . . . I have the key of the Punjab Assembly in one pocket and that of Sind in the other . . . The rightist press is saying I should sit in the opposition benches. I am not Clement Attlee' (Raza 1997: 44).

He was aware that the West Pakistani power élite were not enthusiastic about handing over power to the Awami League and East Pakistan. The military was wary of the Awami League's ultimate objectives, and the strategic and military implications of the 'six-point' plan. Bengali nationalism had become both more strident and vociferous soon after the Indo-Pakistan war of 1965, leading the military to suspect 'the Indian hand'. The military was also concerned with the 'six-point' plan's impact on its budget. The Awami League was not likely to support spending upwards of 60 per cent of public expenditures on an institution which included no more than a token number of Bengalis, and, for all intents and purposes, was not defending East Pakistan (Raza 1997: 46). The powerful West Pakistani commercial concerns that controlled industrial production and jute export in East Pakistan feared loss of their property and influence if the 'six-point' plan were to be implemented. West Pakistan's industrial producers, who sold half of their products in the captive East Pakistan market, were also unlikely to support either reshaping or resizing. To the contrary, they were likely to push for maintaining the *status quo*. Bhutto manipulated these apprehensions to alter the balance of power to his own advantage, conducting a war of manoeuvre over borders that would help him win an incumbent struggle within the existing Pakistan regime. He successfully depicted his own position to be in concert with the interests of the West Pakistani establishment. His plan of action was predicated on questions of nationalism and negotiability of Pakistan's boundaries. He emphasized that the Awami League's demand for reshaping Pakistan was tantamount to resizing it, which allowed him to assume the patriotic high ground. In essence, he adroitly tied his own political fortunes to perceptions of the Awami League's secessionist aims. In this, Bhutto fol-

---

[13] A strong statement to this effect is cited in Syed, A. (1992: 96); also see Wolpert (1993: 153). Bhutto already saw himself as 'heir to the throne' of Ayub Khan—see Sisson and Rose (1990: 57).

lowed in the footsteps of Randolph Churchill, the Marquess of Salisbury, and Joseph Chamberlain in Britain in the 1880s, and Charles de Gaulle in France before 1958, all of whom used the spectre of contraction to advance their political careers just as they opposed it publicly (Lustick 1993: 149–60, 164–5, 179).

Implicit in Bhutto's position was his role as the spokesman of Sind and Punjab. The elections had presented him with an opportunity to wield power at the centre. So long as that possibility held, he was willing to keep Sindhi nationalism at bay, and Sind would remain content with reshaping. He presented the situation as a zero-sum choice. To allow Bhutto to rise to the helm—that is, mollify Sind—must mean to deny Mujib power—that is, inflame East Pakistan—and vice versa. The generals had to choose between Sind and East Pakistan. A situation in which both could be placated was not an option because East Pakistan's numerical strength would have placed Mujib at the helm. Sind would not make common cause with East Pakistan, and the political centre would not be allowed to accommodate both.

Bhutto may have guessed that, faced with a zero-sum choice, the military would choose Sind, but he left nothing to chance. He downplayed Sindhi nationalism at the height of the crisis, and focused the limelight on East Pakistan. He was so successful in this, that, for instance, West Pakistani commercial interests looked to Bhutto to protect their property from the 'six-point' plan, although Bhutto planned to deal with their interests in Sind and Punjab in like manner. Bhutto crafted his position to reflect the views and goals of those who rejected negotiations with East Pakistan, and accepted Mujib as Prime Minister as a prelude to meaningful talks. His posturing as defender of West Pakistan was overt, while his role as champion of Sind was implicit. The military, therefore saw in Bhutto the opportunity to institutionalize a workable arrangement with Sind, which could be left to Bhutto to control, and to suppress East Pakistan, all in the same breath.

It was important that Bhutto's party had done well in Punjab. This gave the military the sense that he was more than a Sindhi nationalist, and would have incentives to work through the political centre. In addition, Bhutto's base in Punjab, from where the military recruited most of its soldiers, made the PPP and the military tacit allies. Bhutto built on the emerging concordat with the military. He would avoid criticizing the military in his public pronouncements, and went out of his way to point out to the generals that they needed him and the PPP to protect Pakistan. The smaller parties of West Pakistan were too divided and weak to serve as the basis for a viable government. Only the PPP would be able to serve that function (Raza 1997: 20–1, 33).

Bhutto had resigned from Ayub Khan's government in 1966 over the Tashkent agreement. Having depicted the agreement as a sell-out he had assumed the posture of a champion of Pakistani nationalism. He used that stature now to question the fidelity of the Awami League to Pakistan, and to put pressure on the military, which had signed the Tashkent agreement, not to sign another 'sell-out'. In this he claimed to be articulating Punjab's interests, serving as its spokesman as well. Bhutto also argued that, since the Awami League had no following in West Pakistan, it could not possibly claim to represent West Pakistan, and hence, its parliamentary majority notwithstanding, it had to rule in alliance with a West Pakistan party, the PPP to be exact, if it was to rule effectively (Taseer 1979: 118). The Awami League was therefore not a national party, and East Pakistan could not speak for Pakistan as a whole. In essence, Bhutto was asserting that there was no such thing as a Pakistani community, and that East and West Pakistan were separate communities, which had to be represented by their own parties. A parliamentary majority by itself was meaningless unless it gave all communities a share of power. Viewing East and West Pakistan as distinct communities, however, undermined prevalent conceptions of national solidarity and identity, and belied Bhutto's own nationalist stance.

Bhutto's game plan was not to allow the National Assembly to convene, and hence prevent the investiture of an Awami League government. He fought for this tooth and nail, at one point going so far as to threaten to break the legs of any member of his own party who attended the National Assembly, if it were to convene (Zaheer 1994: 147). He would relent only if the Awami League reached an agreement with him before the assembly convened; after that the League could not have been restrained because he believed that once the assembly had convened the League could find other West Pakistan parties to work with (Taseer 1979: 121). The Islamist party, *Jama 'at-i Islami*, had already called on General Yahya Khan to hand over power to the Awami League (Nasr 1994: 168) and the Muslim League and National Awami party (NAP), which questioned Bhutto's right to speak for all of West Pakistan, would in time show willingness to work with the Awami League (see Sisson and Rose 1990: 75; Raza 1997: 48; and Salim 1996: 125–48).

The Awami League saw the acceptance of its status as a national party as essential to any future for East Pakistan in Pakistan, and insisted that it had no reason to bargain with PPP when it had a parliamentary majority. To emphasize that his demand was not purely self-serving, Bhutto asserted that without any West Pakistan voice at the helm, the Awami League would produce a new constitution on the basis of the 'six-point' plan that would end Pakistan as a state (Sisson and Rose 1990: 67). By assuming an extreme nationalist position, and casting aspersions on the Awami League, he made it harder for any other party, the military included, to deal with the League.

In essence, here, Bhutto was not negotiating over borders himself, but by depicting the Awami League to be doing so, he was hoping to speak for

Pakistan. He was trying to reverse the calculus of power and the negotiability of borders by turning it into a liability for the Awami League. He was also conducting a war of manoeuvre to prevent the notion of Muslim solidarity providing a viable basis for keeping East and West Pakistan together within the framework of the existing regime. His success in this regard in large measure accounts for the East Pakistan debacle of 1971. His strategy went a long way to prevent public debate over reshaping by depicting the Awami League as unpatriotic, even though his own stance was premised on negotiability of borders, in Sind as well as in East Pakistan. For instance, at the height of the crisis, he would secretly offer Mujib that if he became the Prime Minister of East Pakistan, and Bhutto that of West Pakistan, that they would leave each other alone, a *de facto* contraction of the state from its eastern wing (Zaheer 1994: 157). Championing Pakistani nationalism while in practice manipulating the cleavages that prevented it from integrating all Pakistanis, would thenceforth become a hallmark of West Pakistani politics, and a primary cause of the state's continual struggle to consolidate.

With the PPP and Awami League at an impasse the military sought to resolve the crisis. Bhutto again took no chances. He put pressure on the military not to deal with the Awami League, and to make the opening of the National Assembly conditional on an agreement between PPP and the Awami League. He expressed concern that Yahya Khan had not fully understood the implications of the 'six-point' plan (Raza 1997: 46), hoping to drive a wedge between Yahya Khan and more intransigent elements in the military, just as he presented himself as more concerned with the interests of West Pakistan and better able to defend those interests than the generals. As Yahya Khan prepared to mediate the crisis Bhutto hinted to the military that if the need arose he could make ruling West Pakistan difficult for them. On one occasion, at a public rally, he declared, 'If you are going to talk about Bangla Desh we can talk about Sindh Desh and Punjab Desh' (cited in Wolpert 1993: 150). He was reiterating that the choice between him and Mujib was zero-sum: a choice between Sind and East Pakistan. The allusion to 'Punjab Desh' was to remind the military that he had support in Punjab, and could create problems for the military in its own backyard. Speaking for Punjab, he explained that, even if the military was willing to accept the 'six-point' plan, Punjab was not (Raza 1997: 46); and if need be he would advocate the cause of Punjab before the military, itself a largely Punjabi force.

Bhutto's intransigence appealed to hawkish elements in the military (Sisson and Rose 1990: 77; and see also Choudhury 1974: 190–3). Meetings in late January 1971 between Bhutto and the top command of the military are reputed to have formalized a plan of action, although to the end Bhutto remained wary of a deal between Yahya Khan and Mujib (Raza 1997: 72–3).

By February Yahya Khan had backed away from accommodating Mujib, and was contemplating military action. In all this, Bhutto provided the military with an excuse to postpone the opening of the parliament, and articulated a position that many in the military would have liked to follow, but could not have done without strong popular support. Bhutto provided a political cover for the military's rejection of the 'six-point' plan; it became Bhutto's rejection rather than the military's; and this provided a legitimate pretext for dealing with East Pakistan. Bhutto played a central role in the successful war of manoeuvre that was unfolding. That success, however, was but a battle in a larger war of position that had already begun, and that Bhutto would eventually lose.

Once the convergence of interests between Bhutto and hard-line generals became a tacit alliance, Yahya Khan announced that the opening of the National Assembly would be postponed. Immediately before Yahya Khan's announcement, Mujib had offered the military a compromise plan, which would have turned Pakistan *de facto* into a confederation, but would have left the final shape of the state to future negotiations between the two wings. This, Mujib hoped, would allow the National Assembly to convene. Yahya Khan referred the offer to Bhutto, who rejected it (Raza 1997: 74–81). The leadership of the PPP, which had been asked to respond to Mujib's offer, added that military action in East Pakistan was both necessary and unavoidable (Raza 1997: 78). Bhutto now openly sanctioned military action in place of compromise. He had got his way, and in the process had helped the military move from its initial toying with accommodation and mediation toward an uncompromising position.

Mujib therefore came out of the negotiations empty-handed: the National Assembly was not convened, and he got no concessions on his proposals. The Awami League now assumed an outright secessionist posture, and the generals soon turned East Pakistan into a blood bath. The result would be the permanent loss of that province. Bhutto stuck to his plan of action throughout the civil war and the repression to prevent a resolution that would keep him out of power. He continued to claim to represent West Pakistan, and to threaten the military when he deemed it necessary (Zaheer 1994: 322–52). Consequently, Bhutto's hold over West Pakistan was confirmed—his ascent to the top was now a reality. His success in this regard, and the consequences that it had for Pakistan, shed light on the dynamics of politics in a non-institutionalized state.

Bhutto's approach could be compared to that of de Gaulle in France during the Algerian crisis.[14] Bhutto like de Gaulle understood the advantages of

---

[14] On de Gaulle see Lustick (1993: 257–86).

rapid and total withdrawal from a disputed territory, and of sparing the state a protracted and agonizing security and political crisis. Like de Gaulle, Bhutto had a political agenda, and like de Gaulle before 1958, Bhutto avoided open debate over contraction, and indeed resorted to surreptitious manoeuvrings to force East Pakistan to out itself. However, there is a difference: while de Gaulle ultimately encouraged France to quit Algeria, Bhutto tacitly encouraged East Pakistan to quit Pakistan. Consequently Bhutto did not emerge out of contraction with the same stature, as did de Gaulle.

The Awami League had all along accused Bhutto of doing the bidding of the military, a charge that he was forced to deny on a number of occasions (Wolpert 1993: 149). Others accused him of deliberately pushing East Pakistan out in order to rise to the top.[15] Bhutto's words, '*idhar hum, udhar tum*' (we here, you there) (Wolpert 1993: 146), were widely interpreted to mean that East Pakistan should go its own way (Kasuri 1988). His extreme nationalist stance was seen by others as a calculated strategy to oblige the Awami League to choose secessionism—see Choudhury (1974: 162–3), Mahmood (1984), and Quraishi (1972). That he never opened a public debate about contraction, but relied on the civil war to realize that end, and that the loss of East Pakistan was closely tied to his rise to power, tainted his motives, denied him any benefit of the doubt or credit for his foresight, and eventually compromised his public appeal.

Bhutto was never able to rise above these charges. His ability to act as a national political leader from this point on was compromised. That he had also supported Sindhi demands added to his predicament. It took the full force of the heads of Muslim countries who met for the Islamic Summit in Lahore in 1974 to allow him to overcome opposition to Pakistan's recognition of Bangladesh (Nasr 1994: 180–2). Through his years in office he was accused by his detractors of having sold-out Pakistan for personal gain. Popular beliefs that he had always had an Indian passport, or that his ambitions may have led him to sell-out Pakistan to India, although baseless, are nevertheless significant in what they reveal of his political image. In the final analysis, Bhutto won the war of manoeuvre that assured his rise to the helm in 1971, but ultimately lost the war of position to his own detriment.

The circumstances of Bhutto's rise to power had a direct bearing on what he was able to achieve in office. Pakistan's most important leader since Jinnah, its first democratically elected Prime Minister, and the man who ushered in the most ambitious social programme to date, never left the shadow of the East Pakistan debacle. The extent of damage to Bhutto was such that his daughter's tenure of office too, was affected by it. During her two terms of

---

[15] For a discussion of these charges see Syed, A. (1992: 91–2).

office—1988–90 and 1993–6—Benazir Bhutto was greatly restricted in her handling of ethnic tensions in Sind, and in Pakistan's relations with India. She was forced to adopt more intransigent stances on the Kashmir crisis than was necessary just to rise above the suspicions engendered by her father's legacy.

That legacy has been important in deciding Sind's politics and relations with the political centre after 1971. Bhutto succeeded in institutionalizing an arrangement between Sind and Pakistan, one which has kept Sind under the control of the moderate spokesmen of Sindhi nationalism, who have a stake in Pakistani politics, and as a result have stabilized relations between the province and the political centre. The arrangement did not, however, end negotiations over power and borders between Sind and the political centre. Bhutto's enterprising use of ethnic tensions in Sind in 1969–71, which came to be known as the 'Sind card', became an integral part of political wrangling in the province and at the centre. The centre would feel compelled to continue to deal with Sind in the manner Bhutto had, lest separatism once again gain the upper hand. He was succeeded by three Sindhi Prime Ministers seriatim—Muhammad Khan Junejo (1985–8), Benazir Bhutto (1988–90), and Ghulam Mustafa Jotoi (1990). General Zia ul-Haq (1977–88)—Bhutto's nemesis—retained the pro-Sindhi policies introduced by Bhutto, and in 1983 expanded the scope of quotas that benefited Sindhis in government recruitment (Amin 1988: 176–7).

Bhutto's gambit had failed to remove the negotiability of borders from the political arena. That failure would eventually produce instability. Not only does the spectre of separatism continue to dominate Sind's politics, but also Sind's arrangement with the political centre encourages others to emulate Bhutto's strategy. This has been seen most dramatically in the case of the Muhajirs, who have articulated an ethnic identity and put forth demands for autonomy to rival those of the Sindhis. What appeared as a stable arrangement with Sindhis from 1971 onwards, has since the mid-1980s led to the emergence of mutually exclusive rival claims in that province. Bhutto's strategy may have been fruitful for him and fecund for Sind, but it never resolved the tensions in Sind—rather it fed on them and aggravated them. The festering of ethnic tensions inevitably infested the political process and spilled to other quarters. Bhutto's 'arrangements' escalated tensions between Muhajirs and Sindhis, put greater long-run pressures on the political centre, and aided in the decline in law and order in the province.

Why There Were Different Outcomes in East Pakistan and Sind

Throughout the first two decades of Pakistan's existence, East Pakistan and Sind placed similar demands for autonomy and the redistribution of resources before the state. By the late 1960s the Awami League in East Pakistan and Jiye Sind had both raised the spectre of separatism. But negotiations over borders in East Pakistan led to civil war and secessionism, whereas the centre accommodated Sind—although it did not completely resolve the tensions between Sind and the political centre. This chapter has argued that the political manoeuvrings of Bhutto, and the manner in which he tied the fate of East Pakistan to that of Sind, and then to his own rise to power, explains why contraction occurred in one case, but such a possibility never presented itself in the other. Still, above and beyond Bhutto's strategies there were other intermediate variables at work. These variables, independently as well as in conjunction with Bhutto's manoeuvres, account for the different outcomes in East Pakistan and Sind.

There is little doubt that demography and geography mattered. Whereas East Pakistanis constituted the majority of the population—55 per cent in 1971—in unified Pakistan, Sindhis came third after Punjabis. East Pakistan was separated from the political centre by the breadth of India, while Sind abuts Punjab, and is smaller than the Punjab landmass. Sind provides West Pakistan with its only access to the sea, and as such is of critical economic and strategic value to Punjab;[16] East Pakistan had no such direct value for West Pakistan. Karachi has been the premier commercial, and until recently, industrial centre of Pakistan; East Pakistan's urban and commercial centres did not have the same status. These factors explain the relative bargaining positions of each province, the extent of their manoeuvrability in negotiating over borders, and the kind of responses that they were likely to elicit from the political centre. Sind was less likely to mount a successful separatist movement, but was more likely to be accommodated by the centre. The centre in turn was more confident of suppressing a separatist movement in Sind, but given Sind's economic importance, was also more likely to avoid such a course of action in favour of some accommodation of ethnic demands.

Sindhi nationalism's manoeuvrability was also greatly compromised by the large Muhajir, Punjabi and Baluch—and later Pathan—communities that have predominated in the urban centres of Sind. The migrants are

---

[16] Whenever the question of separatism in Sind arises Punjabis suggest creating a corridor to the Arabian Sea for Punjab.

concentrated in Sind's largest cities, especially Karachi.[17] In Karachi, the provincial capital, Sindhis constitute only the fifth largest community, and in Sind's second biggest city, Hyderabad, they come second after the Muhajirs (Kennedy 1984: 939). In rural Sind, by contrast, Sindhis constitute 82 per cent of the population. The migrant communities have close ties with their provinces of origin, and would have resisted, and in the future will resist secession by Sind. The concentration of migrants in urban centres means that in case of secession, Sind will have to fight to include its main urban centres.[18] Bhutto understood that a Sindhi state was not a realistic or even desirable possibility. Working with the state and within its institutions was the best course of action for Sindhis.

The migrant community in East Pakistan, by contrast, was far smaller in total numbers and as a percentage of East Pakistan's population. With the exception of the few West Pakistani families who were active in commerce and industry, non-Bengalis were not economically or politically significant. The migrant community was neither able to stymie Bengali nationalism in East Pakistan nor effectively resist state contraction. The exception was the handful of wealthy families who did pressure the military to fight separatism.

There was a great difference in the roles that Bhutto and Mujib played in relating local nationalism to politics at the centre. Bhutto was eager to address ethnic issues within the institutional framework of the state. In this he was closer to Suhrawardi than Mujib, who had challenged the institutional frameworks of the state in order to address ethnic grievances. State leaders were willing to accept Bhutto's gambit, but had refused to do so earlier with Suhrawardi. That refusal had radicalized East Pakistani nationalism. Accepting Bhutto's initiative would prevent Sind from traversing the same course. The Punjabi power élite was willing to engage with Bhutto because he posed as a Pakistani patriot, even when he advocated the cause of Sind. Bhutto was able to create a strategic alliance with forces at the centre that opposed East Pakistani secessionism. This alliance included him in the ruling regime, and eventually made him its pivot, despite his ties to Sindhi nationalism. The political centre needed Bhutto to contend with Mujib, and it needed Sind to contend with East Pakistan. Although Sind never posed costs and risks to Pakistan comparable to that posed by East Pakistan, its

[17] According to the census of 1981—the last census taken—the population of Sind was 19.3 million, of whom 10.6 million (55.7%) were indigenous Sindhis—current estimates, however, place the number of Muhajirs at parity with Sindhis. The number of Muhajirs stood at 4.6 million, of whom 3.3 million lived in Karachi. There were also 2 million Punjabis, 1.1 million Baluchis, and 700,000 Pathans, again mostly in Karachi.

[18] When in the 1980s Muhajir nationalism called for a separate Muhajir province, Sindhis had to rely on the political centre to keep Sind intact.

manoeuvrings *vis-à-vis* the state were a source of concern, and as such featured in the power élite's evaluation of its options. Serious turmoil in Sind, especially demands for secession there, would have made a military campaign in East Pakistan unlikely. The military would not have been able to contend with two serious separatist movements at once, least of all because it would not have been able to protect both provinces from Indian intervention. The state would likely have responded more effectively to a Sindhi demand for secession had it ever been put forward. Indeed, had Sind demanded separatism, it is conceivable that the political centre would have quickly contracted out of East Pakistan to crack down on Sind. Bhutto understood this. To him, making common cause with East Pakistan would only help East Pakistani separatism. Helping the centre crack down on East Pakistan would help him and Sind.

Class interests too, tied Bhutto to the centre. Sindhi nationalism was strong among the Sindhi oligarchy, peasants, and middle classes. Sindhi landlords, however, had always relied on central authority—British as well as Pakistani—to keep feudalism in place. These class interests and linkages tied the Sindhi, Baluch, and Punjabi oligarchy together, limiting the scope of local nationalisms. The Awami League in East Pakistan, by contrast, was largely middle class and peasant based, and Mujib was not a member of the oligarchy. Class interests did not tie the spokesmen of Bengali nationalism to the oligarchy in West Pakistan, nor was there a need for state power to enforce feudal rights. Lastly, the military believed that Bhutto could govern (West) Pakistan, but that Mujib could not. By posing as champion of West Pakistani rights, Bhutto had already shown that he could easily rise above Sindhi nationalism, and that his base in Punjab had given him a strong incentive to do so. Mujib would have lost his hold over East Pakistani nationalists had he chosen such a course of action.

Bhutto understood both the potential, and more importantly, the limits of Sindhi nationalism. Once this was clear, he mounted a strategy that would keep Sindhi nationalism in check as he negotiated pay-offs for Sind's neutrality and his own support for the centre. It was his belief that this strategy would more realistically serve Sind's interests, and his own political ambitions. In the process he crafted an intricate strategy of placating his constituency in Sind while assuring the centre of his fidelity to the existing state institutions and ruling regime. He then created alliances with those who objected to either accommodating East Pakistan or contracting out of it. The alliance opened the door to power at the centre for Bhutto, and helped push East Pakistan out.

The Legacy of Dismemberment

The 1969–71 period was traumatic for Pakistan. The two years of struggle ended with a humiliating defeat in a war with India, and the state's failure to thwart Bengali separatism. The outcome would in time, however, strengthen the hold of the West Pakistani ruling political establishment. The crisis would not, however, altogether end the problematic of the negotiability of borders. Continued ethnic tensions, in Baluchistan, NWFP, and especially Sind, would time and again threaten the state with further contraction. The 1969–71 period did not involve an open debate about contraction. Discussions between Bhutto, Mujib, and Yahya Khan occurred behind closed doors, and publicly Pakistan's leaders presented contraction as unimaginable. Yet, East Pakistan became Bangladesh, and eventually Pakistan managed to recognize it.[19]

This reality has led to some discussion among intellectuals about the state's borders. The crux of the discussion has focused on whether contraction is imaginable—in the language of Lustick, it has been over whether Pakistan is at the ideological hegemony stage or not. The answer here is critical, because it will form the basis for any future discussion of contraction. There have emerged two camps in this debate.[20] The first are the Islamists and the right-of-centre intellectuals, who write in Urdu, and are read by lower middle classes; and the second are the secular intellectuals, who write for the most part in English, and are read by the upper classes and the modern segments of the middle classes. The former is closely tied to the Muhajir community, which has for most of Pakistan's history opposed the secession of Sind. The latter is more sensitive to the demands of the country's many ethnic groups, which have often been couched in leftist rhetoric.

The Islamists and right-of-centre intellectuals have since early in the country's history been a part of the project of Pakistan. They depict Pakistan as an Islamic entity, the embodiment of Islamic universalism and brotherhood. In this view, state borders are inviolable; for, anything short of that would question the universality of Islam, the faith, and truth that supersedes all other allegiances in the mind of the faithful. Questioning Pakistan's borders is therefore nothing short of infidelity to Islam. In the works of authors like Muhammad Salahuddin, Altaf Hasan Quraishi, or Siraj Munir, the secession of East Pakistan is explained as a consequence of Indian machina-

[19] Pakistan is contemplating apologizing to Bangladesh for atrocities committed by Pakistan military in 1971 (*Dawn* (Karachi), 28 January 1998).

[20] In Jordan also, two 'publics' are evident in the discussions about severing of ties with the West Bank—see Marc Lynch's analysis in Chapter 11.

tions, and the failures of un-Islamic and self-serving leaders.[21] Their arguments are directed at reinforcing the belief that change in the borders of the 'Islamic state' is unimaginable.

Secular intellectuals on the other hand, have raised the possibility of changes in existing borders. They have underscored the plurality of the Pakistan state, its lack of internal unity, the weak institutionalization of its borders, and the lack of a hegemonic notion of the state, or indeed nation. The Marxist thinker, Tariq Ali, author of *Can Pakistan Survive? The Death of A State*, initiated the discussion here by posing two questions: was it necessary for Pakistan to have been created at all, and will it survive? Arguing that Pakistan was the consequence of British colonial policy, and that it served the interests of the oligarchy, he concludes that there was no (national liberationist) reason that Pakistan should have been created. He then concludes that, since Pakistan has become merely a framework for wielding power by the military and the bureaucratic élite in alliance with the oligarchy and industrial interests, it lacks a *raison d'être*, *and* that it is unlikely to develop one. Ali's argument opens the door to questioning the state entirely—its future, and hence, its borders. A state lacking in a hegemonic notion of statehood or nationhood, and guilty of exploitation, will likely revisit the 1969–71 period (Ali 1983). The historian, Ayesha Jalal, echoes the same scepticism about the idea of Pakistan. She contends that Pakistan is merely a 'conjured' idea with no roots in history, and only tenuous appeal amongst key ethnic groups such as the Pathans (Jalal 1995). She argues that efforts to create a viable 'myth' for Pakistan have so far failed, leaving open questions about the need for the state's creation and its future survival. These works do not address the theory of contraction directly, but question the assumptions about Pakistan's borders and their inviolability that undergird the Islamist and right-of-centre writings, and which formed the basis of state action in East Pakistan. Furthermore, they highlight the reality and possible implications of the non-institutionalized character of the Pakistan state.

An alternative approach among secular intellectuals is to provide the state with a new way of thinking about itself and its borders. Aitzaz Ahsan, a lawyer and PPP leader, has argued that Pakistan was built on the foundation of the Indus basin civilization, and is to be distinguished from the civilizational forces that formed the rest of South Asia (Ahsan 1996). Ahsan's approach acknowledges the failure to date of Islam to glue the disparate units of Pakistan together. The Indus valley myth is not only an alternative path to providing Pakistan with a hegemonic notion of the state, its nation, and its

---

[21] Salahuddin and Munir have written on this issue extensively over the years in the popular weekly, *Takbir* of Karachi; Quraishi's views have appeared in editorials in his popular *Urdu Digest*.

territory, but it is one that is secular. It has the added advantage of explaining why East Pakistan was not meant to be a part of Pakistan, but why Sind is. Ahsan therefore does not question Pakistan's viability, but justifies why it had to be down-sized in 1971. It can be inferred from his line of argument that any part of Pakistan that can be shown not to belong to the Indus basin civilization is a candidate for down-sizing.

The direction of the intellectual debates over the future of Pakistan, and the possibilities for new hegemonic projects that they portend, point to the central dilemma of Pakistan; namely that the issue is not the contraction of a previously institutionalized core out of a territory that it had conquered at some later point in time, but the possible termination of the state itself. In a state that is comprised of disparate units and has no institutionalized core, contraction inevitably involves the question of state survival. Debates about contraction in Pakistan perforce revolve around the foundational myth of the state. To date, such a discussion has not produced the basis for a definition of the state that would remove the negotiability of borders from its politics. Ayub Khan, Bhutto, and later Zia ul-Haq (1977–88), failed to institutionalize Pakistan—or perhaps, given the historical legacy and political reality they faced, they could not have done so. The legacy of the partition of India, the socio-political pacts that formed the state, and the heart-stroke of 1971, combined with the ethnically plural and non-institutionalized character of the state, to entrench the negotiability of its borders.. Pakistan is a special species of polity: in permanent instability, permanently negotiable.

REFERENCES

Ahsan, Aitzaz. 1996. *The Indus Saga and the Making of Pakistan*. Karachi: Oxford University Press.

Ali, Tariq. 1983. *Can Pakistan Survive? The Death of a State*. New York, NY: Verso.

Amin, Tahir. 1988. *Ethno-National Movements in Pakistan: Domestic and International Factors*. Islamabad: Institute of Policy Studies.

Aziz, Kursheed Kamal. 1967. *The Making of Pakistan: A Study in Nationalism*. London: Chatto & Windus.

Barlas, Astma. 1995. *Democracy, Nationalism, and Communalism: The Colonial Legacy in South Asia*. Boulder, CO: Westview Press.

Binder, Leonard. 1961. *Religion and Politics in Pakistan*. Berkeley, CA: University of California Press.

Choudhury, Golam Wahed. 1974. *The Last Days of United Pakistan*. Bloomington, IN: Indiana University Press.

Jahan, Rounaq. 1972. *Pakistan: Failure in National Integration*. New York, NY: Columbia University Press.

Jalal, Ayesha. 1995. 'Conjuring Pakistan: History as Official Imagining', *International Journal of Middle East Studies*, 27: 73–89.

Kasuri, Ahmad Reza. 1988. *Idhar Hum, Udhar Tum (We Here, You There)*. Lahore: Britannica Publishing House.

Kennedy, Charles H. 1980. 'Analysis of Lateral Recruitment Program to the Federal Bureaucracy of Pakistan, 1973–79', *Journal of South Asian and Middle Eastern Studies*, 3: 42–65.

—— 1984. 'Policies of Ethnic Preference in Pakistan', *Asian Survey*, 24, 16: 688–703.

Koelble, Thomas. 1995. 'The New Institutionalism in Political Science and Sociology', *Comparative Politics*, 27: 231–43.

Lustick, Ian. 1993. *Unsettled States, Disputed Lands: Britain and Ireland, France and Algeria, Israel and the West-Bank-Gaza*, New York, NY: Cornell University Press.

Mahmood, Safdar. 1984. *Pakistan Divided*. Lahore: Ferozsons.

Migdal, Joel. 1988. *Strong States and Weak Societies*. Princeton, NJ: Princeton University Press.

—— Kohli, Atul, and Shue, Vivienne, (eds.) 1994. *State Power and Social Forces*. New York, NY: Cambridge University Press.

Moore, R. J. 1988. *Endgames of Empire: Studies in Britain's Indian Problem*. Delhi: Oxford University Press.

Nasr, Seyyed Vali Reza. 1994. *The Vanguard of Islamic Revolution: The Jama'at-i Islami of Pakistan*. Berkeley, CA: University of California Press.

—— 1995. 'Communalism and Fundamentalism: A Re-Examination of the Origins of Islamic Fundamentalism', *Contention*, 4: 123–5.

—— 1997. 'State, Society and the Crisis of National Identity in Pakistan', 103–30 in *State, Society and Democratic Change in Pakistan*, edited by Rasul B. Rais. New York, NY, and Karachi: Oxford University Press.

Oldenburg, Philip. 1985. 'A Place Insufficiently Imagined: Language, Belief, and the Pakistan Crisis of 1971', *Journal of Asian Studies*, 44: 715–23.

O'Leary, Brendan and McGarry, John. 1995. 'Regulating Nations and Ethnic Communities', 245–89 in *Nationalism and Rationality*, edited by Albert Breton, Gianluigi Galeotti, Pierre Salmon, and Ronald Wintrobe. Cambridge: Cambridge University Press.

Quraishi, Altaf Hasan. 1972. 'Suqut-i Dhaka Parda Utha Hey (Curtain Lifts From the Fall of Dhaka)', *Urdu Digest*: 22–40.

Raza, Rafi, 1997. *Zulfikar Ali Bhutto and Pakistan, 1967–1977*. Karachi: Oxford University Press.

Salim, Ahmad. 1996. *Yahya, Mujib, Bhutto Muzakarat ki Andaruni Kahani (The Inside Story of Yahya, Mujib, Bhutto's Negotiations)*. Lahore: Gora Publishers.

Samad, Yunas. 1995. *A Nation in Turmoil: Nationalism and Ethnicity in Pakistan, 1937–1958*. New Delhi: Sage Publications.

Sayeed, Khalid B. 1968. *Pakistan: The Formative Phase, 1857–1948*. London: Oxford University Press.

Singh, Gurharpal. 1997. 'The Partition of India as State Contraction: Some

Unspoken Assumptions', *Journal of Commonwealth and Comparative Politics*, 35: 51–66.

Sisson, Richard, and Rose, Leo E. 1990. *War and Secession: Pakistan, India, and the Creation of Bangladesh*. Berkeley, CA: University of California Press.

Syed, Anwar H. 1982. *Pakistan: Islam, Politics, and National Solidarity*. New York, NY: Praeger.

—— 1992. *The Discourse and Politics of Zulfikar Ali Bhutto*. New York, NY: St. Martin's Press.

Syed, G. M. 1974. *A Nation in Chains*. Karachi.

Taseer, Salmaan. 1979. *Bhutto: A Political Biography*. London: Ithaca Press.

ul-Haq, Mahbub. 1976. *The Poverty Curtain: Choices for the Third World*. New York, NY: Columbia University Press.

Wolpert, Stanley. 1993. *Zulfi Bhutto of Pakistan*. New York, NY: Oxford University Press.

Young, Crawford, and Turner, Thomas. 1985. *The Rise and Decline of the Zairian State*. Madison, WI: Wisconsin University Press.

Zaheer, Hasan. 1994. *The Separation of East Pakistan: The Rise and Realization of Bengali Muslim Nationalism*. Karachi: Oxford University Press.

7

Reifying Boundaries, Fetishizing the Nation: Soviet Legacies and Élite Legitimacy in the Post-Soviet States

Alexander J. Motyl

When the Union of Soviet Socialist Republics (USSR) officially ceased to exist in late 1991, the internal borders of one state automatically became the external borders of fifteen. As all of the newly independent entities had enjoyed the formal status of 'Soviet socialist republics' the USSR's demise compelled the élites in charge of former administrative units to transform them into coherent political organizations with the capacity to administer territories, tax their populations, regulate economies, monopolize violence, and engage in foreign relations. In view of the *leitmotif* of this book—the institutional connection between states, borders, and their peoples—the fact that post-Soviet state-building should have affected, and should have been affected by, the discourse of post-Soviet borders and nations is no surprise. That this discourse should have acquired two peculiar features—the reification of borders by non-Russian élites and the fetishization of the nation by Russian élites—perhaps is.

The Problem

No state borders are natural, of course, and all are, as Ian Lustick suggests, usefully conceptualized as 'institutional features of state' (Lustick 1993: 38; see also Chandler 1998: 15–28). And yet, the boundaries of the USSR's successor states, which, revealingly, are termed 'transparent' by Russians and non-Russians alike, seem especially unnatural. Like most state borders, they are not coterminous with the nations that claim them. Unlike many state borders, however, post-Soviet borders, as the products of Soviet administrative and not planning priorities, fail even to encompass integrated economic spaces. And inasmuch as most of the successor states lack developed state apparatuses—that is, coherent, complex, and institutionalized Weberian organizations—it is not clear that their so-called borders are institutionalized features of any kind of entity. Arguably, the boundaries are just lines, and not borders, as there is little in the way of distinct entities on both sides for the borders to separate.[1]

As awkward amalgams of diverse ethnic groups, as collections of unconnected economic assets, and as politically formless agglomerations of offices and office-holders, most post-Soviet polities might make eminently more sense if they were, to use Lustick's term, 'right-sized'.[2] Indeed, one would expect the option to be the subject of at least some debate, if only because one form of right-sizing, namely 'down-sizing,' or the contraction of boundaries, is not irredentist, and hence not intrinsically destabilizing, while the obstacles to down-sizing should be least formidable in the aftermath of systemic collapse, when behaviours, attitudes, and institutions are fluid and, presumably, more receptive to change. Instead, only Alyaksandr Lukashenka, the mercurial dictator of Belarus, seems to have embraced the logic of voluntary down-sizing. But the extent even of his commitment is unclear, as Lukashenka insists on both a union of Belarus with Russia and the continued retention by both of complete sovereignty—a squaring of the circle that suggests that economic assistance and not political merger is uppermost in his calculations.

For all the other successor states down-sizing is, surprisingly, not an issue. Russian élites preferred destroying Chechnya and committing genocide to withdrawing from an insignificant corner of the former empire. Estonians refuse to consider the possibility that Estonia might be a more efficient and secure nation-state without the troublesome Russian north-east. Ukrainian élites are especially silent about their eastern provinces in the Donbas—a polluted rust belt that serves as the stronghold of anti-reform Communists and is home to a large portion of Ukraine's least loyal, ethnically Russian and Russian-speaking population. Down-sizing is considered even less of an option with regard to the Crimea, the economically impoverished autonomous peninsula claimed by some Russian policy-makers in Moscow, periodically pushed toward independence by indigenous Russophones, and targeted for mass in-migration by Crimean Tatars with destabilizing nationalist agendas—see *inter alia* Starovoitova 1995: 1, 3–4, 7; Taagepera 1993: 223–4; Bukkvoll 1997: 25–60; and AAAS Program on Science and International Security 1995.

---

[1] On the ephemeral nature of post-Soviet states see Motyl (1995).
[2] For a similar point see Chirot (1995: 49).

While down-sizing is on virtually no one's discursive agenda, another form of right-sizing, namely 'up-sizing', the expansion of boundaries or, to use a more traditional term, irredentism, is not. Some Estonians demand that Russia cede territory granted to Estonia by the Treaty of Tartu; Lithuanian nationalists claim Kaliningrad province, currently Russian and formerly Prussian, as historically theirs; Armenians have declared and established by force of arms a mini-state in Karabakh; Tajiks point to parts of Uzbekistan (Baranovsky 1994); see also Harris (1993). Such claims are not surprising in the aftermath of imperial collapse and the unsettled nature of all resultant entities. But what is surprising is that up-sizing has achieved hegemonic status only in Russia. It is only among Russian élites that irredentist language and logic have become entrenched, insistent, and sustained. In this spirit, Russian élites have invented a 'near abroad' populated with Russians and Russian speakers ostensibly languishing under non-Russian rule and pining for a return to the bosom of Mother Russia. North-eastern Estonia, the urban parts of Latvia, much of Belarus, eastern Ukraine and the Crimea, the Trans-Dniester region of Moldova, and northern Kazakhstan are the repeated targets of Russian rhetoric.[3]

Especially striking is the fact that virtually all Russian élites fetishize the Russian nation. Vladimir Zhirinovsky's openly irredentist views typify the extreme right; Gennady Zyuganov's enthusiastic endorsement of Russian patriotism and great-power status is typical of the Communists (Zhirinovskii 1993; Zyuganov 1994). Most importantly, even the mainstream shares this *Weltanschauung*. A programmatic document signed by forty-four of Russia's leading foreign affairs analysts—and ominously entitled 'Will the Union Be Reborn?'—proposes nothing less than a blueprint for integrating most of the former Soviet republics, and Ukraine in particular, in the next ten to fifteen years. The document endorses the construction of a 'genuine federal union of states', while claiming that the 'strategic goal' of integration is 'the economic, political, and spiritual rebirth and rise of Russia', that integration presupposes Russian 'leadership' and that 'all means, including violent ones' may be used in the defence of Russia's 'vital interests' which include 'preventing large-scale forcible violations of the human and national rights' of the Russians living in the near abroad and 'safeguarding the tightest political, economic, and military-political union with Belarus, Kazakhstan, and Kirgizia' (Council on Foreign and Defence Policy 1996: 4–5). Additionally, the document recommends that Russia strive for an economic union among the countries of the Commonwealth of Independent

---

[3] Russian views of the diaspora in the non-Russian republics are discussed in Tolz (1998); Brubaker (1996: 135–45) and Shenfield (1996).

States (NIS), the joint defence of external boundaries, military co-operation, the unity of the civil, legal, informational, and cultural space, a legal basis for the defence of the interests of Russians and emigrants from Russia in the NIS countries, 'real' assistance to the Russian diasporas, the re-establishment of a unified Russian-language television and radio space in the NIS countries, and a system of collective security (ibid: 5). There is no evidence to suggest that the views of the mainstream—or of the extremes—have changed since the document's appearance in May 1996.

Why should down-sizing not be on most élites' discursive agendas, and why should up-sizing dominate Russia's agenda? Why should non-Russian élites reify their borders and Russian élites fetishize their nation? These hegemonic discourses arguably are a product of the different ways in which Soviet legacies, systemic pathologies, and the élite quest for legitimacy have interacted in post-Soviet circumstances. In particular, my argument consists of the following points.

First, Soviet republics were both administrative units and ideologically sanctioned national homelands that provided non-Russian communist élites with power-bases and legitimacy during the USSR's existence and, even more so, at the time of its disintegration in the late 1980s. Because the Russian Soviet Federated Socialist Republic (RSFSR) lacked a comparable institutional and ideological status, Russian communist élites had no ideologically legitimized base to fall back on. Instead, the source of their power and, especially, of their legitimacy turned out to be the Russian nation, which had enjoyed a privileged institutional and ideological status within the USSR.

Second, the legacy of totalitarianism and empire largely determined the course of systemic change in the Soviet successor states. Saddled with fragments of Soviet institutions, and incapable of constructing new ones, most non-Russian polities quickly evolved into agglomerations of competing élites. Only the Baltic states, which escaped the Great Terror and enjoyed a special status throughout Brezhnev's rule as laboratories for experiments involving economic and political decentralization, were partial exceptions to this and some of the other generalizations I shall make (Misiunas and Taagepera, 1983). Russia, in contrast, emerged from collapse with a top-heavy state apparatus that frustrated the revolutionary aspirations of the Yeltsinites, and evolved into an archipelago of coherent political-economic cartels. Both trajectories resulted in a variety of pathologies that confounded expectations of smooth transitions to democracy, capitalism, rule of law, and civil society.

Third, these systemic deformations compelled élites to search for alternative sources of legitimacy. Non-Russian élites developed a cult of statehood that, in the absence of functioning states, boiled down to a glorification of their former status as symbolically sovereign republics and, hence, to a reification of the former republican borders that gave their polities coherence. Incapable of glorifying the post-imperial state apparatus they had shattered or the Russian republic Soviet ideology never fully embraced, Russian élites sought legitimacy by fetishizing the Russian nation. As the primary sources of élite legitimacy, reification and fetishization attained hegemonic status in the political discourses of the post-Soviet polities. In turn, their hegemony limited the kinds of state-building strategies that could be pursued and influenced the kinds of relations that Russia and its neighbours could enjoy.

Soviet Republics

The fifteen polities that succeeded the Soviet Union had all had the status of national republics within the Soviet state. As such, the republics were administrative subunits that also served as the ethnic homelands of the USSR's largest nations and nationalities: the Russians, Ukrainians, Belarussians, Moldavians, Uzbeks, Kazakhs, Kyrgyz, Turkmen, Tajiks, Armenians, Azeris, Georgians, Latvians, Lithuanians, and Estonians. Endowed with flags, hymns, constitutions, capital cities, and other symbolic accoutrements of sovereignty—and with two, the Ukrainian and Belorussian SSRs, seated in the United Nations General Assembly since 1945—the republics stood at the top of the USSR's homeland pyramid. National regions and districts were located at the bottom, while autonomous republics, such as the Yakut, Tatar, and Bashkir Autonomous SSRs (ASSRs), occupied the middle (Hazard 1971).

The position of the RSFSR was anomalous. On the one hand, as the home of central Soviet institutions and the homeland of the Russians, it was in a class of its own. On the other hand, it was also, for that very same reason, something of a residual category. The RSFSR was defined almost negatively, as that part of the Soviet system that had not been placed expressly in the hands of the non-Russians. As the core of the Soviet system, the RSFSR therefore lacked distinctly Russian counterparts to the political, economic, and cultural institutions that the non-Russian republics took for granted—Allworth (1980); Wimbush (1978).

As befitted the boundaries of administrative units, republican borders, as well as the status of some republics, were subject to over two hundred, almost routine, alterations between 1921 and 1980. Most changes involved minor border adjustments; some were substantial. For instance, the Karelian ASSR was created in 1923, upgraded to the Karelo-Finnish SSR in 1940, and then demoted to the Karelian ASSR in 1956. The Moldavian ASSR was formed on the left bank of the Dniester River, as part of Ukraine, in 1924, only to be merged with a full-fledged Moldavian SSR located on territories annexed from Romania in 1940. The Ukrainian SSR was expanded to include formerly Polish provinces annexed by Stalin in 1939–1940 and then, in 1954, was bequeathed the Crimea by Khrushchev. The territory of the later Kazakh SSR went through especially complex permutations involving several name changes as well as transfers and acquisitions of territory (Oliker 1990).

Like the borders themselves, however, these changes were hardly arbitrary. The claim that republican borders were completely 'artificial' rests on the unfounded assumption that non-Soviet borders or borders in general are not, and that the lack of perfect fit between nation and republic is proof of artificiality. The related claim, that Moscow purposefully drew borders solely in order to confound national aspirations and divide nations, is also exaggerated, as Soviet élites spent an inordinate amount of time and energy attempting to align their Stalinist notions of nations with the administrative units supposed to represent them. In the 1920s and 1930s, for instance, Soviet policy-makers, together with legions of demographers and ethnographers, essentially created most of the Central Asian nationalities, going to great pains to categorize them according to appropriate linguistic and ethnic criteria (Kaiser 1994).[4] That such policies were also motivated by political considerations involving the fear of Muslim solidarity goes without saying (Bennigsen and Wimbush 1979); that attempts were made to divide and rule by creating divisions between and among nations and encouraging local élites to compete for scarce resources is also obviously true. We would expect nothing less from Stalin and his successors—or, for that matter, from all policy-makers familiar with gerrymandering.

Soviet Ideology

Official Communist ideology reflected the Janus-faced nature of the republics as both administrative units and homelands. On the one hand, the ideology emphasized that all of the USSR's nationalities had finally found fulfilment and liberation in the Communist motherland. The so-called 'nationality question' had been solved, 'finally and conclusively', by the Communist Party, which enabled the non-Russian nations to attain both national sovereignty and international harmony through the republics. In

---

[4] For a dissenting view, see Connor (1984: 300–2). In my judgement Connor provides little evidence of egregious gerrymandering. See also Brubaker (1996: 26–40).

addition, as class exploitation had been abolished and the state had been transformed into the possession of the 'entire people', the conditions for untrammelled ethnic amity and thoroughgoing national development had been created. Indeed, the Soviet peoples ostensibly enjoyed such harmonious relations with one another that they were increasingly described as 'drawing together' to the point that a 'fusion' or 'merger' was taking place and a new 'international community of peoples, the Soviet people', was in the process of emerging—see Motyl (1987: 71–87); Barghoorn (1956, 1986); Szporluk (1994: 1–9). Although Western specialists tended to ridicule such notions in the 1970s and 1980s, it is ironic to note that, as the continued vitality of a distinctly Soviet political culture and mentality indicates, the 'Soviet people' was not just a figment of Soviet propagandists' overzealous imaginations—see Kljamkin and Kutkowez (1998); Hrytsak (1995: 1, 3, 5, 7); Solovei (1997: 346–58); Simon (1991); and Lewytzkyj (1993).

On the other hand, the ideology, like the republics, contained a dimension that served an imperial purpose. Although all of the nations were equal, one nation—the Russians—enjoyed an exalted status as *primus inter pares*. The Russians had established the Soviet Union, formed the core of the proletarian vanguard, and given birth to the great Lenin. The Russians were the 'elder brother' within the 'family of Soviet peoples', gently guiding their less fortunate siblings along the path of communism and national liberation. The language and culture of the Russians necessarily enjoyed exceptional status within the Union, serving as the vehicles of 'inter-nationality communication' and the 'keys to the treasure-house of world culture' (Motyl 1990: 161–73).

Notwithstanding the ideology's enthronement of Russians and things Russian, it also gave the non-Russians substantial room for manoeuvre. They were, to be sure, second-rank nations, but their élites could rightfully claim, within Soviet limits, what the ideology said was theirs: sovereignty, self-determination, a language, and a culture. In this regard, both the republics and the ideology created sufficient space for the promotion, in appropriate circumstances, of republican interests.

Republican Interests

Such an institutional and ideological arrangement had several long-term consequences. First, despite Moscow's persistent efforts to eliminate what was known as 'localism' and 'bourgeois nationalism,' republican leaders wellnigh inevitably developed loyalties to their bailiwicks. These loyalties were rarely affective, usually reflecting the commonality of interests shared by élites in administratively bounded regions. In a word, local patriotism was a systemic symptom and not just a by-product of nationalism.

Second, the republics came to serve as the institutional vehicles for the development of national identities, generally promoted by, and frequently restricted to, the local artistic and literary intelligentsias whose officially mandated task was to develop culture in a manner corresponding to the dictum, 'national in form, socialist in content'. Unions of writers, artists, journalists, cinematographers, and other 'labourers of culture' were given the resources and possessed the prestige to champion the Soviet national identities placed in their care.

Third, although the intelligentsias, or, more specifically, the dissidents they spawned, often were in conflict with local power-holders, their interests overlapped during periods of decentralization. When central policy-makers enhanced the authority of republican satraps, forging informal alliances with local cultural élites was a convenient means of consolidating their power. Whenever centralization was reintroduced and Moscow reimposed control over its errant republican élites, so too, they reimposed control over their errant republican intelligentsias. Crackdowns on cadres generally coincided with crackdowns on local dissidents (ibid: 87–8, 158–60).

Last but not least, because the official ideology offered them a variety of discursive devices that, while system-supportive, could be used to promote republican ends, both the political and the cultural élites consciously used it to justify their pursuit of local, if not quite national or nationalist, interests. Ivan Dziuba's classic critique of Soviet nationality policy, *Internationalism or Russification?*, was entirely in this vein, claiming that Leonid Brezhnev's policy deviated from true Leninist norms and, hence, should be revised (Dzyuba 1974).

Non-Russian élites thus derived their legitimacy from two, potentially competing, sources. First, as representatives of the Communist Party of the Soviet Union (CPSU), they claimed, with some degree of persuasiveness, to be forging a new, more humane, more effective kind of human community that guaranteed the well-being and security of its inhabitants. Second, as the lords of republican bailiwicks, they claimed to be protectors of their republics' interests and promoters of the indigenous nations' development. These sources were complementary when Soviet rule was more or less effective and decentralization was minimal. When authority decayed or devolved to the republics, however, and the interests of the Union and the interests of the republics began to diverge, reconciling these legitimations became more difficult (Motyl 1990: 59–86). And, of course, when Soviet power began to disintegrate in the mid-to-late 1980s, Soviet-base legitimacy proved increasingly undesirable, and republican élites wrapped themselves in the cloaks of national symbolism.

Russian Communist élites also jumped on the republican bandwagon in the final years of perestroika, with Boris Yeltsin deliberately using the RSFSR as a power-base for his struggle with Mikhail Gorbachev. In particular, the RSFSR's declaration of sovereignty in mid-1989 was an ideologically legitimate way for a republican élite to advance its own interests against the central authorities. But whereas non-Russian élites could use the national dimension of republican status and the Soviet ideology to make the case explicitly for independence, Russian élites quickly came up against an ideological barrier. After all, the ideology sanctified the non-Russian republics within the confines of the ostensibly internationalist Soviet Union, an entity that, it acknowledged, reserved pride of place for Russians and things Russian. There was, however, no place for a Russian state in the ideology and, hence, no ideologically justifiable ways of promoting its interests as a state in general and as an independent state in particular. As the presumption was that the entire Soviet space was Russian, the ideology could not offer much solace to Russian state-builders. It did, however, offer another source of legitimacy—the Russian nation.

Soviet Legacies

Conceptualizing the Soviet political system as both imperial and totalitarian is a useful point of departure. The USSR was an empire in that a Russian 'core'—not, I stress, a Russian state, but a set of authoritative institutions dominated by Russians—exerted dictatorial control over the non-Russian 'peripheries'. Centralized Russian-led organizations ruled both the RSFSR and the republics, while non-Russian organizations vertically dependent on the centre only administered them. In addition, the non-Russian republics, like all peripheries in all empires, interacted with one another politically and economically through the imperial core, which channelled resources and information from the periphery to the core and back to the periphery. Although all of the formally sovereign Soviet republics possessed the defining characteristics of imperial appendages fully comparable with the colonial holdings of other historical empires,[5] there was variation within this seemingly uniform landscape. Ukrainians and Belarussians were granted entry into core institutions; Estonians, Latvians, and Lithuanians enjoyed greatest autonomy within their own republics; Central Asians possessed least.

[5] According to Michael Doyle, 'Empire . . . is a relationship, formal or informal, in which one state controls the effective political sovereignty of another political society' (Doyle 1986: 45). For a more elaborate conceptual discussion, see Motyl (1999).

While empire defined the structure of core-periphery relations, totalitarianism referred to the breadth and depth of state rule. The Party-state exercised virtually total, if inefficiently maintained, horizontal and vertical control over public life (Sartori 1993). Autonomous social, economic, political, and cultural institutions did not exist, except, in incipient form, in the underground. Only the private sphere remained free of state control, as it usually does even in totalitarian systems, unless élites implement policies of terror.[6] The central state's reach was a function of the all-pervasiveness of the Communist Party. The Party's central organs in Moscow ruled both the empire and the totalitarian state; its non-Russian branches supervised the economy, polity, and society at the level of the republics; while its local units penetrated all non-state institutions on the ground. Not surprisingly, the Party justified its dominance with an elaborate ideology that legitimated imperial and totalitarian rule.

Although outwardly alike, Russia and the non-Russian republics were actually quite different at the point of the USSR's collapse. All had been victimized by totalitarianism and therefore lacked the autonomous institutions characteristic of civil society, a market economy, rule of law, democracy, and an independent culture. But Russia inherited both the bulk of the Soviet state—in particular, the central ministries, the army, and the secret police—and the legacy of the Soviet core's national domination. To put the contrast in especially stark, but not inaccurate, terms: with the partial exception of the Balts, non-Russian republics emerged from Soviet collapse without *bona fide* state apparatuses and the skilled élites that go with them, without civil societies, without markets, without democracy and rule of law, without genuinely autonomous cultures and, hence, without mass modern national identities. Russia had a state apparatus, albeit one that was top-heavy and fragmented, as well as the skilled élites to man it, and it possessed a sense of cultural superiority and historical destiny that underpinned both nationhood and empire (Motyl 1997). As I show below, these starting points significantly affected subsequent systemic political trajectories, as well as the discourse of borders.

The Non-Russian Polities

The primary consequence of their status as imperial peripheries was that none of the non-Russian polities inherited effective state apparatuses. Their bureaucracies were shapeless; their ministries were either undermanned or

---

[6] Totalitarianism, in my understanding, refers to the structure of the state. Terror and, hence, state intrusion into the private sphere is a policy that totalitarian élites frequently, but not necessarily, pursue (Motyl 1992: 302–14).

non-existent; and their policy-making and policy-implementing cadres, trained to receive orders vertically, from Moscow, lacked the institutional ties that are a prerequisite of functioning states and effective élites. As state apparatuses, together with militaries, police forces, border guards, and the like, are the necessary conditions of security and survival, the most pressing 'transitional' issue facing the non-Russian élites had to be state-building. A state was the precondition of intermediate goals such as democracy and the market. As clusters of institutions and not merely sets of participatory attitudes and entrepreneurial dispositions, democracy and the market require a rule-governed political base, an effective administrative apparatus and a working government, in order to be viable (Holmes 1995: 77–8; 1996).[7]

But state-building proved extraordinarily difficult in post-totalitarian, post-imperial circumstances, even more so as élites understandably hoped, in defiance of Western historical experience, to construct states without engaging in war.[8] Although all the proto-élites that came to power in the republics were committed to establishing authority, acquiring power, and extending their political reach into the provinces, the malfunctioning economic and political systems they inherited effectively undermined their efforts. With the breakdown of central planning, formerly integrated parts of the Soviet economy fell into the hands of enterprise managers. And with the break-up of the CPSU and the absence of developed party systems, the Party's former republican branches retained much of their influence at all levels of the polity and society. The upshot was the emergence of a particularly resilient political-economic amalgam consisting of powerful managers, old-boy networks, and former Communist *apparatchiks* who, like some of their counterparts in post-colonial Africa and Asia, resisted the centralization of political power and the creation of an effective state.[9]

In turn, the institutional shapelessness of the non-Russian states precluded the development of genuine democratic institutions and encouraged presidential authoritarianism. In the absence of governmental institutions able to enforce rules of the game, the field was open for clan-like groupings of power-holders to seize control of the emerging polities. Democratic rhetoric notwithstanding, genuine democracy could not really take hold, as the *klany*—the terminology, significantly, is local—were usually strong enough to mould emerging democratic institutions to their own ends. By the same token, presidents could accumulate enormous powers by virtue of the fact that parliaments were too undisciplined to balance them effectively.

[7] For one-dimensional definitions of democracy, see Mueller (1996); and see Roeder (1997).

[8] Charles Tilly makes this argument (Tilly 1990/92).

[9] For an overview of these trends, see Karatnycky, Motyl, and Shor (1997). See also Chapter 6 in this volume by Vali Nasr.

Presidents had every incentive to bypass parliament and to form alliances with the power-brokers who ran local fiefdoms and had a stake in the continuation of dilapidated systems that permitted them to live off the polity, economy, and society as comfortable parasites (Easter 1997).

These developments left their greatest mark on the economy and economic reform. Centrally generated laws and decrees had little impact outside capital cities, and more often than not, in the capitals as well. privatization proceeded far more slowly and dysfunctionally than envisioned, because regional bosses either resisted it or exploited it as a means of legally appropriating the assets they already controlled. The scope for crime and corruption was enormous, as local mafiosi with immense resources and influential connections grabbed economic assets and forged alliances with political bosses and regional clans (Goodman 1997). Rudimentary, demoralized, disorganized, and underfunded militaries, militias, and former secret police forces proved incapable of coping with such systemic malfeasance, while frequently transferring their coercive pre-eminence and control of scarce resources into the unrestrained pursuit of self-enrichment.

Under such conditions, non-Russian élites perforce emphasized, even fetishized, state-building for several mutually reinforcing reasons. First, as effective states were the guarantors of élite rule and the preconditions of reform, state-building logically had to be, as indeed it became, a priority. Second, state-building was about the only success, however partial, to which élites could point. Although internally states were anything but Weberian political organizations, externally all had been recognized by the international community, all had acquired seats in a variety of international organizations, and all could boast of the symbolic accoutrements of genuine sovereignty. Third, the other major source of modern élite legitimacy, a pervasive, genuinely popular sense of nationhood, was simply not available to many non-Russian élites. Native culture, native language, and ethnic roots had some intrinsic appeal to local populations, but that was limited, as many non-Russians had been thoroughly sovietized, and had poorly defined notions of who they were.[10] To make matters worse, neither a weak state, nor an enervated economy could promote feelings of national solidarity or pride.

Presidents quickly realized they could draw legitimacy from their association with the state and, more important, from their commitment to statehood. Several examples nicely illustrate the semiotics of their efforts. A lavishly illustrated coffee-table book about Kazakhstan's president, Nursultan Nazarbaev, depicts him as an august state-builder and smiling

---

[10] David D. Laitin provides a wealth of supportive evidence of the tentativeness of Russian and non-Russian national identities (Laitin 1998).

pater familias equally at home in the capitals of the world and in the wheat fields of his domain (Nazarbayev 1995). A collection of Leonid Kravchuk's writings presents him as Ukraine's elder statesman and man of the people (Kravchuk 1992). Cynics might suggest that the photogenic Eduard Shevardnadze purposefully defended the integrity of Georgia by rallying his troops with gun visibly in hand only because foreign photographers were present. Turkmenistan's President, Saparmurad Niyazov, has gone furthest and constructed a veritable 'cult of the personality'.

A 'cult of statehood' thus became enthroned within the official discourse of most non-Russian élites. But the discursive limitations of such a cult soon became apparent. As non-Russian statehood was a 'statehood without a state,' a fragile political condition derived from the status of republics within the USSR and aggravated by the post-Soviet process of reform and non-reform, grounding legitimacy in the republics-turned-states was tantamount to grounding it in nothing more substantial than their symbolic sovereignty. And, as the 'institutionalized feature' of the symbolic sovereignty of Soviet republics was, above all, their boundedness as administrative units, the cult of post-Soviet statehood easily translated into a reification of the boundaries that alone gave the state-to-be political meaning.

The Russian State

In contrast to the non-Russian polities, which inherited fragments of Soviet institutions, Russia acquired the (fragmenting) imperial-totalitarian Soviet state apparatus centred in Moscow, the lion's share of the military, and the core of the former secret police. Although bereft of their peripheral outposts, these core institutions survived more or less intact into the post-Soviet era and fundamentally structured the politics of systemic change in the Russian Federation.

The radical style that propelled Yeltsin to power—assaulting the Soviet Party-state bureaucracy and defining himself as the reformer Gorbachev failed to be—continued as his *raison d'être* into post-Soviet times. Yeltsin's political survival depended on his building democracy, rule of law, civil society, and the market, simultaneously and rapidly, a strategy that amounted to nothing less than attempted revolution.[11] Contrary to Yeltsin's expectations, such a project could not succeed in Russia. Safely ensconced in their positions of authority and wealth, state bureaucrats were either indifferent or hostile to a revolutionary transformation from above, while the state

---

[11] For a typical revolutionary argument, see Sachs (1994). I discuss these issues in Motyl (1994).

apparatus was too strong and the Russian masses too impoverished and disorganized to permit revolution from below. As the minimal necessary conditions of revolution were absent, revolutionary shock therapy perforce failed, and was abandoned by late 1993 (Nelson and Kuzes 1995).

The attempt at revolution did leave its mark, however, both on the state and on the trajectory of change. Two major consequences were democratic deinstitutionalization and political polarization. Yeltsin's push for radical reform necessarily placed him on a collision course with the conservative Supreme Soviet. The armed assault on the parliament building in October 1993 destroyed the emerging institutional balance between the Presidency and the Parliament, with the result that the President subsequently emerged, and was constitutionally enshrined, as the dominant, if not quite fully dictatorial, player in the political arena. In addition, the destruction of the conservative opposition enervated the political centre, while invigorating the extremes—see Reddaway (1993); Rutland (1997); Lynch (1997); Eckstein *et al.* (1998).

The failure of the revolutionaries to capture the state, together with the Presidency's war against the Parliament, also shattered the linkages between and among state institutions and, thus, undermined the President's ability to co-ordinate and direct disparate state agencies. These, in turn, evolved into fortress-like bastions of strategically situated state élites in control of vast public resources. Under conditions such as these, the incipient market could easily be captured by 'comrade criminals' who formed *de facto* alliances with enormously wealthy 'robber barons' and shady financial institutions (Handelman 1994). In contrast to most non-Russian states, therefore, which came under the sway of formless amalgams of bureaucrats in cahoots with clans and criminals, Russia was carved up by élite cartels that, from their base in state institutions and state-controlled enterprises, could lay claim to political-economic spaces within which their interests and authority were paramount (Shevtsova and Bruckner 1997).

Fetishizing the state and its existing boundaries was not an option for Russian élites. The RSFSR was too much of a residual post-imperial category to command much loyalty. More importantly, élite policies—and not, as in the non-Russian states, the legacies of Soviet collapse—had directly contributed to weakening the state apparatus Russia had inherited. Consequently, the élites who had undermined the state were in no position to use it as a source of legitimacy, while the fragmented state they had created could not generate other sources, such as the rule of law, democracy, or prosperity. The humiliated nation was virtually all that remained, especially as a robust imperial ideology targeted it as the source of legitimacy for élites without legitimacy. Perhaps irresistibly, Russian élites were propelled toward championing the Russian nation and, willy-nilly, toward promoting up-sizing.

By mid-to-late 1992, almost all Russian élites adopted the language and logic of Russian greatness, historical destiny, and geopolitical primacy sanctioned by an ideological heritage that had enthroned Russians and things Russian within the former USSR—see Alexandrova (1995: 324–5); Brudny (1998: 259–65); and see also Tolz (1998) and Tismaneau (1998). Discursive neo-imperialism served three mutually supportive ends. First, because of deinstitutionalization, élites could forge a consensus of sorts by accepting a neo-imperial language that established minimal rules of the game for all political agents. Second, the ideology of the imperial nation helped breach some of the élite polarization that Yeltsin's revolutionary assault had created. And third, the language and logic of the fetishized nation provided all élites with a potent source of legitimacy amidst the ruins of post-Soviet Russia.

The neo-imperial discourse adopted by Russian élites necessarily transformed diaspora populations into irredenta longing for inclusion in the nation. As the former core defined itself as a homeland in relation to an irredenta, so, too, the abandoned brethren became, and frequently came to see themselves as, an oppressed minority, as an irredenta longing for return to the homeland—see also Brubaker (1996: 55–9). In turn, Russian policy-makers and publicists developed elaborate schemes for protecting the rights of their 'blood relatives' in the near abroad. The necessity, desirability, and inevitability of some form of 'integration', as a means of simultaneously promoting Russia's strategic interests and defending the abandoned brethren, became a central theme of Russian political discourse.

Internal Consequences

While discourses cannot be conceived as causes of particular effects, and irredentist discourses certainly need not result in irredentist behaviour, they can narrow the range of outcomes considered possible as well as desirable by policy-makers. The two discursive tendencies described above place limits on the ways that state-building can be pursued in post-Soviet polities. In the non-Russian case, the reification of borders has excluded from the realm of respectable political discourse the very possibility of selective, partial, and strategically motivated down-sizing, which, in contrast to the Pandora's Box of irredentism, could conceivably promote the stability and security of states.

The case for down-sizing may be especially compelling for Ukraine, which, other things being equal, would be better off without two of its eastern provinces, Luhansk and Donetsk. Their populations are largely Russian or Russified. Public opinion polls show that they are the least supportive of Ukrainian independence and most supportive of union with Russia (Bakirov and Kushnarev 1996: 202–9). The anti-reform Communist Party of Ukraine has its stronghold in both provinces. Their industrial base consists of hopelessly outdated plants, factories, and coal mines that are an enormous economic drain on Kyiv's ragged resources. The level of pollution in both regions, and thus of health problems, is among the highest in the world. And yet, down-sizing cannot be broached in Kyiv, or, for that matter, in Almaty or Tallinn, where virtually identical conditions hold in northern Kazakhstan and north-eastern Estonia.

The reification of borders has also promoted unitary states. Untouchable borders imply an indivisible national body politic that excludes federal administrative set-ups from serious consideration.[12] Given the enormous regional diversity of many of these polities and the weakness of their central state apparatuses, not only might federalism be an appropriate response to their economic and political challenges, but the pursuit of strong unitary or 'vertical rule' could very well be chimerical. In this sense, Moscow's grant of substantial authority to its regions was at least partly facilitated by the fact that the state's borders are not an élite fetish in Russia.[13]

On the positive side, the reification of borders may have affected the kind of nation-building policies adopted in the non-Russian polities. Inasmuch as borders are inviolable, expanding or contracting them to achieve a closer match between the indigenous nation and its state is discursively impossible. Consequently, the non-Russian élites may have no choice but to live with multinational populations and, perhaps, even to adopt policies inclined toward more inclusive notions of nationhood and citizenship. In turn, such policies will necessarily affect élite recruitment and cadre promotion and, thus, the character of the state apparatus.

In the case of Russia, the fetishization of the nation has come to serve as the lowest common denominator of competing Russian élites. Such a consensus means that the élites running the cartels and the two least democratic of the former Soviet Union's institutions, the army and the secret police, are bound by little more than the discourse of Russian national primacy. While this combination of factors, namely cartellized state institutions, a strong if humiliated army and secret police, and a virtually authoritarian President united by messianic visions of the Russian national mission, may not demonstrably be a non-democratic recipe, they surely fail to facilitate democracy.

---

[12] The Ukrainian Volodymyr Hryn'ov has analysed federalism in Hryn'ov (1995).
[13] Granting regional autonomy has, as I have stressed, roots in Soviet discourse and policy—see Brubaker (1996) and Connor (1984).

Indeed, such combinations are most often associated with bureaucratic authoritarian and/or military rule.

National fetishization could also place Moscow on a collision course with its own non-Russian autonomous republics, which, since the break-up of 1991, have amassed substantial authority over their finances and natural resources. The Soviet Union was able to reconcile Russian rule with non-Russian governance by subsuming both under the aegis of Soviet power and communism. Russia does not, at least not yet, possess an overarching formula that could satisfactorily combine non-Russian autonomy with Russian nationalism. Such a formula may perhaps be found, but the existing neo-imperial discourse will surely be an obstacle to its development (Treisman 1997; Walker 1996). The second war in Chechnya could be a harbinger of things to come.

Conclusion

In sum, two conflicting discourses confront each other in the Soviet successor states. In Russia, up-sizing has come to dominate the political agenda, as imperial collapse and its institutional and ideological legacies have transformed nationhood and the national underpinnings of the state into the central components of élite legitimacy. In the non-Russian polities, down-sizing is not even contemplated, having been transformed into a taboo by a cult of statehood and the reification of state boundaries.

Over time, this contradiction may diminish. If and when national identities and regimes are consolidated, borders may, as Lustick suggests, be open to change. And if and when states, nations, economies, and societies are stabilized, borders need not be the only source of élite legitimacy. For better or for worse, however, as long as the reluctance to consider down-sizing is a function of the Russian insistence on up-sizing, of the fact that the nation is the primary source of legitimacy in Russia, down-sizing will continue to be a non-issue in the non-Russian states.

Down-sizing is unlikely to cross over the 'ideological hegemony threshold' in the non-Russian polities until up-sizing leaves the same threshold in Russia (Lustick 1993). But the second eventuality is unlikely anytime soon for two reasons. First, the degree of élite unanimity is so striking as to suggest a rather longer shelf-life. Second, Russian concern for abandoned brethren in the non-Russian states is also a function of the non-Russian refusal to countenance down-sizing. With such a vicious circle in place, we may expect the tension between down-sizing and up-sizing to continue for some time to come.

The likelihood of continued ideological contestation has important implications. It is hard to imagine a genuine normalization of Russian-non-Russian relations as long as Russians talk of up-sizing and non-Russians refuse to talk of down-sizing. Regardless of who is right and who is wrong, such discursive incompatibility will sow mistrust, as Russians view non-Russians as stubbornly insensitive to the plight of their brethren, and non-Russians see Russians as imperialists and land-grabbers masquerading as defenders of human rights. In turn, the non-normalization of Russian-non-Russian relations could reinforce the discursive practices of both sides, and promote greater efforts to build strong unitary, vertical rule in the non-Russian states and to chip away at the autonomy of the non-Russian autonomous republics within Russia. In these circumstances, democracy is unlikely to flourish, demagogues are likely to emerge, and the potential for violent conflict is likely to grow.

REFERENCES

AAAS Program on Science and International Security. 1995. *Developments in Crimea: Challenges for Ukraine and Implications for Regional Security*, Washington, DC: American Association for the Advancement of Science Program on Science and International Security Directorate of International Programs.

Alexandrova, Olga. 1995. 'Russland und sein "nahes Ausland"', in *Zwischen Krise und Konsolidierung*, edited by Hans-Hermann Höhmann. Munich: Carl Hanser Verlag.

Allworth, Edward, (ed.) 1980. *Ethnic Russia in the USSR*. New York, NY: Pergamon.

Aslund, Anders. 1995. *How Russia Became a Market Economy*. Washington, DC: Brookings Institution.

Bakirov, V. S., and Kushnarev, E. P. (eds.) 1996. *Gorod i gosudarstvo*. Kharkiv: Fort.

Baranovsky, Vladimir. 1994. 'Conflict Developments on the Territory of the Former Soviet Union', 169–203 in *SIPRI Yearbook*, edited by the Stockholm International Peace Research Institute. Stockholm: SIPRI.

Barghoorn, Frederick C. 1956. *Soviet Russian Nationalism*. New York, NY: Oxford University Press.

—— 1986. 'Russian Nationalism and Soviet Politics', 30–77 in *The Last Empire*, edited by Robert Conquest. Stanford, CA: Hoover Institution Press.

Bennigsen, Alexandre, and Wimbush, S. Enders. 1979. *Muslim National Communism in the Soviet Union*. Chicago, IL: Chicago University Press.

Brubaker, Rogers. 1996. *Nationalism Reframed: Nationhood and the National Question in the New Europe*. Cambridge: Cambridge University Press.

Brudny, Yitzhak M. 1998. *Reinventing Russia: Russian Nationalism and the Soviet State, 1953–1991*. Cambridge, MA: Harvard University Press.

Bukkvoll, Tor. 1997. *Ukraine and European Security*. London: Royal Institute of International Affairs.

Chandler, Andrea. 1998. *Institutions of Isolation. Border Controls in the Soviet Union and Its Successor States 1917–1993*. Montreal and Kingston: McGill-Queen's University Press.

Chirot, Daniel. 1995. 'National Liberations and Nationalist Nightmares: The Consequences of the End of Empires in the Twentieth Century', 43–68 in *Markets, States, and Democracy*, edited by Beverly Crawford. Boulder, CO: Westview.

Connor, Walker. 1984. *The National Question in Marxist-Leninist Theory and Strategy*. Princeton, NJ: Princeton University Press.

Council on Foreign and Defence Policy. 1996. 'Vozroditsia li soiuz?', *Nezavisimaia gazeta—Stsenarii*, 23 May.

Doyle, Michael W. 1986. *Empires*. Ithaca, NY, and London: Cornell University Press.

Dzyuba, Ivan. 1974. *Internationalism or Russification?* New York, NY: Monad Press.

Easter, Gerald M. 1997. 'Preference for Presidentialism: Postcommunist Regime Change in Russia and the NIS', *World Politics*, 49: 184–211.

Eckstein, Harry *et al*. 1998. *Can Democracy Take Root in Post-Soviet Russia?* Lanham, MD: Rowman & Littlefield.

Goodman, Andrew. 1997. 'Organized Crime and Corruption in Russia and the NIS: A Framework for Comparative Analysis', *Second Annual Convention of the Association for the Study of Nationalities*, Columbia University, New York.

Handelman, Stephen. 1994. *Comrade Criminal*. London: Michael Joseph.

Harris, Chauncy D. 1993. 'Ethnic Tensions in Areas of the Russian Diaspora', *Post-Soviet Geography*, 34: 233–8.

Hazard, John N. 1971. 'Statutory Recognition of Nationality Differences in the USSR', 83–116 in *Soviet Nationality Problems*, edited by Edward Allworth. New York, NY: Columbia University Press.

Holmes, Stephen. 1995. 'Conceptions of Democracy in the Draft Constitutions of Post-Communist Countries', 71–81 in *Markets, States and Democracy: The Political Economy of Postcommunist Transformation*, edited by Beverly Crawford. Boulder, CO: Westview.

—— 1996. 'Cultural Legacies or State Collapse? Probing the Postcommunist Dilemma', 22–76 in *Postcommunism: Four Perspectives*, edited by Michael Mandelbaum. New York, NY: Council on Foreign Relations.

Hryn'ov, Volodymyr. 1995. *Nova Ukraina: iakoiu ia ii bachu*. Kyiv: Abrys.

Hrytsak, Yaroslav. 1995. 'Shifting Identities in Western and Eastern Ukraine', *The East and Central Europe Program Bulletin*, 5.

Kaiser, Robert. 1994. *The Geography of Nationalism in Russia and the Soviet Union*. Princeton, NJ: Princeton University Press.

Karatnycky, Adrian, Motyl, Alexander J., and Shor, Boris. 1997. *Nations in Transit, 1997: Civil Society, Democracy and Markets in East Central Europe and the Newly Independent States*. New Brunswick, NJ: Transaction Publishers.

Kljamkin, Igor, and Kutkowez, Tatjana. 1998. 'Der postsowjetische "Privat-mensch" auf dem Weg zu liberalen Werten', 96–106 in *Das neue Russland in Politik und Kultur*, edited by Wolfgang Eichwede. Bremen: Edition Temmen.

Kravchuk, Leonid. 1992. *Ie taka derzhava—Ukraina*. Kiev: Hlobus.

Laitin, David. 1998. *Identity in Formation. The Russian-Speaking Populations in the Near Abroad*. Ithaca, NY: Cornell University Press.

Lewytzkyj, Borys. 1993. *Sovetskij narod—Das Sowjetvolk*. Hamburg: Hoffmann und Campe.

Lustick, Ian. 1993. *Unsettled States, Disputed Lands: Britain and Ireland, France and Algeria, Israel and the West-Bank-Gaza*. New York, NY: Cornell University Press.

Lynch, Allen C. 1997. *Does Russia Have a Democratic Future?* New York, NY: Foreign Policy Association.

Misiunas, Romauld J., and Taagepera, Rein. 1983. *The Baltic States, Years of Dependence, 1940–1980*. Berkeley, CA: University of California Press.

Motyl, Alexander J. 1987. *Will the non-Russians Rebel? State, Ethnicity and Stability in the USSR*. Ithaca, NY: Cornell University Press.

—— 1990. *Sovietology, Rationality, Nationality: Coming to Grips with Nationalism in the USSR*. New York, NY: Columbia University Press.

—— 1992. *The Post Soviet Nations: Perspectives on the Demise of the USSR*. New York, NY: Columbia University Press.

—— 1994. 'Reform, Transition, or Revolution', *Contention*, 4: 141–60.

—— 1995. 'The Conceptual President: Leonid Kravchuk and the Politics of Surrealism', 103–22 in *Patterns in Post-Soviet Leadership*, edited by Timothy J. Colton and Robert C. Tucker. Boulder, CO: Westview.

—— 1997. 'Structural Constraints and Starting Points: The Logic of Systemic Change in Ukraine and Russia', *Comparative Politics*, 29: 433–47.

—— 1999. *Revolutions, Nations, Empires: Conceptual Limits and Theoretical Possibilities*. New York, NY: Columbia University Press.

Mueller, John. 1996. 'Democracy, Capitalism, and the End of Transition', 102–67 in *Postcommunism: Four Perspectives*, edited by Michael Mandelbaum. New York, NY: Council on Foreign Relations.

Nazarbayev, Nursultan. 1995. *The President of the Republic of Kazakhstan*. Ankara: Embassy of the Republic of Kazakstan.

Nelson, Lynn D., and Kuzes, Irina Y. 1995. *Radical Reform in Yeltsin's Russia*. Armonk: M. E. Sharpe.

Reddaway, Peter. 1993. 'Russia on the Brink?', *The New York Review of Books*, 28 January: 30–5.

Roeder, Philip G. 1997. 'Why is Russia More Democratic than Most of its Neighbors?', *American Political Science Association Annual Meeting*, Washington, 28–31 August.

Rutland, Peter. 1997. 'Russia's Flawed Market Transition', *American Political Science Association Annual Meeting*, Washington, 28–31 August.

Sachs, Jeffrey. 1994. *Poland's Jump to the Market Economy*. Cambridge, MA: MIT Press.

Sartori, Giovanni. 1993. 'Totalitarianism, Model Mania and Learning from Error', *Journal of Theoretical Politics*, 5: 5–22.

Shenfield, Stephen D. 1996. 'Alternative Conceptions of Russian State Identity and their Implications for Russian Attitudes towards Ukraine', *The Harriman Review*, 9: 142–7.

Shevtsova, Lilia, and Bruckner, Scott A. 1997. ' Toward Stability or Crisis?', *Journal of Democracy*, 8: 12–26.

Simon, Gerhard. 1991. *Nationalism and Policy Toward the Nationalities in the Soviet Union*. Boulder, CO: Westview.

Solovei, Tat'iana. 1997. 'Russkoe i sovetskoe v sovremennom samosoznanii russkikh', in *Identichnost' i konflikt v postsovetskikh gosudarstvakh*, edited by Martha Brill Olcott. Moscow: Carnegie Endowment for International Peace.

Starovoitova, Galina. 'Democracy in Russia after Chechnya', *The East & Central Europe Program Bulletin*, 5.

Szporluk, Roman. 1994. 'Reflections on Ukraine after 1994: The Dilemmas of Nationhood', *The Harriman Review*, 7: 1–10.

Taagepera, Rein. 1993. *Estonia, Return to Independence*. Boulder, CO: Westview.

Tilly, Charles. 1990/92. *Coercion, Capital and European States, AD 990–1992*. Oxford and Cambridge, MA: Basil Blackwell.

Tismaneau, Vladimir. 1998. *Fantasies of Salvation: Democracy, Nationalism and Myth in Post-Communist Europe*. Princeton, NJ: Princeton University Press.

Tolz, Vera. 1998. 'Conflicting "Homeland Myths" and Nation-State Building in Postcommunist Russia', *Slavic Review*, 57: 267–94.

Treisman, Daniel S. 1997. 'Russia's "Ethnic Revival": The Separatist Activism of Regional Leaders in a Postcommunist Order', *World Politics*, 49: 212–49.

Walker, Edward W. 1996. 'The Dog That Didn't Bark: Tatarstan and Asymmetrical Federalism in Russia', *The Harriman Review*, 9: 1–35.

Wimbush, S. Enders. 1978. 'The Great Russians and the Soviet State: The Dilemmas of Ethnic Dominance', 349–60 in *Soviet Nationality Policies and Practices*, edited by Jeremy R. Azrael. New York, NY: Praeger.

Zhirinovskii, Vladimir. 1993. *Poslednii brosok na iug*. Moscow: Pisatel'.

Zyuganov, Gennadii. 1994. 'Derzhava'. Moscow: Informpechat.

8

Turkey's Kurdish Problem: Borders, Identity, and Hegemony

Ümit Cizre

Despite an increasing body of contemporary literature on it, there is still little understanding on the full dimensions of Turkey's Kurdish problem. Objective, creative, and critical scholarship is stunted by a long list of constraints. These include either ideological hostility or excessive empathy with the object of study as well as misrepresentations, distortions, and defensive impulses in both directions. But more importantly, in writing about the issue, social scientists face hard choices between popular perceptions and historical reality. Empirical data derived from opinion polls conducted with Turkish and Kurdish respondents add yet other elements of complexity to the full appreciation of the problem.

One such complexity is defining the territorial parameters of Kurdish nationalism. Most field surveys done or commissioned in the last three years by various civil societal organizations suggest that the majority of Kurdish respondents do not want an independent Kurdish state carved out of Turkey.[1] Whether or not these studies gauge clear opinions or reflect

[1] The PIAR–GALLUP poll conducted in 1994 with 1,000 respondents representing Turkish public opinion and 500 Kurds from urban and rural areas in the south-east shows that 51 per cent of the Kurds surveyed defined the problem as one of 'ruthless repression by the state' in the heavily Kurdish populated region of the south-east. Another 28.1 per cent perceived it as a question of social and economic deprivation. Whereas 6.4 per cent of the Kurds surveyed saw it as an issue of gaining autonomy within Turkish borders, only 4.3 per cent regarded it as an question of carving out a separate Kurdish state. While the overwhelming body of Kurds define the problem as a product of domestic mismanagement and not as an expression of a wish on the part of Kurds to set up an independent state so as to cause contraction of Turkish borders, 48.8 per cent (a plurality) of Turks see the problem to be caused by a terrorist movement which aims to divide Turkey PIAR–GALLUP 1994). The most serious survey evidence which combines empirical and conceptual data to understand and explain the roots and consequences of the Kurdish question from the viewpoint of Kurdish respondents, was published in July 1995. Being sponsored by a powerful and state-friendly economic interest group, the Union of Turkish Chambers of Commerce and Stock

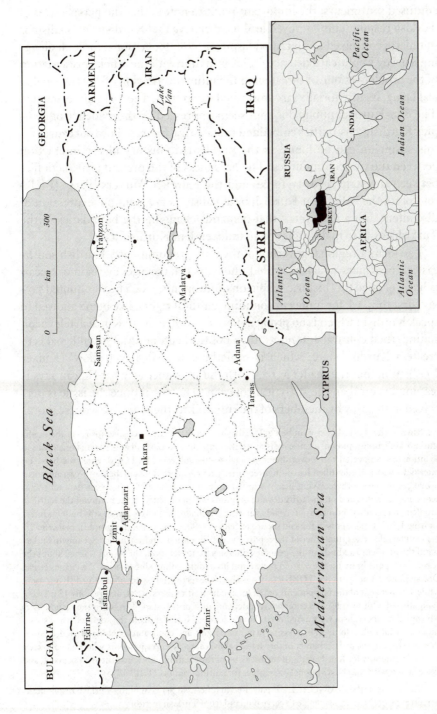

FIG. 8.1 Turkey

confused sentiments, the important point to note is that the perspectives of Turkish respondents surveyed lead us to believe that Kurdish nationalism is popularly conceived as a territory-aspiring, counter-national force challenging Turkey's political existence.[2] This is in tune with the official presentation of the problem as one of threatening the ultimate criterion of Turkey's political being, its territorially circumscribed geography, 'the Turkish rectangle'. The non-Kurdish public does not seem impressed by the evidence of complex Kurdish sensibilities embedded in statistical figures. The root causes for this suspicion can be found in the problematic history of the interaction between the two communities. The harshness of the present armed conflict between the state security forces and the Kurdish Workers' Party (PKK) reinforces the belief that Kurdish nationalism is not a simple expression of discontent, but a movement that demands changing the boundaries of the Turkish entity to make room for an independent Kurdish state.

The former regional governor of the nine predominantly Kurdish southeastern provinces which are ruled under special emergency regime, Necati Bilican, echoed this historic suspicion quite openly, when he was quoted saying 'first they ask for innocent sounding cultural rights, like being allowed to speak Kurdish, which is no problem for us . . . Then, it is a Kurdish television station, then cultural autonomy, then political autonomy. The end goal is to create a Kurdish state, which is something we will never allow' (Kinzer 1997). Whether the reader agrees with the substance of what Bilican says is less important than the analytical concern to note that once the issue is perceived in this way by members of the ruling élite, the official discourse moves

Exchange—the Turkish acronym being TOBB—the report created massive uproar in the media and shocked public opinion because it disclosed the empathy and alarm of a corporatist organization so intimately connected with government, on a taboo-like subject. The TOBB report was based on interviews with self-identified Kurds in three heavily Kurdish provinces in the south-east and three provinces in the south receiving heavy Kurdish migration. It sought to to elicit data on socio-economic variables, and on the attitudes and opinions of respondents on the nature of the Kurdish problem, on identity, immigration trends, language, religion, and terrorism. It was built on interviewing 1,267 respondents in the said six urban centres—90.3 per cent of the sample is male and 9.7 per cent female. The importance of the report lay in its intentions and warnings. Seeking to understand the problem and find out the general principles for its solution, the report warned about the regime's responsibility for the current reality and invited the ruling élite to break the vicious circle. One significant finding of the TOBB study was about the territorial aspect of the Kurdish question: while 42.5 per cent of the respondents opted for a federal administrative structure, only 13 per cent sympathized with the idea of a completely independent Kurdish state. But when the respondents who opted for federalism were asked what they understood by federalism, they defined it as a structure that would allow for freer expression of cultural rights and conditions of living as a Kurd rather than a change in the political unity of the state. A third category of respondents who wished to see a cultural autonomy for Kurds without the break up of the existing state constituted 13 per cent, and associated it with the constitutional guarantees for cultural rights (TOBB 1995).

[2] According to the PIAR-GALLUP poll cited in note 1, 48 per cent of the Turkish respondents perceive the problem as a struggle to carve out land from Turkish territory.

on to the non-negotiability of Turkey's territorial space, on the grounds of preserving Turkey's political life. Even to consider the negotiation of state boundaries in Turkish political syntax is thought to lead to 'wrong-sizing', because it is thought to end in a fatal contraction. This prospect, quite simply, is regarded as putting the life and existence of Turkey in danger.

One definition of the modern state goes straight to the heart of what the majority of Turkish people and state fear: 'the state does not have a territory, it is a territory' (Poggi 1990: 22). Obviously, this approach to defining the state oversimplifies the nexus among people, territory and state by identifying each with the other. It also fails to account for nation- and boundary-defying forms of power, loyalties and differences characteristic of the late modern age. Nevertheless, it strikes the right chord, harmonizing with the popular rejection of the negotiability of boundaries that would spell a death-warrant for the entire life and existence of the Republic. The commitment to this line of thinking is deeply rooted and overwhelming. The ultra-nationalist slogan of 'give land and be rid of' (*ver kurtul*), full of racist overtones, is an inverted form of the official stand and is not sincere. Where contestation over borders has become part of the international landscape, it may be difficult for Western scholarship to understand the depths of extreme nervousness evoked in Turkey by the issue of boundaries. All the more reason, therefore, for scholarly and critical inquiries into the past and present background against which official and popular discourse on boundaries has emerged and is sustained.

This essay will take the official and popular discourse on the idea of non-negotiability of Turkey's boundaries as a given, and will also take it as read that the notion of boundaries is neither anti-political nor anti-social, and that it carries its own philosophical luggage shaped by history. The chapter has two basic objectives. One central concern is to reflect critically on the past and present sources of the Turkish discourse which links immutability of the national borders with existential questions. It is as a result of this posture that any 'adjustment in the size and shape of the state as a strategic response by elites to demands they face that may not be met within the existing borders' (Lustick and O'Leary 1996: 1) is rejected. In doing this, I will identify boundaries with two historical functions: celebration of the likeness of the natives and creation of a distinct political personality for that country by 'domestication of politics' (Wolin 1996: 33). While examining the former function will involve analysing and questioning the creation and construction of the 'hegemonic' idea of Turkey and Turkishness, explaining the latter function will take us to delineating the territorial conditions of existence for Turkey's democracy. Following in the footsteps of Sheldon Wolin who suggests that this latter function turns boundaries into metaphors of integration and exclusion, so that '. . . the reality cloaked in the metaphor of boundaries is the containment of democracy', the notion of Turkey's uncontestable borders will be linked with the justification of a certain democratic imaginary (Wolin 1996: 33). The second organizing theme of the essay is to establish the evolving nature of the expressions of Kurdish distinctiveness from a historical perspective. The terms of these expressions have been reconfigured at different time periods and contexts in interaction with the broader, Turkish, political environment.

Borders as Bounding or Constituting the Nation? Turkey's Grand Right-Sizing of 1919–23 Precluded Further Right-Sizing

Borders took precedence over other attributes of a nation-state in the creation of the Turkish Republic in 1923. There are two reasons why the territorial aspect of Turkish nationalism is most pronounced. The first is related to the memory of historical crises represented by the contractions of the Ottoman Empire preceding the setting up of the Republic. The other is grounded in the identity-driven preoccupation of the Republic that wishes to achieve a political personality distinct from the Ottoman past.

The new entity called Turkey came into existence by a form of right-sizing, that is by the contraction of the predecessor state, the Ottoman Empire. There were a series of right-sizings, contractions in the history of the Empire that are associated in Ottoman-Turkish memory with crisis and debacle: the Balkans and the Arab lands were lost through a series of defeats and withdrawals by Ottoman military and diplomatic power. The Anatolian rectangle was the only context for what was left of the Ottoman boundaries. The dismemberment of the Empire in the last century of its existence turned into a historical scar, redolent of humiliation and failure. The insecurity and anguish occasioned for the subjects of the Empire meant that the idea of contraction, therefore, became at worst a source of major trauma and fears in the popular and élite imagination, and at best, a measure of last resort. The memory of the involuntary Ottoman dismemberment dictated and justified the fundamental rules of Turkey's political life after independence. The habitual language of 'unity and integrity' (*birlik ve bütünlük*), a popular parlance in politics, evokes this memory. David McDowall captures this sentiment when he says that 'it [Turkey] has an emotional and ideological view that its frontiers . . . cannot be changed without threatening the foundations of the Republic . . . The integrity of Turkey within its present borders has acquired an almost mystical quality for those faithful to the legacy of modern Turkey's founder, Mustafa Kemal Atatürk. As a result, the loss of Kurdistan, despite its poverty would be perceived as a grievous blow to the spatial identity of Turkey' (McDowall 1996: 7).

The borders of the new sovereign state to be set up within the Anatolian rectangle were first expressed in the National Pact (*Misak-i Milli*) of 1919–20 as the political mandate of the Turkish nationalist movement. The significance of the National Pact went beyond the putative intention to find a life-space for the remaining elements of the Empire. It embodied two dynamics: it endorsed the reality of the death of the Ottoman Empire through contraction, and yet it confined its territorial engineering to a 'new' sovereign state within a specific part of the imperial geography of the predecessor state. The National Pact, therefore, was a territorial programme for defining a new entity *vis-à-vis* the old one. But the old one was not just an entity to be disregarded, rejected and forgotten. The genesis of modern Turkish ideological developments and state formation had been, largely, within the *ancien régime*.

Indeed, late Ottoman nationalism was instrumental in the emergence of Republic's nationalism. But, the territorial factor significantly served to distinguish official Turkish nationalism from the late Ottoman version. The cultural pan-Turkism of the Young Turks as put forward by some pre-WWI statesmen and ideologues, envisaged a pan-Turkish unity with the various peoples of Central Asia and Caucasus on the bases of ethnic and Islamic criteria. By contrast, early Republican nationalism emphasized the modern concept of civic and social equality regardless of ethnic and religious origins, but they did not completely disown the racial and linguistic component advocated by the prominent theoretician of the Young Turk movement, Ziya Gökalp, who had elaborated some kind of a Turkified Islam as the best recipe for cohesion for the new nation (Lewis 1968: 359). Nor did the Republican concern to set up a secular nation-state 'eliminat[e] Islam from their definition of the concept of nation; in practice, . . . they continued to give a certain consideration to religion.' (Dumont 1984: 30).

If differences between the foundational discourse of the Republic and late Ottoman nationalism were not 'as great as one might expect' (ibid) the most radical departure was on the issue of territory. Pan-Turkism and Islam as ideologies for unifying the mosaic structure of the Empire, 'were both non-territorial; there was no country and no government in the existence defined by either of them' (Lewis 1968: 352), whereas the National Pact attached almost a sacred character to the post-imperial enclave of Anatolia. The 1935 programme of the People's Republican Party, which founded the Republic, declared that 'the fatherland is the sacred country within our present borders' (Kazancıgil 1981: 51).

The strong emphasis on the discourse of territorial identity was also the result of its worrisome lack of emotional appeal. Bernard Lewis reminds us of the lack of a name for Turkey in Turkish (Lewis 1968: 352). Indeed, the National Pact referred not to Turkey and Turks but to the areas inhabited by an Ottoman Muslim majority 'united in religion, in race and in aim' (ibid). Given the weakness of people's existence based on Turkishness, fostering loyalty to the territorial identity of the new construct of Turkey became the crucial underpinning of the Republic's nationalism, intruding into everyday life, penetrating into psyches, turning into an existentialist issue, a matter of life and death. Naming a territorial homeland preceded the formation of national consciousness and a collective conscience: the national territory preceded the nation.

The Turkish rectangle was, of course, portrayed as the cradle of a series of Anatolian civilizations culminating in the Turkish one. This historical geography was employed to delineate not only the external but also the ethnic boundaries of Turks, and to strengthen racial pride and cohesiveness. The Ottoman government had agreed, in the Treaty of Sevres (1920), signed with the Allied Powers, to provide for a Kurdish state. By the time the National Pact laid out the borders of the new state, the nationalist movement had gained sufficient momentum to dictate the conditions of the right-sizing of the Ottoman state to include the predominantly Kurdish areas lying in the eastern flanks of the Anatolian rectangle in Turkey. This claim was based on the Ottoman historical presence and heritage in the historical geography of the region. It was also prompted by political considerations to unite whatever Ottoman Muslim majority was left from the dismemberment process.

Non-Negotiable Borders, National Identity, and the Question of Hegemony

The Kurdish question contests the most critical assumptions of Turkish nationalist doctrine, especially the core principle that there are no identities in Turkey other than the one covered by Turkish national identity. Analysing this assumption offers a theoretical opportunity to link Turkish political identity to the imperatives of the developmental, political role of the 'modern' state and modern nationalisms. This is so, because, since the emergence of a global system of nation-states in the nineteenth and twentieth centuries, the dominant imagination of nationalisms, is, everywhere, the notion of modernity. From the outset, the construction of a homogenous national identity in Turkey was linked with the logic of catching up with the modern

West. Modernity understood as Westernization was connected with economic prosperity and a strong state. A non-negotiable national identity was
thought to secure the conditions of the existence of these two goals. Diversity
and social pluralism were seen as obstacles to the emergence of a modern and
strong state. The crucial point here is that a homogenous national identity
became part of the attempt to extract recognition as a Western nation from
the West. This meant that the 'power' dimension of the Republic became
linked with Westernization, and demonstration of a homogenous national
identity, in turn, had a key role in easing integration with the West on an
equal basis.

Since, however, modernity also entails a discourse of democracy, rights,
and equality of citizens, the goal of controlling the polity could not have been
confined to the imperative of westernizing simply as strengthening the
regime's ability to rule over a unified territory. On the domestic level, westernization was powerfully articulated with Rousseau's conception of
Republicanism which stressed 'the centrality of obligations and duties to the
public realm' and of 'the supreme direction of the general will, the publicly
generated conception of the common good' (Held 1996: 56, 58). The political stratagem of the Kemalists was to reinforce these Rousseauist principles,
by making general will the culmination of the political legitimacy based on
popular sovereignty. Turkish democracy, in consequence, has not emphasized democratic legitimation of governments through their respect for the
rule of law, civil society, and constitutionality. Instead, the ends of the state,
the general will, have held priority above those of the rights of the individuals. Rule by the majority and electoral politics have become proof of the
regime's allegiance to democracy.

The social and historical context of the Republic meant that the national
identity was constructed as a hegemonic ideal at the level of culture and
(westernized) civilization. It also acquired hegemonic significance for the
state because of the weak articulation of this identity with demographic,
social, and historical levels of the society. The national community, from the
inauguration of the Republic, had to be constructed out of an embarrassing
diversity of a demographic reality which was a legacy of the Ottoman mosaic. The confusing range of ethnic, linguistic, and sectarian attachments produced insecurities and anxieties over the question of the constituents of an
identity in an inarticulate and uncertain social world.

Turkish nationalism was formally based on a total repudiation of the past
political and cosmological configuration of the Ottoman Empire. However,
the Ottoman historical legacy continued to shape the national consciousness,
and Islam remained the chief marker of self-identification for the majority.
This was particularly true of the Kurdish communal identity that had a

long-entrenched association with the *Khalidiya* branch of the *Naqshbandi tarikat*—a Sufi brotherhood—dominant in the south-east. The new national identity stood a good chance of being accepted by the Ottoman Muslim population of the Republic if it made Islam the cultural norm of its discourse. But, contrary to the experience of the emergence of Balkan nationalisms, where the church joined forces with the secular élite in instilling a national consciousness against the Ottoman rulers, the Republic was more constrained in its choice of allies.

The legitimizing ethos of Turkish nationalism was not just independence but a total transformation of values in the direction of westernization, understood as the sole route to modernization. Secularism was the pillar, the principle, and the proof of this ethos. It meant disestablishment of Islam as the state religion, and making politics independent of religious considerations, including the religious heterodoxy prevalent among the population. But establishing a positive western-like self was impossible unless the negative and significant other, Islam, was present. In this sense, promotion of a European-like Turkishness has historically involved an open recognition of Islam as a crucial element of Turkish identity. In addition, the Ottoman state tradition of including the highest functionaries of Islam, the *ulema*, within the structure of the state eased the establishment of a similar set-up in the Republic. Establishment Islam became an instrument for articulating a national community. How the state sought to cope with Islam is beyond the scope of this essay. Suffice it to say that state–Islam interaction took a complicated and contingent trajectory over the life of the Republic. For our purposes here, the key problem of Turkish identity lay in developing it in such a way that it could match and overcome the power and salience of Islam. Competing against the stronger traditions and older institutions of Islam became a source of weakness for the attempt to establish the hegemony of the constructs known as Turkey and Turkishness.

Given the fact that the construct of Turkish national identity concealed profound contradictions and antinomies on sociological and historical levels, the Kurdish factor has historically assisted the consolidation and legitimation of state power through providing a testing ground for the Kemalists. As the hegemony of the modern state is made to depend on overcoming political and sociological fragmentation, some imagining of territory-wanting Kurds became instrumental for the master narrative of Turkish nationalism. In short, the imagining of Kurdish nationalism has served to unify the Turkish polity and provide some coherence to Turkish identity. This effect of Kurdish nationalism on Turkish homogeneity bears a striking parallel to the impact Islamism has on closing the ranks of secular minded Turks. In the final analysis, Turkish identity became a constitutive element in the legitimation of the political rule of the Republic. National integration and security became conflated and mutually reinforcing.

Countering and containing Kurdish ethno-cultural existence as distinct from the Turkish one was, then, intimately connected with the aspirations of the state to modernize (westernize) and the unsettled question of hegemony. Pluralism was regarded as disintegrative, sapping the strength of the nation, strength deemed to be essential to achieve with the West. This is the aspect of the Republic that sought to absorb heterogeneity into controlled modernity. Yet, the imperatives of nationalism also bear some responsibility for the definition of Turkish identity that was intolerant of differences. In that sense Turkish nationalism is hardly an aberrant form of nationalism: there is a 'profound dualism at the heart of every nationalism . . . every nationalism contains civic and ethnic elements in varying degree and different forms. Sometimes civic and territorial elements predominate, at the other times it is the ethnic and vernacular components' (Smith 1991: 13). It is this indeterminancy in the dual constituents of nationalism that produces 'the political power of nationalisms [compared with] their philosophical poverty and even incoherence' (Anderson 1991: 5). Membership in a nation is not only defined by civic terms, but also involves participation in a common culture. The contrast between 'civic nationalism', used in the tradition of Hans Kohn to define a Western or modern nationalism as distinct from an 'Eastern' or nasty variety (Kohn 1969; Kohn 1982), is also applicable to the Turkish case. Turkish nationalism also contains two contrasting strands, one highlighting the ethnic singularity of Turkishness and the other that essentially grants equal citizenship rights to all those living on the Turkish territory regardless of their ethnic origin (Sakallioğlu 1996). Indeed, 'the problem is not that Turkey refuses to accept Kurds as Turkish citizens. The problem is precisely its attempt to force Kurds to see themselves as Turks' (Kymlicka 1996: 39) causing, in the process, a suppression of Kurdish historical memory, which in turn produces resentment and resistance.

This dual character of Turkish nationalism reflects the dual models that were simultaneously enforced for building Turkey's political identity since the genesis of the Republic. The first was 'civic integration . . . creating a common civic, national or patriotic identity and citizenship' (McGarry and O'Leary 1994: 102), whereas the second 'assimilation as a model went further and favoured the merging of ethnic identities . . . into a new one' (ibid). As these two models of integration were based on a special understanding of democracy emphasizing the majoritarian logic of electoral politics rather than the 'limited state' concept of Western liberal tradition, their usage in Turkey could be turned into instruments of what McGarry and O'Leary describe as 'hegemonic control' (ibid: 106).

The Nation Made: Reshaping as Integration

How did the official definition of national identity evolve in response to the changing needs of westernization, Kemalist hegemony, and Kurdish challenges? It is fair to suggest that for most of the republican history a homogenizing national identity remained elusive. Nationalism has acted as a conservative force denouncing different foci of loyalty to other than Turkish ethnicity, Sunni Islam, the Turkish language, and Turkish history as heresies. The reshaping of domestic democracy was conceived as, and articulated with, the strategies of national integration and promotion of national unity. National integration in particular was achieved through four basic conduits: electoral participation, military conscription, extensive primary school education, and infrastructural modernization.

Even in the single party period (1923–46), elections were held regularly. And during much of the cold war, Turkey's regular and open multi-party electoral democracy became the most effective means of limiting conflict and legitimating the process of national integration. Trans-community national parties enabled the Kurdish community to transcend narrow local interests and identify their problems with the global discourses of the age, be they capitalism, socialism, or social democracy. In the eyes of the governing élite the low level of threat posed by the Kurdish community was instrumental in ensuring that representative institutions were kept open to them. Compulsory military conscription and the development of a network of primary schools in the remote areas of the country provided some homogenizing experience and a sense of a common larger homeland. The republican progressive view of history dominant among Turkish minds held that traditional loyalties and modes of living could not withstand the onslaught of infrastructural modernization. It found expression in the capitalist integration of the predominantly Kurdish area of the south-east into the mainstream.

In sum, and despite the heritage of resentment within the Kurdish community for the subsumption of their identity within the Turkish national identity, economic modernization during the cold war era provided some shared interests, a degree of equality and a *détente* with the larger community. Kurdish nationalism was not yet capable of disturbing the *status quo* because it was confined to a small educated strata while the less modern and poorer groups were not articulate or mobilized: 'on the one hand, nationalism or at least some degree of Kurdishness constituted their (the Kurdish elites') common ground . . . on the other hand, they were differentiated according to political cleavages that concerned Turkey as a whole . . .' (Bozarslan 1996: 146). That they were able to sustain a double identity, rather than a single discourse committed to Kurdish nationalism, was because of the modicum of security and relative prosperity enjoyed by the Kurds. On the Turkish side, too, the tension between the Western and Islamic facets of national identity did not yet reach the stage of open contestation over what genuinely constituted a 'Turk.' Certainly, the evidence of the 1960s and 70s shows that neither Europeanization nor secularism have ever been clandestine and flimsy aspirations throughout the Republic. The territorial nation-state is popularly rooted and the settlement of 1919–20 is widely regarded as a permanent arrangement.

In the recent post-cold war era, this political configuration was shaken. Two developments have provided the momentum for a redefinition of the constitutive categories of Turkish identity with important implications for the Kurdish issue. First, official nationalism and almost all political poles on the ideological divide have embraced the agenda of a reduced state, popular capitalism, law and order, and global patterns of consumption and life styles. The second force that caused the establishment to reimagine Turkish identity is the ongoing crisis of the model of 'national capitalism' which caused a loss of clear and unambiguous loyalty to the state.

Intense penetrations of modern globalized artefacts and ideas have caused a renewed emphasis on the part of official nationalism on modern/Western aspects of Turkish identity. The old historical concern to gain respect from the West has resurrected itself in the intense struggle to become a member of the European Union. But while, under the global conditions, being considered modern became a central aspect of Turkish modernity and political identity, distinguishing her from the neighbouring countries, pride in the ethnic roots and Sunni Islam were also articulated in the definition of Turkish identity. The neo-conservative tone of the international politics, revival of Islamism, and the escalation of the Kurdish conflict since 1984 provided the impetus for this synthesis. The discourses of a long line of centre-right politicians since the mid-1980s have identified Turkishness with Western values, albeit on a superficial level, as well as with the symbol of the flag, blood and sacrifice, *Ezan* (prayer), and Muslim morals.[3]

What increases the appeal of nationalism for the masses in a global age is the articulation it offers between modern/global values and parochial elements. Emphasizing their ethnic singularity under a global veneer, even the radical ultra-nationalist forces have achieved rehabilitation with the political centre. Political Islam, on the other hand, has become the main beneficiary of

[3] The statements and speeches of the leader of the True Path Party (TPP), Tansu Çiller, who was the Prime Minister of a series of coalition governments formed between the TPP and the Social Democratic Populist Party between 1993–5 are the prime examples of this discourse—see Çiller (1993: 13, 62, 95).

the retreat of the state and the dislocation and disorientation caused by globalism, which are not addressed by the nation-state. Political Islam has put the Western/secular political identity of the Republic under intense pressure. Turkish national identity has become more contestable, but has it really become unambiguous and stable?

The escalation of Kurdish separatist militancy in the last decade and a half adds yet another important dimension to the above problematic, constituting, in Martin Kramer's words a 'violent reminder that Turkey has not achieved full integration as a homogenous nation-state of Turkish speakers' (Kramer 1997: 105). But surely, there is something even more important than this reminder: at certain conjunctures and under certain pressures, new articulations of national identity may become a key to maintaining the non-negotiable character of the boundaries. There may be a democratic opportunity for developing a larger and genuinely inclusive vision of community, which can form the basis of a stable and healthy society.

Kurdish nationalism since 1987 owes much of its militancy to the transformation of official Turkish nationalism in the same period. In contrast with the cold war times when the physical conflict dimension of Kurdish nationalism was almost non-existent, the post-cold war momentum for Kurdish nationalism came from two sources: the force of the official redefinition of the Turkish nation with a strong dose of ethnic homogeneity and the process of global change. The official response to the radicalism of Kurdish nationalism has been to narrow the political space to Kurdish demands, which are now organized on the new basis of an 'identity claim'. This has led to a vicious circle: the political space for the expression of Kurdish identity, interests and ideas is restricted by the failure of traditional political parties in conveying and processing Kurdish demands, and by the closing down of exclusively Kurdish political parties by the Constitutional Court.[4] This created new political opportunities for Kurdish radical nationalism in the 1990s, and at this point, we need to turn to the relevance and implications of the evolution of Kurdish articulations and rearticulations of national identity.

Is Territory the Founding Logic of Kurdish Nationalism?

Of the 20 to 25 million Kurds in the Middle East, some 12 to 14 million live in Turkey, and their current estimated regional concentrations are shown in

---

[4] The first of the series was People's Labour Party—Turkish acronym being HEP—which was founded in March 1990. Being disbanded in July 1993, it was succeeded by Democracy Party (DEP). When this party was banned in June 1994, its place was taken by People's Democracy Party (HADEP). See also the discussion of coercive electoral integration by Brendan O'Leary in Chapter 2.

TABLE 8.1. *Estimated Kuridsh population, by region of Turkey*

Region	Provinces in each region	1965		1990	
		Number (thousand)	% province population	Number (thousand)	% province population
Marmara	1	72.65	1.24	810.13	6.09
Aegean	2	15.77	0.36	296.99	3.93
Mediterranean	3	190.22	4.98	726.55	8.95
Central Anatolia	4	262.64	4.13	579.38	5.53
Black Sea	5	28.72	0.51	37.88	0.50
Eastern	6	1,369.65	38.87	2,230.29	41.96
Southeastern	7	1,192.73	64.24	2,365.04	64.98
Total (% of total population)		3,132.39	9.98	7,046.25	12.60

Source: Mutlu (1996)

Table 8.1. Historically, Kurds have existed throughout written history. The battle of Çaldıran in 1515 marked a watershed in their relationship with the Ottoman political rule: in return for military collaboration with the Ottoman rulers against the rising power of Shi'ism and Persian influence, the pact of Çaldıran guaranteed political autonomy to the Kurds and confirmed the hereditary rights of their princes. The period of stability that followed in the region of what is today known as the south-east of Turkey was disrupted by a number of events, culminating in the destruction of the autonomy of the principalities by the centralization and modernization movement in the Ottoman Empire in the nineteenth century. After the defeat of the Empire at the end of World War I the Treaty of Sevres was signed in 1920. Kurds were promised a scheme of local autonomy for the predominantly Kurdish areas lying east of the Euphrates, and north of the frontier of Turkey with Syria and then-Mesopotamia, with an eventual independence—see Fig. 8.1 and see also the maps in Denise Natali's discussion of the Kurdish question in Iraq, Chapter 9. The Treaty of Sevres, however, was overturned by the Treaty of Lausanne in July 1923 that recognized the sovereignty of Turkey in accordance with the boundaries that Turkey had drawn for itself in the National Pact of 26 January 1920. From Lausanne on, Kurds found themselves living a fragmented existence in Turkey, Syria, Iraq, and Iran.

For various reasons, the question of whether or not Kurdish demands in Turkey contest the territorial framework of the Turkish state is difficult to answer. The issue of territory carries symbolic importance for the Kurdish imagination. The notion of 'Kurdistan' extends 'from the Black Sea near the

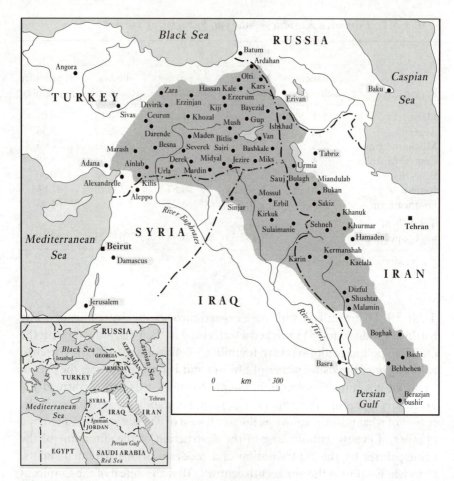

Fig. 8.2 Regions populated by the Kurds in the 1920s

Caucasus to the Persian Gulf as well as the fertile plains to the West'
(Andrews 1982: 17).[5] Kurdish people have existed as a distinct group for
more than two thousand years in the central part of that space: 'there is both
a practical and mythical interpretation of political Kurdistan. The former
affords Kurdistan the borders its political leadership either hopes or believes
it can achieve' (McDowall 1996: 3). Borders that presently span over four
states represent systems of domination for the divided Kurdish nationalist
movements in these countries to challenge.

[5] A more up-to-date imagination of Kurdistan would span an area extending from eastern
Turkey to western Iran, northeastern tip of Syria and northern Iraq.

Have these internationally recognized frontiers kept Kurdish populations apart to the extent of preventing Kurds from extending their emotional allegiance to a greater Kurdistan as 'the imagined homeland'? It can be suggested that 'frontiers have not been wholly disadvantageous to the Kurds' (ibid: 8) in that the permeability of these borders has always allowed a margin of movement for the Kurdish population by cutting across rather than along the linguistic-cultural divisions in Kurdish society (ibid). On the other hand, the diffusion of Kurds in four states has not prevented them from 'double adhesion to two separate entities; the first the state and the second the minority, itself supra-territorial in nature and extending beyond the limits of Turkish political geography' (Bozarslan 1996: 108).

Kurdish demands today are ambivalent messages expressed at different times by different agents and in different modes. On the level of the nation-state when the demands revolve around cultural rights, it is the ethnic singularity of Kurds which emerges as the conscious object. Again at the same level, when demands are centred on material entitlements, social improvement, and legal protection, this discourse is tilted toward a reference to the equality of Turkish citizens. When Kurdish intellectuals and political leaders address themselves to the international community, the discourse becomes adversarial and territorial, challenging the Turkish state on very many accounts. The contents of interviews with Abdullah Öcalan, the leader of the PKK, for example, show big differences depending on the audience. In March 1992, in an interview with a Turkish magazine, he said, 'the PKK is not inevitably insisting on organised violence . . . our goal is not to divide Turkey, but to share it. . . . I do not see it as either reasonable or necessary that a Kurdish region should be detached from the country as if cut by a knife . . .' (Marcus 1983: 242). However, a month later, in an interview in the PKK's European-based magazine, he indicated that he 'had not given up his desire for a Kurdish independent state' (ibid: 243). In April 1998, after the weakening of the PKK as a result of the Turkish military's crackdown, Öcalan seemed to revert back to the message that the PKK does not want to break up the unity of Turkey, and that it would like to start a process of political dialogue with the Turkish state from which the PKK is presently excluded— because of its political violence, and because the Turkish state does not recognize Kurdish political parties—and that all that Öcalan wanted was cultural and political rights.[6]

---

[6] This was reported in an interview by a Turkish daily with Prof. Michael Gunter on his return from a ten-hour interview he had himself conducted with Abdullah Öcalan in Damascus on 13–14 March 1998 (Congar 1998a, b).

The Evolution of the Basis of Kurdish Expressions

Until the limited modernization project of the late Ottoman period was given full impetus in mid-twentieth-century Turkey, Islam was the principal public expression of Kurdish communal identity: the *Khalidiya* branch of *Naqshbandi tarikat* provided the central values and particular ways of thinking and behaving as a Kurd. Kurdish ethnic distinctions overlapped with Islam (Bruinessen 1992: 7). When the secularization policies of the early Republic shattered the power of *tarikats* by closing them, Islam for Turkey's Kurds turned into an 'identity of resistance' (Yavuz 1995: 355), witnessed in a series of revolts between 1925 and 1937.

However, a more substantial and partly voluntary integration of the Kurds into the mainstream in most of the cold war period enabled the Kurdish community to imagine its identity and social existence as less based on Islam and more on the discourses of the age: the emerging secular Kurdish intelligentsia interpreted Kurdishness from the perspective of the key theme of the Turkish political left, distributive justice, and civic and social rights (McDowall 1996: 211). And right-wing Turkish political parties recruited the remnants of the tribal leaders who subordinated their Kurdishness to the state's priorities. Some degree of party political and electoral integration was therefore feasible. In recent Turkish elections Kurds have not homogeneously voted as a bloc, and it would be difficult to tell if they had, but as can be seen in Table 8.2 it is absolutely plain that support for HADEP (Halkın Demokrasi Partisi/The People's Democracy Party), a pro-Kurdish party, in the 1990s was strongly and disproportionately concentrated in provinces with significant numbers of mother-tongue Kurdish speakers; and that participation rates in elections are lower in provinces with significant numbers of mother-tongue Kurdish speakers.

The most recent perspective that dominates the Kurdish nationalist discourse is 'identity'. According to one 1995 report carried out in three predominantly Kurdish provinces in the south-east—Diyarbakır, Batman, and Mardin—and in three provinces in the south which receive intense Kurdish migration—Adana, Mersin, and Antalya—in-depth interviews with one hundred opinion-leaders show that 40.3 per cent of the respondents refer to Kurdish ethnicity as the basis of their identity, while only 22.3 per cent self-identify as Turkish.[7] In yet another report published a year earlier,[8] the percentage who consider themselves Turkish is 21.7. But, when respondents who react to a Turkish identity by not giving any response (30.2 per cent) is

[7] The report was sponsored by the Union of Turkish Chambers of Commerce and Stock Exchanges and published in July 1995.

[8] PIAR-GALLUP (1994: 14). See note 1 above.

TABLE 8.2. *Participation rates and distribution of voting for Kurdish-speaking provinces,[a]* *1991–1995*

| | Election: average participation (%) | | | | | |
| | 1991 National | | 1994 Local | | 1995 National | |
Parties	Turkey	17 Provinces	Turkey	18 Provinces	Turkey	18 Provinces
ANAP	24.0	22.5	21.0	19.0	19.7	16.3
CHP	—	—	4.6	2.8	10.7	5.7
DSP	10.8	2.8	8.8	0.9	14.6	3.2
DYP	27.0	20.8	21.4	22.1	19.2	16.2
HADEP	—	—	—	—	4.2	19.5
MHP	—	—	8.0	5.3	8.2	5.8
RP	16.9	16.6	19.1	27.3	21.4	27.2
SHP	20.8	33.7	13.6	14.2	—	—
Others	0.4	0.6	3.2	6.0	1.6	2.6
Independent	0.1	1.5	0.3	2.5	0.5	3.4
Participation	83.9	80.2	92.2	87.1	85.2	79.9

Key:
ANAP Anavatan Partisi (The Motherland Party)—Center Right
CHP Cumhuriyet Halk Partisi (The Republican People's Party)—Center Left
DSP Demokratik Sol Parti (The Democratic Left Party)—Center Left
DYP Doru Yol Partisi (The True Party Party)—Center Right
HADEP Halkın Demokrasi Partisi (The People's Democracy Party)—Pro-Kurdish
MHP Milliyetçi Hareket Partisi (The Nationalist Action Party)—Turkish Ultranationalist
RP Refah Partisi (The Welfare Party)
SHP Sosyal Demokrat Halkii Parti (The Social Democratic Populist Party)—Center Left (United with CHP in 1994 and resumed its political life under CHP

[a] Kurdish-speaking provinces means those provinces where more than 15% of the population declared Kurdish as their mother tongue during the 1965 census.
Source: Kirişci and Winrow (1997: 142)

added to those who identify themselves simply as 'human beings'—without a national identity—(34.9 per cent) and as a Kurd (18.5 per cent), it becomes clear that an overwhelming percentage (83.6 percent) of Kurds do not consider themselves Turkish. The evidence shows that the official posture that suggests that 'there is no Kurdish problem . . . Turkey has a terrorism problem'[9] cannot be sustained. In reality, nothing in the past was as damaging to state–Kurdish relations as the identity issue. While the past demands of material entitlements could be met without upsetting the *status quo*, the current demand for the recognition of Kurdish identity challenges the pillar principle of the Republic that defines the nation as a homogenous identity

[9] This is a statement made by President Demirel in 1997 (Demirel 1997).

based on a common allegiance to being Turkish. One Kurdish political leader, Şerafettin Elçi, summarizes the new demand: 'Kurds demand the recognition of their identity. There are obviously rights derived from this identity . . . the right to education in their language . . . and the right to organize on the level of political parties and cultural institutions' (interview with Şerafettin Elçi 1995).

This is not to say that there are not a number of serious problems related to the substance of 'identity' and 'ethnic identity' in general. Suffice it to say that the usefulness of identity politics is limited at the outset by the nature of the object it tries to promote: since identities are plural and contextual, there is no good reason to confine the qualities that define identities to 'cultural' ones, nor can identities always be politically peaceful in terms of not excluding the others (Fierlbeck 1996: 20). Still, the real question is not whether a sense of Kurdishness exists; it does. The real issues are two: to translate an existing social reality into part of the public discourse that would keep Kurdish distinctions inside rather than outside Turkey, and to acknowledge that this assertion of identity need have nothing to do with the cultural history or the ethnic significance of Kurds. It has more to do with the larger political context which, by posing a political threat to the cultural freedoms of Kurds has helped to reconstruct their identity on a new basis, precisely because identities have the quality of being capable of being redefined in articulation with a changing historical environment. More correctly, keeping Kurdish distinctions inside Turkey is a search that is reflective of a much wider problem confronting many post-cold war liberal democracies in terms of their attempts to reconcile competing claims for self-defining identities within a unified entity. The logical policy implication here, too, is to develop a liberal, cosmopolitan thinking about civic nationalism rather than adopt non-unitary administrative formulae that might lead to the break up of the Republic.

Why is it ethnicity that has become the chief marker of identity at present? Structural explanations of the Kurdish question focus on the past state policies and overlook the crucial impact of two things that have shaped Kurdish nationalism over the last two decades: the ethnically oriented definition of Turkish identity and intrusion of global ideas and forces. It could be suggested that an uneven modernization of the south-east of Turkey, and the new ethnic turn of Turkish nationalism have provided the context that is receptive to global processes. That this global impetus is mostly on the changing status of territorial and mental boundaries has important implications for the problematic of this chapter.

Globalism and the Shift of Emphasis onto Internal Boundaries

By way of a generalization, it is safe to suggest that with globalization 'boundaries carving up economic life are weakened, [while] the boundaries demarcating cultural and political life appear to be strengthened' (Blaney and Inayatullah 1996: 98). This is obviously linked to the crisis about the loss of state monopoly over the definition of the nation. Contestability of a unidimensional national identity and the emergence of identity politics to gain new rights to promote the constitutional recognition of already existing identities have become parts of the new debate on the redefinition of citizenship and establishment of multiculturalism. Even in the advanced and more democratic societies in the West, there is a steady erosion of the power of the state to attract citizenship loyalty and an intense criticism on the fault-line of the modern liberal state that turns a blind eye to plurality of cultural and social existences. Democracy has come to acquire new meanings associated with uncertainties of commonalities, heterogeneity of political spaces, and contestable foundations of shared understandings of lifestyles. The philosophical boundaries within the nation-states, in other words, have become as important as the external boundaries. Nation-states everywhere try to come to terms with 'the multiple meanings and purposes associated with sovereign boundaries' (Blaney and Inayatullah 1996: 98). This does not mean that the idea of state sovereignty has been abandoned, but that there is a new intellectual possibility for people all around the world to redefine their place-centredness as power relations around them have changed.

Coming back to the Kurdish expressions, it is clear that within the PKK, which has been involved in a bloody confrontation with the state security forces since 1984, the idea of setting up an independent Kurdish state in a classical territorial form is still very much alive. Although there is much popular support for the PKK,[10] it is less rooted in the imaginary territorially

[10] Evidence from the TOBB report in 1995 shows that when questioned on various aspects of the PKK, significant portions of Kurds are either 'silent' or indicate their support for it through indirect ways: while 65.2 per cent did not answer the question on their kinship relations with those who joined the PKK; 25.5 per cent kept silent on the possible objectives of the PKK, and yet 29.9 per cent did not respond to the question why the Turkish Republic could not succeed in defeating the organization. Again a significant proportion (64 per cent) chose to remain silent when they were asked what policies of the PKK they approved of. On the question of whether the government will be able to succeed in wiping out the PKK, while around 10 per cent did not want to answer and 2.6 per cent did not know, an overwhelming proportion (76.8 per cent) of those who responded gave a negative answer. When asked what the objectives of the PKK are, 30.6 per cent connect it with 'cultural and political rights', while only 2.5 per cent with the goal of 'dividing the country and agitating', and 15.3 per cent with setting up an independent Kurdish state. But a more positive image of the PKK is also rejected: a mere 5.6 per cent link it with cultural, political, and human rights and democracy. See TOBB (1995: 18–20).

sovereign Kurdish state than in the wish to break an unhappy *status quo* which has turned 3 million Kurds into refugees and cost 40 billion US dollars and around 20,000 lives on both sides. The incapacity of the Kurdish popular masses to think their way out of their everyday ordeal has not only made them vulnerable to the PKK, it has also paved the way to the entry of global ideas which focus on more democratic arrangements of internal boundaries. The end result of these conflicting pressures has been the use of trans-local and transnational ideas in which human rights, pluralism, cultural rights to education, and broadcasting in Kurdish have become central elements of Kurdish demands in recent years. By the end of 1997–8, however, mass sympathy for the PKK seems to have declined partly because of major military setbacks that the PKK had suffered at the hands of the Turkish army. The disintegration of the core of the PKK leadership militarily has come to mean the disintegration of the core of the PKK's support in the region, and the widespread belief that with the return of some normalcy to the region, it will be difficult for the PKK to keep up the same momentum among its support base.[11]

There are additional reasons to think that the idea of a sovereign Kurdish national territory has been demystified by transnational events. The leading researcher on Kurdish nationalism, Martin van Bruinessen, argues in his recent writings that one essential dimension of the reaffirmation of Kurdish identity has been increased contact and communication among the Kurds of different countries after the Gulf War of 1991 through population displacement (Bruinessen 1996).[12] To van Bruinessen, these two developments have produced paradoxical results: they have reinforced the awareness of a 'common' Kurdish identity embracing all the Kurds in the region, while at the same time increasing the awareness of 'differences' between Kurds of the different states. The result has been the emergence of subnational groups among the Kurds, Alevis, and Zazas developing their separate Alevi Kurdish

[11] Talking about their impressions of an army-organized media tour of the region in November 1997, key journalists (columnists) of the country coming from diverse ideological convictions seemed to agree that as a result of the massive military defeat the PKK had suffered under a Turkish military offensive at the end of 1997, the native population had already cooled off from the PKK, and that the local commanders were now taking advantage of the lull to gain the support of the impoverished Kurds by offering free medical care, humanitarian aid, food, clothes, and consumer goods. The media and the government have also started a campaign to lure businesspeople to the region by offering cheap loans and tax exemptions. For a representative sample of these impressions see Tinc (1997).

[12] In the paper he presented at Princeton University on 22 April 1997, van Bruinessen repeated the same conclusion (Bruinessen 1997). The title of the paper he presented was a significant reminder of the dilemmas faced by the Kurdish identity, 'Kurdish Society in the 1990s: Caught between State, Religion, Nationalist Movement and Intra-Kurdish Ethnic identities'.

nationalism and Zaza identities as distinguished from a comprehensive identity of Kurdishness.

The Diasporic Dimension and Territory in Kurdish Nationalism

One crucial factor that has contributed to the deterritorialization of Kurdish demands has been the transnational aspect of Kurdish nationalism that can be called its diasporic dimension. The escalation of the Kurdish conflict since early 1980s, and the consequent large-scale Kurdish migration to Western and Northern Europe, has created a transnational Kurdish movement connected with 'diasporic public spheres' (Appadurai 1997: 4) in these countries, where Kurdish migrants, refugees, intellectuals, and exiles get involved in a 'long-distance nationalism' (ibid: 22). The interesting point about diasporic or long-distance nationalism is that, according to Appadurai, it operates less on the basis of 'territorial' aspirations than on '. . . the fear and hatred of its ethnic others' (ibid: 165), mainly because it is embroiled with the 'anguish of displacement, the nostalgia of exile, the repatriation of funds or the brutalities of asylum seeking' (ibid). Since this form of transnational nationalism only 'partially' revolves around the idea of a homeland as the substance of territorial affiliation, it is considered to be a 'revolution in the foundations of nationalism' (ibid: 161) which has crept on us 'virtually unnoticed' (ibid). For Stuart Hall as well, diaspora identity is a function of a specific diaspora experience which is mediated and transformed by memory, fantasy, and desire (Hall 1996: 163). Consequently there can be 'no simple return or recovery of the ancestral past which is not re-experienced through the categories of the present' (ibid).

Admittedly, as there is no scientific study made specifically on Kurdish diaspora communities in Europe, we do not have any hard data on the full nature of the Kurdish diasporic identity, and its articulation with territorial elements. On the basis of scant evidence, it seems that there are two conditions for ethnic communities of migrant workers in Europe to turn to home-oriented political goals: they are the establishment of ethnic enclaves which give impetus to the flourishing of lucrative ethnic business, and citizenship granting or denying policies of the host country (Abadan-Unat 1997: 229–51). The ambiguities that surround Kurdish diasporic nationalist aspirations partly stem from the activities of an important group of European-based Kurdish intellectuals who highlight non-territorial principles of solidarity and stressing communal commonalities. Whether they are representative remains to be seen. Technological devices, videos, and internet connections, and the enhanced interest in ethnicity and ethnic artefacts in the West have also been instrumental in highlighting the celebration of Kurdishness in many countries in Europe. Political propaganda and activism, with many supporters within native European populations, have enabled Kurdish causes to gain much sympathy and an important political space in Europe.

The ethnic mosaic of the Anatolian rectangle inherited from the Ottoman Empire has also made the fate of the two communities inextricable: there is a long history of intermarriage, shared political development, and lack of insulation of the two populations from each other. Neither Turkish nor Kurdish history exists in isolation. A Turkish factor has remained integral to the Kurdish sense of self, be it in the form of resentment and resistance, or affection and affinity. This may sound as little encouragement for the peaceful long-term resolution of the present conflict when one remembers over a million mixed marriages between Serbs, Bosnians, and Croatians before the burning of the Yugoslav state. However, the pessimism this fact evokes can be overcome when one remembers that 'it has been the absence of democratic institutions in Russia, the former Yugoslavia, Afghanistan, Somalia, Czechoslovakia and all the other disintegrating multicultural nations that aided and abetted tendencies to ethnic fragmentation and national solution' (Barber 1996: 144). The lesson that this quotation conveys alerts us to the idea that spatial containment of Kurds in the south-east has the potential of sharpening internal boundaries only in the absence of democracy and integrative mechanisms. With the ongoing armed conflict between the PKK and the state security forces causing poverty, hardship, unemployment, and homelessness among the Kurdish citizens of the Republic and the heavy military presence in the region which undermines normalcy, the mental borders between the two communities have been more sharply demarcated. Moreover, the ongoing feud between the Kurdish factions in Northern Iraq testifies to the bitter political divisions and competing loyalties among Kurds which, in the end, seriously hamper a shared idea and vision of a pan-Kurdish state.

Conclusion: *e pluribus unum?*[13]

This essay is an attempt to rethink the connections between the metaphor of boundaries as containers of democracy and the evolution of Turkish and

---

[13] From many, one.

Kurdish identities since the genesis of the Republic. It seems clear that the territorial question, more so for the Turks than the Kurds, is a functional spin-off of contentions that are substantially about power and hegemony in conditions of a historic trend toward social and cultural pluralism in an age of globalizing modernity. The rising appeal of ethnic Kurdish and Islamic fidelities are inextricably intertwined with Turkish nationalist commitments to territorial and political unity and consensuality.

It is important to recognize that neither national identity nor territorial nationalism are illegitimate, pathological, or outdated concepts. What is called into question is the kind of political imagination and understanding of power which sees national identity as 'the only form of life', far superior epistemically to any alternatives. Thus, the problem of nationalism can be solved and national identity can only survive if its meaning is limited: 'national identity, an important support of democratic institutions is best preserved by restricting its scope in favour of non-national identities' (Keane 1995: 201). The new principles of national unity and integrity are debated universally and there is an intellectual consensus that they should draw from the pluralities in the society. The tricky point is that political rights should not be based on cultural and social differences but on a special kind of sameness, rooted in universal principles of equality and freedom. In short, the discomfort and fear about the politics of community-based identities in Turkey can be eliminated when the question of identity is put on the table and analysed from a fresh perspective.

Wishful thinking aside, predictions regarding the future of a change in Turkey's public philosophy are unreliable. This is so because any new move toward establishing a multidimensional nationalism and public imagination requires two simultaneous changes which are difficult, to say the least: the first is 'catching up with' the 'modern' meaning of Western liberal democratic tradition which goes beyond majoritarian arithmetic, while the second is adoption of 'late-modern' components of democracy. Modern democracy presupposes an ethos of democratic legitimacy by which institutions and policies are accepted by even the minority as legitimate simply because they are democratic. The elements in this common conception of legitimacy are accountability and democratic control of the political class through the existence of robust civil institutions including political parties and the supremacy of the rule of law and constitutions. These procedural norms of modern liberal tradition are especially important for developing a critical public sphere for the representation of Kurdish views, and the discussion of new ideas on the Kurdish question without fear of state repression and for a greater public accountability of the public policies on the issue. Catching up with the 'modern' limited state offers possibilities of moderating the nationalist sentiments on both sides as well: '. . . the common values arising out of, for example, union or parent-teacher association or political party membership . . . Difference needs to be offset against common membership . . . rather than being used as an argument for separation' (Barber 1996: 143–4).

In addition, there are post-modern realities in this late modern age that need to be addressed too by the Turkish political class. This is related to the task of drawing common political sentiments from a plurality of cultural and social existences. William E. Connolly (1993: 65) specifies the bases of a new understanding of democracy that democratizes territoriality and nationality in 'late-modern' conditions of uncertainties and paradoxes:

(1) promotion of an egalitarian constitution of cultural life;
(2) establishment of a not too strong sense of shared understandings; and
(3) initiation of a political culture in which a variety of constituencies respond affirmatively to uncertainties and diversities of late modern life by participating in the construction and reconstruction of their identities.

We need to be optimistic about the ability of the Republic to adopt 'modern' limitations of the state in order to adapt itself to a 'post-modern' international environment that, together with other variables, has led the Kurdish question to achieve its present status. *E pluribus unum* is the hope.

But are there concrete grounds for this hope to be realized? The contemporary reality of Turkish politics does not quite generate hopes for a new political wisdom that might easily replace the conventional. Nevertheless, two developments suggest that the unhappy *status quo* is not sustainable indefinitely. The first is related to the growing public awareness that what the Kurds want is what the larger society wants. It has become clear that a central aspect of the Kurdish issue is the conflict between those elements of the regime that advocate modern and post-modern reforms to establish a more open and accountable public space with full regard for the basic rights and freedoms, and those elements that have an interest in resisting these reforms. Curiously enough, it was a road accident on 3 November 1996 in Susurluk, a small township in north-western Turkey, that was instrumental in awakening the public's consciousness to this reality: the identity of the two passengers who died, and the one who was injured, revealed the existence of a criminal triangle of politicians, mafiosi, and security forces engaged in the war against the PKK. It seems clear that the state security forces have been systematically involved in black money laundering, drug-trafficking, and extra-judicial killings. The public anger at the 'Susurluk affair', as it came to be called, turned into an avalanche of societal pressure to reform the justice system, the police, and the bureaucracy, and they called into question the legitimacy of the security operations undertaken in the region in the last decades. Whether the full truth behind the Susurluk affair is ever established or not, the affair has helped to drive home the fact that the Kurdish issue is part of a broader challenge to the state to modernize and democratize itself amidst post-cold war realities.

Secondly, as it becomes clear that the Turkish military has dealt a serious blow to the core of the PKK, including the arresting and trying of its leader Ocalan, it is entirely within the discretion of Turkey's ruling class to move toward a new consensus, based on a more pluralist environment and improved local and national conditions. The power vacuum the PKK will leave behind in the region provides a visible incentive for prudent policy-makers to create a new politics, to respond effectively and efficiently to the contemporary claims of self-defining identities. Life, in other words, is pushing for new solutions, making the ones devised ten or fifteen years ago completely outdated and defunct.

Postscript: After the Capture and Trial of Abdullah Öcalan

After the first draft of this chapter was completed in 1998, Abdullah Öcalan, who stood at the helm of the PKK for 20 years, first became a fugitive and then was captured by the Turkish security forces in Kenya on 15 February 1999. He was subsequently imprisoned in Turkey, tried, and sentenced to death on 29 June. The implications of his dramatic arrest and trial in a State Security Court on a prison island in the Sea of Marmara on charges of crimes against the state, have obvious bearings on the arguments advanced above.

The capture of its most-wanted man, held responsible for the deaths of 30,000 Turkish soldiers, fellow Kurds in the PKK, and civilians on both sides gave a tremendous boost to the self-defined image of the Turkish state. The election victories in April 1998 of the most nationalist Turkish platforms which refused to accept any compromise with Kurdish claims, were partly the result of the frustration and anger felt by Italy's refusal to extradite Öcalan and by the European calls for a fair trial. He had been detained in Rome in November 1998 after he was forced to leave his home base of 18 years, Syria, following an agreement between Turkey and Syria.

The Turkish government chose to use Öcalan's trial to 'teach' the democratic world that the PKK is a vicious terrorist organization, helped out by countries to its east and, most notably, to its west, in financing, training, and finding sanctuary for its members. Trying to embarrass the west by accusing its members of violating the fundamental rule and norm of 'international cooperation against terrorism' did not, however, serve the goal of bridging the gulf between the European Union and Turkey—widening partly because of European discomfort with Turkey's human rights violations. It did bring Turkey closer to the USA: following the American co-operation with the Turkish government in seizing Öcalan in Kenya, 'Turkish policy and opinion makers who until recently attacked Washington for planning to carve up a Kurdish state in the region, directed their anger at the European capitals and expressed gratitude for the American position' (Congar 1999: 46). Buoyed by strong American support and its developing strategic relationship with Israel, Ankara felt confident it could ride the storm within the European Union, including the pleas for clemency after Öcalan's death sentence. On the issue of comparison between the Kosovo Albanians and the Kurds, the Turkish government saw no parallel at all, despite its recognition of the persisting western image of Öcalan as a freedom fighter rather than as a bloody terrorist. Indeed, it indirectly holds the west responsible for much of the bloodshed in Turkey. Ankara's posture toward the Nato intervention in Kosovo—in the name of human rights and humanitarian imperatives—actually sought to draw strength from the controversy surrounding many aspects of the intervention.

Presently the arrest and trial of Öcalan does not seem to augur any significant new opening towards a reconciliation between the Turkish government and Kurdish secessionists. On the contrary, the arrest and trial have been used to reinforce the firmly held official conviction that there is no Kurdish problem but a problem of terrorism that could never have reached such explosive levels without external support. In the perspectives of the establishment and the large segments of the public, the arguments promoted for some time by liberals to the effect that the 'military solution' was bound to fail to stop violence and that what was needed was an overall democratization programme to undermine the PKK's support among the Kurds, have been proved to be invalid, indeed senseless. The liberal advocacy of a critical public sphere for the representation of Kurdish voices, Kurdish language teaching, and Kurdish broadcasting has been dismissed .

Öcalan's rather repentant posture during his trial and his 'moderate' sounding testimony aimed at politicizing the Kurdish question, and at sending different messages to different audiences. Speaking to the European gallery he seemed to be saying that he has now moved to a non-violent discourse and reduced his ambitions to the recognition by the Turkish state of the existence of a separate Kurdish entity within the 'unitary' framework of the constitution, abandoning Kurdish sovereignty aspirations altogether. The implication is that he should now be even more worthy of European support as a peaceful and representative leader, capable of engaging the Turkish government on this new agenda: that his life, that of an indispensable leader, should be spared so that he could mediate a political settlement between the PKK and the Turkish government and thus bring peace.

Within the Kurdish diaspora, however, Öcalan's arrest and trial seems to have had a divisive effect. There are those whose loyalty to the PKK and to the cause of Kurdish independence has hardened because of what they feel has been the unfair treatment Öcalan suffered from European hands which refused to grant him safe sanctuary, and, of course, from the Turkish government. Some diasporic elements, by contrast, appear to have sensed that Öcalan's capture and trial have delivered a major blow to Kurdish nationalism for many years to come. They can be expected to move toward a new search for a peaceful solution to the problem, needless to say, in a yet unclear way. In both tendencies, the centre of their activity has definitely shifted to Europe, which suggests a further internationalization of the Kurdish question that will upset any Turkish governmental calculation that the issue has definitively been resolved.

As regards the PKK, Öcalan's capture, trial, and testimony highlighted the congenital weaknesses of the organization's murky ideology, repressive leadership, and ruthless methods. Öcalan offered his services to the Turkish state to bring down the PKK members from the mountains in three months time if given the chance, that is, if his life would be spared (CNN 1999). His summing up speech emphasized the objections he had raised within the PKK from 1987 to mid-1990s, to its strategies on the grounds that 'these acts of violence were destroying us' (*Milliyet*, 23 June 1999). The speech made visible a gross contradiction between his self-claimed authority to be able to turn the PKK into a peaceful organization in a period of three months, and his confession of his failure to do so in the past. The new wave of violence that the PKK started in major cities after Öcalan's arrest does not add credibility to his openly expressed 'wish' to end the conflict through peaceful methods either. The interpretation that the PKK is simply following the leaders' promise to the Turkish government that was conditional on his life being spared, or the view that there is a leadership struggle within the PKK that presently clouds the formation of clear cut strategy, hold no sway against the popular Turkish belief that violence is the only language the PKK has known since its genesis.

The big question is whether the legacy of insensitivity, violence, and mistrust on both sides, that has plagued the south-east of Turkey for a very long time, will give way to a constructive dialogue. This depends on the extent to which both sides can go through a 'learning' process in a democratic direction, as opposed to a ' teaching' the other side a lesson. The prospects right now are not bright.

REFERENCES

Abadan-Unat, Nermin. 1997. 'Ethnic Business, Ethnic Communities, and Ethno-Politics among Turks in Europe' in *Immigration into Western Societies: Problems and Politics*, edited by Emek M. Uncarer and Donald J. Puchala. London, Washington, DC: Pinter.

Anderson, Benedict. 1991. *Imagined Communities: Reflections on the Origins and Spread of Nationalism*. London: Verso.

Andrews, F. David (ed.). 1982. *The Lost Peoples of the Middle East*. Salisbury: Documentary Publications.

Appadurai, Arjun. 1997. *Modernity at Large*. Minneapolis, MN: University of Minnesota Press.

Barber, Benjamin R. 1996. 'Multiculturalism between Individuality and Community: Chasm or Bridge?' in *Liberal Modernism and Democratic Individuality; George Kateb and the Practices of Politics*, edited by Austin Sarat, and Dana R. Villa. Princeton, NJ: Princeton University Press.

Blaney, David L., and Inayatullah, Naeem. 1996. 'A Problem with Borders' in *Perspectives on Third-World Sovereignty*, edited by Mark E. Denham and Mark Owen Lombardi. Basingstoke: Macmillan.

Bozarslan, Hamit. 1996. 'Political Crisis and the Kurdish Issue in Turkey' in *The Kurdish Nationalist Movement in the 1990s*, edited by Robert Olson. Lexington, KY: The University Press of Kentucky.

Bruinessen, Martin van. 1992. *Agha, Shaikh and State: The Social and Political Structure of Kurdistan*. London and New Jersey: Zed Books.

—— 1996. 'Multiple Shifting Identities: The Kurds, Turkey, and Europe', *Conference on Redefining the Nation, State and the Citizen*, Marmara University, Istanbul, Turkey, 28–29 March.

—— 1997. 'Kurdish Society in the 1990s: Caught between State, Religion, Nationalist Movement and Intra-Kurdish Ethnic Identities'. Paper presented at Princeton University, Princeton, NJ, 22 April.

Chaliand, Gerard (ed.). 1980. *People Without a Country: The Kurds and Kurdistan*. London: Zed Press.

Çiller, Tansu. 1993. *DYP Genel Başkanı Tansu Çiller'in Konuşmaları: 19 Haziran–5 Kasım 1993 (The Speeches of the True Path Party Leader and Prime Minister Tansu Çiller: 19 June–5 November 1993)*. Ankara: Başbakanlık Basım Merkezi.

CNN. 1999. 'Öcalan Pleads for a Chance to Make Peace with Turkey', *CNN Interactive Web Site*, 31 May 1999.

Congar, Yasemin. 1998a. 'Apo'nun Şam Villaları' (Apo's Villas in Damascus), *Milliyet*, 26 March.

—— 1998b. 'Mektup Bekliyor' (Waiting for a Letter). *Milliyet*, 12 April.

—— 1999. 'Do You Understand What I'm Saying?' *Private View*. 3: 40–6.

Connolly, William E. 1993. 'Democracy and Territoriality' in *Reimagining the Nation*, edited by Marjorie Ringrose and Adam J. Lerner. Buckingham: Open University Press.

Demirel, Süleyman. 1997. 'Irk ve Din Partisi Olmaz' (There Cannot be a Party of Race and Religion). *Hürriyet*, 11 September.

Dumont, Paul. 1984. 'The Origins of Kemalist Ideology' in *Atatürk and the Modernization of Turkey*, edited by Jacob M. Landau. Boulder, CO: Westview Press.

Fierlbeck, Katherine. 1996. 'The Ambivalent Potential of Cultural Identity', *Canadian Journal of Political Science*, 1: 3–22.

Hall, Stuart. 1996. 'The New Ethnicities' in *Ethnicity*, edited by John Hutchinson and Anthony D. Smith. Oxford: Oxford University Press.

Held, David. 1996. *Models of Democracy*. Stanford, CA: Stanford University Press.

Hürriyet. 1995. Interview with Şerafettin Elçi.'Turkey is Ours', 26 March.

Kazancıgil, Ali. 1981. 'The Ottoman-Turkish State and Kemalism' in *Atatürk—The Founder of a Modern State*, edited by Ergun Özbudun and Ali Kazancıgil. London: Hurst.

Keane, John. 1995. 'Nations, Nationalism and European Citizens' in *Notions of Nationalism*, edited by Sukumar Periwal. Budapest, London, and New York, NY: Central European University Press.

Kinzer, Stephen. 1997. 'Kurdish Rebels in Turkey Are Down but Not Out', *New York Times*, 8 March.

Kirişci, Kemal, and Winrow, Gareth M. 1997. *The Kurdish Question and Turkey: An Example of a Trans-state Ethnic Conflict*. London, Portland, OR: Frank Cass.

Kohn, Hans. 1969. *A History of Nationalism in the East*. Grosse Pointe, MI: Scholarly Press.

—— (1982). *Nationalism, its Meaning and History*. Malabar, Fla: Krieger.

Kramer, Martin, 1997. 'The Middle East, Old and New', *Daedalus*, 2: 89–112.

Kymlicka, Will. 1995. 'Misunderstanding Nationalism', *Dissent* (Winter, 1995): 130–7.

Lewis, Bernard. 1968. *The Emergence of Modern Turkey*. Oxford: Oxford University Press.

Lustick, Ian S., and O'Leary, Brendan. 1997. 'Rightsizing the State: The Politics of Moving Borders: Theoretical Guidelines for the Participants of Social Science Research Council Workshop 1997', unpublished manuscript, 29 February.

Marcus, Aliza. 1993. 'Turkey's Kurds After the Gulf War: A Report from the Southeast' in *People Without a Country: The Kurds and Kurdistan*, edited by Gerard Chaliand. New York, NY: Olive Branch Press.

McDowall, David. 1996. *A Modern History of the Kurds*. London: I. B. Tauris.

McGarry, John, and O'Leary, Brendan. 1994. 'The Political Regulation of National and Ethnic Conflict', *Parliamentary Affairs*, 46: 94–117.

Mutlu, Servet. 1996. 'Ethnic Kurds in Turkey: A Demographic Study', *International Journal of Middle Eastern Studies*, 28: 517–41.

PIAR-GALLUP. 1994. 'Kürt Araştırması'. Istanbul: Piar-Gallup. 29 September–25 October 1994.

Poggi, Gianfranco. 1990. *The State: Its Nature, Development and Prospects*. Oxford: Polity.

Sakallıoğlu, Ümit Cizre. 1996. 'Historicizing the Present and Problematizing the Future of the Kurdish Problem: A Critique of the TOBB Report on the Eastern Question', *New Perspectives on Turkey*, 14: 1–22.

Smith, Anthony D. 1991. *National Identity*. Harmondsworth: Penguin.

Tinc, Ferai. 1997. 'Güneydoğu Gezisinin Ardından' (After the Southeastern Tour), *Hürriyet*, 23 November.

TOBB. 1995. 'Doğu Sorunu—Teşhisler ve Tespitler'. Ankara: TOBB (Union of Turkish Chambers of Commerce and Stock Exchange). July.

Wolin, Sheldon. 1996. 'Fugitive Democracy' in *Democracy and Difference: Contesting the Boundaries of the Political*, edited by Seyla Benhabib. Princeton, NJ: Princeton University Press.

Yavuz, Hakan. 1995. 'The Patterns of Political Islamic identity: Dynamics of National and Transnational Loyalties and Identities', *Central Asian Survey*, 3.

9

Manufacturing Identity and Managing Kurds in Iraq

Denise Natali

One way to think about regulating ethno-national conflict is to employ
O'Leary and McGarry's taxonomy that distinguishes policies that seek to
eliminate ethnic challenges from those which attempt to manage them
(O'Leary and McGarry 1995). When state élites pursue elimination or management strategies, or a combination of the two, they also decide whether or
not to down-size the state, that is, to reduce the scope—either functional or
territorial—of state institutions and state policies. These strategic choices
have different consequences for the state and its populations. Some may lead
to massacres of entire communities, destruction of land, and economic
decline, while others may encourage political stability and economic growth.
There is no obvious moral hierarchy, as O'Leary and McGarry argue, that
enables us to value integration more than partition, though there is nothing
morally weighty to be said in favour of genocide or expulsions. But even if it
is not possible to construct a universally agreed normative ranking of policy
options, it is useful to identify the conditions in which state élites choose
some policies over others, and the changes in these policies over time. Adding
a temporal dimension to the taxonomy may give insight into patterns of
behaviour between the centre and periphery, constraints of state institutions,
and the role of external influences in managing ethnic challenges.

This chapter examines successive reshaping projects in Iraq—the
attempt by the Iraqi power élite to draw Kurds into the state, recognize the
existence of a Kurdish ethnicity and Kurdish region, while nevertheless
maintaining the idea that the Kurdish people are 'Iraqis first' and that
'Kurdistan' is an integral ethnic and geographical component of Iraq.[1] I

---

[1] In the terminology of O'Leary and McGarry positive Iraqi policy towards the Kurds has
permed elements of integration and territorial autonomy, while negative Iraqi policy has combined
elements of genocide, (internal) expulsion, coercive assimilation, and control. See Brendan
O'Leary's Chapter 2.

analyse centre–periphery relations over a seventy-year period, from the creation of the Iraqi state until the early 1990s. The discourse and policies by successive Iraqi centres toward the Kurdish periphery show that the strategic choices made by the Iraqi élites were a function of transformations of the state. The uneven evolution of Iraq since its formation, from a colonized country to an independent republic, and to a semi-industrialized, Ba'athist, social-welfare state was a changing context in which the incentives for state élites to appeal to Kurds altered. Pushing and pulling these efforts were external influences, internal power-struggles between civilian and military cliques, and tensions within Kurdish communities. But it was the drive of the Iraqi élites to construct an ethnicized, secular-based nationalism within a highly centralized political system that ultimately prevented effective reshaping in Iraq. While opportunities for reshaping existed, the state élites failed to instil a normative sense of 'Iraqiness' among Kurdish communities. As public policies became militant and Arabized, Kurds differentiated themselves from the centre rather than be homogenized in the state as Iraqi citizens. They also divided among themselves, preventing the evolution of a unified Kurdish national identity.

One way to theorize about patterns of behaviour between the centre and periphery is to think of reshaping as part of the state élites' attempts to consolidate their power-base. Centre–periphery relations are closely linked to the pushes and pulls of balancing government factions. If military factions win out over civilian groups, or if conservative Arab nationalists assume control of the parliament defeating leftist challengers, then political power may become centralized and cohesive. State policies are likely to reflect the bloc in power, and to favour some populations over others. They will impact on divisions between Kurds, and reinforce the fractures within the periphery along socio-economic and political lines. If however, political power is more evenly divided between the various factions at the centre, then the chances of political compromise between Kurds and the state increase. Kurds are more likely to accept the state during these periods since political accommodation is more likely under a moderate, decentralized centre than it is under a highly cohesive state. Internal power-plays in the Iraqi core are important in understanding shifts in Kurdish behaviour because they represent changes in the distribution of power and the nature of the state. They are part of the larger process of regime consolidation and centralization that directly impacts on centre–periphery relations (Lustick 1993: 42).

The Transition from Empire to State

The partition of the Ottoman Empire eventually distributed Kurdish communities, territories, water resources, and the petroleum deposits of the fertile crescent into four geographically contiguous sovereign territories: Turkey, Iran, Syria, and Iraq. After the Treaty of Sevres that suggested Kurdish statehood (1920), and the ratification of the Lausanne Treaty (1923), which rescinded the offer, each Kurdish region was legally subsumed into a different administrative and political system. The new state system meant that some Kurds no longer shared a common political centre in Constantinople, but were under different central governments within the boundaries of a new and emergent Middle East state system, albeit one still supervised by the British and French empires. Kurdish regions soon acquired pivotal strategic positions in this underdeveloped zone (see Figures 9.1–9.3).

The creation of Iraq under the British Empire did not immediately alter the patron–client networks and political identities of the late Ottoman system. In the early twentieth century, the heterogeneous, stratified, and undeveloped Kurdish society was still largely traditional—tribal, religious, and local identities remained salient in an exemplary case of Gellner's agraria (Gellner 1983). Socio-economic status was based on distinctions between tribal and non-tribal communities; warriors and tillers of the land; landowners, peasants, and urban groups (Batatu 1978: 58–61; van Bruinessen 1992: 40–1). Although landowners were not homogeneous, the majority consisted of tribal sheikhs. Iraqi Kurds also guarded their ties to Islam and the orders and sects to which they belonged: *Naqshbandiyya*, *Qadiriyya*, *Kaka'i* (*ahl-e haqq*), *Ishna Shari*, and *Yezidi*. Antagonisms between Muslims and the Christian minorities, such as the Chaldaens and Nestorians, persisted into the early twentieth century.

The creation of new sovereign boundaries did not remove the ties that existed between the Kurds, or between Kurdish and non-Kurdish provinces. Given their demographic compositions, political geographies, and resources, Kurdish regions maintained different relations with the state and local populations based on the pre-existing Ottoman *vilayet* system. Some regions were tied commercially and culturally to Persian communities, while others were more integrated with Arabs and Turcomans. Overlapping these local identities was a budding Kurdish nationalist consciousness that emerged in the late Ottoman period.

Under the League of Nations mandate system, Britain took control of Iraq and Palestine while the French settled in neighbouring Syria and Lebanon. Strictly speaking, Iraq was a creation: a novel political system constructed

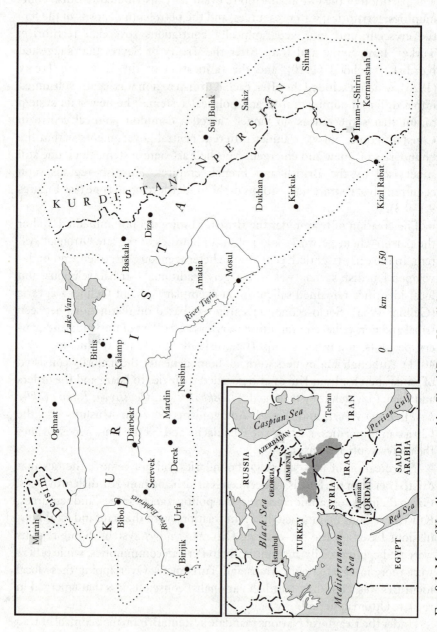

FIG. 9.1 Map of Kurdistan presented by Sharif Paşa, Kurdish representative to the Paris Peace Conference, after the declaration of President Woodrow Wilson's Fourteen Points

FIG. 9.2 Map used by Woodrow Wilson in the Sevres Treaty of 10 August 1920

from three ex-Ottoman provinces. Unlike the Ottomans, the British treated Kurdistan (Mosul province) as a separate entity from Arab Iraq. They organized the new state in two zones: *al-Iraq al Cadjmi*, comprising the northern province of Mosul, predominantly Kurdish but with a Turkish presence; *al-Iraq al-Arab*, the south and central zone of Iraq, that is, Baghdad province, predominantly Arab Sunni; and Basra province, predominantly Shi'a. The High Commissioner assumed direct responsibility for Mosul and treated this 'Kurdistan' as an autonomous entity—evident in British accounting, fiscal, and administrative procedures.

In the unstable post-war context and with the fear of losing the oil-rich Mosul province to Turkey, the British officials made special efforts to pacify Kurdish communities. They recognized the Kurds as a unique ethnic group and acknowledged their nationalist claims. Some foreign officers gained the

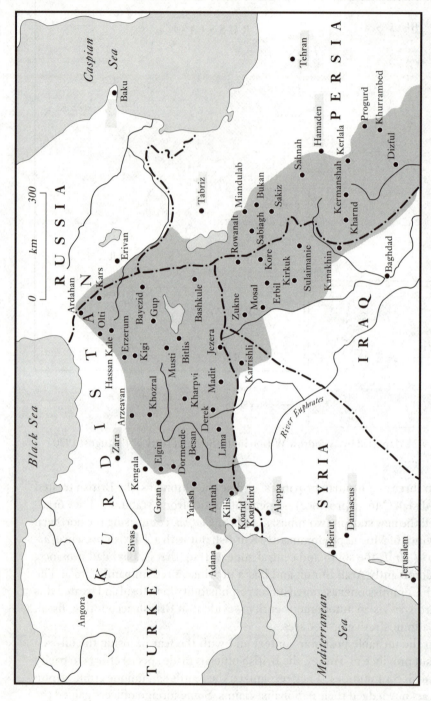

Fig. 9.3 Map of Kurdistan presented by representatives of the Iraqi Kurdish Rizari party to the American legation in Baghdad and the United Nations in 1945

confidence of Kurdish tribal chiefs and sheikhs by offering them political posts, financial incentives, and promising to protect the Caliphate. During his travels with Kurdish notables Major Noel assured an independent Kurdistan with Alexandretta as the seaport. Major Soane spoke directly to the Kurds about their rights to self-determination.

The British attempted to institutionalize Kurdish equality in the new state. The provisional 1921 Iraqi Constitution asserted that Iraq was comprised of two ethnic groups, Arabs and Kurds, and that the Kurdish and Arabic languages had equal status. Iraqi High Commissioner Sir Percy Cox supported these policies by opposing the government's request to hoist the Iraqi flag in Kurdish provinces and refusing to appoint an 'Arabized Kurd' as governor of Suleymaniya province. Additionally, seeking Iraq's admission to the League of Nations the British employed measures that would assure 'minority groups rights' in the new state. Cox welcomed outside intervention, inviting international commissions to Iraq that recognized the quasi-autonomy of local groups (French Governmental Archives 1929).

The large cultural and political opportunities promised to Kurds were limited in time and unevenly implemented, which heightened the ethnic and socio-economic dichotomies in Iraqi and Kurdish society. As the British gained control of the government and settled their territorial claims, they employed new state-building policies that favoured secular communities, Arab nationalists, and tribal-landowning groups. The new Iraqi government was formed from a civil administration of British, Iraqi, and Indian officers. Moulded after the UK's political system, it was a hereditary constitutional monarchy with an elected bicameral legislature. To separate religion and politics, the *sharia* code was omitted from the constitution, although Islam became the official state religion. The *sadah* families retained their religious influence, holding the largest share of positions in the government (Batatu 1978: 189).[2] The British did not build upon traditional Islamic structures nor employ pan-Islamism in their efforts to encourage Iraqi nation-state building. Rather, to bring Iraqi populations together, they attempted to construct a secularized Iraqi identity based on a sense of Iraqi unity (*al-wahda al-iraqiya*).

This idea was particularly challenging given the nature of Iraqi society, or societies, in the state undergoing British tutelage. The population included a mixture of Shi'a and Sunni Arabs, Shi'a and Sunni Kurds, Christians, Turks, Armenians, Jews, and Assyrians. More than half of this heterogeneous population was Shi'a and about one-fifth was Kurdish. Instead of softening or bridging these differences, the British heightened them by elevating Sunni Arabs into positions of power in the government. After appointing the Arab

---

[2] The *sadah* families claim to be of the Prophet's blood.

nationalist, Faisal, a Sunni, as the first king, British officers assigned key posts such as the ministries of education and defence, and the chief of staff to the Sunni Arabs Sati al-Husri, Jafar al-Askari, and Nuri al-Said respectively. By Sunni-Arabizing the government the British had handed power to a group presiding over a population that in its overwhelming majority was nei-ther Sunni nor Arab. Kurds not only lost their own bid for statehood, but were placed in a new context where their former Muslim counterparts were now their overlords. Also, to control unruly tribal groups and Faisal's power, the British played off tribes against one another, instigating land disputes and internal hostilities. In the 1920s, the Royal Air Force and the Iraqi military bombed villages indiscriminately.

Still, Kurdish tribals pledged their loyalty to the government. Coercion, and normative and utilitarian means of compliance helped co-opt tribal and landowning groups. In contrast to the Ottoman reformers, who strengthened the towns at the expense of the tribes, British officials elevated tribal groups while urban centres expanded. Kurdish *aghas* from the leading landowning families were appointed as provincial governors and given relative autonomy (Batatu 1978: 56–61, 90–3). British officials altered the traditional Ottoman land tenure system (*al-tassarif*) so that lands that were formerly the sole properties of the state and frequently redistributed amongst members of tribes became the absolute possessions of tribal chiefs and sheikhs. Certain tribes were excluded from the jurisdiction of central government courts; they were educated in separate schools; they were 'elected' to parliament; and they enjoyed tax benefits. For instance, to spur the production of tobacco, the main cash crop of Kurdistan and Iraq, the revenue department issued over 2,700 new tobacco licenses to merchants in Baghdad and the Kurdish regions. The British also cancelled Ottoman customs taxes that had increased as much as 15 per cent during the war. In consequence, Kurdish *aghas* became some of the wealthiest landowners in Iraq.[3]

If Kurdish politics had been entirely tribal then the majority of Kurds would have been pacified by these policies. Yet this was not the case. As landowners increased their power, peasant communities remained powerless. Also, the policy of elevating tribes counterbalanced the growth of towns and cities whose denizens generally opposed British rule. This situation contin-

---

[3] Material drawn from *inter alia* Anon (1922–3: 11–14); His Majesty's Government (1920: 7–9); Ross (1959: 84); Marr (1985: 65); Lenczowski (1962: 264): McDowell (1996: 297); and Batatu (1978: 56–61, 90–3, and 121). Tribal–state relations were influenced by lucrative tobacco farming. Of the total 3,419,834 *khans* of tobacco (*tutin*) produced in 1922 in Iraq , the bulk was from the Kurdish cities of Suleymaniya (66.8%) from Mosul (19.8%), and from Kirkuk (13.2%). By 1945 about 14,000 of the 16,000 pounds of tobacco produced in Iraq annually was supplied by the Kurdish north.

ued into the 1950s. Even though Faisal added a bureaucratic layer to the government, he ensured that it was tied to the privileged landed stratum. What emerged were two policies in Iraq, one for the tribes and one for the townsmen (Batatu 1978: 93).[4]

Which Iraqi Identity?

Even after Iraq gained nominal independence in 1932, neither the British nor the local élites to whom they transferred power succeeded in consolidating their power-base. Political power waxed and waned between the monarchist—*taba'i* official or imperially dependent nationalists—and those seeking full Iraqi independence; and between communists, Arab, and Kurdish nationalists. Each political tendency that emerged at this time had different interpretations of Iraqi identity, which in turn had different consequences for the Iraqi nation-state building project. Until the early 1940s 'official', monarchist or dependent nationalism (*taba'i*) was predominant among tribal groups, former Sharifian officers, the bureaucratic élite, the Hashemite family, the *sadah* families, and the 'old social classes' who wanted to assure their landowning privileges.

The monarchy's notion of Iraqi identity also appealed to traditional Kurdish leaders because it de-ethnicized the official state nationalism by promulgating the idea of being 'Iraqis first' and recognizing the distinct Kurdish ethnic identity. Until his expulsion from Iraq, Mulla Mustafa Barzani demanded 'Kurdistan for the Kurds under British protection'. The Kurdish ministers without portfolio, Majid Mustafa and Daus al-Haidari, called for Kurdish autonomy that co-operated with Baghdad. While writing about the 'moaning of his heart for the sadness of Kurdistan' Ahmed Begi Jaf remained loyal to the British, who assured his generous salary and political influence as a nationalist leader (Jaf 1969: 134–6).

The Iraqi-first identity also became tied to leftist ideology. Communist and socialist influences emerged in the 1930s, facilitated by the world depression, economic changes that marginalized peasant and urban groups, the influence of the Soviet Union as a model for development, and the formation of leftist groups in Syria, Iran, and Turkey (Laqueur 1957: 175; Ismael 1979; and Batatu 1978: 389–439, 659–99). Communist and socialist ideologies were non-ethnicized and created inclusive spaces for Kurds, Turcomans, and Shi'a Arabs seeking Iraqi independence and socio-economic reform. As with

---

[4] Section 40 of the Criminal Code stated that 'any undesirable townsman can be removed from tribal territories'.

tab'ai nationalism, they helped create collective identities that often became more politically prominent over ethnic identities. For instance, with the rise of the petroleum industry in the 1940s, Kurdish labourers in the Kirkuk and Mosul refineries affiliated with the Iraqi Communist Party (ICP) as part of the new working class and anti-imperialist movement. Leftists temporarily succeeded in 1936, when General Bakr Sidqi, a Kurd, and his Turkish colleague, Hikmet Suleyman, conducted the first military *coup d'etat* in Iraq and removed Arab nationalists from office. Though a socialist he did not make claims to Kurdish nationalism, but displayed Iraqiist tendencies. His was the first in a cycle of *coups d'etat* that would continue until 1942, when the British reoccupied the country under the exigencies of World War II.

A third ideological current was Arab nationalism. It resonated with the core beliefs of most military officers and the *al-Ahd* society within the government. During and after World War II it was influenced by fascism and encouraged by Syrian Ba'athism, the Arab League, and Nasserism in Egypt (see Devlin 1979: 4; Jaber 1966: 23; Wafik 1984; and Tibi 1990). Arab nationalists had distinct ideas about the past, present, and future Iraqi identity based on pan-Arab nationalism (*qawmiyya*) and Iraqi patriotism (*wataniyya*). *Qawmiyya* nationalism was ethnicized—it emphasized the revival of the Arab nation, of which Iraq was considered an integral part. Most members of the Iraq Renaissance Socialist Party (Ba'athists) were *qawmiyya* nationalists, although not all Arab nationalists were Ba'athists. *Qawmiyya* nationalists also employed myths and policies that attempted to deny Kurdish ethnicity. In Ba'athist ideology the Kurds were considered of Arab origin, separated from their true motherland because of colonialism. Ba'athists even claimed that Salahidin, the famous Kurdish warrior, was an Arab.

One of the leading pan-Arabists, Sati'al-Husri, a Syrian-born educator whom the British and King Faisal put in charge of Iraqi education, envisioned a secularized, ethnicized Arab Iraqi identity as necessary to protect Arab culture from imperialism and Zionism. Al-Husri criticized Islamists and Arab nationalists who supported Islam as 'detractors' of Arab nationalist thought—see Yousif 1991: 173; Cleveland 1991: 91–3; Ismael 1979: 63; Wafik 1984: 261; Tibi 1990: 116–23; and Batatu 1978: Ch. 6. His pan-Arabism was influenced by Herderian linguistic nationalism: 'the nation is nothing but a group of people speaking the same language . . . so that every Arabic-speaking people is an Arab people' (al-Husri 1959). Al-Husri introduced Arab nationalist themes to school curriculums and Arabized language and history instruction. After the creation of the state of Israel and the Arab loss in 1948, *qawmiyya* nationalism was outwardly expressed in harsh anti-Israeli and anti-western rhetoric. What emerged was a radical form of nationalism committed to fundamental social change for Arab freedom and unity.

Though *qawmiyya* nationalism was highly exclusionary it did not become a single or dominant ideology among Arabs. Pan-Arabism coexisted with a more moderate strain of Arab nationalism based on the notion of patriotism to the fatherland (*watan*). In addition to the notion of territory, *watan* referred to linguistic and cultural ties between groups living in the same geographical area. *Wataniyya* nationalists supported the idea of an independent Iraq that could exist within a federation of Arab states, but not as part of an Arab union. Their myths about Iraqi identity rested on the idea that Iraqis are the direct twentieth-century descendants of the Mesopotamian and Babylonian civilizations.

These views had more inclusive implications for Kurdish–Arab and centre–periphery relations. Unlike *qawmiyya* nationalists, *wataniyya* nationalists saw themselves as Iraqis first and recognized the local identities of non-Arab ethnic groups (Bensaid 1987: 151).[5] They consisted of moderate and civilian Arab groups who viewed the Kurds as partners, with their own distinct language, culture, and territory. *Wataniyya* nationalists did not attempt to define Kurdish territory as Arab. Consequently, Kurds and leftists saw *wataniyya* nationalism as more politically palatable than *qawmiyya* nationalist discourse. *Wataniyya* nationalism also gained strength because of the secular nationalism of Christian Arabs and European policies that supported regional development and local rather than pan-Arab identities.

In this partially ethnicizing political climate, a moderate Kurdish ethnonationalist current became prominent in Iraqi politics. Just as Arabs attempted to protect their culture against European encroachments, some Iraqi Kurds reacted against growing Arab nationalism. While the British recognized Kurdish ethnic identity and promised cultural freedoms, the Anglo-Iraqi treaty of 1930 made no mention of the Kurds or minority rights in Iraq. Political, educational, and economic opportunities were unequal between Kurdish and Arab provinces, and within Kurdish regions. Of fifty-seven cabinet ministers between 1920 and 1936 only four were Kurds (Hassanpour 1992: 114). Iraqi Kurds were also influenced by Kurdish mobilizations in Syria, Turkey, and Iran during the 1930s and 1940s. They created various clandestine nationalist parties, including the umbrella organization the Democratic Party of Kurdistan (KDP). The writings of Kurdish nationalists such as Mohammed Amin Zeki and Ahmed Begi Jaf were popularized in Iraqi Kurdish circles. Zeki's question 'What race are the Kurdish people, and from where did they come?' generated scholarly attention to the ethnic identity of the Kurds (Zeki 1931: 1).[6] By the mid-1940s

---

[5] The terms *watan* and *wataniyya* have undergone changes in the Arab states in which they are used.

[6] Zeki was influenced by the Young Turk movement of the 1900s and became tied to the Kurdish nationalist circles in Istanbul.

Kurdish nationalism had become a smaller ideological current that coexisted with *tab'ai* nationalism, communism, and Arab nationalism.

Still, Kurdish nationalism was fractured and weak. Although the early Kurdish revolts were defined by their segmented and heterogeneous nature, the mobilizations of the 1940s and 1950s were more complex, reflecting the uneven modernization policies alongside social segmentation. With the development of petroleum reserves, the resources available to state officials expanded, enabling the government to implement programs that mobilized a new urban élite and improved the lot of some unemployed masses.

However, the state officials made no real effort to alter the socio-economic structure of the country. Rather than transform political power by developing industry, they depended upon supportive agricultural policies, which ensured a key role for traditional élites in Kurdish politics and society. Continued support of the traditional stratum allowed the urban–tribal dichotomy to become prominent in Kurdish politics. One of the underlying themes of Kurdish nationalist discourse was the negative role of feudalism in the Kurdish movement. The Kurdish leftist Komeley party referred to Kurdish tribalism as the 'source of all misery and bitter outcomes' (Hassanpour 1992: 63–4). Jaf, a tribal leader himself who benefited from the colonial system, urged Kurds to 'wake up from the hands of ignorance' (tribalism) (Jaf 1969: 23). Faiq Bêkes criticized the backwardness of Kurdish society, blaming tribal sheikhs and landowners for being 'impassioned by money, placing no importance on industry, science, and knowledge . . . and having an idea of honour based on wearing the biggest *jamadani* (turban) to demonstrate their megalomania' (Karim 1986: 66).[7] By the late 1940s, the KDP was split between traditional groups loyal to Barzani, and leftists influenced by Ibrahim Ahmed.

Suppressed Nationalism: Collective Mobilizations

It might have been expected that a Kurdish nationalist movement would have strengthened in this period, especially because Barzani was evicted from the country, the ICP had become Arabized, and the KDP was not invited to join the anti-imperialist United National Front. Yet, by 1958, there was no unchallenged and available political leader, legal Kurdish political party, nor developed Kurdish region that had the economic resources to mobilize Kurdish groups. Nuri Said's imposition of martial law, communist witch-

---

[7] Karim created a section of the book called *Kurdayetî* in which he placed Bêkes's ideas about Kurdish national identity.

hunts, destruction of Kurdish villages, and banning of political parties, including the KDP, suppressed any nationalist programmes. Additionally, there was an absence of political channels—democratic institutions, a civil society, permanent trade unions, interest groups, or free elections—for local populations to legally express themselves.

But even if Kurdish nationalist parties were legalized, it is unlikely that leftist, urban Kurds would have pronounced their Kurdish ethnonational identity. Iraqi politics was not highly ethnicized in the colonial context. That is, while the state élites failed to draw Kurds into the centre, they neither ethnicized or colonized Kurdistan enough to encourage Kurdish ethnonationalism. The traditional stratum retained its role in Kurdish and state politics, urban groups were mobilized, and local populations had spaces to express their Kurdish ethnic identity. Also, the co-existence of competing political currents, the undeveloped nature of pan-Arabism, and the rise of anti-imperialist opposition forces prevented the centralization of Arab nationalist power. As the anti-colonial movement gained force group loyalties shifted, bringing together communists, Arab nationalists, and Kurds together in an opposition group under the banner of Iraqi independence. The anti-imperialist current that became prominent in Iraqi politics, which included the Palestinian liberation struggle, emphasized *wataniyya* nationalism, and had an inclusive element for Kurds and Arabs alike.

Consequently, Kurdish nationalist groups were given some political opportunities to mobilize as an ethnic community. The parameters of inclusion and exclusion in the state were not clearly ethnically defined, but based on the boundaries between the rulers and the ruled. On the eve of the Iraqi revolution, non-tribal Kurds joined Arab nationalists and communists in an anti-imperialist opposition group while some tribes remained loyal to the British.

Independent Republican Iraq

After the revolutionary coup on 14 July 1958, the British were evicted from Iraq and a republic was declared. One of the main concerns of the new leaders was to consolidate political power, particularly because the alliances created between opposition groups soon dissipated. Arab nationalists, communists, and military and civilian cliques commenced new power struggles. The Arab nationalist current also shifted its character. With the rise of the Iraqi Ba'ath party, Nasserism, and the United Arab Republic (UAR) that temporarily unified Syria and Egypt, Arab nationalists insisted pan-Arabism was an integral aspect of Iraqi identity. But tensions within the Arab nationalist current continued to fracture those who supported *wataniyya* and *qawmiyya* nationalisms. Communism also became more salient. Uprisings in Lebanon against the pro-western regime of President Shamun and the 1958 Ba'athist military coup in Syria gave leftist groups a key role in regional affairs. In Iraq, President Abd al-Karim Qasim developed closer ties with the Soviet Union and Comintern countries. Consequently, competing political projects emerged between Arab nationalists, communists, and military and civilian cliques in the government.

The failure of any one faction to gain control over the political apparatus maintained an ambiguous notion of the official state identity and created inclusive spaces for Kurdish groups. The competition between communist and Arab nationalist ideologies was played out by President Brigadier General Abd al-Karim Qasim and Vice President Colonel Abd-al Salam Arif. The crux of their rivalry was the issue of *wahda*, or Arab unity. While Qasim arranged a security pact in Damascus with five liberal Arab states and participated in the UAR project, his leftist leanings and disinterest in Arab union antagonized pan-Arab nationalists (Uriel 1969: 7). Qasim was considered a communist even though he neither joined nor legalized the communist party, though he did elevate communist leaders by giving them high level positions in the government. Arif, however, was a fervent non-Ba'athist pan-Arab nationalist who believed that Iraqi identity should be part of a larger Arab nation. Tensions culminated with Arif's failed assassination attempt on Qasim and his expulsion from Iraq. Qasim then attempted to consolidate his government by gaining popular support.

The winning out of communist and leftist factions, although temporary, checked the ethnicizing tendencies of *qawmiyya* nationalists and permitted opportunities for Kurdish communities. Although Qasim's revolutionary cohort, the Free Officers, were uninterested in Kurdish equality, Qasim made concerted efforts to draw Kurds into the political centre. His ideas of a *wataniyya* identity were published in a 92-page brochure entitled 'The Kurds and the Kurdish Question' in the 1959 Baghdad Review *Editions of the New Culture*. In this publication, the author, Dr Shabur Khobak wrote: 'we must not forget that Iraq is not only an Arab state, but an Arabo-Kurdish state . . . the recognition of Kurdish nationalism by Arabs proves clearly that we are associated in the country, that we are Iraqis first, and Arabs and Kurds later' (Rondot 1958: 50–4). Qasim also attempted to institutionalize Kurdish autonomy. He established a provisional constitution that recognized Iraq's binational character. It stated that the Kurdo-Arab relationship was a 'partnership', despite the larger Arab union in which Iraq was situated. Qasim also made symbolic gestures such as placing the Kurdish sun on the Iraqi national flag, adding the Kurdish dagger crossed with an Arab sword on the Republic's constitution and coat of arms, welcoming Mustafa Barzani to Iraq after twelve years of exile, legalizing the KDP, and releasing Kurdish political prisoners from jail. At the first anniversary celebration of the 1958 revolution, tribal and urban Kurds congratulated Qasim for 'bringing freedom to Kurds and Arabs in the new democratic Iraq'. Barzani, whose expenses were being paid for by the government, supported Qasim.

Much has been written about the political and cultural space Qasim gave to the Kurds: government positions, educational opportunities, and cultural rights, all of which helped to create a positive dialectic between the centre and the periphery—see for example Jawad 1979: 173–4 and Kimball 1972: 214. Equally important however, was how Qasim's policies alienated the traditional Kurdish stratum. Land reforms aimed to break the power of landowners by decreasing the size of plots and their distribution within families. Coinciding with Egyptian and Syrian programmes, these were part of a larger socio-economic restructuring package pushed by the urban bourgeoisie (Marr 1985: 171). Although agrarian reform largely failed at this time, landowners became increasingly hostile to Qasim's government and his urban leftist supporters.

Qasim's policies alienated Arab nationalists and some tribes while strengthening the alliances between leftist groups and the central government. As in the pre-revolutionary period, communists continued to attract non-tribal Kurds because they recognized Kurdish rights within a democratic Iraq. For instance, between January and June 1959 the Baghdad journal *Ittihad al-Shaab*, the Lebanese weekly *al-Hurriya*, and the *Iraqi Review* (in part) reprinted the 1956 ICP manifesto that was dedicated to the Kurdish question. Emphasizing 'Arabo-Kurdish' fraternity, the ICP claimed that 'the common struggle will . . . permit equally the Kurdish nation to prepare the favourable conditions . . . to form an independent state of all the territory of Kurdistan.'[8] Although mentioning Kurdish statehood the ICP did not support an independent Kurdish entity as a political end in itself. Liberating Kurdistan was seen as one step toward realizing the larger goal of world socialism.

Still, urban Kurds responded to this inclusive discourse and joined Arab leftists in an anti-imperialist alliance, just as they had in the pre-revolutionary period. The National Front was not exclusionary and brought Kurds and Arabs together in a political alliance with the government against imperialism. In an April 1959 editorial in the Kurdish journal *Khebat* the KDP, dominated by a leftist politburo, congratulated Qasim for his struggle against imperialism, 'a goal of Kurds and Arabs alike'. The KDP leaders also thanked the Arabo-Kurdish republic for 'carrying the light to other parts of

---

[8] 'Rapport Du Comité Central du Parti Communiste Irakien', *Orient*, 9: 175–81.

Kurdistan, which are submitted to the reactionary regime of Iran and Turkey and to the dictator Gamal Abd al-Nasser'—see 'Nos Buts', *Orient*, 9: 155–7.

The Snake Bites the Snake Charmer

Kurdish urban groups supported Qasim's leftist agenda, but also thought of themselves as Kurds within Iraq. One of the unintended consequences of the state's liberal management policies was that Kurds took advantage of their political and cultural space, perhaps even more so than the Iraqi government expected. Kurds started using their media privileges to emphasize their cultural distinctiveness. In early 1959, numerous articles on Kurdish linguistic unity appeared in the Kurdish press, which attempted to purify the Kurdish language from Arabic influences. They attempted to prove that Kurdish is different from both Arabic and Persian. Others argued that Kurds were the descendants of Aryans, Medes, or of the Sassanids, and not of Arab or Persian stock.[9] Also, at the annual teachers' congress in Shaqlawa, Kurds adopted measures to preserve Kurdish language—the day was 'important in Kurdish history for the freedom of the "sweet" Kurdish language'.[10]

Although Kurdish identity became ethnicized, most Kurdish claims focused on cultural rights: official recognition of Nowruz, the Kurdish new year, inclusion of Shi'a Kurds (*Failis*) within the definition of Iraqi citizenship, and linguistic equality. Territorial separation was not part of Kurdish nationalist mobilizations because most Kurds did not see themselves as a separate political entity from Iraq. The majority of urbanized leftist Kurds continued to affiliate with leftist-leaning Arabs more than with Kurdish tribals, sharing anti-imperialist sentiments and support for socio-economic reform. Qasim's strategy was partially successful in creating a notion of a Kurdo-Arab state, one that was not exclusionary in nature.

Arabizing the State: Aborted Reshaping

This strategy worked to a point, but there was a reaction. External influences and changes in the nature of the state encouraged the pan-Arab nationalist current. The 'reddening' of Iraq worried the American-led, non-communist

[9] 'Nejadî Sasanî Kurd bûn û Fars nebûn', *Hetaw*, Nos. 134–8, Year 5, 20 June 1958. The author argues that Kurds are the offspring of the Sassanids, and attempts to prove their historical roots by referring to variants of the name Kurd, such as Mard, Karduqh, Kermanj, and Scythie.
[10] 'Beşî lawanî dîmukrati Kurdistan', *Hetaw*, No. 147–8, Year 5, 10 January 1959: 1–3. 'Kongrey mamosta w cwananî Kurd le Şeqlawe', *Hetaw*, No. 123, Year 2, 15 September 1959: 1.

bloc and regional Arab states. During this period the United States worked with Nasser as its proxy to fight the communist threat in the Middle East. Moreover, while the pan-Arab nationalists positioned themselves as a political alternative to communism, they gained Soviet support as well. These incidents weakened the communists, caused tensions between the Soviets and the ICP, and gave pan-Arab nationalists a free hand against the leftists. In late 1959 Arab nationalist Free Officers became active in plotting anti-communist schemes such as the abortive Mosul or Shawaf revolt and three-cornered massacres in Kirkuk amongst Turcomans, Kurds, and communists (Rondot 1958: 127–57).[11]

Pan-Arab nationalist and communist power struggles constrained Qasim's reshaping of Iraq. During the early months of the new regime, appeasement strategies were feasible, but pan-Arab military factions were threatened by the growing leftist influence and started to oppose Qasim's rule. In consequence, Qasim chose strategically to retreat from his leftist-leaning agenda, and change his policy toward the Kurds. He arrested communists, imposed martial law, Arabized the names of Kurdish localities, dissolved Kurdish organizations, including the KDP, arrested leading Kurdish nationalists, and started bombing rural areas. Qasim then eased press restrictions on pan-Arabists and appointed the anticommunist, pro-Arab militiaman Ismail al-Arif as acting Minister of Guidance and Minister of Education. Further, he started employing a *qawmiyya* nationalist discourse that negated the ethnic identity of Kurds. After cancelling the Kurdish teacher's conference in 1961 Qasim gave a speech claiming that 'Kurdu' was actually a title bestowed by ancient Kings of Persia upon valiant warriors whose descendants were part of the conquering Muslim army. His references to Iraq as 'one nation rather than a collection of peoples' outraged Kurdish leaders. What followed was a series of media wars in March 1961 between the Arab-nationalist paper *al-Thawra* and the KDP newspaper *Khebat* over the issue of ethnic minorities in Iraq (Hassanpour 1992: 119; Uriel 1969: 333).

Under Arab nationalist influences Kurdish–state relations spiralled downward. Although the Ba'athist military coups in Syria and Iraq fractured Arab unity and challenged the Nasserist currents, they elevated military officers and secular Arab nationalist ideology in the government. In particular, the rise of pro-Nasserist military officer Abd al-Salam Arif to power on 19 November 1963 strengthened the Arab nationalist current and pre-empted

---

[11] The Mosul revolt was conducted by Colonel Shawaf and Free Officers and supported by Nasser to remove Qasim and the communists in Iraq. Shawaf was supported by some Kurdish groups in the Turkish and Iranian border regions.

real reshaping policies. Like other leaders seeking to consolidate their power-base, Arif initially tried to draw Kurds into the centre. He reaffirmed the partnership between Kurds and Arabs in Iraq as 'genuine and basic facts' (Entessar 1992: 117). But while he talked about Kurdo-Arab brotherhood, Arif promulgated *qawmiyya* nationalism as the basis of Iraqi identity. In the Ba'athist newspaper, *Al-Ishtiraki*, in 1964, Arif stressed that Kurdish objectives could not be ascertained without supporting Arabism. He created a new provisional constitution that stated that 'the Iraqi people are part of the Arab people, whose aim is total Arab unity.' Unlike the 1958 constitution, it did not mention the Kurdish role in the Iraqi nation. The fascist ideology of al-Husri was also revived. Pan-Arabist historians such as Mohammed Rashid al-Fil published *The Kurds from a Scientific Point of View* with others at the University of Baghdad, attempting to prove the Arab origins of Kurds (Wafik 1984: 6–8). A combination of eliminationist and control strategies were applied to the Kurdish question: internal expulsions of Kurds from Kirkuk and other sensitive border regions to the south commenced *en masse*, affecting more than 25 per cent of the Kurdish population.

The unexpected death of Arif and the transition of power to his brother Abdul Rahman Arif in 1966 created a fresh opportunity to reconsider centre–periphery relations. While Rahman Arif was an Arab nationalist he was a newcomer who needed to consolidate his support base. He made another attempt to appease Kurdish groups, but the tactics employed were not authentic attempts to make Kurds think of themselves as Iraqis first. Instead they simply stirred interpersonal and interfactional jealousies and kept urban and tribal groups in conflict. For instance, during various negotiations, Barzani, but not Talabani, was summoned to Baghdad. A 'Kurdish' party was created, comprising Kurds and Arabs and promising political autonomy for the Kurds in a democratic Iraq. In fact the 'Kurdish' party was an espionage network run by Baghdad's agents in the north. These superficial divide-and-rule strategies scarcely inspired confidence among Kurdish leaders.

Only when the regime gave the appearance of being serious about Kurdish autonomy could Kurdish–state relations stabilize. One step in this direction was the appointment of Rahman al-Bazzaz as Prime Minister, a moderate civilian leader who claimed that the government 'believed in the settlement of the Kurdish problem by granting the Kurds autonomy'. On 19 June 1966 he introduced the 'Decentralization Administration Project' that promised to create six government-chosen Kurdish 'governorates' that would control their own areas of education, municipal affairs, social welfare, transportation, taxation, and financial administration (Khadduri 1969: 268–71; Ghareeb 1981: 64). This attempt to appease the Kurds went further than any previous efforts. Initially it even gained the support of Kurdish leaders. Barzani called a ceasefire and was willing to negotiate with the government. Yet, pan-Arabist military factions pulled back the over-assertive civilian premier. The pattern of behaviour was similar to that when Qasim was pressured by Arab nationalists to withdraw from his procommunist and Kurdish policies. Like Qasim, Rahman Arif had not created a unified bloc in the government, and was pressured by the more powerful pan-Arab nationalist military factions. He too resiled from authentic Kurdish autonomy, annulled the decentralization plan, and removed al-Bazzaz from office (Hewrami 1966a: 6–7; Hewrami 1966b: 7–15).[12]

As in the later Qasim period, the success of the Arab nationalist militarist current over Kurdish matters was encouraged by external influences. These included the increasing western penetration in the region, the jealousies stirred by external support for Nasserist factions, the Arab–Israeli crisis, the strengthening of regional defence programmes by Israel and Iran, and external assistance to Kurdish factions. External networks fuelled the Kurdish war effort, antagonized Arab nationalists, and heightened divisions between Kurdish communities. One of the conditions of foreign support was that aid would be channelled directly to Barzani, but not to the leftist Talabani faction (Adamson 1965: 208–15; O'Ballance 1973). Also, gross discrepancies between the official discourse and actual Kurdish policies were maintained. While Kurdish autonomy was promised, Kurdish political activities were banned, Kurdish territories were run under martial law, Kurdish villages were bombed, Kurds were arrested arbitrarily, and Kurdish activists were tortured.

Failed Reshaping and Fractured, Variable Ethnonationalism

This stop-and-go pattern of behaviour weakened the credibility of Iraqi reshaping efforts, and alienated Kurds from the state. In one of his initial memorandums to Rahman Arif, Barzani stated that while the decentralization plan 'did not reflect the national rights of the Kurds', he was willing to compromise with Baghdad. He later stated that it was only when 'some government officials changed the strategies by narrowing the Kurdish issue down to reconstruction of the north', that the policies became

---

[12] See Anon (1968: 3–7). Some Kurds criticized al-Bazzaz for 'maintaining the old military party line', claiming that the only reason al-Bazzaz suggested his autonomy plan was because of the Kurdish victory in the 'Battle of Handreen'.

unacceptable.[13] Further, in contrast to the pre-revolutionary period, when government policies elevated the traditional stratum, the Arif governments, like Qasim, threatened landowner power by decreasing the size of private plots and creating state-owned entitlements. From 1958 to 1971, the percentage of land owned by the top 1 per cent of landowners decreased from over 55 to 22 per cent. Thus, it became even more difficult to appease Kurdish tribal groups.

Although benefiting from the government's secularization programmes, urban Kurdish leftists also differentiated themselves from the official state nationalism. Some supported Barzani and entered the war. Others engaged in nationalist writings, which became fully ethnicized and territorialized. Anti-Arab themes became prominent in Kurdish literature. In one of the well-known political poems of this epoch, *Le Bendikhaneda* (In Prison), the author, Qan'a, explains why his nation commits revolutionary acts to achieve liberty. What is significant is that the idea of liberty has changed. The 'stranger' is no longer the imperialist but the Arab, 'who has created the Kurdish malediction through arrest, torture, and assassinations'. The idea of the nation is not Iraq, but Kurdistan. Qan'a states he would rather have death than live without this liberty, because a life of servitude is without honour (Qan'a 1979: 229). Additionally, the writings of celebrated Kurdish nationalists such as Heman from Iranian Kurdistan, and Iraqi Kurds such as Bekhud, Piremard, and Goran, were reprinted and popularized.

The term *Kurdayetî*, or the affirmation of Kurdish nationalist identity, now entered Iraqi Kurdish public discourse (Shakely 1983). It had appeared in a poem called *Kurdayetî* written by Kemal Gir, who was affiliated with the extremist Kurdish nationalist group *Kajik, Komeley Azadî Jiyanawey Yekitî Kurd*, established in the 1940s (Association for Liberty, Life and Kurdish Unity) by Jamal Nebez. In this poem, Gir responds to the communists by establishing *Kurdayetî* as an ideology that cannot be separated from humanism. Although *Kajik* was a marginal group at the time, it posed a challenge to both communism and Arab nationalism. The idea of *Kurdayetî* became popular with Kurdish political leftists. Jelal Talabani gave a series of lectures to Kurdish military cadres in the 1960s and published them under the title of *Kurdayetî*.[14] The theme was that Kurds were ethnically different from Arabs and more nationalistic than the communists.

[13] 'Memorandum From Barzani to the Iraqi Government' (11 November 1966, Baghdad) Translated and reprinted in *The Kurdish Journal*, 3/4 (December 1966): 16–20.

[14] Nebez was a mathematics teacher in Suleymania, influenced by Germany's nationalist socialist ideas. *Kajik* was an extremist group, the only Kurdish party to demand the creation of a Kurdish state including four parts of Kurdistan. After 1975 it changed its name and orientation to the Kurdish Socialist Party (KSP), or PASOK. I thank Halkawt Hakim for discussing this issue in depth with me.

Though Kurdish national consciousness was made salient during the 1960s most urban Kurdish nationalists did not seek secession from Iraq. One Kurdish nationalist criticized the 1960 provisional constitution as an exemplification of growing Arabist chauvinism. While suggesting the Iraqi-first identity he stated:

. . . to say that Iraq is part of the Arab nation is wrong from both a scientific and local point of view. . . . Iraq as a whole cannot be considered part of the Arab nation. Only the historical Arab Iraq, which did not include Kurdistan. . . . Moreover, the non-Arab peoples of the Iraqi republic do not constitute a part of the Arab homeland. Some time in history, Kurdistan became part of the Islamic state, as happened in the case of other Muslim countries. . . . A satisfactory formula should state that the eternal Iraqi Republic identity is formed of a Kurdish part—Iraqi Kurdistan and an Arab part—Mesopotamia. Only the Arab part forms part of the greater Arab nation . . .

(Jawad 1981: 119).

The compatibility of Kurdish and Iraqi identity was also advocated in an internal KDP circular which stated that the first national right of the Kurdish people is '. . . to preserve its distinct identity within the united identity'. The KDP reiterated that autonomy for Kurdistan does not mean separation or a step toward it. Rather 'it only means having a local identity within the Iraqi state' (Jawad 1981: 93). The Barzani faction also expressed these views. The two Kurdish groups remained fractured, however, even though Kurdish ethnonationalism had become prominent. Instead of unifying, Barzani and Talabani turned to regional governments and Baghdad at politically expedient moments to strengthen their own political power.

The Military Authoritarian State

As Kurds were feuding among themselves and against the state, political factions inside the government were waging their own power struggles. By July 1968 the Ba'athist military faction won out once more over the Nasserists and the civilian élites. This *coup d'état*, however, was more than just a regime change. Ba'athist ideology and politics were to fundamentally alter the political, economic, and social structure of Iraq. Ahmad Hassan al-Bakr assumed the roles of President, Prime Minister, nominal head of all branches of the government and its national forces, the Revolutionary Command Council (RCC), and the Regional Command of the Ba'ath Party. Saddam Hussein became the Vice President. To ward off internal challenges and consolidate their rule, al–Bakr and Hussein crippled the leftists by conducting more anti-communist purges and removed most factions that were connected to the former regime. For the first time in Iraqi history, a single political party had gained majority power in the government.

But the Ba'athists had not yet solidified their power, or resolved their own internal factionalization. Power-struggles continued between the socialist-leaning factions and conservative groups. While the communists had been severely weakened, the Kurds continued to disrupt the governability of the northern region. The Kurdish wars, which cost US$270 million annually from 1961 to 1968, drained the government's revenues. Additionally, the Ba'athists were regionally ostracized by Iran, the Arab Gulf states, and Egypt in 1968, and became more isolated when Iran and Syria improved relations in 1974. Increasing tensions between Iran and Iraq stirred Shi'a groups in the Iraqi south and aggravated the Shatt-al Arab border issue. Iran, Israel, and the United States also recommenced their aid to the Barzani faction (Ghareeb 1981: 138–9).[15]

It became politically and economically expedient for the state élites to fight harder for Kurdish support. Following previous appeasement attempts al–Bakr and Hussein tried to make Kurds think they were an integral part of the state. In one speech Hussein employed a *wataniyya* discourse, telling Iraqis 'not to consider himself as a Kurd only or an Arab only, but as an Iraqi with Kurdish nationality, or an Iraqi with Arab nationality . . .' (Hussein 1977: 15, 23). While maintaining Iraq's adherence to Arab union al–Bakr drafted a constitutional amendment stating that, 'the Iraqi people consist of two *main* nationalities: Arab and Kurds' (Ghareeb 1981: 87). High-ranking Ba'athist leaders started taking symbolic tours of the Kurdish provinces, promising to implement development programmes for their 'Kurdish brothers'. Although al–Nayef rejected al–Bakr's attempt to increase Kurdish representation in the government, al–Bakr appointed Kurds to the cabinet. The state's leaders also called for an internal territorial configuration. Hussein promoted the March 1970 Manifesto, or the Autonomy Agreement, as a way of finding a 'permanent solution to the Kurdish problem' (Hussein 1973: 9–18; see also Ghareeb 1981: 90–1). Drawn from the twelve-point al–Bazzaz plan, the document promised limited political self-rule and cultural expression within the given territorial boundaries of Iraq. For nearly two years the regime implemented most of the promises. It expanded Kurds' cultural and

---

[15] See *L'Irak Revolutionnnaire 1968–1973: Le Rapport Politique adopté par le Huitième Congres Regional du Parti Arabe Socialiste Baas Irak*, 107. After the 1968 coup, the United States ended its support for the new anti–American Iraqi government. In return for US$14 million, Barzani was to help overthrow the Ba'athists, refrain from harming Iran or supporting the Iranian KDP, and have no relations with the communists.

political space, gave Kurds administrative rights, and even created another Kurdish province called Dihuk.

Since Kurds were suffering war-fatigue they responded to Iraqi leaders' reshaping efforts. From 1970 until late 1971 Kurdish–state relations were relatively conciliatory. Yet, this period of calm was short-lived. As in previous down-sizing scenarios the state élites recoiled from their policies before implementing real Kurdish political autonomy. During down-sizing efforts they gained Soviet support, strengthened ties with Comintern countries, and improved relations with the Iraqi communist party. Having removed their opposition, by 1974 it was no longer politically necessary to appease the Kurds.

By 1970 the pattern of reshaping behaviour had become clear. After regime changes or when government power is threatened, the state élites attempt to reshape to consolidate their power-base. But given the domination of conservative Arab nationalist, and military factions in the government, the élites are unable, or unwilling to cross the threshold of granting the Kurds political equality. Reshaping is not real but simply a time-gaining tactic used by Iraqi officials.

As they consolidated their rule the Ba'athists centralized their political power under the authoritarian rule of Saddam Hussein. Although he did not assume the presidency until 1979, Hussein had acquired the apex of state power. He appointed his Takriti relations to high military posts, giving militant Sunni Arabs even more control over Shi'as and Kurds. These political transitions coincided with economic alterations in the nature of the state. In particular, the 'petrol-ization' and further socialization of the economy gave the central government novel powers and resources. By 1969 receipts from petroleum constituted nearly 85 per cent of the total value of Iraqi exports. After the 1971 OPEC accords, the full nationalization of Iraqi oil in 1972, and the 1973 oil crisis, Iraqi oil revenues quadrupled, giving the government windfall profits. As a result, Iraq gained independence over its internal affairs, using its new oil revenues to modernize and industrialize the state.

Greater internal economic independence gave the political élites unrestrained power over local populations. As they clan-ized, ethnicized, and centralized their rule, centre–periphery relations became violently antagonistic. Al-Bakr and Hussein talked about Kurdo-Arab unity while telling Kurds they could not disrupt Arab national interests. The Ba'athists claimed that 'they would assimilate Kurds into a crucible of the Arab nation and if necessary, by force' (Hakim 1992: 140). To safeguard their petroleum interests the Ba'athists Arabized Kurdish regions, and in particular Kirkuk. They constructed a series of homes called 'the Arab Circle' around the Kurdish quarters in Kirkuk, reattached parts of the city to other Kurdish lands, deported Kurds from their homes, granted land deeds only to Arabs, and gave Kurdish localities Arabic names.[16]

The rise of Iraq's highly centralized authoritarian regime and increasing reliance on military force was legitimized by shifts in international politics. The Soviet invasion of Afghanistan, the military *coup d'etat* in Turkey (1980), the Shi'a stirrings in the south, the rise of Kurdish nationalism in Turkey, and the Islamic Revolution in Iran encouraged Hussein to further militarize the state. Most important was the descent into the war with Iran. Although Kurdish–Iraqi–Iranian wartime relations are too complex to present here, it should be noted that during the eight-year war (1980–8) American policies became strongly anti-Iranian and anti-Islamic. Western dependence on Middle Eastern oil boosted secular, 'moderate' oil monarchies such as Iraq, Kuwait, and Saudi Arabia (Gause 1994).[17] In 1984, after seventeen years, the USA restored diplomatic relations with Iraq. A lucrative weapons trade developed between Iraq and western defence companies that strengthened Iraqi's military regime. During the war the Iraqi army grew in size from near-ly 200,000 to over one million men (Karabell 1995).[18] This military force gave the regime new options in controlling the Kurds. While Hussein allegedly appealed to his 'Kurdish brothers' his assistant Hassan al-Majid orchestrated the *Anfal* campaign. In 1987 and 1988, the Iraqi military chem-ically attacked over 4,000 Kurdish villages, killing approximately 150,000 Kurdish people and leaving about 180,000 missing (Al-Hafeed 1993: 38–52; Middle East Watch 1993).

Suppressed Nationalism and Economic Opportunism

In a reshaping programme, policies based on coercion and control can annul efforts to appease peripheral groups. That is, gross discrepancies between

[16] Discussions with the representative of New Kirkuk governorate in Suleymaniya, Iraqi Kurdistan, 7 January 1997.

[17] The Kirkuk–Dortyol pipeline that makes deliveries to the Turkish terminal of Yarmurtilik enabled Iraq to export oil without having to traverse Syrian territory.

[18] During the war the American government gave its defence contractors the right to supply marine engines to the Italian navy, which were then transferred to Iraq. The Bush administration supported Hussein as late as April 1990, until the BNP investigation resulted in the suspension of Iraq's US$1 billion credit purchase scheme. One senior administration official stated that 'Everybody knew Hussein's reputation, and no one thought he was a potential member of the Kiwanis Club . . . but could he become a better member of the region? It was worth exploring the possibility, and we didn't have a lot to lose'. When a US delegation led by Bob Dole and Alan Simpson met with Hussein in Mosul on 2 April 1990, Dole stated that 'President Bush assured me that he wanted better relations, and that the US government wanted better relations with Iraq'.

promises and reality can encourage differentiation of peripheral communities from the political centre, despite the use of ethnically inclusive discourses. For instance, even though the Iraqi élites increased Kurdish representation in the government, some Kurds mocked the efforts as 'bizarre action' that 'displayed a few characters whose great great grandparents may have been Kurdish ministers . . . but who are not even remotely connected with the Kurdish movement' (Anon 1968). Kurdish representative Mahmud Othman complained about the gap between the state's official management strategies and the reality: 'In the RCC we have nothing. In the army we have nothing, no key positions. In the security and intelligence services we have nothing. In the Oil Ministry we have nothing. In the Ministry of Foreign Affairs we have nothing. In fact, we hold no key positions. The Kurds have no part in decisions relating to domestic or foreign policies. Everything is done by the Ba'ath party. We have participation on an administrative level only' (Farouk-Sluglett and Sluglett 1990: 309).

The state's policies had become so devoid of credibility that while the government referred to the 1970 agreement as 'the most important accord for Iraqi-Kurd relations' and created the first Kurdish legislative assembly in Iraqi Kurdistan, both Barzani and Talabani refused to participate in the state's United Popular Front. Moreover, by 1970 the reshaping threshold had risen. The Arabization of Kurdish lands territorialized Kurdish identity, tying Kurdish claims to sensitive regions such as Kirkuk (Kutschera 1979: 297).[19] The crux of the Kurdish autonomy issue was no longer about cultural and political rights, but centred on the 'real' ethnic origins of Kirkuk. Petroleum played a key role in this debate. While Hussein was demanding 'Arab oil for Arabs', Kurds were claiming 'Kurdish crude for Kurdistan'.

Most analyses regard the Kurds' refusal to negotiate with Baghdad and the 1975 Barzani-led Kurdish revolt as the height of Kurdish national consciousness. The mobilization was noteworthy because it brought both principal Kurdish groups together under a unified movement. Despite their personal differences, Barzani and Talabani did not compromise over Kirkuk and essential Kurdish lands. Yet, Kurdish nationalist unity was short-lived.

What subsequently happened to Kurdish–state relations after the regime's crack down? What explains the fifteen-year period of quiet in the Kurdish opposition movement, particularly when militant Arab Ba'athism peaked in Iraq? The collapse of the Kurdish resistance created a void in Iraqi

---

[19] During the 1970–4 negotiations Barzani gave Hussein three options on Kirkuk and other sensitive lands: 1) Kirkuk province to remain indivisible, but with regions subsumed to Kurdish organs of autonomy; 2) Kirkuk to be divided in two districts: Hawidja and Karataba for the central government, and the rest, including Kirkuk city, for the autonomous region; and 3) Kirkuk should be divided into the aforementioned two districts while retaining a special status.

Kurdistan. Without external backing and organizational capabilities it was difficult, if not impossible, to resume Kurdish nationalist mobilizations inside Iraq. Additionally, Kurdish activities were restricted by the increasing capabilities of the authoritarian Ba'athist police state. The Ba'athist forces, which became an ideological army *(Jaish al-A'Aqa'idi)*, created an environment of fear throughout the country (Farouk-Sluglett and Sluglett 1987: 89–114; Al-Khalil 1990). In addition to destroying Kurdish villages they forced Kurdish families to resettle in alternative governorates, southern desert areas, or collective towns *(mujamm'at)*, where the regime could exercise greater control over their daily lives.

By the late 1970s, the nature of the state had changed so fundamentally that to be an Iraqi citizen was to be a member of the Ba'ath party. About 80 per cent of all university teachers were Ba'ath party members. School curriculums were changed to include a mandatory course called *'Fekr al-Qair fi-tafsir al-takrikh'* (Regarding the opinions of Saddam on history). In order to graduate, students were required to learn Ba'athist history from a standard university text called *'al-minhadj al-thiqafi al-merkazi'* (The methodology of the central culture).[20] The regime invented new myths of Iraqi history that negated Kurdish culture. One widely popularized myth claimed that the Kurdish New Year *(Nowruz)* was not attributable to the Kurdish hero Kawa, but to an Arab called Jaber Enscira, a compatriot of the prophet.

Even the use of Iraqiist discourse had changed its meaning so that to be *wataniyya* was to be *qawmiyya*. For instance, Hussein developed 'The Re-Writing of History' project *(mashru i'adat kitabat al-tarikh)* as an ideologically-mediated re-examination of the past, including history, national heritage and popular culture. This multi-billion dollar effort highlighted the Mesopotamian antecedents of Iraqi history, and called for ethnic minorities to view themselves as Iraqis first. However, Hussein Arabized Mesopotamian culture by using Arab metaphors to emphasize a localist Iraqi identity. For instance, the Mosul spring festivals pronounced Iraq's historical ties to the Sumerians, Assyrians, and Babylonians, which were Arab symbols (Davis and Gavrielides 1991: 1–35; Baram 1983, 1991). Nowhere in this or other schemes was the Kurds' Median ancestry mentioned as an integral part of Iraqi history. This re-writing of national history and culture did not, needless to say, establish much credibility with the Kurds. Figure 9.4 shows how Iraqi secondary school pupils are instructed in the meaning of the word 'nation'.

---

[20] *Al-minhadj al-thiqafi al-merkazi* (Baghdad: dar al-Howriya, 1990). For students in political science, there was the *al-thiqafa al-qawymiiya* and *Takhri al-merkazi qawmiyya*. Secondary school students used the modified version, *al-takhri thaqqafi*.

This table helps you to form words from the stem nation. List the words and then fill in the blanks in sentences below with suitable words taken from the list you make.

Stem		Suffix	
nation	al	ity	
		iz(e)	d ation
		ist ism	

1   The Arabs are a glorious   ....

2   The ABSP has strengthened   .... in Iraq.

3   The 17th July Revolution has built a strong   .... army.

4   Iraq..   its oil on the first of June 1972.

5   The ....   of oil is one the most important achievements of the Revolution.

6   What is your   .... ? I'm Iraqi.

7   Every nation has the right to   .... its natural resources.

8   The ABSP is a great   .... movement in the Arab Homeland.

FIG. 9.4 Page from an Iraqi secondary school textbook explaining the meaning of the word 'nation' under Arab Ba'athist rule

Given these repressive and racist strategies, why did many Kurds buy into the centre, particularly when militant Arab Ba'athism peaked in Iraq after 1975? The petrol economy created new incentive structures for the state élites to co-opt and control Kurdish groups. From the coffers of their rentier state the regime could employ perverse expenditure mechanisms to make its policies more politically palatable to local populations (Beblawi and Luciani 1987: 16, 51–2; Whittleton 1989; Gause 1994).[21] It placated Kurds by providing them with free monthly food rations, health care, and educational programmes. It offered commercial, banking, and cultural opportunities that allowed merchants, contractors, trading companies, and local businesses to prosper. It supported Kurdish landowners and farmers with agricultural programmes such as wheat-purchase schemes, free fertilizer, and irrigation projects. In some regions Hussein distributed colour television sets to Kurdish civil servants, casino owners, and Ba'ath Party members (Zimmerman 1994).[22] Many Kurds integrated into Iraqi society, taking advantage of the opportunities that were tied to the country's new oil wealth.

These novel public policies altered Kurdish society and its economic relationships. Instead of relying on local Kurdish agriculture to meet increasing consumption patterns, the regime turned to food imports paid for with petroleum rents. Economically disenfranchised rural communities and war-affected populations migrated to—or were forcibly resettled—in the cities, increasing existing urbanization trends (Sherzad 1991). Additionally, modernization and industrialization policies were uneven in their impact. Except for a few factories, mining, and dam projects, Iraqi Kurdistan remained underdeveloped and non-industrialized. Given the particular nature of its capital-intensive chemical industries, Iraq provided high value-added intermediate goods that depended on imported machinery and multinational labour forces, rather than local populations (Stork 1979: 42–8). This situation added more cadres to the urban unemployed and ever-growing service sector.

The displacement of Kurds from their lands broke a key sector of the traditional Kurdish economy and destroyed traditional living patterns. Rather than integrate into the industrial sector, increase their agricultural production, or become Ba'ath party members, most Kurds lived off the government. A 'rent-seeking mentality' emerged among Kurdish communities, that is, income generation was not viewed as part of a process integrated in a chain, but rather, as an isolated activity that brought windfalls quickly. By not having to pay taxes or participate in political affairs, local populations became

---

[21] Rentier states are based on outside sources of revenues and differ from non-rentier states whose income depends on domestic taxation. In a rentier economy the creation of wealth is centred around a small fraction of society, the rest are merely engaged in its distribution and utilization. The government is the main recipient and distributor.

[22] In 1979 the Iraqi regime gave some 30,000 television sets to Iraqi Kurdish refugees from Iran. The populations resettled after the 1988 *Anfal* campaign received no such state assistance. According to my Kurdish informants, the central government's monthly food allocations included wheat flour, sugar, rice, vegetable oil, sugar, tea, shampoo, toothpaste, matches, and heating fuel, to name a few. These rations accounted for nearly 75% of a family's monthly living expenses.

rentiers themselves, simply collecting their take from the state's oil rents (Beblawi and Luciani 1987: 10). Nowhere was the rent-seeking mentality more evident than in the north, where the 'big–daddy syndrome' developed. Dependent on social welfare handouts, Iraqi Kurds changed from a society of producers to one of consumers.

Given the highly fluid context of Kurdish politics it was often economically necessary or advantageous to accept the state handouts. In Iraqi Kurdistan there was an absence of systematic patterns of economic development and political stability. Towns that grew were destroyed. Families that were displaced were resettled elsewhere. Villages that were depopulated were reconstructed, destroyed, and reconstructed again. Refugee groups that were once resettled became internally displaced or part of the diaspora communities. The very turbulence of Iraqi Kurdish politics and society, the underdeveloped nature of the Kurdish economy, and the transiency of Kurdish populations prevented any political institutionalization from evolving in the north. Kurds who bought into the state did so as a way of seeking stability and survival, not necessarily because they viewed themselves as Iraqis first.

Recontextualizing the Reshaping Project

Although the Kurdish issue appeared to have fallen off the political agenda after 1991, Hussein still tried to claim that the Kurds were an integral part of Iraq. During successive anniversary celebrations of the March Manifesto, the government stressed that 'the Kurd is a pure Iraqi' and 'beloved Kurdistan is the cherished part of dear Iraq'.[23] Yet, the Kurds failed to respond to these appeals. Despite the brief attempts to negotiate with Hussein, the breakdown of the Kurdish government, and Kurdish in-fighting, the Iraqi leaders have not been able to cross the threshold of Kirkuk. Hussein's Iraqiist discourse lost its last shreds of credibility as the regime continued to bomb Kurdish regions, burn Kurdish farmlands, attack and assassinate humanitarian relief workers, cut off the electricity to Kurdish regions, and to impose economic blockades between northern and southern Iraq.

Even if the Iraqi élites fought harder for Kurdish support it is uncertain whether they could have co-opted Kurds away from the more economically and politically lucrative incentives offered by regional and international actors. Baghdad's expulsions of Shi'a groups, which included Faili Kurds, from southern Iraq to Iran created new political alliances between Iraqi Kurds, Iran's Supreme Council of the Islamic Revolution (SAIRI) and Shi'a

---

[23] 'Editorial Hails Kurdish Autonomy Anniversary', FBIS, 28 March 1995: 41.

populations in southern Iraq. Additionally, during the 1980s the Turkish government became increasingly active in Iraqi Kurdish affairs as it tried to control its own Kurdish problem and profit from the petroleum agreements arranged with Iraq during the war.[24] Syria's involvement in cross-border Kurdish politics allowed Iraqi Kurdish parties and the *Partiye Karkeran Kurdistan* (PKK), led by Abdullah (Apo) Ocalan, to expand nationalist activities, at least until the Turkish–Syrian agreement was signed in October 1998. The increasing influence of the PKK, the growth of Kurdish diaspora communities, the swelling of refugee groups, and the organization of Kurdish parties brought new pressures to bear on relations between Iraqi Kurds and the regime. Not only were regional states and cross-border Kurdish groups trying to influence Iraqi Kurds, but Iraqi Kurdish leaders were turning to external sources on a regular basis for their own political and economic gain.

External influences gave the Iraqi Kurdish movement semi-legitimacy, increased the significance of Kurdish nationalism, and helped alter the nature of the nationalist claims. American-sponsored democratization efforts had an evident effect on the Kurds, who adopted 'democracy' and 'federation' as part of their own nationalist discourse. Although the US State Department was wary of Kurdish ambitions, other American officials encouraged the Kurds to break away from Iraq. Without American interests, security assistance of the Coalition Forces, and international humanitarian relief aid, Iraqi Kurdistan would not have become a *de facto* autonomous region with its own regional government (Natali 1999).[25] And even though American-led negotiation efforts between Iraqi Kurdish factions emphasized the territorial integrity of Iraq, the effort to prevent the Saddamization of the north reinforces the notion of an Iraqi Kurdish identity separate from Baghdad. After 1991, the Kurds started referring to their territory as 'Free Kurdistan'.

Structural changes in the Iraqi political economy after the 1991 Gulf War created new opportunities for Kurdish communities to mobilize as a nationalist group.[26] The lucrative underground petroleum smuggling economy,

[24] Entessar 1992: 133. In response to the negotiations conducted between Hussein and Talabani in November 1983 Turkish officials increased their military operations, threatened to close the oil pipelines, and pressured Baghdad and Iran to terminate their liaisons with Kurdish groups. The 'hot pursuit' agreement signed between Turkey and Iraq in April 1983 authorized Turkey to conduct cross-border incursions against 'terrorist' groups.

[25] According to Mohammed Tawfik, first Minister of Humanitarian Affairs of the Kurdish Regional Government, one of the reasons Iraqi Kurds staged their own democratic elections in 1992 was that they wanted to receive the backing of the US, which was 'supporting democratic movements in Eastern Europe and in Israel–Palestine'. Other Kurdish informants have made similar statements.

[26] For instance, with the north–south trade route under Hussein's surveillance and Iranian and Syrian borders officially closed, the Turkish border (Habur) was the only legally-opened entrance

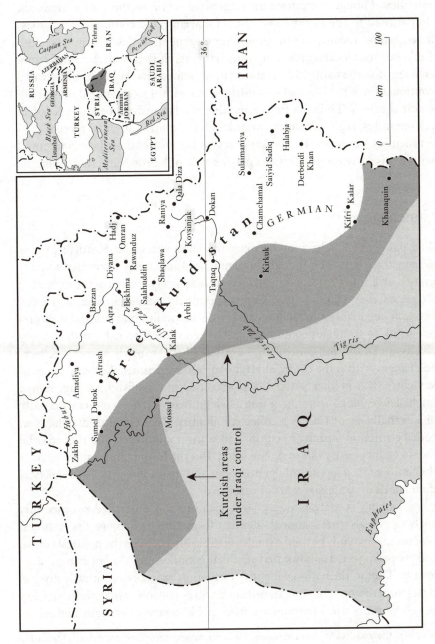

FIG. 9.5 New map of Kurdistan popularized after the 1991 Gulf War

which surged after the Gulf War, gave the Kurdish nationalist élite financial resources to propel their own political party organizations and nationalist activities. Though the Kurds no longer had access to the state's handouts, they turned to the international humanitarian relief community for assistance, whose reconstruction programmes generated new revenue sources. Links between local Kurdish food departments shifted from the central government to international humanitarian organizations. What resulted was a continuation of the big-daddy syndrome but within an expanded network of external actors. These shifts created direct relationships between Kurdish communities, regional actors, international organizations, and foreign governments. Consequently, any future reshaping project must be reconfigured within this increasingly complex playing field of Kurdish and Iraqi politics.

Conclusions

The patterns of behaviour between the state élites and Kurdish groups demonstrate that even though government officials may have tried to integrate Kurds into the Iraqi state, they were ultimately limited in the reshaping strategies they could follow. Centre–periphery relations have alternated between negotiations to facilitate territorial autonomy and cultural rights on one hand, to strategies combining partial genocide, internal transfers, coercive assimilation, and control on the other. These swings have partly reflected changes within the centre at Baghdad, and sometimes the preferences of key élites. But neither pattern has succeeded in establishing a hegemonic, unchallengeable conception of Iraq as a legitimate territory, either externally or internally, or of Iraq as a collective identity. Rentier states may have an added economic capacity to co-opt and control minorities, and they may be able to finance costly internal repression. But the Iraqi regime ran up against the limits of its geopolitical environment and its leaders grossly overplayed their hands in successive wars of conquest.

By looking at state-building strategies in such a detailed manner this analysis reveals that national identity formation is a more finely-tuned process that extends beyond a single relationship between the political centre and its periphery. It shows that national communities do not behave uniformly. That is, the national identity formation process in ethnically diverse states undergoing economic transition involves tensions *within* the periphery as well. Some of these tensions are attributable to power-struggles and socio-

and exit to the land-locked northern region. Turkey became the economic and political lifeline for Iraqi Kurds and Kurdish autonomy became linked to the lucrative petroleum trade at the Turkish border.

economic divisions in heterogeneous, ethnically diverse societies. However, intra-ethnic group identities can become more pronounced if state policies favour, or appear to favour, some groups over others. As a result, differentiation and homogenization can occur within the periphery simultaneously because certain governments may be more beneficial for some communities than for others. As state policies become more finely-grained ethnic groups can become increasingly fractured among themselves. Peripheral groups can obstruct the state's management policies even if these policies may benefit some group members. Further, transnationalization processes after the mid-1980s reveal that any attempt to resolve ethnic group conflicts, and particularly in Kurdistan, must be made within an increasingly complex network of local, regional, and international actors. External penetration in domestic politics makes it increasingly difficult, although not impossible, to manage the Kurdish conflict.

REFERENCES

Abdel-Fadil, Mahmoud. 1987. 'Macro Behavior of Oil Rentier States in the Arab Region', 83–107 in *The Rentier State*, edited by Hazem Beblawi and Giacomo Luciani. London, New York, NY, and Sydney: Croom Helm.

Adamson, David. 1965. *The Kurdish Wars*. New York, NY, and Washington, DC: Praeger.

Al-Hafeed, Salahaddin M. 1993. 'The Embargo on Kurdistan: Its influences on Economic and Social Development', 38–52 in *The Reconstruction and Economic Development of Iraqi Kurdistan: Challenges and Perspectives*, edited by Fuad Hussein, Michiel Leezenberg, and Pieter Muller. Amsterdam: Stichting Nederland Koerdistan.

Al-Husri, Abu Khaldun Sati. 1959. 'Qu'est ce que le Nationalism?', *Orient*, 9: 216–23.

Al-Khalil, Samir. 1990. *Republic of Fear: Saddam's Iraq*. London: Hutchinson Radius.

Anon. 1922–3. 'Review of the Civil Administration of Mesopotamia' in *Al-Iraq Yearbook*. Baghdad: Al-Iraq Press.

Anon. 1968. 'Two Years After', *Kurdica*, 1: 3–7.

Baram, Amatzia. 1983. '*Qawmiyya* and *Wataniyya* in Ba'athi Iraq: The Search for a New Balance', *Middle Eastern Studies*, 19: 188–200.

—— 1991. *Culture and Ideology in the Formation of Ba'athist Iraq, 1968–1989*. New York, NY: St Martin's Press.

Batatu, Hanna. 1978. *The Old Social Classes and the Revolutionary Movements of Iraq: A Study of Iraq's Old Landed and Commercial Classes and of its Communists, Ba'thists, and Free Officers*. Princeton, NJ: Princeton University Press.

Beblawi, Hazem, and Luciani, Giacomo. 1987. *The Rentier State*. London, New York, NY, and Sydney: Croom Helm.

Bensaid, Said. 1987. '*Al Watan* and *al-Umma* in Contemporary Arab Use', 149–74 in *The Foundations of the Arab State*, edited by Ghassan Salamé. London, New York, NY, and Sydney: Croom Helm.

Cleveland, William L. 1991. *The Making of an Arab Nationalist: Ottomanism and Arabism in the Life and Thought of Sati al-Husri*. Princeton, NJ: Princeton University Press.

Davis, Eric and Gavrielides, Nicolas E. 1991. 'Theorizing Statecraft and Social Change in Arab Oil-Producing Countries', 1–35 in *Statecraft in the Middle East: Oil, Historical Memory, and Popular Culture*. Miami, FL: Joint Committee on the Near and Middle East, Florida International University Press.

Devlin, John F. 1979. *The Ba'ath Party: A History From its Origins to 1966*. Stanford, CA: Hoover Institute Press.

—— 1959. 'Discours du President du Conseil D'Irak,' *Orient*, 9: 142–4.

Eaton, Henry. 1965. 'Kurdish Nationalism in Iraq Since 1958', *The Kurdish Journal*, 2/2: 10–14.

Eftekhari, Nirou. 1987. 'Le petrole dans l'économie at la societé irakienne', *Peuples Méditerranéens*, 40: 43–74.

Entessar, Nader. 1992. *Kurdish Ethnonationalism*. London: Lynne Rienner Publishers.

Farouk-Sluglett, Marion and Sluglett, Peter. 1987. 'From Gang to Élite: The Iraqi Ba'th Party's Consolidation of Power, 1968–1975', *Peuples Méditerranéens*, 40: 89–114.

—— 1990. *Iraq Since 1958: From revolution to dictatorship*. London and New York, NY: IB Tauris.

FBIS (Foreign Broadcast Information Service). 1995. 'Editorial Hails Kurdish Autonomy Anniversary', 41.

French Government Archives. 1929. *Le Consul de France à Mossoul à Son Excellence Monsier le Minister des Affaires Etrangères, 9 Décembre 1929*. Paris : Les Archives du Quai D'Orsay (AQD), Levant.

Gause, F. Gregory. 1994. *Oil Monarchies: Domestic and Security Challenges in the Arab Gulf States*. New York, NY: Council on Foreign Relations Press.

Gellner, Ernest. 1983. *Nations and Nationalism*. Ithaca, NY: Cornell University Press.

Ghareeb, Edmund. 1981. *The Kurdish Question In Iraq*. Syracuse, NY: Syracuse University Press.

Hakim, Halkawt. 1992. 'Le Panarabism Irakien et Le Problem Kurde', 124–44 in *Les Kurdes par-dela l'exode*, edited by Halkawt Hakim. Paris: L'Harmattan.

Hassanpour, Amir. 1992. *Nationalism and Language in Kurdistan*. San Francisco, CA: Mellon Research University Press.

Hewrami. 1966a. 'Government By Three', *The Kurdish Journal*, 3 (March): 6–7.

—— 1966b. 'The Evolution of Bazzaz's 12-Point Plan', *The Kurdish Journal* 3 (September): 7–15.

HMG (British Government). 1920. 'Review of the Civil Administration of Mesopotamia'. London: HMSO.

Hussein, Fuad, Leezenberg, Michiel, and Muller, Pieter (eds). 1993. *The Reconstruction and Economic Development of Iraqi Kurdistan: Challenges and Perspectives*. Amsterdam: Stichting Nederland Koerdistan.

Hussein, Saddam. 1973. *Propos Sur Les Problemes Actuels*. Baghdad: Ath-Thawra.

—— 1977. *Saddam Hussein on Current Events in Iraq*, translated by Khalid Kishtainy, London: Longman.

Ismael, Tareq Y. 1979. *The Arab Left*. Syracuse, NY: Syracuse University Press.

Jaber, Kamel S. Abu. 1966. *The Arab Ba'th Socialist Party: History, Ideology, and Organization*. Syracuse, NY: Syracuse University Press.

Jaf, Ahmed Mokhtar Begi. 1969. *Dîwanî Ahmed Mokhtar Begî Jaf*. Hawler: Chapkhaneh Howleer.

Jawad, Sa'ad. 1979. 'The Kurdish Problem in Iraq', 171–82 in *The Integration of Modern Iraq*, edited by Abbas Kelidar. New York, NY: St Martin's Press.

—— 1981. *Iraq and the Kurdish Question*. London: Ithaca Press.

Karabell, Zachary. 1995. 'Backfire: US Policy Toward Iraq, 1988–2 August 1990', *The Middle East Journal*, 49/1: 28–47.

Karim, Mohammed Mala. 1986. *Dîwanî Faiq Bêkes*. Baghdad: Chapkhaney Adib.

Khadduri, Majid. 1969. *Republican Iraq*. London: Oxford University Press.

Kimball, Lorenzo Kent. 1972. *The Changing Pattern of Political Power In Iraq, 1958–1971*. New York, NY: Robert and Sons Publishers Inc.

Kutschera, Chris. 1979. *Le Mouvement Nationale Kurde*. Paris: Flammarion.

Laqueur, Walter Z. 1957. *Communism and Nationalism in the Middle East*. New York, NY: Praeger.

Lenczowski, George. 1962. *The Middle East in World Affairs*. Cornell, NY: Cornell University Press.

Lustick, Ian S. 1993. *Unsettled States, Disputed Lands: Britain and Ireland, France and Algeria, Israel and the West-Bank-Gaza*. New York, NY: Cornell University Press.

Marr, Phebe. 1985. *The Modern History of Iraq*. Boulder, CO: Westview Press.

McDowell, David. 1996. *A Modern History of the Kurds*. London: IB Tauris.

Middle East Watch. 1993. 'The Anfal Campaign in Iraqi Kurdistan: The Destruction of Koreme'. New York, NY, and Washington, DC: Human Rights Watch.

Natali, Denise. 1999. 'International aid, regional politics, and the Kurdish issue in Iraq after the Persian Gulf War', Occasional Paper 31. Abu Dhabi: The Emirates Centre for Strategic Studies and Research.

O'Ballance, Edgar. 1973. *The Kurdish Revolt, 1961–1970*. London: Faber and Faber.

O'Leary, Brendan and McGarry, John. 1995. 'Regulating Nations and Ethnic Communities', 245–90 in *Nationalism and Rationality*, edited by Albert Breton, Jean-Luigi Galeotti, Pierre Salmon, and Ron Wintrobe. Cambridge: Cambridge University Press.

O'Shea, Maria T. 1991. 'Greater Kurdistan: The Mapping of a Myth?', in *Kurdistan: Political and Economic Potential*, edited by Maria T. O'Shea. London: Geopolitics and International Boundaries Research Centre.

Parti Arab Socialist Baas. 1974. 'L'Irak Revolutionnarie 1968–1973 : Le Rapport Politique adopté par le Huitième Congres Regional du Party Arabe Socialist Baas Irak'. Baghdad : Parti Arab Socialist Baas.

Paşa, Sherif. 1919. *Memorandum sur les Revendications du Peuples Kurdes*. Paris: Imprimerie AG Hoir.

Qan'a. 1979. *Dîwanî Qan'a*. Suleymani: Chapkhaney Zenko Suleymani.

Rondot, Pierre. 1958. 'Quelques opinions sur les relations arabo-kurdes dan la Republique Irakienne', *Orient*, 5: 50–4.

Ross, H. Pierre. 1959. 'L'Irak devant la reforme agraire', *Orient*, 9: 81–93.

Shakely, Ferhad. 1983. 'Kurdish Nationalism in Mem U Zin of Ehmedi Khani'. Uppsala: University of Uppsala, Department of Iranian Languages.

Sherzad, A. 1991. 'The Kurdish movement in Iraq 1975–1988', 134–69 in *The Kurds: A Contemporary Overview*, edited by Philip G. Kreyenbroek and Stephan Sperl. London and New York, NY: Routledge.

Stork, Joe. 1979. 'Oil and the Penetration of Capitalism in Iraq: An Interpretation', 38–77 in *Oil and Business in Iraq*. Louvain la-Neuve: Centre de Récherches sur le Monde Arabe Contemporaine, Cahier 4, Institut de Pays en Developement, University Catholique de Louvain.

Tibi, Bassam. 1990. *Arab Nationalism: A Critical Enquiry*. Edited by Marion Farouk-Sluglett and Peter Sluglett. London: The Macmillan Press.

Uriel, Dann. 1969. *Iraq Under Qassem: A Political History, 1958–1963*. Tel Aviv: Praeger Publishers.

van Bruinessen, Martin. 1992. 'Kurdish society, ethnicity, nationalism and refugee problems', 33–67 in *The Kurds: A Contemporary Overview*, edited by Philip G. Kreyenbroek and Stephen Sperl. London and New York, NY: Routledge.

Wafik, Raouf. 1984. *Nouveau régard sur les nationalism Arab: Ba'ath et Nasserism*. Paris: L'Harmattan.

Whittleton, Celine. 1989. 'Oil and the Iraqi Economy', 54–72 in *Saddam's Iraq: Revolution or Reaction?*, edited by Committee Against Repression and for Democratic Rights in Iraq (CADRI). London: Zed Books.

Yousif, Abdul-Salaam. 1991. 'The Struggle for Cultural Hegemony During the Iraqi Revolution', 172–96 in *The Iraqi Revolution of 1958: The Old Social Classes Revisited*, edited by Robert Fernea and William Louis. London and New York, NY: IB Tauris.

Zeki, Mohammed Amin. 1931. *Kurd û Kurdistan*. Mahabad: Entesharat Siryan.

Zimmerman, Ann. 1994. 'Kurdish Broadcasting in Iraq' *The Middle East Report*, 24/4: 20–3.

10

Indigestible Lands? Comparing the Fates of Western Sahara and East Timor

Stephen Zunes

While over one billion people have been successfully decolonized over the past fifty years, Western Sahara and East Timor are still recognized by the United Nations as non–self-governing territories. They are two of the relatively few cases where colonial rule was not ended peacefully or with the consultation of the indigenous population as required by international law. They remain the two largest territories still under the United Nations Committee on Decolonization. Within five weeks of each other in late 1975, on the verge of internationally recognized independence, both Western Sahara and East Timor were invaded and annexed by large neighbours. Both invasions were extremely brutal, prompting large-scale refugee flight in the case of Western Sahara and being accompanied by widespread massacres in East Timor. While both seizures were challenged by United Nations Security Council resolutions, the permanent members, France, the UK, and the USA blocked effective enforcement action. Despite the fact that the take-overs were blatant violations of international norms, they largely festered in obscurity because of the countries' small populations, remote locations, and the potential embarrassment to major powers allied to the occupying governments. While both occupying states clearly had the 'available power resources' traditionally defined to maintain control (Lustick 1993: 38), and most observers believed that these take-overs were permanent, East Timor is now free of Indonesian control and Western Sahara's occupation may also be reversible.

This chapter compares and contrasts the issues behind both disputes and the contending forces that have attempted to influence the outcome, and tries to draw some lessons regarding territorial expansion and eventual contraction. Both countries were relatively small territories ruled by minor colonial powers which held onto their possessions until the mid-1970s, one to two decades after independence had been granted to most African colonies and nearly two to three decades after independence had been granted to most Asian colonies. Both peoples had distinct ethnic and linguistic identities from their larger neighbours before their respective European conquests, yet their sense of distinct nationhood was reinforced through their contrasting colonial experiences: not only did the Sahrawis and East Timorese live under different and longer-term colonial administrations, but they experienced less absolutist styles of rule with less disruption to traditional economies and ways of life.

In both cases, the take-overs were élite-driven nationalist initiatives, though in very different forms. The Moroccan irredentist cause has had a far more longstanding, solid, and consistent level of support, growing out of a popular nationalist movement. Indeed, the take-over of Western Sahara involved the mass mobilization of Morocco's own population in the 'Green March'. Internally the incorporation of the 'Sahara provinces' was recognized and enthusiastically supported almost universally. Indonesia's take-over of East Timor, while generally supported by informed—or, one could argue, misinformed—sectors of society, by contrast, never had as widespread or as vehement a level of popular support. It never ranked nearly as significant a chapter in Indonesia's modern history as was Morocco's expansion to the south—an event depicted on currency and postage stamps, emphasized in school textbooks, and regularly featured in patriotic celebrations.

The opportunity to expand their states' boundaries, particularly in the case of Indonesia, was occasioned by the belated collapse of the European empires in Portugal and Spain and their respective transitions from authoritarian government to liberal democracies. Neither conquest went as quickly or as easily as the invading governments' political and military leadership imagined. The level of military or political resistance to integration was not anticipated. Both conquests were eventually militarily victorious throughout most of the respective territories, but large numbers of young conscripts from both Morocco and Indonesia had to be sent to fight and maintain control over a population in lands which their governments claimed had enthusiastically welcomed the take-over.

Despite these similarities, the Moroccanization of Western Sahara has been far more successful than the Indonesianization of East Timor, largely because of the much smaller population of the former, and the fact that Moroccan settlers are now the clear majority within Western Sahara and most of the Sahrawi population is in exile. Neither regime succeeded, however, in convincing the majority of the indigenous population to identify with the new masters. The great advances in building a modern industrial infrastructure within the territories, particularly by Morocco, appear to have done little to win over the hearts and minds of the natives. Enormous costs were incurred in building up the infrastructures, as well as substantial losses of men and materiel in the guerrilla wars that followed the invasions. However, it is unclear whether this hardened the attitudes of the occupiers, fixating them on the 'sunk costs' they had already incurred, or whether it led them to realize that the long-run costs of conquest outweigh the long-run benefits. In the case of Indonesia, the military and its allied militias engaged in a scorched earth policy as they departed, pillaging and razing much of the East Timorese capital of Dili and other towns and cities. The 'civilizing mission' of the occupations was not accepted by most of the native populations, but it has helped maintain popular support within the core of the conquering state, reinforced by the large-scale use of settlers to change the demographics, a policy that has been particularly successful in Western Sahara.

One key difference between the two cases is that while there was little open controversy in either country regarding the integration of the territories, the legitimacy of the Moroccan regime is far more closely identified with the fate of Western Sahara. In Lustick's terms the annexations, by the late 1980s, appeared to be on 'a regime level', but there is far more at stake for Morocco—the status of the Sahara provinces has become much closer to that of 'ideological hegemony'.[1] A look at a map indicates the relative size of the territorial expansions—see Fig. 10.1. Abandoning the Western Sahara would reduce Morocco's territory by almost one-third. The resources Morocco has put into its annexation, financial, human, diplomatic and military, are proportionately far more than that expended by Indonesia, a state with ten times Morocco's population. While the conquest of Western Sahara has been the most pressing foreign policy issue for the Moroccan government, East Timor always ranked well behind broader foreign relations questions for Indonesia, particularly those related to its ambitious but struggling international economic agenda. In consequence Indonesia was more amenable to international pressure to withdraw from East Timor if and when valued economic and strategic partners and international organizations could link their ongoing co-operation to territorial compromise.

Indonesia, however, had greater initial success diplomatically than Morocco, reflecting the former's greater economic and strategic importance. While seventy-five states have recognized independent Western Sahara,[2] known as the Sahrawi Arab Democratic Republic, or SADR, only fifteen, mostly poor African states have formally recognized an independent East Timor. Western Sahara has full membership in the Organization of African

---

[1] See discussion in Chapters 3 and 13.

[2] Pressure from France and other allies of Morocco has led several to since rescind such recognition.

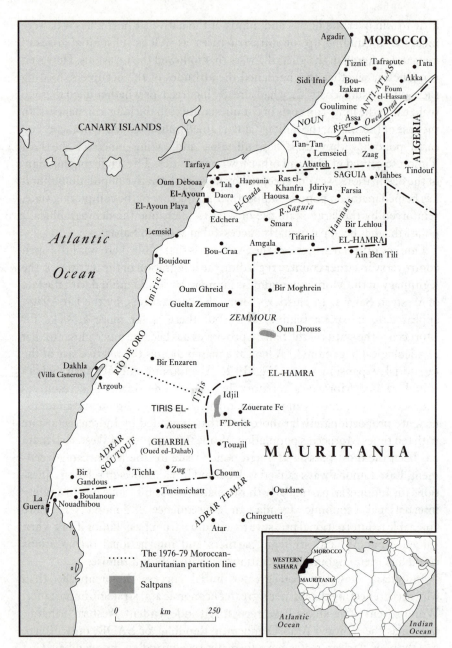

F̶ɪɢ. 10.1 Territorial expansion into Western Sahara

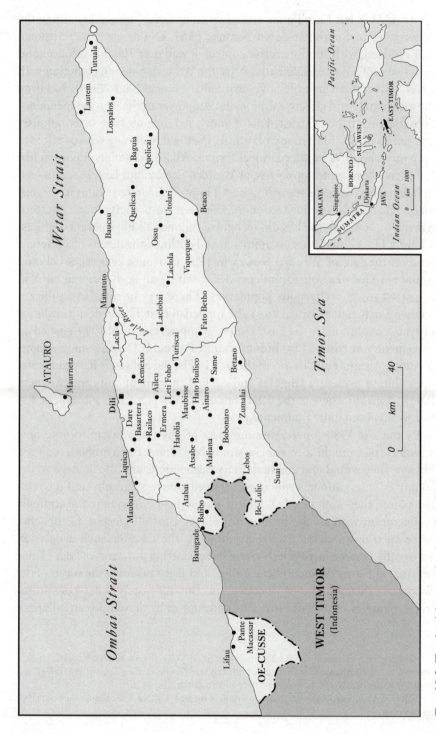

Fig. 10.2 Territorial expansion into East Timor

Unity (OAU), but East Timor was never considered for membership in the Association of Southeast Asian Nations (ASEAN) or any other regional body. Indeed, with administrative control of well over 100,000 refugees and an active professional diplomatic corps, the Western Saharans function with a real 'government-in-exile'. Western Sahara's neighbour Algeria has been the most active and effective diplomatic supporter of the pro-independence Polisario Front; by contrast, East Timor's neighbours have ostentatiously ignored its claims.[3] For many years only Portugal made any serious effort to keep the issue alive in international forums. Major non-aligned powers like India have been quite supportive of Western Sahara, but largely acquiesced to Indonesian concerns regarding East Timor. The United States has recognized Morocco's administration of, but not sovereignty over, Western Sahara; by contrast, the US did recognize Indonesia's incorporation of East Timor.[4] The United Nations approved and outlined the details of a referendum on the fate of Western Sahara in 1991 that most observers believed would have led to a vote for independence—if it had been free and fair and restricted to the indigenous population. There was no similar significant momentum for such a procedure to be applied in East Timor, despite calls for just such a solution by the East Timorese opposition, until 1999—when an agreement was reached by Indonesia and Portugal. Despite some serious divisions within the Polisario in the late 1980s, the Sahrawis have generally been able to present a singular and unified movement to represent them internationally, whereas the East Timorese independence movement has historically been more fragmented.

By the late 1980s, increasing numbers of observers began to note how withdrawing from these territories would be a rational step for both regimes, because they would end costly military occupations and the damage to the countries' international reputations. Indeed, given geography and the relative power, they would likely be able to develop close economic and strategic co-operation without the burden of military control. Despite factors that make such down-sizing extremely difficult, the case for such a decision apparently became increasingly compelling, shifting the status of East Timor into that of Lustick's 'incumbency stage' and also weakening the status of the Western Sahara in the Moroccan eyes. But ultimately what constitutes 'right-sizing' is a subjective matter—determined by those who can influence

---

[3]   Indeed, it was extremely difficult for south-east Asian NGOs to even discuss the East Timorese situation in an organized setting. Scheduled international forums on East Timor were banned and participants deported by both Malaysian and Filipino authorities.

[4]   The USA has noted, however, that the wishes of the East Timorese population were not taken into account.

the policies of the states in question, not by what outside observers may contend is the rational, legitimate, or moral course to take.

Historical Background

The distinct national identities of the peoples of Western Sahara and East Timor by comparison with their respective Moroccan and Indonesian conquerors are based in part on authentic cultural and ethnic distinctions, but their manifestations as modern nationalist movements are largely accidents of history. The former colony of Spanish Sahara encompassed 127,000 square miles in north-western Africa, the boundaries of which came about as part of a series of agreements with the French, who controlled neighbouring lands, at the beginning of the twentieth century. Like many similar agreements between colonial powers in Africa, the lines had no significant correlation with geographic or ethnic boundaries. At the time of the Spanish withdrawal in 1975, there were believed to be well under 150,000 Sahrawis, consisting of three sub-ethnic groups: the Requibat, the Teknas, and the Oulad Delim, whose ancestors have been inhabiting the land for more than a millennium. Though they have all maintained ties with people in the neighbouring states, they have collectively exhibited a history of nomadic independence and a fierce resistance to colonialism. Their ancestors resisted attempted conquests by Romans, Vandals, and the Byzantines. As a distinct people, the Sahrawi date from the fourteenth century with the intermarriage of desert Berbers with the Maquil Arabs (Harrell-Bond 1981: 3). From the fifteenth century, the Spaniards had a series of forts along the coast; they formalized their control in the Congress of Berlin in 1886 but did not have full control of the interior until the mid-1950s. Until that time, most Sahrawis continued to live a largely nomadic existence.

The island of Timor, along with other parts of the East Indies, was the subject of competing colonial interests of the Netherlands and Portugal as far back as the sixteenth century. By the mid-nineteenth century, Timor had been formally partitioned, with the Dutch controlling most of the western half of the island and the Portuguese controlling the eastern half, along with an enclave on the north-west coast, totalling approximately 13,000 square miles. The divisions coincidentally approximated the pre-colonial division of the island between two confederations of kingdoms (Barbedo de Magalhaes 1990: 17). Despite 400 years of formal colonialism, Timor's kingdoms preserved a high level of autonomy for much of that period, maintaining their historic trade links with other islands of the archipelago. These kingdoms consisted of loosely-knit localized territorial groups with a hierarchy of clans, ruled by chiefs who received tribute and arranged marital alliances with neighbouring clans (Taylor 1991: 2). Though Portuguese rule included many of the standard abuses by European imperial powers, there was also a degree of benign neglect. Portuguese became the common language among educated East Timorese and increasing numbers of the indigenous population converted to Catholicism, but the colonial imprint, as in Western Sahara, was weaker than in many colonized parts of the world.

The East Timorese are primarily of Melanesian stock, though Malays and, more recently, Chinese, Arabs, Africans, and Portuguese added to the racial mix, with a population approximating 600,000 at the time of the Portuguese withdrawal. There were virtually no cultural, ethnic, or religious linkages with the Javanese, who have always dominated Indonesian politics and society and who control the country's government and armed forces. Pre-colonial ties were limited to some trade. Even during the height of Javanese power between the tenth and fifteenth centuries, there was no political or even significant cultural influence.

Were it not for the continued Spanish repression and the strong national-ist reaction that ensued, Western Sahara might have been integrated into Morocco as a hinterland of traditional peoples with minimal contact with the government but falling short of establishing a distinct national identity—as happened with nomadic peoples of southern Algeria and their relationships with the government in Algiers.[5] Spain in fact traditionally emphasized the cultural and ethnic distinctiveness of the Sahrawis, influenced by the desire to resist Moroccan and Mauritanian irredentism especially during the latter years of their colonial rule (Harrell-Bond 1981: 1). But the Sahrawis' distinct identity was hardly an artificial creation: their nomadism, as well as their clothing, diet, dialect, poetry, pigmentation, and facial features, clearly dis-tinguish them from their Moroccan counterparts. Similarly, it has been argued that were it not for the experience of differing colonial masters, East Timor would have become part of the Republic of Indonesia along with West Timor and surrounding islands with only limited resistance, despite distinct ethnic differences from the Javanese controlling the central government. However artificial colonial boundaries may have been, centuries of control by European powers still played a major role in sharpening distinctions between those on either side of colonial borders—distinctions that change the focus of trade, transportation, and élite education.[6] The Moroccans and Indonesians apparently failed to fully recognize that however modest their

---

[5] Occasional acts of resistance by the Tuaregs and others have occurred but there is no seces-sionist movement to speak of.

[6] As one might expect from Gellner's theory of nationalism (1983), and see Chapter 2.

territorial claims may have appeared, integration would not come without resistance. In 1973, a group of Sahrawi nationalists formed the Polisario Front, which developed a moderately leftist nationalist movement that forged ties within all three major ethnic groupings and between both young radicals and traditional elders. Independent reports by the UN and other outside entities noted that the clear majority of Sahrawis supported independence under the Polisario (United Nations 1975: ch. 13, Annex: Report of the UN Visiting Mission to Spanish Sahara). Similarly, and not long afterwards, the East Timorese Fretilin movement grew out of a social democratic grouping and emerged as the leading revolutionary nationalist movement pursuing the struggle for independence in that country, a cause which also was supported by the vast majority of the population (Taylor 1991: 35).

Origins of Aggrandizement

Western Sahara has long been part of the Moroccan vision, most explicitly articulated by nationalists in the 1950s, of *Le Grand Maroc*, a 'Greater Morocco'. That vision has at times also included territorial claims for all of Mauritania, western Algeria, western Mali, and the extreme north of Senegal. The Moroccans claimed that all of these territories had at one time or another been under Moroccan control. This conception was most clearly articulated by Allal el-Fassi, the principal leader of the Istiqlal Party, who, upon his return from exile in 1956 just after Moroccan independence from France, insisted that only parts of the historic Alawite empire had been freed. At first, his rather grandiose claims were not taken too seriously, but his party soon endorsed the idea. King Mohammed V decided not to allow the chief nationalist party to outbid the monarchy so, by the end of 1957, claims for a Greater Morocco became official government policy.

To make such territorial aggrandizement possible, Morocco threatened to seize part of neighbouring countries by force. In 1962–3, Morocco clashed with newly-independent Algeria, taking advantage of the chaos following Algeria's bloody revolution by seizing a number of border towns before being forced to withdraw. Morocco initially opposed Mauritania's independence, successfully blocking its membership in the United Nations for more than a year and delaying recognition by several allied countries. Morocco also opposed Mali's independence, though less vigorously. Not surprisingly, Morocco interpreted the imminent imperial withdrawal from Western Sahara in the mid-1970s, then known as Spanish Sahara, as part of its reclamation of territory from Spanish colonialists, beginning with the return of northern Morocco—save the two *presidios* of Ceuta and Melila—soon after independence from France in 1956, of the Tarfaya region in 1958,[7] and of Ifni in 1969.[8]

By contrast to the clearly articulated irredentist vision in Morocco, there was never much effort, in word or in deed, by the Indonesians to indicate an interest in taking over what was then known as Portuguese Timor during the first twenty years of Indonesian independence. While the unification of the entire Dutch East Indies under Jakarta's rule has been a demand of virtually every Indonesian nationalist, and President Sukarno for a time led Indonesian claims for such adjacent British possessions as Malaysia, Singapore, and Brunei during the 1950s and early 1960s, the small Portuguese colony was never much of an issue. When East Timor first became an item in international forums on decolonization in the early 1960s, the Indonesians explicitly discounted any territorial claims, though there were some contradictory statements which did indicate some interest among some sectors of the Indonesian leadership (Taylor 1991: 20–1). Even during the struggle with the Dutch over Irian Jaya in the early 1960s, the question of East Timor was never raised. By the late 1960s and early 1970s, however, following Sukarno's ouster, the army's intelligence agency, BAKIN (*Badan Koordinasi Intel*), began covert support for a pro-integrationist group in East Timor. The official line at that point was still that of 'non-interference' in the country's affairs. There appears to have been internal disagreements within the Indonesian government regarding their position, with BAKIN leading the lobbying for annexation. BAKIN's role proved to be decisive, however, as its officers and their network of allies formed the backbone of Suharto's 'New Order', and were thus able to influence government policy (Taylor 1991: 23, 25, 30). Indonesia's military regime appears to have been motivated by the desire to consolidate the fragile national unity of the country through an example of strength and firmness against East Timorese efforts at independence (Barbedo de Magalhaes 1990: 23). Ongoing divisions within the Indonesian government became apparent in 1999, when the civilian president BJ Habibie agreed to an internationally-supervised referendum on the fate of the territory. The military formally backed his decision, but then supported and engaged in massacres of independence supporters and widespread pillage and destruction of property.

---

[7]   The Tarfaya region, located south of the Draa River, had traditionally not been considered part of Morocco. Ethnically and culturally, the inhabitants are essentially the same as those in Western Sahara, and are separated from their patrimony by an arbitrary horizontal line. Despite this the Polisario, in their own 'right-sizing' considerations, have renounced any claims on the region.

[8]   Ironically, in 1959, and again in 1962, Spain offered the Spanish Sahara to Morocco in exchange for dropping their claims on the presidios, but Morocco refused, since the territory was thought by both countries to be of little value (Lalutte 1976: 8).

An important motivating factor for the take-over in 1975 was the regime's concern over the possibility of a leftist revolutionary government amidst their archipelago. While East Timor's poverty and small size certainly did not render the country a threat, its possible external affiliations as well as the prospect that it could serve as both an exile base and a model for a wider left-wing resurgence was most troublesome to the Indonesian authorities (Leifer 1983: 155). Suharto's New Order was not ready to risk the existence of an independent state capable of encouraging a new challenge to its authority, particularly after the Communist scare of the early 1960s. Vietnam, Laos, and Cambodia had come under the control of Marxist-Leninist revolutionaries in the months preceding the invasion of East Timor, as had the former Portuguese colonies of Mozambique, Angola, and Guinea-Bissau. Yet most analysts believe the decision by Indonesia to seize the territory took place in the summer of 1974, before these revolutionary triumphs, before the leftward turn in the Portuguese revolution, and before the transformation of Fretilin from a social democratic party to a more explicitly leftist revolutionary movement. At the very least, however, these developments gave the Indonesians a stronger excuse to rally support from both domestic sources and foreign powers concerned with Communist advances to oppose independence (Barbedo de Magalhaes 1990: 22–3).

Regime Stability

Despite their recent liberalization, Morocco and Indonesia were authoritarian states for much of the period of their occupations. Consequently, both governments were able to 'remove potential intractable questions of the composition of the political community from the political arena' without much difficulty and were able to include the annexation of the territories in question as part of their nations' 'presumptive beliefs' (Lustick 1993: 38). At the same time, both states had some limited trappings of democracy and a need to appease certain sectors of the population beyond élite circles, even prior to Suharto's overthrow in 1998 and the death of King Hassan II in 1999. This raises interesting questions as to what motivated these two governments to seize the respective territories in 1975 and to rally the population to their expansionist aims, and why withdrawal from these territories was seen as problematic.

For most of its time since independence, the Moroccan government has not been completely stable. Were this otherwise, it is doubtful that the monarchy would have caved in to ultra-nationalist sentiments to mount its invasion of Western Sahara and its serious consequences of increasing the country's economic woes, facing international isolation, and allowing for the killing and maiming of thousands of young Moroccans. In the early 1970s, the level of apathy and cynicism among the Moroccan public was quite palpable. Hassan's efforts at legitimizing himself through elections backfired when they were blatantly rigged. His new constitution was far less democratic than the one promised by his father in 1955. There were serious coup attempts in 1971 and 1972 from which he barely escaped with his life. The opposition refused to join in coalition and his government was widely seen as unable to address basic economic and social problems. Outbreaks in 1973 of small-scale guerrilla warfare by elements of the opposition pointed to the failure of the 1970 constitution to guarantee political freedom, as well as continued corruption, slow economic growth, retarded social change, the domination of the economy by French and other foreign interests, and continued Spanish colonial presence in the presidios, the Zarffarine Islands, and the Spanish Sahara. There was a sense of malaise in the country, particularly among students and intellectuals. The questionable loyalty of the armed forces had not abated. It was in this context that King Hassan forcefully claimed the nationalist banner. It was not the first time he had used war as a legitimating tool: soon after his ascension to the throne, the border war with Algeria also helped rally support around the new king.

The Moroccan leadership saw Western Sahara, at least in part, as a question on which to test national resolve and distract attention from domestic problems. Taking over the Western Sahara from the vacating Spaniards became, for King Hassan, the substitute for the unrealized goal of a 'Greater Morocco'. By depicting his war against the Sahrawis as a war against European colonialism, Hassan was able to come across as a liberator rather than an invader and, at the same time, squash domestic criticism of his close ties to Western interests. Nationalists pushed the greater Morocco idea; Hassan decided to use it to counter charges that his was a neo-colonialist regime. The 1975 crisis with Spain over the fate of the territory led virtually every segment of the Moroccan community to pledge its loyalty to the king (*bay'a*). The Moroccan opposition was largely co-opted by the Green March.

It would be overly-simplistic, however, to conclude that King Hassan simply stirred up the Sahara question to rescue himself from the crisis confronting his throne in the early 1970s. Much had to do with the timing of the Spanish decision to grant Western Sahara independence and, at times, Hassan may have been as much a follower as a leader of public opinion. But he could have worked out a face-saving compromise short of a full-scale invasion, which could have mollified the military and public; he did not. There was great enthusiasm for invasion from the population, opposition parties, and the media. Indeed, not only was there remarkable unity among virtually all sectors on the Sahara question, despite enormous differences on other issues, it remains virtually the only policy matter that unites Morocco's legal political parties. Moroccans have tended to blame the lack of greater international support for the take-over on inept diplomacy, not on the possibility that the Moroccan position might be illegitimate. Most Moroccans accepted without question that their territorial integrity took precedence over self-determination and international law. This sense of national unity then allowed Hassan to grant greater political liberalization for a short period, as even the socialist and communist opposition embraced the forcible annexation of Western Sahara.[9]

While most Moroccans supported the war effort publicly, the exact scale of support is hard to gauge. Hassan ruled it illegal to oppose or even debate Moroccan claims to Western Sahara; violators usually ended up in prison.[10] Such limits on debate indicate both that Western Sahara has not been part of political discourse and that the regime is not confident of complete public support.[11] The largest opposition bloc, the socialists, have historically been more hardline than the King on the issue, denouncing the idea of a referendum on Western Sahara and other efforts by the OAU and the UN for a peaceful and negotiated solution (*Philadelphia Inquirer*, 19 January 1982). This may be an opportunistic posture—to appear patriotic enough to avoid excessive repression, and to hang a possible defeat around the neck of the monarchy—so the socialists' support may not be that deep-rooted. Though the opposition parties led the irredentist sentiments, the resulting war and occupation has strengthened the regime and its authoritarian reach. Says Sidi Omar, of the Moroccan Human Rights Association, 'The Western Sahara is a political question that helps the Moroccan authorities resolve internal issues. It is on the dark side of politics' (Huband 1996).

If King Hassan provided open and highly public leadership on the Sahara issue, Suharto was publicly more cautious on East Timor, especially when compared with some of his more hawkish generals—in part to help obtain the silent approval of his Western supporters, and to limit the risk of endangering his future access to Western military hardware (Budiardjo and Liong 1984: 19). His rule seemed quite secure after the terror of the mid-1960s and he never felt a strong need to play the nationalist card for domestic consumption. He and his generals led a massacre of at least half a million left-wing

[9] For example, in April 1979 Morocco's entire political élite, ranging from conservative monarchists to the Communist party, formed the National Defence Council in support of the take-over of Western Sahara (*New York Times*, 1 May 1979).

[10] 'UN Visit Raises Hope for End to Sahara War', *New York Times*, 6 December 1987.

[11] This means that the application of Lustick's theory of state expansion and contraction is somewhat problematic in authoritarian regimes—where formal closure of discussion on certain topics cannot be taken as an indicator of 'ideological harmony'.

opponents and ethnic Chinese in the mid-1960s and jailed hundreds of thousands more. With virtually all the opposition killed, exiled, jailed in remote island gulags or cowering in submission at the time of the collapse of the Portuguese empire, Suharto had no great need to appease nationalist critics.

While there was no popular outpouring in Indonesia in support for the state's take-over of East Timor, the government's position was widely accepted internally. The level of Timorese resistance and the scale of the massacres and forced starvation—estimated to be as high as 200,000 (Center for Defense Information 1983)—remains to this day unknown to the vast majority of Indonesians. Within Indonesia, during the final years of the Suharto regime, when some space opened for talking about controversial political topics, the two areas that were essentially off limits were the Suharto family's business dealings, and East Timor. After his overthrow in May 1998 *both* these themes became admissible, the first dramatically so.

Despite being granted scholarships to Indonesian universities and other incentives to buy their loyalty, few Timorese gave up on the nationalist cause and many became involved in underground pro-independence organizations within Indonesia proper and were therefore kept under a very close watch. The government often hired students from West Timor and other nearby islands to engage in public demonstrations for integration and to even attack pro-independence East Timorese (Confidential sources, based on interviews with East Timorese students in May 1997). Still, this did not stop these students from organizing politically; the mid-1990s saw a series of brief but dramatic occupations of foreign embassies in Jakarta by East Timorese youth seeking political asylum (Jardine 1996: 402). Following the downfall of Suharto, demonstrations became open and defiant, both in East Timor and within Indonesia itself.

There was a rather dramatic growth in awareness of the East Timor situation among pro-democracy activists in Indonesia during the 1990s, in part because of networking by East Timorese within Indonesian dissident circles; there have been few if any cases where an occupied people have been as successful in organizing support within the population of their occupiers. Among more mainstream opposition elements, however, the concern was focused primarily on improving human rights conditions, rather than recognizing the East Timorese people's right to self-determination. Indeed, some Indonesian pro-democracy activists resented international concern over East Timor, and were frustrated that the oppression of 600,000 Timorese received more attention in the international community than the oppression of 220 million Indonesians. Many on the left-wing of the Indonesian opposition, such as the People's Democratic Party (PRD), openly supported East Timorese independence. The far more significant opposition movements led by Megawati Sukarnoputri criticized the repressive and over-centralized governance of the Suharto regime in East Timor, but still favoured the country's integration into Indonesia.

The democratic movement in Indonesia included many strong nationalists. In the Indonesian context this meant support for unifying all the islands, which, for most, included East Timor. Covert intervention by the United States in the late 1950s against the nationalist Sukarno government focused upon encouraging secessionist movements in north-western Sumatra and other outer islands (Kahin and Kahin 1995). Thus, centralized rule from Java and bitter opposition to independence or even to federal forms of autonomy became ingrained in the national consciousness and transcended the ideological spectrum.[12] In the 1950s and early 1960s, the charismatic Sukarno used anti-imperialist rhetoric as a substitute for coherent economic or political planning and all internal opposition was defined as a threat by external neo-colonial interests (Taylor 1991: 20). Later, as in Western Sahara, the fact that the colonial power of the disputed territory was a fascist European state, helped give the appearance of a moral imperative for Indonesia to 'liberate' the country.

Changing International Dimensions

Morocco and Indonesia were successful in their efforts at territorial expansion largely because of the acquiescence of great powers, and, by extension, the United Nations Security Council. The efforts of the United States and others to minimize pressure on Morocco and Indonesia meant that the Security Council could only pass resolutions 'deploring' the invasions—relatively weak language for such situations. However, the resolutions did call for the withdrawal of Moroccan and Indonesian forces and a negotiated settlement, reaffirming the right of self-determination for both peoples and calling for an end to the fighting. This was stronger language than that used for the Chinese occupation of Tibet, where no action was taken, and for the Israeli occupation of the Sinai Peninsula, Gaza Strip, West Bank and the Golan Heights, where withdrawal was linked to security guarantees being provided by neighbouring states. However, it was far weaker than language used following Iraq's invasion of Kuwait and, more importantly, no enforcement mechanisms, such as economic sanctions, were included.

Both American and French diplomats privately acknowledged that a major reason for not opposing Morocco's irredentism in Western Sahara was

---

[12] See the discussion in Chapter 2 on resistance to federalism in post-colonial states.

the fear that it would lead to the collapse of their ally King Hassan, a concern which continues for the monarchy as a whole. Consequently, they were unwilling to be forceful, even when the Moroccans began delaying and sabotaging the 1991 agreement for a referendum. More recently, changes in global politics, such as the fall of Communism and the international debt crisis, have significantly reduced the political leverage of non-aligned Third World countries at the United Nations, traditionally the strongest supporters of Sahrawi self-determination. The West, which has been far more tolerant and sometimes outright supportive of Morocco and its irredentist designs, now has more clout in the United Nations and other international forums. Similarly, while the country's international relations have been damaged by its colonial ambitions, Morocco is still able to work closely with Algeria on areas of mutual concern, prompted by the growing need for closer economic co-operation, despite harsh differences on Western Sahara (Zunes 1995). Support for Morocco's position in the United States, France, and other Western powers actually increased in the early 1990s despite the end of the cold war, because the king's regime was seen as a bulwark against radical Islamists in the region. The Western Saharans initially were more successful than the East Timorese in the diplomatic field because of the active support of their influential neighbour Algeria. However, the Polisario's ally has been far too distracted by its internal crises to muster effective leadership. Not long after the 1991 agreement for a ceasefire and the holding of a referendum, the flow of arms from Algeria, already reduced, essentially halted.

Yet there are other forces at work which have provided a degree of diplomatic leverage on Morocco. In addition to the widespread recognition of an independent Western Sahara, annual resolutions in the General Assembly led to lopsided majorities supporting self-determination. Morocco's takeover of Western Sahara is significant because thus far it is the only successful violation of the OAU's principle forbidding the altering of colonial boundaries by force.[13] Indeed, Morocco withdrew from the OAU in protest at the regional body's recognition of the SADR in 1982, the only occasion in which a country has formally left the organization. King Hassan and his son have had to be sensitive to pressure from the international community and reduced support from Morocco's financial supporters in the Arab Gulf when the Saudis became less willing to continue bankrolling the occupation forces, particularly when oil revenues declined, and they had to increase their own military spending to counter perceived threats from Iraq and Iran. Lastly, the desire to have Morocco's take-over of Western Sahara legitimized in the eyes

---

[13] Morocco and Somalia were the only African states to dissent from this principle upon the adoption of the OAU charter in 1963.

of the international community, even if it meant risking the loss of the territory, was apparently very important to King Hassan, who studied politics and law at the Sorbonne—whether his successor will have the same normative constraints remains to be seen.

While the international community has not allowed Morocco's Western Sahara policy to interfere substantially with normal relationships, it has arguably played a role in restricting closer ties in this era of economic interdependency. The Arab Maghreb Union, an economic treaty linking Morocco with four other countries in north-west Africa, has not progressed nearly as far as Morocco would desire partly because of Algerian and Mauritanian opposition to Morocco's ongoing occupation. More importantly, as with Turkey and its occupation of northern Cyprus, the occupation has become perhaps the major obstacle to closer co-operation with the European Union—with which Morocco has long desired full membership.

Indonesia initially had an easier time than the Moroccans in the international arena. During the late 1970s and 1980s, increasing numbers of governments effectively recognized Indonesia's take-over, most crucially Australia, which had offshore oil interests in the Timor Gap. The United States, the ASEAN nations and most Islamic countries also threw their support to the Indonesians. Annual General Assembly resolutions at the United Nations calling for East Timorese self-determination ended in 1982 when it became doubtful that there would be enough votes to pass. The work of small groups of human rights activists in Europe, North America, and Australia kept the issue alive in subsequent years.

The widespread pandering of foreign governments to Indonesian designs in East Timor did not mean, however, that the strong moral and legal arguments in favour of East Timorese independence did not eventually prove decisive. The awarding of the 1996 Nobel Peace Prize to two East Timorese activists[14]—and, to a lesser extent, fallout from a well-publicized massacre in 1991[15]—mobilized public opinion in democratic countries in support of the East Timorese cause. Though an international solidarity movement does exist for Western Sahara, primarily in Europe, it pales in comparison with the movement in support of East Timor, which grew dramatically in the 1990s, and helped encourage greater media coverage of the human rights situation. By 1997, after years of silence, editorials in influential Western media such as the *New York Times* and *The Economist* finally called for self-determination for East Timor (Jardine 1996: 403). These movements successfully

[14] Catholic Bishop Carlos Xemenes Belo and East Timor's *de facto* foreign minister Jose Ramos Horta.
[15] Known as the Santa Cruz massacre, at least 271 peaceful demonstrators were massacred by Indonesian soldiers before foreign journalists at a cemetery in Dili.

pressured the United States and other influential governments to reluctantly threaten sanctions in response to the post-referendum massacres in
September 1999, which forced Indonesia to accept international peacekeeping forces.

While most Islamic polities have sided with Morocco or remain neutral
regarding Western Sahara, the Roman Catholic Church took an increasingly
active role in supporting the rights of the East Timorese, the vast majority of
whom were Catholic and under the rule of the world's largest Muslim country. As the only major pre-invasion public institution of East Timorese civil
society to survive the years of occupation, the Church became the centre of
the unarmed resistance. The Portuguese and other governments became
more emboldened to press the issue at international forums (ibid: 400). In
Australia, the United States and several EU states, opposition parties on
both the left and the right challenged their governments' support of the
Indonesian regime over the East Timor issue. Australia finally called for East
Timorese self-determination and, in December 1998, the European Union
adopted a resolution supporting a referendum. Meanwhile, the US Congress
also passed resolutions supporting a referendum. It became difficult for
Indonesian leaders to visit a major western state without being dogged by
both pro-Timorese demonstrators and reporters questioning the country's
East Timor policy.[16] Public opposition in the United States to Indonesia's
occupation of East Timor was largely responsible for the government cancelling its request for the purchase of US fighter jets and military training in
May 1997[17] and proposed arms transfers to Indonesia became major political
battles in several countries. Indeed, the United States, which provided 90 per
cent of the weapons used in Indonesia's initial invasion, eventually prohibited the use of US weapons by Indonesian forces in East Timor. Furthermore,
profound dissatisfaction with the Indonesian regime's reluctance to abide by
suggested reforms by the International Monetary Fund lessened American
support. The US refused to link a bailout with the situation in East Timor
but the perceived need to appease the Indonesians lessened. The US also did

[16] Suharto initially cancelled his scheduled appearance at the Vancouver meeting of the Asia-
Pacific Economic Conference (APEC) in the autumn of 1997, concerned over the threatened large-
scale demonstrations, including civil disobedience, by Canadian human rights demonstrators. Only
when Canadian authorities convinced him such protests would be controlled and kept at an enormous distance from the meetings, did he consent to participate. Heavy-handed tactics by Canadian
authorities against pro-East Timor demonstrators, revelations of co-ordination with Indonesian
authorities, and the subsequent cover-up became a major scandal for the government of Prime
Minister Jean Chrétien.

[17] Congress might not have been able to block the sale, or the request for training, but there
would have likely been an embarrassing series of hearings on Capitol Hill—spearheaded by liberal
Democrats concerned about human rights issues and conservative Republicans seeking to embarrass the Clinton Administration over its close ties to Suharto.

not want to see its ally weakened or distracted by East Timor in the wake of the far more significant economic crises. The end of the cold war and the increasing political moderation of Fretilin undoubtedly eased US concerns about an independent East Timor—as did the passage of the Law of the Sea Treaty, which allows for US submarines to pass unimpeded through such deep water ocean corridors as the Ombai-Wetar Straits north of East Timor, an issue which apparently concerned the US in 1975 (Taylor 1991: 403).

This moral pressure proved increasingly embarrassing for Indonesia, as well as for foreign companies seeking investment opportunities in the country, and foreign governments seeking close diplomatic, military and economic ties. That and the forced resignation of Suharto helped to create the momentum for a diplomatic solution to the problem. Already facing enormous criticisms internationally for its domestic political repression, its labour practices, environmental policies, and response to the economic crisis, moderate elements within the Indonesian leadership hoped that agreeing to a withdrawal from East Timor after a referendum would prove to be a relatively painless way of assuaging international pressure. Indeed, some analysts trace the increased possibility of Indonesian compromise over East Timor back to the 1988 decision to open up the territory to outside observers and foreign investors, which in turn was a response to negative international publicity about the repression of the population (Feith 1992). The severe repression that followed the 1999 referendum was led by elements of the military indifferent to international public opinion. Even they backed off, however, when the Clinton Administration, under growing popular pressure at home, announced the severing of military co-operation nine days into the post-referendum attacks.

Audie Klotz, in her pioneering work *Norms in International Relations: The Struggle Against Apartheid* (1994), argues that while many international relations theorists 'emphasize the difficulties of co-ordinating multilateral policies and the primacy of material interests', it was normative values manifested on a global scale that led to South Africa's diplomatic, cultural, and economic isolation. This was made possible through 'the loose coalition of governments, non-governmental organizations, and individuals that made up the trans-national anti-apartheid movement' who successfully 'globalized' their concerns as an influential political force, and that could be replicated elsewhere. While most realist perspectives suggested little promise for Indonesian or Moroccan compromise on their territorial conquests, Klotz notes how 'norms constrain states' behaviour through reputation and group membership, and that norms constitute states' definitions of their own identities and interests'. She reminds readers in her conclusion how the history of decolonization 'demonstrates the power of weak and non-state actors to

transform both global norms and the distribution of social power in the international system' (ibid: 4, 6, 166, 173). The greatest external pressure for territorial compromise for Morocco in Western Sahara and Indonesia in East
Timor has come from NGOs and the Third World. This pressure—in the
case of East Timor—eventually influenced the policies of major Western
powers and the United Nations, which, in turn, forced the Indonesians to see
territorial compromise as the wisest course of action. Whether a similar
mobilization could also prove decisive in the case of Western Sahara remains
to be seen.

Potential for Right-Sizing

Whatever the similarities and differences between these two cases, both
Morocco and Indonesia, despite occupying virtually all of the respective
territories, failed to win over the majority of the populations to support
incorporation. Both, despite some level of acquiescence by some foreign governments, were unable to establish durable international legitimacy. And,
questions emerged as to whether the élites' political and economic gains from
the occupations outweighed the serious political and economic costs. There
is therefore a logic that would counsel that 'right-sizing' the relevant states
would require granting these territories their right to self-determination,
and withdrawing to within their own legitimate boundaries. Legally speaking, and from the perspective of the majority of populations in the territories
in question, challenging Moroccan and Indonesian control is part of a legitimate anti-colonial struggle for liberation. However, the population of the
occupying power generally saw this resistance as that of an illegitimate secessionist movement.[18]

The decisive factor, however, in affecting the destinies of these territories
remained the perceptions of the Moroccan and Indonesian regimes—however legally or morally problematic this might seem. Ian Lustick cites
Andrew Mack's thesis regarding the 'asymmetric' stakes in struggles
between small states and large states in colonial or neo-colonial situations
because so much more is at stake for the colonized power. As Lustick
observes, this thesis may not apply if both the leadership and much of the
population of the large state fail to see themselves as colonizers. What is at
stake is more than just the instrumental values of the territory in question
but, given that the boundaries have become 'institutionalized features of
states', the entire distribution of power within the state system. For Morocco,

---

[18] As did the media within sympathetic countries like the United States.

control of the Western Sahara has become the major legitimizing cause of the monarchy developed in combat with Moroccan nationalists, for whom it is also perhaps the major legitimizing formula. In Indonesia, while East Timor *per se* did not have close to the same importance, the unity of the country as a whole and the suppression of secessionist movements on the outer islands remain key concerns of present and future state managers. While the East Timorese struggle for independence did not constitute, legally speaking, a secessionist movement, the fear of a dangerous precedent weighs heavily on the Indonesian leadership. Losing East Timor opens up questions of the shape of the country as a whole, challenging the prevailing ideology of national unity. 'The territorial shape of a state . . . helps determine what interests are legitimate, what resources are mobilizable, what questions are open for debate, what ideological formula will be relevant, what cleavages could become significant and what political allies might be available' (Lustick 1993: 41). Many speculate that the horrific repression in East Timor in 1999 which followed the 30 August pro-independence vote was a calculated warning by the Indonesian military to what secessionist movements within Indonesia might expect if they also opted for independence.

In both Indonesia and Morocco, for most of their periods of occupation, it appears that control of the territories was at least at the regime stage, where disengagement would mean struggle over the integrity of the regime itself. This continues to be true in Morocco. However, the Indonesian regime collapsed anyway, thus providing room for territorial compromise. The death of King Hassan may not have the same regime-imploding consequences as the resignation of Suharto. Neither incorporation ever reached the ideological hegemony stage. Lustick (1993: 41) argues that control of a territory has crossed the ideological hegemony threshold only when 'its status as an integral part of the state, not as a problematically occupied asset, becomes part of the natural order of things for the overwhelming majority of the population whose political behaviour is relevant to outcomes in the state'. Given the authoritarian nature of both governments during this period, the percentage of the population whose 'political behaviour is relevant' in such decisions was rather limited. This differentiates my cases with Lustick's three cases—the UK, France, and Israel—which were all democracies or publicly liberal regimes with extensive suffrages. During the Suharto years, there was an effective prohibition of discussion of state contraction of any kind. In Morocco, public discussion on the status of Western Sahara is effectively prohibited. That such discussion has to be banned at all may be indicative that those in power are not confident that the ideological hegemony threshold has been crossed. At the same time, the majority of the population does not question incorporation—though, if allowed the free exchange of ideas, attitudes might shift, as occurred in Indonesia. Should the population of the occupying power, for example, learn the real beliefs of the overwhelming majority of those in the territories, that there has been substantial loss of life of state soldiers as well natives, that enormous economic resources have been squandered in conquest and control, and that large segments of the international community view their action as illegitimate, it could change attitudes.[19] Increasing democratization and access to international communication may enhance just such possibilities.

In times of crisis and large-scale disruption, the politically-relevant percentage of the population, even in the most autocratic societies, can grow dramatically. The very small size of the territories at issue relative to the population of the conquering state makes it relatively easy for the regime to simply suppress the pro-independence opposition. What might lead to a change would be that the costs of suppressing violent or nonviolent resistance would become prohibitive, either militarily or in infrastructural expenditure. Another possible shift could come as a result of international pressure, for example, through the threat of international sanctions or a decline of international credibility or influence. Either could 'break apart hegemonic conceptions within the political class of the central state' (Lustick 1993: 448).

While the potential for such right-sizing came to pass in Indonesia, great obstacles remain in Morocco. Ongoing Moroccan efforts to delay the referendum or stack the voter rolls in its favour may indicate a continuing unwillingness to risk giving up the territory. However, if one assumes Morocco may indeed eventually be willing to take such a risk, it could be because the new king, Mohammed VI, is more attuned to liberal democratic ideals and recognizes the need for a more co-operative relationship with the Europeans and his North African neighbours. While the Moroccans have backed out of previously scheduled referenda with little negative consequences, it may be more difficult now and in the future. The US in recent years has appeared to me more willing to encourage Moroccan compliance with its agreements and to end its damage to the United Nations' reputation at a time when the US wants to use the UN to advance its agenda elsewhere (Brazier 1997). With the end of the cold war, the threat of a fundamentalist take-over in Algeria diminishing, and Morocco no longer needed as an intermediary in the Arab-Israeli talks, and with the growing political moderation of the Polisario Front, the US can afford to push harder than it had previously.

---

[19] A democratic society, even a highly-educated one, does not necessarily care about such issues. Few Americans, for example, fully appreciated how unpopular certain US foreign interventions were by the population affected or by the international community, such as the Contra War against Nicaragua. For a provocative analysis of this phenomenon, see Chomsky and Herman (1988).

Morocco has relinquished claims on territory on several previous occasions. It quietly renounced its demands to parts of Mali and Senegal in the early 1960s. It finally recognized Mauritania in 1969, nine years after its independence from France, and reiterated its support for Mauritanian sovereignty in 1974 as part of the negotiations leading up to the partition of Western Sahara. A 1972 agreement with Algeria relinquished claims on the Tindouf region and other areas of dispute with its neighbour.[20] However, these compromises were in large part an effort to help secure the Western Sahara. At no point has Morocco voluntarily given up territory already under its control. Tactical shifts on the diplomatic front, while sometimes dramatic, appear to have in no way lessened the Moroccan conviction that control of Western Sahara is justified.

Success in legitimizing Morocco's control of Western Sahara was in part an effort by King Hassan to enhance his claim as the 'reunifier of the Kingdom.' Most of the late king's reign centred on this enterprise. An end to Moroccan control of Western Sahara would have ended the truce the monarchy had with the organized opposition. Indeed, there had long been an assumption in some diplomatic circles in Rabat that the monarchy would fall if it lost the referendum (Murphy 1991). In effect, the regime was too weak to take such a risk. The question is whether the new king, less closely identified with the irredentist campaign than his father, will thereby have more leverage to right-size his state or whether the control over Western Sahara is still at a sufficiently hegemonic level to make such territorial compromise impossible. Saharan policy has always been centred on the monarch—in contrast with occasional periods of liberalization where the Prime Minister and other segments of government are able to exercise authority. The tendency in any centralized bureaucracy, particularly an authoritarian one, to please those ranked above suggests that bad news and pessimistic predictions do not necessarily meet the king's ear on every occasion. Thus, a discourse on the possibility for contracting state boundaries as a rational strategic choice may be more likely to occur in a more open and pluralistic political system than currently exists in Morocco. Conversely, however, a decision of the king to go ahead with a referendum could be based on what could be a naïvely optimistic belief that the majority of the Western Saharan population would support incorporation.

The military, always a key element in Moroccan politics, is still divided on what to do next. For years, there have been rumours of purges and even a possible coup attempt. Some suggested that King Hassan pursued the war in

---

[20] Despite such agreements, Moroccan maps, even in government offices, still display an ill-defined border on the east.

order to keep most of his armed forces out of the country so they would not attempt another overthrow. The few military units left inside Morocco itself leave their garrisons only without ammunition and only if accompanied by loyalist gendarmes (Randal 1984). Given that the army has risen from 56,000 members in 1975 to over 200,000 because of the war, integration of demobilized soldiers into the economy could be dangerous (Westervelt and Reichman 1989). Hassan even feared an over-zealous military might attempt an attack on the western Algerian region around Tindouf, both to crush the centre of Polisario resistance and seize Algerian territory long claimed by Morocco. Therefore, he kept a tight rein on the military, even those fighting in the Sahara.[21] It is unclear whether King Mohammed will feel more confident.

Some Moroccan citizens want more resources shifted from the Western Sahara to Morocco proper, but many observers believe that the national will could sustain the costs of the occupation indefinitely, particularly since the 1991 ceasefire indicated Polisario's military weakness. The opposition parties are still solidly behind annexation and grass roots pressure for an end to the war is not strong enough to resist the political repression. With the occupation so closely ingrained in Moroccan nationalism and the monarchy concerned to preserve itself as the powerful governing institution, the only likely way for Morocco to withdraw—even if it lost a fair referendum—would be under international pressure. Indeed, the new king and military might even welcome such pressure to justify a withdrawal from Western Sahara before a very disappointed and potentially angry population.

Irredentist sentiments are still overwhelming in Morocco and among its settlers in Western Sahara. Pro-independence Sahrawis are mostly in exile, and those that remain in Western Sahara are outnumbered by Moroccan settlers and are kept in check by a brutally effective occupation force. With Algeria preoccupied by its domestic crisis, military support for a renewed war by the Polisario remains doubtful, and no other party can be expected to provide the needed assistance. The entire Western Sahara population, including exiles, is a bare 3 per cent of the total Moroccan population.

The biggest obstacle to withdrawal may be within Morocco itself—popular opinion, well-manipulated by the crown and other political élites, sees Western Sahara as an inherent part of the Moroccan nation-state. With the mainstream opposition taking at least as hard a line toward Western Sahara as the monarchy, greater democracy would not necessarily mean greater likeli-

---

[21] Even Moroccan prisoners of war are not welcome to return. When the Polisario offered an unconditional release of two hundred Moroccan POWs in June 1989 as a good will gesture coinciding with the United Nations Secretary General's peace making visit to Rabat, the king refused repatriation efforts by the International Committee of the Red Cross (ICRC).

hood of territorial compromise. Whether these factors outweigh the factors working against continued Moroccan control and whether the monarchy could manage to survive a defeat in a referendum, remains to be seen. By contrast, among the minority of Indonesians supportive of East Timorese independence, there was a widespread belief that freedom for East Timor and democracy for Indonesia were inextricably linked. Not only did Indonesia's democratic opening provide for the necessary political opening for advocates of East Timorese independence, but having a democratic republic on the archipelago was seen as a possible inspirational precedent for pro-democratic forces throughout the other islands. Thus, unlike Morocco, the Indonesian opposition included both elements favouring East Timorese freedom and—even among those supportive of annexation—a more flexible attitude towards self-governance. Some US officials speculated that Suharto was the only one strong enough to compromise on East Timor against the wishes of the military.[22] Unlike Morocco, where the military is a potential rival to the ruler, Suharto was a military man himself and so tightly controlled promotions and assignments that he was thought to be far more secure than King Hassan, and less likely to be forced from office, regardless of what happened to East Timor. However, the decision by President Habibie to allow the East Timorese their right of self-determination created a showdown between military and civilian elements within the regime, which was ultimately won by the civilians, a situation possible only after Suharto's downfall.

The only elements of Indonesian society that appeared to genuinely benefit from the incorporation of East Timor were those connected to conglomerates invested there and beneficiaries of the Timor Gap oil and gas exploitation; the power of both of these elements declined, however, as a result of the economic crisis and calls for reform. The only other Indonesian group with a direct stake in the situation were the Indonesian settlers who migrated either on their own or with strong government encouragement; however, these were mostly poor people who do not have much political clout and, in any case, the East Timorese leadership has explicitly rejected any immediate repatriation. In anticipation of the referendum, Indonesia suspended its transmigration programme in mid-December 1998.

Even during Suharto's final years, there was increasing public recognition of the failures of the government's Timor policy—some Javanese intellectuals began to raise the possibility of right-sizing to the borders of the old Dutch administration (Aditjondro 1997: 4–5, 7–8). Cracks in the armour were also evident in a series of riots in East Timor's urban areas in 1994 and guerrilla fighters were able to attack a series of targets in both rural and urban

---

[22] Background briefing, US Embassy in Indonesia, May 1997.

areas simultaneously in May 1997, surpassing in strength what most observers thought they were capable of. While there continued to be repression by Indonesian forces in East Timor, including the massacre of scores of peasants in November 1998 and a rise in killings by Indonesian-backed pro-integration Timorese paramilitaries, Indonesian officials began to allow large public pro-independence demonstrations, and a number of jailed independence activists were released. Indonesian Christian leaders, initially pleased that the annexation of East Timor raised the percentage of the Christian minority in the country, began to speak out against the repression. While few in the Indonesian government or business community openly supported independence, influential sectors of neighbouring states became increasingly supportive of withdrawal. For example, an April 1997 survey in the *Far Eastern Economic Review* noted a majority of subscribers in every country surveyed, outside of Indonesia, supported East Timorese independence. Some in the military began to recognize the futility of a military solution (Aditjondro 1997: 8–9). Like France's Charles De Gaulle, a new generation of military leaders apparently decided to cut the country's losses by scapegoating the old discredited leadership.

Conclusion

The initial success of Moroccan and Indonesian expansionism was based on a number of factors. One was the more prudent ambition of territorial expansion compared with previous irredentist claims, for example, Sukarno's claims against Malaysia, Singapore, and Brunei sparked an international crisis in the mid-1960s, claims abandoned under Suharto's New Order.[23] Hassan's confining of the project of *Le Grand Maroc* to Western Sahara enhanced the credibility of his government's territorial ambition, and appeared less threatening to those countries affected by the previous much grander schemes. What to outsiders appeared to be a form of aggressive expansionism and settler colonialism was portrayed as an important anti-colonialist struggle within both Morocco and Indonesia. Western Saharan and East Timorese nationalists were portrayed as lackeys for the former colonial power and/or of a new imperialism: Algerian, in the case of Western Sahara and 'communist'—Soviet or Chinese, depending on the audience and time period—in the case of East Timor. Both Hassan and Suharto were particularly successful in neutralizing much of the potential opposition from

---

[23] Indeed, Sukarno's claims led many to suspect that the British played a role in the 1965 coup which toppled Sukarno in favour of Suharto and other rightist generals.

both domestic left-wing critics and neighbouring states by making any dissent against the ongoing occupations appear as tantamount to a betrayal to the anti-colonialist and nationalist cause.

The occupying powers did not have to worry about enforcement of UN Security Council resolutions against their occupations, particularly since they were both allied with the world's one remaining superpower. While the United States raised concerns about the human rights situation in East Timor and Western Sahara, successive administrations refused for many years to call for self-determination in either territory.[24] Indeed, following the 1975 invasions, then-US ambassador to the UN Daniel Patrick Moynihan bragged how, under State Department instructions, he had made the UN 'utterly ineffective' in bringing them to a halt (Moynihan 1978: 247). While the oil reserves in the Timor Straits and the phosphate and other mineral resources in Western Sahara influenced nearby powers to acquiesce in the Moroccan and Indonesian expansions,[25] economic factors appear to have had little to do with these states' decisions to invade. They appear to have been based more upon largely political and strategic considerations, which may be less pressing in the twenty-first century than they were in the mid-1970s.

In both countries, the commitment to annexation was at least on a regime level and unquestionably popular with the core public, particularly in Morocco. Outside of small, youthful leftist student movements, which were quickly suppressed, little opposition was voiced in either country, though the level of repression to such dissident voices made it difficult to gauge. However, in neither of the occupied territories was incorporation ever accepted. Even the US embassies in Rabat and Jakarta, respectively, which largely supported the occupying powers, acknowledged that a majority of Sahrawis and East Timorese supported full independence.[26] The generation that has grown up under occupation appears to be at least as supportive of independence as their parents. In addition, both the Fretilin and the Polisario have introduced novel democratic institutions derived from indigenous cultural values among populations they control, and recognize—and have built

[24] During his first year in office, President Carter ordered an increase in military aid to Indonesia of 79%, including deliveries of counter-insurgency aircraft which allowed the Indonesians to dramatically expand the air war with devastating consequences. When asked about US law prohibiting such arms transfers to such aggressor state, a State Department official stated that since Indonesia had annexed East Timor, the conflict was no longer an invasion but an internal rebellion.

[25] Indonesia's awarding of exclusive rights to Australian oil companies for exploration in the Timor Gap was instrumental in Australia's decision to formally recognize Indonesia's annexation. Similarly, as part of a secret annex to the Madrid Accords, Morocco had to pay the Spaniards $(US)90 million for 65% of the phosphate consortium Fosbucraa while Spain retained a 35% interest in the mining company and port facility, as well as fishing rights (*Wall Street Journal*, 26 July 1976).

[26] Interviews by SZ with US diplomatic personnel in Rabat (June 1990) and Jakarta (May 1997).

upon—traditional political alliances.[27] However supportive the population of the occupying powers may have been of their governments' irredentist designs, efforts to achieve ideological hegemony have failed in the territories themselves. As a result, Indonesia lost East Timor and Morocco's hold on Western Sahara will not be secure until it can establish its legitimacy among the population of an occupied territory. And, as long as citizens in countries allied to the occupying powers feel moved to challenge their governments' acquiescence to ongoing violations of international norms, the fate of such territories will not be settled in the eyes of the international community, which—in this increasingly interdependent world—may also play a major role in determining how a government may decide it is in its best interest to down-size its boundaries.

REFERENCES

Aditjondro, George. 1997. 'Challenges and Prospects of the Indonesian Pro-East Timor Movement'. Unpublished paper, Newcastle University, New South Wales, Australia. 15 January.

Barbedo de Magalhaes, Antonio. (1990). *East Timor: Land of Hope*. Oporto: University of Oporto.

Brazier, Charles. 1997. 'Light in the Darkness', *New Internationalist*, 26 (December).

Budiardjo, Carmel and Liong, Liem Soei. 1984. *The War Against East Timor*. London: Zed Books.

Center for Defense Information. 1983. 'A World At War'. Washington, DC: Center for Defense Information.

Chomsky, Noam and Herman, Edward. 1988. *Manufacturing Consent: The Political Economy of the Mass Media*. New York, NY: Pantheon.

Feith, Herb. 1992. 'East Timor: The Opening Up, the Crackdown and the Possibility of a Durable Settlement', 63–80 in *Indonesia Assessment 1992: Political Perspectives on the 1990s*, edited by Harold Crouch and Hal Hill. Canberra: Indonesia Project, Department of Economics and Department of Political and Social Change, Research School of Pacific Studies, Australian National University.

Gellner, Ernest. 1983. *Nations and Nationalism*. Oxford: Basil Blackwell.

Harrell-Bond, Barbara E. 1981. 'The Struggle for the Western Sahara, Part I: Prelude'. American Universities Field Staff Reports No. 37.

Huband, Mark. 1996. 'Forgotten Victims Languish in Tussle Over W. Sahara', *Christian Science Monitor*, 10 May.

---

[27] While the anniversaries of incorporation are, and have been marked by large and carefully-orchestrated official celebrations within the territories, there appears to have been virtually no genuine spontaneous participation.

Jardine, Matthew. 1996. 'Pacification, Resistance and Territoriality: Prospects for a Space of Peace in East Timor', *GeoJournal*, 39(4).

Kahin, Audrey and Kahin, George. 1995. *Subversion as Foreign Policy: The Secret Eisenhower and Dulles Debacle in Indonesia*. New York, NY: WW Norton.

Klotz, Audie. 1994. *Norms in International Relations: The Struggle Against Apartheid*. Ithaca, NY: Cornell University Press.

Lalutte, Pauline. 1976. 'Sahara: Notes Towards an Analysis'. MERIP Reports, March. Washington, DC: Middle East Research and Information Project.

Leifer, Michael. 1983. *Indonesia's Foreign Policy*. London: Routledge and Kegan Paul.

Lustick, Ian. 1993. *Unsettled States, Disputed Lands: Britain and Ireland, France and Algeria, Israel and the West Bank-Gaza*. New York, NY: Cornell University Press.

Moynihan, Daniel Patrick. 1978. *A Dangerous Place*. Boston, MA: Little, Brown and Co.

Murphy, Kim. 1991. 'Moroccan Throne Appears at Stake in a Historic Western Sahara Vote', *Los Angeles Times*, 9 November, A 16.

Randal, Jonathan C. 1984. 'Morocco's Unrest Has its Roots in Economic Woes'. *Washington Post*, 27 January, A 19.

Tanter, Richard. 1998. 'The Peace Process in East Timor'. *Inside Indonesia*, 53: On-line version.

Taylor, John G. 1991. *Indonesia's Forgotten War: The Hidden History of East Timor*. London: Zed Press.

United Nations. 1975. 'Report of the Special Committee on the Situation with Regard to the Implementation of the Declaration on the Granting of Independence to Colonial Countries and Peoples (covering its work during 1975)'. New York, NY: United Nations.

Westervelt, Eric and Reichman, Jill. 'Shifting Political Sands Blur the Dream of a Grand Maghreb', *Towards Freedom*, 38(2): 4.

Zunes, Stephen. 1995. 'Algeria, the Maghreb Union, and the Western Sahara Stalemate', *Arab Studies Quarterly*, 17(3): 23–36.

11

Right-Sizing Over the Jordan: The Politics of Down-Sizing Borders

Marc Lynch

The severing of ties between Jordan and the West Bank in 1988 represents an important case of 'right-sizing the state'.[1] After years of maintaining a claim to the unity of the two banks of the Jordan, the eponymous state unilaterally abandoned its claim to the West Bank. Unlike some other cases in this volume, the decision to sever ties followed primarily from international concerns. The institutionalization of the new borders, however, emerged from élite politics within a transforming public sphere. Key élites, particularly Transjordanian nationalists, took advantage of this opening to assert a domestic order congruent with an East Bank polity. Élites of Palestinian origin largely acquiesced in this new construction of state identity, because it responded to longstanding PLO demands and because of its instrumentality in advancing Palestinian interests in the peace process. Through public deliberation in a liberalizing public sphere, élites arrived at a consensus that the new conception of Jordanian borders best served both Jordanian and Palestinian interests. The new borders became institutionalized in the discourse and practice of the state, legislation, and the key components of organized civil society. Over the course of the 1990s, Jordanian official and popular positions alike rejected every initiative towards the renewal of political unity between Jordan and Palestine: during periods of Jordanian strength and periods of Jordanian weakness; during periods of optimism in the peace process and periods of pessimism; and even after the death of King Hussein and the ascension of his son, Abdullah, to the throne.

---

[1] There is no implication that the new size of the state is objectively normatively 'right' or 'correct'—though there must always be some who make this claim. 'Right-sizing' refers to the conclusions drawn by political agents themselves in the course of public political deliberation about the appropriate borders of the state. This chapter develops and draws on ideas published in Lynch (1999).

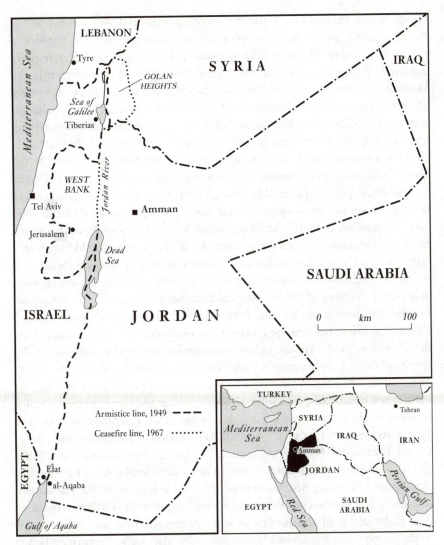

Fig. 11.1 Jordan

The right-sizing of the Jordanian state offers an intriguing example of the voluntary surrender of the claim to territory. Even though Jordan lost the territory in question to Israel in the 1967 war, the West Bank remained an integral part of the domestic consensus on Jordanian borders, identity, and interests. The claim to speak on behalf of the West Bank and the attempt to regain control over it was a deeply held, fundamental part of Jordanian foreign policy, consistently maintained in the face of substantial opposition.

Nevertheless, the combination of the severing of ties and the liberalization of the early 1990s produced a fundamentally new conception of the borders of the Jordanian state. By early 1992, the status of these new Jordanian borders approached what Lustick calls 'the regime threshold'. Most importantly, the kinds of arguments about the West Bank heard in the Jordanian public sphere changed. Instead of considerations of economic or political benefit, characteristic of politics during the 'incumbency' stage, Jordanians now argued that any ties to the West Bank posed an existential threat to fundamental Jordanian interests and even to the survival of the Jordanian state. By the early 1990s, revision of Jordan's borders to include the West Bank ceased to be a 'normal' policy option. The new consensus on Jordanian state borders solidified over the ensuing years, and was thoroughly ratified in the 1994 Jordan-Israel peace treaty. Amid profound political opposition to that peace treaty, one argument which was not heard was that Jordan should have negotiated for the Palestinians and sought a sovereign role in the West Bank.

This consensus continues to face serious problems, however, which work against the crossing of the 'ideological hegemony' threshold. No consensus on the citizenship status and legitimate social power of Jordanians of Palestinian origin has emerged comparable to the consensus on Jordan's borders. Even as public sphere debate produced a powerful consensus on the irreversibility of the severing of ties, bitter battles continued over the ability of Jordanians of Palestinian origin to participate in politics. Should they be considered Jordanians, with full rights to organize and participate politically, or should they be considered Palestinians, fundamentally outside the Jordanian system? The very future of Palestinians in Jordan remains unresolved, because the Oslo accords and the Jordanian–Israeli peace treaty defer discussion of the Palestinian refugees to the multilateral talks. The failure to this point of the peace process to produce a viable solution to the Palestinian question prevents the complete institutionalization of the Jordanian borders. The right-sizing of the Jordanian state interacted with two other major 'right-sizing' struggles, involving generally the same territory: Israeli debates over the future of the Occupied Territories, and the Palestinian debate over the appropriate territorial locus of their demands for self-determination. As long as the status of the West Bank remains unresolved, some degree of uncertainty about its relationship to Jordan will remain. The passing of King Hussein and the ascension to the throne of his son, Abdullah, and his Palestinian-origin wife, raises these questions anew. These ongoing discursive and political battles have prevented the question of state borders from passing from the regime stage to the ideal hegemony stage—for an important recent discussion see Hamarneh, Hollis, and Shikaki (1997).

The Severing of Ties: Overview

Before 1989, Jordanian–Palestinian relations had been intensely contested in international arenas, but firmly excluded from Jordanian public debate.[2] Contentious debate in the Arab and Palestinian public spheres forced a steady reduction in the Jordanian claim to the West Bank, as Jordanian arguments failed to convince Arab publics of either the legitimacy or the utility of its claim. In the Jordanian public sphere, on the other hand, identity and borders stood as the reddest of red lines, discussed publicly only within the bounds of a severely circumscribed official discourse. From 1950 to 1967, the Jordanian state actively sought to assimilate Palestinians into Jordanian citizenship and resisted any assertion of Palestinian nationalism. Indeed, the attempt to annex and assimilate the Palestinian territories of the West Bank after 1950 represents an important case of attempted territorial expansion which deserves analytical attention in its own right. Despite the sharp contestation of Jordan's Arab identity throughout the decades of the 'Arab cold war', the 1950 borders achieved close to hegemonic status. Even the PLO, formed in 1964, generally focused their efforts on Israel and not on the West Bank, while Israeli actors arguing for territorial expansion were marginalized during the 1950s and 1960s.[3]

After Israel captured the West Bank in 1967, the PLO's struggle for Palestinian representation redefined the terms of debate, with the status of the West Bank becoming a central concern for inter-Arab debates.[4] The bloody conflicts between the Jordanian military and the Palestinian Resistance Movement in 1970–1 greatly enhanced separatist sentiments among both Jordanians and Palestinians. In 1972, King Hussein advanced a federal proposal, the 'United Arab Kingdom', which would recognize two autonomous regions, Jordanian and Palestinian, under a central federal government. This federal proposal clearly marked the two regions as distinct entities, even as it called for political unity, and therefore should be seen as a first step towards right-sizing. After several years of fierce argumentation, the 1974 Rabat Arab Summit decision declaring the PLO the sole legitimate representative of the Palestinian people established a new Arab consensus that Jordan reluctantly accepted. Despite token gestures towards

---

[2] For relations between Jordan and the PLO through the 1980s see Bailey (1984); Mishal (1978); Day (1986); Sayigh (1987); and Brand (1988).

[3] One exception to this assertion is the discussion of a 'Palestinian Entity' between 1959 and 1961, in which the West Bank was mooted as a possible location for the entity, against strong Jordanian objections.

[4] Gresh (1988) presents an overview of Palestinian debates about the location of the Palestinian state—see also Tessler (1994).

'Jordanization', Jordan did not abandon its ambition to reclaim the West Bank. The loss of Arab recognition of its right to negotiate for the return of the West Bank did not constitute 'right-sizing' in the minds of most Jordanian élites, but rather represented an external constraint to be manipulated and challenged. The Arab consensus did provide an important alternative conception, however, which gained increasing acceptance in Arab and international discourse. By the late 1980s, even hard-core advocates of unity could hardly claim an uncontested, 'natural' relationship between the East and the West Banks. Jordan continued to claim a prominent role in any peace settlement, despite this shifting external conception, asserting fundamental interests in the West Bank. Jordanian official discourse continued to include the West Bank in the framework of Jordanian identity and borders. In 1985, Jordan and the PLO agreed upon a confederal framework for a peace settlement with Israel, a constitutional framework that admitted more independence between Jordanian and the Palestinian states and therefore further established a conception of an East Bank Jordan. While Jordan abandoned co-ordination with the PLO in early 1986 and renewed its bid for influence on the West Bank, confederation remained the official PLO position.

The royal speech of 31 July 1988 announcing the severing of legal and administrative ties between Jordan and the West Bank set in motion a process of élite struggle oriented towards establishing a new consensus on Jordanian state identity (Robins 1988; Susser 1990). Despite its domestic implications, the severing of ties should be seen primarily as an international gambit, adopted by the King and a few close advisors in response to the Palestinian Intifada, changes in Israeli discourse about Jordan, and the failure of peace negotiations. The major political debates that drove the severing of ties took place in international public spheres, not domestic. The formal Arab consensus position on the Intifada at the Algiers Summit starkly demonstrated the non-viability of the Jordanian position.

The sudden change in the proclaimed identity and borders of the state, in the absence of a public space within which to negotiate new norms, undermined the stability of the regime. While the centralization of foreign-policy-making in Jordan allowed the King to make a dramatic, sudden decision on the location of state borders, it was the liberalization of the political system and the opening of the public arena to political debate which enabled the institutionalization of the new borders. Between August 1988 and April 1989, the severing of ties incubated, exacerbating contradictions whose public, collective interpretation was repressed. In April 1989, the Jordanian south erupted in protests and riots, which shook the foundations of the Hashemite regime. While the uprisings have often been interpreted as a direct response to increases in the price of bread, they must be understood in the context of the widespread perception of corruption and authoritarian behaviour by the government. The major demands of the protesters focused upon account-ability, public freedoms, and the closing of lines of communication between the government and the citizenry.[5] Only after the uprisings of April 1989 did the new politics of identity emerge from the private salons into the public sphere: the severing of ties made identity politics necessary, but only the opened public sphere made identity politics possible. A specifically Jordanian public space emerged, embodied in an open press, elections, and a con-tentious public discourse, in which the focus upon 'domestic' issues rein-forced the idea of the new borders. The emergence of this public sphere had a direct impact on identity politics: contentious public debate forced actors to articulate claims and positions in ways which produced outcomes unintend-ed by any specific élite actors—even the King. Élite actors seized upon the opportunity provided by the foreign policy initiative to advance their con-ceptions of the appropriate political structures of the emerging 'new Jordan.' Arabist public sphere debates ended the hegemonic conception of Jordan's borders; the severing of ties represented the official acceptance of this Arabist consensus; and the opening of the Jordanian public sphere provided the structural conditions for a war of position over the new borders.

The Public Sphere and Right-Sizing

This analysis of the politics of Jordanian state contraction suggests the theo-retical significance of the public sphere—see Habermas (1989) and (1996)—for 'wars of position' over state borders. In Lustick's framework, the structure of the public sphere itself remains constant. Presumably because of the institutionalized democracy in the states he considers, the question of the existence of a viable, effective, and relatively free public sphere coterminous with state borders does not arise. In many developing countries, where con-siderations of border revision may coincide with moves towards liberaliza-tion or democratization, the existence, location, efficacy, and character of the public sphere can have a significant impact on the fortunes of right-sizing projects. Conceptions of borders and the shape of the public sphere are mutually constitutive, structuring the political debates over identity, inter-ests, and political order. In Jordan, the appearance of an open print public sphere was a necessary condition for the negotiation of consensus on the revised borders. The liberalization of 1989 produced a lively independent press and an openly contested political arena. As the arena for public debate

[5] Analysis and documents were published in *al-Urdun al-Jadid* (1989).

opened, political entrepreneurs responded to the new political opportunities by advancing competing frames interpreting the meaning of the new borders. In the course of these debates, élites converged around a formula, 'Jordan is Jordan and Palestine is Palestine,' which incorporated the East Bank borders as a baseline. This consensus was formally ratified in the 1991 National Charter, and became the shared reference point for political debate in the 1990s.

A public sphere can be defined as 'a contested participatory site in which actors with overlapping identities . . . engage in negotiations over political and social life' (adapted from Bohman 1996; Calhoun 1992). The struggles over the definition of state borders and state identity do not take place in a vacuum. The public sphere provides the structural arena within which actors engage in communicative action oriented towards consensus. Shared beliefs about state identity, national interests, and the legitimacy of the political regime are produced through this public discourse. Public debate oriented towards consensus takes place in multiple, overlapping arenas; it cannot be taken for granted that the 'domestic' public sphere is primary or even obvious (Lynch 1999). The emergence of a public sphere corresponding to a particular conception of borders is a crucial dimension in the process of institutionalization or deinstitutionalization of borders. For much of its history, Jordanian policies and identity have been debated primarily in Arabist public spheres, with great overlap with the Palestinian arena. The rise of a Jordanian public sphere in the early 1990s coincided with a sudden sharp decline in the relevance of these competing public spheres. The Gulf crisis effectively closed the Arabist public sphere, as Jordan found itself isolated from the Arab mainstream because of its refusal to join the war coalition against Iraq. The Madrid peace process and the Oslo Accords, marginalizing the other traditional competitor to the primacy of the Jordanian public sphere shattered the Palestinian public sphere. As a result, in the early 1990s the Jordanian public sphere became the primary site of norm, identity, and interest formation for most Jordanian élites.

Indicators of Change in the Public Sphere

Identity politics between the severing of ties and the April 1989 uprisings demonstrates how the structure of the public sphere constrains actors. Despite the sharp impetus to public debate about the new situation, actors remained bound by the existing media outlets and discursive red lines. The shock undermining hegemonic norms, and political entrepreneurs willing to thematize the issue were not enough to overcome state repression of the public sphere. The sharp distinction between public and private discourse, seen in the frank and open debate in the political salons and tribal *diwans*, suggests the importance of these limitations on public debate. Public sphere restrictions did not prevent people from privately interpreting the significance of the severing of ties, but they blocked the public interaction from which new collective understandings might emerge.

Blocking such public discourse required direct state intervention. For a short period immediately after the severing of ties, the Jordanian press did form an arena for vigorous public debate. The early exchanges in the press vividly reveal the confusion which the severing of ties wrought among Jordanians and their eagerness to discuss it publicly. On 3 August, Fahd Rimawi broke the initial stunned silence, urging Jordanians to 'make open what is now whispered' (Rimawi 1988). According to Rimawi, the sharp divergence between the public sphere calm and the furious agitation in the private political salons posed a great danger to the stability of the system. The press quickly filled with essays both supporting and attacking the decision to sever ties, with anger evenly divided between the PLO which had demanded separation and—less directly—the Jordanian regime for acceding to it.

After this outburst, the state resorted to exceptional measures to shut down the public sphere and stifle the escalating debate. The Economic Security Committee, a martial law institution, reorganized the press by replacing the chief editors and imposing tight censorship, on the grounds that press reporting was shaking public confidence in the Dinar and thereby endangering the security of the country. In the context of this enforced public silence, three phenomena emerged. First, many Palestinians began to transfer financial capital out of the country in anticipation of a move to strip them of their citizenship rights. At the same time, Palestinian workers in the Gulf began to avoid Jordanian banks when remitting their wages to families in Jordan or in the Occupied Territories. These uncoordinated but widespread measures proved disastrous for the Jordanian economy. The value of the Dinar collapsed to roughly half of its value against foreign currencies. This economic impact was not as inevitable as it is sometimes made out in retrospect. The economic consequences of the severing of ties followed from the uncertainty tied to the absence of an open public sphere in which its meaning could be clarified, debates, and interpreted.

The second phenomenon, the spread of rumours and underground pamphlets, followed directly from the silence of the official media and the escalating political repression. 'Black pamphlets' circulated widely in Amman, accusing public officials of corruption and calling for public freedoms. While both rumours and pamphlets are familiar features of Jordanian society, this period saw an unprecedented level of such activity. In the absence of credible information, the historically grounded distrust of the regime's intentions in the Palestinian community inclined many to believe the worst. The impact of these black pamphlets was not confined to the Palestinian community, however; Transjordanians were also affected by the economic collapse, repression, and rumours of high level corruption. Most Jordanians of all origins perceived a breakdown in the lines of communications between state and society.

Third, the severing of ties emboldened and politically legitimated the Jordanian exclusivist trend. A Transjordanian, 'East Bank-first' trend had long operated beneath the surface, as Transjordanian élites, reportedly with the support of Prince Hassan, urged King Hussein to abandon his interest in the West Bank and to concentrate on the development of the East Bank (Day 1986). These Transjordanian élites saw the severing of ties as a victory and an opportunity to establish a new political order. If Palestinian interests could be defined out of the national consensus, then the field would be left open for the hegemony of the Transjordanian élites. Given the resentment of Palestinian domination of the private sector, simmering communal tensions, memories of Black September, and long-standing suspicions of the political loyalty of Jordanians of Palestinian origin, this gambit fell on fertile soil.

The uprisings which broke out in the southern cities in April 1989 posed a potent challenge to the regime. Because they were driven by Transjordanian tribes rather than by Palestinian refugees, they could not be dismissed as external agitation. Indeed, Palestinians largely refrained from protesting. In response, the Jordanian regime began a democratization process aimed at restoring its badly frayed legitimacy (Mufti 1999). The combination of elections, reining in of Public Security Directorate abuses, and widened press freedoms did not lead to real democracy, given the realities of monarchy. But it had the singular and striking feature of opening up a domestic print public sphere. This opening finally allowed the contradictions of identity, long suppressed and now exacerbated by the severing of ties, to be worked out in public. Cautiously at first, and then bursting forward headlong into the semi-official daily press and into the proliferating independent weekly press, open discussion of identity transformed the Jordanian political arena. This press opening offered a public arena during a crucial transitional period in which the meaning and political significance of the identity of citizens of various origins could be articulated and contested.

The press served as the primary site for political argumentation. The semi-official daily press opened its doors to a wide spectrum of political opinion, although the extent of pluralism varied considerably and their editors occasionally responded to Palace directives to end debates on controversial issues. The independent weekly press pushed more vigorously at the traditional red lines, breaking taboos and providing a forum for serious debate about Jordanian–Palestinian relations. While the weeklies were often used by actors intent of inflaming communal tensions, this should not diminish their substantive contribution on rational public debate. The weeklies proved less responsive to gag orders from above and forced 'private' issues on to the public agenda. The opening of the press was not matched by comparable changes in television or radio. Political opposition and contentious debate were to a large degree simply excluded from television, which remained a state monopoly. While people watched TV, they did not view it as a site for political information or debate: 64 per cent of Jordanians, according to one survey, relied on the press for political information, compared with only 10 per cent who preferred TV (Muhadin 1992). Analysts and participants decried this ongoing control of television, repeatedly calling for the Jordanian 'glasnost' to extend to the electronic media, but had little success.

The discussion of identity in the Jordanian public sphere did not entail the mobilization of social movements based on identity. These battles were carried out in the press, not in the streets, which Lustick (1993: 122) argues is characteristic of 'wars of position'. The absence of riots, violent acts, mass protest marches, and other examples of disruptive collective action leads some observers to conclude that Jordanian society did not react to the severing of ties in any politically meaningful way. This conclusion does not withstand scrutiny. In the 1990s, identity, and specifically the question of Jordanian–Palestinian relations, went from being the most taboo of subjects to the most profoundly discussed of topics. This public debate questioned the fundamental assumptions of Jordanian identity. The debate was taken seriously enough by the regime to warrant repeated interventions by the King calling for national unity, including the direct application of pressure on newspaper editors to stop publishing 'divisive' articles. When debate became too heated, King Hussein intervened by declaring that 'whoever harms our national unity will be my enemy until Judgment Day,' which would temporarily end the controversy. The contentiousness of the debate, the prominence of the participants, the seriousness with which the political élite and the Palace viewed it, and the observable impact on state policy all point to the political relevance of the public sphere.

From 1990 to 1995, the independent press thrived, as political weeklies filled the marketplace. Virtually all political viewpoints found a platform, invigorating the political life of the kingdom. As Jordan moved towards peace with Israel, however, the government began to clamp down on the opposition press. After a period of escalating harassment and arrests of journalists, the government finally issued a temporary Press and Publications Law in the summer of 1997 which closed down most of the weeklies in advance of the elections (Human Rights Watch 1997). While the Supreme Court declared this Press Law unconstitutional in early 1998, after the elections, and many of the closed weeklies resumed publishing, the chilling effect on the public sphere was clear. Jordanians warned of the return of a sharp gap between public and private discourse, the closing of lines of communication between the government and society, and the dangers of a closed public sphere. The outbreak of serious riots in the southern cities in 1996 and 1998, in the context of this repression, strengthens the argument developed here. The status of the Jordanian public sphere can therefore be divided into three distinct periods: the period of closure and repression prior to 1989; the open and active public sphere of 1990–5; and the increasing repression after 1995.

Political Identity Entrepreneurs

The dynamics of competitive framing provided clear incentives for political entrepreneurs to take ever more extreme positions on Jordanian–Palestinian relations—see *inter alia* 'Ayad (1995); Hourani and Abd al-Rahman (1997); Lynch (1998). Transjordanian exclusivists, the first to take advantage of the new freedoms, tended to drive the political debate. Because of Palestinian reluctance to assert a Palestinian identity within Jordan, Jordanian exclusivists possessed an inherent advantage in this struggle. The memory of the 1970 civil war, combined with the experience of Lebanon, acted as a brake on more extreme identity politics. Palestinians generally argued for an inclusivist conception of identity in Jordan which would allow them to participate as Jordanian citizens without surrendering their Palestinian identity. Since the severing of ties explicitly made the East Bank the exclusive focus of state identity, Transjordanians held a stronger position in interpreting the change. By the early 1990s all mainstream Jordanian parties and movements had in practice converged around an East Bank conception of the political arena, even those such as the Muslim Brotherhood which continued to preach for unity. Political competition was as often intra-communal as intercommunal, with struggles among Transjordanian movements driving much of the political debate.

The first trend among Jordanian exclusivism was pro-government, representing the state élite, and drawing support from the Transjordanian-dominated army and state bureaucracy. The largest Jordanian exclusivist party, *al-Ahd*, led by Abd al-Hadi al-Majali, represents this position. *Al-Ahd* quickly acquired a reputation as the 'state's party,' supporting the government along a wide range of controversial issues, including the peace treaty, normalization, economic reform, and the electoral law. Numerous other

Jordanian exclusivist parties formed, usually built around a prominent personality and often with tribal affiliations. In June 1997, eight of these centrist parties united into the National Constitutional Party, amidst great fanfare in the official media, with the implicit goal of achieving a majority in the 1997 Parliamentary elections. While it failed in this endeavour, Majali did become the speaker of the new Parliament. *Al-Ahd* and the NCP advocate a statist nationalism, which takes an exclusivist form. Jordanian identity means 'accepting the political form of the Jordanian state . . . whoever lives on Jordanian land is Jordanian as long as he [sic] accepts the constitution and the Jordanian identity' (al-Majali 1992). Whatever one's private sense of identity, one must publicly profess a Jordanian identity: 'Jordan . . . is a homeland [*watan*] for all Jordanians and all Palestinians who choose to live in it . . . all of us are citizens of the Jordanian state except the one who wants to incite events and declare openly his Palestinian identity' (al-Majali 1994: 12). Interestingly, this formula provides an opportunity for a permanently settled Palestinian population to participate in Jordanian politics, as long as they accept the priority of the Jordanian identity. Nevertheless, this version of Jordanian nationalism is clearly exclusivist in its conception of domestic order, and strongly supports the East Bank borders.

Competition between different strands of 'Jordanian exclusivism' is a major component of the strategic framing process. A more radical Jordanian exclusivist position based on a tribal Jordanian national identity also asserted itself after the severing of ties, even more forcefully embracing the East Bank borders. This movement tries to articulate the interests and grievances of the poor tribal areas. Ahmed Awidi al-Abaddi—Member of Parliament 1989–93, 1997–present—has been its most assertive public voice, advancing a primal Jordanian claim on the land and the state.[6] Abaddi's ideology expresses hostility to Palestinians and ethnic non-Jordanians regardless of their political positions. Unlike *al-Ahd*, which relies upon a sharp public/private distinction and will accept those Palestinians who are loyal to the Jordanian state, Abaddi rejects any deviation from criteria of blood and tribe.[7] Radical Jordanian exclusivists oppose the Jordan-Israel peace treaty, which *al-Ahd* and the NCP support, because it contains no provision for the return of the Palestinians. The newspaper *al-Mithaq*, beginning in 1997, relentlessly

---

[6] Interview, Ahmed Awidi al-Abaddi, Amman, May 1995. For a discussion of al-Abaddi's belief system, see Shryock (1995). Abaddi has recently been involved in a sensational sex scandal, in which his Parliamentary immunity has been lifted; at this point, it is unclear whether this was politically motivated.

[7] This reliance on tribe and attachment to the land was particularly threatening to King Hussein, since the Hashemite family came from the Hijaz to rule the Transjordan mandate; Abaddi's criteria of 'five generations' would have excluded the King and his sons from the Jordanian identity.

drove home its opposition to any peace plan which involved the resettlement of Palestinian refugees in Jordan.[8] The radical exclusivists criticize the disproportionate allocation of public resources to Amman, home of the Palestinian bourgeoisie, at the expense of the development of the tribal areas. Most Jordanian public figures express fear of and, often, contempt for radical Jordanian exclusivism, but the increasing power of these ideas should not be underestimated. No successful political party yet represents this trend, but its contours can be clearly seen.

In contrast to the proliferation of Jordanian exclusivist parties, Palestinians generally preferred either to participate in ideological parties—Islamic Action Front, Communist Party—or to abstain from politics. The long tradition of underground Palestinian political organization, largely within the framework of PLO factions, had difficulty translating into the new Jordanian political arena. While some Palestinian organizations formed Jordanian parties after 1990, Yasir Arafat's *Fateh*, the largest and most influential Palestinian movement in Jordan, did not. The most important of those factions which did organize as a Jordanian party, *Hashd*, the offshoot party of the Democratic Front for the Liberation of Palestine (DFLP), advanced one of the most forceful inclusivist identity claims within the boundaries of the East Bank. This is not an extreme of Palestinian exclusivism to match the Jordanian extreme: no party could legitimately take such a position in the new Jordan. *Hashd* sees the 'call to establish special Palestinian organizations in Jordan . . . [as] a call to divide the ranks of the national [*wataniyya*] movement in the country.'[9] The severing of ties 'prepared the way for reordering the relations between the two brotherly Jordanian and Palestinian peoples on the basis of equality and brotherhood and independence . . . [and] solidarity against the common enemy' (al-Zibri 1993). The Palestinians in Jordan are both an integral part of the Palestinian people and an indivisible part of Jordan, and no conception of identity which cannot resolve both of these facts can prove satisfactory. This inclusivist conception, based on the assertion of the shared class interests of the Jordanian and Palestinian masses, has deep roots in the discourse of the Palestinian Left, while consciously trying to adapt to the severing of ties and an East Bank Jordan.

Such Palestinian parties have struggled to find a legitimate place in the Jordanian arena and placed only a small number of members in Parliament. The splits took place along lines similar to those in the Jordanian community, as Palestinian élite interests diverged from those of the Palestinian refugee community. While leftist Palestinian parties attempted to represent the

---

[8] Personal interviews, Nahid al-Hattar, May–June 1997; and *al-Mithaq* archives.
[9] *Hashd* Central Committee, Political thought paper, September 1992.

interests of the deprived classes, and took a strong oppositional stance towards the peace process, prominent members of these parties defected, looking to form a moderate inclusivist coalition. In 1997, a number of prominent Palestinian figures identified with élite Palestinian interests attempted to form a United Democratic Party which would take a moderate position on the peace process and work for democratic reform and an inclusivist conception of citizenship inside of Jordan. As with the radical Jordanian exclusivists, these efforts failed to coalesce into a political party. Nevertheless, the outlines of such a political grouping, representing a loyal Palestinian élite, could be perceived in these discussions.[10]

The primary challenge to the exclusivist consensus came from Arab nationalists and Islamists, who criticized the separation of Jordan and Palestine as an artificial division of the Arab nation. The Islamist defence of unity was reinforced by strong organizational ties with the West Bank: the severing of ties made an exception of Islamic *waqf* institutions, and Jordanian Islamists consistently placed Palestinian issues at the forefront of their political agenda.[11] Ibrahim Ghousha, Hamas representative in Jordan, argued that 'we are in favour of unity . . . The severing of ties was a temporary measure . . . it is the right of the Palestinian identity to make itself prominent and the right of the Jordanian identity to make itself prominent, but we search for a wider Islamic identity.'[12] Fahd Rimawi, editor of a prominent Arabist weekly, argues that the process of intermingling of populations has progressed to the point where it is impossible to really speak of two peoples. For political purposes, he recognizes the utility of the assertion of such separate identities but, he contends, the vast majority of 'Jordastinians' have little use for these formulations. The primary use of the identity differentiation, in Rimawi's view, is to prevent the consolidation of a united opposition front and to further the agenda of prioritizing Jordanian state interests over Arab nationalist interests. Rimawi remained unfazed by rancorous identity debates, dismissing them as futile attempts by self-interested chauvinists to invoke a nonexistent reality (Fahd Rimawi, personal interviews, May 1995; see Rimawi 1990). Although Arabism remains important for Jordanian identity and discourse, especially with regard to relations with Iraq, Arabist parties have become rather marginal within the reconfigured Jordanian arena—as in the

---

[10] Taher al-Masri, a key member of this élite, spent much of the summer trying to form a coalition with Ahmed Obaydat, a prominent Transjordanian former Prime Minister. This form of loyal opposition, with an inclusivist Jordanian–Palestinian character, would represent a major development in the party spectrum. As the *Jordan Times*, 25 March 1998, noted, however: 'Report on a new center-left political party . . . is wishful thinking.'

[11] See Robinson (1997b) for a discussion of the Palestinian Islamist movement and its changing relationship with the Jordanian Muslim Brotherhood.

[12] Interview, Ibrahim Ghousha, al-Bilad, 17 May 1995.

Arab world in general—and were targeted by the regime as Iraqi agents and repressed after the southern uprisings of 1996 and 1998.

Finally, a centrist position, heavily represented in the daily press, relies upon the concept of citizenship to overcome identity-based differences—see al-Hattab (1993a) for a good example. This position accepts the consensus on the revision of state borders while rejecting the exclusivist vision of identity for domestic politics. Such an identity-blind position appeals to many members of the Palestinian-origin élite. This position also most accorded with the public position of the late King Hussein throughout the 1990s, who invoked a Jordanian citizenship 'blind to roots and origins.' Both the Constitution and the National Charter guarantee full rights to all citizens regardless of roots or origins, and King Hussein publicly resisted the attempts to assert an exclusivist definition of identity by key members of his ruling coalition. The monarchy is generally seen as the major check on identity struggles, because the King can offer a unifying national figure and can in principle prevent the capture of state power by either constituency. The King's private position was less clear, however, as he was often accused of using identity politics to divide popular opposition and appeared to tolerate the development of exclusivist parties (Brand 1995).[13]

An intriguing dimension of this identity discourse is that the severing of ties posited a distinction between Jordanian and Palestinian which had an increasingly tenuous basis in demographic and social reality. Empirically, Rimawi's observation about the growing 'Jordastinian' social reality, especially in Amman, seems accurate. Taher al-Masri, one of the poles of the nascent élite inclusivist coalition, pointedly ridiculed calls to define membership in the Jordanian identity by noting that this would demand 'categorization of Jordanians by criteria that are apparent only to him' (Masri 1997). As events in the former Yugoslavia tragically demonstrate, the 'realities' of intermarriage and daily toleration do not necessarily prevent the powerful discursive power of demands to articulate distinct national identities. Jordanians of all origins refer to that experience, along with Lebanon's and their own in 1970, to warn against the dangers of communal outbidding and extremism.

The population of the refugee camps and their potential return to Palestine represents the primary 'sticky' fact with which all political entrepreneurs must contend. While located in Jordan, the refugees maintained a claim to Palestinian identity and the right to return. Nevertheless, they had—in principle—all the rights and responsibilities of any other Jordanian citizen. The distinction between 1948 refugees and 1967 refugees, not to

---

[13] Adnan Abu Odeh, personal interview, Washington, December 1995.

mention the large number of citizens who migrated voluntarily to the East Bank prior to 1967 and the hundreds of thousands of returnees from Kuwait and Saudi Arabia in 1990–1 is crucial; significant differences between these groups make it foolish to speak of any 'Palestinian' position or identity. The wealthy Palestinian bourgeoisie which controls economic life in Amman has little in common other than ascribed identity with the impoverished residents of the camps. Were the Palestinians to win the right of return, it is generally assumed that a significant portion of the Palestinian élite of Amman would choose to stay.[14] For radical Jordanian exclusivists, the future status of the refugees represents the most compelling reason to demand public articulation of Jordanian identity policy; élite inclusivists generally prefer to avoid such discussion about their future, instead demanding assurances that their citizenship rights will be respected.

Right–Sizing the State and Domestic–International Interaction

While Jordanian right-sizing involved both international concerns and domestic power relations, the evidence indicates that the King's inner circle was more interested in the international dimension than the domestic.[15] The severing of ties served as a challenge to the PLO, as a rebuttal to Israeli pressure, as a response to American failures in the peace process, and as a tactical move in the Arab arena. The decision was framed by the failure of the Peres-Hussein agreement and the outbreak of the Palestinian Intifada in late 1987. Right-sizing the state initially aimed at strengthening Jordanian positions within international and regional arenas. The absence of serious political debate inside of Jordan before the decision, and the high levels of repression in that period, suggest that domestic entrepreneurs did not drive the decision.[16] Only after the severing of ties did élites mobilize to interpret the meaning of the decision for the domestic structures of the state.

The Jordanian government explained the severing of ties in exclusively international terms. Jordanian spokesmen emphasized that the decision aimed at strengthening the Palestinian identity and making it more prominent in the international arena. Hussein emphasized that the measures were not directed at Jordanian citizens: 'our measures related to the West Bank are

---

[14] See Artz (1997) for a discussion of the questions surrounding the return of Palestinian refugees.

[15] Masri, Abu Odeh, Marwan Dudin interviews cited above.

[16] For discussion of the closed condition of the public sphere before 1989 see 'A policeman on my chest, a scissors in my brain,' *Middle East Report*, November–December 1987.

connected only to the occupied Palestinian land and its people, and not to Jordanian citizens of Palestinian origin . . . they have full rights and responsibilities of citizenship like any other citizen . . . they are an indivisible part of the Jordanian state.' At this point, the main domestic consideration was to insulate the state from any possible negative repercussions. The Jordanian decision to abandon its claim to the West Bank and to pursue a redefinition of state identity around the East Bank responded to a set of international challenges and opportunities. In order to gain these advantages, it was necessary to win Arab consensus in support of the disengagement. Jordanian government therefore took a series of increasingly costly steps to win this support, culminating in the recognition of the Independent State of Palestine. These steps helped to lock in the disengagement in the short term, providing the space for the domestic debates which followed.

Of the international threats and opportunities, perhaps the most prominent was the claim by influential Israeli actors that Jordan lacked a national identity and that a Palestinian state should therefore be created on the East Bank. According to some on the Israeli right wing, most prominently Ariel Sharon, the only obstacle to creating such a Palestinian state, presumably accompanied by a mass transfer of Palestinians across the river, was the Hashemite monarchy.[17] If the Palestinian state were created in Jordan, the international community might be more willing to accept Israeli annexation of the West Bank. The demographic majority of Palestinian-origin Jordanians, combined with longstanding Revisionist historical claims on the East Bank, underlay the claim that Jordan comprised a *de facto* Palestinian state and should formally become so. While few believed that Israeli action in this direction was imminent, it posed an unnerving challenge which could not be ignored. To combat the 'Jordan is Palestine' argument, Jordan needed to both prove the existence of Jordanian identity and reconcile the place of Palestinians within it.

In contrast to the claims by leftist Palestinian factions in the 1970s about the unity of Jordan and Palestine, the PLO since the 1980s has consistently rejected the 'Alternative Homeland'. This reflected the internal debates over the location of Palestinian self-determination, with the 1974 Rabat consensus and the shifting focus of diplomatic struggle towards the West Bank and Gaza reducing Palestinian interest in the East Bank. By the 1980s, no major Palestinian figure expressed interest in establishing Palestinian rule in the East Bank. Such a Palestinian state would undermine the Palestinian claim to a state in the West Bank and Gaza, and would in no sense satisfy Palestinian

---

[17] Lustick (1993) discusses the debate in terms of the challenge to the hegemonic discourse in Israel. For a lengthy presentation of these views, see Israeli (1991); Shindler (1995); and Klieman (1981).

aspirations for self-determination. The Alternative Homeland was therefore overwhelmingly viewed as detrimental to Palestinian national interests. Transjordanians and the Hashemite regime, of course, considered the idea an existential threat and firmly opposed it. One should not underestimate the extent to which the Jordanian regime and Transjordanian exclusivists found the identity threat useful, however. Decision-makers may have felt some threat, especially since Hussein did not have the working relationship with the Likud leadership that facilitated his dealings with the Labor Party, and because of the influx of Soviet Jews which seemed to be creating greater Israeli hunger for territorial expansion. But the 'threat' was arguably more important as a strategy in the field of identity politics inside of Jordan. The appropriation of the fear of the Alternative Homeland became a master stroke binding the hands of Palestinian origin citizens. Once consensus was secured about the threat to both Palestinian and Jordanian interests by any Palestinian political presence in Jordan, it became virtually impossible for Palestinians to mobilize as Palestinians. This served to legitimize the political dominance of the Transjordanian state élite. Whatever Sharon's intentions in challenging Jordanian identity, the impact was in fact to strengthen that identity.

The Palestinian Intifada, most frequently cited as the proximate cause of the severing of ties, did lead to shifts in Jordanian policy. The Intifada was in part directed against the Jordanian role as part of an Israeli/Jordanian condominium in the West Bank, expressing the overwhelming Palestinian popular rejection of the Jordanian role.[18] Unable to claim popular support inside of the West Bank, Jordan lost a major justification for its ongoing attempts to play such a role. This popular rejection undermined any remaining Jordan belief that it could hope to regain its control over its lost territories. There was some fear that the Intifada could spread to the East Bank, because of the number of Palestinians resident in Jordan and the repressive political conditions of the day.[19] By the summer of 1988, Jordanian security services seemed to have societal unrest pretty well in hand, however, and it is unlikely that Jordanian leaders felt any existential threat. Still, given Jordan's claim to the West Bank, the Intifada could reasonably inspire the oppressed Palestinian in Jordan. The Jordanian regime needed a formula by which the Intifada could be separated from the political and social demands of Jordanians of Palestinian origin. The severing of ties facilitated such a formula. If the West Bank, Palestine, were recognized as separate from the East Bank, Jordan,

[18] An oft-cited opinion poll from 1988 shows that 72% of West Bank Palestinians considered the PLO their legitimate leader, compared with 3% who favoured King Hussein (Shadid and Seltzer 1988).

[19] See Andoni (1990); and Brynen (1991).

then Jordanians could legitimately support the Intifada as an external event while still marginalizing Palestinian political activity in the East Bank. Palestinian leaders in Jordan accepted the justification for avoiding such political activity, and their acceptance of these boundaries powerfully reinforced the new Jordanian consensus.

The severing of ties, therefore, responded to international challenges and opportunities. The stagnation of the peace process, including the failure of the Peres-Hussein agreement, left jordan with little hope for diplomacy. The Arabist consensus in support of the Intifada affirmed the PLO's role in the West Bank at the expense of jordan, while the leadership of the Intifada also vocally expressed its preference for the PLO. The Intifada facilitated a convergence of interests between Palestinian élites, who sought Jordanian support for the uprising, and Transjordanian élites, who wanted to prevent Palestinian political mobilization in the Kingdom. The Alternative Homeland threat perhaps seemed more dire as the Intifada stymied Israeli efforts at control and increased the possibility that extreme possibilities might be entertained. 'Right-sizing' served to strengthen Jordan's position in the international arena and to protect it from manifest international threats. At the same time, however, it set in motion a largely unintended process by which the new borders became deeply institutionalized and the internal identity politics of the Kingdom changed dramatically.

After the Separation: Identity Politics and Defining Borders

After the severing of ties, the southern riots, and the liberalization of 1989, Jordanian institutions were reconstructed around the new borders. Changes in state institutions quickly proved that this severing of ties was more serious than the similar moves after the 1974 Rabat summit. The measures served to consolidate the international acceptance of the reality of Jordan's decision. State institutions were the first to be reconstituted. The National Charter and the key legislation of the liberal era, the Political Parties Law and the Press and Publications Law, extended the new conceptions into civil society. Civil society institutions, particularly the Professional Associations, resisted the trend, but their resistance and the public dialogue surrounding it actually helped to consolidate the broader consensus. Once articulated, the new borders set in motion a process of élite contestation to interpret their political meaning. The opening of the public sphere in 1989 transformed the nature of that struggle and provided the conditions of possibility for the consolidation of a new public consensus. By 1992, I argue, conceptions of Jordan's borders crossed the regime threshold, with the Palestinian and Jordanian agreements with Israel over the next few years further consolidating these borders. Indeed, the Jordanian–Israeli treaty formally demarcated Jordan's western border for the first time. The crisis of the peace process, combined with the continuing uncertainties about domestic order, prevented the crossing of the hegemony threshold.

State Institutions

The reconstruction of state institutions progressed quickly after the royal speech. The Ministry for Occupied Territory Affairs was abolished, replaced by a Palestinian bureau in the Foreign Ministry. Every state agency underwent a comprehensive review of its policies in order to conform with the new concept of Jordan, changing regulations on everything from drivers' licences to marriages and family unification. Most importantly, new regulations on passports declared that only regular residents of the East Bank would be recognized as Jordanian citizens, carrying full (five year) passports. From the date of the decree, permanent residents of the West Bank were to be considered 'Palestinian' and residents of the East Bank 'Jordanian.' The status of residents of the refugee camps remained highly sensitive, since refugees officially maintained a Palestinian identity and the right to return. The high sensitivity to any move towards 'resettlement' ensured that this would remain a hole in the official specification of identity.

The dissolution of Parliament, with its West Bank representation, and the drafting of an East Bank electoral law for new elections, marked a particularly significant step. Such dissolution had long been considered a point of no return in terms of relations with the West Bank. The demarcation of electoral districts exclusively on the East Bank solidified the reality of the new borders for all political actors. Three national elections have since been held, sufficient to fully internalize this reality. Because the electoral districts were drawn in order to overrepresent Transjordanian constituencies and underrepresent Palestinian population centres, and Palestinians voted in far lower numbers than did Transjordanians, these Parliaments have given shape to a specifically Jordanian political community. Intense debates over the electoral law, including both the districting and the principle of 'one vote' in multiple member districts, and the predominance of tribal voting in the latter two national elections, undercut the political representation function to some degree, but not its significance in representing the borders of the Jordanian state.

The Jordanian National Charter, produced by an appointed but broadly representative royal commission in 1991, provided a formal consensus on the boundaries of 'national action' in all spheres of political life. This Charter sought to draw clearly the lines between Jordanian and non-Jordanian, between legitimate and illegitimate activity and succeeded to a large degree in obtaining consensus around these principles.[20] The Charter recognized the legitimacy of both Palestinian and Jordanian identities, but rigorously limited Jordanian public action to those individuals and groups with an explicitly Jordanian identity. The Charter consensus takes as basic that 'Jordan is Jordan and Palestine is Palestine,' and that the political activity of each should be confined to its distinct arena (al-Fanik 1990).[21] Palestinians should participate in the new Jordanian politics as individuals, but not as Palestinians. This consensus served the interests of both major élite con-stituencies: Palestinians were guaranteed an end to Jordanian efforts to com-pete with the PLO; and Jordanians received Palestinian acquiescence to their domination of Jordanian political institutions.

Political Parties

The principles of consolidating the new Jordanian borders also directly gov-erned the licensing of political parties in the early 1990s. As political parties were either new creations or reconfigured underground parties, they were quite responsive to the new identity norms. All major political parties in Jordan accepted the new consensus on borders. The Political Parties Law emphasized that licensed parties must not have any organizational or politi-cal ties to any Palestinian faction. 'A stand against parties with external ties . . . is now a national consensus with which nobody can differ,' wrote one influential columnist (Daoudiya 1992). Parties tied to Palestinian factions obtained licences only by accepting the principle of a sharp distinction between Jordanian and Palestinian. The acceptance and application of the new identity norm in such political parties is an important example of how the disengagement between 'Jordan' and 'Palestine' became embedded in Jordanian domestic institutions.

The arguments over the licensing of *Hashd*, the DFLP offshoot, became a litmus test in the struggle to define the identity politics of political parties. In April 1991, Jordanian chauvinists lashed out at the newly restructured party: 'Is it logical that there be a Jordanian party with the goal of guaranteeing the right of part of the Jordanian people to preserve a non-Jordanian identity and

---

[20]   See Rimoni (1991); and Hourani and Dabass (1996).

[21]   Abd al-Hadi al-Majali claimed that 'Jordanian–Palestinian relations are the most important dimension of the Charter' in a public lecture, *al-Rai*, 20 May 1991. In May 1990, *al-Dustur* published a five part survey of the opinion of Charter Committee members on the Jordanian–Palestinian question, flagging this as a primary area of concern.

to express it in a framework that is not the Jordanian state?' (al–Fanik 1991a). As parties began to apply for licences in late 1992, the debate over *Hashd*, and by extension all Jordanian parties with a Palestinian character, escalated dramatically: 'In this new era . . . with a National Charter aimed at eliminating the phenomenon of dual loyalty and dual nationality . . . is it rational to license a party that has a non–Jordanian nationality and has loyalty to something other than Jordan?' (Akour 1992b). When the Interior Ministry rejected its application, a fierce public debate produced a consensus in favour of granting the licence on democratic grounds, despite deep unease on identity grounds. Public opinion could be mobilised behind the right to form opposition parties against the preferences of the Interior Ministry, but few would stand up to call for the right of Jordanians of Palestinian origin to organize as and be represented by Palestinian parties. The Interior Ministry eventually relented and granted the licence (Akour 1992a).[22]

In February 1993, Fahd al–Fanik argued that 'the democratic process of Jordan will influence *Hashd* more than *Hashd* will influence it, and the result will be the focus of *Hashd* on Jordanian national issues . . . from a Jordanian perspective' (al–Fanik 1993a). This acceptance demonstrates the logic of the public sphere, in which participation in shared institutions would produce a shared identity. *Hashd* found it increasingly difficult to maintain a balance between its Jordanian identity and its ties to its parent Palestinian organization. After the defection of several key party members over the question of DFLP control of the party, questions resurfaced about the party's independence. In July 1995, the Interior Ministry took *Hashd* to court over its 'foreign connections'. While observers worried about government intolerance of political parties, few publicly objected to the characterization of Palestinian organizations as 'foreign.'

More important than the details of the party's struggle for legal recognition is what this case reveals about identity politics in the new Jordan. First, the primary arena for contesting interpretations was the Jordanian press, which offered platforms for a wide range of positions. Defenders and opponents published dozens of articles in both dailies and weeklies. The strongly felt need to establish consensus on norms governing political identity drove public figures from all positions to participate in this debate. Second, the identity debate often involved other issues but was not reducible to them. For example, the 1994 and 1995 eruptions coincided with a general state offensive against independent political organizations. Third, the debate was primarily driven by the Jordanian exclusivists, the identity position most empowered by the new normative structure.

[22] See also Fara'na (1992) and al–Khalil (1992).

Inclusivists were almost always on the defensive when identity politics came to define the political situation. Their only acceptable appeals, to toleration, democracy, and national unity, paled in the face of the sensational discourse of exclusivist patriotism. Only when the terrain of struggle could be shifted away from identity and towards some issue, like normalization, which could unite Jordanians of all origins, could these actors reclaim the offensive. Finally, the splintering and clear weakness of all parties with a Palestinian character powerfully demonstrates the difficulties of Palestinian political participation within the new borders.

The Islamist movement, the largest and best organized political movement in the kingdom, rejects the emphasis on Jordanian/Palestinian cleavages, presenting an inclusivist identity claim. The Islamists have been the least firm in their endorsement of the East Bank borders. In November 1994, the Islamist weekly emphasized that 'the physical unity of the two banks cannot be ended,' while its chief political editor asserted that 'the Jordanian identity and the Palestinian identity are in confrontation with the Zionist enemy and are not meant to deepen separation and chauvinism' (al-Mayateh 1994). While the Muslim Brotherhood has long been an integral part of the Hashemite ruling coalition, its status as the premier opposition party after 1989 led it to become increasingly 'Palestinianized' (Robinson 1997b). For Palestinians, unable to organize under that identity, Islamist ideology offers an inclusivist framework conducive to political action.

In practice, however, the Islamist movement clearly demonstrated its willingness to accept the reality of the severing of ties and to distinguish between the Jordanian and the Palestinian arenas. While Hamas maintained offices in the Muslin Brotherhood compound in Amman, this does not translate into organizational unity. Identity tensions emerged in the Islamist movement in the mid-1990s, as relations between the government and the Islamists deteriorated. Calls by Islamist leaders such as Abdullah al-Akaylah and Bisam al-Amoush for a focus on Jordanian interests and an end to the subordination of Islamist politics to 'a Palestinian agenda' ignited significant dissension within the Islamist movement. Hawkish leaders and much of the membership rejected the 'separatism' of such appeals to focus on national issues. In mid-1999, the Muslim Brotherhood reportedly locked its doors to Hamas spokesman Ghousha and began urging its members to 'either renounce their links with Hamas or lose their membership in the Brotherhood' (Hattar 1999).[23] The split between reformists and radicals over IAF policy and

---

[23] Abdullah al-Akaylah's interview in *Islamic Action*, December 1996, and a series of articles by Bisam al-Amoush, *al-Rai*, January 1997, called for the Islamist movement to redirect its attention towards 'Jordanian' issues and to participate in the coming elections. Islamist 'hawks,' often of

participation in the elections reflected, at least in part, a conflict between the more traditional, reformist Jordanians and the more radical Palestinians.

The Press

The independent and party press underwent a similar process after the passage of the 1993 Press and Publications Law. Again, the dominant theme in public debate was the need for all publications to be 'really' Jordanian, with no external ties or support. Once again, Palestinians were the major target, although penetration by other Arab states also figures into the debates. Like the state, the Parliament, the Professional Associations, and political parties, the press became a site for establishing the new Jordanian state borders and attendant political identity. Every prospective editor and owner of a newspaper or magazine had to demonstrate his independence, financial and political, from any foreign—Palestinian—source. Proposed revisions of the Press and Publications Law in 1996 went even farther, altering the requirement that editors and owners be 'resident in Jordan' to a requirement that they be 'Jordanian'.[24] Perhaps because of these ownership provisions, several best selling weeklies regularly ran sensationalist stories inflaming Jordanian–Palestinian differences and favoured columnists known for their Jordanian exclusivist views. Even liberals who valued the contribution of the weekly press to democratization expressed unease about their tendency to exaggerate identity-based conflicts. In July 1994, during a period of particularly intense Jordanian–Palestinian press debates, the editor of a major daily proposed a 'Law to Protect National Unity' which would make writing essays which 'create fears and doubts and arouse divisions' a criminal offence (al-Sharif 1994). In late 1996, Nahid Hattar, a prominent intellectual in the new Jordanian nationalist movement, was arrested on charges of harming national unity for a controversial essay entitled 'Who is a Jordanian?' The resulting uproar captures much of the liberal dilemma. Even as they worried about state intervention to control open debate in the public sphere, they equally worried that 'the topic of "who is a Jordanian" threatens to destroy our democracy' (Fara'na 1995).

Professional Associations

Deeply embedded societal institutions, especially those with entrenched interests in the West Bank, resisted the attempt to impose major change in

Palestinian origin, reacted fiercely, expelling Amoush and Akaylah from the party. For the hawks' reaction, see interviews with Himam al-Sa'id, *Shihan*, 3 May 1997, and Abd al-Man'am Abu Zant, *al-Hadath*, 6 May 1996 ('God help those who would Jordanize the Islamist movement!').

[24] Draft Press and Publications Law text in *al-Sabil*, January 1996.

identity norms from above. In October 1988, the state-appointed editor of the leading daily newspaper, Rakan al-Majali, used the severing of ties to unleash a fierce assault on the political role of the Professional Associations.[25] These Associations had long been a centre of opposition political activity in Jordan, because of the illegality of political parties and the severe constraints upon political organization. While there had always been a Jordanian–Palestinian subtext to the politics of the Associations, because of the Palestinian domination of the private sector and the professions, Majali's attack made this dimension explicit. Association leaders responded legalistically, that their constitutive laws clearly included the West Bank branches, with dual headquarters in Amman and Jerusalem, and could not be changed without constitutional revisions. The severing of ties, which had not followed constitutional procedures, should only be considered 'political speech' rather than binding legislation.[26]

The resistance presented by the Associations helped to consolidate the East Bank consensus even as it challenged it. The battle over the Associations continued through the 1990s, weaving together themes of political opposition, identity, and the boundaries of Jordanian political action. In late 1992, the participation of West Bank lawyers in the Association elections drew fire, with articles such as the bluntly titled 'Sever the ties, oh lawyers!!' (al-Fanik 1992b). After harsh criticism of the participation of several members of the Jordanian Engineers Association in a PLO conference on establishing independent Palestinian Associations, Engineers Association President Layth Shubaylat defended continued unity in terms of supporting Palestinian political aspirations rather than in terms of defending a Jordanian claim on the West Bank.

During the confrontation over the peace treaty with Israel, the issue exploded again. The Associations had quickly emerged as a centre of opposition to normalization, with the elected councils of every major Association adopting binding resolutions forbidding their members from dealing with Israel (al-Mayateh 1995; Faisal 1995). In early 1995, Association elections again returned strongly anti-normalization councils. The government challenged the results of several elections on the grounds that West Bank Palestinians had participated. The Minister of Justice defended the decision to challenge the West Bank lawyers' participation as 'an issue of state sovereignty,' citing the incompatibility of the West Bank participation with the

---

[25] The initial article, along with the unpublished responses by the Association presidents and other political activists, were collected and published in *al-Urdun al-Hadid* 12/13 (1989).

[26] See Lawyers' Association President Kamal Nasir's explanation in *al-Dustur*'s roundtable, 'Opening the file on the Professional Associations,' 28 November 1995.

new Jordanian identity. Most members of the political public recognized the importance of the Associations as the testing ground of competing visions of Jordanian identity and entered the fray, defending or rejecting the Association's right to keep its West Bank ties. In the summer of 1996, the Palestinian Authority again proposed independent Palestinian Associations, but retreated after a Palestinian delegation visited Amman, on the basis that independent Associations should await an independent state (*al-Rai*, 19 July 1996). The ongoing organizational ties to the West Bank by the Associations therefore represents a hole in the reconstruction of Jordanian identity, but the ferocity of the battles over the issue and the consensus among Association leaders that the ties would end as soon as the Palestinians were able to establish independent Associations, supports the overall trend towards separation.

The Peace Process and Jordanian Identity Politics

It has never been possible fully to insulate the internal politics of identity from foreign policy, although the severing of ties might be interpreted precisely as an attempt to build such insulation. The peace process, which since the mid-1970s has focused on the future status of the West Bank and Gaza, represents the formal intersection of the Jordanian, Israeli, and Palestinian 'right-sizing' projects. Jordanian positions on a final settlement on the West Bank can therefore be taken as a crucial leading indicator of the Jordanian conception of its borders and identity. All Jordanian peace initiatives prior to 1988 envisioned some Jordanian role in the West bank: the 1972 'United Arab Kingdom,' linking the East and West Banks in a federal system; the 1985 Jordan–PLO confederation agreement; the 1987 Hussein–Peres agreement. After 1988, on the other hand, Jordan rejected every proposal which included a Jordanian role in the West Bank. This consistent rejection suggests that the change which took place went deeper than a tactical revision of Jordanian priorities. The opposition to any Jordanian role in Palestine, visible in the response to several confederation initiatives in the 1990s, demonstrates that Jordanian conceptions of the borders of the state passed beyond the regime threshold and moved close to the ideological hegemony threshold without passing through it. Since this point, relations between Jordan and the Palestinian National Authority have often been tense and conflictual, particularly over the Jordanian role in Jerusalem. What is most important, however, is that Jordanian–Palestinian conflict in this period focused on distributional issues rather than existential issues. Conflict over the distribution of benefits in the January 1994 Economic Protocols, for example, differs in kind from the existential struggles for representation which dominated relations prior to 1988. King Hussein and his governments have consistently supported the PNA in its negotiations with Israel, have regularly consulted with Arafat, and have repeatedly insisted that the idea of confederation should be tabled.

When Arab-Israeli peace negotiations began in Madrid in 1991, Jordan provided an 'umbrella' for Palestinian participation.[27] Because Israel refused to negotiate directly with the PLO, Jordan offered the only mechanism by which the Palestinians could participate. The Palestinians formed a distinct and autonomous grouping within the Jordanian delegation. Within the Jordanian public sphere, the relationship between the Jordanian and Palestinian delegations emerged as divisive. Because of the changes wrought by the severing of ties, Jordan refused to negotiate for the Palestinians and consistently insisted that the Palestinians represent themselves. Jordanians accepted the joint delegation formula only with reservations: '[because] the form of Palestinian representation will determine the final settlement . . . and failure in the peace talks would threaten Jordan . . . this is a Jordanian internal issue' (al-Udwan 1991). Jordanian exclusivists protested the subordination of Jordanian interests to the needs of the Palestinians. Since the disengagement had ended Jordanian–Palestinian unity, 'the delegation does not represent anybody . . . it is not Jordanian and it is not Palestinian' (al-Fanik 1991b; Masarweh 1991). The joint delegation could be acceptable to the emergent Jordanian consensus only to the extent that the Palestinian delegation quickly and firmly established its functional independence.

As negotiations proceeded, numerous proposals suggested some form of Jordanian–Palestinian confederation. In response, the Jordanian press, political parties, and official spokesmen converged around a consensus position on confederation: any talk of confederation is before its time until the Palestinians possess a fully sovereign state.[28] Jordanians rejected any form of solution which would restore the pre-disengagement conception of Jordan. Fahd al-Fanik spoke for this increasingly powerful trend when he bluntly asserted that 'I think that confederation is suicide for Jordan' (interviewed in *al-Sabil*, 26 October 1993). The deepening of the consensus can be observed in the way that the arguments against confederation in the Jordanian sphere shifted over time. Whereas in 1990 the primary arguments were tactical, emphasizing negotiation positions, by early 1992 the Jordanian public cast

---

[27] Ashrawi (1995) offers the perspective of a Palestinian member and al-Majali (1995) gives a Jordanian view.

[28] My files include hundreds of press essays on the subject, which form the basis for the analysis presented here. The sheer volume of commentary on this 'sensitive' issue is in itself an important indicator of the change in the public sphere in terms of identity discourse.

the objection to confederation in terms of an existential threat to Jordanian interests and security. Relations with the West Bank, long seen as a primary Jordanian interest, now came to be understood as the greatest potential threat to Jordanian survival.

A pivotal moment in the articulation of a new consensus came in March 1992, when a confederation proposal floated by Israel and PLO figures emerged as a way out of the blocked Washington negotiations. The loud Jordanian public outcry startled most observers and almost certainly played a decisive role in killing the idea (al-Fanik 1992a; Shaqir 1992; Zibri 1992). For several weeks, discussion of confederation dominated the public arena, with opinion running almost unanimously against. Exclusivists such as Fanik led the debate, but Arabists, Islamists, Palestinian activists, and liberals all accepted the basic premise that confederation should not be considered until after the Palestinians had achieved a sovereign state. Confederation before Palestinian sovereignty was seen as a threat to Jordan, in that it would facilitate turning Jordan into Palestine, and allow Israel to block the creation of a Palestinian state. Where the pre-1988 consensus had assumed the political and economic benefits of a prominent role in the West Bank, the 1992 consensus revealed a conviction that any ties to the West Bank could prove an existential threat to Jordan. The public rejection of confederation in March 1992 stands as an important indicator that the new Jordanian borders had crossed the regime threshold, such that the state's hands were tied in terms of even considering a revision of Jordanian borders to reclaim the West Bank.

Every confederation proposal floated in the following years met with a similar response: immediate, hostile, near-unanimous rejection by the Jordanian public sphere. In August 1993, for example, just before the revelation of the Oslo negotiations, a confederation proposal attributed to Hanan Ashrawi again ignited fierce denunciations in the Jordanian public sphere: 'We must ask: has Jordan withdrawn from its decision to sever ties after King Hussein vowed Jordan would never do so?' (al-Akour 1993a; al-Mayateh 1993a). Commentators stressed the danger to Jordan inherent in any role in the West Bank as often as they cited the need to respect Palestinian independence—a telling change in strategy. One senior writer convincingly claimed a popular consensus for this rejection: 'it is well-known that both Jordanian and Palestinian political circles reject confederation as a conspiracy on Jordan' (Hijazi 1993). This effective consensus seriously constrained any movement towards restoring ties even under propitious circumstances, not only because of public resistance but also because of these new conceptions of Jordanian interests. One Yarmouk University opinion poll in February 1993 found that 54 per cent of Jordanians opposed any form of unity between

Jordan and Palestine, a rather shocking result in the context of four decades of continuous Jordanian assertion of its claims to the West Bank (Sharida 1993).[29] Even more telling is the response to this poll, in which numerous commentators came forward to defend the emphasis on Jordanian national interests in the face of a sceptical reaction.

The revelation of the secret talks at Oslo in August 1993 shattered the generally positive relations which had been built between Jordan and the PLO, unleashing a new round of identity debates (Tal 1993). The formation of the joint delegation had, for all of its drawbacks, facilitated an effective discourse in Jordan of co-ordination [*tansiq*] with the PLO. This co-ordination put the regime on the side of major forces in the political public which had traditionally been relatively hostile or suspicious. By working closely with the PLO, Jordan showed itself to be supporting the Palestinian cause and foregoing any ambitions in the West Bank. The Oslo negotiations, not only outside the framework of the joint delegation but by all accounts unknown to most Jordanian decision-makers, could only be interpreted as a premeditated deception.[30] Despite Jordanian shock and anger, Israeli acceptance of a political role for the PLO clearly supported the Jordanian separation from the West Bank. A consensus quickly emerged that in light of the Palestinian action, Jordan could now look to its own interests. The publicly defended need to defend the interests of the down-sized entity moved the consensus on Jordan's borders farther past the regime threshold.

Oslo immediately affected the Jordanian elections scheduled for November 1993, as calls went up demanding their postponement until matters became more clear. Jordanians worried that the election campaign would be dominated by a Palestinian debate over Oslo to the exclusion of Jordanian issues (al-Qullab 1993; Mohasna 1993). The fact that this did not happen provides important evidence about the increasing autonomy of the Jordanian public sphere. Even more pressing, the prospect of an imminent return of Palestinian refugees to Palestine clouded the election. Their participation in the elections might be taken as a renunciation of their right to return, while their exclusion from the elections would be seen as undemocratic. Jordanian exclusivists contested the right of Jordanians of Palestinian origin to participate in electing a Parliament whose country they might soon abandon. This argument foundered upon the fact, quickly becoming self-evident, that Israel would not soon permit a collective return (al-Fanik 1993b; al-Mayateh

---

[29] For discussion, see al-Kaylani (1993). The methodology and findings of this survey are not beyond question, but the appearance and the reception of the poll deserve attention.

[30] Abd al-Salam al-Majali and Jawad Anani asserted in *al-Rai*, 4 April 1995, and *al-Sabil*, 11 January 1994, respectively, that they had no prior knowledge of the Oslo deal.

1993b; Fara'na 1993a). Even were such return possible, some writers emphasized that the Jordanians of Palestinian origin would still be Jordanians, whose nationality could not simply be stripped from them. The core question stood out starkly for all who confronted the question of the future of Jordanian citizenship and identity politics: 'are Jordanians of Palestinian origin who can't return Jordanians or Palestinians?' (al-Hattab 1993b).

The elections also raised the issue of the candidacy of Jordanians of Palestinian origin for Parliamentary seats. An advertisement in support of the candidacy of Hamada Fara'na from the people of several Palestinian villages enraged exclusivists, one of whom fumed that 'he is nominating himself for elections in Jordan, not in Palestine . . . how is it possible for the people of those villages to be represented in the Jordanian Parliament?' (al-Akour 1993b). Fara'na responded angrily that he fulfilled all the legal requirements of Jordanian citizenship, but his critics 'call on the government to strip me of my citizenship rights' (Fara'na 1993b).[31] While Fara'na did not win a seat in Parliament, fourteen Jordanians of Palestinian origin did. That more than half of these Palestinians were from the Islamic Action Front aided regime efforts to portray the opposition as Palestinian (al-Za'atra 1993).[32]

In the peace treaty signed by Jordan and Israel in October 1994, Jordanian bargaining focused on such state interests as border revisions and water rights, resolutely excluding consideration of refugee ('Palestinian') issues. This explicit focus on the interests of the East Bank helped to consolidate the consensus on Jordanian borders. In justifying the treaty, official Jordanian discourse heavily emphasized the achievement of Israeli recognition of the legitimacy of the Jordanian entity. The front page editorial of the leading daily on the day of the signing ceremony shouted 'Jordan is not Palestine!!', asserting that the treaty 'silences the Israeli idea . . . that Jordan is the eastern extension of the Hebrew state, which was a source of Israeli aggression and threat . . . this treaty means that Jordan is Jordan and Palestine is Palestine' (*al-Rai*, 24 October 1994). A leading advocate of the treaty asserted that 'the main reason for the peace treaty was, in fact, to end the threat of the Alternative Homeland' (al-Fanik 1994b). In other words, the international legitimation of 'right-sized' Jordan—within East Bank borders, with a Jordanian identity, and under Hashemite rule—stood as the key accomplishment of the treaty. As various dimensions of the treaty's economic and political results came under fire, the recognition that 'Jordan is Jordan' occupied an ever more central position in the regime's justifications (Wardum 1994).

---

[31] Fara'na won a seat in 1997.
[32] On the election, see Riedel (1994).

Still, the idea of the 'Alternative Homeland' threat could not die so easily, given its utility for the Jordanian exclusivists in the domestic political arena. The concept remained the guarantor of the exclusivist vision of identity politics. As early as a month after the signing ceremony, Fanik warned that 'the Alternative Homeland could still happen if Jordanians find they don't have real sovereignty in Jordan' (al-Fanik 1994b).

Complicating the attempt to fully consolidate the new Jordan, the treaty deferred the question of refugees to the multilateral negotiations, implicitly excluding the issue from the bounds of Jordan's self-interest. Since the right of return of the refugees had always been a key issue between Jordan and Israel, many citizens wondered if there had in fact been secret agreements for the resettlement of the Palestinian refugees in Jordan. Official denials of such secret deals did little to assuage popular concerns. President Clinton reinforced these fears when he addressed the Jordanian Parliament, comparing Jordan to the United States as 'a country of immigrants.' Was this meant to encourage the refugees to accept a final status as 'immigrants' to Jordan? Jordanian exclusivists reacted even more sharply, noting that the American 'country of immigrants' had been built on the subjugation of the continent's original inhabitants, a fate 'native' Jordanians had no interest in sharing (al-Fanik 1994a). For the new Jordanian nationalists, the fear that Jordan had secretly agreed to begin implementing the resettlement of the Palestinians in Jordan became something of an obsession.[33] In the debate over the peace treaty, the regime relied heavily upon the assertion of distinctly Jordanian interests. Since the PLO had made its independent decision at Oslo, no Jordanian could any longer refer to Palestinian interests in public discourse. By forcing all public debate to be cast in terms of the interests of East Bank Jordan, the regime and opposition together reinforced and more deeply embedded this conception of Jordanian borders and identity.

Jordanian–Palestinian relations inside of Jordan since the peace treaty have developed in the context of profound polarization between the government and political society. The government became increasingly repressive and defensive in the face of widespread dissatisfaction with the peace treaty with Israel, the turn against Iraq, and the imposition of unpopular economic reforms. It is often suspected that the government attempted to manipulate communal tensions in order to hinder the emergence of a united opposition coalition. The opposition coalition certainly perceived such an agenda behind the eruptions of identity politics: 'we reject allowing parochialism and sectarianism to emerge . . . it is our duty to cement unity and close ranks

---

[33] The newspaper *al-Mithaq* best expresses this Jordanian nationalist interpretation of the peace treaty and its implications.

to confront the enemy . . . we should unite the people and not divide them.'[34] The exclusivist National Constitutional Party was the only major party to support the peace treaty. While no effective opposition Jordanian radical party emerged, the Jordanian community was far from united in support for the peace treaty. Radical Jordanian nationalists targeted the NCP for its support of unpopular government policies, and even seemed willing to consider alliances with Palestinian parties opposed to the peace treaty. The period since the peace treaty, then, can be characterized as one in which the consensus on borders has not been challenged, while debates over identity have interacted with the struggle over the peace treaty.

Exclusivist-driven identity debates escalated despite warnings by King Hussein of the urgent need to preserve national unity. Exclusivists and inclusivists alike convincingly responded that Jordan could not seriously plan for the future until the ultimate citizenship of Jordanians of Palestinian origin had been settled. While inclusivists suggested that the only legitimate assumption was that they would continue to be Jordanian citizens, the debate was largely shaped in terms of the exclusivist agenda. By May 1995, radical exclusivists openly argued that 'Jordan welcomed [the Palestinians] and the only loser has been Jordan' (al-Abaddi 1995). While regime spokesmen rejected the extension of the discursive separation of Jordanian and Palestinian interests to the domestic sphere, many Jordanian exclusivists were less shy about making this connection. If there were distinct Jordanian and Palestinian identities and distinct Jordanian and Palestinian interests, how could any Jordanian citizen legitimately claim a Palestinian identity?

While Jordanian exclusivists warned that the severing of ties would soon be reversed, this should not be interpreted as a sign of a weakening consensus. On the contrary, the exclusivists used this appeal to the consensus on borders as a weapon in the real battle over the political order inside of Jordan. With every challenge, the government had more forcefully to commit itself to never rescinding the severing of ties. Jordanian exclusivists discounted all evidence of the institutionalization of the new borders, while seizing upon every piece of contrary evidence as a sign of impending disaster. In November 1995, Jordanian exclusivists protested loudly about the offer of Jordanian passports, but not citizenship, to certain West Bank residents (Hawatmeh 1995). Jordanian exclusivists interpreted the move as a feint towards rescinding the severing of ties, despite explicit official denials, and responded forcefully enough to draw a public condemnation from the usually supportive Palace. Ahmed Awidi al-Abaddi announced plans—which

---

[34] Opposition coalition statement as published in *al-Majd*, 11 February 1997 (FBIS-NES-97-030).

were not realized—to collect 1 million Jordanian signatures on a protest petition.[35] *Al-Mithaq* provided a running commentary on the regime's alleged intentions to shift power to the Palestinian élite: the peace treaty, which would lead to the resettling of the refugees; privatization, which would take economic power out of the hands of the Jordanian-controlled public sector and place it in the hands of the Palestinian-controlled private sector; the granting of passports to West Bank residents. All of these campaigns reinforced the East Bank borders, while working to discourage Palestinian political activity.

While the formula of separation between Jordan and Palestine, with possible confederation held out as a distant possibility, is now well-entrenched among the political élite, there is to this point less reliable evidence about how widely this conception is held among the general population. Divergence between élite and mass opinion can be seen in an unprecedented 1995 opinion poll which found a sharp divide between élite opinion leaders and the general public on the question of Jordanian–Palestinian relations (Hamarneh 1995). The élite sample proved far more inclined to Jordanian or Palestinian exclusivism, to total separation between the two entities, and to the promotion of distinct national identities and interests. The popular sample, on the other hand, was far more sympathetic to close relations between the two identities and entities and generally rejected the claims on Jordanian chauvinism. For example, when asked about the degree to which the groups had emerged into a single identity, 69 per cent of the popular sample replied that there had been a great deal of integration, while only 49 per cent of Jordanian-origin élites thought so. Only 30 per cent of the popular sample suspected Jordanians of Palestinian origin of dual loyalties, compared to 54 per cent of Jordanian-origin élites who harboured such suspicions. A December 1997 CSS opinion survey, which did not distinguish between élites and mass opinion, found that 84 per cent of Jordanians supported some form of Jordanian–Palestinian unity, with a shocking 63 per cent supporting federal unity (Hamarneh 1998).

Opinion leaders reacted to the surveys with great hostility. The finding of general support for close Jordanian–Palestinian co-operation rather than for the pursuit of narrowly-defined Jordanianism contradicted the project of Jordanian exclusivism. Even more dangerous, the finding of sharp differences between élites and the majority of the people cast doubts upon the representativeness of the Jordanian public sphere. The disjuncture between élite and mass views should not be used to discredit the importance of the shifts in

---

[35] Reported in *al-Hadath*, November 1995; personal interviews, Nahid Hattar, June 1997.

Jordanian identity norms, however. Élite opinion leaders drive political discourse in Jordan, and their perspective on the future of Jordanian–Palestinian relations is most likely to determine whatever consensus and policies emerge. The findings of a general opinion poll tell us nothing about which groups are more likely to be mobilized for political action around an issue.

The escalating use of Jordanian–Palestinian relations as a 'wedge' issue in political action suggests that it will be of greatest importance to precisely those individuals and groups most likely to engage in political action. An important example of the use of Jordanian–Palestinian differences as a wedge to divide the opposition can be seen in the activities of Abd al-Hadi al-Majali (National Constitutional Party). In January 1997, Majali delivered an inflammatory lecture on 'Jordanian national identity and the question of mixed political loyalties'.[36] Majali's thematization of communal identity came in direct response to the emergence of an opposition coalition bridging Jordanian–Palestinian lines, which had recently organized a successful boycott of an Israeli Trade Fair. Taher al-Masri, a key figure in the efforts to form an inclusivist élite coalition, responded to Majali with an impassioned call on all Jordanian citizens to denounce exclusivist ideas. In early February, the opposition leader Layth Shubaylat, who represents an inclusivist mass public opinion, published an open letter to the King begging him to intervene to protect national unity, take a stand against the resettlement of refugees, and prevent 'power centres in the state apparatus' from fostering divisions in Jordanian society (see Shubaylat 1997). King Hussein intervened, again calling for an end to discussion of Jordanian identity until after a Palestinian state had been successfully established.

Such differences suggest that exclusivism is primarily driven by élite political entrepreneurs who have not succeeded in mobilizing mass opinion around Jordanian–Palestinian differences. The high level of intermarriage, interaction, and shared lives of Jordanians and Palestinians, especially in Amman, produces rather different results than the print public sphere pushing towards chauvinism and narrowly defined national identities. What is more, the prominence of economic concerns and opposition to the peace treaty push towards class and political coalitions rather than communal ones. Many citizens seem to distinguish quite clearly between a territorial conception of a right-sized Jordan and the ethno-nationalist conception of a Jordanized Jordan.

After the death of King Hussein and the ascension to the throne of his son Abdullah, speculation about Jordanian–Palestinian confederation briefly

---

[36] Majali's speech published in *al-Rai*, 20 January 1997; Masri's response published in *al-Rai*, 30 January 1997; Majali's response to Masri in *al-Rai*, 1 February 1997.

returned to the political arena. With the sudden, drastic change in the leadership of Jordan, analysts perceived the opportunity for equally dramatic change in Jordan's foreign policy. Many speculated that Abdullah's Palestinian-origin wife would provide both an opportunity and an incentive for the new King to appeal to Palestinians. Abdullah called publicly for the full equality of all citizens, and made a stir with a surprise inspection of the Allenby Bridge which drew attention to the ongoing movement of peoples between the East and West Banks. Furthermore, the passing of the King allowed Palestinians to relate to the new King as a blank slate, without the accumulated grievances of decades of political competition. Finally, some speculated that Arafat would view the young Abdullah as a more easily manipulated or dominated figure, with whom a political confederation could be tolerated. Arafat made an appeal for confederation within days of the ascension of the new King. As the analysis of this paper predicted, however, Arafat's call met with a universally negative reaction: 'Jordanian deputies, political parties from across the political spectrum and newspapers joined forces in criticising Arafat's trial balloon' (*Jordan Times*, 28 February 1999).

At the level of foreign policy, Jordanian–Palestinian relations remained relatively strong despite the domestic turmoil.[37] This success can be directly attributed to the consolidation of the new hegemonic conception of Jordanian borders in the Jordanian public sphere. As this conception became more deeply embedded, Palestinian fears of Jordanian intentions on the West Bank diminished.[38] Jordanian–Palestinian clashes over the Jordanian role in Jerusalem in the summer of 1994, and in the Islamic *waqf* institutions in early 1995, were resolved as Jordan severed its ties with these remaining institutions. By 1994, most Jordanian–Palestinian conflict revolved around distributional, economic issues, in which the idea that the Jordanians might have ambitions on the West Bank did not appear as a significant concern. The election and subsequent policies of Benjamin Netanyahu placed considerable stress on the Jordanian–Palestinian relationship, but did not succeed in driving a wedge between them. If anything, it powerfully demonstrated the common threat posed by the potential collapse of the peace process and drove the two sides to closer co-ordination. The Hebron negotiations, for example, involved Jordanian interventions on behalf of the PNA, and King Hussein repeatedly attempted to press Israel to be more forthcoming on Palestinian interests. Hussein consistently declared his support for a Palestinian state, and reacted furiously when Netanyahu attempted to justify his policies

---

[37] For a more conflictual view, see Jarbawi (1995).

[38] But such fears did not completely disappear. For example, the 23 April 1996 issue of the Islamist weekly *al-Sabil* claimed to have possession of an internal PA document accusing Jordan of 'dreaming of ruling the West Bank'.

towards the Palestinians in terms of the Jordanian fear of a Palestinian state. Overall, the relationship between Jordan and the PNA supports the argument that the East Bank consensus has become deeply institutionalized and accepted both internally and externally.

Conclusion

In this chapter I have argued that the Jordanian regime severed ties from the West Bank in 1988 primarily for foreign policy reasons, but that the opening of the public sphere in 1989 produced political dynamics which led to profound changes in identity norms. Jordanian–Palestinian relations became the principal public obsession of the political élite, after years of their being the principal taboo of public life. Remarkably quickly, a consensus was achieved in favour of the new definition of Jordan's borders, even though no similar consensus could be reached over the status of Palestinian-origin citizens. Building on this consensus, Jordan moved away from its demand for a political role in the West Bank, adopting the position that it would not consider even confederation until after the formation of an independent Palestinian state. The PLO-Israeli Declaration of Principles and subsequent peace agreements, and then the Jordanian–Israeli peace treaty, consolidated this consensus, rendering a reversal of the severing of ties extremely unlikely. Since 1990, even proponents of unity speak only of confederation, a far cry from the hegemonic assertion of Jordanian–Palestinian unity within a single state. The institutionalized consensus on the shape of Jordanian borders makes it highly unlikely that any Jordanian government would accept a renewed role in the West Bank even if offered. The political struggles over the distribution of power and benefits within these borders have not produced such a consensus, however, and the question of communal or political (regime/opposition) mobilization will continue to dominate Jordanian politics for the foreseeable future. Jordan's borders have been right-sized, without comparable consolidation at the domestic level.

REFERENCES

al-Abaddi, Ahmed Awidi. 1995. 'The nation and nationalism merchants', *Shihan*, 27 May.
al-Akour, Salameh. 1992a. 'Why all this crying about national unity?', *Sawt al-Shaab*, 23 December.
—— 1992b. 'Words on party licenses', *Sawt al-Shaab*, 3 October.
—— 1993a. 'Confederation once more', *Sawt al-Shaab*, 26 July.

al-Akour, Salameh. 1993b. 'Why exchange Palestine for Jordan?', *Sawt al-Shaab*, 6 October.

al-Fanik, Fahd. 1990. 'The Charter and Parties', *al-Rai*, 15 March.

—— 1991a. 'Citizenship, not resettlement', *al-Rai*, 19 April.

—— 1991b. 'Does Jordan have interests?', *al-Rai*, 29 November.

—— 1992a. 'So-called confederation', *al-Rai*, 1 April.

—— 1992b. 'Sever the ties, oh lawyers!!', *al-Rai*, 3 December.

—— 1993a. 'Hashd faces a choice', *al-Rai*, 13 February.

—— 1993b. 'No to postponement', *al-Rai*, 21 September.

—— 1994a. 'At Jordan's expense!', *al-Rai*, 5 November.

—— 1994b. 'Dangers', *Shihan*, 10 December.

al-Hattab, Sultan. 1993a. 'Citizenship or origins?', *al-Rai*, 19 November.

—— 1993b. 'Priorities', *al-Rai*, 10 October.

al-Kaylani, Musa. 1993. 'We don't want the Palestinians', *al-Dustur*, 15 February.

al-Khalil, Samih. 1992. 'National unity it's not a line that can be drawn in the newspaper', *al-Dustur*, 25 December.

al-Majali, Abd al-Hadi. 1992. 'Interview', *al-Rai*, 26 December.

—— 1994. 'Interview', *Rasalat Majlis al Umma*, June.

al-Majali, Abd al-Salam. 1995. 'Memoirs', *al-Rai*, 1–4 April.

al-Mayateh, Samih. 1993a. 'Confederation: why now?', *al-Dustur*, 2 August.

—— 1993b. 'Why postpone?', *al-Dustur*, 24 September.

—— 1994. 'External funding', *al-Sabil*, 5 December.

—— 1995. 'The attack on the Associations is the other face of authoritarian democracy', *al-Sabil*, 24 October.

al-Qullab, Saleh. 1993. 'The ball is in our court', *al-Dustur*, 30 September.

al-Sharif, Nabil. 1994. 'A National Unity Law', *al-Dustur*, 12 July.

al-Udwan, Taher. 1991. 'Palestinian representation and Jordanian interests', *al-Dustur*, 22 July.

al-Za'atra, Yasir. 1993. 'Half of the Palestinian Ministers are ours', *al-Sabil*, 30 November.

al-Zibri, Tisir. 1993. 'On the concept of citizenship', *al-Dustur*, 12 May.

Andoni, Lamis. 1990. 'Jordan', 165–94 in *Echoes of the Intifada*, edited by Rex Brynen. Boulder, CO: Westview.

Arzt, Donna. 1997. *Refugees into Citizens*. New York, NY: Council of Foreign Relations.

Ashrawi, Hanan. 1995. *This Side of Peace*. New York, NY: Simon and Schuster.

'Ayad, Khalid. 1995. 'The File on Jordanian–Palestinian Relations', *Majellah al-Dirasat al-Filastiniyya*, 24: 89–154.

Bailey, Clinton. 1984. *Jordan's Palestinian Challenge, 1948–1983: A Political History*. Boulder, CO: Westview Press.

Bohman, James. 1996. *Public Deliberation*. Cambridge, MA: MIT Press.

Brand, Laurie. 1988. 'Identity suppressed, identity denied', in *Palestinians in the Arab World*. New York, NY: Columbia University Press: 149–85.

—— 1995. 'Palestinians and Jordan: Crisis of Identity', *Journal of Palestine Studies*, 24: 46–61.

Brynen, Rex. 1991. 'Palestine and the Arab state system: permeability, state consolidation, and the Intifada', *Canadian Journal of Political Science*, 24: 595–621.

Calhoun, Craig. 1992. *Habermas and the Public Sphere*. Cambridge, MA: MIT Press.

Daoudiya, Mohammed. 1992. 'The Jordanian parties law', *al-Dustur*, 23 January.

Day, Arthur. 1986. *East Bank/West Bank*. New York, NY: Council on Foreign Relations.

Faisal, Toujan. 1995. 'Will the Associations pay the price of their positions?', *al-Sabil*, 21 November.

Fara'na, Hamada. 1992. 'Party licenses and democracy', *al-Dustur*, 22 December.

—— 1993a. 'Elections are a national obligation', *al-Dustur*, 4 October.

—— 1993b. 'Jordanians and Palestinians . . . response to Akour', *al-Dustur*, 11 October.

—— 1995. 'Democratic burdens', *al-Dustur*, 25 November.

Gresh, Alain. 1988. *The PLO: The Struggle Within*. London: Zed Books.

Habermas, Jurgen. 1989. *The Structural Transformation of the Public Sphere*. Cambridge, MA: MIT Press.

—— 1996. *Between Facts and Norms*. Cambridge, MA: MIT Press.

Hamarneh, Mustafa. 1995. 'Jordanian–Palestinian Relations: The Internal Dimension'. Amman: University of Jordan, Center for Strategic Studies.

—— 1998. 'Jordanian–Palestinian Relations'. Amman: University of Jordan, Center for Strategic Studies.

—— Hollis, Rosemary, and Shikaki, Khalil. 1997. *Jordanian–Palestinian Relations: Where To?* London: Royal Institute of International Affairs.

Hattar, Saad. 1999. 'The MB and Hamas: A bond not easily broken', *Jordan Times*, 3 May.

Hawatmeh, George. 1995. 'Caught between two moods', *Middle East International*, 17 November.

Hijazi, Arafat. 1993. 'Confederation: a trap for Jordanians or for Palestinians?', *Sawt al-Shaab*, 15 August.

Hourani, Hani, and Abd al-Rahman, Asa'ad. 1997. *Jordanian–Palestinian Relations: Reality and Future Prospects*, unpublished manuscript, New Jordanian Research Centre, Amman.

—— and Dabass, Hamed. (eds.) 1996. *The National Charter and the Democratic Transition in Jordan* [in Arabic]. Amman: Al-Urdun al-Jadid.

Human Rights Watch. 1997. 'Jordan: Clamping Down on Critics', Human Rights Watch/Middle East 9/12: October.

Israeli, Raphael. 1991. *The Palestinians between Israel and Jordan*. New York, NY: Praeger.

Jarbawi, Ali. 1995. 'The triangle of conflict', *Foreign Policy*, 100: 92–108.

Klieman, Aaron. 1981. 'The Search for Durable Peace: Israel, Jordan and Palestine', *Washington Papers*, 83.

Lustick, Ian. 1993. *Unsettled States, Disputed Lands: Britain and Ireland, France and Algeria, Israel and the West-Bank-Gaza*. New York, NY: Cornell University Press.

Lynch, Marc. 1998. 'Jordan's Competing Nationalisms', in *Middle East Studies Association Annual Meeting*, Chicago: Middle East Studies Association, University of Arizona.

—— 1999. *State Interests and Public Spheres: The International Politics of Jordanian Identity*. New York, NY: Columbia University Press.

Masarweh, Tareq. 1991. 'It represents nobody', *al-Rai*, 14 December.

Masri, Taher. 1997. 'Response to Majali', *al-Dustur*, 18 January.

Mishal, Shaul. 1978. *East Bank/West Bank*. New Haven, CT: Yale University Press.

Mohasna, Mohammed. 1993. 'The Jordanian elections', *Sawt al-Shaab*, 21 September.

Mufti, Malik. 1999. 'Elite bargains and the onset of political liberalization in Jordan;, *Comparative Political Studies*, 32: 100–29.

Muhadin, Zakria. 1992. 'An Opinion Survey' [in Arabic]. Amman: Mu'assisat.

Riedel, Tim. 1994. 'The 1993 Parliamentary elections in Jordan', *Orient*, 35: 51–63.

Rimawi, Fahd. 1988. 'The importance of the other opinion', *al-Dustur*, 3 August.

—— 1990. 'National Unity', *al-Dustur*, 11 June.

Rimoni, Issa. 1991. *The Long Road to the Jordanian National Charter* [in Arabic]. Amman: Shuman Foundation.

Robins, Phillip. 1988. 'Shedding Half a Kingdom', *British Bulletin of Middle East Studies*, 16: 162–75.

Robinson, Glenn. 1997a. *Building a Palestinian State*. Bloomington, IN: Indiana University Press.

—— 1997b. 'Can Islamists be democrats?', *Middle East Journal*, 51: 373–87.

Sayigh, Yazid Yusif. 1987. *Jordan and the Palestinians* [in Arabic]. London: Riyad al-Ris.

Shadid, Mohammed, and Seltzer, Rich. 1988. 'Political attitudes of Palestinians', *Middle East Journal*, 42, 16–32.

Shaqir, Muna. 1992. 'Confederation: why is it desired now?', *al-Dustur*, 22 March.

Sharida, Mohammed. 1993. 'Jordanian–Palestinian unity?'. Irbid, Jordan: Yarmouk University Center for Jordanian Studies.

Shindler, Colin. 1995. *Israel, Likud and the Zionist Dream*. New York, NY: St. Martin's Press.

Shryock, Andrew. 1995. 'Popular genealogical nationalism', *Comparative Studies in Society and History*, 37: 325–57.

Shubaylat, Layth. 1997. 'Open Letter to the King "On National Unity"', *Shihan*, 8 February (letter dated 3 February).

Susser, Asher. 1990. 'In Through the Out Door', *Washington Institute for Near East Policy*, Washington Papers 19.

Tal, Lawrence. 1993. 'Is Jordan doomed?', *Foreign Affairs*, 72: 45–58.

Tessler, Mark. 1994. *History of the Israeli–Palestinian Conflict*. Bloomington, IN: Indiana University Press.

Wardum, Bater. 1994. 'The personality of Jordan after the treaty', *al-Majd*, 26 December.

Zibri, Tisir. 1992. 'Confederation between principled position and conditional tactic', *al-Dustur*, 24 March.

12

'Right-Sizing' or 'Right-Shaping'? Politics, Ethnicity, and Territory in Plural States*

Oren Yiftachel

Introduction

The territorial dimension of state politics has recently become a central topic in the social sciences[1] raising timely and critical questions on issues taken for granted by previous research. In particular, the work of Ian Lustick and his 'right-sizing' model of state expansion and contraction, provides a sound conceptual framework for this scholarly debate. Using Lustick's model as an analytical point of departure, this chapter pursues two objectives. First, theoretical aspects of the 'right-sizing' model are reviewed and discussed, and second, three cases of bi-ethnic states, Lebanon, Cyprus, and Belgium, are briefly analysed and compared to illustrate the chapter's theoretical arguments. The three cases provide useful grounds for examining state territorial politics, mainly because their—internal or external—borders, and their pubic policies toward peripheral groups, have changed on several occasions. As such, they form an appropriate basis for testing key aspects in the processes defined as the 'right-sizing' and 'right-shaping' of ethnically plural states. The overall purpose is to reflect theoretically and empirically on the process of stabilizing state borders in constant 'dialogue' with Lustick's pioneering work.

Based on the theoretical discussion and on evidence gathered from the three cases, the chapter argues that we need to extend Lustick's model and

* The comments made on earlier drafts by Ian Lustick, Brendan O'Leary, and Thomas Callaghy are highly appreciated. I am grateful for the hospitality of the Department of Political Science, the University of Pennsylvania, where I was a Fulbright Fellow during 1996–7, and where this chapter was first written.

[1] See e.g. Lustick (1985, 1993); McGarry and O'Leary (1993); Murphy (1989, 1996); Taylor (1993, 1994, 1995, 1996a, b, c); and Yiftachel (1997).

introduce notions of 'right-shaping' the plural state to complement its 'right-sizing'. 'Right-sizing' emphasizes external state borders and majority-centred rationales, and hegemony, while 'right-shaping' denotes the combined spatial, political, and institutional content of governance, and the more subtle issue of intrastate borders, identities and uneven institutionalization. In other words, 'sizing' primarily refers to the demarcation of state borders by the political centre, whereas 'shaping' is concerned with the nature of majority-minority relations *within* these borders.

'Right-shaping' the state, in my view, needs to combine enlightened public policies and institutional design with a thorough understanding of the impact and meaning of ethnic geographies. Peaceful integration of a given territory into a plural state depends on both policies and geographies that cultivate legitimacy, while protecting minority identity, rights, and equality. This is particularly relevant in the current 'epoch of ethno-nationalism', during which ethno-territorial identities have consolidated, and increasingly influence the power and policies of state élites *vis-à-vis* peripheral minorities. A ceaseless dialectical process determines the political stability of plural democracies—and therefore their sizing and shaping—in which forces emanating from the state's political centre interact with those emerging from the ethnic peripheries. The prefix 'right'—as in 'right-sizing' and 'right-shaping'—in my discussion denotes a movement towards democratic stability, while 'wrong' connotes the opposite. An integral part of the chapter's argument, then, is that the 'right-shaping' of plural states entails policies which promote—although they may not fully achieve—democratization and mutual recognition between majorities and minorities.

Two central disciplines that implicitly address the state-sizing issue, political science and political geography, have remained largely isolated from one another, with very little cross-fertilization or scholarly dialogue. Indeed, political science literature has rarely problematized the political geography of states as a fundamental variable in explaining their stability, integrity, or collapse. Conversely, political geographers have paid only scant attention to the institutionalization of territory and its population as an effective stage of the state-building process. This chapter attempts to address this deficiency, by drawing on literature from both political science and political geography.[2]

---

[2] Further definitions are in order here. 'The state' is the agglomeration of public institutions and agencies whose laws and policies are imposed over the territory within its borders. 'Nation-building' is the deliberate effort to construct an overarching collective identity based on a putative common national—most often ethnic—sentiment, culture, and heritage. 'State-building' is a complementary project, aimed at forging social solidarity and loyalty around state-institutions, territory, and common interests. State-building does not always overlap with nation-building, since peripheral ethnic minorities are often excluded from the state-imposed definition of 'the nation',

Theoretical Foundations

State, Nationalism, and Space

The analysis presented here rests on several theoretical underpinnings. First, it perceives nation- and state-building projects to commonly embody elements of ethnic and class oppression. This is expressed through state-building practices and hegemonic discourses which usually reflect the interests of dominant élites—see Giddens (1985); Tilly (1975, 1984, and 1990/92); Mitchell (1991). However, élite control is often contested, resulting in political mobilization among minorities, ideological groups, and the poor. Therefore, social change in general, and policy changes in particular, are generated by the interaction of forces emanating 'from above' by these élites, and the resistance to these forces emerging from below (Kirby 1993; Tilly 1985).

Second, among the collective identities constructed by and within modern states, and especially following WWI, ethno-nationalism should be seen as a dominant order around which most other collective identities develop. This dominance has caused national identities to be considered 'banal' (Billig 1995), but because of this very 'banality', they are also *dynamic* in scope and modes of expression. This is because the hegemonic nation-building discourse continuously remoulds the self-identity and 'collective imagination' of homeland ethnic minorities. Being constantly exposed to ethno-national discourses, such minorities are likely to develop ethno-national consciousness, and may consequently destabilize existing political structures with campaigns for autonomy, regionalism, or sovereignty (Anderson, B. 1991, 1996; Hechter and Levi 1979; Connor 1994; Smith 1995).

Third, the concept of *active space* teaches us that the links between space, collective identities, and group relations must be seen as dynamic and reciprocal (Jackson and Penrose 1993). That is, while social processes create spatial outcomes, the territorial shape of these outcomes also influences the social, economic, and political picture. Here we depart from the traditional social science approach, which treats space as 'flat' acting simply as a container of social change.

---

but remain citizens of the state. 'Ethnicity' is defined as a social bond based on belief in a common cultural past at a specific place. 'Plural society' is interchangeable with 'deeply divided society', denoting a polity composed of two or more non-assimilating ethnic groups. Finally, ethnic 'territorial integrity' entails the secure existence of a community within its collective region(s), and the protection of this region from encroachment and dislocation.

'Right-Sizing' or 'Right-Shaping' the State?

State-building is driven by the economic and spatial control sought by élites. It is legitimized through the construction of hegemonic national identities which portray the economic, cultural, and social interests of the élites as 'national', and therefore beyond challenge. Ian Lustick's original work draws on the experiences of Britain–Ireland, France–Algeria, and Israel–West Bank to construct a model of state-building, with specific applicability to territorial expansion and contraction (Lustick 1993).

In summary, Lustick argues that the processes of incorporating a new territory into existing states (expansion) and the shedding of this territory (contraction) are marked by three broad stages separated by two thresholds: those of 'regime; and 'ideological-hegemony'. Hegemony is perceived in its Gramscian sense of a 'moment' when a totally dominant set of beliefs and practices prevails in society, and prevents the emergence of significant challenge or resistance. Full incorporation of a territory would thus entail its 'climbing' over the regime and ideological thresholds, and its integration as part and parcel of the undisputed state entity, as perceived by the political centre. Implicit in Lustick's model is that full incorporation would also entail the extension of this hegemony over the residents of the incorporate territory—with or without their consent—a process leading to relative democratic stability. Conversely, Lustick describes the process of retreat from such territories as a far more politically difficult and socially disruptive 'backward' movement across these two thresholds. Such movement occurs because of political conflicts which threaten: the incumbent rulers and government élites; these élites and the state regime; and the élites, the regime, and the hegemonic sets of ideologies and beliefs which frame the society in question. Failure to incorporate a territory is thus explained by the inability of interested élites and groups to construct a hegemonic moment in which withdrawal from the territory in question is not even entertained as a viable political option. The failure to reach a hegemonic moment is therefore likely to result in political and territorial instability of the expanded state.

Lustick's work provides a very useful point of departure but two key factors in the reciprocal state-territory nexus are underplayed by the model: the nature of public policies and the impact of ethnic geographies. First, he focuses chiefly on political struggles at the core as key determinants of the state's territorial integrity and political stability. This largely overlooks the mobilization of population inhabiting the incorporated territories, and particularly ethnic minorities. The reaction of minorities to control from the central state may vary greatly according to state policies, with oppressive policies usually leading to escalating inter-ethnic conflict, whereas accommodating policies generally result in increasing legitimacy of the central state (Hechter and Levi 1979; Shafir 1995).

Second, while Lustick has problematized the location and institutionalization of state borders, he does not sufficiently account for the critical influence of ethnic geographies and identities on the continuing struggle over these borders. More specifically, Lustick's model underplays issues such as: the regional concentration or dispersal of ethnic groups, the urban processes or ethnic mixing or segregation, or the impact of distant and neighbouring ethnic diasporas—see for example Jackson and Penrose (1993); Keating (1996); Mikesell and Murphy (1991); Williams and Kofman (1989).

Yet the geography of ethnic groups is intimately linked to the development of collective identities. This has assumed greater political significance with the emergence of ethno-nationalism as a dominant world order, a discourse, ideology, and reality that affects ethnic groups in a variety of settings and circumstances. Needless to say, not all ethnic groups are able or willing to launch a national struggle, although their identity is nonetheless deeply affected by the prevailing division of the world into ethnic nations. This is particularly the case with 'homeland ethnic groups', which tend to develop non-assimilating territorial identities framed within the global logic of self-determination (Connor 1994: 346; Smith 1986, 1995). Hence, a model explaining state expansion and contraction must include the political geography of ethnicity, which often influences the mobilization of peripheries and thereby the political stability of states.

This topic leads us to a further difficulty in Lustick's model: the application of a Gramscian notion of hegemony-construction to the case of multi-ethnic and multinational polities. Gramsci formulated the concept to explain political and class domination in a different setting, namely that of the Italian Risorgimento at the latter half of the nineteenth century and the beginning of the twentieth century, during which parallel processes of state-building and nation-building extended a capitalist-nationalist hegemony *over the Italian people* and not over other peoples. The hegemonic moment, *à la* Gramsci, is marked by a distorted but widely accepted fusion of philosophy and practice *within* the sphere of a society in question. It is an order in which a certain social structure is dominant, with its own concept of reality determining most tastes, morality, customs, and political principles (adapted from Gramsci 1971). Given the economic, political, and cultural power of the élites, a hegemonic order is likely to be reproduced, unless severe contradictions with 'stubborn realities' generate counter-hegemonic mobilizations.

Therefore, for Gramsci the external boundaries of 'society' are not all discussed, implicitly assuming, in the Italian case, that hegemony has the potential to reach all Italian speakers. Gramsci does account for the power of nationalism, but Italian nation-building during the Risorgimento is for Gramsci a historical process enhancing the construction of socio-economic and national hegemony within Italy. Lustick's model, on the other hand, extends the (potential) construction of hegemony across ethno-national boundaries, and identifies the 'hegemonic moment' by lack of a concerted challenge to the socio-political order. While the broadening of hegemony analysis to other contexts is indeed stimulating and promising, Lustick's specific use of the concept sidesteps the inherent problem of state expansion which brings two or more distinct ethno-national societies under one regime.

It is argued here that in such multi-ethnic settings the preservation of state territorial integrity ('right-sizing') does not only depend on the construction of hegemony among the majority and its political class, but equally depends on the nature of policies towards the peripheral minority ('right-shaping') and on the subsequent political geography of ethnic relations. This is the case because the hegemonic order in question is over state territorial *sovereignty*, and not a certain socio-economic order—as, for example, is the case with liberal or capitalist international hegemonies. Given the hope of most (mobilized) homeland ethnic groups to obtain sovereignty under the nation-state global order, the extension of state hegemony over peripheral ethnic groups is particularly difficult. If 'right-sizing' is not accommodated by 'right-shaping', then a situation termed by Gramsci (1971: 166) as 'incurable contradiction' may arise, and undermine the stability of the political order.

The difficulties of extending a core-initiated hegemony over minority territory is made clear by Gramsci's analysis (1971: 105–6) of Serbia's attempt to become the hegemonic 'Piedmont of the Balkans'. These attempts failed because 'both in Croatia and in the other non-Serb regions we find that there is an anti-Serb intellectual bloc . . .'. Here Gramsci noted that opposition to Serbian hegemony did not come from the traditional rural élites, who were co-opted by Serbia, but mainly from non-Serbian—chiefly Croatian—peasants and their intellectuals. Gramsci noted that the difference between Piedmont and Serbia was not only related to class-consciousness or ethnic geography, but, critically, was also historical. Here he observes: 'that Serbia did not succeed is due to the fact that after the war [WWI] there occurred a political awakening of the peasantry such as did not exist in 1848 [in Italy]' (ibid: 105). Although Gramsci does not explicitly refer to ethno-national consciousness, it appears that the reference to 'political awakening', which militated against Serbian hegemony, relates to the rise of territorial ethno-nationalism during the period in question.

It is acknowledged here of course that the extension of hegemonic control in any setting necessitates the 'conversion' of peripheries which are often culturally different to the expanding centre. This is because societal 'centres' and their borders are never 'given' or primordial. But the extension of an all-powerful state hegemonic order appears limited to populations with a degree of cultural similarity, which can 'absorb' the hegemonic order. Here the comparison between southern Italy—culturally distinct from the dominant north, but similar enough to be integrated—and Croatia—possessing deep historical and cultural differences from Serbia—is illustrative: the Italian élites managed to incorporate the south, while their Serbian counterparts failed *vis-à-vis* Croatia. This does not indicate of course that ethnic differences between groups are primordial, but rather that during the Italian Risorgimento, northern élites could exploit a vague sense of overarching, if weak, *Italian-ness*—based on the common territory, and a common written language among the many dialect groups—and institutionalize the new Italy around these 'Italian' groups. But a similar attempt to construct a hegemonic Yugoslavia was far more difficult in a setting marked by greater social distance, and during a more nationalist historical period.

Needless to say, control over new ethnic territories can be maintained through coercion or benign incorporation. But the infiltration of stabilizing hegemonic norms and beliefs throughout a multi-ethnic society is unlikely when ethno-nationalism is a dominant global ideology and practice, because it is unlikely to be accepted—or successfully imposed over—the various ethnic peripheries.

We need, therefore, to explore deeper to explain the maintenance of territorial integrity and political stability in plural societies. Based on the foundation of Lustick's work, but extending it to address the absences highlighted above, it is suggested here that these clues lie in the 'right-shaping' and not merely the 'right-sizing' the state. In particular, we shall explore two key factors for political stability: public policies and ethnic geographies.

Shaping Plural Democracy

Public Policy

The literature on public policy and democratic stability in plural societies has been rich and varied. The liberal approach was dominant until the 1970s, arguing that individual assimilation and cross-cutting cleavages provide a key to achieving political stability (Deutsch 1966; Glazer and Young 1983; Gordon 1964, 1975). It was heavily criticized in later decades, and found particularly irrelevant to our case-studies of non-assimilating homeland minorities (see Connor 1994). Another approach sees territorial partition as a conflict-resolution option, although it has rarely been practised by governments in plural states (Waterman 1996). Given our interest in the democratic stability of plural (deeply divided) states, two main state-shaping approaches have remained most relevant: accommodation and control.

Accommodation

In contrast to the assimilative-liberal approach, policies of accommodation are premised on inter-ethnic compromise and the mutual recognition of non-assimilating ethnic identities. A variety of approaches and methods of inter-ethnic political accommodation has been discussed—see for example McGarry and O'Leary (1993); Nordlinger (1972); and Lustick (1997)—with a particularly prominent model being consociationalism (Lijphart 1977).

The consociational model legitimizes ethnic cleavages, and attempts to satisfy the socio-economic and identity needs of ethnic groups through a process of élite bargaining, power-sharing, participatory politics, and appropriate institutional design. Four principal regime practices characterize consociationalism: power-sharing, proportionality, segmental autonomy, and mutual veto rights (ibid). Stability in consociational regimes is secured through the creation of a broad overarching loyalty, and through compromise among segmental élites on key constitutional and public policy issues. Examples of effective consociational regimes are Switzerland, Canada, and Belgium. Several newer democracies, such as Malaysia, Spain, and Romania, and most recently Northern Ireland (O'Leary 1999), have implemented elements of consociationalism in their attempts to reach a stable political order.

Despite its normative and explanatory appeal, the consociational model has been criticized as being simplistic, ambiguous, and unsuitable for societies suffering 'institutional underdevelopment' (Crighton and MacIver 1991; Halpern 1986). It has been repeatedly criticized for confusing normative and explanatory arguments, and glossing over the pervasive maintenance of stability through control, domination, and coercion, both by majorities over minorities, and by élites over their 'own' segmental constituencies (Lustick 1979, 1997).

Control

Political stability is also preserved through the imposition of control over ethnic minorities. In some plural—particularly post-colonial—societies, formal democratic procedures merely obscure a state shaped by control and oppression. 'Legitimate' democratic methods of majority rule can thus lead to a tyranny of the majority. States dominated by one ethnic group while maintaining some democratic procedures on an *individual* level were labelled as 'ethnic democracies' (Smooha 1990); or 'ethnocracies' (Yiftachel 1997a).

Three principal control practices are typically used by governments of such 'ethnocracies': political surveillance, economic dependence, and territorial containment (Smooha 1980; Yiftachel 1992a). Clear differences thus exist between the role of the states in consociational and control regimes: in the former the state acts as an even-handed protector of the partner groups and their cultures, while in the latter the state becomes 'a legal and administrative instrument of the superordinate segment' (Lustick 1979: 330). Examples of the use of the control approach in plural democracies include pre-1968 Northern Ireland, Sri Lanka, and Israel, where the state's apparatus serves almost exclusively the interests of the 'ruling' ethnic group, while maintaining the appearance of a formal democracy—see respectively O'Leary and McGarry (1996: chs. 3–5); Arasaratnam (1986, 1987); and Lustick (1976).

Regarding the efficacy of the two policy approaches, most studies have argued that accommodation and consociational policies tend to increase the prospects of long-term stability of plural democracies, whereas ethnic control policies tend to exacerbate long-term conflicts—see for example Esman (1987); Hewitt (1977); Gurr (1993); Rudolph and Thompson (1985); Yiftachel (1992b); Lane and Ersson (1990); and Zariski (1989). Although most of these scholars are aware of the criticisms levelled at the consociational model, they note that under consociational policies, gaps and disparities between ethnic groups tend to diminish over time, because of the principles of proportionality and mutual recognition built into the system. On the other hand, state-shaping based on control policies tends to intensify these disparities, and thereby increases the frustration and militancy of disgruntled minorities, and the likelihood of open ethnic conflict—for a sweeping review, see Gurr (1993).

The Role of Ethnic Geographies

The discussion of public policies alone, while highlighting vital aspects of maintaining stability, often lacks a serious discussion of spatial factors. As argued elsewhere (Yiftachel 1997a, b) the analysis of plural states must unravel the multiplicity of spatial and social boundaries, existing 'above', 'below' or 'across' international borders. These boundaries stem from historical residential patterns and from struggles over land control and political power; they hold 'in place' certain social and ethnic structures and hierarchies which we must integrate into the quest to understand ethnic relations and political stability in plural societies. The territorial dimension of sizing the state is only one of several spatial factors affecting the cohesion and integrity of the plural state.

The significance of spatial factors, and particularly that of ethnic geographies, also stems from the all-important identity function of the modern 'nation-state'. The present dominant nation-state world order assumes an ideal overlap of ethnicity, territory, and government (Billig 1995). This logic has been increasingly 'diffused' by the processes of colonialism and globalization (Anderson, B. 1991; Smith 1995). However, the expression of ethnonationalism varies dramatically across space, as it meets the rigid and often incompatible grid of existing state boundaries, creating 'an intensifying crisis of the nation-state hyphen' (Anderson, B. 1996: 5).

Nonetheless, the fundamental rationale of self-determination—which depends on ethnic territorial control—still constitutes a most powerful driving force for non-assimilating groups, placing persistent pressures on plural states to accommodate their identity concerns (Anderson, B. 1996; Connor 1994). Ethnic geography is thus a critical factor constraining the range of possibilities available to peripheral groups: do they have the necessary basis for pursuing self-determination? If not, what can they achieve within their geographic setting? Put differently, we need to *breathe life* into the territory in question, and find its ethnic composition and collective meaning to assess the central state's ability to integrate peripheral regions. Two key spatial dimensions impact significantly on state-building and public policy.

First, the degree of *ethnic separation or mix*, which is often determined by state policies, has a direct bearing on political stability. Ethnic regional concentrations are often viewed as potential bases for minority secession, and are thus feared by most state-shapers. However, this is rarely the case in consociational polities, where the protection of territorial integrity of peripheral 'homeland' groups generally enhances the prospects of peaceful ethnic coexistence (Lijphart 1977: 45). Comparative examples clearly illustrate this point. In the relatively stable cases of Switzerland, Spain, and Canada, ethnic 'homelands' are clearly defined (Murphy 1989: 420). In contrast, in Northern Ireland, Sri Lanka, and Malaysia, where ethnic communities have been physically intermingled, open conflicts have erupted—see Arasaratnam (1986); Boal, Douglas, and Orr (1982). This phenomenon can also be observed in recent events in Eastern Europe, where the process of democratization has exposed the fragility of social order in ethnically mixed states and regions, such as Bosnia, Croatia, and Nagorno Karabakh. The problematic consequences of ethnic spatial mix are linked to the concept of ethnic territoriality, which is perceived to be threatened by the usually coerced mix between ethnic groups (Sack 1983, 1986).

A second spatial factor relates to the *trans-statal distribution of ethnicities*. Here the changing scales of majority-minority relations are politically significant: a minority within a state can be part of a powerful regional (transborder) majority, with direct implications to its status within the state (Shafir 1995). This is reinforced by Crighton and MacIver (1991: 138–9), who note that 'protracted ethnic conflicts' are directly correlated with the 'fear of extinction' experienced by state majorities, who are surrounded by larger ethnic entities affiliated with an internal minority. Here, too, shapers of public policies must fathom the local, state, and trans-state association between territory and identity, and the impact they have on ethnic politics.

'Right-' and 'Wrong-Shaping' the State: Lebanon, Cyprus, and Belgium

We now turn to a brief exploration of the cases of Lebanon, Cyprus, and Belgium and examine their attempts to shape stable democratic regimes. The three states are relevant for our discussion because they all went through internal boundary and policy changes, allowing us to test key dimensions of the 'right-shaping' of plural states. In addition, the three states share certain geopolitical characteristics, such as a relatively small size, a unitary regime, and proximity to states governed by groups affiliated with the local ethnic minority.

Lebanon (1943–85)

Lebanon is composed of seventeen different ethnic-religious groups, although all groups—except arguably the small Druse community—are either Christian or Muslim. Apart from religion, the main divisions between the Lebanese sects are cultural, characterized by a relatively Western orientation of the country's Christians, as opposed to a more Arab orientation of their Muslim counterparts. Lebanon was resized in 1920s when the 'original' polity was extended by the then French rulers to incorporate several new and predominantly Muslim regions. It was estimated that in the early 1940s, 30 per cent of the population was Maronite Christian, 20 per cent Sunni Muslim, 18 per cent Shiite Muslim and 11 per cent Greek Orthodox. In total, Christians outnumbered the Muslims by a ratio of 6:5. It is widely agreed that since then, the proportion of the Muslim communities has increased markedly and reached about 60–3 per cent of the population by the mid 1980s (Kliot 1987: 62).

In 1943, while gaining independence from French rule, Lebanon adopted the accommodation approach and was shaped as a classical consociational democracy. This political arrangement was based on an unwritten 'national pact' which shared power between the country's four main sects: the President was to be a Maronite, the Prime Minister a Sunni, the Chairman of the Legislature a Shiite, and the Deputy Prime Minister a Greek Orthodox. Executive power was thus finely balanced between the élites of the four communities, and two main religions. The Lebanese cabinet, the country's main decision-making body, was composed through proportional representation of the main sectional interests according to the proportions agreed in 1943. The electoral system was a combination of the plurality and proportional systems, guaranteeing a representation of most sectional interests from each constituency (Lijphart 1984), and ensuring an overall ratio of six Christians to five Muslims in the parliament. Other consociational mechanisms included a large degree of social, religious, and cultural autonomy to the various sects, proportionality between the sects in civil service appointments, and a right of all the main sects to veto major policies or legislation (Kliot 1987; Rabinovich 1984).

It could be expected, at least according to consociational theory that the shaping of Lebanon would usher in a period of relative political stability (Smooha and Hanf 1992: 21). However, although the consociational setting did temper some long-standing historical tensions, it was still subject to continuous threats and challenges. These stemmed from internal and external factors. A short civil war in 1958 was triggered by the insurgence of disgruntled Muslims in the country's deprived regions (Smooha and Hanf 1992; Kliot 1987). This war was settled only with the intervention of US troops who came to the aid of the Christian President.

Following several key changes—including population movements, increasing Muslim demographic power, growing assertion of disenfranchised Palestinian refugees, and increasing external intervention in Lebanon's ethnic relations—tensions between the Muslims and Christians increased, erupting into an all encompassing civil war in 1975. The associated collapse of social and political order since 1975 put an end to a gallant attempt to shape Lebanon as a consociational democracy in an unstable geopolitical environment. As noted by Lijphart (1977: 150) 'the Lebanese consociational regime established a remarkable, although obviously far from perfect, record of democratic stability'. The enduring appeal of the ethnic accommodation approach was illustrated again at the end of the Lebanese civil war, when the restoration of political order, enshrined in the 1989 Taif peace agreement, was based again on consociational methods. The new agreement—which still falls short of restoring full democracy in Lebanon because of persisting Syrian and Israeli intervention—took into account the demographic and geographic changes which had taken place in the country (Smooha and Hanf 1992).

Let us return to the 1975 collapse of the Lebanese consociation. What were the main explanations provided by scholars for the 'wrong-shaping' of

Lebanon and its subsequent deterioration into open ethnic conflict? First and foremost, the key consociational principle of proportionality eroded over time. The gradual but undeniable demographic increase of Muslims *vis-à-vis* Christians did not find expression in the composition of state institutions, which remained rigidly structured along the provisions of the 1943 national pact (Khalaf 1987; Kliot 1987). This, in effect, entailed the transformation of ethnic relations in Lebanon *from accommodation to control*, as the Christian community which was gradually becoming a minority hung on to its constitutional powers. Needless to say, this meant that the Lebanese system was gradually losing its legitimacy among Muslim communities, a process exacerbated by continuing class tensions between the generally privileged Christians and deprived Muslims (Khalidi 1979).

Second, Lebanon's geography of ethnicity was not conducive to any ethno-territorial solution, as historical processes of settlement, invasion, and succession found expression in a pattern of highly mixed regions (Khalidi 1979). The roots of the problem relate to the resizing of the state in 1920 when new Muslim regions were incorporated. This created a much more heterogeneous composition of the population, and put in motion a process of increasing spatial mix, as the various ethnic groups were being integrated into the Lebanese economy (see Fig. 12.1). Several ethnic enclaves exist in Lebanon, particularly following the development of territorially-based militias during the civil war, but they are not distinctive enough to allow the solution of territorial federalism (Kliot 1987), or for the protection and enhancement of ethnic identities and cultures which has become the standard aspiration of homeland ethnic minorities during the ethno-national era. In addition, the gradual transformation of the regime from accommodation to control, and the attempts of Christian élites to hold on to their privileges, meant that the Muslim regions incorporated in 1920 were not fully integrated into Lebanese society. This appears to be a case of 'incorporation without integration' (cf. Lustick 1993) or in our language here, a both 'wrongly-sized' and 'wrongly-shaped' plural state.

Third, Lebanon's trans-statal geopolitical position was critical to its ongoing problems. Situated between Syria—which has since 1943 claimed historical rights to Lebanon as part of 'Greater Syria'—and Israel—which occupied parts of southern Lebanon—exposed the state to constant intervention of external powers, a problem exacerbated by its military weakness. In addition, Lebanon's geographical position placed its Christian, and particularly Maronite, community in a classical position of a 'threatened majority' against the occasional surfacing of pan-Arab nationalism and pan-Islamic sentiments (Crighton and MacIver 1991). This can partially explain their unwillingness to change the country's national pact, fearing a

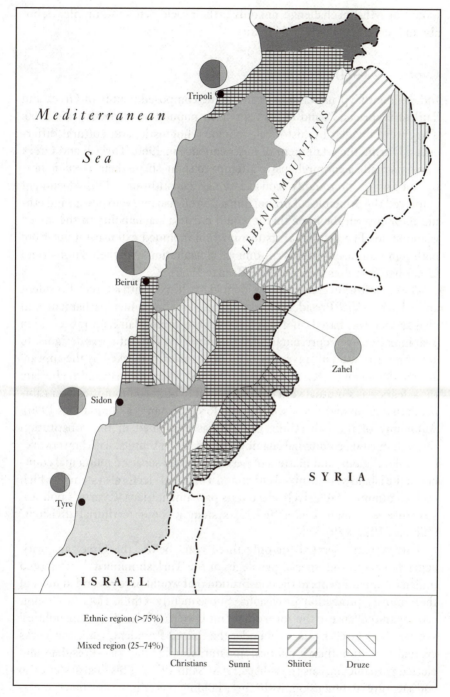

FIG. 12.1 The pattern of ethnic distribution in Lebanon

mounting Muslim challenge, not only to their socio-economic privileges, but also to their ethno-territorial identity.

Cyprus (1960–74)

Independent Cyprus was a bi-ethnic state, composed mainly of Greek and Turkish Cypriots, 78 and 18 per cent of the population respectively in 1960. They were divided by historical, religious, linguistic, and cultural differences. During the attainment of independence in 1960, Turkish and Greek Cypriots made a comprehensive attempt to right-shape their nascent state, by forging a thoroughly consociational constitution. This document employed the principles of proportional power-sharing, veto power, and ethnic autonomy, in the hope that it would create a stable polity in the mixed island-state. The process of its formulation included extensive input from both communities, as well as continuous consultation with their Turkish and Greek patron-states (Joseph 1985; Raanan 1980).

The constitution created a presidential executive, with a Greek President and a Turkish Vice President. Representation in the cabinet, parliament, and civil service was based on a seven (Greek) to three (Turkish) ratio, which guaranteed an overrepresentation of the minority. This ratio was designed to allay minority fears of 'a tyranny of a Greek majority masked by the appearance of democracy' (Kyridikes 1968). An additional mechanism to alleviate these fears was a mutual veto power granted to both communities over cabinet decisions on matters of security and foreign affairs (Koumoulides 1996). Autonomy of the two ethnic groups was enshrined in the constitution through separate communal chambers for each community, with powers over cultural, religious, and matters of personal status; separate municipal councils in the island's large mixed cities; and a national electoral system in which each community exclusively elected its parliamentarians. Cyprus's political structure was shaped as a 'federal system without territorial divisions' (Lijphart 1977: 159).

This system operated for only three years before the Greek majority, aggrieved about the 'special privileges of the Turkish minority', attempted unilateral amendments to the constitution that would have rescinded most of the minority-protection provisions. Subsequently, ethnic riots broke out, causing the collapse of the government into two parallel and separate political systems. The Greeks remained under the elected President, while the Turks created their (unofficial) political apparatus under the Vice-President and elected parliamentarians (Kyridikes 1968; Salih 1978). This dual system also had a territorial dimension, with Turks holding power in several newly created Turkish enclaves. This non-agreed system lasted until 1974, when a Greek

Cypriot effort at unification with Greece caused another wave of ethnic upheaval. It prompted Turkey to invade the island and create a Turkish statelet along its northern coastline. The invasion was associated with large scale population-displacement, after which the previously intermingled Greek and Turkish communities became totally separated into two distinct regions. Since 1974, Cyprus has been a resized state under a *de facto* partition, although no country except Turkey has recognized the 'Turkish Cypriot Republic' established in the island's north (Kliot and Mansfeld 1996).

Cyprus, like Lebanon, represents a failure in the consociational shaping of the polity, although, significantly, in Lebanon the model operated quite successfully for three decades, whereas in Cyprus it lasted only three years. Several arguments are advanced to explain this 'wrong-shaping'. First, Greek Cypriots were never fully in favour of the consociational agreement which they perceived as unfairly benefiting the Turks. The Greeks unilaterally rescinded the proportionality and mutual-veto agreements. They saw these agreements as effectively blocking the possibility of '*Enosis*': the Greeks' dream of fully mobilizing their ethno-national identity and uniting with Greece. Consequently, the state reverted in 1963 *from consociation back to control*, a move that caused obvious resistance among the Turks (Raanan 1980; Salih 1978).

Second, the geography of ethnic relations in pre-1963 Cyprus was marked by a high degree of spatial mix, in nearly all of the island's regions. This presented difficulties in the shaping of the country's consociational regulations. To complicate matters further, the island's six largest cities were mixed, although most towns and villages were segregated—see Fig. 12.2. Following the 1963 riots, the Turks retreated into more confined enclaves, where they could carry out their life under the (unofficial) Turkish-Cypriot authorities. This process of ethnic separation was completed in 1974, in the aftermath of Turkey's invasion (Kliot and Mansfeld 1996; see Fig. 12.2). In our language the Cypriot state was resized, following unsuccessful reshaping attempts.

A further geopolitical cause of the problems of political stability in Cyprus, like Lebanon, was the island's location and its military weakness which exposed it to continuous external intervention particularly from Greece and Turkey. While this had occurred for hundreds of years (Doob 1986), it became a seriously destabilizing factor only since independence, as both communities were vying to control the new repository of power, the state (Koumoulides 1996; Kliot and Mansfeld 1996).

Yet the key point for our interest in 'right-shaping' the plural state remains the inability of Cyprus to manage its communal relations within a spatially-mixed structure. Again, we need to draw here on the diffusing and incessant

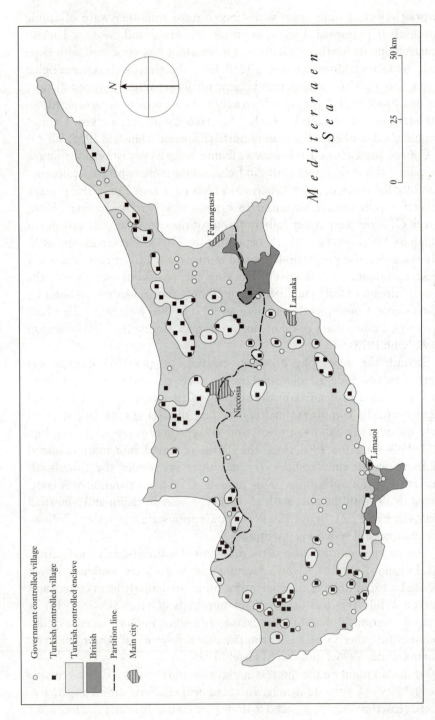

Fɪɢ. 12.2 The geographical and settlement distribution of Greeks and Turks in Cyprus

power of ethno-nationalism, which mobilized both communities to aspire for 'pure' ethnic territory. This created insurmountable problems for 'right-shaping' a geographically mixed polity. In the 1990s, negotiations for future inter-communal agreement hinge on a federal-type solution, whereby the territorial integrity and thus collective identity of Turkish Cypriots would be protected (Kliot and Mansfeld 1996).

Finally, the case of Cyprus, like Lebanon, demonstrates the high cost associated with a reversal of the 'consociational state-shaping process'. The amendments made by the Greek majority in 1963 constituted an attempt to reverse the process of majority-minority proportionality and revert *from accommodation to control*. The reintroduction of control policies was indeed one of the principal factors in the collapse of the Cypriot state (Raanan 1980). The high cost of the consociational reversal also highlighted again the limits to élite control: when Greek élites sought to deepen their domination over the Turkish minority, their move led to the *de facto* partition of the state. In our current language we can note then, that the 'wrong-shaping' of Cyprus led to the resizing of the state.

Belgium (1963–93)

Like the previous two cases, Belgium is essentially a bi-ethnic state, composed of Dutch-speaking Flemish (58 per cent), and French-speaking Walloons (40 per cent) and a small community of German speakers (2 per cent). The main divisions between the two groups are ethnic, linguistic, and regional (see Fig. 12.3). The spatio-regional separation between the two communities has sharpened in recent years because of the 'politics of language' which has dominated the country since the turn of the century (Murphy 1995). It is the changing location and content of internal boundaries between the two communities which make Belgium an illuminating case of both 'right-sizing' and 'right-shaping' a plural state.

The state of Belgium was formed in 1830 in an act of secession from the Dutch kingdom by the mainly Catholic southern regions. The state became a constitutional monarchy, dominated by the Francophone Walloons who were concentrated mainly, but not exclusively, in the Belgian south, later to be named Wallonia. In contrast, the Dutch speaking Flemish community traditionally resided in the rural northern Flanders region (see Fig. 12.3). During the nineteenth century the Walloons formed the demographic majority of the country, and maintained their privileged position through strong links with one of the great powers of the time, France. Flemish élites during this period also adopted French as the main political, cultural, and economic language. The highly centralized and unitary political structure

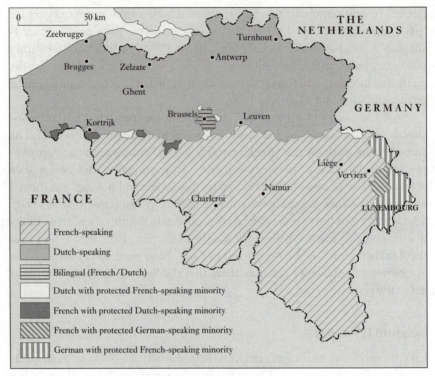

FIG. 12.3 The pattern of ethnic distribution in Belgium

adopted by the Belgian state further reflected and reinforced Walloon domination and control.

But as noted by Hossay (1996), Belgium's state-building occurred when nationalism was gradually replacing religion as the main kernel of European collective identity. Given this context, Belgium did not develop into a homogeneous nation-state, but rather as a 'state of two ethnic nations'. The growing influence of European ethno-nationalism, and the continuing dominance of the Walloons spawned resistance among the Flemish, who began to develop communal consciousness, and rival the French for control of the country's politics, economy, and culture. This was augmented by the changing of the demographic balance, with the Flemish reaching parity with the Walloons during the 1930s, because of higher fertility rates.

The Flemish challenge to Walloon control spawned a gradual process of ethnic accommodation, embodying several key elements of consociationalism. The process witnessed the Belgian regime being decentralized from a unitary central government into the two communities. It began very slowly around the turn of the century, when the Flemish won the right for education in Dutch, and continued with the ever more conspicuous presence of a separate, and increasingly powerful, Flemish entity in politics and among the country's élites. The most significant phase of this process occurred during the three decades between 1963 and 1993, on which this section focuses.[3]

In 1963, the government decided, for the first time, to institutionalize regional identities by creating an official political and geographic division between the two ethno-lingual groups, and by offering duplicated facilities and services for each area. The Brussels area, situated well within Flanders, but having a decisive Francophone majority, was declared a third administrative region (De Rigger and Fraga 1986). In 1971, following increasing inter-ethnic hostility around the demarcation of language areas, with a watershed conflict concerning the University of Louvain, the Belgian constitution was amended to facilitate the devolution of the unitary state. The responses of the central government were, in the main, aimed at accommodating Flemish grievances and protecting the identities of the two communities, rather than deepening the control of the dominant group, as had been the case in Lebanon and Cyprus.

The constitutional amendments of 1971 were moderate, but introduced the notion of regional autonomy and provided an institutional setting for autonomy. Accordingly, in 1974 two separate regional councils, and two Ministerial Committees, were established in Flanders and Wallonia. In addition, in 1973, linguistic parity was ensured in the central government through legislation, adding a further consociational mechanism—inter-ethnic coalition—to the process of ethnic accommodation. This executive parity augmented the general principle of proportionality which already prevailed in Belgium through a proportional representation electoral system, and widespread practices of proportional appointments to the central public service.

In 1980 further constitutional reforms were introduced, attempting to respond to another wave of inter-ethnic tension, and frequent incidences of governmental collapse. These mainly stemmed from Flemish demands for ethno-regional control over language, culture, and development. The amendment entailed the upgrading of the regional councils in Flanders and Wallonia to the status of 'regional assemblies', with increased powers to enact cultural, educational, public health, and development legislation. Each

---

[3] In widely quoted critiques of consociation published in 1975 (Barry 1989/91a, b) claims that the restructuring of Belgium did not represent ethnic consociationalism, because accommodation was struck between multi-ethnic party élites which cut across the ethnic divide. However, the evidence shows that Barry may have confused form with content, as the essence of Belgian constitutional change has revolved around the accommodation of ethno-regional rights. More importantly, most Belgium-wide political parties have since been divided into Flemish and Walloon subsections.

region became governed by a regional executive with increased financial and policy-making powers (Europa World Yearbook 1997).

The pressure for constitutional reshaping of the Belgian state did not end there. As Murphy (1995) shows, the devolution process was a major engine in the construction and consolidation of ethno-regional identities. This created further constitutional demands for devolution, and Belgium began, in the late 1980s, another major 'reshaping' phase: a transformation into constitutional federalism. Further legislative, executive and financial powers were transferred to the regions, most notably in the areas of education, economic, and (international) trade policies. The changes also included the creation of a regional assembly for the Brussels region which previously had a lower status. The first Belgian federal constitution came into effect in 1989, and despite persistent difficulties such as the rise of extreme Flemish nationalism, and the unresolved status of Walloon suburbs around Brussels, the transformation into federalism was completed in 1993.

The Belgian federal state is now comprised of the largely autonomous regions of Flanders, Wallonia, and (bilingual) Brussels. The three regions have directly elected assemblies, with provisions for both geographical and non-geographical ethno-lingual autonomy and responsibility. Regional and community administrations were to assume sole responsibility for legislation and policies in the areas of culture, educational, environmental, housing, transport, public works, and partial responsibility in the areas of economic development and trade (Europa World Yearbook 1997; Thomas 1990). While it is too early to reach a conclusion on the merits of the new Belgian regime, and further disintegration may be possible, the events of the last few years suggest that a federal Belgium may be politically stable. Overt tensions and violence between the two communities have subsided, and the spectre of premature governmental collapses has also decreased. Therefore, and unlike the two previous cases, Belgian institutional design and public policies have moved the regime *from control to accommodation*, with Belgium's recent political history illustrating the effectiveness of accommodation and consociational theories. More specifically, the stabilization of Flemish-Walloon relations can be attributed to the two key factors on which we have focused the examination of 'right-shaping' the state: public policy and ethnic geography.

First, the policies of the Belgian government since 1963 have been consistent in the accommodation of what was widely perceived as justifiable Flemish demands for proportionality in the distribution of political resources, and for ethno-regional autonomy. The Belgian state recognized that the consolidation of ethno-lingual identities is inevitable and was able to facilitate the process, thus 'shaping' it in a manner conducive to the maintenance of political and social stability. Second, the Belgian government was attuned to the significance of regional geography, and to the importance attached by the two ethnic communities to ethno-regional autonomy and their territorial integrity. The two ethnic regions in Belgium, and especially Wallonia, are quite recent geographic entities, but once these regions assumed the role of ethnic homelands, they became a safe and cherished foundation for identity-maintenance and identity-construction. This has a crucial stabilizing function in an era when the fulfilment of ethnic and national self-determination is one of the major engines of political change. The protection of regional autonomy has thus contributed to Belgium's relative stability, in sharp contrast to the territorial encroachments in Lebanon and Cyprus which led to conflict and instability.

Lastly, Belgium's geopolitical setting was favourable, and particularly the lack of external intervention. This allowed the state to gradually arrive at ethnic accommodation based on genuine inter-ethnic negotiation, thereby receiving wider legitimacy among the populace. Again, this stands in contrast to the cases of Lebanon and Cyprus where policies were often influenced or imposed by external powers. Hence, the transformation of Belgium between 1963 and 1993 demonstrates the possibility of 'right-shaping' the state, to enhance democratic stability in deeply divided settings.

Conclusion: Towards 'Right-Sizing' and 'Right-Shaping' the State

What lessons, then, can we draw from the cases of Lebanon, Cyprus, and Belgium about the 'right-shaping' and 'right-sizing' of plural democracies (see Table 12.1)? First, drawing on Lustick's 'right-sizing' model, we can note that all three cases represent failed hegemonic projects. The three dominant ethnic groups could not assert their control over peripheral groups, despite dominating the state apparatus. A key factor here is the historical period: whereas in Lustick's analysis, the establishment of British and French hegemonic control over Ireland and Algeria, respectively, occurred before the consolidation of ethno-nationalism among the Irish or Algerians, in the three cases studied here, state-building took place in a period when ethno-nationalism was a dominant global ideology and practice, impeding the extension of central control over peripheral minorities and their territories. More specifically two key factors for the 'right-shaping' of plural states are appropriate: public policies and ethnic geographies.

As regards public policies and associated institutional design, in two of the cases, Lebanon and Cyprus, it appears as if consociationalism failed to

TABLE 12.1. *The state, ethnic spatial relations, and democratic stability in Lebanon, Cyprus, and Belgium*

	Lebanon (1985)	Cyprus (1964)	Belgium (1997)
Public Policy	From consociation to control	From consociation to control	From control to consociation
Proportionality	Decreasing	Decreasing	Increasing
Majority's regional status	Christians 1.7% in Middle East	Greeks 6% in Turkish region	Flemish 11% in French region
Trans-statal influence	Very high—Syria, Israel, Palestinians	Very high— Turkey, Greece	Low
Internal spatial relations	From mix to enclaves	From mix to separation	From enclaves to separation
Minority identity	From ethnic to mini-national	From ethnic to mini-national	From ethnic to ethno-national
Democratic stability	Fragile, collapsed in 1975	Fragile, collapsed 1963–74, destroyed in 1974	Fragile 1963–80, increasingly stable since

stabilize ethnic relations. This runs counter to influential political theories, which recommend accommodation and consociationalism as a suitable option for shaping the plural state (Lijphart 1977, 1996; Rudolph and Thompson 1985). It was mainly the violation of the principle of proportionality by the dominant groups in Lebanon and Cyprus, that caused escalating tensions and instability. Conversely, a consistent momentum towards proportionality took place in Belgium, partially explaining its relative political stability. This demonstrates that a critical 'right-shaping' component is inter-ethnic *proportionality*. The reversal of a momentum towards proportionality possesses grave consequences to democratic stability in plural states.

The impact of proportional power-sharing is an illustration of the importance of public policies and institutional design for the 'right-shaping' of plural states. It highlights the destabilizing impact of minority mobilization against violations of 'right-shaping' policies. Hence, the three cases show that other dimensions should supplement a central pillar in Lustick's (1993) 'right-sizing' model, concerning the ultimate power of the political centre to determine the fate of incorporated territories. The cases support the theoretical assertion made earlier that in certain political-geographical settings, clear limits constrain the power of the majority and its political class to determine the state's size and shape. In both Lebanon and Cyprus it was intensive and violent unrecognized majority and actual minority resistance which eventually reshaped and resized the state. Even in the more stable Belgium, resistance launched by the subordinate Flemish community made inroads into earlier Francophone domination. This caused a gradual resizing of internal ethnic and administrative regions, and a movement towards 'right-shaping' of the state's public policies and institutions.

A further lesson we can draw from the three cases is on the impact of ethnic geography. In the cases of Lebanon and cyprus the aggrieved minorities possessed links with their ethnic brethren in nearby states, thereby complicating the majority-minority balance of power within the state. The encroachment into minority territories, as well as the spatial ethnic mix in Lebanon and Cyprus presented further difficulties in the attempts to preserve their consociational democracies. In Belgium, the state recognized the importance of territorial integrity and autonomy for the two ethnic communities and moved to protect and enhance these principles.

The comparison highlights, then, that two key principles of inter-ethnic accommodation, namely proportionality and minority territorial integrity, were violated in the 'wrong-shaped' and unstable Lebanon and Cyprus, but protected and enhanced in 'right-shaped', more stable, Belgium. In other words, it was not consociation which caused instability in Lebanon and Cyprus, but rather a retreat from it! To further explain this phenomenon, we need to reiterate the powerful impact of ethno-nationalism which, as mentioned earlier, is a most potent force shaping contemporary state politics (Connor 1994). The impact of ethno-nationalism frequently finds expression in the consolidation and political mobilization of ethnic minorities within plural states. These minorities often develop ethno-regional identities which maximize their self-determination capacity within a constraining political structure. This is most commonly achieved by protecting and enhancing a homeland region as a safe foundation for their communal and cultural development (Shafir 1995; Yiftachel 1997b).

As we have seen in all three cases, even a hegemonic discourse among the majority group—Greek Cypriots, Lebanese Maronites, and Walloon Belgians—which portrayed the state as 'their own', did not deter the minority from mobilizing a struggle for political, territorial, and cultural rights. This often led to the reshaping and even resizing of the state, often with severe consequences for both the majority and the minority. In sum, struggles over hegemony in the political centre have been extremely significant, but their analysis cannot be complete without considering the causes and consequences of counter-mobilization in the ethnic periphery, and particularly ethnic pursuit of proportionality and ethno-territorial autonomy.

Remaining at a theoretical level, Gramsci's hegemonic analysis may be highly useful for understanding the diffusion and reproduction of supremacy in societies where no deep internal ethnic or national cleavages exist. A genuine 'hegemonic moment' exists only when peripheral groups aspire to assimilate, integrate, and mobilize within a dominant and taken-for-granted social order. This is so even when the political centre itself is not fixed, and is subject to internal struggles and transformations, as is often the case. In the era of ethno-nationalism, during which 'homeland' ethnic identities have hardened and consolidated, the extension of hegemonic control from a state's centre over ethnic minorities is thus unlikely. In such historical and geographic settings, the peaceful integration of minorities and their territories appear to depend not only on the construction of an all-embracing hegemonic discourse at the political centre, but equally on the enactment of enlightened public policies which would accommodate the periphery.

The lessons derived thus shed light on significant links between the 'rightsizing' and 'right-shaping' of plural states. It appears as if 'right-shaping' policies, and particularly those stressing power-sharing, proportionality, and ethnic territorial integrity, have the potential to legitimize central state control over peripheral ethnic territories. The legitimacy awarded to the regime by the periphery, in turn, enhances the construction of hegemony at the centre regarding the territorial extent of the state. Conversely, in the absence of 'right-shaping' policies and appropriate institutions, such legitimacy is withdrawn from the state, with adverse consequences to social and political stability.

In summary, states incorporating sizeable 'homeland' minorities during the last century have generally witnessed a *dialectical* dynamic in which forces emanating from both centre and periphery interact in an evolving political process. The dynamics of this struggle ultimately shape the state's internal politics and determine its level of democratic stability and territorial integrity. Lebanon, Cyprus, and Belgium illustrate the importance of inter-group proportionality, the limits to majority power *vis-à-vis* non-assimilating ethnic minorities, the improbability of a hegemonic majority control extending over homeland minorities in the epoch of ethno-nationalism, and the critical link between ethnic territory, identity, and political mobilization.

The 'right-shaping' and 'right-sizing' of plural states thus depends on 'breathing life' into the territories in question, and on understanding the evolving histories, identities, and aspirations of the inhabitants of these territories. In the light of these observations, Lustick's ground-breaking model should be extended to incorporate these additional components, and account for the improbability of 'right-sizing' the state without a parallel process of 'right-shaping' its policies and institutions. This endeavour can be greatly enhanced by a more intense dialogue between the rich traditions of political geography and political science. Lustick's pioneering work forms an ideal foundation on which to construct such a dialogue.

REFERENCES

Anderson, B. 1991. *Imagined Communities: Reflections on the Origins and Spread of Nationalism*. London: Verso.

—— 1996. 'Introduction', 1–16 in *Mapping the Nation*, edited by G. Balakrishnan. London: Verso.

Anderson, M. 1996. *Frontiers: Territory and State Formation in the Modern World*. Cambridge: Polity.

Arasaratnam, S. 1986. *Sri Lanka after Independence: Nationalism, Communalism, and Nation Building*. Madras: University of Madras.

—— 1987. 'Sinhala-Tamil Relations in Modern Sri Lanka', 33–54 in *Ethnic Conflict: International Perspectives*, edited by J. Boucher. Newbury Park: Sage.

Barry, B. 1989/91a. 'The Consociational Model and Its Dangers', 136–55 in *Democracy and Power: Essays in Political Theory 1*, edited by B. Barry. Oxford: Oxford University Press.

—— 1989/91b. 'Political Accommodation and Consociational Democracy', 100–35 in *Democracy and Power: Essays in Political Theory 1*, edited by B. Barry. Oxford: Oxford University Press.

Billig, M. 1995. *Banal Nationalism*. London: Sage.

Boal, F. W., Douglas, J. N. H., and Orr, J. A. E. 1982. *Integration and Division: Geographical Perspectives on the Northern Ireland Problem*. London, New York, NY: Academic Press.

Connor, W. 1994a. *Ethnonationalism: The Quest for Understanding*. Princeton, NJ: Princeton University Press.

—— 1994b. *The Politics of Ethnonationalism*. Nevada, NV: Nevada University Press.

Crighton, E., and MacIver, M. A. 1991. 'The Evolution of Protracted Ethnic Conflict: Group Domination and Political Underdevelopment in Northern Ireland and Lebanon', *Comparative Politics*, 23: 127–42.

De Rigger, M., and Fraga, L. 1986. 'The Brussels Issue in Belgian Politics', *Western European Politics*, 9: 376–92.

Deutsch, K. 1966. *Nationalism and Social Communication: An Inquiry into the Foundation of Nationality*. Cambridge, MA: MIT Press.

Doob, L. W. 1986. 'Cypriot Patriotism and Nationalism', *Journal of Conflict Resolution*, 30: 383–96.

Esman, M. 1987. 'Ethnic Politics and Economic Power', *Comparative Politics*, 19: 395–418.

Europa World Yearbook 1997. 'Belgium: Introductory Survey', 556–66.

Giddens, A. 1985. *The Nation State and Violence: Volume 2 of A Contemporary Critique of Historical Materialism*. Oxford and Cambridge: Polity Press.

Glazer, N., and Young, K. (eds.) 1983. *Ethnic Pluralism and Public Policy: Achieving Equality in the United States and Britain.* London: Heinemann.

Gordon, M. M. 1964. *Assimilation in American Life: The Role of Race, Religion and National Origins.* New York, NY: Oxford University Press.

—— 1975. 'Towards a General Theory of Racial and Ethnic Relations', 84–111 in *Ethnicity*, edited by N. Glazer and D. P. Moynihan. Cambridge, MA: Harvard University Press.

Gramsci, A. 1971. 'Selections from the Prison Notebooks', edited by Q. Hoare and G. Howell-Smith. London: Lawrence and Wishart.

Gurr, T. 1983. 'Settling Ethnopolitical Conflicts', in *Minorities at Risk: A Global View of Ethnopolitical Conflicts*, edited by T. Gurr. Washington, DC: United States Institute of Peace Press.

Halpern, S. 1986. 'The Disorderly Universe of Consociational Democracy', *West European Politics*, 9.

Hechter, M. 1978. 'Group Formation and the Cultural Division of Labour', *American Journal of Sociology*.

—— and Levi, M. 1979. 'The Comparative Analysis of Ethnoregional Movements', *Ethnic and Racial Studies*, 2: 260–74.

Hewitt, C. 1977. 'Majorities and Minorities: A Comparative Survey of Ethnic Violence', *Annals of the American Association of Political and Social Sciences*, 433: 150–60.

Hossay, P. 1996. ' "Our People First!" Understanding the Resonance of the (Belgian) Vlaams Blok's Xenophobic Programme', *Social Identities*, 2: 343–64.

Jackson, B., and Penrose, J. (eds.) 1993. *Constructions of Race, Place and Nation.* London: UCL Press.

Joseph, J. S. 1985. *Cyprus: Ethnic Conflict and International Concern.* New York, NY: Peter Lang.

Kats, A. 1977. 'The Geographical and Settlement Distribution of Greeks and Turks in Cyprus' (in Hebrew), *Marhavim*, 2: 104–10.

Keating, M. 1996. *Nations Against the State: The New Politics of Nationalism in Quebec, Catalonia, and Scotland.* New York, NY: St. Martins Press.

Khalaf, S. 1987. *Lebanon's Predicament.* New York, NY: Columbia University Press.

Khalidi, W. 1979. *Conflict and Violence in Lebanon.* Cambridge, MA: Harvard University Press.

Kirby, A. 1993. *Power/Resistance: Local Politics and the Chaotic State.* Bloomington, IN: Indiana University Press.

Kliot, N. 'The Collapse of the Lebanese State', *Middle Eastern Studies*, 23: 54–74.

—— and Mansfeld, Y. 1996. 'The Political Landscape of Partition: The Case of Cyprus', *Political Geography*, 15.

Koumoulides, E. D. 1996. *Cyprus in Transition 1960–1985.* London: Trigraph.

Kyridikes, S. 1968. *Cyprus: Constitutionalism and Crisis Government.* Philadelphia, PA: University of Pennsylvania Press.

Lane, J. E., and Ersson, S. O. 1990. *Politics and Society in Western Europe.* London: Pinter.

Levi, M., and Hechter, M. 1985. 'A Rational Choice Approach to the Rise and Decline of Ethnoregional Political Parties', in *New Nationalisms of the Developed West*, edited by E. Tiryakian and R. Rogowski. Boston, MA: Allen and Unwin.

Lijphart, A. 1977. *Democracy in Plural Societies: A Comparative Exploration*. New Haven, CT, London: Yale University Press.

—— 1984. 'Proportionality by non-PR Methods: Ethnic Representation in Belgium, Cyprus, Lebanon, New Zealand, West Germany and Zimbabwe', 111–23 in *Choosing an Electoral System: Issues and Alternatives*, edited by A. Lijphart and B. Grofman. New York, NY: Praeger.

—— 1996. 'The Puzzle of Indian Democracy: A Consociational Interpretation', *American Journal of Political Science*, 90: 208–68.

Lustick, I. 1976. 'Arabs in the Jewish State: A Study in the Effective Control of a Minority Population'. Berkeley, CA: University of California.

—— 1979. 'Stability in Deeply Divided Societies: Consociationalism Versus Control', *World Politics*, 31: 325–44.

—— 1985. *State-Building Failure in British Ireland and French Algeria*. Berkeley, CA: University of California Press.

—— 1993. *Unsettled States, Disputed Lands: Britain and Ireland, France and Algeria, Israel and the West-Bank-Gaza*. New York, NY: Cornell University Press.

—— 1997. 'Lijphart, Lakatos and Consociationalism', *World Politics*, 50: 88–117.

McGarry, J., and O'Leary, B. 1993. 'Introduction: The Macro-Political Regulation of Ethnic Conflict', 1–47 in *The Politics of Ethnic Conflict Regulation*, edited by J. McGarry and B. O'Leary. London and New York, NY: Routledge.

Mikesell, M. W., and Murphy, A. B. 1991. 'A Framework for Comparative Study of Minority-Group Aspirations', *Annals of the Association of American Geographers*, 81: 581–604.

Mitchell, T. 1991. 'The Limits of the State: Beyond Statist Approaches and Their Critics', *American Political Science Review*, 85: 77–96.

Murphy, A. 1989. 'Territorial Policies in Multiethnic States', *Geographical Review*, 79: 410–21.

—— 1995. 'Belgium's Regional Divergence: Along the Road to Federalism', 73–100 in *Federalism: The Multiethnic Challenge*, edited by G. Smith. London: Longman.

—— 1996. 'The Sovereign State System as a Political-Territorial Ideal: Historical and Contemporary Considerations', 81–120 in *State Sovereignty and Social Construct*, edited by T. Biersteker and C. Weber. Cambridge: Cambridge University Press.

Nordlinger, E. 1972. *Conflict Regulation in Divided Societies*. Cambridge, MA: Center for International Affairs, Harvard University.

O'Leary, B. 1999. 'The Nature of the Agreement', *Fordham Journal of International Law*, 22: 1628–67.

—— and McGarry, J. 1996. *The Politics of Antagonism: Understanding Northern Ireland*. London and Atlantic Heights, NJ: Athlone.

Raanan, G. D. 1980. 'Cyprus, 1974 to 1977: Problems of Conflict in a Multiethnic Country', 172–214 in *Ethnic Resurgence in Modern Democratic States*, edited by U. Raanan. New York, NY: Pergamon.

Rabinovich, I. 1984. *The War in Lebanon 1976–1983*. Ithaca, NY: Cornell University Press.

Rudolph, R. R., and Thompson, R. J. 1985. 'Ethnoterritorial Movements and the Policy Process: Accommodating National Demands in the Developed World', *Comparative Politics*, 17: 291–311.

Sack, R. D. 1983. 'Human Territoriality: A Theory', *Annals of the Association of American Geographers*, 73: 55–74.

—— 1986. *Human Territoriality: Its Theory and History*. Cambridge: Cambridge University Press.

Salih, H. I. 1978. *Cyprus: The Impact of Diverse Nationalism on a State*. Atlanta: University of Georgia Press.

Shafir, G. 1995. *Immigrants and Nationalists: Ethnic Conflict and Accommodation in Catalonia, the Basque Country, Latvia, and Estonia*, Albany, NY: State University of New York.

Smith, A. D. 1986. *The Ethnic Origins of Nations*. Oxford: Basil Blackwell.

—— 1995. *Nations and Nationalism in a Global Era*. Cambridge: Polity Press.

Smooha, S. 1980. 'Control of Minorities in Israel and Northern Ireland', *Comparative Studies in Society and History*, 22: 126–35.

—— 1990. 'Minority Status in an Ethnic Democracy: The Status of the Arab Minority in Israel', *Ethnic and Racial Studies*, 13: 389–413.

—— and Hanf, T. 1992. 'The Diverse Modes of Conflict-Regulation in Deeply Divided Societies', *International Journal of Comparative Sociology*, 33: 26–47.

Taylor, P. J. 1993. *Political Geography: World-Economy, Nation-State and Locality*. London: Longman.

—— 1994. 'The State as Container: Territoriality in the Modern World System', *Progress in Human Geography*, 18: 151–62.

—— 1995. 'Beyond Containers: Internationality, Interstateness, Interterritoriality', *Progress in Human Geography*, 19: 1–15.

—— 1996a. 'Embedded Statism and the Social Sciences: Opening Up New Spaces', *Environment and Planning A*, 28: 1917–28.

—— 1996b. 'Territorial Absolutism and Its Evasions', *Geography Research Forum*, 16: 1–12.

—— 1996c. *The Way the Modern World Works: World Hegemony to World Impasse*. Chichester: John Wiley & Sons.

Thomas, P. 1990. 'Belgium's North–South Divide and the Walloon Regional Problem', *Geography*, 75: 36–50.

Tilly, C. 1975. 'Reflections on the History of European State-Making', in *The Formation of National States in Western Europe*, edited by C. Tilly. Princeton, NJ: Princeton University Press.

—— 1984. *Big Structures, Large Processes, Huge Comparisons*. New York, NY: Russell Sage Foundation.

—— 1985. 'Models and Realities of Popular Collective Action', *Social Research*, 52: 717–47.

—— 1990/92. *Coercion, Capital and European States, A.D. 990–1992*. Oxford and Cambridge, MA: Basil Blackwell.

Waterman, S. 1996. 'Partition, Secession and Peace in Our Time', *Geojournal*, 39: 345–52.

Williams, C. H., and Kofman, E. 1989. *Community Conflict, Partition and Nationalism*. London, New York, NY: Routledge.

Yiftachel, O. 1992a. 'The Concept of "Ethnic Democracy" and Its Applicability to the Case of Israel', *Ethnic and Racial Studies*, 15: 125–36.

—— 1992b. 'The State, Ethnic Relations and Democratic Stability: Lebanon, Cyprus and Israel', *Geojournal*, 21: 212–21.

—— 1997a. 'Israeli Society and Jewish-Palestinian Reconciliation: "Ethnocracy" and Its Territorial Contradictions', *Middle East Journal*, 51: 505–19.

—— 1997b. 'The Political Geography of Ethnic Protest Nationalism, Deprivation and Regionalism among Arabs in Israel', *Transactions: Institute of British Geographers*, 22: 91–110.

Zariski, R. 1989. 'Ethnic Extremism among Ethnoterritorial Minorities in Western Europe', *Comparative Politics*, 21: 253–72.

13

Conclusion: Right-Sizing and the Alignment of States and Collective Identities

Ian S. Lustick

The post-World War II order that most of the world understood itself to inhabit after 1945 is gone. This scary but familiar and relatively stable world was overturned by an interrelated series of sudden and massive political transformations. The most important of these was the collapse of the Soviet Union. The full impact of this enormous change in the structure of the inter-state system is yet to be fully understood.

The most obvious result was an abrupt halt to the cold war. Just over one decade ago, the externally ordered regime of political power that had dominated but stabilized the lineaments of political space in Eastern Europe, the Balkans, and central Asia disappeared, opening up fundamental questions of state boundaries, political community, and regime type in a broad swathe of Eurasia. The end to a global Soviet–American rivalry substantially decreased political involvement and political supervision by Great Powers over clients in outlying areas. This development destabilized different regions by removing props from weak regimes and encouraging ambitious counter-élites and rival governments to challenge prevailing arrangements.

Partially independent of these developments, and largely preceding them, has been the rise to prominence of religious fundamentalist movements— Islamic, Hindu, Christian, and Jewish—in the Middle East, South Asia, some parts of Latin America, and in the United States. These movements have brought radical change or civil war to Iran, Sudan, Sri Lanka, and Algeria and have powerfully affected political systems in countries such as Guatemala, Israel, Egypt, Pakistan, and Nigeria. In the former Soviet bloc, countries such as Azerbaijan, Yugoslavia, Georgia, Tajikistan, Chechnya, Indonesia, and the former Czechoslovakia have been literally torn apart by disputes over how to organize, share or dominate political space. In even more extreme cases, such as Somalia, Liberia, Rwanda, Zaïre/Congo, and Afghanistan, the very existence of states has been put into question as a result of the collapse or failure of all central institutions. Where institutions remain substantially viable, we still witness tremendous pressures arising from the potent mobilization of ethnic, national, or religious groups such as the Basque in Spain, the Albanians in Macedonia, the Kurds in Turkey, Kashmiris, Sikhs, and Bengalis in India, and Indians in Mexico. In other cases, the end of the cold war helped accelerate changes that have moved protracted conflicts toward promising but still unsettled futures. Blacks and Whites in South Africa, Irish nationalists and Ulster unionists in Northern Ireland, and Israelis and Palestinians in the West Bank and Gaza have engaged in intensive and complex processes of bargaining over how to redesign political institutions and control of territory so as to adjust the form and content of states to the substance and relative power of rival political communities.

Some effects of the end of the cold war and of the revitalization of suppressed national, religious, and other identities are less apparent. Demands for regional autonomy or independence by groups caught within political systems still powerful enough to suppress them and minimize their international visibility include Shi'a Muslims in Iraq, Kurds in Iran, Tibetans and other groups under Beijing's control, and various peoples within Indonesia's jurisdiction, aboriginal populations in Canada and various Latin American countries, and a variety of ethnic and religious groups in Southeast Asian countries such as Burma, Malaysia, and the Philippines. In Europe, on the other hand, pressures for changes in the mapping of state authority and community identity may be less intense, but the transparency of the systems involved and the growth of larger loyalties and overarching institutions associated with the European Union, heighten awareness of demands raised by regional groups and ethnic minorities: Corsicans and the Breton in France, the Welsh and Scots in Great Britain, the Catalans in Spain, Hungarians in Slovakia, etc.

Whether these forces demanding change and disturbing the political order stem from the end of the cold war, the rise of religious fundamentalism, or the transfer of authority from individual state governments to supra-national regimes, it has become very clear that one of the most important challenges of the post-cold war period is to develop new perspectives on how to cope with the inevitability of change in the way state and nations/peoples are matched with one another. This means understanding the hegemonic and contingently naturalized character of territorial and other boundaries. For new hegemonic boundaries will be essential to achieve democratic—or any other—stabilizations. Although their importance will eventually be tied to the invisibility of their constructedness, they must still be analysed and manipulated as contingent products of processes and projects of political institutionalization.

In the final analysis, both states and nations (or peoples) are institutional-ized features of our world which serve more or less effectively, under varying conditions, to afford human communities the structure and stability they need. If important circumstances change we cannot be too surprised if these institutional categories do not. But even if states and nations do survive, as it seems they will, it would be utterly surprising if all the *particular* correspon-dences in the boundaries and attendant identities of states and nations that preceded these upheavals survive.

It is within this larger set of questions, about aligning, de-aligning, and realigning political institutions and collective identities that the work reported in this volume should be understood. By asking about how and under what cir-cumstances central states might change their shape in response to ethnic upheavals and regionalist demands, we have sought to expand options for align-ing identities and states without encouraging premature deconstruction of the boundaries that remain natural in the minds of those who live within them.

Two False Inevitabilities

As I commented in Chapter 3, observers of protracted and polarizing disputes of the sort that have afflicted Sri Lanka, Kashmir, Northern Ireland, the West Bank, the western Sahara, Kurdistan, Cyprus, southern Sudan, Somalia, Tajikistan, Ngorno-Karabakh, and the former Yugoslavia, cluster in their dispositions toward the future around two inevitabilities. On one side a tendency crystallizes to view the past as having led, beyond some tragic turning point, to an inexorably dismal future. On the other hand, there are those whose rationalist or idealist focus on a specified and mutually satisfying outcome blind them to the enormous obstacles that real historical processes have placed in the path of such tantalizing resolutions.

From the perspective of observers who emphasize entrenched interests and irreversible institutional facts as barriers to any creative efforts to ame-liorate disputes, the notion of thresholds of institutionalization should hold appeal as a kind of opportunity. Both analytically and emotionally, it suggests the possibility of sudden, substantial, and even transformative change. The crucial element is to develop a base of knowledge, accumulated and refined through cross-cultural comparison, about the dynamics of movement across these thresholds and the signs of their political proximity. Only thus can the foundation be laid for reasoned and realistic action rather than faith-based commitments or pessimistic paralysis.

On the other hand, from the perspective of those fixated on the irrational-ity or even insanity of violence-prone disputes and the intellectual availability of arrangements that could alleviate or eliminate them, the two-threshold theory of institutionalization presented in *Unsettled States, Disputed Lands* (*USDL*) (Lustick 1993) is cautionary. By understanding the way contingency congeals into hardened political institutions—institutions which resist incremental retreat—those whose projects claim to reflect the long-term interests of all sides to a conflict, or the long-term forces at work, can still appreciate the enormous barriers to change that institutions can represent. For these actors and observers the theory of institutionalization thresholds is important for two different reasons. First, no resolution of a conflict can be achieved, and no effective action toward its achievement can be plotted, unless a path from 'here' to 'there' is understood as politically viable by élites willing and able to carry out the necessary policy changes. But no design of these pathways will be possible if the sometimes sharply, sometimes slowly changing slopes of the terrain to be traversed are not well mapped and if the political tasks at different points along the way are not distinguished from one another.

Another contribution of this theory to political right-sizing is that once deinstitutionalization has been accomplished, and a wider array of options is made feasible by the transformation of hegemonic or regime-level problems into incumbent-level problems, processes of reinstitutionalization will be required. So even for those whose immediate interest may be in down-sizing—territorially or functionally—they will also need to think, eventually, of how the new smaller or more limited sectoral authority structure can be institutionalized, that is, moved across the regime and then hegemonic thresholds in the state-building direction.

Expanding the Universe of Cases

One of Marx's most quoted aphorisms is that 'Men make their own history, but not just as they please. They do not choose the circumstances for themselves, but have to work upon circumstances as they find them . . .' (Marx 1926: 23). Something like this is true of theories. Theories or models explain outcomes and contribute to the production of new insights and more interesting questions, but robust theories and models do so in circumstances not of their own choosing. As summarized in my contribution to this volume, the two-threshold theory of state expansion and contraction that I developed and tested in *USDL* used British–Irish, French–Algerian, and Israeli–Palestinian histories as vehicles for these purposes. These settings were chosen because variation in patterns of outcomes across time in each of these relationships can be compared while maintaining a high degree of control over cultural, international system, demographic, and regime-type variables. This kind of control allowed the potent aspects of the theory to make themselves visible. Predicted patterns within the large arrays of 'cases', which comprised treatment of the British–Irish, French–Algerian, and Israeli–Palestinian relationships, were clear enough to be corroborated despite the complexities and simplifications inevitably attending any such wide-ranging and temporally expansive comparative study.

The present collection of work on countries that did not figure centrally in *USDL* is an opportunity to deploy the overall perspective developed in that book, and some specific portions of its argument, 'in circumstances not of their own choosing'. One key element in that perspective is appreciation of the political implications—both the opportunities and the dangers—associated with the theoretically unarguable and currently palpable fact that boundaries of states are malleable. The contributors to this volume were members of an inaugural workshop on 'Right-Sizing the State' project that began under the auspices of the Social Science Research Council workshop in May 1997. Each author studies a country or countries whose inhabitants are confronting ethnic, religious, and/or national problems that have a crucial territorial dimension. In each case these are problems about the shape and size of states that have produced, and/or threaten to produce, large-scale violence and disruption. To what extent, these authors have asked, and in what ways, might strategic, purposeful change in the size of a state—and especially contraction in the size of a state—present itself as a feasible or preferable route to preserving or enhancing prospects for democratic stability?

Each author has asked questions of their cases that *USDL* helped frame and which the theoretical apparatus in that book purports to help address. In addition to the cogent analysis of the individual cases, this collection gives substantial support to the theoretical perspectives encouraged by *USDL* and to many of the general propositions it contains. At the same time, many of these essays echo traditional and prevailing prejudices against adjustments in the territorial location of boundaries—against transfers of territory or acquiescence to the demands of secessionist movements. Most of the contributions also highlight a number of themes which were not crucial to the treatment of the British–Irish, French–Algerian, and Israeli–Palestinian relationships, but which bear directly on any right-sizing project.

The authors whose studies conclude most clearly that territorial right-sizing, via strategic acts of state contraction, have been or would be optimal responses to protracted or looming problems, are Alexander Motyl in his treatment of the general condition of the non-Russian successor states to the Soviet Union, Gurharpal Singh in his analysis of India's relationship to Kashmir and Punjab, Stephen Zunes in his discussion of both the

Moroccan–Western Sahara relationship and the Indonesia–East Timor issue, and Marc Lynch in his study of Jordanian developments subsequent to the country's 'disengagement' from the West Bank.

Motyl describes the Russian Federation as suffering from overwhelming demands on its tattered apparatus. In its decrepit state it falls back on one thing it does have to infuse its authority with a measure of legitimacy and purpose—Russian nationalism and a strong commitment to the Russians of the 'near abroad' and, perhaps, to the territories they inhabit. On the other hand, most of the breakaway Republics are almost purely creatures of a legacy of Soviet 'nationalities' policies. Without effective governing bureaucracies or established national movements, their boundaries in Motyl's view are virtually all that they have, aside from fear of Russian irredentist activity. Motyl's analysis is that to build stable and democratic national polities, many of these states should relinquish regions containing angry or separatist-inclined ethno-national groups. But he warns that this will not happen, that the successor states will not down-size until Russia is strong enough to forswear up-sizing.

Gurharpal Singh's discussion of the Indian case is similar. Singh warns that the recurrence of cycles of violence in response to ethno-political mobilization under separatist banners is because of the institutional dependence of the Indian state on conceptions of itself which insist that maintenance of its original borders be treated as a sacrosanct principle. By camouflaging the actual political core of the Indian polity as rule by a dominant North Central Hindu/Indian population, this principle has preserved the reputation of India as an adaptive reshaping state in response to demands for democratization or devolution coming from linguistic and other groups in the core, meanwhile concealing the systematic refusal of such demands when raised by groups in the periphery. Singh suggests, as does Motyl, that looming threats of violence and prospects for long-term democratic stability will require the Indian state to be stripped of its hegemonic commitment to the post-partition borders, permit sensible state contractions in Kashmir, Punjab, and perhaps elsewhere, and thereby put a halt to recurring cycles of violent separatist activity. Unlike Motyl with regard to Russia, Singh sees India as a state strong enough to problematize its size without risking its internal coherence. He also sees, in the Hindutvist movement, something that Motyl does not describe as present in the Russian political landscape—a rival set of ideas for legitimizing authority that could make strategic contraction of *state* borders a discussible and even implementable option. The key here is that in contrast to the Congress Party and its secular allies, the precise boundaries of the Indian state as created in 1947 are not as crucial to those guided in politics by community appeals as they are to those guided by purely statist appeals.

Stephen Zunes shows quite clearly that Indonesia's take-over of East Timor and Moroccan efforts to incorporate the Western Sahara as integral parts of the Moroccan state produced protracted and violent conflicts. Resistance to right-sizing (down-sizing) solutions in these cases is explained by the institutionalization of expanded boundaries past the regime threshold. For Suharto, before that dictator's recent overthrow, and for the Moroccan monarchy, maintaining Indonesian and Moroccan rule of these outlying territories was, and for the Moroccan monarchy still is, an issue threatening the stability of regimes within which they and the élites associated with them have enjoyed their positions and exercised their power. In accordance with Zunes's argument, we saw, after the reintroduction of democracy in Indonesia, not only open discussion of the future of East Timor but considerably more openness in that country toward state contraction as a solution. Indeed, despite threats of separatism in many other areas of the archipelago, Jakarta finally did leave East Timor. The dramatic shift in opportunities for solving the East Timor problem via state contraction that occurred in the wake of regime change in Jakarta is strong evidence in support of the argument I make in my contribution to this volume regarding thresholds as barriers to change which conceal opportunities for dramatic and rapid right-sizing. Comparing the Indonesian case to the Indian and post-Soviet cases as presented by Singh and Motyl we can imagine that right-sizing policies favoured by the authors in both those cases may indeed be not as fanciful as most observers think. What is crucial is regime change that de-links state institutions to particular boundaries, or a strengthening of a regime so that it need not rely as much as previously on particular territorial boundaries.

Indonesia, India, and the Soviet successor states thus provide excellent examples of the 'inside-out' effect—of how boundaries, and changes in boundaries, reflect developments, levels of institutionalization, and shifts in the constellation of power within the states whose territorial extent they purport to describe. The same is true of Morocco, and of Jordan, as described by Marc Lynch. But these latter cases also highlight 'outside-in' dynamics—the manner in which changes or imagined possible changes in the location of boundaries can produce profound shifts in the internal politics of states. Thus in Morocco, nationalist opponents of the monarchy have latched on to the Western Sahara issue, presenting themselves as 'more nationalist than the king', precisely, suggests Zunes, in order to delegitimize, challenge, and then overthrow the monarchy when right-sizing via state contraction from the Western Sahara is attempted. On this view, Hassan's tactical success in leading the 'Green March' in 1975 to extend his state's rule of the Western Sahara was a strategic blunder for him and is regime. If, in Indonesia, change in the regime was a prerequisite for change in the size of the state, in

Morocco, where incorporation of the Western Sahara has approached or crossed the hegemony threshold, movement toward deinstitutionalizing Moroccan rule there may be the best opportunity, or the only way, to achieve a change in the regime.

In Lynch's fascinating study of the effect of Jordanian right-sizing—disengagement from the West Bank—he shows how the late King Hussein's decision to remove the Palestinian West Bank from the official compass of the Hashemite Kingdom had powerful incumbent- and regime-level consequences for Jordanian politics. Indeed what Lynch shows is that deinstitutionalizing Jordanian rule of the West Bank set the stage for what he describes as a successful reinstitutionalization of a rather different regime. Aside from its smaller territorial extent, the 'new' Hashemite Kingdom of Jordan—with the explosive issue of Palestinian/West Bank/PLO aspirations for dominance within Jordan itself largely removed—has a relatively thriving public sphere, at least for the print media, with new opportunities for Islamist political expression, a hegemonically established smaller boundary—the East Bank only—and a new set of 'Transjordanian' opportunities for political ascendancy in Amman. Lynch suggests that the Jordanian case shows how regime-recomposition—at least with respect to the creation of a public sphere—may be not only a path toward deinstitutionalizing a regime-embedded state border, but a consequence of it and a contributing factor toward reinstitutionalizing a right-sized version of the state.

Despite the approbation offered by Singh, Zunes, Motyl, and Lynch for right-sizing projects—and implicit acceptance of right-sizing options by Callaghy and O'Leary—most of the contributors reflect in some way the prevailing resistance to changing the established external borders of states as a response to political strain.[1] For the most part these authors analyse and recommend reshaping projects—entailing devolving powers and authority from the central state to regional or communal structures in various spheres—as a substitute for resizing the territorial boundaries of the state as a whole. Yiftachel argues strongly that consociational patterns of shared authority among command élites, restricted state authority, and internal boundaries for rival communal groups hold out the possibility of maintaining state borders intact with high levels of democratic stability. He points to Belgium, as have Arend Lijphart and others, as an instructive example of how consociational techniques and institutions have enabled that country to sustain high levels of democratic stability without contracting its borders to separate Walloon from Flemish populations. At the same time he documents the

---

[1] For particularly influential statements, see Horowitz (1985: 589–92); Lijphart (1985); and Laitin (1998: 344–5).

failure of consociationalism in Cyprus and Lebanon by emphasizing the unwillingness of élites within the dominant communal segments in those countries—Greeks and Christians—to restrain their hegemonic ambitions—ambitions frustrated by the limitations on state authority that are inherent in consociationalism. For Yiftachel, wrong-shaping in Cyprus and Lebanon led to a Turkish invasion and forcible resizing. In Lebanon, wrong-shaping produced system collapse and, perhaps, *de facto*—Syrian and Israeli enforces—partition.

In Tom Callaghy's treatment of Laurent Kabila's disappointing performance following his take-over of the failing Zaïrean state, he draws attention to opportunities Kabila missed to reshape the state, renamed Congo. Callaghy observes that instead of permitting a governing group of élites to emerge, which would entail sharing power with the National Conference and with tribes, communal, and regional groups not his own, and opening the door to a serious rival in Tshisekedi, Kabila adopted 'the common practice of African leaders of falling back on the deeply embedded patterns of a patrimonial administrative state . . . moving relatives and members of his own Balubakati clan, ethnic group, and region into key positions' (Chapter 4: 000). In the absence of a coherent right-shaping strategy that would align Congolese territorial boundaries with the actual political reach of the government, Callaghy warns that the regime Kabila founded must find a way to reshape the Congo appropriately or set the stage for a *de facto* and probably violent resizing process.

This notion, apparent in both Yiftachel's and Callaghy's analyses, of a kind of trade-off between the likelihood of resizing and the implementation of appropriate reshaping, is also present in Denise Natali's surprising account of variation in the policies different Iraqi regimes and leaders have promoted toward the presence and political status of Kurds in Iraq. She shows a repeated pattern of overtures toward the reshaping of Iraq in directions that would accommodate the Kurdish presence in the country by incorporating Kurds and the Kurdish identity into the institutionalized conception of the state—either through schemes for Kurdish autonomy or by reshaping Iraq from a Sunni Arab political formula with aspirations to join a Pan-Arab, Ba'athist-led super state, into an Arab-Kurdish Iraqi state. Natali shows that these functionally down-sizing programmes were repeatedly interrupted, ineffectively implemented, or cancelled whenever the regime in Baghdad decided it no longer needed to accommodate Kurdish aspirations or when it was in such desperate straits that it had to gain exclusive access to oil resources in the Kurdish region or align itself with external, militantly Pan-Arabist forces. Failure of these reshaping projects to be fully and successfully implemented then set the stage for violent and prolonged conflict between the regime and the Kurdish population, including the genocidal Anfal campaign and the Kurdish revolt during the Gulf War. As a result of international intervention, Iraq was then resized, creating a small but politically important Kurdish semi-independent area in the north of the country.

Although Vali Nasr's primary focus is on the chronically problematized status of Pakistan's territorial borders, he also uses this trade-off idea. Nasr explains Bangladeshi secession—forcible resizing—as the result of a failure of Karachi élites to respond effectively to East Pakistani demands for a reshaping of the state which would have provided more resources and more authority to East Pakistani Bengalis. Similarly Motyl also mentions that the strong tendency in many post-Soviet titular Republics toward authoritarian 'Presidential' regimes is directly related to the inability of those states to right-size toward smaller arenas within which a more competitive form of democratic politics would not pose threats of anarchy or civil war. Ümit Cizre, who strongly argues that any resizing of the Turkish state would be catastrophically wrong—for Kurds and others in the country—holds out a civic nationalist reshaping of the Turkish regime as the only hope for democratic stability in that country. She is categorical in her insistence that to change the regime in this way will require preserving the territorial boundaries of the state as hegemonically institutionalized.

But in these studies the relationship between resizing and reshaping takes on other dimensions in addition to that of a trade-off between two alternative strategies. Yiftachel emphasizes that any right-sizing project, and especially state expanding projects, require right-shaping in the direction of extending more powers and rights to inhabitants of target territories if the new boundaries are to be hegemonically established. Although I disagree—in some respects—with his reading of Gramsci, I agree that responding effectively to sustained peripheral demands for political involvement and representation is an important requirement for core states to protect their institutionalized incorporation of such territories against counter-hegemonic movements. In my analysis of the French–Algerian relationship I observed that the explosive pressures that led to the 1954 revolt and the subsequent contraction of the French state from Algeria were the result of the failure to promulgate and implement any of the generous proposals for right-shaping the French–Algerian polity. These proposals were designed to devolve real power to Muslims in the Algerian 'departments' of France. In my treatment of Ireland, on the other hand, I argued that after the Great Famine, in the 1840s, Britain had lost all hope of satisfying Irish aspirations short of state contraction. In that context, the Irish home rule movement of the late nineteenth and early twentieth century was much more a stepping-stone to independence and camouflage for the secessionist ambitions of its leadership than it was a proposal to stave off resizing with reshaping. A similar analysis is offered by Singh, who explains the reshaping proposals of secessionist groups in the peripheries of the Indian state as tactical exploitations of the official rhetoric that supports reshaping in response to communal demands. Singh argues that, similar to most Irish home rulers, these groups pose as right-shapers while developing the mobilizational capacity for achieving central state right-sizing—'right' from their point of view—once the hegemony of Indian beliefs in the permanence of India's current territorial boundaries is success-fully challenged.

In the three relationships which formed the comparative core of *USDL*, international factors played a significant role in producing pressures toward state contraction. They insinuated new ideas that rationalized right-sizing movements or undermined efforts to habituate metropolitan inhabitants to claims about the full absorption of outlying territories— especially Algeria and the West Bank and Gaza. Nonetheless international factors tended to play a subordinate role in my accounts of these cases. In the chapters of this volume, however, it is striking how centrally important international factors are, reflecting, perhaps, intensified forces of globaliza-tion, greater communicative interpenetration, the increasing density of international political relations, and the smaller size and greater vulnera-bility of some of the states analysed relative to their international environ-ment—at least when compared to Britain and France in the late nineteenth and early and mid-twentieth centuries. International factors appear most prominently in these treatments, either as cultural influences that require states to present themselves to the world and their own inhab-itants in particular ways, or as direct pressures arising from economic, political, or military disparities.

For example, both Indonesia and Morocco have demonstrated a willing-ness to apply massive force ruthlessly against resisting populations who rep-resent a tiny fraction of their own demographic bulk. But Zunes also shows that not just local preponderance, but great power policies and preferences during the cold war were permissive causes of Moroccan and Indonesian attempts at upsizing. In the end, however, it seems that for Zunes, inter-national factors are the key elements explaining the *failure* of Indonesia and Morocco to seal the integration of East Timor and the Western Sahara. Morocco ran up against a strong norm, fully backed by the Organization of African Unity, against any changes in the territorial boundaries of post-colonial Africa and a norm supporting democratic processes for expressing aspirations of national self-determination that has produced sustained United Nations and United States efforts to organize a referendum in the disputed territory. In East Timor, a significant factor keeping that territory's fate from being sealed under Indonesia's hegemonic incorporation was the global reach of the Catholic church and the visibility and encouragement it gave to co-religionists active in the independence movement.[2]

Singh and Cizre emphasize the penetration into India and Turkey of globalized norms of secularism, free market capitalism, and civic/liberal notions of individual and group rights. Both describe these aspects of contemporary international political culture as impacting powerfully on the politics of moving borders. Just as Raymond Cartier's profit-and-loss attitude toward French colonial holdings influenced attitudes in France toward African colonies including, eventually, Algeria (Lustick 1993: 106, 323–4), so does Singh argue that in India the instrumentalizing and rationalist perspectives associated with global capitalism are creating an ideational basis for the success of future right-sizing, state contraction, and secessionist projects in India. He points specifically to competition among Indian states to attract foreign investment and a general trend toward economic liberalization which displaces the Nehruvian state's centralized control of the Indian economy and devolves economic power to individual states. In Turkey, Cizre argues that penetration by globalized reflections of Western culture has intensified the Turkish regime's emphasis on its secularist, Republican, and majoritarian foundations, effectively ruling out territorial contraction or even autonomy as a response to Kurdish demands for self-determination. At the same time, she observes that liberal and even post-modern aspects of international political culture, along with a vigorous transnationally active Kurdish diaspora, challenge the Turkish state to move toward a civic and inclusive version of its nationalist ethos in order to achieve democratic stability within its existing boundaries.

Separatist issues in India and Turkey are located near the ideological hegemony threshold, where discursive barriers to addressing these questions explicitly are most salient. In this context, amidst subtle but high-stakes wars of position, international political culture plays a critical role. Indeed, international political cultural factors, or regionally specific cultural influences, are also prominent in the contributions of Lynch, Natali, Callaghy, and Zunes. But where the fate of a particular territory is already present on the agenda of a polity, more direct pressures, constraints, and incentives, emanating from outside the boundaries of the state, are more likely to be influential. This is clearly the case in Lynch's analysis of Jordan, Natali's discussion of Iraq, and Callaghy's treatment of Congo.

[2] An interesting reflection on the pervasiveness of anti-colonialist international norms is that both Indonesia and Morocco have explicitly characterized their efforts in these outlying territories as anti-imperialist—as have, of course, both the Fretilin movement in East Timor and the Polisario in Western Sahara.

According to Lynch, Jordan's act of state contraction from the West Bank, 'followed primarily from international concerns', even if the reinstitutionalization of its smaller shape arose from political dynamics internal to the country. The independent factors he identifies as crucial are the 1987–93 Palestinian Intifada on the West Bank and Gaza—which might or might not properly be treated as 'international'—in the failure or Great Power-sponsored multilateral peace-making efforts toward the Arab–Israeli conflict, and, especially, Israeli political discourse which promoted highly threatening notions of Jordan—the East Bank—as an artificial state and the proper and future repository for Palestinians and Palestinian nationalism. Natali explains the Qasim regime's decision to abandon its bold reshaping of Iraq into a socialist Arab-Kurdish state as Qasim's response to Nasserist, Pan-Arab pressures, and the influence of strongly anti-communist regimes in Kuwait and Saudi Arabia. Callaghy begins his account of the Congo by reminding his readers of the extent to which international forces, especially during the cold war, created a network of support for Mobutu's 'lame Leviathan' regime in Zaïre. In his account of the end of the Mobutu regime in Zaïre and its replacement with Laurent Kabila's 'Congo', he stresses the end of the cold war as creating conditions under which regional forces connected to Zaïre's uncertain future could be unleashed. He makes it clear that Mobutu's fall and Kabila's success were in substantial measure the result of Ugandan-supported Tutsi intervention from Rwanda, along with assistance from Angola, Zambia, and Zimbabwe. His discussion of prospects for democratic stability in Congo turns on whether necessary reshaping—democratization and ethnic inclusion—projects can be implemented to stave off a resizing of the country that will otherwise occur. Callaghy's assessment is that Congo is unlikely to reshape precisely because of the relative weakness and ineptitude of international pressures in that direction and because of support the regime can draw to resist intervention from surrounding states.

The borders of three of the states considered by the contributors to this volume were born out of dramatic upheavals that marked them with peculiar significance. In Turkey, according to Cizre, the exceedingly strong resistance to thinking about right-sizing or state contraction as responses to chronic internal disturbances is linked to a rigidification or hegemonic fetishization of the borders as established for Turkey by Atatürk following the demise of the Ottoman Empire. Having accepted a massive loss of territories that had been under Ottoman suzerainty, and having mobilized the Anatolian peasants for a successful war against Greeks and other Europeans set upon dividing much of the Anatolian rectangle among themselves, the Republic established by Atatürk was based on political myths and psychic conceptions that revolved centrally around the mystification of the Anatolian rectangle as an irreducible 'Turkey'—however non-Turkish many of the inhabitants within this landscape be. Singh cites a similar rigidification of boundaries in the Indian case. The trauma of partition, according to Singh, produced a Hindu dominated Indian state exquisitely sensitive to the catastrophic centrifugal implications of communally-based separatism. Its response was to fetishize the boundaries of the state, however accidental they were, as the permanent and unchangeable container of an Indian community whose claim to unity amidst diversity constitutes its most important political identity.[3] Associated with this argument is Singh's fascinating contention that it is precisely the Hindutvist movement, which shifts explicit attention to the Hindu identity of India rather than to its 'civic' identity, which has the most potential to embrace state contraction solutions to the Kashmir and Punjab problems.

If the trauma of the subcontinent's partition produced rigidity and an exclusion of boundary change from the agenda of Indian politics, it seems to have had nearly the opposite effect for Pakistan. As Vali Nasr notes, the tumultuousness of Pakistani political life, including the war, the Kashmir conflict, the secession of East Pakistan, and a succession of separatist threats in West Pakistan—Sindi, Baluch, and Pathan—are unsurprising in light of the theoretical perspective of *USDL* and Pakistan's failure to remove the question of the boundaries of the state from the centre stage of its political life. Indeed what Nasr observes is distinctive about Pakistani politics is the very 'normality' of explicit political competition based on threats of secession or demands for rather profound resizing and reshaping measures. In the language of the *USDL* model, the secession of East Pakistan represented the failure of an overextended Punjabi dominated West Pakistan hegemonic project that institutionalized itself past the regime threshold within West Pakistan. Influenced, as Nasr points out, by Ali Bhutto's own extravagant political strategy, Karachi refused Bengali proposals for reshaping the state. The result was a violent resizing of the state—the secession and emergence of Bangladesh. The question of the borders of the state within the smaller Pakistan then emerged, not as embedded hegemonically or at the regime level, but as a perennial problem and resource for contending élites. Since the creation of Bangladesh, in other words, the shape of the Pakistani state has been located within the incumbent stage—to the left of the regime threshold. As Nasr shows, virtually every ambitious Pakistani politician, and especially Ali Bhutto, has used expectations (fears and hopes) about the real possibility

---

[3] On this particular point, see also Srirupa Roy's dissertation in progress, entitled 'Divided We Stand: Diversity and National Identity in India, 1947–1997' (Department of Political Science, University of Pennsylvania).

of change in the shape of the state to advance their own careers within a quite weakly institutionalized Pakistani state.

A range of other patterns and propositions advanced and discussed in *USDL* find significant support in the cases analysed in this volume. Motyl makes a strong argument for the centrality of state shaping issues, contending that the trajectories of almost all the post-Soviet successor states can only be understood and intelligently discussed if the boundaries of these states are understood as problematically institutionalized features of political life. Zunes echoes another important argument in *USDL* about the plausibility of counterfactuals regarding British absorption of Ireland and French absorption of Algeria. I maintained that neither of these projects were impossible, but that by extending the state's imperial ambitions well beyond Ireland and Algeria, and then claiming for those vast areas the same integral status as Ireland and Algeria, that Britain and France both severely undermined the prospects of hegemonically institutionalizing their rule of Ireland and Algeria. In this vein Zunes argues that the substantial success Indonesia had, and Morocco has had, in making their rule of East Timor and Western Sahara appear as irreversible, is due in part to Indonesia's decision not to pursue claims against Malaysia, Singapore, and Brunei, and Morocco's decision to relinquish claims to Mauritania.

Similar to the way that I showed European historicist ideas contributed to the beginning of a war of position in Britain over the Irish question, and to the way that post-World War II anti-colonialist and Federalist ideas shaped French discourses about Algeria, so do Cizre and Singh both identify new ideas from abroad as crucial ingredients in burgeoning wars of position in Turkey and India over right-sizing and right-shaping proposals. As other observers of Turkish affairs have noted, Islamist ideas, linking Kurds and Turks together as Muslims, and drawing on related 'neo-Ottomanist' perspectives within the intelligentsia, could be important ingredients in an incipient war of position over right-sizing or right-shaping solutions to the Kurdish problem. Likewise, Zunes suggests that the one group in Morocco capable of providing an alternative interpretation of the state's vocation that could integrate a contractionist solution to the Western Sahara problem are the Islamists. As seen above, Singh gives the same importance to Hindutvist ideas and overarching identities for reinterpreting India in a manner that could rationalize state contraction. Callaghy, on the other hand, points to Kabila's failure to advance any new formula as a candidate for hegemonic institutionalization as part of his reason to expect severe instability and violent resizing in the Congo.

All of the contributors identify discrepancies between official beliefs about the reality, appropriateness, or permanence of state borders and various, underlying realities. But several essays focus on the absence of entrepreneurs willing to take the risks necessary to build right-sizing hegemonic projects based on reinterpretations of those discrepancies. Indeed one can reformulate Motyl's argument as one focusing on the timidity of Russian and titular republic élites—fearing political oblivion if they offer rational solutions ruled out by prevailing discourses. Singh emphasizes the same factor, the absence of risk-taking entrepreneurs, as the single most important factor preventing the development of a full-blown war of position in India over right-sizing possibilities. Lynch places great stress on the energy and effectiveness of Jordanian political entrepreneurs who have vigorously exploited new opportunities in the post-disengagement era to reinstitutionalize a contracted image of the Jordanian state. Nasr portrays Bhutto as very similar to Randolph Churchill, Salisbury, and Joseph Chamberlain in late nineteenth century Britain, or to de Gaulle during the Fourth Republic—ambitious élites who exploited the problematization of the status of outlying territories in order to make opposition to down-sizing a winning political issue. Cizre makes a similar point when she explains the significance for Turkish neo-conservative élites for whom the figuring of Kurdish and Islamist 'threats' provides exactly the right kind of enemies for an integralist, Republican, and secular Turkey.

However, exploring cases 'not of the model's choosing', contributors to this volume have also identified important ways in which the categories, expectations, and hypotheses advanced in *USDL* could be amended or extrapolated. In his analysis of the particularly fluid situation in Zaïre/Congo in the late 1990s, Callaghy points to the problem of conceiving of movement across the model's thresholds as necessarily defining discrete chronological phases. His case leads him rightly to emphasize that wars of position, wars of manoeuvre, and incumbent-level struggles *can* all proceed simultaneously, and perhaps usually do. The ways in which these kinds of struggles may sort themselves into characteristic sequences would thus represent important hypotheses and distinguishing aspects of different cases.

The British, French, and Israeli states analysed in *USDL* were chosen, in part, because as relatively open parliamentary democracies they made it easier to use public opinion data and the discourse of competing élites to measure changing beliefs, fears, and objectives. But based on his study of the opportunities which emergence of a public sphere in Jordan provided to those who successfully campaigned to reinstitutionalize a contracted state boundary, Lynch points out an important implication of this feature of the cases covered in *USDL*. Lynch suggests that without a well-institutionalized public sphere, wars of position over re- and deinstitutionalization efforts would be much more limited. Indeed it may well be that a strong civil society may be an important requirement, not so much for contracting out of a disputed territory, but for reinstitutionalizing the new, smaller—or bigger, in the case of upsizing—shape of the state as a deeply embedded and stabilizing feature of the polity.

A prominent criticism of *USDL* has been its primary focus on politics in the core. A number of researchers have sought to extend the model more explicitly in the direction of recognizing the importance of differences and developments among the 'native' population in the outlying territory. While acknowledging that the 'gross discrepancies' required to enable movement toward state contraction are produced by large-scale mobilization in the periphery—the Irish Land War, the Home Rule Party, the Algerian insurrection, and the Intifada—the model in *USDL* does more or less assume such 'heroic' manifestations but then proceeds to understand likely trajectories based on struggles in the core. The role of political forces—apart from settlers—emanating from the periphery thus tends to be 'negative'—a factor, which if absent, would rule out state contraction. Yiftachel, Zunes, and Natali, on the other hand, devote some positive attention to the dialectical contribution of desires and mobilization in the periphery. Considering East Timor and Western Sahara, Zunes is forthright in his argument that stabilizing expanded Indonesian and Moroccan borders will be impossible without satisfying the requirements of the native populations in the outlying territories. In this context, Yiftachel—Cyprus, Lebanon, and Belgium—and Natali—the Kurdish issue in Iraq—especially emphasize that the sincere implementation of reshaping mechanisms can open real prospects for preventing state contraction, prolonged violent struggle, or forcible resizing.

Regardless of the particular usefulness or awkwardness of the theory of boundary institutionalization presented in *USDL* and examined here, the studies in this volume provide strong evidence that a well-developed concept of boundary institutionalization and a well-supported theory of how states can strategically contract, territorially or functionally, would have important policy implications. As awareness of the constructedness—as opposed to the primordial nature—of collective identities percolates from academia into the corridors of power, it is crucial that both scholars and policy-makers understand that neither identities *nor* state boundaries are 'priors' of political life, whose irrationalities in the face of changed circumstances must forever close our minds to prudent adjustments. The challenge will be to use this knowledge to achieve peaceable transitions where violence would otherwise occur without encouraging destabilization of boundaries—boundaries whose sturdiness or even invisibility as political constructs allows life in most places to proceed without the affliction of questioning the basic alignment of state and collective identity.

REFERENCES

Horowitz, Donald. 1985. *Ethnic Groups in Conflict*. Berkeley, CA: University of California Press.

Laitin, David. 1998. *Identity in Formation. The Russian-Speaking Populations in the Near Abroad*. Ithaca, NY: Cornell University Press.

Lijphart, Arend. 1985. *Power-Sharing in South Africa*. Berkeley, CA: University of California Press.

Lustick, Ian. 1993. *Unsettled States, Disputed Lands: Britain and Ireland, France and Algeria, Israel and the West-Bank-Gaza*. New York, NY: Cornell University Press.

Marx, Karl. 1926. *The Eighteenth Brumaire of Louis Bonaparte*. New York, NY: International Publishers.

NAME INDEX

SUBJECT INDEX